# International M&A,
# Joint Ventures
# & Beyond

# International M&A, Joint Ventures & Beyond

## Doing the Deal

### Second Edition

**David J. BenDaniel**
**Arthur H. Rosenbloom**
**James J. Hanks Jr.**

**John Wiley & Sons, Inc.**

0471022242X

This book is printed on acid-free paper. ∞

# About the Authors

**David J. BenDaniel** is the Berens Professor of Entrepreneurship at the Johnson Graduate School of Management, Cornell University. He attended the University of Pennsylvania, where he received a B.A. and an M.S. in physics, and the Massachusetts Institute of Technology, where he received a Ph.D. in engineering. As a visiting fellow and lecturer at the Harvard Business School, he taught the management of technological innovation; he has also served as a visiting professor at Keio University in Japan. He has worked as senior vice president for venture capital at American Research and Development/Textron, as group vice president for technology components for Exxon Enterprises/Exxon Corporation, and as manager of the Technical Ventures Operation of General Electric Company; and he has served on the boards of over 20 business ventures. Professor BenDaniel's work includes publications in international mergers and acquisitions, business valuations, and mathematics. He is senior fellow of the university-wide Entrepreneurship and Personal Enterprise Program at Cornell University.

**Robert T. Bossart** is of counsel at Greenberg Traurig LLP (New York). He specializes in corporate and international tax matters for U.S. and non–U.S. multinationals. He also serves as a member of the firmwide international tax specialty team. With more than 20 years of experience with multinational corporations in the industrial products, consumer products, and services industries, he has frequently advised in mergers and acquisitions, structuring and restructuring, financing considerations, transfer pricing issues, advance pricing agreements, strategic repatriation planning, and revenue agent examinations. Mr. Bossart is a member of various CPA and legal professional societies. He is also a director of the International Tax Institute and a member of the International Fiscal Association. Mr. Bossart is a frequent speaker to industry and trade groups, including the Tax Executives Institute and the World Trade Institute. Mr. Bossart is both a certified public accountant and an attorney. He holds a B.S. in economics from the Wharton School of the University of Pennsylvania, an M.B.A. in accounting from Johnson Graduate School of Management of Cornell University, a J.D. from Fordham Law School, and an LL.M. in tax law from New York University Law School.

**Kenneth D. Brody** is the cofounder of Taconic Capital Advisors LLC, an investment firm focused primarily on equity arbitrage, and the founder of Winslow

Partners LLC, a private investment firm. Mr. Brody served as president and chairman of the Export-Import Bank of the United States from 1993 to early 1996. Prior to his government service, Mr. Brody spent 20 years at Goldman Sachs & Co. He was a general partner and a member of the firm's management committee. Mr. Brody is a member of the boards of directors of Federal Realty Investment Trust and Quest Diagnostics Incorporated. He serves on a number of investment committees, including the American Red Cross. Mr. Brody is also a member of the Council on Foreign Relations. Mr. Brody received a B.S. with high honors in electrical engineering from the University of Maryland and an M.B.A. with high distinction from the Harvard Business School.

**Robert F. Ebin** is a partner in the Manhattan law firm Sussman Sollis Ebin Tweedy & Wood, LLP, concentrating in corporate and commercial transactions; public and private debt and equity issuances; bank financings; mergers, acquisitions, and strategic alliances; and cross-border business ventures. Over the past 30 years he has counseled clients in dozens of transactions in each of these areas, as well as in the licensing and protection of intellectual property and unfair competition. Mr. Ebin is a graduate of Brown University (A.B. 1962) and Columbia University School of Law (LL.B. 1965, cum laude), where he was a Harlan Fiske Stone Scholar and a founding editor of the *Columbia Journal of Transnational Law*. He also attended the M.B.A. program of the Graduate School of Business of New York University, where he concentrated in finance. Mr. Ebin has served as outside general counsel and member of the boards of directors of public and private companies, including Magna Software Corporation (New York City), RSR Corporation (Dallas, Texas), International American Homes, Inc. (West Orange, New Jersey), and Transcontinental Properties, Inc. (Los Angeles, California). He is currently a member of the Association of the Bar of the City of New York and the New York State Bar Association. He has been a member of the Midtown Securities Group and the Swedish-American and Danish-American chambers of commerce. Mr. Ebin has organized and given seminars and speeches and has published articles on subjects including cross-border strategic alliances (New York City, 1994, and Copenhagen, 1992) and acquisitions of U.S. businesses and U.S. real estate (Stockholm, 1988 and 1989; Malmo, 1988; London, 1989; and Copenhagen, 1990).

**Alexander E. Fisher** is a principal in Fisher, Harris, Shapiro, Inc., and president of A. Fisher Co., both of which are located in New York City. He has a B.S. in economics from the Wharton School of the University of Pennsylvania and a J.D. from Columbia University School of Law. His specialty is the creation of alternative risk strategies, particularly those relating to multilocation risks from multicorporate organizations.

**James J. Hanks Jr.**, is a partner in the Baltimore office of the 425-lawyer firm of Ballard Spahr Andrews & Ingersoll, LLP. He received an A.B. from Princeton University; his LL.B. from the University of Maryland Law School, where he was an editor of the *Maryland Law Review*; and his LL.M. from Harvard University. During the 1967–1968 term, Professor Hanks served as law clerk to Judge Charles Fahy of the United States Court of Appeals for the District of Columbia Circuit. In private practice, he represents publicly and privately held corporations and other entities in securities offerings and other financing transactions. He has represented buyers or sellers in over 250 mergers or acquisitions, including several valued at over $10 billion. Professor Hanks has testified in both federal and state courts as an expert witness on corporation and securities law matters. He frequently serves as independent counsel to boards of directors and board committees in connection with major transactions, stockholder litigation, and conflicts of interest. He is also an adjunct professor of management at Cornell's Johnson Graduate School of Management, where he teaches International Mergers and Acquisitions, and an adjunct professor of law at Cornell Law School, where he teaches a course in U.S. and European corporate governance at the Cornell Law School-Université de Paris I (Sorbonne) Summer Institute in Paris. He is also an adjunct professor of law at Northwestern Law School. Professor Hanks is the author of *Maryland Corporation Law* and the coauthor, with Bayless Manning, of the third edition of *Legal Capital*. He is also the author of many law review articles and a frequent speaker on corporation law issues. He has been actively involved in the revision of the Model Business Corporation Act and is a member of The American Law Institute.

**Scott L. Hoffman**, former managing partner of the Global Energy & Project Finance Group of Nixon, Hargrave, Devans & Doyle LLP (now Nixon Peabody LLP), Washington, D.C., is a partner in the law firm of Evans, Evans & Hoffman, LLP, Richwood, Ohio, where he practices in the area of project finance. He has been active in the development and financing of domestic and international energy and infrastructure projects. He has represented senior lenders (as agent, lead lender, participant, and syndicate group member), subordinated lenders, investment banks, and equity investors in a wide variety of project financing. Mr. Hoffman is the author of *The Law and Business of International Project Finance, Second Edition* (Transnational Publishers, 2001) and numerous articles on project finance. An honors graduate of Ohio Northern University, Mr. Hoffman received his J.D. with honors from Syracuse University, where he was managing editor of the *Syracuse Law Review*.

**Roy W. Hoffman, CPA**, is the managing director in charge of the International Services Group in the New York office of American Express Tax and Business Services, Inc. Mr. Hoffman specializes in financial and management consulting to foreign-owned ventures. Mr. Hoffman has more than 25 years of experience advising clients on accounting, business management, and personal finance issues. He has counseled many large and small foreign clients who have created U.S. subsidiaries or have acquired U.S. operations. These clients include public and private companies and government and quasi-government entities. His international and national client roster spans a wide range of industries, including manufacturing, import/export, freight forwarding, law, fashion, and jewelry. Active in his industry, Mr. Hoffman is a member of the New York State Society of Certified Public Accountants (NYSSCPA) and the American Institute of Certified Public Accountants. He serves on the Cooperation with Investment Bankers and Stock Exchanges Committee of the NYSSCPA. Mr. Hoffman has an M.B.A. from Baruch College, City University of New York; an M.A. in history from C.W. Post College on Long Island; and a B.A. from Allegheny College in Pennsylvania.

**Richard M. Inserra** is assistant treasurer, Risk Management and Insurance, for Union Carbide Corporation. Mr. Inserra's responsibilities include the risk financing and risk management strategies for Union Carbide's worldwide operations. Before joining Union Carbide, Mr. Inserra was vice president, Risk Management and Business Analysis, for Triangle Industries, Inc., a Fortune 200 company. Positions with increasing levels of responsibility prior to Triangle were at American Can Company, NL Industries, Inc., and Nabisco, Inc. Mr. Inserra has earned an M.B.A. and a post-M.B.A. in management information systems from Iona College. He was named "Risk Manager of the Year" by *Business Insurance* in 1984.

**Vladimir L. Kvint** is a professor of management systems and international business at Fordham University's Graduate School of Business and has served as adjunct professor of international business at the Leonard N. Stern Graduate School of Business at New York University. Dr. Kvint is the president of the International Academy of Emerging Markets. He has a D.Sc. in economics and a Ph.D. in management economics, an M.S. in mining electrical engineering, and an honorary doctorate from the University of Bridgeport. Since 1989, he has been a consultant on emerging markets to many U.S. and European companies. Previously, he occupied a number of high-ranking positions in the former Soviet Union, including chief of department, USSR Academy of Sciences, for projects related to regional technological programs, and chief of department, Organizational Management of Norilsk, Russia's largest enterprise, with 150,000 employees. Between 1992 and 1998, Dr. Kvint was a director of emerging markets at Arthur Andersen. Between 1998 and 2000, he was a director at Metromedia International Telecom, Inc. In 2001, he won a Fulbright scholar award in economics. He has also published more than 250 articles, is author or coauthor of 18 books, is a member for life of the Russian Academy of Natural Sciences, and is a member of the Bretton Woods Committee.

**Yonghong Mao** is a director in Financial Investment Services for Standard & Poor's. She has a B.S. in mathematics from Wuhan University in China and an M.S. in applied mathematics from Brigham Young University and recently received a Ph.D. in statistics from the Stern School of Business at New York University.

**Paul McCarthy** is a partner at Baker & McKenzie, Chicago, Illinois. He holds a J.D. from the University of Michigan Law School, an M.C.L. from the University of Chicago Law School, and a B.A. from Cornell University. He specializes in

U.S. and international mergers, acquisitions and joint ventures, partnership and limited liability company law, and international compliance programs. Mr. McCarthy spent six months on Legal Staff of the European Economic Community and was a professor of law at Boston University Law School from 1968 to 1972 and at Haile Selassie University Faculty of Law, Addis Ababa, Ethiopia, from 1966 to 1968. He is a member of the Chicago and the American Bar Associations.

**Richard F. McClurg** is a consultant in human resources with a broad domestic and international background. His international experience includes residence in Europe and extensive work in the Middle East, Africa, and Latin America with acquisitions and new ventures. Prior to becoming a consultant, Mr. McClurg worked for Union Carbide Corporation in a variety of human resources capacities. He holds a B.A. from Washington and Jefferson College and a J.D. from the University of Michigan Law School.

**Jane W. Meisel** is a tax partner at Arthur Andersen LLP, concentrating on U.S. and international acquisitions. Previously, she was international tax counsel at Debovoise & Plimpton. She graduated from Barnard College, magna cum laude, with honors in history; holds an M.A. from Columbia University; and received a J.D. from Columbia Law School, where she was an editor of the *Columbia Law Review*. She also received a master's degree in taxation from New York University. She has written numerous articles for the *International Tax Review*.

**Laurance R. Newman** is the president of Access Management, a Wisconsin-based management consulting firm that works with companies and their management in the development and execution of global business strategies. He is also the senior adviser to the Mertz group—an organization specializing in middle-market acquisitions and divestitures. Most recently, he was president and CEO of Rexworks, Inc., a Milwaukee-based public company that manufactures large industrial machinery for the cement and waste-reduction industries. Mr. Newman is also the retired executive vice president of SC Johnson & Co. In his career with SC Johnson, he served as senior vice president, Worldwide Services Business, and as senior vice president, Corporate Development, responsible for SC Johnson's merger and acquisitions activities and for joint ventures, new businesses, and licensing programs worldwide. In addition, he had responsibility for Johnson's Asia-Pacific operations and its global cleaning businesses. Johnson Wax is a private, global company participating in over 45 countries around the world with annual revenues of over $5 billion. Mr. Newman has been involved in over 45 acquisitions and divestitures, as well as many licensing and joint venture projects. He holds a B.A. and an M.B.A. from Northwestern University.

**Richard Porter** is a human resources consultant specializing in working with global companies on their people-related issues. He has a wealth of practical experience in postmerger integration work, as well as lecturing and writing on the subject. Most recently he was the global head of human resources for Young &

Rubicam Advertising, an agency with operations in more than 80 countries. Previously he served in a number of international human resource appointments for Guinness and United Distillers Inc., part of the Diageo Group of companies. He is an economics graduate of the University of Strathclyde and holds a master's degree from the Institute of Human Resources Management in London. He is also an international fellow at Tulane University's A. B. Freeman School of Business.

**Arthur H. Rosenbloom** is managing director of CFC Capital LLC, a firm specializing in securities valuation, litigation support, merger and acquisition advisory, and private placements of debt and equity. He was formerly chairman of the board of Patricof & Co. Capital Corp., a New York City–based firm similarly engaged. Mr. Rosenbloom holds a B.A. from Bucknell University, an M.A. from Columbia University, and a J.D. from the Cornell Law School. Mr. Rosenbloom's merger and acquisition advisory and valuation work has involved him with companies as diverse as Blockbuster Video, VNU, American Express, Act III Communications, Hyatt Corp., Continental Airlines, Trans Union Corp., Singer Corporation, and Axel Johnson Inc. His contributions on investment banking-related topics have appeared in *Inc.*, *Forbes*, *Business Week*, *The Harvard Business Review*, *Matthew Bender Corporate Counsel's Annual Mergers and Acquisitions Magazine*, *D&B Reports*, and the *National Law Journal*. He has been coeditor of the *Matthew Bender Federal Tax Valuation Digest* and the Prentice-Hall *Handbook of International Mergers and Acquisitions*. Mr. Rosenbloom has lectured on going-concern valuations and merger and acquisition matters before the American Institute of Certified Public Accountants, the Financial Executives Institute, and forums under the auspices of the Wharton School of the University of Pennsylvania, Cornell's Johnson Graduate School of Management, and Cornell Law School. He is an adjunct professor at the Stern School of Business at New York University and a fellow at NYU's Center for Law and Business, a joint venture between NYU's law and business schools.

**Roy C. Smith** has been on the faculty of the Stern School of Business at New York University since September 1987 as a professor of finance and international business. Prior to then, he was a general partner of Goldman Sachs & Co., specializing in international investment banking and corporate finance. Upon his retirement from Goldman Sachs to join the faculty, he was the firm's senior international partner. During his career at Goldman Sachs, Professor Smith set up and supervised the firm's business in Japan and the Far East, headed business development in Europe and the Middle East, and served as president of Goldman Sachs International Corp. while resident in the firm's London office from 1980 to 1984. In addition to various articles in professional journals and op-ed pieces, he is the author of *The Global Bankers* (E. P. Dutton, 1989), *The Money Wars* (E. P. Dutton, 1990), *Comeback: The Restoration of American Banking Power in the New World Economy* (Harvard Business School Press, 1993), and *The Wealth Creators* (St. Martin's Press, 2001). He is also coauthor with Ingo Walter of *Investment Banking in Europe: Restructuring in the 1990s* (Basil Blackwell, 1989),

*Global Financial Services* (Harper and Row, 1990), and *Global Banking* (Oxford University Press, 1996). Professor Smith received his B.S. from the U.S. Naval Academy in 1960 and his M.B.A. from the Harvard Business School in 1966.

**David R. Tillinghast** is a partner in the New York office of Baker & McKenzie. He represents a broad spectrum of U.S. and foreign companies, both publicly and privately held. His practice includes the tax aspects of domestic and international transactions, including mergers and acquisitions, securities offerings, investment funds, joint ventures and leasing, and project and other types of financings, as well as transfer pricing and related issues. Mr. Tillinghast served as a member of the Permanent Scientific Committee of the International Fiscal Association from 1983 to 2000 and as its chairman from 1995 to 2000. He has also served as reporter for the American Law Institute project on the international aspects of U.S. income taxation, as chairman of the Committee on Foreign Activities of U.S. Taxpayers of the American Bar Association, and as chairman of the Committee on Taxation of the Association of the Bar of the City of New York. He has published a book entitled *Tax Aspects of International Transactions* and prepared the chapter entitled "Tax Considerations in Merging or Acquiring U.S. Enterprises" in the *Handbook of International Mergers and Acquisitions.* He was formerly Special Assistant International Tax Affairs (the position presently titled International Tax Counsel) of the U.S. Department of the Treasury. The *National Law Journal* reported that "he is generally regarded by his peers as the country's top international tax lawyer." In 1996, the New York University School of Law Master's Program in International Taxation established in his honor the David R. Tillinghast Lectures on International Taxation. Mr. Tillinghast is a graduate of Brown University, cum laude with honors in philosophy, and Yale Law School, where he was note and comment editor of the *Yale Law Journal.*

**Roberta J. Waxman-Lenz** is an independent consultant on financial and economic issues. She has worked for the World Bank in Kazakhstan on a project to restructure and liquidate large industrial enterprises. Prior to this she worked for Ernst & Young in Kazakhstan on its Mass Privatization Project. She focused on the development of a National Securities Commission and designed a corporate governance training program. Ms. Waxman-Lenz worked as a financial analyst/ investment manager at the Central Asian-American Enterprise Fund, reviewing business plans of Kazakhstan companies to assess their potential for financing, and at the U.S. Export-Import Bank as a financial economist, covering Central and Eastern Europe and the former Soviet Union. Her activities entailed analyzing economic conditions and private sector developments in the region to assist in making lending policy decisions. She has also been an analyst in the International Division of the U.S. Department of Treasury. She holds an M.A. from The Johns Hopkins School of Advanced International Studies.

**Cynthia N. Wood** received a Ph.D. from the University of Virginia and completed postdoctoral work at Johns Hopkins University. She also studied at the University of Salamanca in Spain. Dr. Wood has extensive experience as a management consultant, specializing in change management, organizational development, international mergers and acquisitions, and executive training. Clients have included food and beverage companies, automobile manufacturers, paper bag manufacturers, and software companies. She has worked for the American Management Association, PRC, and for Richard A. Eisner and Company. Dr. Wood regularly makes presentations to management groups, including the International Society for the Advancement of Management and the International Academy of Business Disciplines.

 **Preface**

**W**e have assembled an experienced team of hands-on practitioners to provide their knowledge for *International M&A, Joint Ventures, and Beyond: Doing the Deal.* The corporate principals, legal and financial advisers, government officials, investment and commercial bankers, and business school professors for whom this work is intended will, we hope, view this book as a roadmap—one that sets forth the general issues in most cross-border transactions and allows for an insightful solicitation of other expertise on the particular problems associated with a given deal. If we have succeeded in providing such a map, our journey in preparing it will have been worthwhile.

The globalization of the deal business proceeds apace, as increasingly competitive business environments and high potential rates of return cause growing numbers of companies to look outward at transactions beyond their national borders. In addition to a continuation of vibrant U.S.–U.K. deal flow (e.g., British Telecom–MCI), transactions until recently quite unimaginable are taking place daily, including significant U.S. investments in Japan and privatizations in Kazakhstan and other regions of the former Soviet Union. While political tensions may cause ebbs and flows in the deal stream (e.g., possible human rights issues in Taiwan, Hong Kong, and in mainland China), and while certain regions will take longer to benefit from this phenomenon than others will (e g., some central African countries), the trend is perfectly clear—more cross-border mergers and acquisitions, joint ventures, strategic alliances, and project financings in more places than ever before, with increasing involvement in them by middle-market and smaller companies. According to *Mergerstat Review*, in the most recent five-year period, there have been 3,638 inbound acquisitions (foreign buyers of U.S.–owned companies) and 5,936 outbound acquisitions (foreign sellers to U.S.–owned companies). The total dollar value of these transactions in both directions was close to $143 billion. This total of 9,574 transactions divided into the total of $143 billion of deal price suggests an average price of $14.9 million, making this cross-border M&A phenomenon a decidedly middle-market one. In addition, there have been myriad joint ventures and strategic alliances for which no public computations are available.

Against this backdrop, the need for a work of this kind has become increasingly clear. There is, to our knowledge, no U.S. text dealing exclusively with cross-border deals. In attempting to fill the void, we have addressed the principal functional areas that impact cross-border transactions. Not surprisingly, the strategic planning, legal, tax, accounting, insurance, negotiating, financing, people/organizational, and postmerger integration areas covered here are precisely the same ones found in domestic transactions. But international transactions create levels of complexity not found in purely domestic ones. These include the inability, absent special circumstances, to do tax-free exchanges in some jurisdictions; dramatically different ways of dealing with purchase goodwill in others; and the burdens associated with time, distance, political risk, currencies, language, and conflicting cultures. It is the need to work through the complications associated with cross-border deals that, we hope, will give the work its importance.

Country-to-country differences are most pronounced in cross-border transactions involving companies in emerging markets whose legal, tax, accounting, and business regimes are, at least for the time being, asynchronous with those of many Western countries. Here, the litany of potential deal stoppers is long. Contradictory laws at the same level of government, contradictory laws at different government levels (national versus local), laws that change in the middle of a deal, and laws that will be put on the books postdeal (e.g., antipollution regulations) are surely among the most vexing. Creditors' rights in countries without anything like a Uniform Commercial Code or a well-developed bankruptcy law, problems in enforcing judgments, the absence of generally accepted accounting principles in many places, and tax regimes and tax compliance issues that vary dramatically from country to country are also worrisome. Woven into some of the text (but by no means comprehensively) are tips on how to proceed with transactions in such places—the ultimate challenge to the intellect and the ingenuity of the cross-border dealmaker.

These troubling issues notwithstanding, we confidently predict that a world grown smaller with the proliferation of modern communications and larger in the conceptualization of marketplaces will be characterized by increasing numbers of cross-border deals as we go forward in the new millennium. Along with our readers and students, we hope such deals will make the world a more prosperous and harmonious place.

DAVID J. BENDANIEL
ARTHUR H. ROSENBLOOM
JAMES J. HANKS JR.

*Ithaca, New York*
*New York, New York*
*Baltimore, Maryland*
*March 2002*

 # Acknowledgments

**A** work of this sort would never have seen the light of day without hours of devoted labor from a number of people, for many of whom this acknowledgment and the satisfaction of a job well done are the only rewards.

To Orietta Ramirez, Esquire, of CFC Capital LLC and to Colleen Homan of the Johnson Graduate School of Management, Cornell University, thanks for your many hours of reformatting and loving attention to the countless ministerial details.

To Greg Hubbell, a Cornell M.B.A. student, thanks for riding herd on the authors; and to Don Schnedeker, our Johnson School head librarian, for compiling the book's references.

To Melissa Scuereb, our editorial assistant at John Wiley & Sons, special mention for your careful edit of the text and thoughtful, elucidating questions and comments.

To Bill Falloon of John Wiley & Sons, praise for your gentle application of pressure as the book wended its way from conception to realization.

To our chapter authors, accomplished professionals all, our appreciation for the generous outpouring of your time and talent for which this acknowledgment is the most modest of thank yous. We would like to welcome two new authors, Roy W. Hoffman, who provided an expanded and very up-to-date accounting chapter, and Richard F. McClurg, who wrote an entirely new chapter on human resource issues that reflects his vast experience.

Finally, to our wives and families, thanks for your forbearance in forgoing the social and recreational hours that were put on hold during the course of our work on the text.

D.J.B.
A.H.R.
J.J.H.

# Contents

# List of Exhibits

# International M&A,
# Joint Ventures
# & Beyond

# PART ONE

# Critical Issues in Planning and Implementation

In Chapter 1, Laurance R. Newman, who has over 30 years' experience in the planning and implementation of international deals at SC Johnson & Co., covers the general strategic issues associated with international mergers and acquisitions (M&A) activities for corporate growth.

The author advocates a global development program as a central element of corporate strategy with international acquisitions, joint ventures, and/or strategic alliances as vehicles for growth. It is suggested that a review of this excellent planning material would be useful before reading the chapters that follow it.

# Strategic Choices

*Laurance R. Newman*

Internal and external corporate growth has long been a preoccupation of the financial and the business communities of the world. If a company is identified as a growth company, it becomes more attractive to its owners if it is private and to the investment community if it is public.

## THE QUEST FOR CORPORATE GROWTH

To achieve corporate growth, companies throughout the world are becoming less and less insular. They view the world as a totally integrated business community. Their vision of corporate growth transcends national borders and encompasses developed and less-developed countries.

It has been a number of years since Kenichi Ohmae described the growing realization that the world business and economic community is truly a triad, managed by the industrial complexes of Japan, North America, and Western Europe. The interaction of these large industrial masses shapes the destiny of most corporations. A company's future will, in the long run, be determined by the ability of that company's management and board to understand the interaction among these colossuses. The understanding of global economic impact and of how this impact relates to a business decision made in Chicago, Kiev, Dusseldorf, or Seoul is a requirement for survival in today's increasingly competitive economic environment.

Winning in the marketplace by creating sustainable competitive advantage and market leadership and dominance is the critical attribute of a successful company from both a financial perspective and a Wall Street perspective. Whether you review studies of profitability and market dominance generated by the Marketing Science Institute or study the market-winning strategies of General Electric, winning in the marketplace is critical to success. Global branding and the globalization of attitudes, behavior, and technology have required many local (i.e., European or United States) companies to seek worldwide expansion strategies to exploit their locally developed products (Coca-Cola, Pampers), distribution systems (Wal-Mart), or technologies (Lucent, Nortel, Alcatel).

Those companies with a global vision are better suited to weather rapid changes in a global marketplace. Those that operate solely on an ad hoc reactionary basis are likely to see their revenues and profits fluctuate violently.

As important and forward looking as Ohmae's triad concept was for global strategic thinking, it was only a few years later that worldwide changes reemphasized the importance of a strategic framework in competing globally. Beginning with the demise of the former Soviet Union and the abandonment of state-controlled economic activity, the 1990s launched an era of the global marketplace. Highlighted by trends embracing capitalist and free market doctrine, developing economies have been growing at two, three, and four times the growth rate of the economies of Europe and Japan and the United States. When these circumstances were combined with China's and India's commitments to economic reform, companies with worldwide strategies were forced to consider an additional two billion potential customers as part of their marketplace.

Exhibit 1.1 shows the world environment and potential business reaction in a four-factor series of linkages that must work together to provide a company with a properly flexible strategic direction in a changing business environment. (This exhibit has been modified from the traditional strategic four-factor diagram.)

The strategic management of most businesses generally requires mastery of four key linkages: resources, strategic planning, organization, and strategic control. The formulation of clear mission objectives is the means for conquering the demands put on an organization. If one plans to manage an enterprise of multinational dimensions, this understanding is necessary for survival. A number of years ago, one could hardly envision a global marketplace consisting of cars from Japan, steel from Korea, or soft goods from China. The strategic diagram described in Exhibit 1.1 allows consideration of those factors in developing current and future product lines and gives recognition to the changing nature of the external environment. It also considers one's organization and how it needs to be adapted to fit the changing links in its strategic management. Proper controls are critical if one plans to manage a far-flung, diverse business organization.

EXHIBIT 1.1

**The Shape of Global Competition in the 1990s**

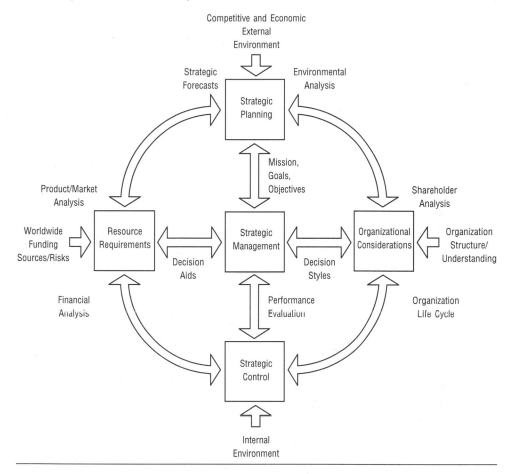

Many U.S. multinationals and their non–U.S. counterparts manage a significant number of critical business units throughout the world. Most of the employees of such companies do not speak the language of the country in which the company is headquartered. A strategic vision and a strategic plan allow these companies to effectively manage the timing and the use of resources to optimize short- and long-term yield. Organizational strategy flows from a desire to meet a predetermined corporate purpose. To achieve that purpose, top management, and sometimes the controlling shareholders, must have a long-term design. This design will include visions of a company's markets, its geography, its environment, and its purpose. A corporate strategy requires a comprehensive plan that takes into account the allocation of available corporate resources to meet that organization's basic mission and priorities.

## CORPORATE STRATEGY

Corporate strategy, according to most practitioners, is the pattern of decision making in a company that:

- Shapes and reveals its objectives, purposes, or goals.
- Produces policies and plans for achieving these goals.
- Defines the business in which the company intends to be and the kind of economic and human organization it seeks to be.

Corporate vision, objectives, and strategies can be viewed in some hierarchal context as Maslow's famous traditional hierarchy of human needs. Exhibit 1.2 shows how an organization can order these parameters.

Of critical importance in this hierarchy is the feedback element, which, in practice, is not limited to performance measurement. Only through written feedback does one have an opportunity to retest, reevaluate, and readjust goals. In forming its strategic plan, every company should evaluate its past and current performance. Such a written evaluation enables management to compare its accomplishments against its objectives. Did it accomplish its strategies? Were assumptions about the world environment correct? Are the timing and the vision appropriate? Each evaluation is a way of measuring the company's ability to achieve its vision in a timely and orderly fashion. If the report indicates significant shortfalls, one must retest the strategy and vision and ask:

- Did we miss because the environment or the economic conditions changed?
- Did we miss because we misunderstood the market?
- Did we miss because we are not as adept as our competitors in attacking and managing a competitive marketplace?
- Did we miss because our vision of the future was at a pace that is faster than the environment itself?

In the consumer products world, many product-technology innovations were far ahead of their time. For example, liquid and low-suds detergents have been out for a number of years, but only in the past 10 years have they made significant impact on the market.

## GLOBAL DEVELOPMENT PROGRAM

There are three key questions that must be addressed:

1. *What business am I in?* The classic railroad or transportation business model quoted in so many business cases is critically pertinent as one considers the global corporate growth. If the railroads had realized that they were in the transportation business, their strategy would have mandated development of buses, planes, and possibly automobiles.

EXHIBIT 1.2
**Hierarchy of Objectives**

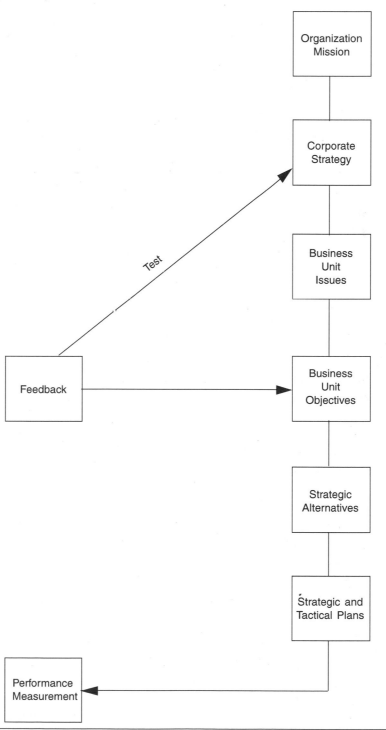

2. *Where are my current markets going?* Are they growing? How are they growing—in market potential, distribution, frequency of usage, and other elements?

3. *What is my sustainable competitive advantage?* Construct for your company a matrix chart by marketplace, product, or geography, and address the issues described in Exhibit 1.3.

4. *What do I do better than my competitors and what do my competitors do better than I do?* Are we being realistic about our own capabilities? Is our valuation internal, or do our customers evaluate our performance?

5. *What would my customers do if I went out of business?* If customers have instant choices that satisfy their needs, what sustainable competitive advantage do we truly have?

Another approach to measuring how you are doing is the adoption of a balanced scorecard to measure your corporate performance. In a recent article in *CFO,* the author interviewed Kaplan and Norton about the results in the marketplace since they published their article in the *HBR* in January 1991. Their thesis is that "there were significant shortcomings to using only financial metrics to judge corporate performance and urged companies to use such factors as quality and customer satisfaction as well."

A recent study by Bain found that about 50 percent of the Fortune 1000 companies were using a balanced scorecard model to enhance performance measurement.

Exhibit 1.4 gives a more comprehensive list of questions that might be asked about one's business plans or the business plans of a company that one might acquire.

## Acquisitions Only as a Tactic

It may appear strange to the reader that thus far acquisitions or joint ventures have not been discussed. It is intentional. Most of the chapters in this book deal with

EXHIBIT 1.3

**Matrix Chart**

|  | High | Medium | Low |
|---|---|---|---|
| 1. Product differentiation |  |  |  |
| 2. Barriers to entry |  |  |  |
| 3. Market growth rate |  |  |  |
| 4. Future demand curve |  |  |  |
| 5. Capital intensity |  |  |  |

EXHIBIT 1.4

**The Strategic Business Plan: A Customer-Based Vision**

1. Why have a strategic business plan?
2. Why might preplanning be more important than the plan itself?
3. What are nonfinancial benefits of customer-based planning?
4. Why does top-down, bottom-up, top-down planning produce better results?
5. What comprises a self-examination health care checkup?
   - Strategic questions.
   - Tactical questions.
   - People resources.
   - Focus.
6. What are key preplanning management questions?
   - What business are we in?
   - What is our primary competitive strength?
   - What is our primary competitive weakness?
   - What is our most significant business opportunity over the next three to five years?
   - What is our most significant business threat over the next three to five years?
   - What are our core competencies?
   - What core competencies must be significantly improved for us to be more competitive in the next three to five years?
   - What is our sustainable competitive advantage in each of our key business segments?
   - What are the competitive advantages that our primary competitors have developed?
   - Can we define our business in developmental terms—core, developing, and emerging?
   - How should we allocate resources among our opportunities—sum of the digits or par weighting?
   - Why have we not been as successful (or unsuccessful) over the past 36 months?
   - What should we have done differently?
7. What areas should we question as we prepare to write the plan?
   - The business.
   - The end benefit, services, or technology that we sell.
   - How to win or continue to win in these business segments.
   - The critical steps required to win.
   - Risk discussion.
8. What are the key customer-driven elements of the plan?
   - Clearly understood business definition.
   - Market definition.
   - Business characteristics.
   - Customer and potential customer analysis.
   - What does it take to win?
   - Primary competitors.
   - The competitors strengths and weaknesses.

*(continued)*

EXHIBIT 1.4
_(continued)_

- Our competitive advantage in this segment.
- Metrics of success.
  a. Volume.
  b. Market share/penetration.
  c. Dollar sales.
  d. Profit/ROA, and so on.
  e. Customer satisfaction.
  f. Competitor behavior.
  g. Risk assessment.
9. Does the plan clearly define what we want to do and how we are going to do it?
- Key objectives.
- Key tactics.
- Drilled-down tactic blowout.
- Time of tactics.
- Person(s) responsible.
- Barriers to success.
- Expected competitive response.
- Resources required.
10. Have we communicated to the people who have to deliver the objective?
11. Have we established clear milestones that are formally reviewed?
12. Is compensation tied to plan results, not to activities?

the transaction and all the business and legal ramifications of its execution. They are the means to implement a preexisting business strategy. This chapter is designed to take you through the strategic process, step by step, so you know why you are making an acquisition or a joint venture and how that transaction fits your strategy. Many of you have been involved in business deals. Think for a second. Was the deal driven by a predetermined strategic plan? Was it opportunistic? Was it both? Was it neither? _Transactions per se should never be a strategic goal of any organization._ They should be the result of a well-studied program to identify various alternatives to achieve a corporation's predetermined goal. Many companies espouse a strategy that results in a plan to do a deal rather than to properly delineate and define their corporation's objectives. Transactions are but one means to achieve identified strategic objectives. Many times in business plans, operating groups use the word _transaction_ to represent the difference between how far their current business plan will take them and the outer edge of their assigned corporate goal (i.e., gap filling).

Before determining if external expansion is a viable alternative for achieving a corporate strategy, managers must start with a mission, either at the corporate level or at the business unit level. A mission describes your vision. It describes your world audiences. It talks about where you are going, how you will get there, and what the world is going to look like when you achieve the result. It identifies the needs of the company's multiple constituencies: its customers, shareholders, employees, and the world in which it transacts business. Given a mission statement, one can turn attention to the objectives that enable the mission to be accomplished.

While it is unfortunate when a company does a deal without a strategy, it may be worse when a company pursues second- or third-rate entry points to a market because of a declared strategy and the inability to execute that strategy properly.

Firms must have a business growth strategy. Firms look for and need to explore growth opportunities on a global basis. A number of strategic analyses have identified the primary four components that contributed to growth-gap analysis between a company's sales potential and its current performance.

1. *Product line gap.* Closing this gap entails completion of a product line, either in width, depth, or geography, by introducing improved or new products.
2. *Distribution gap.* This gap can be reduced by intensifying coverage and exposure and expanding distribution. This is especially true for global business development.
3. *Usage gap.* To increase users, a firm must induce current nonusers to try the product or service and current users to increase their frequency of usage/purchase.
4. *Competitive gap.* This gap can be closed by making inroads into the market position of direct competitors as well as of those who market allied products or services.

When you perform this gap analysis, it is critical to identify your company's gap potentials. In identifying those potentials, you must consider their alternative executions. *This is where deal making can play a critical role.* Do you really have the ability, the internal resources, or the patience to expand your product line in Japan or in Germany or in the United States? How can you sell products in Southeast Asia without a sales force? Do you recognize the problem of importing products into Brazil? All of these must be examined as you look at the choice between internal growth and external growth.

The gap analysis should take into account the elements set forth in Exhibit 1.5 when considering organic versus external growth.

## INTERNATIONAL TRANSACTIONS AND DEAL MAKING

In evaluating international business deals, foreign currency risks become an issue; but with the globalization of the financial markets, there is increasing ability for a strong company to borrow in local currency to do a deal in Japan, the United Kingdom, Germany, the United States, and Italy; even the former Soviet Republic and Eastern Europe are becoming real possibilities.

As more fully described in Chapter 7, many multinationals have discovered

## EXHIBIT 1.5

**Analysis of Organic versus External Growth Alternatives**

| | Domestic Market | | | Foreign Target Markets | | |
|---|---|---|---|---|---|---|
| | Low | Medium | High | Low | Medium | High |
| 1. Market share | | | | | | |
| 2. Relative market share | | | | | | |
| 3. Product quality | | | | | | |
| 4. Market growth | | | | | | |
| 5. Vertical integration | | | | | | |
| 6. New product activity | | | | | | |
| 7. Research and development and sales | | | | | | |
| 8. Marketing and sales | | | | | | |
| 9. Productivity | | | | | | |
| 10. Capacity utilization | | | | | | |
| 11. Investment intensity ratio | | | | | | |
| 12. Inventory level | | | | | | |

that it is easier to raise capital (or debt) in foreign markets and have sought listings on the international exchanges. For example, there are currently around 520 foreign companies listed on the U.K. exchange, including 43 of the top 100 U.S. industrial companies and 9 of the 10 largest U.S. commercial banks.

Banking connections and relationships need to be developed globally, not just in one's corporate locale. By developing and nurturing these relationships, one obtains better access not only to potential merger partners but also to the financing and the financing skills necessary to fund the transaction.

## International Transaction Climate Perspective

This section, while hardly definitive, is intended to provide perspectives that can guide and direct preliminary evaluation of geographic areas that may hold interest for cross-border transactions.

### *United States*

The U.S. deal process is finely honed and driven by financial players. Focus is on return on investment (ROI) or return on equity (ROE). Leveraged buyouts, restructurings, or consolidation are normal business activities. The recent economic slowdown and collapse of the dot-com companies have and will provide some interesting cherry-picking purchase opportunities. Money tends to be plentiful, government and union involvement are very limited, and exposure risks of international currency and foreign cultures are minimum.

### Asia

Asians are not a monolithic group. This is rather obvious, but what are the differences? In their language, customs, and religion, the Chinese and the Koreans are as different as the Irish, the Italians, or the Eastern Europeans. Deal-making activity and the infrastructure to execute it are extremely limited today but will grow as the Asian firms become more attractive acquisition targets.

### Japan

Japan's internal business culture is changing, not by leaps and bounds but slowly and steadily as Japanese managers begin to see cross-border transactions as offering viable economic benefit. Most of the major Japanese banks have developed merger-and-acquisition (M&A) departments. They are designed primarily for cross-border transactions because Japan recognizes the need for a global presence. The skills and analytical abilities that allow a Japanese company to make a friendly takeover bid in North America or Europe are going to be applied to the Japanese market in time. The head of Merrill Lynch Capital Markets in Japan, in a 1987 article in a Japanese merger-and-acquisition magazine, indicated that he thought a friendly takeover bid in Japan would come within a year. Historically, Japanese acquisitions were done very privately and very quietly by one company taking over a financially distressed smaller company for the benefit of its employees. The Japanese Ministry of Finance has authorized a study by a university professor to determine the potential effects of M&A on the economy, on employment, and on cultural attitudes. An outcome may result in the government recognizing the potential benefits of acquisitions within Japanese business. The issue of limited acquisition potential in Japan exists today despite many well-publicized deals.

In Japan, 30 percent of the shares may effectively convey control. Culture and experience dictate that first a relationship or an alliance must be developed with a company before one can discuss acquisition, perhaps distribute products for it, or work together with the company on a joint venture or a coventure. Junzo Sawamura, chief manager, Capital Services Consulting Division, Mitsubishi Bank, has indicated that a U.S. company must be patient enough to spend at least six times as much time to acquire a business in Japan as it would in the United States or in Europe. Do most Western multinationals have the patience to do this?

Notwithstanding considerable writing on the growth and the flourishing of M&A activity in Japan, and despite the optimism relating to its expansion, as of yet, little has happened. Kenji Suganoya, general manager of Yamaichi's Corporate Planning Department, has indicated that, in the Japanese tradition, "to sell a company in Japan is considered shameful in much the same way as [the failure

that caused] an ancient war lord [to] kill himself for surrendering his castle or
. . . a captain [to] choose to go down with his ship." In addition, the debt-equity
ratio of Japanese companies averages about 80 percent despite considerable recent
improvement, compared to only about 50 percent for U.S. companies. Japanese
companies, therefore, are more dependent on their banks. The banks become key
investors and, in fact, are heavily involved in the company's decision-making
process. Nevertheless, many Japanese bank M&A people believe the boom will
hit Japan. The collapse of the Japanese economy during the late 1990s resulted
in unheard of layoffs, loss of regional power, and failure of significant sectors of
the Japanese financial community. These changes have allowed many U.S. and
European companies to acquire Japanese financial assets (insurance companies,
banks, finance companies, and real estate) at fire sale prices . . . they believed.
In Japan, patience will continue to be a key operating word.

### Europe

After the United States, Europe has been the most active participant in cross-
border transactions over the past few years. As U.S. companies recognized that
a global perspective was critical for the expansion of their operations, Europe
became a key target. The continued evolution of the European Union (EU) allowed
U.S. cross-border transactions to participate in a Pan-European setting. The growth
of multilanguage labeling and advertising through the sky-channel (satellite driven,
multicountry, multilanguage TV) and other such multicultural devices allows
companies to look at acquisitions in Europe on a base that is broader than country
by country.

Though a cross-border transaction from the United States to Europe antici-
pates a more Pan-European business and marketing environment, it is very important to recognize that the United States of Europe does not exist. Countries and
cultures in Europe are still very different from each other. Traditions and cultures
will not change but will slowly evolve over time. Technical and legal barriers may
be dropped between countries, but emotional, ethnic, and cultural barriers will
remain for a considerable period of time.

The most important caveat in a cross-border transaction in Europe is to make
sure that your company understands the cultures of the countries in which you
are going to do business. Germany is not Italy. Italy is not France, and neither
relates directly to Spain or the United Kingdom in terms of business pace, business
culture, and the modes of executing business transactions. For example, do not
expect to do European business planning during the month of August when most
of Southern Europe is closed. You will not change that culture.

### Germany

Many German companies evolved post–World War II and are still run by entrepreneurs or their families. German banks are heavily involved and exercise a great
deal of corporate direction and control. Acquisitions are both difficult and expensive. The combination of the aging of many of the senior German family members

with a significant change in the German capital gains law have placed many untouchable Germany companies on the sale block.

### Italy

Italy is probably the most entrepreneurial country in Europe. Companies grow and flourish despite the many changes in Italian governments. Businesses tend to be adventuresome, to take risks, and to explore new frontiers of fashion and creativity. Separating the entrepreneur from the company is very difficult.

### France

France is evolving from a very insular country into one willing to tolerate foreign investment. Recent acquisitions by Henkel and others have set new patterns for the participation of significant foreign investment. The establishment of the right relationship and contacts in France through French intermediaries is absolutely critical to establishing a dialogue with a target company. It is important to understand potential government intervention in issues of redundancy and plant closings. Also, rights and privileges of the workers' council should be anticipated and accounted for.

### Spain

With Spain's recent involvement in the EU, acquisition activity has increased dramatically. In evaluating acquisitions in Spain, it is important to determine whether the Spanish entity to be acquired will remain competitive once all the trade barriers have been dropped. Can one support the cost structure and the market share in a new business environment? Many Spanish companies may be available because the owners recognize a dramatic change in the business culture and climate. Study the market carefully and proceed cautiously in Spain.

### United Kingdom

The United Kingdom has been most like the United States in terms of the process and structuring of deals. U.K. companies have been involved in significant restructurings over the past many years, which have also seen the privatization of major government corporations in automotive, aircraft, and similar industries. The financial infrastructure and the U.K. stock market support acquisition activity within the country. The government has supported major restructuring that results in viable economic business operations. The investment banking community is also more highly developed in the United Kingdom than in other European countries. U.K. accounting practices related to goodwill (a charge against retained earnings rather than against net income as is the practice under U.S. GAAP [generally accepted accounting principles]) have made U.K. companies very successful bidders in cross-border activities, especially in the U.S. market. The recent change in how a U.S. company's goodwill will be handled will level the accounting impact of U.K. versus U.S. purchases.

## Benefits of International Transactions

Earlier in this chapter, transactions were mentioned as alternative strategies by which to accomplish a corporate objective. Transactions may be needed because most corporations, particularly global ones, cannot realize all of their growth by internal means. Most corporations do not have the experience, the infrastructure, or the resources to allow the simultaneous planting of a flag in a number of countries around the world. Hence, deals become a viable avenue for the execution of this strategy. It is critically important that companies recognize the increasing necessity of developing a global view of the world and global business strategies.

A cross-border transaction can bring the corporation a series of benefits:

- Identified ongoing business with *brand franchises, successful products,* and known *brand names.*
- *New distribution systems,* especially in parts of the world where it is critical to have a complete infrastructure, including a sales force.
- *Manufacturing facilities,* especially in transporting difficult or costly products where it is critical to have a facility near the customer.
- *New customers* in new markets.
- *New technology* by which to enter or to serve an identified market.

## Role of New Products as a Source of or for the Acquired Company

The role of new products in an acquisition is especially important in emerging business like telecommunications, e-businesses, and financial services

Many times one of the key reasons for an acquisition is to provide either a source or a market for new products either from or for the acquirer. If this is the case, understanding of the new product fit, skills, plans, and history is very important in understanding acquisition of value.

An assumption that the acquisition will be a critical source of new technology for the parent company or that the acquired company will be a great source for use of the acquirer technology must be thoroughly tested.

The creation of new products and the upgrading/revising of old products is the lifeblood of a growing, learning organization. In the past few years companies have been investing billions of dollars in the restructuring of their new product process and program. The objectives are driven by recognition that:

- The life cycle of a new product/service has been dramatically reduced.
- Time to market—from ideation to market—has to be reduced by an order of magnitude of at least 50 percent to 100 percent.
- Return on investment must be achieved in a much shorter time frame (i.e., 12 to 24 months rather than a more traditional 36 to 42 months) in a more competitive, shorter-life-cycle world.

- In-depth end-user understanding, analysis, and testing is critical for market success and end-user acceptance.
- The marketplace is changing so rapidly (i.e., telecommunications) that the prediction of future change direction might be more important than the skill to develop the new technology today.

In Exhibit 1.6 there is a list of questions that you might ask about new products and their process in both the acquirer and the potential acquiree (please note in Exhibit 1.6 some questions and issues to be raised as you review new products plans of both companies).

## New Opportunities in International Transactions

Because incremental per-share earnings increases are very important to both the acquiring company and Wall Street, the recent discussions and proposals by the U.S. accounting standards board regarding the handling of acquisition goodwill could provide a positive earnings uptick for many transactions. If the impact of goodwill write-off against current earnings was reduced or eliminated, it would enhance per share earnings.

### EXHIBIT 1.6

**Proactive New Product Development**

1. Why have a new product development program?
2. What are the critical business strategies for this organization and how do new products fit?
3. How does new product development enhance customer value?
4. How does this organization deliver value?
5. What does customer-focused, new product development require?
6. What are various types of new products?
7. What are critical steps in the new product development process?
8. How do you set clear objectives?
9. Is your testing process clear and predictive?
10. What are product launch steps?
    - Testing.
    - Scenario planning.
    - Test markets.
    - Entry points.
    - Competitive response.
11. What are critical elements of launch?
    - Pricing.
    - Promotion.
    - Sales force and channel management issues.
    - Monitor, track, adapt.
    - Roles and responsibilities in the launch.

## Problems in International Transactions

### Culture Shock

Be sure to understand the culture, the people, the country, and the business environment of the potential acquisition. The Japanese and the Chinese are very different, as are the Koreans and the Taiwanese. The Germans and the French are as different as the Spaniards and the Norwegians. Differences in history, culture, business practices, and style will affect such areas as approaching a target, the role of the intermediary, negotiating style, pricing practices, and willingness to allow significant precontract and preclosing due diligence. Understand the goals of the participant in the European Union, what has transpired to date, and how the history has and will affect the parties to the transaction. While the process of adaptation is ongoing, most European companies have made significant changes in how they go to market and manufacture products.

### Management Distance

Des Moines, Iowa, is not Paris, France. They are apart, in distance and in culture. Thus, management must be comfortable handling an operation very far from its home base and understand that business practices in Paris are very different from those in Des Moines, in style, timing, and sophistication. Add to these the adverse impact of time zone differences, and one can readily understand why communication between the parties is more difficult than in a domestic transaction.

### People Problems

Many countries have an additional player in people management: militant unions, workers' councils, and countrywide labor problems. Each of these may signify people-management issues different from those at home. It is important to understand these issues and to have a plan to manage their impact and to account for their extra costs.

### The Importance of People Due Diligence

For years organizations that provided intellectual services noted that their inventory and critical assets left the building each evening. This is becoming more and more true of every organization today. A growing part of understanding the value of a potential acquisition candidate is a thorough analysis of the important members of the management team—their strengths, weaknesses, and leadership skills and their willingness to continue after the closing.

People due diligence is even more critical in a cross-border transaction when you do not have an established presence in the country that you will be entering. In many European and Asian markets historical relationships still continue to have an important influence on both customer and vendor selection. Knowing which people to keep, how to keep them, and how to properly exit redundant employees with dignity becomes a critical program element in many countries to retain appropriate standing in the business community.

The less the cross-border acquisition brings you a trophy brand, the more critical this type of due diligence becomes. Many acquirers today are using professional headhunter firms to conduct sophisticated research on key "keeper" management teams and critical functional managers.

In the recent Daimler/Chrysler merger, it became apparent that the expectations of the German buyers of the American Chrysler managers have been seriously compromised, resulting in a total redo of the management team. Did their personnel due diligence predict this outcome?

### Lack of Local Business Knowledge

The more one knows, the more one knows how little one knows. Do not assume a knowledge of what appears to be a similar business in a foreign country. Having produced widgets for 50 years in Canberra does not assure the ability to understand widget production in Capetown or Cape Canaveral. Be sure, before closing a transaction, to truly understand the business in that country.

### Poor Knowledge of Industry and Geography

Many foreign transactions fail because one of the parties wrongly assumes that it knew the other party's country and industry. The average days' receivable in Industry X in Venezuela is 197 days, not 31 days as in the United States. Such circumstances have a major bearing on an investment cash flow and payback schedule.

These kinds of collections issues might have a major effect on the cost and productivity of the sales force if a high percentage of their time is devoted to collections. In many countries it is also required to assign a high percentage of incentive pay to collections, in addition to sales rewards.

## DEAL-MAKING STRATEGY

Entry strategies in overseas markets begin with a look at some numbers. If the market leader in the segment one proposes to enter grows with the market and if the market is growing at 20 percent per year, a target company half the size of the leader must grow two-and-a-half times faster than the leader and the market (i.e., at 50 percent per year) in order to catch up to the leader within five years. A company one-fourth the size of the leader must grow nearly four times faster than the leader (almost 80 percent per year) to catch up within five years. *This suggests that companies with low relative market shares in otherwise attractive foreign markets are poor acquisition candidates.* The work on market share structure developed by the Marketing Science Institute says that when the market leader is strongly entrenched, it has a low probability of being unseated without a new technology, new service elements, or some new device to create significant differentiation, such as the impact of Federal Express and the fax machine on business communications. The recent decline in the pay phone business, for example, is a direct result of the growth of cell phones. The phenomenon is illustrated in Exhibit 1.7. The number 1 brand, with sales of $100 million this year, is projected to grow to $250 million in five years at a compounded growth rate of 26 percent per year. The number 2 and 3 brands, with sales of $50 million and $25 million, respectively, must grow at 50 percent and 78 percent per year in order to generate sales of $250 million in five years.

The number 2 brand is likely to have half the share of the number 1 brand, and brand 3 is usually relatively unprofitable. This is especially true in a stagnant business. Acquiring the number 3 brand with no new technology or no unique synergy is probably an exercise in futility.

If an acquisition, a joint venture, or a strategic alliance is a true tactical choice for a corporate growth strategy, each party must be willing to walk away from it if the appropriate candidate to meet strategic needs cannot be found.

*Successful transactions today, especially in cross-border deals, involve a number of dynamic markets that one must consider at the same time.* A business deal with one of the leading companies in any of the dynamic markets would provide a satisfactory execution of a predetermined strategy. The deal should not pull the company into a strategic direction that was not planned, but one should not become wedded to a single strategy that has little likelihood of working.

Many transactions are partly opportunistic, but opportunistic deals should be made within a framework of agreed-to, well-thought-out business development strategies. Otherwise, the transaction is not opportunistic but random. Many opportunities require quick development of the relationship necessary for an ultimate purchase. This is especially true with the M&A auctions that have become so popular since the mid-1980s. Having an agreed-to, approved plan from management concerning how to approach a strategic market or markets is absolutely critical to the effective and proper execution of an acquisition program.

Understanding the competitive environment and understanding any of the companies that might be opportunistic acquisition candidates allowed GE to make a $45 billion bid for Honeywell in 36 hours. Time will tell if they were prepared enough or if they understand the business as thoroughly as required. A recent article noted, "On a Thursday afternoon last October 2000, Jack Welch caught wind of United Technologies Corp's negotiations to acquire Honeywell International Inc. for $40 billion in UTC stock and charged up his troops to steal the deal. By Friday General Electric's company chairman had personally faxed Honeywell an 11th-hour offer valued at $45 billion in GE stock." Since then a third party intervened, and the deal cratered. A very proactive and protective EU antitrust authority has recently joined the bargaining table.

EXHIBIT 1.7

**Market Share Rank**

| Sales ($M) | Company | | |
| --- | --- | --- | --- |
| | Number 1 | Number 2 | Number 3 |
| This year | $100,000,000 | $50,000,000 | $25,000,000 |
| 5 years out | $250,000,000 | $250,000,000 | $250,000,000 |
| Compound growth rate | 26% | 50% | 78% |

## Points to Consider in Planning the Deal

### *Why Not Just Export?*

Many young and growing companies are innocents abroad. Many push exports even when the foreign currency has been devalued. On the other hand, many successful global companies find export markets exceptionally difficult to penetrate. They have found that using local nationals to manage their foreign businesses gives them a better chance to build a long-term business franchise within the culture of the local country, thus demonstrating that putting the right product at the right place at the right time in an overseas market is better than shipping a home-based product to a foreign market.

### *Examine the Planning Process*

There is no greater comfort in an external expansion program than being equipped with a reliable business plan. Try to look out at least five years, and project earnings and cash flow. Remember, when choosing a partner, each firm inherits the other's cash flow issues.

It is helpful to have a sophisticated planning process in place. Those who do not are at a decided disadvantage and run the risk of entering a partnership long on memories but short on prospects. The decision-making process in business relates to the future, not to the past.

Those unused to a planning process often ask, "How can one project five years out with any certainty?" Reliability in planning is derived empirically. A first attempt will be ragged at best; one learns from each planning cycle. There is no time like the present to begin—and it is a better alternative than "gut feel," crystal balls, or Ouija boards. Any deal that fits two companies together, either formally or informally, requires the parts to mesh as a well-designed puzzle. A history of accurate planning on both sides will instill a sense of confidence in the financial projections and the risk profile.

Before embarking on an overseas expansion program, examine your company's strengths and weaknesses. One strength might be its ability to make rapid decisions in a fast-changing, competitive environment. A weakness might be the lack of capital to support the company's next needed surge of growth. The strength-and-weakness analysis helps in selecting a partner that complements your company's skills or shores up its weaknesses or allows your strengths to shore up weaknesses of the target.

Also, consider your firm's business style and its decision-making tempo. Some call it "temperamental fit." Practically all pharmaceutical companies entered the cosmetics business in the 1960s and were disillusioned by those moves in the 1970s. One reason for this failure is that a good pharmaceutical product takes years to develop, whereas a cosmetics product must often be developed in a matter of months. Much of a pharmaceutical company's market planning can be done at a different pace and reviewed only once or twice a year, a luxury not available in a cosmetics company. Some decisions of great strategic importance have to be made quickly, lest the competition get to the marketplace first.

Distinctions between the business styles of companies from different countries and how they affect deals are made elsewhere in this book. Another difference is the one between a financially oriented company and an operationally oriented one. The financially oriented management style features a hands-off attitude toward day-to-day operations. The operationally oriented company is characterized by a top management group deeply involved in the operations. Most conglomerates are financially oriented. Financially oriented companies are usually aggressive deal makers, tend to favor debt as consideration to drive up the return on equity, and are attracted to deal structures that minimize taxes.

Certain companies usually make suitable partners for financially oriented companies and others do not. For example, financially oriented companies and smaller high-tech companies rarely mix well. The financially oriented company often looks for stability and debt service coverage. If problems arise with the subsidiary, it wants easy access to people who can offer a quick fix. High-tech companies typically do not fit that pattern. Financially oriented companies are often good international acquirers because they are comfortable in managing by the numbers from a distance.

Operationally oriented companies subordinate the making of deals to concerns about how to manage the new subsidiary or joint venture. They tend to look for growth stability. In an acquisition, they are often meddlesome. This meddlesome nature suggests that an operationally oriented company should not stray too far from its basic business. If a company is very operationally oriented and *needs* to participate in the day-to-day decision making, it is likely to be quite frustrated with an overseas acquisition. We have recently seen the development of sophisticated financial buyers who have the skills to both buy and operate their investments with seasoned experienced managers. These are not the old leveraged buyout (LBO) firms but a new breed of business managers called PEGs (private equity groups).

Assuming that your strategic development program has identified international transactions as means to a given corporate strategy, it is important to answer a series of questions.

## Who Is Responsible?

Developing and executing a successful international business deal is an entrepreneurial line function, no matter how the individual charged with the program is shown on the corporate organization chart. An individual must be identified and charged with responsibility for the program. He or she will require a wide diversity of international business skills, including analytical ability and negotiating skills, as well as the interpersonal skills to orchestrate a large variety of multicultural technical specialists to aid in the evaluation and the execution of an acquisition or a joint venture. Many companies find it difficult to identify a single individual who possesses enough broadly based skills to be able to take total leadership for an international transaction. Hence, many operate with a small cadre of business specialists who execute the program together.

For example, SC Johnson centralizes responsibility for the identification, the evaluation, and the execution of all its acquisitions worldwide within its corporate group in Racine, Wisconsin, in concert with local and regional operating managers. The company accesses local operating management and other technical groups to support the process, but it gives the responsibility to a group of people who have developed a reasonably high skill in acquisitions.

### Where?

Identify the targets as part of the strategy for a particular country or region. This is critical to orchestrating the appropriate search techniques to identify potential candidates.

### What Deals to Make?

The determination of what you are trying to achieve in terms of product, company/partner, or country is contingent on the answer to this question. Consideration of volume levels, market position, technical competence, manufacturing characteristics, distribution and warehousing skills, and employee relations are all important.

Given a company plan and an assessment of strengths and weaknesses, it is time to talk about screening candidates for deals. Some companies determine the attractiveness of candidates on purely financial bases, such as size of revenues and profits, profit margins, and rates of return on assets and equity. Others prefer to give prime consideration to operational elements directed to the business characteristics of the seller. A screening approach that takes both such concerns into consideration is optimal. Exhibit 1.8 is an example of a screening chart that allows evaluation of several companies on various weighted criteria.

You should spend a long time studying the criteria you want and paring down the list of companies to a manageable number (six, perhaps). Then go to work wooing them. It is amazing how successful one can be if proper research is done. This method will not result in instant gratification. Patience is necessary, for good deals take time to develop.

Tyco, a U.S.–based diverse holding company, has made over a hundred acquisitions since 1994. Their CEO has provided the following guideline for successful acquisitions:

- We don't do acquisitions that are accretive right away.
- We get costs out as quickly as possible—even in two weeks.
- We push hard for revenue enhancement.
- We only do acquisitions of businesses we know and understand.
- We do not push acquisitions down from corporate; they must come up from the operating divisions.

### Why Should One Do a Deal?

It would seem that this question is somewhat redundant if you have worked through an appropriate strategic plan. The process of re-asking it provides a double-check on your strategic direction. For example: Why should *A*, a U.K. company, acquire a potato chip company in the United States? Answer: To provide

## EXHIBIT 1.8

**Screening Chart**

| Criteria | Weight | Companies* A | B | C | D | E | F |
|---|---|---|---|---|---|---|---|
| Expands corporation into its designated field | 5 | | | | | | |
| Offers diversification into a new attractive market | 3 | | | | | | |
| High-technology business and protectable product assets | 4 | | | | | | |
| Business not subject to cycles | 3 | | | | | | |
| Good sales growth prospects | 5 | | | | | | |
| Good historical profitability | 4 | | | | | | |
| Makes significant contribution to earnings | 4 | | | | | | |
| Market leader with its major products | 5 | | | | | | |
| High levels of R&D commitment | 4 | | | | | | |
| Controllable size | 3 | | | | | | |
| Managerial reputation | 4 | | | | | | |
| Good investor relations | 3 | | | | | | |
| Weighted Total | | | | | | | |

*Rate each company on 0–10 scale, with 0 the lowest and 10 the highest for each criterion; multiply each rating by the weight; then add column to find the weighted total.

a distribution system for store-delivered snacks that are a technical strength of *A*. Why should *B*, a U.S. company, acquire a pasta company in Northern Italy without a factory? Answer: To provide additional volume opportunities for an underused manufacturing facility in Milan. Ask the question and answer it as an important double-check to your strategic thrust.

## How to Go About It

This quantitative answer to "how to go about it" will help add structure to the search. The answer should define the species and the amounts of payment.

1. Is there a financial limit (e.g., $3 million or $300 million)?
2. What structure is acceptable?
   • 100 percent ownership.

- Controlling ownership. A U.S. company may want 51 percent or more for control (public vs. private).
- A joint venture with a participating partner.
- A local joint venture with a nonparticipating partner.
- A collaboration agreement (alliance).

3. Will the deal be friendly or hostile? A hostile bid is increasingly common in Europe, perceived as almost totally irresponsible in Japan, but fairly commonplace in the United States.

Understanding government regulations that may control or restrict the acquisition are very important. Finalize a list of key candidates, and develop a marketing program to contact and to open negotiations with potential candidates. Understanding your corporation's patience and tolerance levels is important to the development of the target list and to the closing of a transaction. Time differences, cultural barriers, and other elements of international acquisitions will extend the life of the deal. As was mentioned earlier in the chapter, consider whether your corporation will tolerate a one-to-four-year process time.

In larger companies, sponsorship of an acquisition can be a tricky affair. More deals are thwarted from lack of sponsorship than for any other reason. Sponsoring managers often are unaware of the time it takes and the frustrations one encounters in an acquisition; it is easy to lose interest. Thus, the operating group responsible for sponsoring a particular overseas target must be excited about the potential of the transaction and its ability to address the company's strategic needs. In an international business deal, the sponsor is often a local affiliate, particularly when the overseas target is to be integrated into the buyer's operation. Sometimes the sponsor is the regional or corporate group, if the acquisition represents a new thrust into the country or business and will be managed independently from other operations.

The workload of an active buyer can be another problem. Activity comes in waves and is hard to organize. Many successful companies are advocates of frequent and open communication about pending deals with the organization's appropriate stakeholders. However, this varies by business culture. Most management does not like surprises and wants to know about and participate in the acquisition or the venture projects under development.

## Finders and Intermediaries

Companies are solicited daily with deal suggestions from customers, suppliers, managers, commercial and investment bankers, and business brokers. To maximize deal flow, it is important to be prepared to respond promptly to such suggestions with reasons to support the decision to go forward or not to proceed. One cannot execute this well unless the strategy development and the screening process have been solidly carried out.

It is important to have an approved corporate policy on compensation of *intermediaries* (here defined as the people who put the parties together, as distinguished from the term *investment bankers*, which is here defined as the people involved in assisting the parties in structuring and negotiating the transaction and possibly raising the financing required to close the deal). This policy should be promptly placed in the hands of the intermediaries involved. Keep a log of all suggestions coming in.

Instruct all company managers to refer unsolicited proposals to the person responsible for corporate development or M&A. Tell your managers that they will be responsible for the second fee should a doubling occur. Always inquire pointedly about the relationship between the intermediary and the prospect, and make a careful judgment about whether you are getting the right story. It pays to ask the unknown intermediary for references, including deals he or she has completed, and the names of satisfied clients.

It is important when dealing with an intermediary that you clearly determine whether the buyer or the seller will be responsible for the fee. Never use an intermediary in any significant way until you have a clear understanding of how the fee will be calculated, what triggers payment or money due, or what part of the total financial transaction is subject to any fees.

Intermediaries can play a key role in international transactions. Many companies use them to provide critical interface. For example, in Japan, asking a company if it is for sale is a terrible affront and indicates that you think it is a failure or in financial trouble. However, a board member of the target company could be gently asked over cocktails whether the company has ever considered the possibility of a collaboration with another company. If the answer is yes, the dialogue can begin. The right contact is very important in an international transaction. Be patient. Many times the negotiation of a simple letter of intent or term sheet may take many months. Whether to use an intermediary may depend on the facts related to a particular transaction. Consider the following when the target is:

- *A non–U.S. affiliate of a U.S. company.* An investment banker or other intermediary will probably be very helpful. A local investment banker may be extremely helpful in understanding the company.

- *A non–U.S. public company.* Because of the existence of public shares (even though the purchase may involve private and/or public shares), an intermediary and an investment banker may both be very important. They could be the same person; it is possible that the intermediary who can facilitate the introduction to the company will not be the investment banker you want to handle a tender offer.

- *A non–U.S. private company.* Local intermediaries are very important. In many countries in Asia, South America, and Southern Europe, they are absolutely critical in arranging for and nurturing the negotiation. As suggested earlier, their purpose is not to participate in the negotiations but to support and facilitate the process. Deal structure may be critical because of tax considerations and government regulations.

In any transaction, legal, financial, and appraisal advisers should be involved as quickly as possible; they usually are worth their cost and are far less effective when they get into a deal late in the process.

## Recommendation Document

Once a letter of understanding, a nonbinding letter of intent, or a heads of agreement (an outline of the principal points in the transaction) is negotiated, it is important to develop a single, concise, well-written acquisition or joint venture recommendation document. This document should be approved by the appropriate executive committee and in most companies, depending on the size of the transaction, by the board of directors. The document should contain the following nine areas of discussion:

1. Recommendation.
2. Strategic objectives that led to the transaction.
3. The company to be acquired, joint ventured with, or invested in and its characteristics.
4. The strategic fit of the target to the strategic plan objectives of the acquiring company.
5. Discussion of price and value, including return on investment, return on assets, profit margins, and earnings per share effect.
6. Discussion of business, government, or cultural characteristics of the country or company that are different from those found in the country of the acquiring company.
7. Discussion of planned changes in governmental structure that may affect the cost or the competitive situation of the target business: happenings in the EU, the decapitalization effect of South American currency revaluation, Hong Kong becoming part of mainland China, and so on.
8. Discussion of an integration plan as an essential part of any business deal. It is easy to make deals but much tougher to operate companies. Without a strong vision of the operation and the posttransaction consequences, it will be very difficult for the acquiring company to effect its strategy. Before agreeing to do a deal, a plan should be in place regarding:
   - Who stays/leaves/joins the company or joint venture.
   - How it is to be run.
   - Cost implications of having the acquiring company's employees in an overseas company.
   - How, if at all, to integrate the target into the operation of the acquiring company.
   - What functions or people are likely to be redundant.
   - How to handle potential problems with workers' councils, unions,

governments in the target's country or that of the acquiring company; posttransaction integration issues.

9. Discussion of how to handle a variety of issues:
   - Currency fluctuations and currency controls (especially critical in a first cross-border deal).
   - Repatriation of earnings and dividends.
   - Possible need for additional capital.

For a further list of issues to consider when performing due diligence, see Exhibit 1.9.

## PRIVATIZATION—A DEAL-MAKING OPPORTUNITY

A new trend is sweeping the world—one that is happening primarily outside of the United States. A trend involving infrastructure sales in key industries (telecommunications and transportation) and basic product categories (steel, mining, or chemicals) is increasingly in evidence. The privatization of these critical country industries is "denationalization." In many instances, to enter these local critical categories outside the United States will require the acquisition of a government-owned company through a stock offering, an outright purchase, or a joint venture.

(Please note that your plan might have to accommodate the time, costs, and

EXHIBIT 1.9

**Nonfinancial Due Diligence**

1. The risks of poor due diligence.
2. The drivers of the business that might be acquired.
3. Critical marketing due diligence issues.
   - Market.
   - Brand.
   - Advertising.
   - Distribution.
   - Sales organization.
   - Competitor.
   - Innovation.
   - Brand replacement.
   - Brand value improvement.
4. Customers.
   - Buying behavior.
   - Reason for buying.
   - Expected changes in behavior.
   - Expectations.

- Value equation.
- Available substitutes.
- Competitive conflicts.
5. Vendor.
   - Reason for selection.
   - Reliability of supply.
   - Reliability of price.
   - Competitive problems.
   - Importance as a customer under new model.
   - Opportunity for concessions.
6. The new organization.
   - Understanding the people.
   - Understanding the formal and informal organizations.
   - Selecting the new organization.
   - Selecting the new management team.
   - Clear buyer-owned integration plan.
   - Third-party evaluation of key players on both an absolute and a relative basis.
   - Process to move fast and to make mistakes early.
7. Government and government agencies.
   - Current relationships.
   - Open issues.
   - Historic problem.
   - Plan for winning, or at least not losing.
   - Impact of sale/purchase of line or division.
8. Community.
   - How the acquiring company is viewed.
   - How the acquiring company wants to be viewed.
   - Historic issues/problems.
   - Willingness or experience with community relationships.
9. The infamous Street.
   - Assumed reaction.
   - Preemptive strike.
   - Damage control (for example, P&G/Gillette)
   - Clear plan.

---

issues related to mismanaged public entities and issues related to fixing problems, solving infrastructure, and dealing with nonfunctioning government employees.)

Exhibit 1.10 depicts the dramatic trend in privatization from 1989 to 1994. Key divested sectors have been telecommunications and power utilities. Consortiums of U.S. and European companies have been major players in these purchases.

The world is privatizing. As may be seen in Exhibit 1.11, government-owned entities (including many in the United States) are up for sale throughout the world. There are still many large government-owned companies available around the

EXHIBIT 1.10

**Global Trends**
Worldwide Sales of State-Owned Enterprises
(In billions of U.S. dollars)

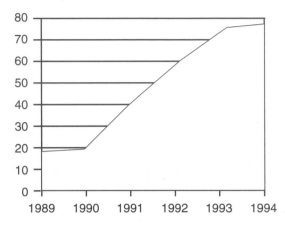

### Privatization by Industry

| Industry | Volume (US$ Millions) | Percent of Total |
|---|---|---|
| Telecommunications | $13,975.6 | 22.2 |
| Power utilities | 11,573.7 | 18.4 |
| Energy | 10,611.2 | 16.8 |
| Tobacco | 7,775.7 | 12.3 |
| Insurance | 7,482.1 | 11.9 |
| Banking | 4,465.6 | 7.1 |
| Vehicles | 2,094.7 | 3.3 |
| Steel | 1,899.1 | 3.0 |
| Mining | 1,661.5 | 2.6 |
| Coal | 1,497.4 | 2.4 |
| Total | $63,036.6 | 100.0 |

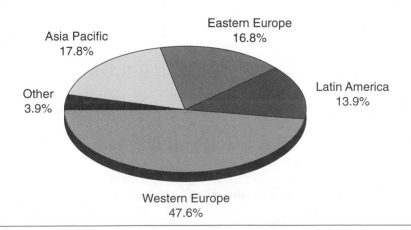

## EXHIBIT 1.11

## Examples of Global Privatization

| Company | Business | Buyer |
| --- | --- | --- |
| **Argentina** | | |
| Aerolineas Argentinas | Airline | Iberia (Spain) |
| **Brazil** | | |
| Cia. Siderurgica Nacional | Steelmaker | Group led by Banco Bozano Simonen (Brazil) |
| **Canada** | | |
| Teleglobe | Telecommunications | Memotec Data |
| **Chile** | | |
| Entel | Telecommunications | Telefonica de Espana (Spain) |
| **China** | | |
| Jilin Chemical | Chemicals | Public offering |
| **Colombia** | | |
| Colombiana Automotriz | Automaker | Mazda/Sumitomo |
| **France** | | |
| Renault | Automaker | Public offering |
| Thomson | Electronics | Waewoo |
| **Germany** | | |
| Salzgitter | Steelmaker | Preussag (Germany) |
| **Hungary** | | |
| FAU | Bottler | PepsiCo International (United States) |
| **Jamaica** | | |
| Tel of Jamaica | Telecommunications | Cable and Wireless |
| **Japan** | | |
| Japan Tobacco | Tobacco production sales | Public offering |
| East Japan Railway | Railroad | Public offering |
| **Lithuania** | | |
| Klaipeda Tobacco | Tobacco | Phillip Morris |
| **New Zealand** | | |
| Tel New Zealand | Communications | Bell Atlantic/Ameritech |
| **Poland** | | |
| FSM | Automaker | Fiat |
| **Taiwan** | | |
| China Steel | Steel | Public offering |
| **United Kingdom** | | |
| British Coal | Coal | RJB Mining |

world that have not yet been privatized. In addition, many of the early public offering privatizations offer an opportunity for market entry through the purchase of public shares.

Government privatization is a nontraditional way to view the process of growth through transactions. Of course, a deal involving a government entity requires patience, a willingness to make capital infusion, and possibly retraining of an entire workforce.

## JOINT VENTURES AND STRATEGIC ALLIANCES IN THE ERA OF GLOBALIZATION

As is more extensively reflected in the chapters of this book covering the particular topics, international joint ventures and strategic alliances, in one form or another, are being announced daily. Many observers considered them to be a major trend in the business world of the 1990s. Their proliferation is prompted in part by the fact that often the merits of a purchase of control do not outweigh the risks, the financial commitments, and the management difficulties, which may be mitigated by the formation of a strategic alliance. In addition, the trend allows companies to expand into new markets that were once inaccessible (i.e., China, the former Soviet bloc countries, India) or where local laws and regulations virtually dictate the inclusion of a local partner. However, the proliferation of international strategic alliances since 1990 appears to be more influenced by a broader set of phenomena associated with the globalization of business and commerce. (Please note in Exhibit 1.12 a detailed checklist of some of the issues and dos/don'ts of joint ventures.)

In addition to the opening of formerly closed and controlled economies, there has been the development of electronic financial transactions and telecommunication linkages that result in instant information and awareness everywhere. Concurrently, political leaders in developing economies have been aggressively embracing capitalism as the means by which to advance social and political agendas.

These technical and social changes, combined with an increase in the pace of change and of competition from outside one's home market, perhaps most persuasively explain this growing trend. The ability to offer old products in new markets, to afford the advantages of defensive positioning of products and services, and to leverage on an overseas partner's strengths are what have prompted companies like IBM, Northwest Airlines, Verizon, and others to employ this deal form. Although often difficult to manage, subject to the changing vagaries of international markets, and not always easy to terminate, international joint ventures (IJVs) and strategic alliances will be very much in the picture in the twenty-first century.

EXHIBIT 1.12

**Joint Venture and Strategic Alliance**

1.  Why do them at all?
    *   Mitigation of risk.
    *   Globalization.
    *   Inaccessibility of new markets.
    *   Formally closed or semiclosed economies.
    *   Instant global information.
    *   Global branding.
    *   Increased pace of change.
2.  Motivation to form strategic aliances.
    *   New opportunities for old products.
    *   Geographic expansion.
    *   Defensive positioning.
    *   First their rights.
    *   Reduction of competitive threat.
3.  Critical scope issue in the new global economy.
    *   Limitations on the JV scope geography.
    *   Limitations on the JV business or technical scope.
4.  Key issues in partner selection.
    *   Knowing your partner.
    *   Compatibility of culture and values.
    *   Avoiding competition.
    *   Establishing a 50/50 mentality.
    *   Understanding what each of you does best.
    *   Allowing the joint venture management freedom to operate successfully.
    *   Looking out for signs of trouble—solving them quickly.
    *   Leveraging key internal or external expertise in putting a JV together.
5.  Longer-term issues.
    *   Instability of management/management succession.
    *   Business industry instability—buggy whip or zap mail.
    *   Difficulty in termination—change of worlds; 10-year rule.
6.  Partner's complementary strength.
    *   Control flow possibly following strength—majority versus super majority, winning versus gamesmanship.
    *   Geography.
    *   Technology.
    *   Distribution.
    *   Manufacturing scale.
    *   Financial resources.
    *   Shelf presence (i.e., freezer case).

EXHIBIT 1.13

**Postmerger Integration**

1. What are the critical issues?
2. How do you access the importance of the critical issues?
3. What should you have done before you closed?
4. What is more important—speed or correctness?
5. How do you solve conflict?
6. How do you pick the winners versus the losers?
7. What is more important—team harmony or team competence?
8. How do you get the teams involved in designing their new world?
9. How do you manage both content and process?
10. How do you organize to get the integration done?
11. How do you manage success?
12. How do you reward success?
13. How does the Street measure success?
14. What do you do if the Federal Trade Commission (FTC) becomes your partner?

## SUMMARY

International deal making is complex and challenging; but if properly executed and properly integrated, the resulting transactions can add significant volume and profit to a predetermined strategic plan for a company. Keys to success include the following:

- Orchestrate the strategy carefully.
- Develop a strong proactive plan to identify, contact, and convince acquisition, joint venture, and strategic alliance candidates of the benefit of a transaction with your company.
- Close only at a price that provides sufficient return on assets or return on investments to execute a long-term strategic vision.
- Perform a thorough due diligence.
- Negotiate an agreement that offers the best possible protection.
- Execute a well-thought-out posttransaction integration plan (please note additional thoughts in Exhibit 1.13).

Following each of these steps offers the best opportunity for a successful international deal that will serve a company's strategic needs for many years.

# PART TWO

# Legal Aspects

In Chapters 2 and 3, Paul McCarthy of the international law firm of Baker & McKenzie covers the legal aspects of acquiring U.S. and non–U.S. companies. (Throughout the book, these may be called inbound deals and outbound deals, respectively.)

For the inbound deals treated in Chapter 2, the author discusses the regulatory framework in the United States; structuring the acquisition; the documentation preferred in the United States, including the commonly expected clauses of an acquisition agreement; the principal legal concerns of the buyer for which due diligence is required; the acquisition vehicle; and the closing.

For outbound deals, treated in Chapter 3, the author describes the more complex regulatory framework of most non–U.S. jurisdictions; the structuring of acquisitions as share acquisitions, asset acquisitions, or mergers; the documentation, which is often much simpler in transactions involving only foreign nationals; due diligence issues; organizing the foreign acquisition vehicle; and the closing (or simultaneous closings in several jurisdictions).

Both chapters have extensive checklists.

# Legal Aspects of Acquiring U.S. Enterprises

## 2

*Paul McCarthy*

The optimal acquisition structure for U.S. targets depends in part on the nature of the entity that owns the target (typically a corporation), the target's business and financial condition, and the buyer's business objectives. An acquisition by a non–U.S. party will encounter relatively few regulatory constraints, although the United States has enacted a review procedure for acquisitions by non–U.S. interests that may affect national security. An acquisition may take the form of a share purchase, an asset purchase, a merger, or a combination of these, depending on the interests of the buyer and the seller. Acquisition agreements in the United States are usually rather extensive, functioning as a means of structuring and accomplishing the acquisition, producing substantial disclosure concerning the target business, and allocating the risks of the business between buyer and seller.

## REGULATORY FRAMEWORK

### Governmental Approvals

Foreign acquisitions of U.S. businesses are assisted by a general absence of government regulation of foreign investment and an absence of a general system of exchange controls in the United States.

## General

There is no general system of licensing or regulating foreign investment or foreign acquisitions in the United States. However, the Exon-Florio amendment to the 1988 Omnibus Trade Bill authorizes the president to review certain acquisitions, mergers, and takeovers of U.S. companies or businesses by non–U.S. entities. The president is empowered to suspend or prohibit any such acquisition, or order divestment of the acquired company if the acquisition has been completed, if the president finds credible evidence that the non–U.S. person might take any action that threatens to impair the U.S. national security. The president has delegated the authority to investigate to the Committee on Foreign Investment in the United States (CFIUS), an interagency group.

The definition of *national security* has been left vague, listing just three "factors to consider" in making a determination:

1. The domestic production needed for projected national defense requirements.
2. The capability and capacity of domestic industries to meet national defense requirements, including the availability of human resources, products, technology, materials, and other supplies and services.
3. The control of domestic industries and commercial activity by non–U.S. citizens as it affects the capability and the capacity of the United States to meet the requirements of national security.

The third factor could be interpreted to include even nondefense industries, and many acquisitions of companies having no connection to the defense industry have been reported to CFIUS.

The Exon-Florio amendment applies to any transaction that could result in non–U.S. "control" of a U.S. person or entity. This includes the power to make significant decisions, even where only a minority interest is acquired.

The Exon-Florio provisions impose strict time limits for the investigation and review procedures. Review will begin on receipt by CFIUS of either "voluntary" notice from the parties involved or notice from an appropriate agency of the U.S. government. This notice must now contain a significant amount of prescribed information, including the latest available transaction documents. CFIUS has 30 days to decide whether the transaction should be investigated. If CFIUS finds that an investigation is warranted, it has 45 days to conduct the investigation, during which it may request additional documents and personal appearances by the parties, and make its decision. An investigation is mandatory where a foreign government–controlled entity acquires control of a U.S. company and CFIUS concludes that the transaction "could affect national security." The president then has 15 days to review and approve the decision. Transactions will be allowed to proceed without interference unless action is taken by the government within these time periods. However, unreported transactions will continue to be subject to review at any time. Therefore, in case of doubt, it will make sense to report any sizable transaction to CFIUS before proceeding with an acquisition.

### Exchange Controls

The United States exercises few controls over foreign exchange transactions by U.S. citizens or non–U.S. persons. No approval of the Treasury Department or other finance authorities is required to make an investment. A non–U.S.-owned enterprise is free to invest capital and to remit profits and repatriate capital abroad without any license or restriction. Interest and royalties paid to a non–U.S. parent are free of restriction. However, the U.S. government monitors foreign exchange transactions of substantial size. Although this monitoring is only for informational purposes, failure to make full and accurate disclosure where required could result in serious criminal penalties under money-laundering and other federal statutes.

### Reports

Foreign-owned enterprises are required to make periodic, direct investment reports to the U.S. Department of Commerce pursuant to the International Investment Survey Act of 1976 if 10 percent or more of a substantial enterprise is foreign-owned. Non–U.S. investment in real estate requires additional reports, particularly to U.S. tax authorities, under the Foreign Investment in Real Property Tax Act. The acquisition of 200 acres or more of agricultural land must be reported to the U.S. Department of Agriculture. Real estate acquisitions may also give rise to other, nonfederal, reporting obligations. A non–U.S. buyer of industrial property in a rural area should be careful to ascertain whether any portion of the property purchased can be considered agricultural property, but no specific report is necessary for acquisition of nonagricultural land.

## Restricted Industries

Non–U.S. ownership of certain restricted industries is limited or regulated by the federal or state government. These include the defense, banking, insurance, domestic air or water transportation, fishing, and radio and television broadcasting industries.

### Defense and Other Government Contractors

Foreign-owned U.S. firms are free to bid on contracts with the federal and state governments. Buy–U.S. requirements tend to consider where the item is produced rather than who owns the product. However, an enterprise that is non–U.S. controlled or influenced is unlikely to receive a security clearance and so will not be able to contract with the Department of Defense. (An exception is sometimes available for Canadians and U.K. citizens.) A non–U.S. equity interest of more than 5 percent creates a presumption of non–U.S. control, although the degree of actual control will be the decisive factor. Even loans or licenses from non–U.S. citizens may constitute non–U.S. control in some circumstances. Thus, acquisition by a non–U.S. buyer could severely damage a company that depends on defense business, but such disqualification can be avoided. For example, foreign-owned stock of the whole company or, more likely, the stock of the subsidiary that actually engages in defense business may be placed in a voting trust controlled by U.S. citizens, or the company may be managed by a board of directors having a majority of U.S. citizens. Other methods of decontrol may also be available. While such solutions satisfy legal requirements, they can result in significant operational and managerial problems on issues such as the need to report to two boards of directors or one board plus the trust.

### Banking

Banking in the United States is regulated at both state and federal levels. A non–U.S. bank may establish either a federal or a state branch to engage in banking directly so long as it is subject to examination by federal and/or state banking authorities and meets other specified regulatory criteria. In addition to establishing a branch in the United States, a non–U.S. bank may also establish an agency (i.e., an entity that can provide lending products but cannot generally accept deposits) or a representative office. A non–U.S. bank may also acquire an existing U.S. bank provided it obtains approval of federal banking authorities. If the target bank is state chartered, it will also be necessary to obtain the consent of state banking authorities. Most state laws do not restrict foreign ownership of state banks, and state regulatory authorities are increasingly willing to approve takeovers by non–U.S. persons. A non–U.S. acquirer must comply with the Bank Holding Company Act of 1956, which places certain restrictions on both the domestic banking and the domestic nonbanking commercial activities of the non–U.S. acquirer and the target bank. The recently enacted Gramm-Leach-Blitely Act of 1999 has significantly expanded the nonbanking activities in which banks, including non–U.S. banks, can engage (e.g., insurance, merchant banking, and other financial activities); however, banks in the United States are still generally prohibited from engaging in general commercial activities. A non–U.S. bank's worldwide structure and long-range plans should be examined in detail before it attempts to establish a presence in the United States or to acquire a U.S. bank.

### Investment Banking

Investment banking is strictly regulated in the United States. However, the acquisition of an investment banking firm does not require advance government approval, and foreign nationals are not restricted from owning such firms. Many engage in investment banking activities in the United States directly or through U.S. subsidiaries. A foreign-owned firm may be registered as a broker-dealer with the Securities and Exchange Commission (SEC) and may be a member of U.S. stock exchanges and the National Association of Securities Dealers (NASD).

### Insurance

Insurance is largely regulated at the state level. The acquisition of an insurance company normally requires state government approval. No state imposes a citizenship or residency requirement on ownership of an insurance company, although some impose citizenship requirements on directors. Approval of an acquisition is subject to substantial financial disclosure by the acquirer. Even with such disclosure, insurance company acquisitions are sometimes rejected by state insurance commissioners, often without explanation.

### Public Utilities

Because they are so closely regulated by the states, the acquisition of a public utility would require state government approval.

### Communications and Power

Non–U.S. individuals and firms may not obtain a license to engage in radio or television broadcasting from the Federal Communications Commission (FCC), although they may be permitted to operate a private communication system. An FCC license may be granted to a U.S. corporation only if all of its officers and directors are U.S. nationals and not more than 20 percent of the stock is owned or controlled by non–U.S. persons. The acquisition of more than 20 percent of a corporation engaged in the telegraph business is similarly restricted. There are no comparable restrictions on the foreign acquisition of a telephone company. Some states prohibit an out-of-state corporation from engaging in a local telephone business (although many states are now trying to end barriers to out-of-state competition), but such restrictions almost never extend to the citizenship or the residency of the shareholders. There is no federal or state restriction on non–U.S. participation in or ownership of other communications businesses, such as newspaper publishing.

Non–U.S. ownership or control of nuclear power facilities is prohibited, but non–U.S. persons may control corporations engaged in other power-generating businesses, such as hydroelectric facilities.

### Transportation

Non–U.S. persons are restricted from participation in domestic maritime and air transportation and may be limited under state law from engaging in railroad transportation.

Maritime shipping between two U.S. ports is limited to U.S. built and registered vessels owned by U.S. citizens. No foreign corporation may participate in this business. A U.S. corporation will qualify so long as its chief executive officer (CEO) and a majority of a quorum of its board of directors are U.S. citizens and at least 75 percent of its equity is owned and controlled by U.S. citizens. A U.S.–registered vessel may be sold or mortgaged to a non–U.S. person only with U.S. government consent. Non–U.S. persons are free to engage in international maritime transport with the United States.

Domestic air transport may be engaged in only by domestically registered aircraft. Only U.S. citizens, partnerships in which all partners are U.S. citizens, and U.S. corporations in which the CEO and two-thirds of the directors are U.S. citizens and 75 percent of the voting stock (but up to 49 percent of the equity) is held or controlled by U.S. citizens may register an aircraft. Surprisingly, this limitation extends beyond commercial aircraft to private aircraft as well. The acquisition of more than 10 percent of a domestic air carrier's shares is subject to Federal Aviation Agency (FAA) approval. A foreign-registered aircraft may be authorized to transport goods and people internationally if the carrier is technically qualified and if the transport is in the public interest, which usually means that the country of the aircraft's registration affords reciprocal privileges to U.S.–registered aircraft or that there is a treaty between the United States and the country of registration.

Federal law does not limit non–U.S. ownership of railroads, but some state laws prohibit any out-of-state railroad company from operating within the state. Some states also restrict the nationality or the residence of directors of railroad corporations and, in one case, non–U.S. shareholding.

### Other Maritime Activities

Only U.S.–registered vessels may engage in domestic towing, salvage, or dredging operations. Only U.S. persons, or corporations that meet the same requirements as for vessels that participate in domestic maritime transport, may register such vessels. The same management and ownership requirements apply to vessels fishing within U.S. territorial waters. Non–U.S. vessels may fish within the 200-mile or continental-shelf limit of exclusive U.S. fishing rights, subject to control by the Department of Commerce.

### Real Estate

There is no federal law that limits non–U.S. ownership of real estate, but several states have such prohibitions. For example, Iowa limits the right of non–U.S. persons to own agricultural property. Most such laws are rather archaic and are unlikely to be enforced. A non–U.S. company can circumvent these laws through proper structuring of ownership, such as holding the land through a U.S. corporation. Nevertheless, few investors are willing to risk forfeiture of ownership, however remote the risk may seem.

### Natural Resources

There is no general limitation on non–U.S. exploitation of natural resources in the United States. However, substantial amounts of exploitable land are owned by the federal government. Although federal lands may be leased for removal of oil, gas, coal, and other minerals only to U.S. citizens, partnerships, or corporations, there is no limitation on non–U.S. shareholding or control of such U.S. businesses. Similar rules apply to federal leases of timberland and of the outer continental shelf. Restrictions and reporting obligations also may apply with state-owned property. Some states restrict non–U.S. real estate investment to certain-size tracts.

## Other Regulations and Legal Considerations

Other legal matters that a non–U.S. buyer must consider in connection with an acquisition of a U.S. company include antitrust notification requirements, federal and state securities regulations, and regulations regarding mergers.

### *Antitrust Regulation*

U.S. antitrust law prohibits any acquisition or merger that would have the tendency to lessen competition or to create a monopoly. However, this restriction has rarely been used to block acquisitions if the buyer is foreign and has no existing operations or only limited operations in the United States.

If a U.S. acquisition meets certain minimum size levels (in general, a value of $15 million or more) and the parties are of a certain size (with sales or assets of $100 million or more in the case of one party and of $10 million or more in the case of the other party), a Hart-Scott-Rodino premerger notification must be filed with the Department of Justice and the Federal Trade Commission (FTC). Detailed financial and descriptive information concerning the "ultimate parent" of the acquiring and the target corporations, their product lines, and the transaction itself must be included. The ultimate parent will be the corporation that is highest in the chain of ownership if the actual buyer is a subsidiary. If the ultimate parent corporation is privately owned (as would be the case with many family-owned enterprises), the ultimate parent may be the family itself. Although the notification may appear burdensome and unnecessarily intrusive, buyers can normally comply with the law by disclosing only a reasonable amount of business information.

The parties must wait 30 days to complete the acquisition, although early termination may be requested. It is not permissible to proceed with the acquisition prior to expiration of the waiting period even if the transaction is made expressly subject to divestment in case the government later objects. Managerial and financial control of the target must remain with the seller until expiration of the waiting period. However, the effective date of the acquisition may be made retroactive to a date prior to such expiration, thereby giving the buyer the financial benefit of the target company's operations during the waiting period if the transaction ultimately proceeds.

The Department of Justice or the FTC may request additional information at any time during the waiting period, in which case the waiting period will be suspended until the information is provided. Such a "second request" can be very burdensome and time-consuming. Therefore, the parties are usually quite willing to discuss the transaction and to provide additional information to the government. Parties should ensure that all information provided is accurate and complete, especially if the timing of the acquisition is important.

Hart-Scott-Rodino filings are confidential. U.S. government authorities will not even confirm or deny if a filing has been made. Therefore, filing a notification should not jeopardize an acquisition or create unwanted publicity in the United States or in the buyer's home country.

### Securities Laws

The purchase and sale of securities, including the shares of a corporation and ownership interests in many other entities, are strictly regulated by both federal and state governments.

*Issuance of Shares.*   A non–U.S. corporation may issue shares or other securities in the United States to finance an acquisition. This would typically be the case with an acquisition in which the buyer exchanges its shares for the shares or assets of the target company. Shares or other securities must be issued pursuant to a registration statement filed with the SEC, unless an exemption from registration is available. The most commonly used exemption in acquisitions is the *private offering* exemption, that is, an offering to a limited number of knowledgeable investors. In any case, the buyer is required to make full disclosure concerning its business affairs and financial condition to the seller, even in a private transaction. Strict antifraud provisions apply to any issuance or sale of shares or securities.

*Tender Offers.*   A Williams Act notice must be filed with the SEC once 5 percent or more of any class of a publicly held target's securities are acquired. This must include a statement of the purchaser's intentions. A tender offer is regulated by federal securities law, including the antifraud rules.

Certain states have adopted legislation to make hostile tender offers to domiciliaries more difficult. Corporations have adopted restrictions in their articles of incorporation and have taken other defensive measures for the same purpose.

### Mergers

It is often simpler to merge with a public corporation than to tender for its shares, although, as described under "Mergers, Disadvantages," a merger is more time-consuming. A *merger* is a joining together of two or more corporations by operation of law. A non–U.S. buyer will not merge directly with the target but will typically establish a U.S. subsidiary to act as the merger partner. A merger with a public company will require the approval of the target's shareholders and so will be subject to securities law regulations. Public shareholder approval must be obtained through a proxy statement that must contain certain prescribed information, including financial information on the proposed merger partner and often on its non–U.S. parent.

## STRUCTURING AN ACQUISITION

Many factors must be considered in structuring the acquisition of a U.S. corporation. Many of these factors apply in domestic transactions, although they tend to be more complicated in an international acquisition.

## Shares or Cash

The use of cash to acquire shares or assets or to effect a merger offers no legal difficulties. This is the form normally used by a non–U.S. buyer.

There may be tax advantages (especially to the sellers) to using shares or other securities to acquire the shares or the assets of a target enterprise. The use of shares for this purpose is subject to securities law regulation. As noted earlier, shares or other securities may be issued only pursuant to a registration statement unless an exemption from registration is available. In addition, the target's shareholders will be interested in taking shares only if there is a significant public market for the shares offered. This is a severe limitation on the possibility of non–U.S. buyers using shares unless they have shares or other securities traded on a U.S. stock exchange or on Nasdaq (including perhaps American Depository Receipts [ADRs]) or if the seller is willing to accept securities traded on a foreign exchange.

## Acquisition Vehicle

A non–U.S. buyer may acquire shares or assets directly. As noted earlier, more often, a non–U.S. buyer will establish a U.S. acquisition vehicle in the form of a partnership, a limited liability company, or a corporation to acquire assets and, often, shares.

### *Partnership*
A U.S. partnership may be a general partnership, with unlimited liability for all partners, or a limited partnership, with limited liability for the limited partners. Corporations may be partners in either type of partnership. A partnership will often be used if the acquired business is to be conducted as a joint venture because such a structure may offer tax advantages for both U.S. and non–U.S. participants. A partnership may be used if the target business primarily involves real estate or natural resources. An investment in partnership form may also have advantages for investors from certain countries, such as Germany, where income earned through a U.S. partnership may not be subject to taxation in the investor's own country.

### *Limited Liability Companies*
Limited liability companies have come into use in the United States only in the past decade, but they are now used regularly in place of corporations in U.S. practice. A limited liability company offers the informality of a partnership while (as the name implies) providing a limitation on the liability of all of the members to their investment in the company. A limited liability company may be taxed in the United States as if it were a partnership, which can be very advantageous to a non–U.S. acquirer. A limited liability company is also very attractive for joint

ventures or for any situation in which the target is to be owned by two or more unrelated parties.

### Corporation

A corporation is the traditional acquisition vehicle used by non–U.S. buyers. There is but a single form of share company in the United States, the corporation. A corporation may be organized in any state. (There is no national business corporation law.) Delaware corporation law is particularly flexible; and because it has few mandatory provisions, many U.S. corporations organize under that law. A U.S. corporation may be organized very quickly because organization does not require prior approval of any governmental authority, nor does it involve prolonged review or processing of documents or outside valuation of contributions. There is no limitation on non–U.S. persons acting as shareholders in a U.S. corporation except for certain regulated industries discussed earlier. The organization of a U.S. corporation is discussed later in this chapter.

### Holding Company

A new corporation or a limited liability company may be used to acquire shares, thereby establishing a holding company structure. A U.S. holding company may be used if assets are to be acquired or if the acquisition is to be effected through a merger. Such a structure is permissible and comparatively simple in the United States because a U.S. corporation (and some limited liability companies) may have a single shareholder. U.S. corporate members of the corporate group may file a consolidated income tax return. A holding company structure is likely to give the non–U.S. buyer greater flexibility in tax and business planning in the future, especially if it plans to make other U.S. acquisitions.

## Share Acquisitions

The acquisition of shares or membership interests is the simplest form of acquisition, especially if there are only a few shareholders and all are willing to sell. As in any other sale of securities, the seller will be subject to the antifraud provisions of U.S. securities law, but it is customary to include the same full set of disclosure provisions in either a share or an asset acquisition agreement.

### Advantages

Where shares are acquired, all assets remain in the target company and few transfer documents are required. Thus, the acquisition may be completed fairly quickly, even if a public tender offer is required, as discussed later. Transfer taxes may be limited or avoided; but because such taxes are relatively low in most states (Florida is an exception for real estate), the transfer tax issue is less of an advantage in the United States than in most other countries. The target company will retain all of its assets, including its licenses, permits, and franchises. In an asset transaction, these can be difficult to transfer because of the need to obtain consents from the issuing government agencies. In a share acquisition, important contracts and leases may be unaffected by the transfer. These matters must be investigated, however, to make certain that the mere change of control of the target will not bring about termination of permits or contracts.

### Disadvantages

In a share acquisition, the target company will usually retain its tax attributes, both favorable and unfavorable, assuming that the business is continued. A higher purchase price paid for the business may not be reflected in the tax basis of the target corporation's assets after the acquisition, unless the seller consents to certain elections. Because these elections are usually disadvantageous to the seller, they are rarely made. The target corporation will retain all of its tax and other liabilities, whether disclosed or undisclosed, although, in a U.S. transaction, the seller will typically indemnify the buyer against certain undisclosed liabilities of the target, as discussed in the later section on acquisition agreements.

## Asset Acquisitions

### Advantages

If assets are acquired, the buyer's tax basis in the acquired assets may be increased to reflect the actual purchase price. Also, not all the assets of the target corporation need be purchased. Thus, if one is interested in only one line of business or one division of a corporation, an asset purchase is the most straightforward way to accomplish the transaction, although in certain cases it may also be possible for the target corporation to rid itself of the unwanted business or assets prior to a share acquisition. However, both the legal and the tax aspects of a demerger (or corporate split) are complicated in the United States.

Another benefit of an asset acquisition is that not all liabilities need be acquired. However, certain liabilities may pass to the acquirer in any case. For example, certain state property taxes will constitute a lien on the assets acquired. Environmental liabilities may become the responsibility of any subsequent owner. Substantial pension liabilities may pass to the purchaser under some circumstances. A few states will impose responsibility on the acquiring corporation for product liability claims, even for products sold prior to the acquisition. In the United States, the seller will usually indemnify the buyer against any such liabilities in the acquisition agreement, which may be sufficient protection if the seller is financially sound.

In a few states, assets may also remain subject to attachment by creditors of the seller for a period of time after the transaction is closed unless certain bulk sales procedures, including notices to all creditors of the seller, are followed. These procedures are quite inconvenient and are often ignored when the seller is a substantial corporation, in which case the buyer will rely on the seller's indemnification against any claims of creditors. A number of states have abolished such bulk sales laws. If the selling corporation is insolvent, great care must be taken to avoid any charge of fraudulent conveyance (a disposition of assets while a company is insolvent or one that causes it to become so, or for inadequate consideration), which can be actionable by a company's creditors.

### Disadvantages

An asset acquisition is more complex than a share acquisition because all assets must be transferred. Consents to the transfer of certain valuable assets, such as licenses, permits, or contracts, may not be obtainable or may be obtainable only at a significant price. However, it is not usually difficult to obtain consents from public or private parties merely because the ultimate buyer is a non–U.S. person. Favorable tax attributes of the target corporation will normally be lost.

## Mergers

All state laws provide for the merger of corporations, and most states now provide for the merger of limited liability companies and other entities (including a merger of different forms of entity). In a merger, two entities are joined by operation of law; that is, all assets and liabilities become the property of the surviving entity (or a new entity) solely by filing a certificate of merger. Normally, one entity disappears and the other continues as the successor to both lines of business. To be effective, a merger requires the consent of the board of directors and the shareholders (in a corporation) or the members (in a limited liability company) and a public filing with the state. Any form of consideration may be used in a merger. Thus, equity interests in the target may be converted to cash, to equity interests in the acquiring entity, or to equity interests in any other entity. The target entity may also be the survivor, often termed a reverse merger, with its shares or interests converted to the right to get cash or other property.

### Advantages

The principal advantage of a merger is that the transfer of assets and the exchange of target corporation shares are automatic. Shareholders of the target corporation have no option to retain their shares (although dissenting shareholders may have the right to obtain an appraisal of their shares and to recover the appraised value in lieu of the amount offered to them in the merger). No separate transfer documents are required. Transfer taxes normally do not apply in a merger.

Valuable permits, contracts, and the like may also be easier to transfer in a merger than in an asset sale, but these do not remain in the same corporate entity unless the merger is accomplished by merging the buyer's subsidiary into the target corporation. Such a reverse merger is possible in the United States, leaving the target as the surviving corporation. In this case, it is still possible to eliminate the target's shareholders by automatically converting their shares to cash or to shares in the buyer or any other corporation, as discussed earlier.

### *Disadvantages*

A merger with a publicly held corporation may be time-consuming because of the need to hold a meeting of the shareholders and to comply with U.S. proxy rules. If the publicly held target is attractive to other potential bidders, the delay in effecting a merger may allow these other bidders to compete for the target, increasing the price of the shares and, possibly, frustrating the acquisition. Non–U.S. clients are often reluctant to battle, or even compete, with other bidders. In such cases, a friendly tender offer for sufficient shares to approve a merger may be effective. This may be completed quickly. If the tender is successful, timing will no longer be important, and any remaining shareholders can be eliminated through a "cash out" merger of the acquisition vehicle with the target.

## Financing an Acquisition

It is increasingly common to finance an acquisition with the target's assets or future profits. This is called a leveraged buyout (LBO). The assets of the target company may be pledged to a bank or other financial institution, or the buyer may issue high-interest, subordinated debt instruments, normally referred to as *junk bonds*. Such bonds constitute securities and must be registered with the SEC unless an exemption from registration is available. Unlike the case under many European corporate laws, the use of the target's assets is not illegal or even disreputable in the United States. Nonetheless, non–U.S. buyers rarely use local U.S. debt financing (leveraged or otherwise) for an acquisition, although this is affected by interest rates in the United States.

Non–U.S. buyers are more likely to use shareholder loans to finance an acquisition, especially if they have borrowed in their own countries, which is another form of leveraged buyout because it is the target that will effectively repay the borrowing. Because dividends are not deductible by the U.S. corporation payer, it is generally advantageous to treat payments to non–U.S. shareholders as interest. However, such loans must bear a U.S. market interest rate, must be treated as loans, and must not constitute too great a portion of the company's financing versus its share capital. Interest payments (and dividends) to non–U.S. residents may be subject to U.S. withholding tax.

## DOCUMENTATION

### Letter of Intent

The letter of intent sets out the principal points on which the parties have agreed. It is useful in identifying important issues between the parties. Its disadvantages are that it may delay the preparation and the signing of a definitive contract or, in the case of public companies, may prematurely trigger the need for disclosure.

Except for certain matters, such as confidentiality, standstill, and the like, a letter of intent is typically made not legally binding between the parties. However, in the United States, the parties are considered to be morally bound, and a U.S. party will be most reluctant to make important changes in the terms set out in the letter of intent absent a significant change in the target or in the circumstances of the transaction. A letter of intent may also create legal liabilities if one of the parties fails to negotiate the definitive agreement in good faith. Thus, it is important that all matters of importance to the non–U.S. buyer, especially the material terms and the structure of the transaction, be considered and reviewed with legal counsel before a letter of intent is signed.

## Acquisition Agreement

With or without a letter of intent, the parties and their attorneys must prepare and negotiate a definitive acquisition agreement. It should set out all of the rights and obligations of the parties, both before and after the closing. A non–U.S. buyer should expect a complete explanation of all aspects of the agreement because that is the key element in the transaction. A non–U.S. buyer should never fear to appear unsophisticated and should take nothing for granted. Many non–U.S. buyers make unwarranted assumptions based on business and legal practices in their own countries. Good lawyers always try to explain all elements of the acquisition agreement and related agreements in terms that take into account the buyer's own experience and to draft documents that are easier for the client to understand, avoiding unnecessary "lawyer's" terminology. Nonetheless, questions from clients are always appropriate and welcome.

Acquisition agreements in the United States tend to be fairly long. The principal features of a U.S. acquisition agreement are described in the following paragraphs.

### Subject of Acquisition

The property to be acquired by the buyer, whether assets, shares, or a combination of both, should be specified. Any assets or businesses to be excluded must also be identified. If a merger is contemplated, this will be described.

### Price

The price paid for a U.S. enterprise may be fixed, subject to adjustment, or contingent. The cash price in a share acquisition or a merger may be fixed, although the seller may represent that the target's net worth, or other financial statement item, will be a certain minimum, with postclosing downward (or sometimes upward) adjustments to the price for amounts above or below such a figure. In such case, net worth or other financial measuring rods would be determined by a postclosing audit. Such audits, often by an independent accounting firm, are quite customary in the United States and would only rarely be resisted by a U.S. seller. An audit affords the non–U.S. buyer substantial protection, but an audit should only supplement the buyer's own preclosing due diligence investigation.

In an asset transaction, the seller's cash is normally excluded. The price paid for property, plant and equipment, and non–balance sheet intangibles, such as intellectual property, will be fixed; but the price for current assets, particularly inventory and receivables, will depend on the level of such assets as of the closing. These and any other items subject to adjustment will be determined by an audit conducted immediately after the closing.

If a target's earnings history is short or subject to question, the parties may make part of the purchase price contingent on future earnings performance. Such an "earnout" arrangement (see Chapter 12, Pricing and Negotiations) is fraught with difficulty because the buyer will wish to operate the purchased business freely, but the seller will have a continuing interest in it and so wish to impose significant limitations on the buyer.

### Allocation of Price

In an asset transaction it is advantageous to allocate the purchase price to specific assets so as to avoid the parties' taking inconsistent positions. The parties will normally agree to use these allocations for all tax purposes. The parties are not completely free to make any allocation they wish, for allocations are subject to challenge by tax authorities, who have an interest in allocating as much of the purchase price as possible to nondepreciable items, or items depreciable only over long periods, such as goodwill.

### Payment

An acquisition agreement normally calls for payment by wire transfer at the closing, although bank (cashier's) checks are sometimes used. The mechanics of payment are discussed in the section Closing at the end of this chapter.

A portion of the price may be paid on a deferred basis through the issuance of a promissory note. This will permit the purchase to be more easily financed out of the assets and future profits of the acquired business. It may also provide a means for satisfying any claims that the buyer may have after the closing. Therefore, a non–U.S. buyer should always consider this possibility, even though it may not be customary in the buyer's own country.

### Assumption of Liabilities

In a sense, all liabilities are assumed in a share transaction or a merger because after the closing the buyer will own the debtor corporation or a successor in interest to it. Normally, only the target's assets are exposed to such liabilities, although this may be of little solace to the buyer if undisclosed liabilities appear after the closing. As noted earlier, this risk is somewhat mitigated by the seller's indemnity against any undisclosed liabilities that one customarily finds in U.S. acquisition agreements.

In an asset acquisition, the liabilities to be assumed and those to be excluded should be described in considerable detail. The buyer will have to assume the obligations under all contracts assigned to it. The buyer should also consider assuming trade payables because it is the buyer who will have the greatest interest in seeing that suppliers of goods and services are paid. The amount of the liabilities assumed should be considered a part of the overall purchase price. Generally, liabilities not specifically assumed by the buyer are retained by the seller.

### Representations and Warranties

Representations and warranties are usually quite extensive and cover the areas of greatest concern to the parties. These areas are discussed in the next section, Principal Legal Concerns of the Buyer. Acquisitions in the United States are made on the basis of full disclosure of all aspects of the purchased business. Representations and warranties are designed to provide disclosure of information about the target enterprise but they, along with the indemnification provisions, also allocate the risks of the business between the parties and can form the basis of claims after the closing.

### Covenants

Any matters to be carried out between the signing of the contract and the closing (or beyond it) will be set forth as the specific covenants of one party or the other. The most significant such covenant is the one that requires the seller to conduct the business in the ordinary course between contract and closing. It will typically prohibit the seller from engaging in any major transactions without the advance approval of the buyer.

### Conditions

The preconditions to closing the transaction will be set forth in the acquisition agreement. Typically such conditions are the continued accuracy of the seller's representations and warranties, the performance of the seller's covenants, the rendering of legal opinions, the execution of ancillary agreements, the absence of any material adverse change in the seller's business, and the obtaining of any key consents or approvals to the transaction.

### Closing

The transfer documents to be executed and delivered at the closing, as well as the method of payment of the purchase price, should be specified. The mechanics of closing a U.S. acquisition are described in the section at the end of this chapter.

### Indemnification

An indemnity is a form of guaranty under which one party undertakes to reimburse another party for a specified loss or liability the other party may suffer. Insurance is a common example of indemnification. Indemnity provisions are commonly used in the United States to allocate risks of a target business between seller and buyer.

If a public company is acquired, in most cases, it is impractical to obtain any continuing indemnity from the public shareholders after the closing; and the target's management and controlling shareholders, if any, will generally refuse to accept the responsibility alone. In this situation, the representations and warranties will expire at the closing, and there will be no ongoing indemnity obligation. The burden is on the buyer to verify all facts about the target prior to the closing. The buyer will be aided in this by the fact that the target has been subject to the public disclosure obligations of U.S. securities law.

If the target is privately owned, the acquisition agreement will require the seller to indemnify the buyer for any misrepresentations or breaches of warranties or covenants. The buyer will be subject to a similar obligation in favor of the seller. The indemnification provisions will allocate responsibility for the conduct of the business both before and after the closing. An indemnification provision will also specify the period following the closing during which one party will be responsible to the other party. The seller has a natural desire to end its indemnification obligations as soon as possible. "Survival" periods are typically between one and three years, but one full year of operation plus a complete audit are essential (and usually sufficient) to identify possible indemnification claims. Environmental indemnification obligations and claims with respect to title to the shares or membership interests or, perhaps, assets are often unlimited in time. Indemnification provisions may specify that claims may be made only after all claims reach a certain minimum level. Once this level is reached, the agreement may permit a party to assert all claims or only those in excess of the minimum. It is increasingly common for an agreement to provide a maximum claim that may be asserted, usually somewhere between 50 percent and 100 percent of the purchase price.

## Other Agreements

The acquisition agreement may provide for a variety of ancillary agreements to be signed at the closing. These may include a noncompetition agreement, employment agreements with one or more of the sellers or key employees of the target, and ongoing leases and licenses. These are discussed in the section Closing.

## PRINCIPAL LEGAL CONCERNS OF THE BUYER

The representations and warranties in the acquisition agreement focus on the matters of greatest legal and business concern to the buyer. As noted previously, representations and warranties are designed to elicit information about the target company. Thus, they play a vital role in the buyer's investigation of the target. The disclosures made in the acquisition agreement will be based in part on the due diligence investigation performed by counsel and others for the seller and will be further verified by the investigation of the buyer and its counsel. This investigation may be more far-reaching than would be encountered in the non–U.S.

buyer's home country. The expense involved should be weighed against the added protection afforded the buyer.

## Corporate Authority and Organization

The seller will represent that the selling entity is properly organized and that the individuals acting on its behalf are duly authorized to do so. There is no commercial register or the equivalent in the United States. Therefore, the buyer and its counsel will independently verify the seller's authority through examination of the target's books and records, as well as through public filings of publicly held targets. A share acquisition agreement will contain a representation that the target corporation is properly organized. In addition, the buyer will rely on the opinion of the seller's legal counsel concerning the seller's organization and authorization. Typically, buyer's counsel will independently verify the validity of the original organization of the target corporation only in a share acquisition. In other cases, the buyer will rely on the seller's representations and the opinion of seller's counsel.

## Financial Statements

The acquisition agreement will state that the financial statements that have been presented to the buyer (which may or may not be attached to the agreement) have been prepared in accordance with generally accepted accounting principles (GAAP) on a basis consistent with prior periods and "fairly present" the financial condition of the target. Financial representations will be included even if all financial statements have been audited by a reputable accounting firm. Usually, they will contain specific representations as to certain assets, such as inventory and accounts receivable.

## Compliance with Law

### Environmental Compliance
In the United States, the buyer will inherit legal responsibility for any environmental problems existing on any property purchased, whether the transaction is in the form of an asset acquisition, a share acquisition, or a merger. Environmental liabilities represent one of the most significant traps for the unwary buyer. Therefore, the buyer will want full disclosure of any such problems. These will include any failure by the business to comply with environmental laws or with any environmental permits for day-to-day operations. Of equal concern are any hazardous waste materials that may be stored or buried on any real property. The

removal of such waste can be incredibly expensive. In many industries, it may be appropriate to have a so-called Phase 1 environmental audit of the premises and a Phase 2 or Phase 3 audit that includes soil borings and air and water tests to ascertain the presence and extent of any problems. (However, Phase 2 and 3 environmental audits trigger disclosure obligations.) The buyer will want to confirm that any waste materials that have been carried off the premises have been handled and disposed of in accordance with applicable legal requirements. A purchaser may become liable for the improper off-site disposal of waste material by a predecessor or even by an unrelated third party, such as a waste disposal service retained by a previous owner of the business. Environmental permits or licenses will have to be transferred or new ones obtained in the case of an asset acquisition. It will be necessary to consult with environmental authorities to be certain that the permits will be respected on the change of ownership in a share acquisition. In certain states, such as New Jersey and Connecticut, the advance approval of state authorities may be required in order to complete the acquisition. Because environmental liabilities are so extensive in scope, the seller's environmental indemnities are usually unlimited in amount and time.

## Other Licenses and Permits

Although the regulation of businesses is relatively limited in the United States, most businesses operate with a variety of governmental licenses and permits, some of which are primarily designed to raise money for local governmental authorities. These include general business licenses, building permits and certificates of occupancy relating to structures, boiler permits and other permits to operate certain forms of machinery and equipment, and vehicle licenses and registrations. In addition, specific governmental licenses and franchises may be necessary for certain kinds of businesses. It may be possible to transfer these licenses and permits to the buyer in an asset acquisition. More often, however, new licenses and permits must be obtained. Arrangements for the transfer or the obtaining of such licenses must be made so that they are in place at the closing if the business is to continue without interruption. Even vehicle licenses may present problems because their transfer may take some time.

Government licenses and permits are generally not assignable, even though material to the business. They may terminate in the event of a material change in control of the target, although such termination is more often imposed by practice on the local level than by statute. In any case, the buyer will want to be certain it can obtain its own licenses and permits prior to the closing. The agreement will generally call for disclosure of the licenses and permits used by the business and will have a representation as to assignability.

## Compliance with Other Laws

The buyer will wish to confirm that the business operates in compliance with zoning laws and other local laws regulating the use of real estate. Zoning law compliance is not always covered by title insurance. The buyer will be concerned about compliance with federal occupational safety and health laws. It is unlikely that the seller will be able to give absolute assurance of such compliance, but the buyer will want to know that the seller is at least not aware of and has not received notice of any violations. The buyer may also want some assurance that the seller is not aware that it has violated any laws relating to equal employment opportunity, hiring, or other laws affecting employment and employment practices.

These compliance matters may be the subject of specific provisions in the indemnification section of the agreement. Even if it is not possible for the seller to give absolute assurance of compliance in certain areas, the seller can expressly retain responsibility for noncompliance. This allocation of risk and responsibility is one of the major negotiating points in any U.S. acquisition.

## Employees

### Employment Protection

Unlike many non–U.S. jurisdictions, there are no U.S. statutes requiring that employees be retained or given specific severance pay on termination of employment in an acquisition, although, as described later, federal and some state laws require advance notice if an entire plant is to be closed. Employees have no right to review, to approve, or even to be consulted about an acquisition of their employer. Employees do not automatically become the employees of the acquiring corporation in an asset purchase, although they will in a share acquisition or a merger. However, a non–U.S. buyer should not assume that it has an entirely free hand in dealing with employees. Most U.S. employers have adopted employment policies that may legally bind successors. These will often provide for some form of termination compensation unless the employees are offered employment with substantially the same salary and, perhaps, the same benefits by the acquiring corporation. For this and other reasons, the seller will often insist that the buyer agree to employ its existing workforce and may want to specify the terms and conditions of that employment. As with other economic issues, these matters will be negotiated between the buyer and the seller. Related matters, such as accrued vacation pay, will have to be dealt with because the employees will expect to retain these accrued benefits after the closing. A non–U.S. buyer especially will not want to appear to be insensitive to employee expectations.

### Labor Agreements

In a stock purchase or a merger, the buyer is bound by any collective bargaining (i.e., labor) agreement to which the target corporation is a party. A purchaser will be bound in an asset acquisition only if it expressly assumes the collective bargaining agreement. A collective bargaining agreement will bind only one company and its employees, not an entire industry. A buyer will usually want to take advantage of the anxiety of the target's workforce to renegotiate the terms of employment. Consequently, it will generally resist assuming any collective bargaining agreements. The buyer will, however, be required to recognize any existing labor union and to bargain with it in good faith. Many non–U.S. buyers will find U.S. labor unions easier to deal with than their non–U.S. counterparts.

## Termination Notice

The federal government and some state governments, as well as many collective bargaining agreements, require advance notice when industrial plants are closed. Depending on the degree of continuity in an acquisition, such statutes or contract provisions may apply to the buyer. Federal law also requires that a terminated employee be allowed to continue any employer-sponsored health program for a period of time but at the cost of the employee.

## Pensions and Other Benefits

If the target has maintained any employee benefit programs, including pension plans, responsibility for continued adequate funding of these obligations may pass to the buyer, even in an asset acquisition. Such plans are subject to extensive federal regulation. A buyer of a business may incur significant obligations created prior to the acquisition, including making up any underfunding of the pension plan. In an asset acquisition, the seller would generally want the buyer to continue its existing pension plans because termination of a plan can be expensive and time-consuming. Termination is avoidable only if the buyer is willing to have a plan that is more or less comparable, although not necessarily identical, to the seller's existing plan. In any acquisition, experts (lawyers and actuaries) hired by the buyer should examine in detail the target corporation's pension plan to avoid having the buyer incur substantial unexpected liabilities.

## Material Assets

### Physical Facilities

The buyer will want to obtain clear title to any plants or other real estate owned by the target because these are material to the operation of the business. Title to real estate is transferred by a deed, which is publicly recorded. (Title certificates are also used in certain locations.) There is no notary of the kind found in many civil law countries. In most U.S. states, title to real property is investigated and insured by title insurance companies. The title company will insure clear title, subject to certain specified exceptions, such as identified mortgages, easements, and servitudes. If significant real estate is owned by the target, title insurance should be obtained even if shares are being acquired and no real property is actually being transferred. The buyer should obtain a survey of the property that indicates the location of all buildings, easements, servitudes (such as utility lines), and other matters affecting the physical layout of the property and that discloses any difficulty with access to the property. As noted earlier, the buyer may also wish to obtain an environmental audit. The buyer will want to ensure that the property is being used legally and in compliance with all building codes and zoning ordinances; these will be covered by title insurance only if specifically requested and paid for. In an asset acquisition, the transfer of real estate will require the payment of state and local transfer taxes; but with certain exceptions, these tend to be far lower in the United States than in most other countries.

### Intellectual Property

In many businesses, intellectual property constitutes a substantial component of value. The buyer will want to conduct a thorough investigation of title to all intellectual property, including trademarks and patents, and ensure that title to such property can be effectively transferred to it in the case of an asset acquisition. A non–U.S. buyer may be particularly interested in the extent of foreign protection of the acquired intellectual property. The buyer will also want to be assured that all necessary consents to the assignment of any intellectual property licenses have been obtained. This may be necessary even in the case of certain stock acquisitions if the license is terminable upon a material change in control of the target enterprise.

A major issue often encountered with non–U.S. buyers is the seller's unwillingness to warrant that its patents are valid because such a warranty goes far beyond a mere representation of good title. A significant number of challenged patents are ruled invalid in the United States, and so a warranty of validity will generally be resisted by U.S. sellers.

### Agreements and Licenses

Agreements and licenses that are material to the success of a business may be jeopardized by an acquisition. (For example, following the foreign acquisition of Firestone, General Motors announced that it would no longer purchase tires from Firestone as original equipment on its automobiles.) An acquisition agreement will require disclosure of any contract above a certain size or extending beyond a certain duration to alert the buyer to the commitments to which the business is subject and to advise the buyer of the consents that must be obtained to assume such agreements or leases. The other party to such contracts or leases may be reluctant to consent to assignment without compensation if, for example, the rent or other compensation is below market. Thus, the acquisition agreement may contain additional representations regarding assignability and a lack of knowledge by the seller that any material business will be lost solely as a result of the acquisition.

## Liabilities

### Product Liability

A principal concern of any buyer of a U.S. business is strict liability for personal injuries resulting from products manufactured and sold by the business. As in most other countries, the manufacturer or seller of a product in the United States is liable for damages sustained as a result of the manufacturer's or seller's negligence. However, under the U.S. doctrine of strict liability, one who sells a product is liable for any physical harm caused to the ultimate user or consumer or to its property if the product at the time of sale is in a defective condition (such that it is unreasonably dangerous to the user); if the seller is engaged in the business of selling the product; and if the product may be expected to and does reach the user without substantial change. Combined with the propensity of U.S. juries to award substantial damages, the doctrine of strict liability makes product claims a material cost of doing business in the United States. Any buyer will want to obtain some assurances from the seller that such exposure will not be unreasonable in amount. The buyer will want to investigate the historical experience of the seller to ascertain whether the business itself involves undue risks.

In a stock purchase or a merger (or in an asset acquisition in a few states), the buyer will be concerned about assuming responsibility for products sold prior to the closing. Although the seller may represent that it knows of no such liabilities, there is no way the seller can give complete assurance in this regard. Therefore, the parties will want to allocate responsibility as part of the indemnification provisions. Typically, sellers remain responsible for any products sold or shipped prior to the closing, and buyers are responsible for products sold or shipped after the closing. Indemnification for product liability will often be either unlimited in time or limited to the applicable state statute of limitations. This latter limitation is not very meaningful because it generally begins to run only at the time the person is injured, which may be long after the product is sold or shipped.

### Tax Liabilities

In an asset acquisition, the buyer will almost never become directly liable for taxes based on the operation of the business prior to the closing. However, certain ad valorem taxes (those based on the value of property) may constitute a lien on the assets purchased. In this case, and in the case of a stock acquisition, it is normal for the seller to accept complete responsibility for tax liabilities attributable to the operation of the business prior to the closing and to indemnify the buyer against any such liabilities. Such indemnification generally runs for the period of the statute of limitations.

### Other Liabilities

In the United States, the seller will often represent that there are no undisclosed liabilities of the business, contingent or otherwise. If the target nonetheless has any undisclosed liabilities, they will usually be the responsibility of the seller pursuant to an indemnification. In an asset acquisition, the buyer will expressly not assume any liabilities other than those specifically identified in the agreement.

## No Material Change

The seller will generally represent that there has been no material adverse change in the operations or the financial condition of the business since the date of the most recent financial statements or some other cutoff date. In addition, lack of any material adverse change will often be a condition of closing. A typical provision in an acquisition agreement will limit the seller's right to conduct the business between contract signing and closing other than in accordance with past practice and in the ordinary course of business and will prohibit the seller from making any material change in the business, from making any major purchases or investments, from incurring any significant obligations or liabilities, or from changing compensation or other employee benefits without the consent of the buyer.

## OTHER LEGAL MATTERS

There are a number of other legal matters that may be of concern in an acquisition.

## Distributors and Agents

Acquisition agreements typically require disclosure of all material distribution and sales representative agreements and arrangements. Unlike the practice in many other countries, in most states the buyer is free to terminate distributors and sales representatives without being liable for mandatory termination compensation payments. Few states have statutes requiring such compensation. However, there is a general trend in the United States against arbitrary or abusive terminations. Thus, a buyer should be careful to document that any such terminations are made pursuant to a reorganization of the acquired business's distribution arrangements. The buyer should also be sure that such terminations are not motivated by matters constituting antitrust violations. For example, it would be illegal to terminate a price-cutting distributor in an attempt to control pricing.

## Immigration

A non–U.S. acquirer will often contemplate sending its own executives and skilled technical experts to assist with the operation of the acquired business after the closing. These individuals may easily visit the United States on temporary business visas (a B-1 visa) for short periods of time. In the case of a transferring executive, appropriate visas are available, but obtaining them may be somewhat time-consuming. Any important personnel transfers should be planned with the help of experts well in advance of the closing.

## Importation of Parts and Components

All matters pertaining to the importation of merchandise into the United States fall within the exclusive jurisdiction of the federal government. Many products imported into the United States are subject to the payment of import duties, generally payable on an ad valorem basis and determined by their specific classification. The customs authorities have the right to challenge any claimed valuation, particularly where the transaction is between a non–U.S. parent and a U.S. subsidiary. If a non–U.S. buyer plans to use an acquired corporation, for example, to assemble parts and components imported from abroad, it will want to ascertain early on that it will be able to import the parts and components without being subject to quotas (which is almost certainly the case) and to obtain some guidance as to the import duty cost of such importation.

There are a number of special forms of customs entry, such as foreign trade zones, that may be of particular interest to a non–U.S. buyer. Products of non–U.S. origin may be shipped to a foreign trade zone located in the United States without making a formal customs entry or paying any U.S. customs duties. Such products may be stored, sold for export, or assembled while located within the zone and then reexported, all without incurring any U.S. customs duty.

A non–U.S. buyer may encounter certain restrictions on imports into the United States, particularly antidumping and countervailing duties. These are imposed when products are imported at what the U.S. Customs Service considers an unjustifiably low price. In some cases, quotas may be imposed on certain products. If the acquired business will be dependent on imported materials or components, the non–U.S. buyer should review its plans and anticipated pricing with customs counsel prior to proceeding with an acquisition.

## ORGANIZING THE ACQUISITION VEHICLE

Whatever the form of the acquisition, it is likely that the buyer will want to organize a U.S. limited liability company or a corporation to act as the acquisition vehicle. (Some investors may prefer a form of partnership because of the tax or other advantages available in their own country.) The acquisition vehicle will be organized before the closing and probably prior to signing the acquisition agreement. Alternatively, the acquisition agreement may be signed by the buyer and assigned to the acquisition vehicle prior to the closing. Organizing a U.S. limited liability company or a corporation involves a number of steps.

## Initial Decisions

The principal matters to be determined by a non–U.S. buyer in order to organize a U.S. liability company or a corporation and prepare it to operate are the name of the entity; the state of organization; its principal place of business; its initial capital; the identity of the members or shareholders; the number, the names, and the addresses of directors and officers (which may be omitted in the case of a limited liability company managed by one or more "managers"); whether the entity will operate after the closing; its fiscal year; and any banking relationship. With certain exceptions, a limited liability company or a corporation may choose any name, so long as it is not confusingly similar to that of another limited liability company or corporation. The state of organization will usually be the same as the principal place of business, although as noted earlier, Delaware is a popular choice for state of organization.

## Public Filings

A U.S. corporation is formed by filing a certificate or articles of incorporation (the terminology depends on the state of incorporation—both terms are substantially equivalent) containing information required by state corporate law. Typically, this contains only the name of the entity, its principal place of business in the state, and its authorized and issued capital shares (discussed in the later section Corporate Structure and Management). In the case of a limited liability company, a certificate of formation or articles of organization containing similar information, will be filed in the state of organization. The articles may include the names of the initial directors or the manager and other matters of concern to the shareholders or members. The articles or certificate will be signed by one or more incorporators, who need not be shareholders or members. This is particularly convenient for a non–U.S. investor because this document often must be notarized, something that can be difficult if it has to be done outside the United States.

## Organizational Meetings

In the case of a corporation, unless the directors are appointed in the certificate or articles, the incorporator or shareholders will hold an initial meeting to elect the directors. The directors will then hold a meeting to elect the officers, to accept share subscriptions, to authorize their issuance, to select a fiscal year, and, normally, to authorize the opening of a corporate bank account. At the initial or a subsequent meeting, the directors will also approve the acquisition of the target and the execution of the acquisition agreement and related documents. A written signed "consent" resolution may substitute for any of these meetings.

If the buyer entity is a limited liability company, the members will normally enter into an "operating agreement" to govern the operation of the limited liability company. This will cover many of the matters covered in the bylaws of a corporation and many of the matters that would take place at an organizational meeting, such as the appointment of the managers and the approval of the proposed acquisition transaction. Even if there is only one member, this document will still be referred to as an "agreement" but will be legally effective even though there is only one party to it.

## Capital and Financing

U.S. corporations may issue common and preferred shares. Common shares fully participate in the economic life of the corporation. Preferred shares typically carry preferences for dividends or distribution of assets on dissolution. Shares may be voting or nonvoting but may not be in bearer form. Shares may be issued for cash, for personal or real property, or for services already performed or to be performed. No public appraisal or court approval is required to value contributed property. To provide flexibility, it is normal to authorize more shares than will initially be issued. No fixed percentage of the authorized shares must be subscribed or paid for.

The interests of the members in a limited liability company may be represented by certificates; or, more commonly, those interests may merely be reflected in the operating agreement or perhaps in a membership register maintained by the company (the latter is not mandatory). As with shares, membership interests may be issued for cash, for personal or real property, or for past or, in many states, future services. In Delaware, interests may also be issued for no consideration. Members and membership interests may be given differing rights to participate in profits, distributions, and equity of the company, and these need not correspond to voting power. Interests may be made nonvoting.

## Corporate Structure and Management

A corporation consists of three principal organs: the shareholders, the board of directors, and the officers.

### Shareholders

As noted earlier, a U.S. corporation may have a single shareholder. Shareholders elect directors and approve extraordinary acts and transactions, such as a merger, the sale of substantially all assets, or the dissolution of the corporation. They may approve amendments to the articles of incorporation or the bylaws. Shareholders normally do *not* declare or approve dividends or approve the company's financial statements.

### Board of Directors

A U.S. corporation is managed by its board of directors, although they may delegate substantial authority to its officers. Directors declare dividends and recommend such actions as a merger or a dissolution to the shareholders. The corporation may have a single director, although a larger number is more common. Directors need not be shareholders, and so qualifying shares are never needed. Generally, directors need not be U.S. citizens or residents of a particular state. An exception exists for companies in the regulated industries noted earlier.

Directors of U.S. companies act as a body and do not represent the corporation individually. There is no managing director of a U.S. corporation. Directors may not meet through proxies, but they may meet through a conference telephone call and may act through written consent resolutions signed by all of the directors. Corporations may not act as directors.

New statutes governing closely held companies permit the shareholders to manage the corporation and to dispense with the board of directors, but these are not often used by non–U.S. investors.

### *Officers*

Typically, the officers consist of a president, one or more vice presidents, a secretary, and a treasurer. The officers are elected by the board of directors and may be removed at any time. The president is normally the chief operating officer (COO) of the corporation. A vice president will act in the absence of the president. The secretary may be called on to confirm the authority of the president or another officer to act for the corporation. The treasurer supervises the financial affairs of the corporation. A corporation may also have a chairman of the board of directors, who may or may not be an officer of the corporation.

## Management of a Limited Liability Company

A limited liability company must have members, but its management structure may be determined in whatever manner the members desire. The members may manage the company directly, or they may provide for the election of a manager or a board of managers to conduct the affairs of the company. They may choose a corporation-type management structure, with both a board of directors and officers.

The members hold the ultimate authority in the company and have to approve any extraordinary action, such as a merger or a sale of substantially all assets. They may act through meetings, written consents, or conference telephone calls, and they may delegate as much power as they wish to the manager or the board of managers. The managers may also represent the company in dealings with third parties.

## CLOSING

The closing of a U.S. acquisition will be organized primarily by legal counsel for the buyer and the seller. A closing will typically involve the following matters.

## Transfer Documents

The transfer documents to be executed and delivered at the closing will depend on the nature of the transaction. In a stock purchase, the seller will deliver certificates representing all of the shares in the target corporation accompanied by an executed "stock power" (or power of attorney) authorizing the transfer of the shares on the books of the target. Membership interests not represented by certificates will be transferred by a form of assignment.

In a merger, the parties will execute a formal plan of merger (in most states) for filing with the secretaries of state of the jurisdictions in which the respective corporations are organized. This document may be considerably shorter than the definitive merger agreement. It may have to be notarized. These formalities will be accomplished immediately prior to the closing, and the plan of merger may be sent ahead to the appropriate state capital(s) to be ready for filing on the day of the closing.

An asset acquisition is more complicated. Real estate will be transferred by deeds for each parcel. Deeds typically will have to be notarized and recorded in the locality in which the real estate is located. Recording will be completed on the date of the closing or shortly thereafter. At the closing, the title insurance company will execute and deliver a binder insuring title to the real estate. Personal property will be transferred by bill of sale, which requires no formalities. Agreements and other intangibles will be transferred by a form of assignment, which may be combined with the bill of sale. Separate assignment documents may be required for patents and certain other assets, some of which are subject to formal requirements.

## Payment

In an international acquisition, payment is more often effected by wire transfer than by cashier's check. The disadvantage of a cashier's check is that it will have to be deposited for collection, and so funds may not be available to the seller on the day of closing. This can cause the loss of a substantial amount of interest. Wire transfers make funds immediately available once the transfer is acknowledged by the seller's bank, but delays sometimes occur. International wire transfers are more likely to be delayed on a Monday or a Friday because of the large volume of other transfers and transactions on those days. Therefore, whenever possible, it is preferable to close in the middle of the week. If the closing must be held at the beginning or end of the week or if timing is crucial, payment may be made by a federal funds cashier's check, which is somewhat inconvenient for the buyer to obtain but which provides immediately available funds to the seller.

## Other Agreements

A number of ancillary agreements may be executed at the closing. These are likely to include the following.

### Noncompetition Agreements

There are business and tax reasons why the buyer would want the seller and key seller personnel to agree not to compete with the target business for some period of time after the closing. Such agreements are generally enforceable if they are reasonable and designed to preserve the benefit of the acquisition to the buyer.

### Employment Agreements

It is not unusual for the seller of a privately held business, and possibly family members, to have been employed by the corporation prior to the acquisition. A significant consideration in agreeing to sell the business may be some assurance of continuity of employment. In acquisitions of professionally managed entities, the buyer will want to ensure that certain key individuals will be available to operate the target business after the closing. This is most often true of top executives and important technical personnel. In these cases, either the buyer or the seller may require that employment agreements be executed with such key persons at or prior to the closing.

### Leases and Licenses

It may not be possible to transfer to the buyer all of the tangible and intangible property necessary to operate the business. For example, the seller may continue to use key software or technology in its retained businesses. In such cases, tangible property may have to be leased and intangible property licensed to the business.

### Service Agreements

If the buyer is purchasing a portion of an integrated business, the buyer may not receive a fully stand-alone operation. In this case, the seller may have to provide postclosing services to the buyer on a short-term or occasionally long-term basis. Computer access is a common example of such a postclosing service provided by the seller.

## Other Documents

Other documents may also be delivered at the closing. These include legal opinions from counsel for both parties. It is normal to deliver a certified copy of the certificate or articles of incorporation of the target company to the buyer as well as a certificate issued by the appropriate secretary of state indicating that the target company is in "good standing" in its state of incorporation. It is also customary for the target (and for the buyer) to deliver a certificate affirming that all representations and warranties in the acquisition agreement are true and correct as of the day of closing. The officers and directors of the target in a stock acquisition will deliver written resignations. This is not necessary in an asset acquisition because employees are not automatically transferred with the business.

## Consulting an Attorney

The point at which a non–U.S. buyer should consult a U.S. attorney will also vary. If there is any significant question about the legal permissibility of the acquisition, an attorney will become involved after the buyer has conducted an initial investigation into the business and financial aspects of the target and has determined that the acquisition is desirable from a business point of view. A non–U.S. buyer should bear in mind that such a purchase is a significant transaction in an unfamiliar environment, one in which acquisitions are quite complicated and where the pitfalls are many. A U.S. attorney should be consulted before any document is signed, including the letter of intent, and prior to deciding on the form and the structure of the transaction.

## U.S. ACQUISITION LEGAL CHECKLIST

The following checklist represents matters typically addressed by attorneys in the course of an acquisition. The approach to a given acquisition will vary with circumstances, but the matters covered are set out in more or less chronological order.

# Checklist: U.S. Acquisitions

I. Initial due diligence.
    A. Preliminary investigation of business.
        1. Financial statements.
        2. Business operations.
    B. Confidentiality agreement.
        1. Access to information about target.
        2. Confidential treatment of target information.

II. Regulatory considerations.
    A. Foreign investment approvals.
        1. CFIUS investigation, national security.
            a. Notice requirements.
            b. Investigations and time limits.
        2. Government restrictions on non–U.S. ownership.
            a. Defense, federal.
            b. Banking and other financial institutions, state and federal.
            c. Insurance, state.
            d. Air and maritime transport, federal.
            e. Ownership of ships and aircraft, federal.
            f. Communications and power, federal.
            g. Railroads, state.
            h. Towing, salvage, and dredging, federal.
            i. Fishing, federal.
            j. Natural resources, federal.
            k. Agriculture, state.
            l. Other real estate, state.
    B. Other limitations and notices.
        1. Hart-Scott-Rodino premerger notice.
        2. Takeover and public tender legislation.
            a. Federal, Williams Act.
            b. State legislation.
         3. Other securities law considerations.
            a. Proxy rules, merger.
            b. SEC registration or exemption if shares or other securities are used as consideration.
    C. Bulk transfers.
        1. Notice to creditors.
        2. Other formalities.

III. Structuring the transaction.
    A. Purchase price.
        1. Shares or other equity securities.
        2. Cash or debt securities.
    B. Acquisition vehicle.
        1. Non–U.S. parent.
        2. New or existing local subsidiary.
            a. Formalities to establish new corporation.
            b. Time requirements for new corporation.
    C. Form of acquisition.
        1. Share or membership interest acquisition.
            a. Simplicity.
            b. Continuity of business.
            c. Contracts, permits, and tax attributes.
            d. No transfer taxes.
            e. Assume liabilities.
        2. Asset acquisition.
            a. Complexity.
            b. Transfer taxes.
            c. No continuity of contracts, permits, or tax attributes.
            d. Assume only transferred liabilities.
        3. Merger (often not available).
            a. Simplicity/complexity.
            b. Some continuity of business, contracts, or permits.
            c. Possibly avoid transfer taxes.
            d. Assume liabilities.

IV. Principal documentation.
    A. Letter of intent.
        1. Outline of transaction.
        2. No-shop (no overt solicitation of other buyers).
        3. Access to information.
        4. Confidentiality.
    B. Acquisition agreement.
        1. Description of transaction.
            a. Transfer of assets, shares, or merger.
            b. Price and payment terms.
            c. Price allocations in asset transfers.
            d. Price adjustment.
        2. Liabilities assumed in asset transfers.
        3. Representation and warranties (see Legal due diligence, V).
        4. Covenants.

       a.   Conduct of business.

       b.   No-shop.

       c.   Confidentiality.

       d.   Standstill.

       e.   Consents to assignment and nonassignable contracts.

       f.   Future employment of key personnel.

  5.  Conditions to closing.

       a.   Representations true and covenants performed.

       b.   No adverse change in business.

       c.   Related agreements executed.

       d.   Legal opinions.

       e.   No litigation affecting transaction.

       f.   Government approvals (Hart-Scott-Rodino, etc.).

       g.   Other consents and approvals (material contracts, leases and licenses, loan agreements, etc.).

       h.   Transfer or issuance of material permits.

  6.  Closing (see VII).

  7.  Indemnification.

       a.   Coverage.

       b.   Threshold or deductible amount.

       c.   Survival of obligations (time limits).

  8.  Dispute resolution and governing law.

       a.   Arbitration/mediation/conciliation.

       b.   Choice of forum.

C.  Other agreements.

  1.  Noncompetition agreement.

       a.   Parties covered.

       b.   Scope (time, field, and geography).

       c.   Legality and enforceability.

       d.   Tax elements.

  2.  Employment agreements.

       a.   Key employees.

       b.   Selling shareholders.

       c.   Tax elements.

  3.  Leases and licenses.

       a.   Nontransferable or nontransferred property.

       b.   Commingled property.

  4.  Services agreement.

       a.   Transition to permit target to achieve stand-alone capability.

       b.   Essential commingled services.

  5.  Parent or other guaranties.

6. Ongoing supply or distribution agreements.
7. Escrow agreement(s).
8. Intellectual property agreement(s).

V. Legal due diligence (normally also covered by representations and warranties).
   A. Corporate matters.
      1. Organizational documents (articles of incorporation and bylaws).
      2. Corporate records (minutes of shareholders and directors meetings, stock transfer records).
      3. Annual and other reports (include proxy statements and 10-Ks and 10-Qs if a public company).
      4. Lists of shareholders, officers, directors, auditors.
      5. Capitalization.
         a. Number of shares.
         b. Identity and status of shareholders.
      6. Identification of and information concerning subsidiaries.
   B. Corporate authorization.
      1. Shareholder and director approval requirements.
      2. Resolutions.
      3. Shareholder and voting agreements.
   C. Financial matters.
      1. Financial statements.
         a. Five years' audited financial statements (if available) including balance sheets, income statements, consolidated and consolidating statements, and other financial information.
         b. Most recent unaudited financial statements.
         c. Projections, if any.
      2. Identification of bank accounts.
      3. Financings.
         a. Loan and credit agreements and other lending documents.
         b. Financing leases, sale and leaseback transactions, installment purchases.
         c. Recorded and unrecorded security interests, Uniform Commercial Code searches.
         d. Compliance reports to lenders.
      4. Reports to and from, and correspondence with, auditors.
      5. Tax matters.
         a. Copies of federal income tax returns for five years.
         b. Audit reports.

        c.  Notices from Internal Revenue Service (IRS).

        d.  Settlement documents.

D.  Government reports and filings.

    1.  Material permits and licenses.

    2.  Reports to and from government agencies.

    3.  Correspondence with government agencies.

    4.  Government applications.

    5.  Other evidence of compliance with laws, regulations, and so on.

E.  Material agreements.

    1. Joint venture or partnership agreements.

    2. Long-term agreements.

    3. Significant personal property leases.

    4. Material insurance policies.

    5. Agreements or arrangements with officers, directors, or other affiliates.

    6. Customer lists.

    7. Noncompetition agreements.

    8. Guaranties.

    9. Product warranties.

    10. Other material contracts.

F.  Intellectual property.

    1.  Patents.

    2.  Trademarks.

    3.  Computer programs.

    4.  Copyrights.

    5.  Know-how.

    6.  Licenses.

    7.  Infringement claims.

G.  Real estate.

    1.  Title insurance.

    2.  Surveys.

    3.  Deeds or equivalent.

    4.  Mortgages.

    5.  Leases.

H.  Employee matters.

    1.  Employment contracts.

    2.  Employee benefit documents (pension plans and related trust documents, insurance policies, etc.).

    3.  Labor contracts.

    4.  Employee lists.

    5.  Employee records (payroll, turnover, etc.).

   I.  Environmental matters.
  1. Government reports (see V, D).
  2. Environmental audits and surveys (internal and external).
  3. Environmental permits and authorizations (reports and records).
  4. On-site survey and testing.

   J.  Litigation and liabilities.
  1. Copies of all judgments, decrees, or orders that bind target.
  2. Description of all current and threatened litigation, including names of attorneys to contact.
  3. Description of government investigations in past five years (see also V, D).
  4. List and description of product liability claims in past five years.
  5. Copies of significant court filings in any pending litigation.
  6. Name of responsible insurance company, if any.

**VI.**  Organization of acquisition vehicle.
  A. Formalities.
    1. Reserve corporate name in relevant states.
    2. File certificate or articles.
  B. Capital.
    1. Prepare and execute share or membership certificates.
    2. Enter issuance in stock record books.
  C. Management/corporation.
    1. Hold organizational meetings of shareholders and directors.
    2. Adopt bylaws.
    3. Elect directors.
    4. Elect officers.
    5. Authorize acquisition and execution of acquisition documents.
  D. Management/limited liability company.
    1. Adopt operating agreement.
    2. Elect manager(s), if any.
    3. Elect officers, if any.
  E. Other organizational matters.
    1. Obtain taxpayer's identification number.
    2. Prepare minute books.
    3. Qualify corporation to do business in necessary states.

**VII.**  Closing.
  A. Transfer of documents.
    1. Deeds.
    2. Bills of sale.

      3.   Assignments of agreements.

      4.   Assignments of intangible assets.

B.  Payment.

      1.   Wire transfers or cashier's checks.

      2.   Promissory note.

C.  Corporate formalities.

      1.   Shareholder and director approval.

      2.   Election of new directors.

D.  Other matters.

      1.   Related agreements—obtain.

          a.   Noncompetition agreements.

          b.   Employment agreements.

          c.   Leases and licenses.

          d.   Service agreements.

      2.   Obtain legal opinions.

      3.   Update certificate or articles; ensure acquisition contract representations are true and correct as of closing.

      4.   Obtain certified articles of incorporation and good-standing certificates.

      5.   Obtain resignations of officers and directors.

# Legal Aspects of Acquiring Non–U.S. Enterprises

*Paul McCarthy*

**T**he acquisition of a business outside the United States will involve most of the complexities inherent in acquiring a U.S. enterprise, along with a few surprises. In the international context, additional obstacles and considerations will arise, some because of rules imposed by many non–U.S. jurisdictions and others because they are inherent in any international acquisition. These additional obstacles may take the form of:

- Investment approvals.
- Exchange control approvals or consents.
- Tax clearances.
- Clearances under local or international competition laws.
- Unusual problems arising in the due diligence investigation of a foreign target.
- Necessity of agreeing on an allocation of the purchase price among assets located in various jurisdictions.
- Burdensome mechanics required to comply with local law or practice relating to the documentation necessary to effect the acquisition for local purposes.

All of these factors will be further complicated if the acquisition is multinational (that is, it must comply with the laws of several non–U.S. jurisdictions).

As in a domestic context, an acquisition may take the form of a share purchase, an asset purchase, or a merger, although the last of these is considerably less common abroad. Although acquisition agreements tend to be shorter outside the United States, they are becoming more like U.S. agreements in many jurisdictions. It is likely that a U.S. acquirer will continue to look to the acquisition agreement as a means of obtaining substantial information about the target company and of allocating business risks between buyer and seller.

## REGULATORY FRAMEWORK

The acquisition of a non–U.S. company will generally be subject to numerous government approvals and notices, including:

- Foreign investment approvals.
- Exchange control approvals.
- Antitrust or competition clearances or consents.
- Tax clearances, filings, or payments.

These may vary depending on the nature, the size, and the structure of the business conducted and the manner in which it is acquired, as well as on the size of the enterprise. The revenues, assets, business, and structure of the acquiring entity may often be relevant as well.

### General Requirements

In some cases, an approval, a clearance, or a consent may have to be obtained in advance of the acquisition. In other cases, it is necessary only to notify the appropriate governmental authority. In some cases, failure to obtain a required governmental approval may make the acquisition void or voidable. In other cases, the failure may not affect the validity of the acquisition, but it may deny the buyer the right to remit earnings or repatriate capital or cause it to lose tax or other benefits or incentives.

As in the United States, there are certain industries that are considered particularly sensitive. These include such industries as banking, communications, computers, defense, public utilities, shipping, and transportation. Outside of these sensitive industries, government approvals may be fairly routine. However, even routine approvals may be quite time-consuming, requiring anything from two weeks to six months. In controversial situations, approvals may take longer and may even be unobtainable or obtainable only subject to unacceptable conditions.

Government approvals are of such importance that they should be considered in detail during the course of negotiations and prior to the execution of a definitive acquisition agreement. The parties must pay particular attention to filing deadlines.

It is desirable for the parties to agree in advance which party will be primarily responsible for obtaining relevant approvals, although both parties should cooperate in this endeavor.

In a multinational acquisition, the parties should consider whether it will be appropriate to delay all closings until all government approvals are obtained or whether it will be possible to proceed with the acquisition of entities in some countries while leaving other acquisitions for a delayed closing after all approvals have been received. If an entity is vital to the entire enterprise, the entire transaction will have to be made subject to obtaining all necessary approvals for its acquisition. Where a particular entity is not vital to the enterprise as a whole or where approval is highly likely but time-consuming, a bifurcated closing (or series of closings) may be appropriate. It may also be appropriate to provide for a reduction in the purchase price if a required approval is not obtained. In any case, the acquisition agreement should make the closing in a given country subject to obtaining all necessary government approvals in that country. It would often be a violation of foreign law to sign an unconditional acquisition agreement.

The need for government approvals may also affect the structure of the acquisition. For example, the acquisition of shares in a holding company that owns shares in a local company may not be subject to the same approval requirements as a direct acquisition.

## Approvals and Notifications

### Foreign Investment Approvals

Many countries impose approval requirements on foreign purchasers simply because they are nonresidents of the country in which the target enterprise is located. In a simple, small acquisition, the approval process will ordinarily take several weeks. In a large, complex transaction, the process may take several months. Of course, in certain countries, obtaining approval for even a small acquisition may be time consuming.

Many countries restrict foreign ownership of commercial ventures regardless of the industry involved, although some are becoming more liberal. For example, India used to limit foreign equity participation in industrial companies to 40 percent. Now, however, up to 51 percent may be acquired with automatic approval in many industrial sectors, and approval may be granted for acquisitions of 100 percent. Varying restrictions appear throughout Latin America, the Middle East, and Asia. For example, in Korea, the acquisition of an equity interest in any existing local enterprise is, in principle, permitted. In practice, 100 percent foreign ownership in a local enterprise is permitted except for (1) certain specific business sectors subject to specified foreign ownership limitations (e.g., foreign ownership is permitted up to 49 percent of the shares with voting rights issued by a facility-based telecommunication company regulated under the Telecommunications Business Act) and (2) those companies designated as "public interest companies" by the Minister of Finance and Economy of Korea from among the local enterprises that are listed on the Korean Stock Exchange or registered with the KOSDAQ (in which case foreign ownership in respect of shares with voting rights is permitted up to 40 percent of the total issued shares, provided that the portion of shareholding interest that constitutes "foreign direct investment" pursuant to the Foreign Investment Promotion Act is excluded in calculating the limitation ratio). In yet other countries, such as Indonesia, the percentage of foreign ownership may determine the kinds of activity (such as local distribution) in which local enterprises may engage.

### Exchange Control Approvals

In some countries, foreign direct investment is subject to foreign exchange control approval. Without such an approval, it may not be possible to repatriate profits, capital, interest, or royalties. In such cases, the transfer of funds in connection with a business acquisition will often require such approval.

For example, there are no exchange or foreign-investment controls in Italy. Thus, profits may be freely repatriated subject to the applicable withholding tax. The only exceptions are investments in the banking and the insurance sectors (where authorization is required), specific sectors where restrictions apply (e.g., airlines), and investments in financial and securities investment companies (which must be reported to the Bank of Italy and are specifically regulated). Foreigners may freely purchase real property, provided that their countries' laws offer the same opportunity to Italians.

Most other Western European countries no longer impose such requirements. The United Kingdom, for example, abolished all such restrictions in 1979. Prior government exchange control approval is required in some countries outside Western Europe and Japan, including most countries in South America. India has recently liberalized its system, but the Reserve Bank still exercises considerable control over capital movements.

The ease of obtaining foreign exchange approvals may depend on whether the seller is already in full compliance with local exchange control laws. Therefore, the buyer should always request a representation to that effect from the seller, especially a non–local seller. If the seller is not in full compliance and does not hold all appropriate approvals, it may be time-consuming (or impossible) to obtain approval for the acquisition.

### Restricted Industries

As noted earlier, any acquisition that results in the transfer of an enterprise from local to foreign control may come under intense governmental scrutiny if a particularly sensitive industry is involved. This has been especially true in France where, with respect to such areas as electronics, data processing, and defense, approval may not be available at all or may be made conditional on continued substantial French participation.

### Reports

In certain countries, no prior approval is needed for an acquisition, but the government must be notified after the fact. Among these is Venezuela. Other countries only require a report of an indirect acquisition (that is, an acquisition of an entity that owns a local company).

## Other Regulations and Legal Considerations

A number of other legal issues should be considered in connection with an acquisition outside the United States, including competition law and labor law compliance.

### Competition Law (Antitrust)

In the European Union (EU), the need for prior clearance with the European Commission depends on whether the acquiring company and the target meet (on a worldwide level and at the EU level) certain financial thresholds. The thresholds are 5 billion euros (roughly US $4.3 billion at 1 euro − US $0.85) of gross sales revenues of the acquiring entity plus the target on a consolidated basis at the worldwide level, and 250 million euros of gross sales revenues of the acquiring entity plus the target at the EU level.

In 1997, an alternative set of the financial thresholds was added. An acquisition, a merger, or another form of concentration has an EU-wide dimension where:

1. The combined annual worldwide gross sales revenues of the acquiring entity plus the target is more than 2,500 million euros; and
2. The annual EU-wide gross sales revenues of each of the acquiring entity plus the target exceed 100 million euros; and
3. In each of at least three member States of the EU,[1] the combined annual gross sales revenues of the acquiring entity plus the target exceed 100 million euros; and
4. In each of those three member States, the annual gross sales revenues of each of the acquiring entity plus the target exceed 25 million euros.

Unless each of the acquiring entity plus the target achieves more than two-thirds of its annual EU gross sales revenues within one and the same member State.

---

[1]Austria, Belgium, Denmark, Finland, France, Germany, Greece, Ireland, Italy, Luxembourg, Netherlands, Portugal, Spain, Sweden, and the United Kingdom. Norway, which is a member State of the European Economic Area, is also included for the purpose of the application of the financial thresholds for merger control purposes.

For EC competition law purposes, if the combined market share of the parties prior to the acquisition is less than 20 percent, there will normally not be any problem.

If the acquisition does not have a European dimension and does not meet those thresholds, a prior filing with the German Cartel Office is required if the acquisition has an effect on the German market and if the worldwide revenues of the acquiring company plus the target are sufficiently large. France has recently made competition clearance mandatory as well. The decision to grant approval depends on the parties' market shares in Germany. This approval can take up to four months, but quicker approval is often forthcoming in noncontroversial situations. The circumstances of an acquisition may also make it advisable to obtain competition law approval in the United Kingdom. This can usually be obtained in one to two months. Many countries outside of the EU, including Canada and some Latin American jurisdictions, now have competition law notice requirements, either pre- or postclosing. In Brazil, virtually everyone must file (with a very early filing deadline) even though there are little in the way of assets or business in that coutnry.

A Hart-Scott-Rodino filing may be required in the United States if the target company holds operating assets in the United States or has aggregate sales to the United States of more than US$25,000,000 in its most recent fiscal year.

### Employment and Labor Law

Employees receive far greater legal protection in many countries outside the United States, particularly in the case of dismissal, than in the United States. This will make it appropriate to include quite explicit covenants, representations, and warranties on these points in the purchase agreement. European sellers of businesses consider employment matters to be quite significant and so devote a substantial amount of attention to these concerns during negotiations. These matters are briefly discussed later under "Employees" in the section Principal Legal Concerns of the Buyer.

As in the United States, the employees of most foreign targets will learn of the acquisition only after the deal is struck. However, in certain European countries, employees are given a role in conducting the business, particularly where works councils have been established; and this role may be important in the case of an acquisition. For example, in the Netherlands, the proposed acquisition of a company or business that normally employs 50 or more employees must be presented to the works councils (if installed) of both the acquirer and the target in order to obtain their advice on the proposed transaction. The management of the acquirer and the target company must each request this advice from its respective works council in sufficient time to allow serious consideration to be given to the proposed transaction and for the works council's advice to be conveyed to management (the works council is not given a veto over the transaction). If the works council's advice is not followed, the parties involved must wait at least one month before closing the transaction. Within this one-month period, the works council may appeal against the decision to the Enterprise Chamber of the Amsterdam Court of Appeal. The Chamber assesses whether the parties could reasonably have reached their decision had they weighed the interests involved. If the Chamber finds that the parties could not reasonably have come to their decision, it may issue an order requiring the parties to revoke the decision in whole or in part, to prohibit its further implementation, and to reverse any measures already taken. Although this rarely happens, buyers generally find it in their interest to become involved in the dealings with the works council to ensure good labor relations after the acquisition is completed.

Similarly, it may be appropriate or even required for the works council to be consulted before a French company is acquired, at least if the employees or their conditions of employment will be affected by the acquisition. The same is true for a number of other countries, both inside and outside of Western Europe.

## STRUCTURING THE ACQUISITION

### Shares or Cash

Cash is the normal consideration used in an acquisition of a non–U.S. target. Shares and other securities are rarely used. If shares of the U.S. parent are used, the buyer must comply with local securities laws. Such shares may be used without filing a registration statement with the Securities and Exchange Commission (SEC) as long as certain steps are taken to ensure that the shares (or other securities) are not redistributed to the United States. However, the sellers may want to obtain securities for which there is an established market, and it may be that the only market available for such trading is a U.S. stock exchange. In this case, the shares should be registered either upon issuance in connection with the acquisition or subsequently upon their resale in the public markets. Alternatively, the sellers may not require registration in the United States if the U.S. parent's shares are traded on other stock markets, such as London or Tokyo.

### Acquisition Vehicle

The vehicle used to acquire the non–U.S. target will depend on the buyer's overall tax planning and on the structure of the target company. If the target company is operating in a variety of jurisdictions through local subsidiaries, it may be possible to acquire each subsidiary or to acquire the shares of the company that is the parent of those subsidiaries. Such an indirect acquisition may be advantageous in avoiding foreign investment (but not competition) requirements in some countries. The organization of a foreign acquisition vehicle is discussed later in the section Organizing the Acquisition Vehicle.

## Share Acquisitions

As in the United States, this is the simplest form of acquisition.

### *Advantages*

All assets remain in the target corporation, so few transfer documents are required. Transfer taxes may be limited or avoided. This is particularly important in many countries because such taxes may be substantial. Stamp duties may still apply, however, and other transfer taxes may be payable regardless of the form of the acquisition. The target corporation will retain all of its assets, including licenses, permits, and franchises, which might otherwise be difficult to transfer. The same is probably true with contracts and leases.

### *Disadvantages*

The target corporation will retain all of its negative tax attributes and exposure to prior unpaid taxes. The target will also retain all of its liabilities. Discovery of such liabilities may be more difficult in a non–U.S. context, as discussed under "Representations and Warranties" in the section "Documentation."

## Asset Acquisitions

### *Advantages*

Not all of the assets of the target need be purchased. Thus, if a single line of business is being sold, the transaction will have to be structured as an asset acquisition unless preclosing reorganization is implemented. Also, not all of the target's liabilities need be acquired. However, in many foreign countries, the sale of substantially all of the assets constituting a business (what would be referred to in the United States as a bulk transfer) will be more complex than would be the case in the United States. For example, in many European countries, the sale of a business means that the employees of the business automatically become employees of the buyer. In Brazil, if certain transactions are characterized appropriately, it may be possible to transfer the employees directly to the buyer, who assumes all their past liabilities; or the parties may agree to have the seller terminate all or part of its employees, who will receive a severance indemnification and who may be immediately rehired by the buyer without any latent severance liabilities.

### *Disadvantages*

As in the United States, an asset acquisition can be more complex than a share acquisition. Assets, such as licenses and contracts, may require third-party consents in order to be transferred. As noted earlier, transfer and other taxes can be substantial in many countries.

## Mergers

Mergers are not available in all countries. Even where available, they may differ substantially in theory and practice from those in the United States. For example, in Canada, a merger is considered to be the joining of two separate businesses that continue together after the merger. One company is not considered to be the survivor while the other disappears. (However, this theoretical difference appears to have little significance in practice.) In addition, mergers may be subject to public notice and appraisal requirements and to waiting periods.

Where a merger is available, its principal advantage is the same as that in the United States. The transfer of assets from the target to the buyer is automatic, although certain filings may have to be made to record the transfer. This may greatly facilitate the transfer of valuable permits and contracts. However, there is probably no country in which a merger may be structured with the flexibility available in the United States. Few countries allow the variety of consideration provided for in the United States, nor are reverse mergers generally known. By contrast, demergers (or corporate splits or spinoffs) are often easier in other countries than in the United States.

## DOCUMENTATION

### Letter of Intent

The letter of intent sets out the principal points on which the parties have agreed. It is useful in identifying important issues between the parties. Its disadvantage lies in that it may delay preparing and signing a definitive contract. A letter of intent is not legally binding between the parties, but it may create an obligation to bargain in good faith. Parties outside the United States feel free to propose departures from the letter of intent to a greater extent than would a U.S. party. Nonetheless, all matters of importance to the parties, especially the structure of the transaction, should be considered and reviewed with counsel and other consultants before a letter of intent is signed. Disclosure of the signing of a letter of intent is not normally required outside the United States even for a publicly traded company.

### Acquisition Agreement

Acquisitions in many countries involving only nationals of those countries and relatively small enterprises are often done without the formalities followed in the United States. In particular, acquisition agreements may be much shorter, often without any contractual representations and warranties. If a sophisticated buyer is involved, however, the acquisition agreement will be similar to that used in the

United States; it will have a more detailed treatment of those areas, such as employees, that constitute more substantial buyer risks outside the United States.

In the case of a multinational acquisition, it is often advisable to use two types of agreement: (1) a master agreement that governs the transaction as a whole and (2) local agreements that govern only the transaction in each country. This approach avoids inconsistencies and permits the local agreements to be shorter than they might otherwise be, thereby simplifying translation and similar problems in the event that the agreement has to be registered with local authorities. It may also avoid having each local taxing authority try to reallocate the purchase price to increase local income or transfer taxes. The principal features of a non–U.S. master agreement and local agreements are described in the rest of this section.

### Price and Payment

As in the United States, the price may be either fixed or subject to adjustment. The purchase price as well as the amount allocated to each transaction will be set out in the master agreement and the amount allocated to the local transactions will be repeated in each local agreement.

In an asset transaction, the price paid for fixed assets will be set, whereas the price for current assets will be determined by the level of those assets at the closing. This will normally be established through a postclosing audit. An earnout arrangement for determining the price is quite rare outside the United States.

The allocation of the price among various countries may be significant. The agreement should provide that the parties will follow these allocations for tax purposes in every jurisdiction. The per-country allocation provision appears only in the master agreement. It may also be advisable, in certain countries for transfer tax purposes, to allocate the price in the local agreement among the various assets purchased in an asset transaction.

Payment will normally be made by wire transfer. If local asset agreements are used, payment may have to be made simultaneously in a number of jurisdictions. This will require substantial coordination, with inevitable delays.

### Assumption of Liabilities

All liabilities are included in a share transaction or a merger, although it is more frequently the practice that the seller will indemnify the buyer against certain liabilities, particularly those that, at the closing, are undisclosed or contingent. In an asset transaction, the buyer will have to assume responsibility for all agreements and leases assigned. The buyer will also normally assume responsibility for trade payables because it is the buyer that has the greatest interest in seeing that suppliers of goods and services are fully paid. Certain other liabilities, such as those for employees, may transfer to the buyer automatically.

### Representations and Warranties

A representation and warranty is a statement that something is true or correct (e.g., the target's financial statements have been prepared in accordance with generally accepted accounting principles [GAAP]). The representations and warranties will cover the main areas of concern to the parties. They are discussed in greater detail in the later section Principal Legal Concerns of the Buyer. The notion of full disclosure is less common outside the United States, although sophisticated sellers will not be surprised by the extent of the representations. On the other hand, if a family-owned company is being acquired in Europe, the sellers may flatly refuse to provide the extensive representations common in the United States. In that case, the buyer will have to choose with care the particular matters it wishes covered and independently investigate any other important matters, although here, too, difficulties may be encountered. Sellers outside the United States are often less willing to make full disclosure on matters they consider sensitive. A multinational acquisition normally includes the representations and warranties only in the master agreement.

### Covenants

A covenant is a promise to act or to refrain from acting (e.g., target will not dispose of its assets except in the ordinary course of business between contract and closing). As in the United States, covenants often cover those matters that ought to take place between the signing and the closing, as well as obligations relating to the postclosing period. Thus, the seller is required to conduct the purchased business in the ordinary course and will be prohibited from engaging in any major transaction without the consent of the buyer. In a multinational transaction, most pre- and postclosing covenants will appear only in the master agreement. However, it is often useful to include covenants that describe local matters in local agreements as well, in order to provide an explanation of what takes place. For example, the local agreements might describe the transfer of local employees, the treatment of benefits, and the like.

### Conditions

Typical conditions to closing are the obtaining of any required government and other approvals, the execution of ancillary agreements, and, sometimes, the absence of any material adverse change in the business. Legal opinions are not always provided in cross-border transactions. In acquiring a family-owned business, the buyer should not be surprised to find the seller reluctant to provide such opinions. For instance, a French entrepreneur will not be accustomed to relying on attorneys to anywhere near the same extent as people do in the United States. The same is true in Japan; but attorneys are used as counselors more frequently in England and Germany. In a multinational acquisition, there is no need to include the conditions in the local asset agreement. A comprehensive provision in the master agreement will suffice.

### Closing

The master agreement and local agreements will describe the mechanics of closing. The typical legal mechanics of non–U.S. closings are described in the later section Closing.

### *Indemnification*

In an acquisition between sophisticated parties, an indemnification provision of the kind used in the United States may be included. In a multinational acquisition, this will generally be included only in the master agreement because it will likely be the ultimate parent to which the buyer will look for indemnification. As in the United States, the indemnification provisions are designed to allocate the risks of the business between buyer and seller. In the case of the acquisition of a family-owned business, an indemnification provision may be very difficult to obtain because it is totally unfamiliar to the sellers.

Also, an indemnification may be interpreted more narrowly abroad. An indemnification provision may not be enforced if it is shown that the buyer knew of the misrepresentation or, in some cases, if the buyer should have or could have known. The notion of caveat emptor is often applied even in a sale of shares.

Even if an indemnification provision is included in the acquisition agreement, consideration has to be given to the practical aspects of being able to enforce such a provision. In many countries, such as Spain and Italy, simple litigation can take 10 years or longer. In other countries, the judiciary may be tainted by corruption. In these circumstances, a seller (even a major corporation) having an indemnification obligation may refuse to honor it, knowing that the buyer has no practical remedy. In such countries, some form of holdback or bank guaranty, combined with international arbitration, will have to be considered if indemnification is to have any practical value.

## PRINCIPAL LEGAL CONCERNS OF THE BUYER: DUE DILIGENCE

As in the United States, the representations and warranties in a non–U.S. acquisition agreement are designed in part to cause the seller to disclose material information of greatest concern to the buyer. In certain cases, because of local custom, these representations and warranties will be less extensive than in the United States. Moreover, even if an unsophisticated seller is willing to make certain representations, it may not fully appreciate all their ramifications. Therefore, the buyer should independently verify as much as possible about the target with the assistance of local attorneys and consultants. (In this as in many other areas, general experience and familiarity with international transactions will not suffice.) The buyer should be aware that the sources of such information may differ substantially from those available in the United States. Not only will the information itself and the willingness of the seller to disclose it fully differ, but what is most important with a foreign target may be quite different from what would be important in the case of a U.S. target. It is always a mistake to simply use U.S. concepts in representations, warranties, or legal opinions, without taking account of local differences. Examples of these differences are set out in the succeeding paragraphs.

The existence of a commercial registry in most civil law countries means that certain information about a target may be publicly available. In many jurisdictions, the commercial registry information on a share company will include the name of the company; its principal place of business; its capital (including issued but not fully paid-in capital); and the directors of the company, their authorization to represent the company, and any restrictions on that authority. In England and many other countries, annual financial statements will be on file at the companies register.

The principal concerns of a buyer of a non–U.S. entity are most likely those discussed in the following paragraphs.

## Corporate Organization and Authority

The buyer will want to confirm that the target company is properly organized, particularly in a share acquisition. However, the means of ascertaining this may differ substantially from the means used in the United States. For example, in France, one can confirm that the company is enrolled with the commercial register and can obtain an extract from the commercial register indicating what the company's capital is and who has the authority to act for the company. It may be possible to obtain an official copy of the memorandum of association in many, though not all, countries. In some countries, this may be certified by the commercial register or, as in Belgium, by a notary.

There is no concept of "good standing" in most countries. Good standing in the United States generally means that all franchise taxes have been paid and all filings have been made. In many countries, there are no ongoing franchise fees or taxes, and no periodic filings are required. This is the case, for example, in Germany. Therefore, including a representation or seeking a legal opinion that a company is in good standing is meaningless and should be avoided. If the buyer insists on some equivalent of good standing, it is possible for the seller to state that there exists no condition or circumstance that would permit the dissolution of the company without further administrative action or notice on the part of shareholders, creditors, or the local court.

## Employees

As noted earlier, the protections provided by employment law are considerably more extensive in many developed countries than in the United States. The best-known case is Japan, where employees have customarily enjoyed the right of lifetime employment (although this custom has given way in many places in the face of Japan's ongoing economic difficulties). However, in many countries, much of this is regulated by law, independent of any particular arrangements with the employer. Therefore, it is not sufficient to rely on representations and warranties in the acquisition agreement, although appropriate provisions should be included to provide for the parties' respective responsibilities vis-à-vis employees. The buyer should seek competent advice from qualified local counsel about the implications both of the transaction and of acquiring the employees of the target.

## Employment Protection

Often, the employees of a target company will automatically transfer with the business and it will not be necessary for the buyer to offer employment or to take any other steps in this regard other than confirming the transfer of employment. With these employees, the buyer will inherit all attendant liabilities, especially when they retire or are terminated. In some countries, such as France and Germany, the buyer must continue the employment on terms no less favorable than those offered by the seller. Otherwise, the employees will be considered to have been terminated and may be entitled to substantial termination compensation from the seller. Once these responsibilities have been identified and quantified, it is possible to assess whether one should seek to have the seller retain some of them. For example, in Italy, the employee has a right to an indemnity upon termination of employment, even by voluntary retirement or termination for good cause, the indemnity being dependent on length of service. Standard U.S. pension representations might not pick up this liability. In some countries, like Brazil, it may be possible in an asset acquisition to treat the employee as having been terminated and to give him or her the right to receive this sort of indemnity immediately.

## Employee Benefits

The handling of employee-benefit matters may be simpler in other countries than it is in the United States. In some Western European countries, such as France, pensions are largely statutory and are paid out of government-operated funds. There actually is no pension fund to transfer and no pension liability to assume. All such liabilities are held by the government and are funded by taxes similar to U.S. Social Security taxes, although the benefits tend to be far more extensive. In Germany and several other countries, private insurance is used to fund pensions. It will be necessary to obtain the cooperation of the target's insurance company to be certain that there is no gap in coverage.

In the United Kingdom, there are pension schemes quite similar to the defined-benefit and other pension plans found in the United States. These are closely governed by myriad tax and pensions laws. Adequate and extensive provisions may be required to ensure that the buyer acquires the assets necessary to discharge the responsibilities it is assuming. However, such assets may be transferred only to a new pension plan and then only with the consent of each employee.

## Labor Agreements

A labor union is a significant factor in the acquisition of any business. Even in an asset transaction, the buyer may be required to assume all obligations under a collective bargaining agreement. In some countries, the collective bargaining agreement is negotiated between the union and a group of employers. In that case, the buyer will have little or no opportunity to renegotiate the agreement at the time of the acquisition.

## Compliance with Law

### *Environmental Matters*

In many countries, environmental regulation has not reached the level it has in the United States. Asian countries have been notorious in ignoring environmental concerns. In Europe, however, governments have begun to regulate the disposal of waste and the cleanup of hazardous sites to a degree approaching that of the United States, albeit without the same litigation costs. Awareness of problems in the environmental area has been on the rise even outside Europe, and one can expect greater regulation in the future. It is, therefore, prudent to investigate any target for potential environmental difficulties. On the one hand, it may be easy to get a seller to assume continued responsibility for environmental matters arising out of the operation of the business prior to the closing because that exposure appears to be slight today. On the other hand, such a proposal will be viewed by the seller as rather unusual and may arouse suspicion and even hostility.

### *Licenses and Permits*

As in the United States, businesses are required to operate under a variety of governmental permits and licenses. If anything, such regulation is more extensive and stricter abroad than it is in the United States. If shares are acquired, the target will typically come with permits and licenses intact, provided that all governmental authorizations have been obtained previously. This assumes that the particular business is not restricted with respect to foreign ownership or change in ownership. If this is not the case, governmental consent will ordinarily be required for the target to continue to use such permits and licenses.

In the case of an asset transfer, as in the United States, permits and licenses may not be assignable, and new permits and licenses must be arranged for at or prior to the closing. Obtaining new permits may be quite time-consuming.

If there is a change in the management of the target, the new managers may be required to have permits to operate. In France, if the managing director or manager of a French share company or limited liability company is not a citizen of an EU country, a commercial card must be obtained. This will take some months, and so adequate preparation should be made to avoid delays. As a general rule, in Europe, work permits must be obtained; and, in some cases, residence permits must be secured for new expatriate managers who are not EU nationals.

## Liabilities

### *Product liability*

It is still true that product liability claims outside the United States are far fewer, and judgments smaller, than in the United States. This is due in part to cultural norms. In the United States, money is considered an appropriate compensation for many injuries. In many other countries, however, there is a much smaller likelihood of someone bringing a lawsuit in response to an injury, even where someone appears to be at fault. In Japan, bringing a lawsuit is socially discouraged. The doctrine of strict liability is the norm in the EU in regard to personal injury claims, but this is only gradually being adopted in most other countries. Even where lawsuits are successfully prosecuted, the size of the awards is unlikely to approach those in the United States. Nonetheless, one can expect a gradual increase in the likelihood of product liability claims in various countries, particularly in the EU, in light of the EU directive on product liability law.

### Tax Liabilities

If shares are acquired, the target corporation will carry with it all of its tax attributes, positive and negative. Tax avoidance and even fraud are common in many countries. For example, due diligence in an acquisition of one substantial Italian company revealed that the target maintained three separate (and inconsistent) sets of books. The U.S. buyer had to correct these practices after the closing because the target would have to be integrated into the U.S. company's accounting system and, as a subsidiary of a U.S. company, it would always be more visible to local tax authorities. However, correction entailed substantial tax costs for prior years for the target company, costs that the seller was most reluctant to assume. In fact, the seller did not wish to see these matters disclosed to the tax authorities at all. It is less likely that the buyer in an asset acquisition will assume any income tax liabilities, and the buyer will be free to set up its own accounting system. However, certain assets may be encumbered with tax liens, the existence of which may be very difficult to ascertain, and this liability may have to be covered through indemnities or escrows.

### Other Liabilities

The notion of full disclosure is viewed as a bit unusual outside the United States. Therefore, a request for a representation that there are no undisclosed liabilities in the business, contingent or otherwise, may make a non–U.S. seller somewhat uncomfortable. However, such a representation is, if anything, more important in this context. No one wishes to purchase a business on a caveat emptor basis. An appropriate indemnification or escrow provision should also be included, especially if the seller is reluctant to make a representation on a broad basis; and consideration should be given to remedies for indemnification, as discussed earlier.

## Financial Statements

Accounting practices vary greatly from country to country, and the presentation of financial information may seem unfamiliar to a U.S. buyer. Nonetheless, there are generally accepted accounting principles in most Western countries and in many parts of Asia. Therefore, the seller should be required to confirm that the financial statements it has presented to the buyer have been prepared in accordance with such principles. This will often not be the case with closely held companies.

There will then be little choice for the buyer other than to prepare closing financial statements under the supervision of an accounting firm. Although the balance sheet may be audited, it is inherently less reliable than audited statements prepared by accountants familiar with the target, and with the full cooperation of the target's management.

The seller of a privately owned firm will often resist any substantial reliance on outside experts. This will vary from country to country. In Germany, for example, businesspeople often rely on lawyers, tax advisers, and accountants. Therefore, there is a greater likelihood that audited financial statements will be available for the target's past operations and that preparation of an audited closing financial statement will be acceptable to the seller. By contrast, French businesspeople rarely rely on outside experts, and then do so primarily for such extraordinary matters as litigation. In one instance, the seller of a French company refused to agree to an audit of the company's books as a partial determinant of the purchase price and even refused to deal with the buyer's attorneys and accountants. Although this reluctance was undoubtedly due in part to a desire to avoid disclosing inadequacies in the target's inventories and other accounting matters (concerns often present with a U.S. seller of a family-owned company), the psychological aspects of the matter were quite significant. Therefore, care should be taken at the letter-of-intent stage to spell out in detail exactly what will be done with respect to such matters. The buyer should not rely on the inclusion of even a well-known accounting term like "certified" in describing closing financial statements. It is useful to have the seller's financial statements translated into a U.S. presentation by an accountant knowledgeable in both accounting systems.

## Material Assets

### *Physical Facilities*

The buyer will want to be certain that it has title to any plants or other real estate owned by the seller or target corporation. Title insurance is virtually unknown outside the United States, although it is occasionally used in Canada. In most common law jurisdictions, the buyer will rely on an opinion of its counsel based on an examination of the records at the registry of deeds or the equivalent. In civil law countries, real estate will often be transferred by notarial deed, in which case, the notary plays a function far beyond that of a notary public in the United States. The notary functions as a government-appointed attorney, acting in effect for both parties, to ensure that proper title has been conveyed. The notary will also deal with all other formalities of transfer. It is up to the notary to ensure that there are no material encumbrances on the property.

Transfer taxes tend to be far more significant outside the United States. As one might expect, the stated consideration for the transfer may come under some scrutiny.

### *Intellectual Property*

Intellectual property may be a very important part of the target's business. Intellectual property systems vary substantially from country to country. In many countries, registration of a trademark, for example, is of vital importance in protecting one's rights. Without registration, all rights to enforce a trademark against third parties may be lost. At the same time, actual local use of the trademark may not be a prerequisite to registration. This is the case, for example, in Japan. Therefore, it is important for the buyer to ascertain that all of the intellectual property necessary to operate the business is not only transferred to the buyer but is also properly registered.

In Great Britain and other Commonwealth countries, a registered user agreement must be executed and entered into by any party that uses a trademark of which it is not the owner. If not handled properly, the trademark could be lost. The buyer will want to look into all of these matters to ensure that the intellectual property it believes it is getting will be transferred in a form fully enforceable against third parties.

In most countries, unless specifically restricted, an agreement is assignable. A principal exception is an agreement that is, by its very nature, personal to the other party, as, for example, in the case of an employment agreement with respect to the employee. These rarely arise in acquisition situations. In an asset transaction, all agreements will have to be scrutinized to determine whether there are any limitations on their assignability. An agreement or a license abroad rarely provides for termination solely because of a material change in ownership of one of the parties. However, such a restriction is possible as a matter of contract or regulatory law, and all material documents must be scrutinized to ascertain this.

## ORGANIZING THE ACQUISITION VEHICLE

One encounters a variety of business forms outside the United States. In France, the commercial code provides for no fewer than eight forms of business organization, of which seven have separate legal personalities. The rules governing such entities will be crucial if, as is often the case, the buyer must organize a local company to hold acquired shares or assets. An acquisition vehicle will generally be in corporate-like form, either a corporation in common law countries (principally Great Britain, Canada, Australia, India, Pakistan, Hong Kong, Singapore, and other former British colonies) or, in many civil law countries (which include Western Europe, South America, Japan, and Korea), a share company or a limited liability company. These acquisition vehicles are discussed in the following paragraphs.

## Corporations: General

Corporations in Great Britain and other Commonwealth countries are similar to those in the United States, although there are more mandatory provisions in British company law than in U.S. law. In many civil law countries, a limited liability company tends to be used for smaller enterprises. A share company will be used for larger enterprises, particularly those whose shares are held by the public. The rules applicable to limited liability companies tend to be flexible, and these are particularly useful for wholly owned subsidiaries. By contrast, share companies are subject to numerous formalities and restrictions. However, their shares may be freely traded.

The following discussion describes a generic share company and a generic limited liability company organized in a civil law country. The specific rules applicable to these companies in particular jurisdictions vary substantially and should be reviewed in detail with competent local counsel.

## Share Companies

Share companies are similar to U.S. corporations, but there are many more mandatory procedures and rules governing share companies than there are for U.S. corporations.

### Formation

A share company will be formed when its organic document is enrolled with the commercial register in the location of its principal place of business. Unlike the United States, where Delaware corporations are common, there is currently no "Delaware" in Europe. A share company whose principal place of business is in Germany would not be organized in France, for example.

It may take considerable time to organize a share company in many foreign jurisdictions. There may be bureaucratic delays from several weeks to several months between the filing of the appropriate documents and the organization of the company. This delay factor should be borne in mind if a buyer contemplates organizing an offshore company to facilitate an acquisition. Attorneys in some countries keep "shelf" (nonoperating) companies available for their clients; but acquiring such companies inevitably involves some risks if the company had operated previously or had been originally organized for another shareholder. Shelf companies should be obtained only from attorneys who are very well known to the client.

### Capital

The capital of a share company is represented by shares, which are typically freely transferable, subject only to any applicable securities laws. Shares may be issued for cash or for property. It is generally necessary to obtain a public appraisal or court approval to establish the value of any contributed property, which considerably complicates the acquisition of assets and their contribution to a newly organized local subsidiary.

In a number of jurisdictions, shares may be represented by bearer certificates. Shares have a specified par value; no-par shares are generally unknown.

## Corporate Structure

A share company consists of two constituent parts: (1) the shareholders and (2) the directors. Most civil law countries require that there be more than one shareholder (usually three to seven). There is usually no limitation on foreigners acting as shareholders, although foreign investment in some countries may require some form of government approval. Shareholder meetings may be held by proxy and are often represented by fictitious "minutes" of a meeting that has taken place only on paper. Consent resolutions of the kind used in the United States are generally unknown.

The directors in many share companies function as both officers and directors do in a U.S. corporation. Thus, the directors both manage the share company and represent it in its dealings with others. In some countries, such as Germany, there are two boards of directors, one performing a supervisory function and the other managing day-to-day affairs. In France, the board of directors may supervise the management of the company while the managing director conducts the company's affairs.

Many countries require that a majority or some other fixed number of directors be citizens of the country. In France, a new managing director or manager who is not a citizen of an EU country must obtain a commercial card before acting in this capacity. This can be a time-consuming matter. Directors may delegate their authority to others and so may act through proxies, although in some countries proxies may be given only to another director. Alternative directors are sometimes used as well. Directors do not generally act through written consent resolutions.

## Limited Liability Companies

The SARL in France, the GmbH in Germany, and the Yuren Kaisha in Japan are examples of limited liability companies. There is no equivalent to the limited liability company in England. A limited liability company, for many purposes, is more flexible than a share company.

### Formation

A limited liability company will typically be organized through the enrollment of a deed or an agreement among the participants with the local commercial register.

### Capital

The capital of a limited liability company will normally be characterized as interests or quotas rather than as shares because a share denotes something that may be freely traded and is often certificated. Quotas may not be freely traded and are represented only on the company's register of quotaholders, not by certificates. A limited liability company will typically be required to have more than one quotaholder, although the number of required quotaholders may be less than the number of shareholders required for a share company. Quotas may be issued for cash or for personal or real property. As with a share company, contributions in kind must go through some form of public appraisal or court approval to value the contributed property.

### Corporate Structure

A limited liability company will have two principal organs: (1) the quotaholders and (2) the managers. In most countries in Western Europe and in Japan, there is no limitation on domestic or foreign corporations or on individuals acting as quotaholders in a limited liability company except in certain restricted industries. However, foreign investment in this or any other form may be subject to prior government approval.

Like the directors of a share company, the managers of a limited liability company act both as directors and as officers of the company in that they are authorized to represent the company individually. Their authority may be limited by an appropriate notation in the commercial registry, and this will be binding on third parties who deal with the company. However, it is customary for managers to enjoy fairly wide powers in managing the business.

## CLOSING

### Mechanics of Closing

The legal mechanics of closing an acquisition abroad may be quite complicated, involving a number of formalities, documents, and filings. In a multinational acquisition, it will be necessary to provide a means to have simultaneous closings in several different countries because certain acts will have to be carried out within the country in question. Often this can be done through the use of informal escrows or preclosings, whereby the local closing takes place one or two days in advance of the master closing. All of the executed documents will then be left with a local attorney pursuant to a letter agreement to be delivered to the parties when the attorney is notified that the master closing has taken place.

Even a closing of the sale of shares in a single country may involve complications unfamiliar to a U.S. buyer. For example, in purchasing a French share company, whether alone or as part of a larger transaction, it is customary to transfer the shares in a transfer document signed with certain specific language, that is, *"bon pour transfer de* (number) *actions de capital."* In other countries, such as Austria, the transfer document must be by means of a notarial deed, that is, a formal document executed in front of a notary.

A transfer document will have to be signed by an authorized representative of the transferor, often in the country in question. It is normal to use a formal power of attorney, legalized before a consulate whenever possible.

In many jurisdictions, such as France or the Netherlands, quotas may not be represented by certificates that may be transferred by endorsement or delivery. Where ownership is evidenced only by an entry in the share or quota registry book of the company, in some countries, the transfer will have to be recorded in the share or quota registry by a representative of the transferor or transferee for the transfer of ownership to be effective, whereas in other countries notification of the transfer to the issuing company within a certain number of days after the closing may be sufficient. Director or shareholder approval may be required, especially if there is a shareholder agreement in effect.

Share transfers can be made even more complicated when the number of shareholders is large. In a French share company, for example, there must be at least seven shareholders, often requiring nominee shareholders. A director of a share company must become a shareholder within three months of appointment as a director, further increasing the potential number of nominee shareholders. Such nominee shareholdings must all be transferred at the closing.

The seller's representatives as directors or managers will usually be required to resign, effective at the closing, but subject to the election of new directors or managers. The seller should bear responsibility for any indemnities that must be paid to resigning directors or managers. Because new directors may have to be elected by the shareholders, it will be necessary to have a shareholders' meeting at the time of the closing. Notice requirements should be observed. Because a notice period may be fairly long, this requires advance planning.

As previously noted, many countries require that directors must be shareholders (or become shareholders within a certain period of their appointment). These qualifying shares of directors should be made subject to executed transfer documents held by the company so that their shares may easily be transferred if they cease to be directors. The appointment and the resignation of directors at the closing may also have to be published or filed with the local commercial register.

## Other Agreements

A number of ancillary agreements may be executed at the closing.

### Noncompetition Agreements

As in the United States, there are sound business reasons why the buyer will want the seller to agree not to compete with the acquired business after the closing. The enforceability of such agreements will depend on local law, although most countries will enforce them if they are reasonable in duration and geographic scope. Any tax benefits derived from the use of such a covenant will depend on local law.

### Employment Agreements

It is likely that the buyer will want some assurance that key employees will remain with the business. This may be accomplished in part through a representation in the agreement that the seller is not aware of any plans of key employees to leave and by a covenant that the seller will not offer employment to these key employees for some period after the closing. If the buyer wants greater assurance, it may make it a condition of closing that key employees enter into formal employment agreements. Written employment agreements are generally more common outside the United States, and so this should be relatively easy to accomplish.

Although such agreements are not specifically enforceable, most employees can be expected to honor their commitment, particularly since the agreement will provide them with assurance of continued employment.

### Leases and Licenses

If the seller is going to retain some tangible or intangible property of significance to the business, it will be necessary to empower the acquired company to use it under a license or a lease. Appropriate forms of agreement are known in most countries; but if the agreements call for payment outside the country in which the leased facility is located or the licensed trademark or technology is used, exchange control or other government approval may be required and payments may be subject to withholding taxes. Local formal requirements should also be respected, such as a registered user agreement for trademarks in the United Kingdom and many Commonwealth countries.

## NON–U.S. AND MULTINATIONAL ACQUISITION CHECKLIST

The following checklist indicates, in more or less chronological order, the principal matters addressed by attorneys in the course of an outbound acquisition. The point at which attorneys should become involved varies. However, anyone contemplating an acquisition abroad is likely to encounter rules and practices that are not only different, but also unlikely to be anticipated. Therefore, an attorney experienced in cross-border transactions should be consulted at the very outset.

# Checklist: Multinational and Other Non–U.S. Acquisitions

I. Initial due diligence (nonlegal, done by buyer).
   A. Preliminary investigation of business.
      1. Financial statements.
      2. Business operations.
   B. Confidentiality agreement.

II. Regulatory considerations.
   A. Foreign investment approvals.
      1. Government restrictions on foreign ownership.
      2. Government approvals and notices.
         a. Advance notices and waiting periods.
         b. Postclosing notices.
   B. Exchange control approvals.
   C. Antitrust limitations and approvals.
      1. Mandatory.
         a. EU: premerger notice to Commission.
         b. Germany: Cartel Office approval.
         c. Other countries.
      2. Advisory.
         a. United Kingdom.
         b. Other countries.
   D. Consultation with employees.
      1. Netherlands: works council.
      2. France.
      3. Other countries.

III. Structuring the transaction.
   A. Purchase price.
      1. Shares or other equity or debt interests.
      2. Cash or notes.
   B. Choosing acquisition vehicle.
      1. Foreign parent.
      2. New or existing local subsidiary.
         a. Formalities to establish new entity.
         b. Time requirements for new entity.
   C. Choosing form of acquisition.

1. Equity acquisition.
   a. Relative simplicity.
   b. Continuity of business.
   c. Contracts, permits, and tax attributes.
   d. No transfer taxes.
   e. Assume all liabilities.
2. Asset acquisition.
   a. Complexity.
   b. Transfer taxes.
   c. No continuity of contracts, permits, or tax attributes.
   d. Assumption of only some liabilities.
3. Merger (sometimes not available).
   a. Simplicity/complexity.
   b. Some continuity of business, contracts, and permits.
   c. Possible avoidance of transfer taxes.
   d. Assumption of all liabilities.

IV. Principal documentation.
   A. Letter of intent.
      1. Outline of transaction.
      2. No-shop (no overt solicitation of or discussion with other buyers).
      3. Access to information.
      4. Confidentiality.
   B. Purchase agreement: single country transaction.
      1. Description of transaction.
         a. Transfer of assets, equity, or merger.
         b. Price and payment terms.
         c. Price allocations (asset transfers).
         d. Price adjustment.
      2. Liabilities assumed (asset transfers).
      3. Representations and warranties (see V).
      4. Preclosing covenants.
         a. Conduct of business.
         b. No-shop.
         c. Confidentiality.
         d. Other.
      5. Other covenants.
         a. Transfer of employees.
         b. Obtaining of consents and approvals.
      6. Conditions to closing.
         a. Government approvals.
         b. Transfer and issuance of material permits.

      c.  Other consents and approvals (material contracts, leases and licenses, loan agreements, etc.).

      d.  No adverse change in business.

      e.  Legal opinions (not always available).

      f.  Representations true and covenants performed.

      g.  No litigation affecting transaction.

      h.  Related agreements and documents executed.

  7.  Closing (see VII).

  8.  Indemnification (less common outside the United States).

      a.  Coverage.

      b.  Threshold and deductible amounts.

      c.  Survival of obligations (time limits).

      d.  Remedy (hold back, escrow, bank guaranty).

  9.  Dispute resolution and governing law.

      a.  Normally local law.

      b.  Choice of forum—arbitration.

C.  Master and local agreements (multinational acquisitions).

  1.  Master agreement.

      a.  Description of overall transaction.

      b.  Overall price.

      c.  Allocation of price among jurisdictions.

      d.  Representations and warranties.

      e.  Preclosing covenants.

      f.  Other covenants.

      g.  Conditions to closing.

      h.  Coordination of local closings.

      i.  Indemnification.

      j.  Dispute resolution and governing law.

  2.  Local agreements.

      a.  Description of local transaction.

      b.  Local price.

      c.  Payment mechanism.

      d.  Covenants, if any, applicable only to local transfer.

      e.  Local closing mechanics.

      f.  Governing law—usually same as master agreement.

D.  Other agreements.

  1.  Noncompetition agreement.

      a.  Parties covered.

      b.  Scope (time, field, and geography).

      c.  Legality and enforceability.

      d.  Tax incidents.

    2. Employment agreements.
       a. Key employees.
       b. Sellers.
       c. Tax matters.
    3. Leases and licenses.
       a. Nontransferable property.
       b. Commingled property.
    4. Services agreements.
       a. Transition to permit target to achieve stand-alone capability.
       b. Essential commingled services.
    5. Parent or other guaranties.
    6. Ongoing supply or distribution agreements.
    7. Escrow agreement.

V. Legal due diligence (These are normally also covered by the representations and warranties.).
  A. Corporate matters.
    1. Organizational documents (statutes, etc.).
    2. Corporate records (minutes of past meetings, etc.).
    3. Annual and other reports.
    4. Lists of shareholders, officers, directors, auditors.
    5. Capitalization.
       a. Number of shares.
       b. Identity and status of shareholders.
       c. Any noncash consideration paid for shares (possible appraisal).
    6. Identification of and information concerning subsidiaries.
  B. Corporate authorization.
    1. Shareholder and director approval requirements.
    2. Resolutions.
    3. Powers of attorney.
    4. Shareholder and voting agreements.
  C. Financial matters.
    1. Financial statements.
       a. Five years' audited financial statements (if available), including balance sheets, income statements, consolidated and consolidating statements, and other statements.
       b. Most recent unaudited financial statements.
       c. Projections.
    2. Identification of bank accounts.
    3. Financings.
       a. Loan and credit agreements and other lending documents.

       b.   Financing leases, sale and leaseback transactions, installment purchases.

       c.   Recorded and unrecorded security interests and title retention arrangements.

       d.   Compliance reports to lenders.

    4.   Reports to and from and correspondence with auditors.

    5.   Tax matters.

       a.   Copies of income tax returns for five years.

       b.   Copies of other significant tax returns.

       c.   Audit reports.

       d.   Settlement documents.

D.  Government reports and filings.

    1.   Material permits and licenses.

    2.   Reports to and from and correspondence with government agencies.

    3.   Government applications.

E.  Material agreements.

    1. Joint venture or partnership agreements.

    2. Long-term agreements.

    3. Significant personal property leases.

    4. Material insurance policies.

    5. Agreements or arrangements with officers, directors, or other affiliates.

    6. Customer lists.

    7. Noncompetition agreements.

    8. Guaranties.

    9. Product warranties.

  10. Other material contracts.

F.  Intellectual property.

    1.   Patents.

    2.   Trademarks.

    3.   Computer programs.

    4.   Copyrights.

    5.   Know-how.

    6.   Licenses.

    7.   Registered users.

G.  Real estate.

    1.   Evidence of title.

    2.   Deeds or equivalent.

    3.   Mortgages and hypothecations.

    4.   Leases.

    H. Employee matters.
        1. Termination rights and indemnities.
        2. Individual and general agreements.
        3. Labor unions and agreements.
        4. Employee benefits.
    I. Environmental matters.
        1. Regulatory reports.
        2. Internal reports.
        3. On-site survey and testing.
    J. Litigation.
        1. Copies of all judgments, decrees, or orders applicable to target.
        2. Description of all current and threatened litigation, including names of attorneys to contact.
        3. Copies of significant court filings.
        4. Name of responsible insurance company, if any.

VI. Organize acquisition vehicle.
    A. Formalities.
    B. Capital.
    C. Management.

VII. Closing.
    A. Transfer documents.
        1. Execution of documents.
        2. Formalities (notarial deed, etc.).
        3. Mandatory or customary language on transfer documents.
    B. Governmental formalities.
        1. Notices.
        2. Filings.
            a. Foreign investment.
            b. Exchange control.
            c. Tax.
    C. Corporate formalities.
        1. Notices to or filings with corporation.
        2. Shareholder and director approval.
        3. Nominee shareholders.
        4. Election of new directors and officers.
    D. Other documents.
        1. Related agreements.
        2. Legal opinions.
        3. Certification of representations as true and correct as of closing.

# PART THREE

# Accounting and Tax Aspects

In Chapter 4, Roy W. Hoffman of American Express Tax and Business Services, Inc., provides a remarkably comprehensive discussion of the accounting aspects of cross-border deals. In the first part of the discussion, a thorough comparative analysis of similarities and differences of the generally accepted accounting principles (GAAP) in different areas of the world is presented. Then the author gives a detailed treatment of the process of due diligence. Following that, an analysis is provided of postdeal control objectives from an accounting perspective, which lead to procedures for managing the business in different countries and cultures. The financial reporting and auditing requirements for numerous representative national jurisdictions are presented.

In Chapters 5 and 6, David R. Tillinghast of Baker & McKenzie and Robert T. Bossart of Greenberg Traurig and Jane W. Meisel of Arthur Andersen cover the tax aspects of inbound and outbound deals, respectively.

In discussing inbound deals, Tillinghast describes in detail the commonly used forms of transactions. He then covers the issues in structuring the form of each of these transactions for U.S. tax purposes, as well as the tax aspects of certain important special issues, such as covenants not to compete and interest on money borrowed to finance the purchase. An extensive checklist is provided to guide the foreign acquirer on U.S. tax matters.

For outbound deals, the Bossart-Meisel team covers a variety of tax concerns that either do not exist or exist to a substantially lesser degree in a domestic acquisition. These include U.S. tax accessibility and tax deferral, U.S. foreign tax credit rules, the usual forms for offshore transactions (taxable stock acquisitions, taxable asset acquisitions, and tax-free exchanges), and overseas financing considerations. A checklist is provided here, as well.

# 4

# Accounting Aspects of International Mergers and Acquisitions

*Roy W. Hoffman*

In a mergers and acquisitions (M&A) environment, accounting is a vehicle to communicate the economics of a target business to a purchaser and to the potential financing sources for proposed transactions.

The association of accounting with mergers and acquisitions is a most natural and important one. The successful consummation of an acquisition transaction is based, in part, on the ability of a seller to communicate information about a target to a purchaser and the purchaser's ability to interpret, synthesize, evaluate, and react to such information. Accounting is a principal vehicle for communicating this information and for moving the negotiating parties closer to the closing of their deal. The postclosing process also depends on accounting, particularly the internal accounting controls necessary to monitor and to manage the acquired operations, consistent with generally accepted accounting principles (GAAP), which support the issuance of financial statements for different purposes and to different users. Accounting, therefore, is like many other things in life: It is often hard to live with but definitely impossible to live without.

The first section of this chapter, Understanding Financial Information, presents a comparative analysis of similarities and differences in the GAAP followed in various countries around the world. Next is the discussion, Evaluating the Target, in which elements of due diligence are described and examples of information that should be obtained from the target company and critically reviewed are provided. Finally, Postacquisition Considerations summarizes control objectives and procedures to be implemented for managing the business and for external financial reporting and audit requirements in a number of different countries.

## UNDERSTANDING FINANCIAL INFORMATION

Once one acknowledges that accounting is a communications vehicle, or a language, it is easy to identify an immediate problem in pursuing acquisitions on an international basis—the lack of a common language to link countries. This dilemma is real whether one is talking about a spoken language or a written one. Like a tourist who is not fluent in the language, a purchaser not well versed in the local GAAP that underlie financial information of a target company is at a great disadvantage.

Prospective purchasers must make informed investment decisions based on available data and have the ability to compare specific acquisition opportunities with others. Hence, they require transnational information to be understandable and comparable. The differences in GAAP between countries can have a significant effect on proposed transactions. Some of the variations are so great that prospective buyers in a particular country will not consider certain types of acquisitions in another. Thus, in countries where goodwill is required to be amortized against income over a period of years, companies can be discouraged from making acquisitions where a premium might have to be paid over net asset value to obtain strategic market position, undervalued or hidden assets, or exceptional earnings performance. Alternatively, a company that does not consolidate its foreign subsidiaries may be free to make its decisions on the basis of the investments' economics alone. One of the criteria, therefore, in identifying an international acquisition candidate is to determine whether local accounting policies treat such a transaction in a favorable way.

What follows here is a brief overview of some of the major and most frequently encountered areas of difference between U.S. GAAP and the accounting principles followed elsewhere around the world. A summary of this overview appears as Appendix 4.1.

### Accounting for Long-Term Investments in
### Share Capital of Other Entities

In the United States, the method of accounting for investments in other companies is generally based on the percentage of voting securities of the investee held by the investor. The degree of interest or influence is usually determined on the basis of the percentage of voting securities held. In rare circumstances, other factors may override the holdings test (e.g., if the investment is temporary in nature or if the investee cannot repatriate earnings because of foreign laws). The three methods primarily employed in the United States are consolidation, equity method, and fair value method.

### Consolidation

When the investor controls more than 50 percent of the voting securities of another company, the investee company is referred to as a *subsidiary* and is usually considered to be a part of a parent. Line-by-line consolidation of the subsidiary's financial statements with the financial statements of the parent is considered to be the most informative disclosure and is usually necessary for fair presentation under U.S. GAAP. The U.S. Securities and Exchange Commission (SEC), however, does not permit consolidation if the investor is a registrant and owns 50 percent or less of the voting securities of another company. Significant intercompany transactions between the parent and its subsidiaries are eliminated in the consolidated financial statements.

### Equity Method

When the investor holds 20 percent to 50 percent of the investee's voting securities or has a subsidiary that is not consolidated, the investment is generally stated at the underlying net asset value, with the equity in the investee's earnings or loss included in the investor's income statement for the current period (equity accounting). Any dividends received are treated as an adjustment to the basis of the investment. This method of accounting for 50 percent-or-less owned companies and nonconsolidated subsidiaries is followed by the United Kingdom and Canada, but it is not acceptable in many other countries.

### Fair Value Method

When the investor holds less than 20 percent of the voting securities of another company, the investment is generally stated at cost. Dividends declared or paid by investee companies that are carried at cost are included in the investor's earnings for the current year. Under Statement of Financial Accounting Standards (SFAS) No. 115, investments in debt securities intended to be held to maturity should be measured at amortized cost. Trading securities and available-for-sale securities should be measured at fair value, and realized gains and losses are included in earnings. For trading securities, unrealized holding gains and losses are included in earnings; these gains and losses are reported in equity until realized for available-for-sale securities. Timing of the recognition of dividend income differs in certain foreign countries where dividend income is recognized in each year, regardless of whether the dividends have been formally declared or paid.

## Translation of Foreign Currency Financial Statements and Accounting for Foreign Currency Transactions

The accounting policies of recognition and accounting for foreign exchange gains and losses vary significantly from country to country. Current U.S. practice under SFAS No. 52, issued by the Financial Accounting Standards Board (FASB), distinguishes between translation adjustments and transaction gains and losses. Translation adjustments arise when a foreign entity's financial statements are translated into U.S. dollars at the current exchange rate. Translation adjustments are not included in determining net income for the period. They are accumulated as a separate component of equity until disposal or substantial liquidation of the related foreign entity takes place.

Transaction gains and losses arise when exchange rate changes affect transactions of the enterprise. Transaction gains and losses are generally recognized as income in the accounting period in which they arise.

The accounting policies of many countries allow for either deferral of unrealized exchange gains or losses or capitalization of such gains and losses as part of the related asset. Some countries apply historical or current exchange rates, depending on the nature of the account or transaction, and recognize all gains and losses in the current period. Other countries require that only realized gains and losses be recognized in the accounts; still others require the recognition of unrealized losses (but not unrealized gains) in addition to realized gains and losses.

## Investment in Debt Securities

U.S. accounting principles require that debt securities intended to be held to maturity be stated at amortized cost. Such investments may not be written up to appraisal or market values, although these values must be disclosed in the notes to the financial statements. If the security is determined to be permanently impaired, it should be written down as net realized value. There is no provision for any subsequent write-up should appreciation occur.

In the United States, amortization is calculated using the *effective interest method* (also called present value amortization), which reflects a periodic interest amount equal to a constant percentage carrying value. The *straight-line method*, by contrast, reflects an arithmetic non-present-valued interest calculation and is also permitted in certain other countries, notably France and Japan.

## Deferred Income Taxes

U.S. GAAP require that income taxes be provided against current-period income as reflected in the financial statements, even though all or some of such income will not be reported for tax purposes in the current period and taxes will not be payable currently. This means that, even though some current-period accounting income is not currently taxable, income tax expense must be provided in the financial statements against income on which taxes are currently payable and income on which the tax liability is deferred regardless of the length of that deferral (the *deferral method*).

In Brazil and Japan, the concept of deferred taxes is recognized for consolidated financial reporting purposes only. Individual accounts in these countries record only the amount of tax currently payable or record income taxes solely on a cash basis. In France, the United Kingdom, and Germany, other methods of deferred taxation are permitted, most notably, the *liability method*, which focuses on differences between accounting and taxable income in the balance sheet as opposed to the deferral income.

## Fixed Assets and Depreciation

In the United States, fixed assets such as furniture, equipment, and leasehold improvements are recorded at historical cost and are depreciated on a systematic basis over the remaining useful life of the asset (or terms of the lease, in the case of leasehold improvements). In Brazil, it is accepted practice to write up longer-term assets to higher values that reflect inflation indexes provided by the government. The United Kingdom and France permit assets to be written up to appraised value. Depreciation in such cases is based on the value of the assets new.

## Research and Development Costs

In the United States, research and development (R&D) costs are generally expensed in the period incurred. France and Japan permit deferral of R&D costs (including costs of personnel, materials, equipment, facilities, and intangibles directly related to R&D activities) to future periods that may benefit from R&D activities.

## Inflation Accounting

A subject of much debate throughout the world has been the question of how to account for the impact of inflation. In the United States, SFAS No. 89 encourages, but does not require, that information be disclosed by public companies with assets in excess of $1 billion or inventories and property, plant, and equipment in excess of $125 million. Income is adjusted for the impact of changing prices for specific goods and services used by the company (current cost) and purchasing power gain or loss on net monetary items. If included, the inflation-adjusted data disclosed by public companies must be presented as supplementary information to the basic financial statements. The basis financial statements continue to be prepared on the basis of historical cost.

SFAS No. 89 applies only to U.S. public companies and has not been extended to foreign issuers by the SEC. However, the SEC requires foreign private issuers with financial statements denominated in the currency of a country that has experienced a cumulative inflationary effect of 100 percent over the most recent three-year period to present supplementary information that quantifies the effects of changing price on the company's financial condition and results of operations. In Canada, inflation accounting is required for public companies having a specified minimum amount of assets.

Requirements for disclosure of the impact of inflation differ widely in other countries. Australia, Germany, and Japan have no requirement for disclosure of inflation-adjusted financial information. Brazil allows for the write-up of certain assets (usually long-term assets) on the basis of certain inflation indexes provided by the government and other sources. The depreciation account reflects the adjusted asset values and, accordingly, may result in the reporting of current or replacement costs in the income statement. There also are countries that either require or permit disclosure of inflation-adjusted financial statements prepared on bases different from constant-dollar or current cost (as specified by SFAS No. 89).

## Capitalization of Interest Expense

U.S. accounting principles require the capitalization of interest costs as part of the historical cost of certain "qualifying" assets if the asset requires a period of time to get it to the condition and to the location of its intended use, assuming interest costs are incurred during that period. In general, capitalization of interest costs applies to major assets constructed for a company's use or assets intended for sale or lease that are constructed or produced as discrete projects, like ships or aircraft.

In France, the interest costs incurred during construction or production of such assets are considered to be period costs. Therefore, the interest costs are charged to income rather than capitalized as part of the cost of the assets, although interest related to the financing of costs of certain internal construction may be capitalized.

## Accounting Changes

In the United States, a change in an accounting principle or its method of application is reported, in most cases, in the income statement in the period during which the change occurs. The effect of the accounting change on periods prior to the change is presented as a cumulative amount, net of tax, below income from continuing operations. In the United Kingdom, a prior period adjustment is permitted where there is a change in accounting policy (as opposed to an accounting estimate) and the comparatives are restated.

## Debt Issue Expense

U.S. accounting principles require the deferral and amortization of debt issue costs. The SEC also requires that some portion of lump-sum fees paid to investment banks in takeover or leveraged buy-out (LBO) transactions be included in debt issuance costs. Thus, debt issue costs are recorded as deferred charges and amortized to income over the life of the debt. In Brazil, Australia, and Japan, the amortization periods are limited irrespective of debt maturity dates. In Germany, the full amount of debt issue costs is charged against earnings in the year incurred.

U.S. GAAP also specify the accounting treatment for any discount or premium arising on the sale of long-term debt. Debt discount or premium must be reported as a direct deduction from or addition to the liability and may be amortized as interest expense or interest income over the life of the debt. The method of amortization must produce a constant rate of interest on the amount of debt outstanding in any period.

## Accounting for Business Combinations (Mergers and Acquisitions)

A business combination occurs when one entity acquires part or all of another entity for cash, shares, or other consideration. The principal authoritative literature applicable to accounting for business combinations in the United States is represented by Statements 141 and 142 of the Financial Accounting Standards Board. FASB 141, "Business Combinations," is effective for all business combinations occurring after June 30, 2001. FASB 142, "Goodwill and Other Intangible Assets," is effective in fiscal years beginning after December 15, 2001; however, early application of FASB 142 is permitted for certain entities with fiscal years beginning after March 15, 2001, provided that the first interim financial statements have not yet been issued. The authoritative literature prior to the June 2001 issuance of FASB 141 and 142 was Opinion 16 of the former Accounting Principals Board (APB) for business combinations and Opinion 17 for intangible assets.

APB 16 acknowledged two distinct types of business combinations: (1) pooling of interests and (2) purchase. The opinion identified 12 criteria, grouped into three broad categories, to test whether a particular combination should be accounted for as a pooling of interests. If the combination met all 12 criteria, pooling-of-interests accounting was required. The pooling-of-interests method was defined as accounting for a business combination as a uniting of the ownership interests of two or more companies by exchange of equity securities. FASB 141, which supersedes APB 16 in its entirety, requires all business combinations to be accounted for by a single method called the purchase method. This change put the United States more in step with how business combinations are accounted for outside of the United States. Use of the pooling-of-interests method is rare in many jurisdictions and prohibited in others, including France, Australia, and Germany.

## Application of Purchase Accounting

### *Standard Historical Cost Principles*

Under purchase accounting, the cost of an acquired entity becomes the new basis for recording the investment in the net assets of the target. This concept is reasonably consistent around the world where purchase accounting is applied. If the purchase price consists of consideration other than cash, the cost of such consideration is determined by its fair market value or the fair market value of the net assets received from the acquiree, whichever is more readily determinable.

### *Cost of an Acquired Entity*

There are three general categories of costs that ultimately determine the total acquisition cost to be accounted for under the purchase method:

1. The up-front purchase price to be paid to the seller by the closing date of the transaction.
2. Contingent future consideration based on the occurrence of events identified in the acquisition agreement.
3. Transaction costs of consummating the acquisition that will be paid to parties other than the seller.

The *up-front price* can be either a fixed amount stated in the acquisition agreement or an amount based on a formula applied to certain financial data at or prior to the closing date. In either case, any consideration that must be exchanged between buyer and seller after the closing date is characterized as contingent consideration.

*Contingent consideration* usually results from one of the following postclosing events: (1) an audit of the target's financial statements, as of the closing date and/or for the period ending at such date, that determines that adjustments to the up-front price are required pursuant to a contractual formula applied to such financial statements; (2) achievement of contractually specified earnings levels (an earnout formula); or (3) the nonachievement of contractually specified market values for securities issued to the seller as part of the up-front price. Contingent payments are not recorded as a component of the cost of an acquired entity until resolution of the uncertainty giving rise to the contingency is reasonably assured.

*Transaction costs*, frequently as high as 5 percent or more of the purchase price, encompass a wide variety of services necessary to consummate the acquisition and include commissions to finders or other intermediaries; fees to investment bankers, attorneys, accountants, actuaries, engineers, or other outside consultants; and commitment or origination fees and other costs relating to financing the acquisition.

## Allocating Costs to Net Assets

The valuation of the assets and liabilities of an acquired business by the acquirer is the essence of and often the most difficult consequence of accounting for a business combination under the purchase method. The previous carrying values of the target's assets and liabilities give way to what could be an entirely new series of values, based on the total acquisition cost (including transaction costs) allocated to individual assets and liabilities based on their relative fair market values. The former stockholders' equity of the acquired company is eliminated.

All of the assets acquired and liabilities assumed are reviewed to determine their fair market values at the acquisition date. The most typical valuation concepts are:

- *Cash and accounts receivable.* Most frequently, these are valued at their carrying values prior to acquisition, assuming that such assets can be converted into other liquid assets at the option of the holder within a reasonably short period. Receivables should be valued after considering allowances for returns, discounts, unearned interest, and bad debts.

- *Marketable securities.* At fair value.

- *Inventories.* For finished goods, the standard is net realizable value less a normally expected gross profit (for work in process, the standard is also adjusted for costs to complete). For raw materials, the standard is current replacement cost. In almost all situations, any LIFO (last-in, first-out) reserve maintained by the target prior to the acquisition is eliminated.

- *Intangible assets' fair value.* Intangible assets can be trademarks, customer lists, and license agreements, for example.

- *Property, plant, and equipment.* These are booked at current replacement cost for "similar capacity" (that is, adjusted to used-asset market).

- *Accounts payable and accrued expenses.* These are booked at carrying values prior to acquisition, assuming cash payments to be made within a reasonably short period.

- *Notes payable and long-term debt.* These are booked at the net present value of cash payments to be made using a current interest rate applicable to the type of debt being assumed.

- *Pension plan obligations.* These are carried at the excess of deficiency of assumed projected benefit obligations based on the actuarial present value of pension benefits attributed to the pension benefit formula used to service the plan assets transferred to the acquirer. This calculation gives rise to a recorded liability or an asset. The data necessary for valuing the net liability or asset should be reviewed by a consulting actuary.

- *All other liabilities.* The net present value of future cash payments using an appropriate discount rate is the standard.

Once all of the target company's assets and liabilities have been individually fair valued, the net fair value is compared to the total acquisition cost. In many situations, a difference between the two represents the excess of acquisition cost over the net fair value of assets acquired, resulting in goodwill. Goodwill is no longer amortized but is evaluated for impairment on an annual basis and also between the annual evaluations when other factors exist (for example, a significant adverse change in the business climate that may indicate goodwill impairment).

In some countries, goodwill is recognized only on the acquisition of an enterprise and represents the excess of the purchase price paid over the *book value* of the net assets acquired, not an adjusted value as in the United States. Some countries require write-off of goodwill against current earnings over a period of time, whereas others, like the United States, permit goodwill to be carried indefinitely as an intangible asset without amortization.

When the difference between the total acquisition cost and the fair value of the net assets acquired results in an excess of fair value over cost, a careful evaluation of the reasons for the apparent "bargain purchase" must be made. Noncurrent assets (other than noncurrent marketable securities and deferred tax assets) should be written down to the extent of the excess of fair value over cost, and any remaining excess should generally be recognized as an extraordinary gain in the period the business combination is completed.

## Accounting for Contingencies

Contingent consideration is one of the components used in arriving at the total acquisition cost to be accounted for when such contingency contribution is either paid or becomes payable to the seller and when cash or other assets of the acquirer (other than its own shares of stock) are the medium of payment. This most frequently is classified as additional goodwill. Often, however, contingencies exist that cannot be resolved prior to the consummation of the acquisition. Litigation and governmental investigations into environmental concerns are examples. SFAS 141 requires that such items be considered in the fair valuing of the assets and liabilities of the acquiree as follows:

- After evaluating the contingency, one determines whether the creation or the impairment of an asset or the incurring of a liability is probable and whether the result can be quantified.
- If a resulting asset or liability is determined within one year after the closing, an adjustment is made to the allocation of the total acquisition cost based on the fair value of the asset or the liability arising from resolution of the contingency.
- If, after the allocation period, an asset is created or impaired or a liability is incurred as a result of the resolution of a preacquisition contingency, it is accounted for in the period of resolution through a credit or charge to earnings.

## Purchase Accounting and Income Taxes

SFAS 141, Business Combinations, requires that amounts assigned to assets acquired and liabilities assumed in a purchase business combination be at fair value. Frequently, fair value will differ for book purposes from the tax bases of the assets acquired and the liabilities assumed, for example, because the transaction is nontaxable.

Current practice holds that the tax basis of an asset or a liability should not be considered in determining its fair value for purposes of allocating the purchase price to specific assets and liabilities. Assets acquired and liabilities assumed are recorded at their "gross" fair value. Differences between the assigned values and the tax bases of assets acquired and liabilities assumed in purchase business combinations are regarded as temporary differences. Accordingly, assuming likely realization, deferred tax assets and liabilities are recognized for differences between the assigned values and the tax bases of assets acquired and liabilities assumed in a purchase type transaction.

When the purchase price exceeds the fair value of identifiable net assets acquired, the result is:

- Assign fair values (irrespective of the tax bases) to identifiable assets acquired and liabilities assumed.

- Compare the assigned fair values of the identifiable assets and liabilities with their tax bases to determine the temporary differences.

- Recognize deferred tax assets and liabilities for the future tax consequences of the deductible and taxable temporary differences between the assigned values and their tax bases.

- Recognize a deferred tax asset for the tax benefits of operating loss and tax credit carryforwards for tax purposes acquired in the combination.

- Recognize a valuation allowance for all or some portion of the deferred tax asset for acquired deductible temporary differences and acquired carryforwards to reduce that deferred tax asset to the amount that *more likely than not* will be realized in the future by the consolidated entity.

- Record goodwill for the difference between the purchase price and the values assigned to identifiable assets and liabilities, including the deferred tax assets (net of any valuation allowance) and deferred tax liabilities.

## General Comments

We have covered the broad areas in U.S. accounting principles and practices. The methods differ from those of other countries. Differences also exist in disclosure requirements between the United States and other countries.

A target's financial statements should conform to the accounting policies used by the acquirer. Such a process may not be easy because records may be inadequate or because the need to revise several years' historical accounts could be a time-consuming job. This exercise should be completed as early as possible within the overall acquisition process.

When acquiring a non-U.S.-based listed or private company, it may also be necessary to conform the accounts of the acquirer with those generally accepted in the country of the target. This would typically be the case if common stock was being issued by the acquirer in exchange for shares in the target. In the United States, a foreign buyer must be prepared to revise its own accounting policies to produce financial statements in conformity with U.S. GAAP, or to provide disclosure reconciling the non–U.S. accounts to those that would be generally accepted in the United States (this is discussed later).

## International Accounting Standards

The International Accounting Standards Committee (IASC) was set up in 1973 by professional accountancy bodies in nine countries: Australia, Canada, France, Germany, Japan, Mexico, the Netherlands, the United Kingdom, and the United States.

### *Objectives*

The objectives of the IASC were:

- To formulate and publish in the public interest accounting standards to be observed in the presentation of financial statements and to promote their worldwide acceptance and observance.
- To work generally for the improvement and the harmonization of regulations, accounting standards, and procedures relating to the presentation of financial statements.

In 2001, the IASC was restructured and the International Accounting Standards Board (IASB) was formed. The IASB assumed standard-setting responsibilities effective April 1, 2001. The IASB wishes to promote convergence of accounting standards around the world.

### *Standards*

Current international accounting standards deal with most of the topics that are important internationally in the financial statements of business enterprises.

- They require a consolidated balance sheet, an income statement, a cash flow statement, and industry and geographical segment information.
- They deal with the recognition and the measurement of inventories, depreciation, research and development costs, income taxes, property, plant, equipment, leases, revenue, retirement benefit costs, government grants, goodwill, borrowing costs, and investments.

- They deal with presentation of the income statement and balance sheet, extraordinary items, current assets, current liabilities, and government assistance.
- They require disclosures of income statement and balance sheet items, contingencies, post–balance sheet events, related parties, and related-party transactions.
- They deal with mergers and acquisitions, investments in affiliates, and interests in joint ventures.
- They deal with disclosures in the financial statements of banks and similar financial institutions, financial reporting in hyperinflationary economies, and reporting by retirement benefit plans.

International accounting standards apply to the financial statements of any commercial, industrial, or business enterprise. The IASB Framework, which reflects more up-to-date thinking, refers to commercial, industrial, and business reporting enterprises, whether in the public or the private sector. The application of international accounting standards to business enterprises will be achieved through conformity with international financial reporting standards (IFRS).

Individual countries may decide to limit the applicability of the requirements of a standard when incorporating those requirements into national standards or law. For example, some countries may exempt small enterprises, and some countries may limit the application of the requirements to companies whose securities are listed on stock exchanges or to consolidated financial statements.

It is sometimes argued that international accounting standards are developed for the financial statements of listed companies or even of just those companies with listings on foreign capital markets. It is also argued that the standards should apply only to consolidated financial statements, because the separate legal entity financial statements are often governed by national accounting requirements that are influenced by tax considerations. The committee believes that implementation difficulties in some countries should not block the use of international accounting standards in other countries. Therefore, the committee seeks to develop international accounting standards that can be applied in all financial statements of all business, although some countries may exempt or limit the application of the standards.

## The SEC and Foreign Securities Issuers

The SEC was created to establish more efficient capital markets by providing adequate protection for investors, hence increasing their confidence. It is the policy of the SEC to fulfill its role primarily through regulations that require full, fair, and adequate disclosure of information to investors on securities issued and traded in the public market.

Non–U.S. issuers are generally treated like domestic ones. They are confronted with no special barriers if they wish to enter U.S. capital markets. This is consistent with the free enterprise philosophy of the United States, which has traditionally held that free market forces should determine the direction of capital flows throughout the world so that economic efficiency is maximized. This philosophy permits U.S. investors the freedom to invest their money wherever they desire. Accordingly, the SEC permits foreign companies to enter U.S. capital markets freely if they are willing to comply with its requirements to provide full, fair, and adequate disclosure.

Foreign issuers may find the disclosures required by the SEC burdensome, both because the SEC requirements are usually more extensive than disclosure requirements in other countries and because there are differences in accounting principles between the United States and other countries. To alleviate this burden, the legislation that created the SEC was amended in 1964 to permit the commission to grant certain special exemptions to the issuers of foreign securities provided that these exemptions do not diminish protection of U.S. investors.

As a result, some of the reporting requirements of foreign issuers are less stringent than those for domestic issuers. The commission has occasionally relaxed specific rules when asked to do so by foreign registrants on the grounds that hardship would result from compliance.

In addition, the SEC has adopted certain changes to reporting requirements for foreign registrants and has released additional proposals to: (1) extend certain of the foreign registrant accommodations to U.S. registrants; (2) further streamline reporting requirements for both domestic and foreign registrants; (3) reduce, for foreign issuers, the requirement to reconcile to U.S. GAAP for certain items (e.g., business combinations and foreign currency translation) if home-country accounting principles comply with international accounting standards.

How to enable foreign issuers to overcome the substantial problems of adapting their practices to U.S. requirements without increasing the risk to investors has traditionally been approached by the SEC from different perspectives on accounting versus auditing issues. On accounting matters, the commission is flexible. U.S. GAAP are not imposed on foreign companies. Instead, foreign issuers may file financial statements based on foreign accounting principles as long as a reconciliation of their financial statements to U.S. GAAP is included when there are material differences between the foreign principles and U.S. GAAP. The reconciliation is generally presented in the footnotes to the foreign issuer's financial statements.

## EVALUATING THE TARGET

After a target's financial information has been translated by the purchaser from an accounting point of view, the next step to consider in the acquisition process is the qualitative evaluation of the target, or *due diligence*. A due diligence review is a challenging and interactive exercise in which the acquisition team conducts an investigative analysis of the operating and/or financial areas of the target's business. The review is international to the extent of the geographical dispersion of the target's operations, assets, and markets and can be an integral part of the planning of multinational corporate and tax structures of the combined company. Its overall objective is to assist the purchaser in assessing the risks, the rewards, and the opportunities of a potential merger or acquisition. The review procedures vary and must be adapted to meet the needs of almost each acquisition. In addition to in-house personnel designated by the purchaser, the acquisition team frequently includes accountants, lawyers, and other outside specialists.

## Scope

The scope of a due diligence review may be narrow or broad. The most typical narrow-scope review is initial fact-finding. Initial fact-finding may be limited, for instance, to obtaining information about the target company's operations by discussions with target company management and its accountants and by a review of accountants' working papers. This level of due diligence may be useful when an acquirer is in the early discussion states of a potential transaction and needs general information about the company being considered.

A broad-scope due diligence review, whether performed in stages or with all procedures authorized at the outset, may include expanded fact-finding or procedures designed to provide conclusions or recommendations. The following procedures are typical of expanded fact-finding:

- Make inquiries or seek other corroborating evidence supporting target management's comments about the company's operations, interim financial information, employment contracts, sales backlog, and so on.
- Perform fact-finding procedures with respect to the target's
  —Ownership and management.
  —Products, markets, and major competitors.
  —Status of litigation, if any.
  —Sales methods, product distribution, salespeoples' compensation, pricing policies, and terms.
  —Product development efforts.
  —Relative position in the industry (comparative data on sales, backlog, earnings, dividends, and certain key ratios, usually covering the past several years).
  —Principal suppliers and terms.
  —Age, capacity, and use of property, plant, and equipment; capital commitments; and future capital requirements.
  —Subsidiaries and the amount and the method of handling intercompany transactions.
  —Long-range plans and budgets; relationships with stockholders, creditors, customers, and the community.
  —Personnel administration, interdepartmental coordination, organization, labor market, employee contracts, strike record, and so on.

The following examples illustrate due diligence review procedures designed to provide conclusions or recommendations.

- Evaluate the target's marketing, planning, administrative, or other functions.
- Apply specific procedures to identified elements, accounts, or items of the target's financial statements.
- Assess the adequacy of data processing operations in meeting the needs of the target.
- Apply specific procedures to all or part of the company's system of internal accounting controls.
- Read projected income statements, cash flow projections, or other prospective information.
- Perform an in-depth review of the target's employee benefit plans.
- Perform an in-depth review of the target's tax posture.
- Perform an in-depth review of the tax aspects of a proposed acquisition or merger.
- Perform a fair market value analysis of the company.
- Provide assistance or advice on the strategy for negotiating an acquisition or merger.

## Procedures

Fact-finding is the means most often used to obtain requested information about a target. It includes:

- Systematic inquiry—asking the right questions.
- Observation and critical analysis—evaluating responses to inquiries in light of other data gathered, knowledge of the industry, and a general understanding of business risks and the ways they interrelate.
- Follow-up—making additional inquiries and seeking corroborating evidence when necessary.

Because of the flexible nature of a due diligence review, the fact-finding process cannot be standardized. The manner in which such efforts progress depends on the needs of the acquirer. The extent of corroborating evidence sought, if any, depends on judgment, the circumstances, and whether such evidence is required as part of the predetermined scope of the review. The approach followed should never be mechanical; the acquisition team should always be able to react to additional information as it is uncovered.

Obtaining information on a target company through inquiry and observation can be difficult. Even the most experienced review team should be alert to certain pitfalls. For various reasons, the target company's management may view the due diligence process as somewhat adversarial, despite previously positive negotiations, causing it to be uncooperative or inclined to color the facts to present the company in its best possible light.

In addition, the process of inquiry requires the experience of asking the right questions along with an intuitive grasp of how deeply one can probe without disrupting the process being made toward an acquisition, merger, or other agreement. Some of the more frequent pitfalls encountered are discussed in the next section.

## Frequent Pitfalls in Evaluating a Target

### *Omitting Key Questions or Question Areas*
Perhaps the most important qualitative characteristic that ought to be possessed by the due diligence team is business acumen developed over time through involvement in other fact-finding missions. Without experience, it is difficult to ask the right questions; over time, however, the members of the team should have acquired a natural understanding of how potential business risks interrelate. Consider the case of a manufacturer who sells machinery through independent dealerships. Inquiries about these dealerships should focus on the terms of dealership agreements, on floor-planning arrangements, on customer financing on which the company is directly or contingently liable, and on the size and the financial stability of the dealers themselves, along with the possibility that the company may be forced to acquire one or more dealerships in order to sustain its marketing efforts.

### *Failure to Utilize Appropriate Industry or Technical Expertise*
Inquiries often cover areas requiring a specialized understanding of scientific terms, producing processes, unusual industry conditions, and so on. Whenever possible, the team should prepare for these areas by involving the appropriate specialists prior to initial fact-finding. For example, a manufacturer of precision aircraft parts may use numerous metal-forming operations to create each product. The effectiveness with which these operations function may be measurable only by an industrial chemist.

### *Vague or Unclear Responses*
Inquiries may be hindered by management's inability or unwillingness to fully respond to questions. Company managers also may be concerned that a specific answer would be in conflict with previously obtained information. Sometimes, but not always, persistence in follow-up inquiry can overcome this problem.

### *Incomplete Information*
Target company management may seek to increase the perceived attractiveness of the company by providing partial responses to questions. For example, it may state

that overall employee turnover has declined 20 percent in the past year without mentioning that a key level of skilled employee has actually experienced increased turnover. An alert inquirer can often pursue question areas to minimize such hidden information.

### Incorrect Information

Unless the team is charged with the verification of certain information received, it may be impossible to determine whether responses are accurate. The inquirer should at all times be observing events that may be in conflict with the answers or information being received. Whenever possible, the inquirer should also ask several managers to provide their perspectives on a given area of inquiry.

### Responses in Inappropriate Form

Very often, in an attempt to save time, management will react to a request for information by providing documents or answers that do not directly satisfy the request. Management may supply voluminous legal documentation that must be scrutinized at length in order to uncover the information desired. This presents the team with the choice of devoting extra time to this task or redirecting management to respond more precisely.

### Lack of Cooperation

The ostensible willingness of a company's management to permit business inquiries to be made by outsiders does not ensure the management's cooperation. During the inquiry process, managers must discharge their day-to-day responsibilities simultaneously with responding to information requests. In the case of a prospective acquisition, managers may feel their positions are endangered through cooperation. The result can be an unwillingness to participate satisfactorily in the due diligence review.

### Demand for Further Commitment Prior to Proceeding

The target's management may not be expecting the depth of review typically found in a good due diligence effort and may decide to cut off the inquiry and require that, for additional time to be devoted to describing the company, a formal agreement be reached.

### Limitations on Access to People or Operating Locations

Management may decide that, rather than cut off inquiries or refuse to answer all questions, it will limit the team to one or several persons at a single location, possibly away from the heart of operations. If the review is intended to be an in-depth fact-finding mission, such limitations can undermine the acquirer's objectives. Access to the right persons in an organization and direct observation of operations and productive facilities are almost always crucial to a satisfactory description of the business.

## Delays in Response

The pitfalls just mentioned can surface in the form of slow responses to requests for information. For example, interim financial statements available within a few days or a week of the period covered may be withheld for several weeks. Such delays can create severe difficulties in meeting contractual deadlines relating to a transaction.

Below are examples of common mistakes that can be made when performing fact-finding. This list is not comprehensive.

- Considering the cash flow potential of different business segments without understanding the tax treaties between various countries that could impact the ability of repatriate earnings.

- Evaluating operational efficiency without considering severance statutes in different countries.

- Obtaining a summary of pension assets and vested benefits without information as to the underlying assumed rates of return on plan assets.

- Analyzing overall employee turnover without regard to specific employee classifications.

- Failing to consider the impact of socioeconomic or political changes on future operating potential.

- Observing general cleanliness, safety features, and work flow without noticing the employee.

- Inquiring as to the reputation of past accountants without obtaining an explanation as to why they were dropped.

- Discussing methods of buying and selling commodities of financial instruments without inquiring about whether appropriate protective financial steps (like hedging) are taken.

- Failing to follow up on pending items.

- Failing to inform the purchaser of delays in obtaining information on which the seller may wish to rely during negotiations.

- Obtaining internal projections without their underlying assumptions.

- Listing the selling shareholders without investigating their relationship to one another and/or their motivations in considering a sale.

- Analyzing past tax returns without asking if they have been audited.

- Comparing relative product contributions to revenues on a dollar basis without considering relative unit sales.

- Failing to establish a clear, initial understanding on the seller's part as to the specific objectives for the due diligence review.

## What to Look For

The end product of the due diligence process is a level of comfort for the acquirer concerning the quality of the operation being acquired. In evaluating a prospective target, it is often difficult to separate the financial and the nonfinancial areas of investigation, because there are numerous overlaps. For example, the evaluation of the target's management and staff personnel is a nonfinancial consideration but the amount of their compensation and fringe benefits is clearly a financial concern. Since accounting tends to have a quantitative emphasis, the focus will be on the financial aspects of evaluating the target, specifically on the assets, liabilities, and operations reported on its financial statements.

The checklist at the end of this chapter outlines the types of information about the target that the acquisition team normally needs to obtain. What the purchaser is looking for in accumulating and studying such data can be highlighted below for major financial statement captions.

## POSTACQUISITION CONSIDERATIONS

To this point, the accounting aspects of mergers and acquisitions have been associated with events and processes that have occurred prior to the actual consummation of the transaction: First, there is a need to understand the accounting bases for financial information about the target that has been provided to the purchaser. Then, once the purchaser relates the accounting principles and methods underlying such information to his or her own country's GAAP, the due diligence process accelerates in a substantive way and the assets, liabilities, and operations of the target are evaluated qualitatively by the acquisition team.

If the purchaser and the seller are able to agree on all of the terms and conditions for a deal, a written agreement is executed and a closing date is scheduled. The closing date for an acquisition has a twofold significance: First, it signifies the official transfer of ownership of the target from the seller to the purchaser. Second, it confirms the responsibilities of the purchaser to integrate the newly acquired entity into its own operating and/or reporting systems. Some acquired companies will be operated as fully self-sufficient, stand-alone businesses, whereas others will be completely merged or otherwise operationally combined with the purchaser's existing business and will lose all or part of their previous identity.

Because many international acquisitions result in acquired companies operating as individual freestanding entities (particularly true in the case of acquisitions of U.S. companies by non–U.S. acquirers), a great deal of effort will be required to ensure that the acquirer can monitor the financial position and the results of operations of its new business from a distance, even though representatives from the parent will often be permanently on site. To react quickly to sudden changes in sales volumes, production costs, or local and/or global economic conditions, the new acquisition will need to be well controlled and organized, that is, conducive to reliable financial reporting. Thus, the concept of *internal* control within the new company will be discussed next. The final section will be described as *external* financial reporting responsibilities and audit requirements that the new company may face in a number of different countries around the world.

## CONTROL—AS EVIDENCED IN FINANCIAL REPORTING AND AUDIT REQUIREMENTS

Commitment to control at the highest levels of an organization is what sets a positive "tone at the top" about control. The "tone at the top" will be reflected in setting priorities and allocating resources to achieve control. The importance of control will be clear to all members of the organization and they will behave accordingly. Putting it differently, if good control is not important to top management, it may not be important to others in the organization.

The reporting process of a company involves obtaining input from transaction records as the basis for making accounting entries to a general ledger and ultimately preparing financial reports. In multinational organizations, preparation of internal and external financial reports or statements typically requires consolidation and other procedures, such as translation of financial statements into the reporting currency of the parent company.

In the pages that follow, the financial reporting requirements, authoritative sources for acceptable accounting principles, and objectives for independent audits are summarized for the United States, Brazil, Canada, Mexico, Denmark, France, Germany, the Netherlands, Spain, the United Kingdom, Australia, Hong Kong, Japan, Singapore, Israel, and Saudi Arabia.

Note that the summaries included here were compiled within the 24-month period prior to the publication of this book. The reader should inquire, therefore, about more recent legislation or regulations that would impact the discussion that follows.

### United States

#### Public Companies
*Statutory Reports.* Companies whose securities are listed on a national securities exchange, those with securities traded over the counter and with total assets of over $3 million and with 500 or more holders of one class of equity securities, or companies with over 300 holders of a class of securities registered under the Securities Act of 1933 must file annual and quarterly reports with the SEC. The form and content of the financial statements as well as any required schedules are prescribed in Regulation S-X. The annual report on Form 10-K must contain a comparative balance sheet as of the end of the most recent and preceding fiscal years. Comparative income statements and statements of cash flows must be included for the most recent and two preceding fiscal years. Notes to the financial

statements are required as of the end of the two or three most recent fiscal years, depending on the nature of the note. Annual financial statements must be audited, and quarterly financial statements must be reviewed under Statement on Auditing Standards No. 71, "Interim Financial Information." Annual financial statements and schedules must be in English. Consolidated or combined financial statements are required, although there are limited circumstances under which certain subsidiaries might not be consolidated.

***Tax Returns.*** Returns must be filed annually with the Internal Revenue Service (IRS). Tax returns must be prepared in compliance with the rules and regulations encompassed by the Internal Revenue Code. Auditor involvement is not required, and returns are strictly confidential.

## Foreign Companies

Foreign companies are generally treated like domestic companies. They are confronted with no specific barriers if they wish to enter U.S. capital markets. As earlier indicated, because some foreign companies may find SEC requirements more extensive than disclosure requirements in their own countries and because of differences in accounting principles, the SEC can grant certain special exemptions to foreign companies, provided these exemptions do not diminish the protection of U.S. investors. The SEC adopted changes to reporting requirements for foreign registrants in 1994. These changes are: (1) foreign registrants are now permitted to file disclosure documents in draft form and on a nonpublic basis; (2) the SEC will accept, without a reconciliation, a statement of cash flows prepared in accordance with International Accounting Standard (IAS 7) instead of SFAS No. 95; (3) first-time registrants with the SEC will be required to provide a reconciliation to U.S. GAAP of only the two most recent fiscal years and any interim period financial statements required to be included in the document; and (4) a number of required schedules have been eliminated.

***Statutory Reports.*** Non–U.S. companies are automatically subject to the registration and reporting provisions of the Securities Exchange Act of 1934 if they have total assets in excess of $3 million and a class of equity securities held by 500 or more people, of whom 300 or more reside in the United States. Such companies automatically become subject to the 1934 act by taking any of the following three actions: (1) listing a class of securities on a U.S. national securities exchange, (2) registering an offering of securities pursuant to the Securities Act of 1933 when there are more than 300 shareholders on a worldwide basis for a class of securities, and (3) electing to comply with the 1934 act although the asset and security holder tests are not met. A non–U.S. company subject to the 1934 act must file the appropriate forms required under the act or establish an exemption from the act's requirements. Absent an available exemption, the non–U.S. company must comply with the 1934 act by filing the appropriate forms to meet both the registration and the continual reporting requirements of the act. The form used by most non–U.S. companies to meet their initial registration and annual reporting requirements is Form 20-F. Form 20-F requires disclosure of certain items of financial and nonfinancial information about the registrant, including specified financial statements, footnotes, accountants' report, and financial schedules. The 1934 act requires companies to file interim reports during the year on Form 6-K, disclosing information about the registrant that has been disclosed publicly in its home country. Non–U.S. companies considered equivalent to U.S. domestic companies (because of ownership of 50 percent or more of their shares by U.S. residents, the extent of their U.S. operations, or the composition of their board of directors) are required to file the same reports within the same period of time as U.S. registrants. Financial statements filed as part of Form 20-F may be based on the accounting principles followed in the registrant's home country. However, if there are material differences between the foreign accounting principles and U.S. GAAP, a reconciliation to U.S. accounting principles and SEC Regulation S-X must also be filed. Fiscal-year financial statements required in either a registration statement or an annual report filed with the SEC must be audited by an independent public accountant. The audit examination of a non–U.S. company must satisfy the same requirements as the audit of a domestic company; that is, the SEC must be satisfied that generally accepted U.S. auditing standards were applied in the accountants' audit of the financial statements for all periods presented.

### Audits and Accounting

*Independence.* Certified public accountants must be independent of the corporation. This is required by the SEC, the American Institute of Certified Public Accountants (AICPA), and the various state boards of accountancy.

*Auditors' Reports.* These generally state whether the financial statements "present fairly" the financial position, results of operations, and cash flows in conformity with GAAP applied on a consistent basis.

*Authoritative Sources.* Generally accepted auditing standards (GAAS) are prescribed by the AICPA. GAAP are prescribed by the FASB.

## Brazil

### Companies Subjected to Some Degree of "Public Accountability"

*Statutory Reports.* The corporations in reference are comprised of:

- Listed companies (called "open capital" corporations), whose quarterly and annual financial statements must be filed with the Securities Commission (CVM—after the name in Portuguese: Comissão de Valores Mobiliários), the annual financial statements having to be published.
- Banks and financial institutions, regulated by the Central Bank of Brazil (BACEN), where the semiannual and annual financial statements must be published and filed with BACEN.

- Other companies, such as insurance companies, pension plan funds, healthcare enterprises, and others, that are regulated by governmental agencies and that have a number of requirements regarding chart of accounts, accounting criteria, financial statement formulas, and information filing.

The current format of financial statements, including explanatory notes, is regulated in detail by the Corporate Law, as are the methods for recognizing and measuring assets and liabilities. These rules are mandatory for corporations (listed or not) that have to publish their annual financial statements. Publicly held corporations are required to follow more comprehensive rules set out by CVM and by the Brazilian Institute of Accountants (IBRACON—Instituto Brasileiro de Auditores Independentes)—and companies that submit their financial statements to annual audit tend to do the same. Financial statements published by corporations subjected to some degree of public accountability have to be audited. Interim fi-nancial statements are to be submitted to a limited review by independent accountants, quite similar in scope to the one required by the SEC in the United States.

Under Corporate Law and CVM regulations, publicly held corporations must prepare and publish consolidated statements when these two conditions are met cumulatively: (1) the holding company has power to elect the board of directors of the investee, whatever the percentage of interest held; and (2) more than 30 percent of the investor shareholders' equity is in voting shares or quotas issued by affiliates and subsidiaries (15 percent if the investment in each subsidiary individually is taken into consideration).

Other companies may and do prepare consolidated financial statements, although they are not legally required to do so. CVM has the authority to decide whether companies should be included or excluded from consolidation. When the business of corporations within a group is so different that they cannot reasonably be treated as a single undertaking, they can be excluded from consolidation.

The consolidation procedures follow generally accepted standards internationally, such as elimination of intercompany balances, investments in subsidiaries against the respective shareholders' equity, intercompany profits on goods originated in related companies and still retained within the group, and disclosure of minority interest income and equity. Disclosure of information on the subsidiaries also follows generally applied patterns.

In acquiring control of a subsidiary, a company should show in its accounting records the amount of the subsidiary's assets at accounting records' value, any cost excess or shortfall being shown as positive or negative goodwill on acquisition, the expending and taxation deductibility of this amount being subject to certain conditions.

Due to inflation pressure during the 1980s, publicly held corporations were required to prepare fully indexed, constant-currency financial statements, expressed in year-end purchasing power, using an official index, the IGP-M (General

Consumer Price Index) as of 1986. This was discontinued for financial statements for years beginning after January 1, 1995.

***Tax Returns.*** Corporations pay income tax based on their trading profit as reported in the income statement for the fiscal year, which ends on December 31, regardless of the fiscal year of the company. The accounting pretax income is adjusted by the effects of various criteria acceptable for income tax purposes, which leads to the taxable income (known under the fiscal rules as the "real" income). Such adjustments arise from accruals on nondeductible expenses and inclusion or exclusion of nontaxable revenue, which give rise to permanent and temporal differences. These are controlled in a special fiscal book, the Taxable Income Calculation and Control Ledger (LALUR—*Livrode Apuraçao do Lucro Reãl*), and the corresponding effect should be treated, in certain cases, as deferred income tax. Criteria for charging income tax to the current year or for deferring it are fairly consistent with internationally accepted rules.

### Other Companies

***Statutory Reports.*** Private (not listed) corporations must publish annual financial statements (no requirement to audit such statements exists) in both the Official Gazette (Diário Oficial) and a newspaper within the region where they are domiciled at least five days before the date of the annual shareholders' meeting, which, in turn, must be held no later than 120 days after the year-end.

The type, form, and content of a corporation's financial statements are prescribed by the Corporate Law (Law 6.404/76). The financial statements also have to comply with the standards set forth by the accountancy authoritative body, the Federal Council of Accountancy (CFC—Conselho Federal de Contabilidade), and, for publicly held companies, with CVM regulations. As per the Corporate Law, the financial statements should comprise:

- Management's report.
- Balance sheet (Balanço Patrimonial).
- Income statement (Demonstração do Resultado).
- Statement of changes in shareholders' equity (Mutações do Patrimônio Líquido).
- Statement of changes in financial position (Origens a Aplicações de Recursos).
- Explanatory notes, including the main accounting policies adopted by the company.

Private corporations are also required to publish summarized minutes of the annual shareholders' meeting and any other shareholders' meetings and to file copies of these documents with the Registrar of Commerce.

The accounting practices referred to earlier mainly refer to a corporation (SA—Sociedade por Açoes), although most of them are also applicable to and are followed by the other types of companies permitted by Brazilian legislation, such as limited liability partnerships (called "limitadas," as from the designation of "sociedade de responsabildade limitada"). Limited partnerships and sole-proprietor companies are, in principle, not obliged by law to follow the rules and principles set forth by Corporate Law, nor is it mandatory for them to publish their periodic financial statements. However, the accounting profession has, in practice, imposed such generally accepted criteria and practices to almost every enterprise in the country, regardless of its corporate form. These exempt companies are also influenced by criteria established by tax laws and regulations.

The Brazilian law requires the use of the expression "limitada" or "Ltda" at the end of the name of a company that is incorporated as a limited liability partnership. The capital of such companies is divided into nominative quotas, rather than shares, the trading of such quotas usually being subject to approval of the other partners. These companies do not need to meet the filing and publishing requirements mentioned earlier, but they are required to file their Articles of Incorporation and any subsequent amendments thereto with the Registrar of Commerce.

## Audits and Accounting

***Independence.*** Independence is required by the Code of Ethics, issued by the CFC and by CVM regulations. As per the latter, listed corporations' auditors are not allowed to render advisory services to their audit clients, in order to avoid an independence issue.

***Auditing Standards and Accounting Principles.*** IBRACON, affiliated with the International Federation of Accountants (IFAC), is the professional body that develops accounting principles and audit standards through a committee called the Comissão Nacional de Normas Técnicas (CNNT), the National Committee on Technical Rules. As that committee has no legal authority to empower such principles, these criteria and practices are usually submitted to the CFC to be issued under the form of an authoritative resolution.

U.S. GAAP and International Accounting Standards Board (IASB) Pronouncements have significant influence on the Brazilian principle setters, mainly because of the large volume of investments made and activities carried out by foreign companies in this country. In general terms, Brazilian accounting principles follow international standards, which is increasingly enhanced by active participation of Brazilian accounting professionals in international bodies and committees.

It is the understanding of IBRACON that internationally accepted accounting principles (especially those issued by IASB) are to be adopted by Brazilian enterprises and accountants when there is no applicable local rule.

***Auditors' Report.*** Financial statements of publicly held corporations, financial institutions (banking industry), public utilities, and government-controlled companies, as well as other organizations, must be audited. Many of the largest private companies' financial statements are also audited. The independent accountants' report on the financial statements of a corporation must be signed either by an individual auditor alone or in conjunction with a registered firm of independent auditors. To audit a publicly held corporation, the auditor must also be registered with the CVM.

IBRACON, in conjunction with CFC, issues ethical rules and requirements with which auditors and accountants must comply in their professional practices. This ensures that an auditor is independent, has no personal or family interest in the audited company, and is technically and legally able to carry out audit work. In practice, a firm of auditors, rather than an individual, is appointed by either the board of directors or the administrative counsel of the company.

The auditor's report must:

- Identify the company and the audited financial statements.

- State that the responsibility for issuing the financial statements lies with the management and that the auditors are responsible for expressing an opinion thereon.

- State that the audit was conducted in accordance with generally accepted auditing standards and describe the main procedures prescribed thereunder.

- State, in the opinion paragraph, that the financial statements examined conform with GAAP (called Fundamental Accounting Principles in Brazil) and whether the effects of inflation have been fully disclosed. As the Corporate Law has banished any kind of inflation accounting as of January 1, 1996, this must be disclosed.

- Date the report and disclose the auditor registration number with the CFC.

Qualified opinions and disclaimer of opinion must be clearly stated, along with the reasons therefore, in the auditor's report.

## Canada

### *Public Companies*
***Statutory Reports.*** Businesses can be incorporated under either the federal Canada Business Corporation Act (CBCA) or under any one of the ten provincial and two territorial corporation statutes. Securities acts in the provinces have differing definitions of public, or reporting, companies. Generally, they include companies that offer their securities to the public and must have three directors, the majority of whom are Canadians. The legislation also specifies reporting, disclosure, and audit requirements. The requirements for a company incorporated in Ontario are presented here and are similar to the requirements of other provinces. All public corporations incorporated federally are subject to disclosure requirements and must file their financial statements (which become open to public inspection) with the director of Consumer and Corporate Affairs. A public company is generally required to file an annual report with provincial securities regulatory authorities

within 140 days of the corporate year-end. A copy of the annual report must also be sent to each shareholder at least 21 days before the annual meeting. There are also requirements for public companies to distribute interim financial statements to shareholders. The Securities Act requires that comparative financial statements be prepared and that they include a balance sheet, a statement of earnings, a statement of retained earnings, a statement of cash flow, and explanatory notes. Management, not the auditor, has primary responsibility for the preparation of accurate and complete financial statements. Financial statements must be prepared in accordance with GAAP as set forth in the handbook of the Canadian Institute of Chartered Accountants (CICA). The auditor generally reports only on the current year. The annual financial statements must be audited, but not the interim statements. Reports are usually in English. However, financial statements that are filed or distributed in Quebec generally must be in French, and Quebec shareholders can request such statements in French or in English. Each public company must file separately. Consolidated statements are generally required.

*Tax Returns.*   Returns are filed annually with Revenue Canada, which also collects corporate income tax imposed by all of the provinces (except Ontario, Quebec, and Alberta, which require the filing of a provincial corporate tax return). Revenue Canada is not involved in the creation of tax legislation and regulations. Those are developed by the federal Department of Finance. Proposals for legislative change, which are produced regularly, must be enacted by Parliament in the form of amendments to the Income Tax Act. Changes to income tax regulations are passed by approval of the federal cabinet.

A corporation must file an income tax return within six months of the end of its fiscal year-end. A corporation may choose its own fiscal year, but once chosen, the year-end cannot be changed without Revenue Canada's permission. Nonresidents file a return only in respect of their employment in Canada, business carried on in Canada, and dispositions of taxable Canadian property. Provincial capital tax returns are required in British Columbia, Saskatchewan, Manitoba, Ontario, and Quebec. Returns must be completed in the form prescribed by the Income Tax Act and must be accompanied by financial statements for one year and the auditors' report, if any.

## Private Companies

*Statutory Reports.*   Statutory reports must be filed by companies registered under the CBCA. Private companies may have one or more directors. The CBCA generally requires that comparative financial statements be prepared, although the auditor only reports on the current year. The Income Tax Act requires that the statements include a balance sheet, an income statement, a statement of retained earnings, a cash flow statement, and notes. Financial statements must be prepared in accordance with the *CICA Handbook.* Unaudited financial statements may be issued if shareholders are in agreement and if the statements are accepted for filing tax returns. Consolidated financial statements are generally required. No specific chart of accounts is mandated, but there are specific record-keeping requirements. Filings may be in English or in French. In addition, if a company provides interim financial statements or related documents to shareholders, to a public authority, or to a stock exchange, these materials must also be filed with the director of Corporate and Consumer Affairs.

### Audits and Accounting

*Independence.*   In order to issue an audit report, chartered accountants must be independent of the corporation. The CBCA disqualifies any person from being an auditor who is not independent of the corporation being audited, its affiliates, and the directors or officers of the corporation and affiliates.

*Auditors' Reports.*   The reports state whether the financial statements "present fairly" the corporation's financial position, the results of operations, and the cash flow in accordance with GAAP applied on a consistent basis.

*Authoritative Sources.*   The *CICA Handbook* is the authoritative source for accounting principles and auditing standards. Industry standards are also highly considered.

## Mexico

### Accounting Aspects of International M&A Mexico

In Mexico, the Mexican Institute of Public Accountants (MIPA) is a federation that groups institutes and colleges established in different cities throughout the country. The existence of MIPA means that the profession is self-regulating with respect to the acceptance of accounting principles, auditing standards and procedures, and rules of professional ethics.

MIPA is responsible for issuance of GAAP to be used in Mexico. All the references herein are based on the official documents of MIPA.

### Listed Public Companies

*Statutory Reports.*   In order for a stock company to be able to issue shares for placement to the general public, authorization must be obtained from the National Banking and Securities Commission (CNBV), and the shares must be registered on the Mexican Stock Exchange.

Listed companies are required to supply periodic information (some of it quarterly) to the CNBV, to the shareholders, and, if applicable, to the stock exchange. The financial statements of a listed company must be examined by a public accountant and by an appointed statutory auditor (comisario, usually the company's independent public accountant). The comisario has certain legal powers and responsibilities, including attendance at all board meetings.

The reports include the balance sheet, income statements (if necessary, a note giving figures for the earnings per share), statement of changes in stockholders' equity, statement of cash flow, and footnotes disclosure, all usually covering two years.

All records must be registered in pesos and written in Spanish.

*Tax Returns.*   Corporations are subject to income tax at the current rate of 35 percent on their computed taxable income. Taxable income is arrived at using a method that takes into account inflation's effect. The most common adjustments to the financial statement net income made in arriving at taxable income are:

- Inventory purchases are deductible, instead of cost of sales.
- Inflation gain or loss from monetary assets and liabilities is included in taxable income.
- Interest and exchange fluctuations are included or deducted from taxable income in real terms.
- Depreciation is applied using the straight-line method and then adjusted by inflation.
- Tax losses carried forward may be indexed by inflation.

A company distributing dividends must calculate corporation tax of 35 percent on the amount of dividend grossed up by a factor of 1.5385. If dividends are originated from the Net Fiscal Profits Account (CUFIN), dividends are free of tax. However, if dividends are paid to individuals or foreigners, a 5 percent withholding tax must be paid.

### Private Domestic Incorporated Companies

*Statutory Reports.*   Same requirements as for public companies except that reports need not be published nor audited by an independent accountant. (Private companies would be subject to an audit for tax purposes depending on the level of income of prior years.)

*Tax Returns.*   Same as for public companies.

### Audits and Accounting

*Independence.*   The MIPA has issued a document called "Code of Professional Ethics," which defines whether an independent accountant is working independently or not.

*Auditing Standards and Accounting Principles.*   As previously stated, all standards and principles are ruled by the MIPA.

*Auditors' Reports.*   Any company may apply for an audit report, including confirmation of compliance with federal taxes and other contributions, to be submitted for review by the Secretariat of Finance and Public Credit. Most companies provide such a report to avoid lengthy direct audits by the tax authorities.

Auditors' reports must attest that the financial statements "present fairly" the financial position and the result of operations of the company.

# Denmark

## *Public and Private Limited Companies*

*Statutory Reports.* Companies have to make annual financial statements with comparative figures containing an income statement, a balance sheet, notes, a director's report, and an audit report. The audit report, prepared by a qualified auditor, includes the total financial statement as well as the director's report.

The report requirements increase with the size of the company. The standards for reporting are similar to International Accounting Standards and are from 2002 market value. The value for subsidiaries is equity value. The reports can be in languages other than Danish.

Consolidated statements are required by law for holding companies and their subsidiaries, except where the holding company is itself a subsidiary of a bigger group.

The reports must be filed with the Danish Commerce and Companies Agency within five months after the year-end, and thus they are available for the public.

The primary difference between public and private limited companies is the size of the share capital, which amounts to DKK 500.000 for public limited companies and DKK 125.000 for private limited companies.

*Tax Returns.* Tax returns are filed annually and are due on July 1. The audited financial report must be sent to the tax authorities. Law requires no auditor involvement.

Resident companies where the effective management is in Denmark, are fully liable to taxation of their global income. Nonresident companies are only taxable of the Danish branch income.

The corporation tax is 30 percent of the taxable income, which also includes capital gains, except for shares owned for more than three years.

Dividends from foreign subsidiaries where the Danish parent company holds at least 25 percent of the share capital are tax exempt. Distribution of dividends is tax exempt if the holding is situated in a country with which Denmark has a double taxation treaty.

Denmark has also enacted CFC rules, whereby low-taxed financial income earned by foreign subsidiaries under certain conditions is regarded as income for the Danish holding company.

Mergers can be carried out tax exempt. Acceptance in advance has to be obtained from the tax authorities.

Taxes are paid in two advance installments with a final payment in the following year.

## *Audits and Accounting*

*Independence.* Independence is required by law and by auditing laws.

*Auditors' Reports.* Auditors must state whether the financial report presents a "true and fair view" and whether it has been prepared in accordance with the law and company statutes.

*Authoritative Sources.* These are the Danish Company Accounts Act of June 7, 2001, and the Danish Accounting Standards issued by the professional organizations, the continuing obligations for companies admitted to the stock exchange, the insurance standards, and bank standards.

## France

### All Commercial Business Entities

*Statutory Reports.* Statutory reports must be prepared for shareholders. The reports comprise historical financial statements for two years, including a balance sheet, an income statement, and a funds statement, together with notes to the financial statements, prepared in accordance with the Business Act and the General Accounting Plan (Plan Comptable Général), pursuant to the European Union Fourth and Seventh Guidelines.

A directors' report to shareholders, or its equivalent, is also required. The reports must be in French, records must be retained for 10 years, and specific charts of accounts are mandated for specific industries. The statutory reports, based on historical financial information, are required to be audited and reported on by the statutory auditor (*commissaire aux comptes*) for all corporate entities. The statutory auditor is appointed at the general meeting of shareholders for six years. A listed company whose accounts are consolidated is required to appoint at least two statutory auditors. The same requirement exists if a company solicits funds from the public. Any operation that involves soliciting funds from the public requires issuance of a prospectus (Note d'Information) whose contents have received approval of the Commission des Operations de Bourse (C.O.B.), which is the French equivalent of the SEC.

Société à Responsabilité Limitée companies (SARLs), or private limited liability companies, are subject to audit when they meet two of the following three conditions: (1) 50 employees, (2) 1.5 million euros in assets, and (3) 3 million euros in turnover.

For other entities, audits are required depending on certain differing criteria with respect to balance sheet amounts, net sales, and number of employees. In addition to information for shareholders and to meet public filing requirements, entities that meet certain criteria are required to prepare information (principally for distribution to the Worker's Committee) relating to current and projected debt and to provide income and funds statements.

The statutory auditor is required to review this information and to report on it as necessary. Similarly, entities with over 300 employees must also establish a "social report" on employee matters for submission to the Worker's Committee and to employment authorities. This also requires review by the statutory auditor.

*Tax Returns.* Returns are filed annually within three months after the closing of the fiscal year and sent to the French tax center. An audit is not required. The returns must be prepared on special preprinted tax declaration forms, which include a statutory balance sheet and an income statement together with supporting analyses and certain information contained in footnotes referred to in the statutory reporting section. Permission can be requested from the tax authorities to file on a group basis. The French tax consolidated regime is applicable only in case of prior election, and particular conditions must be respected. Consolidated or combined statements are not required.

## Publicly Quoted Companies and Groups

***Statutory Reports.*** Requirements, in addition to the requirements described for commercial business entities, are summarized as follows. For listed companies, audited consolidated financial statements must be joined to the *Document de référence* transmitted to the C.O.B. Those companies, including their subsidiaries for which the balance sheet total exceeds 3 million euros, must publish in the Bulletin d'Annonces légales obligatoires (BALO) a balance sheet, an income statement, and a list of their shareholdings in other companies.

Consolidated financial statements are required by law for listed and public holdings companies and for all limited companies that meet, during two consecutive years, two of the three following criteria: (1) 500 employees, (2) 15 million euros in assets, and (3) 30 million euros turnover.

In addition, quoted companies must publish unaudited interim financial information in the BALO that includes quarterly sales for the period, with cumulative figures for the year (and comparative figures) and an interim six-month report. The statutory auditor is required to review and to report on the semiannual information, which includes a consolidated balance sheet and an income statement together with notes to the financial statements.

## Audits and Accounting

***Independence.*** This is required and is defined both by law and by the ethics code of the profession.

***Responsibilities of Auditors.*** These are prescribed by statute and are wide ranging. In addition to determining whether the financial statements and financial information provided to the shareholders are fairly stated, the auditors must report to the board on irregularities discovered, make recommendations on accounting principles, and report to legal authorities on any misdemeanors discovered.

***Auditors' Reports.*** These must present two standard types of audit opinions: (1) the general report on the financial statements and financial information provided by the board of directors and (2) the special report on related-party transactions. In the general report, the auditors attest to the compliance with the legal requirements, the use in good faith of accepted valuation principles, and the presentation of a "true and fair view."

***Authoritative Sources for Accounting Principles.*** Sources include the "Code de Commerce" and the General Accounting Plan (Plan Comptable Général).

The evolution and the new accountancy rules are set by the Committee of the Accountancy Regulation (Comité de la Réglementation Comptable), whose regulations are applicable to the companies.

Different professional groups provide pronouncements from the Conseil National de la Comptabilité, the Ordre des experts Comptables, the Compagnie Nationale des Commissaires aux Comptes, and the C.O.B., as well as other material by various groups of accountants.

## Germany

### Public and Private Limited Companies

***Statutory Reports.*** Audited financial statements are required annually for public and private limited companies (GmbHs and AGs, respectively) that meet at least the size criteria defined for medium-sized companies by the German Commercial Code (Handelsgesetzbuch) for two consecutive balance sheet dates (DM = deutsche mark):

|  | *Company Size* | | |
|---|---|---|---|
|  | *Small* | *Medium* | *Large* |
| Total assets | < DM 3.4 million | < DM 13.7 million | > DM 13.7 million |
| Turnover | < DM 6.9 million | < DM 27.5 million | > DM 27.5 million |
| Average number of employees | < 50 | < 250 | > 250 |

Regardless of the size criteria, if the limited company is a certain listed company or has issued certain types of securities publicly traded, the company may be treated as a large-sized company.

The basic *filing and publication requirement* is that large limited companies and other enterprises subject to the Disclosure Law (Publizitätsgesetz) must publish their audited financial statements in the Federal Gazette as well as file them with the trade register. Businesses subject to the Disclosure Law are all those meeting at least two of these three requirements: (1) over 5,000 employees, (2) over DM 63.9 million total assets, and (3) over DM 127.8 million turnover.

Listed companies must also deliver the required number of printed financial statements and the report of the executive board to the stock exchange and the banks. Medium-sized corporations must file their audited accounts with the trade register, whereas small corporations file unaudited accounts.

The publication and/or filing of the financial statements together with the business report and, for AGs only, the report of the supervisory board (which explains how the board has supervised management during the year and whether it agrees with the financial statements) has to take place after the approval by the shareholders at the annual general meeting (but within 12 months following the balance sheet date). The same filing requirements apply for group financial statements.

Holding companies are required to produce and to publish *group financial statements* incorporating the results of majority-owned subsidiaries worldwide (control concept) or subsidiaries under uniform control of the holding company. Holding companies that are themselves wholly owned subsidiaries (subholding companies) of a European Union (EU) company are exempt from this requirement, provided that the group accounts prepared by the parent are published in German.

German subholding companies may also be exempt from preparing their own group financial statements even if the parent company is located outside the EU but does produce and publish in German group financial statements that contain the same information as required by the EU Eighth Directive.

Exemption will also be given if, during two consecutive financial years, the financial statements for the parent and the subsidiary companies do not exceed two of the following three limits:

|  | Sum of Individual Financial Statements | Consolidated Financial Statements |
|---|---|---|
| Total assets | DM 16.5 million | DM 13.7 million |
| Turnover | DM 33.0 million | DM 27.5 million |
| Average number of employees | 250 | 250 |

The *form and content of financial statements* for a limited company are laid down in the third book of the Commercial Code. The financial statements have to be prepared by the executive directors, who are responsible for the company's activities. They are generally composed of a balance sheet and income statement, notes to the financial statements, and a business report (Lagebericht), which is intended to complement and complete the picture provided by the financial statements and to provide a commentary concerning the development of the company during the year, its position at the end of the year, and the likely future risks in the development of the business.

*Tax Returns.*    Returns are filed annually and are due May 31. Income has to be declared on a calendar-year basis. In cases where a company's fiscal year is not the calendar year, the company must report the income of the fiscal year ended in the calendar year for which a return is filed. The returns are accompanied by a balance sheet and an income statement. An audit is not required for tax purposes. The return must be in German. Additionally, although consolidated returns are not per se allowed by German tax law, the tax treatment of *Organschaft* (single-entity relationship for tax purposes) provides similar relief. Under the Organschaft treatment, income or loss of a controlled company (Organgesellschaft) is attributed to the controlling company (Organträger).

## Audits and Accounting

*Independence.*  Requirements for auditors are set out in the bylaws of the Wirtschaftsprüfer Chamber (Germany's analogue to the AICPA) and in the Commercial Code.

*Auditors' Reports.*  Auditors must state in their reports whether the accounting records, financial statements, and management report comply with the law and with company statutes. The financial statements and management report must present, in compliance with required accounting principles, a true and fair view of net worth, financial position, and results of operations. Furthermore, the auditor has to state that the management report gives a complete picture concerning the development of the company during the year, its position at the end of the year, and the likely future risks in the development of the business.

*Authoritative Sources for Accounting Principles.*  These are the Commercial Code, Corporation Law, the Limited Liability Company Law, the Disclosure Law, the Credit Institute Law, and the Insurance Law, as well as the pronouncements by the German Institut der Wirtschaftsprüfer and the German Accounting Standards Committee.

# The Netherlands

## Public and Private Limited Companies

*Statutory Reports.*  All public and private limited companies should prepare annual financial statements within five months after year-end. This period can be extended to 11 months. Limited companies should also prepare accounts for filing at the Trade Register of the Chamber of Commerce. For companies not exceeding certain size criteria, the contents of the statutory accounts as well as the accounts for filing purposes can be limited. The statutory accounts must be presented to the annual general meeting of shareholders. Audits are compulsory for medium sized and large companies. Exemptions from the legal provisions for annual accounts and audits are possible if a parent company, inter alia, files a statement at the Trade Register, mentioning that it will be fully liable for the obligations of its subsidiary.

In general, in the notes to its annual accounts, an enterprise that, solely or jointly with another group company, heads a group shall include consolidated financial statements, showing its own financial information together with that of its subsidiaries in the group and of other group companies.

A part of a group may be excluded from the consolidation, provided, inter alia, the financial information that the legal entity should consolidate has been included in the consolidated annual financial statements of a larger entity and that these accounts have been prepared in accordance with the provisions of the Seventh Directive or, if these provisions need not be observed, in an equivalent manner.

Small groups are exempt from preparing consolidated financial statements.

Consolidation is generally carried out by the full consolidation method so that the net asset value of the parent company itself is nearly always equal to the consolidated net asset value.

If certain provisions are satisfied, the financial information relating to joint ventures may be included in the consolidated financial statements on a proportional basis, pro rata to the percentage interest held therein.

In choosing an accounting principle, a company shall follow the general provisions that the annual financial statements shall fairly, clearly, and systematically reflect the amount and the composition of the assets and liabilities at the end of the financial year and the result for that period and the items of income and expenditure on which it is based.

Principles that may be considered are the acquisition price or manufacturing cost and, with respect to tangible and financial fixed assets and stocks, their current value.

Generally, if the current value basis would more successfully fulfill the central requirement of providing a true and fair view, the company must use this basis in preparing the annual financial statements.

In the statutory balance sheet, investments in subsidiary companies and participating interest should be valued at their net asset value, while the notes to the accounts should provide additional information about these investments.

***Tax Returns.*** Annually, all limited companies should file corporate tax returns supported by a copy of the balance sheet and the income statement at the Dutch Inland Revenue. Tax returns relate to the same period as the company's financial year. The Articles of Association of the company should specifically mention the financial year-end in case this would not be equal to the calendar year. No audit is required for the annual corporation tax return. Tax returns should normally be filed within five months after the financial year-end. This period, however, can be extended. In that case, the company should prepare a provisional tax return. Based on this information, the Inland Revenue will raise a provisional assessment. When settling the provisional tax assessment with the definitive assessment, special interest-calculation rules will be applicable.

## Audits and Accounting

***Independence.*** Requirements for auditors are set out in the bylaws governing the rules of professional conduct and practice of the Dutch accountancy bodies.

***Auditors' Report.*** The financial statements of all legal entities other than those classified as small are required to be audited. Audits may also be carried out by duly authorized foreign accountants.

The auditor's report states that he or she has performed an audit of the financial statements. The auditor's conclusion is directed toward the truth and fairness of the financial position and result, as presented in the financial statements. The auditor also verifies that the financial statements are in compliance with the legal requirements that deal with the financial statements.

*Authoritative Sources for Accounting Principles.* The financial statements should be prepared following accounting principles generally accepted in the Netherlands. These principles are set out in Guidelines for annual reporting (Richtlijnen).

These Guidelines have been developed as a result of consultation between the Dutch Institute of Registered Accountants (NIVRA—Netherlands Instute van Registeraccountants) and the representative bodies of employers and employees, all of whom participate in the Council for Annual Reporting. Judgments of the Enterprise Division of the Amsterdam Appeal Court and the Supreme Court rulings are incorporated in the Guidelines, insofar as they are considered to be generally applicable. The international standards of the IASC are also included, insofar as they can be considered acceptable to Dutch accounts. The Council for Annual Reporting has prioritized the implementation of new and revised IASC standards in the Dutch Guidelines.

## Spain

### *Public and Private Companies*

*Statutory Reports.* All mercantile companies, including consolidated groups, are required to prepare annual accounts and to then file them with the Mercantile Register. Annual accounts must be filed with the Mercantile Register within one month of their approval by the company's general shareholders' meeting. The Mercantile Register will keep annual accounts for six years during which time they are public. The lack of filing proper accounts could imply the impossibility to file certain corporate documents into the Mercantile Register, stopping part of the company operations.

Company directors are responsible for the preparation of annual financial statements, which include balance sheet, profit-and-loss account, and the annual report (Memoria).

For both the balance sheet and the profit-and-loss account, comparative figures are required. All these documents can be submitted in euros or in pesetas.

The annual report includes a description of the company's accounting policies and a source and application of funds statement. Annual financial statements are enclosed with a director's report. An analytical profit-and-loss account is optional.

Small companies are allowed to present abbreviated accounts if at least two out of the following three limits are not surpassed: (1) assets less than 395 million pesetas, (2) sales less than 790 million pesetas, and (3) an annual average number of employees of fewer than 50.

An audit report from the annual accounts must also be included, except for those companies allowed to fulfill abbreviated balance sheet and annual report. (This exception does not apply when a specific regulation establishes the need of the audit.) Auditors must be appointed by the general shareholders' meeting. The appointment, which is for between three and nine years, must be made prior to the end of the period to be audited. Auditors may be reappointed on an annual basis after completing their first period of duty.

Foreign companies owning branches in Spain must file their annual accounts in Spain, or if there are equivalent filing requirements, they must certify the filing of the accounts in their country.

***Tax Returns.*** A company's tax returns are filed annually, according to the company's accounting year (not necessarily the calendar year), within a month after the approval of the annual accounts by the company's general shareholders' meeting. The meeting must be held within six months after the end of the fiscal year.

Tax forms include their own balance sheet and profit-and-loss account. The disclosure of the information may differ from that included in the annual accounts.

The calculation of the tax basis is performed regarding general accounting principles. Differences with tax regulations may generate temporary or permanent differences, which must be disclosed in the tax return.

## Audits and Accounting

***Independence.*** Independence is required by law and by the Spanish accountancy bodies.

***Auditors' Reports.*** Auditors must express in their reports an opinion on the annual accounts as a whole, based on their work as carried out in accordance with generally accepted auditing standards. This work includes the examination, on the basis of selective tests, of the evidence underlying the annual accounts and the evaluation of the presentation of those statements. This work also includes an examination of the accounting policies applied and the estimates made.

***Authoritative Sources for Accounting Principles.*** The Código de Comercio is the basic rule in mercantile law in Spain. Although it dates from 1885, it has been subject to revisions and has been adapted to European Union directives. Main accountancy requirements are also covered by the Texto Refundido de la Ley de Sociedades Anónimas (1989) and Ley de Sociedades de Responsabilidad Limitada (1995).

The development of accountancy practice is included in the Plan General de Contabilidad (PGC), whose last modification dates from 1990. Main accounting principles are set out in the PGC. There also are some adaptations of the PGC to specific sectors.

The authority in charge of the regulation and development of accounting rules is the Instituto de Contabilidad y Auditoría de Cuentas (ICAC), depending from the Ministerio de Economía y Hacienda. Specific regulations are also built up by such controlling bodies as Comisión Nacional del Mercado de Valores (Stock Exchange Authority) or Dirección General de Seguros (Insurance Authority), among others. Tax regulations have a great importance, although the last modification of Company Tax regulations gives preference to accounting standards. ICAC is also the regulating authority of the audit professional practice, approving audit standards and controlling audit professional bodies.

Auditors must be registered, after having passed the necessary qualification tests, in the official register (Registro Oficial de Auditores de Cuentas—ROAC), which is controlled by the ICAC. Audit companies also must be included in the register.

Individual auditors and audit companies may join professional bodies and usually do, even though the affiliation is not obligatory. In Spain, there are three professional bodies: (1) Instituto de Auditores Censores Jurados de Cuentas de España (IACJCE), (2) Registro de Economistas Auditores (REA), and (3) Registro General de Auditores. All these professional bodies have strict ethical standards that ensure the independence and technical ability of auditors. Both the ICAC and the professional auditing bodies have the right and the responsibility to verify the technical quality of all work and to ensure that their members accomplish audit standards. ICAC is also in charge of publication of the audit standards.

## United Kingdom

### *Public and Private Companies*

*Statutory Reports.* Reports of all companies (limited and unlimited) must be sent to all shareholders and debenture holders and must be presented before the shareholders at a general meeting, usually the annual general meeting. An audit, by a qualified auditor, of the financial statements contained in the reports is required for all companies with turnover in excess of £1 million. (There are circumstances when companies with turnover below this level are also required to be audited.) Limited companies must also file the statutory reports with the Registrar of Companies; these reports are available for inspection by the public. Companies that are statutorily defined as small or medium (in terms of specified balance sheet totals, sales, and number of employees) may take advantage of provisions (abbreviated accounts) that allow less-detailed reports to be filed, but the full report must be prepared for shareholders. The reports must include annual financial statements with comparative figures comprised of a balance sheet, a profit-and-loss account, a cash flow statement (which is required unless the company is defined as small), and audit report and supporting notes. A directors' report to the shareholders is also required; this is not subject to audit, but it is reviewed by the auditors for consistency with the financial statements. Consolidated financial statements are required, unless the company is itself a wholly owned subsidiary of a member state of the EU or the group is defined as small or medium within designated parameters. Accounting standards require that consolidated accounts include associated companies using the equity method of accounting and joint ventures using the gross equity method. Reports must be in English. It is not possible to file on a group basis, and each company in a group must file its own financial statements. Specific record-keeping requirements are prescribed by law. The U.K. Listing Authority requires listed companies to publish biannual interim financial statements, which need not be audited. The interim statement and the annual statutory report must be filed with the U.K. Listing Authority.

***Tax Returns.*** Tax returns supported by a copy of the audited financial statements are filed annually for corporation tax purposes with the Inland Revenue for a company's accounting period. No auditor involvement is required by law. Under the Corporation Tax Self-Assessment system a company must normally file a corporation tax return, with supporting documentation such as accounts, 12 months after the end of its accounting period. Payment of tax is normally required within nine months of the year-end, with interest running on any amount eventually agreed to have been overpaid or underpaid. Companies with large profits are required to pay their tax on account in quarterly installments.

## Unincorporated Branches of Overseas Companies

***Statutory Reports.*** The statutory report of the overseas company rather than the branch is required to be filed with the Registrar of Companies. The accounts can be in the format required by the relevant overseas legislation. No audit is required. If the reports are in a language other than English, a certified translation into English must also be submitted on filing with the Registrar of Companies.

***Tax Returns.*** Requirements are the same for public and private companies, except that the accounts to support the tax return are the accounts of the branch only.

### Audits and Accounting
***Independence.*** Independence is required by both law and the U.K. accountancy bodies.

***Auditors' Reports.*** These are required by law to state whether the financial statements present a "true and fair view" and have been prepared in accordance with the Companies Act 1985.

***Authoritative Sources of Accounting Principles.*** These are the Companies Act 1985, Financial Reporting Standards issued by the Accounting Standards Board, Statements of Standard Accounting Practice issued by its predecessor body, pronouncements of the Urgent Issues Task Force, the continuing obligations for companies of the U.K. Listing Authority, and Statements of Recommended Practice for specific types of entity, such as charities and pension schemes.

## Australia

***Statutory Reports.*** In Australia the level and the nature of statutory reporting is dependent on the size and the complexity of the company structure. Exhibit 4.1 shows the broad categories of companies.

EXHIBIT 4.1

**Corporate Entities**

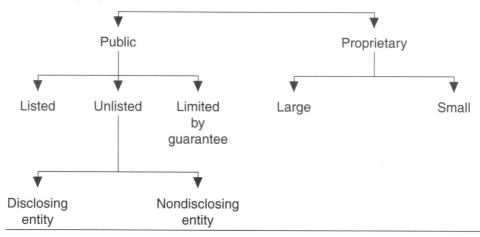

All public entities must prepare financial statements in a statutory format and will generally be required to lodge those financial statements with the Australian Securities and Investments Commission (ASIC).

To the extent that the company is a listed public company, the financial statements and reports must comply with all applicable accounting standards, the Stock Exchange listing rules, and all other miscellaneous accounting and disclosure provisions. In addition all entities that are listed and unlisted disclosing entities must produce abbreviated half-year financial statements. Disclosing entities also have a continuous disclosure requirement to make public disclosure of all price-sensitive information that is not generally available to the public. This information will be disclosed either to the Australian Stock Exchange (ASX), in the case of listed companies, or to the ASIC, in the case of an unlisted disclosing entity. Once lodged with the ASIC or ASX, all information can be accessed by the public.

Public companies that are unlisted and companies limited by guarantee must produce annual financial statements that comply with all applicable accounting standards and lodge these financial statements with the ASIC within four months of the year-end.

Proprietary companies that are large must prepare and lodge financial statements with the ASIC within four months of the year-end. A company is considered large if it meets any two of the following three tests: (1) gross consolidated turnover in excess of $A10,000,000, (2) gross consolidated assets in excess of $A5,000,000, and (3) total group employees of 50 or more. There are no requirements for a small proprietary company to produce annual financial statements.

Care should be taken when analyzing a proprietary company's financial statements to review the level of compliance with accounting standards. Some proprietary companies deem themselves to be "nonreporting" entities, which entitles them to set their own compliance regime; and, therefore, compliance with accounting standards is not required.

***Tax Returns.***   Each company in Australia is allocated an ABN (Australian business number), an ACN (Australian company number), and a tax file number. All companies other than those specifically excluded have a balance date of June 30 each year. An annual tax return is required to be lodged for the company each year outlining its assessable income and deductible expenses. Tax is paid at a uniform rate on all taxable profit. The rate is currently 30 percent. All capital profits are included within the same tax return.

In addition to the annual tax return, all companies are required to lodge a Business Activity Statement (BAS), in which they account to the revenue authorities in respect of the goods and services tax (GST) collected and employee tax deductions withheld. Most companies lodge and pay their BASs on a quarterly basis; but large organizations (i.e., those with an annual turnover of $A20,000,000), lodge and pay monthly.

## Audits and Accounting

***Audit Requirements.***   All public companies and large proprietary companies are required to appoint an auditor. All subsidiaries of foreign corporations are deemed to be large regardless of their actual size. The ASIC has a class-order discretion to grant audit relief in certain circumstances upon application by the company.

***Auditor Qualifications.***   An auditor's qualifications are outlined in both the Corporations Law and the professional bodies code of ethical conduct. The predominant theme in these pronouncements is to ensure that the auditor maintains his or her independence and has achieved a suitable level of educational and professional qualifications.

***Auditors' Reports.***   There are generally two types of audit opinions expressed by auditors on financial statements.

1. *Audit report.*   This report is a positive statement forming the opinion that the financial statements have been prepared in accordance with applicable accounting standards and the provisions of the Corporations Law and that they are prepared so that the financial statements are true and fair.
2. *Review report.*   This report is a negative assurance statement that is usually applied to abbreviated half-year financial statements. The report expresses that nothing has come to the auditor's attention that would indicate that the financial statements are not in compliance with standards and not giving a true and fair view.

***Accounting Standards.***   Australia has become involved in the worldwide trend toward globalization of accounting and auditing standards. Compliance with Australian standards will on the whole ensure compliance with International Accounting Standards.

## Hong Kong

### *Companies Incorporated under the Companies Ordinance*

*Statutory Reports.* These are required annually for all companies incorporated in Hong Kong under the Companies Ordinance. Every company incorporated elsewhere that is carrying on business in Hong Kong must register with the Registrar of Companies under Part XI of the Companies Ordinance as a "branch" within one month of the establishment of a place of business in Hong Kong. On registration, the overseas company is required to deliver to the Registrar of Companies a certified copy of the company's documents of incorporation, particulars of the directors and secretary, and details of the representative authorized to accept notices in Hong Kong. Public companies also file their reports with the Registrar of Companies. The reports contain audited financial statements for the current year, with corresponding amounts for the preceding year, including a balance sheet, an income statement, a cash flow statement, and notes. The cash flow statement is not required for companies with annual turnover or gross income of less than HK$20 million. Private companies, which include banks, insurance companies, shipping companies, and charitable and nonprofit entities, are exempt from certain disclosure requirements. The reports should be presented at an annual general shareholders' meeting held not more than nine months after the fiscal year-end (six months for public companies and members of groups that include public companies), although an extension can be granted by the Court. There is no mandatory financial year-end. A directors' report is also included, but it is usually not audited. Other disclosure requirements are specified by the Companies Ordinance and the Listing Rules of the Hong Kong Stock Exchange (Listing Rules) in case of listed companies. If the report of a public company is not in English, a certified translation in English must be filed. If a company has subsidiaries, audited group financial statements (usually in consolidated form) are required unless the holding company is as of year-end a wholly owned subsidiary of another corporate body. Record-keeping requirements call for proper books of accounts to be kept at the registered office of the company or at such other place as the directors believe appropriate. These books must be preserved for seven years. If the books are kept outside Hong Kong, financial statements disclosing the financial position of the business must be sent to Hong Kong at intervals not exceeding six months.

*Tax Returns.* Returns are filed annually with the Inland Revenue Department, which issues standard forms to taxpayers for completion and return to the department. For companies incorporated in Hong Kong, audited financial statements must be submitted with the profits tax returns unless their total gross income for the basis period does not exceed HK$500,000. Income derived from sources outside of Hong Kong, regardless of residency status, is generally not assessed to tax in Hong Kong. Consequently, there are only limited provisions for granting double tax relief for foreign taxes paid. Auditors may act as tax representatives for clients. The returns must include financial statements that cover the basis period relevant to the year of assessment, including a balance sheet, an income statement, and notes. A cash flow statement is not required, but one is usually included if it has been prepared. For the profits tax returns, a prescribed form must be completed that presents certain general information on the company and its transactions with nonresidents. A computation of assessable profit together with supporting schedules must be prepared. Assessable profits are arrived at in accordance with GAAP as adjusted to comply with the requirements for the Inland Revenue Ordinance. It is not possible to file on a group basis because taxes are assessed on each entity and there is no group relief.

## Audits and Accounting

*Independence.*   This is required by the Companies Ordinance and by the Hong Kong Society of Accountants (HKSA).

*Responsibilities of Auditors.*   Responsibilities include reporting to shareholders on whether the audited financial statements have been properly prepared in accordance with the Companies Ordinance and whether they present a "true and fair view."

*Authoritative Sources for Accounting Disclosure Requirements.*   Sources include the Companies Ordinance, Listing Rules, and, for accounting principles, the Hong Kong Society of Accounts (HKSA), which functions pursuant to the Professional Accountants Ordinance and is the only body authorized to regulate accountants.

## Japan

### Public Limited Companies

*Statutory Reports.*   These must be filed semiannually with the Ministry of Finance (MOF), under the requirements of the Securities and Exchange Law, and with the securities exchanges. All companies listed on the Japanese stock exchanges and nonlisted companies that file registration statements with the MOF must appoint both a statutory auditor and an independent auditor. The independent auditor examines the financial statements and information of an accounting nature, and the statutory auditor examines all other areas. A full-scope audit is required for the annual financial statements, and an interim examination is performed in connection with the semiannual statements. In the interim report, the auditor indicates whether the semiannual statements provide "useful information relative to the interim period constituting part of a fiscal year." These requirements apply to all listed companies and to unlisted companies that issue new shares to the public or whose shareholders have sold their shares to the public (50 or more people) in amounts aggregating 100 million yen or more during the past two years.

There are, however, some exceptions to the general requirements. Financial statements that are filed with the MOF may or may not be audited by an independent certified public accountant (CPA), depending on the form of company organization. The most common form in Japan, for businesses required to register with the MOF, is the *kabushiki kaisha* (joint stock corporation). An examination and an auditor's report are required of an independent certified accountant only if the financial statements have not been approved at the general meeting of stockholders that follows each accounting period. If so, the audit requirements apply only to the parent company's financial statements, which are considered the primary financial statements. However, audited consolidated financial statements, in the form of an attachment to the annual report, must also be filed annually with the MOF and with the securities exchanges. The reports must present an MOF-approved form of a balance sheet for two fiscal year-ends and an income statement for two fiscal periods. A statement of cash flows is a part of the financial statements of Japan. Statements of profit appropriations for two fiscal periods are also required, and a two-year comparative statement of manufacturing costs is attached to the income statement. Notes to the financial statements cover two fiscal periods. Fourteen special schedules are required for one fiscal period only. A business report that accompanies the financial statements must contain information as a description of the company's principal business and locations, capital investments, relationships with a parent company or subsidiaries, a discussion of results of operations and the status of assets (covering at least the past three years), outstanding problems, the major shareholders, any investments the company has in these shareholders, and events subsequent to the balance sheet date. The independent auditor's opinion covers information of an accounting nature that appears in the business report. It is presumed that the statements will be in Japanese, although there is no requirement that foreign languages not be used.

***Tax Returns.*** Returns are filed in accordance with the requirements of the Japanese tax laws, semiannually and annually. Financial statements should be attached to the tax returns, which are filed with local tax authorities. As taxable income is calculated based on book income and as tax laws prescribe that certain deductions would be allowed "if recorded in the accounts," tax laws have strongly influenced the evolution of accounting practice in Japan. The methods of recording various allowances and calculating depreciation that result in the most favorable tax treatment, for example, are generally used and are applicable in preparing financial statements as well.

## Limited Companies
***Statutory Reports.*** These must be prepared at least once a year, in accordance with the Japanese Commercial Code. The audited financial statements are to be maintained at the company's head office for five years for inspection by shareholders and creditors and at branch offices for three years. An audit of the financial statements by an independent auditor is required of all limited companies with capital stock of more than 500 million yen or total liabilities of 20 billion yen or more. Financial statements and a statutory auditor's report are to be maintained at the head office of the company for inspection by shareholders and creditors.

A company may voluntarily appoint a number of statutory auditors, in accordance with its articles of incorporation. For companies with capital of over 500 million yen, the statutory auditors must examine areas in addition to financial statements. A notice, including financial statements and a statutory auditor's report (as well as that of the independent auditor, if applicable), is to be sent to shareholders two weeks before the annual meeting. The reports include financial statements as prescribed by the Japanese Commercial Code, consisting of a balance sheet for one fiscal year-end and an income statement for one fiscal period. A proposal of profit appropriation should also be included, and certain information, including significant accounting policies, must be disclosed in footnotes. Eleven special schedules are required, as well as any other schedules considered necessary under the circumstances.

## AUDITS AND ACCOUNTING

*Independence.*   Requirements for CPAs are specified in detail under the Japanese CPA law and related regulations. In general, neither auditor nor spouse can have any interest, financial or otherwise, in a company the auditor is to audit.

*Responsibilities of Auditors.*   These are specified for statutory auditors and independent auditors and differ depending on whether a company being audited reports under MOF requirements or under the requirements of the Japanese Commercial Code (JCC) for limited companies. The financial statements prescribed by the JCC must be attested to by the company's statutory auditor and by an officer of the company, who need not be and in most Japanese companies is not a CPA.

*Auditors' Reports.*   These must state whether, in the auditors' opinion, the financial statements "present fairly" the company's financial position and the results of its operations.

*Authoritative Sources for Accounting and Auditing Standards.*   Sources include the MOF (for reporting under the Securities and Exchange Law), the Corporate Accounting Deliberation Board (an advisory board to the MOF), the Ministry of Justice, and the Japanese Institute of Certified Public Accountants. In addition, financial statement and schedule forms are issued by the government ministries responsible for certain industries, including construction, shipbuilding, securities, railroads, automotive transportation, banking, maritime operations, insurance, electric power, and gas.

*Special Comment.*   It is sometimes possible for firms engaged in international operations to adjust their financial statements to U.S. GAAP, particularly if they are affiliated with U.S. companies. In addition, it is not unusual for companies with European affiliations to follow International GAAP or U.S. GAAP reporting.

In such cases, a company must issue another report in accordance with the JCC, if the company meets the statutory size requirements or if local shareholders request such a report.

## Singapore

### *Companies Incorporated under the Singapore Companies Act*

*Statutory Reports.* These are required annually for companies incorporated in Singapore under the Companies Act (Chapter 50), that is, public listed companies and private limited companies except exempt private companies (companies that have no shares that are beneficially held by any corporation and have not more than 20 members). An exempt private company does not need to file the audited financial statements with the Registrar of Companies if it is able to file a solvency certificate signed by the Company Secretary and by the independent auditor stating that there are reasonable grounds to believe that the company is able to meet its liabilities as and when they fall due. Public listed companies also file their report with the Registrar of Companies. These are available for public inspection. The directors are responsible for the presentation of a company's financial statements, which give a true and fair view of the state of its financial affairs. The reports contain audited financial statements for the current year, with corresponding amounts for the preceding year, including a balance sheet, a profit-and-loss account, a statement of changes in equity, a cash flow statement, and notes to the financial statements. The balance sheet and the profit-and-loss account must be accompanied by the directors' and the auditors' reports as well as by a statement signed by the directors that the financial statements show a true and fair view and that there are reasonable grounds to believe that the company will be able to pay its debts as and when they fall due. The cash flow statement is not required for companies with annual sales or gross assets of less than SGD 5 million, for companies that are wholly owned subsidiaries of a company incorporated in Singapore, or for exempt private companies unless such entities are required to publish financial statements under regulatory requirements. The reports should be presented at an annual general shareholders' meeting held not more than six months after the financial year-end, although the Registrar of Companies may grant an extension on application. The first annual meeting of a company incorporated under the Singapore Companies Act is to be held within 18 months of the company's incorporation and, subsequently, once in every calendar year at intervals not exceeding 15 months. Every public listed company must also submit to its shareholders and to the Singapore Exchange Securities Trading Limited (SGX-ST) the annual report not later than five months after the end of the financial year. A financial statement for a half-year and a full year should be provided to the Exchange for public release immediately after the figures are available and, in any event, not later than three months after the relevant period. Quarterly announcements will be from January 1, 2003, onward and announcements within 60 days of quarter-end. There is no mandatory financial year-end. For annual reports, a directors' report is also included but is usually not audited. The financial statements must be stated in Singaporean currency, and comparative figures must be shown as required by the Ninth Schedule of the Companies Act. Holding companies must publish group financial statements, normally in the form of consolidated financial statements, dealing with the group as a whole. Many companies also publish a chairman's statement. The SGX-ST-listed companies have to disclose certain additional financial data, such as earnings per share, segmental information, information on business activities, and details concerning directors and officers. If the report of a public company is not in English, a certified translation in English must be filed. If a company has subsidiaries, audited group financial statements (usually in consolidated form) are required unless the holding company is as of year-end a wholly owned subsidiary of a Singapore company. Record-keeping requirements call for proper books of accounts to be kept at the registered office of the company or at such other place as the director believes appropriate. These books must be preserved for seven years. If the books are kept outside Singapore, financial statements that disclose the financial position of the business must be sent to Singapore at intervals not exceeding six months.

*Tax Returns.*   Returns are filed annually with the Inland Revenue of Singapore, which issues standard forms (Form C) to taxpayers for completion and return to the department. For companies incorporated in Singapore, audited financial statements must be submitted with Form C. The tax system in Singapore operates on a territorial basis. In other words, income is payable as income accrued in or derived from Singapore or received in Singapore from outside. Income derived from sources outside of Singapore, regardless of residency status, is generally not assessed to tax in Singapore. Consequently, there are only limited provisions for granting double tax relief for foreign taxes paid. Auditors may act as tax representatives for clients. The returns must include financial statements that cover the basis period relevant to the year of assessment, including a balance sheet, a profit-and-loss account, and notes to the financial statements. A cash flow statement and a statement of changes in equity are not required but are usually included if they have been prepared. For Form C, a prescribed form must be completed that presents certain general information on the company and its transactions with nonresidents. A computation of chargeable income must be prepared. Chargeable income is arrived at in accordance with GAAP as adjusted to comply with the requirements for the Inland Revenue Authority of Singapore and the Singapore Income Tax Act. It is not possible to file a tax return on a group basis because taxes are assessed on each entity and there is no group relief.

## Audit and Accounting

*Independence.*   This is required by the Singapore Companies Act and by the SGX-ST, as well as by the Securities Council in the case of audits of security dealers.

*Responsibilities of Auditors.*   Responsibilities include reporting to shareholders on whether the audited financial statements have been prepared in accordance with the Companies Act and the Statements of Accounting Standards in Singapore and giving a true and fair view of the state of affairs of the company, the results, changes in equity, and cash flow of the company and whether they present a "true and fair view."

***Authoritative Sources for Accounting Disclosure Requirements.*** Sources include the Singapore Companies Act and, for accounting standards and guidelines laid down in the Statements of Accounting Standards issued by the Institute of Certified Public Accountants of Singapore and the SGX-ST for public listed companies. Pursuant to the Accountants Act of 1987, the Public Accountants Board is the only body authorized to regulate accountants.

### Alternative Entities to Be Used in Singapore

Every person carrying on a business in Singapore must register as an entity. There is no foreign shareholding restriction of ownership. Foreign entities can incorporate companies that are 100 percent owned.

The three options are:

1. Branch of an overseas office—a branch is an extension of the head office and is not limited in liability as compared to a PTE Ltd. company.
2. PTE Ltd. company as a subsidiary of an overseas company—as a PTE Ltd. company, the liability of the entity in Singapore is limited to the share capital put in. The requirements of a PTE Ltd. company are:
   - Two directors; at least one shall be a resident of Singapore.
   - Two natural persons to be subscribers to the Memorandum & Articles, normally the two directors.
   - Shareholders can be a company.
   - Minimum share capital paid up is $2.
3. Representative office—this is actually not an entity, and the activities are limited and subject to the approval of the trade development board.

## Israel

### Limited Companies

As with most countries throughout the world, many entrepreneurs prefer to organize their businesses or enterprises as limited liability companies (corporate entity with share capital, whereby the additional liability of its members is limited to any unpaid amount for the shares issued) for many reasons.

A company is considered incorporated only if it has been registered with the Companies Registrar in the Ministry of Justice. To register, it must apply to the Companies Registrar, enclosing the company's statutory document—the Articles of Association, signed by its founders. The Articles contain the rules and bylaws for the company's management, the powers and responsibilities of its shareholders and of its directors, the company's various organs, the means for implementing these rules, and the procedure by which the Articles may be amended, without causing a cessation in the company's operations.

***Statutory Reports.*** Both public and private companies must be registered with the Companies Registrar.

An annual information report must be filed every calendar year. A private company has to file this report with the Companies Registrar and must also file with the Israel Securities Authority and the Tel Aviv Stock Exchange (TASE). The report is to contain detailed information, including:

- Location of the office where registered.
- Number and amount of the authorized issued share capital.
- Mortgages and liens on the company's assets.
- Names of shareholders and details of their holdings.
- Names of directors and of the company's secretary.

The annual information report of a public company is more detailed.

***Tax Returns.*** Israeli corporations are subject to a tax of 36 percent on taxable income. Israeli companies are taxed on income from all sources, worldwide, including capital gains. The tax year of a corporation is the calendar year. Israeli corporate income tax returns are due within five months following the close of the taxable year (December 31). An extension may be requested for periods of up to an additional eight months. For public corporations, the entire estimated tax liability must be paid together with the extension request. All tax returns must be accompanied by a financial statement and an adjusted statement for income tax purposes, which were audited by an Israeli Certified Public Accountant.

Estimated taxes must be paid in 10 fixed installments or in 12 installments based on the individual percentage of revenue.

### Public Companies

A public company, as defined in the Companies Law, is a company whose shares are sold or issued to the public through the TASE. Sometimes the shares are issued through other stock exchanges or on the over-the-counter market, these two being mainly in the United States, England, and Europe. The TASE is the only trading place in Israel for securities issued by public companies and government bonds. A company that issues its shares to the public does so in compliance with the Securities Law. Trading in securities and raising capital from the public are regulated by the Securities Law, under which the Securities Authority was established to protect the interest of investors.

***Statutory Reports.*** In order to issue securities to the public, the issuer must issue a prospectus according to specific requirements.

Public companies, including those who offer their shares to the public without being listed, are obliged to comply with additional presentation and disclosure requirements imposed on them by the Securities Law and various securities regulations. The general principle underlying these requirements is to provide all the necessary information that will enable the holders of a company's listed securities and the public to appraise the condition of such a company.

Publicly traded companies are required to file their annual financial statements with the Israel Securities Authority and with the TASE within three months following their financial statement date. Their financial statements are to be denominated in Israeli currency.

A company listed on the TASE is required to issue a quarterly interim condensed financial statement. Essentially, the statement consists of a balance sheet, a statement of profit and loss, a statement of changes in shareholders' equity, a statement of cash flows, and a selected number of notes to the financial statements, which are accompanied by a review letter of the company's auditors and also a director's report.

Public companies listed on the TASE must file the following additional reports and documents with the Companies Registrar and/or the Israel Securities Authority:

- Changes in the Memorandum and Articles of Association (only Articles of Association for companies incorporated after February 1, 2000).
- Details about those who hold 5 percent or more of the voting rights or shares of the company, including any changes in such holdings.
- Any material agreement into which the company has entered.
- Salaries of the five highest paid officers and directors.
- Any benefits and transactions with those who hold 5 percent or more of the issued capital stock.
- Change of auditors.
- Changes in the capital stock.
- Composition of the board of directors.
- Conflict of interest.
- Private placements.

## Private Companies

Any limited company that is not a "public company" is a "private company." A private company must file a statutory annual information report with the Companies Registrar and also submit to its shareholders its annual financial statement, audited by a certified public accountant. Certain private companies have to file a balance sheet only.

## Foreign Companies

A foreign company wishing to do business in Israel must register with the Companies Registrar, which requires the filing of its Articles of Association, which includes the names of its directors and other relevant information.

Foreign companies wishing to issue shares on the TASE must issue a prospectus containing annual audited financial statements and unaudited interim financial statements for recent quarters, provided in separate English and Hebrew copies. Companies incorporated in the United States are permitted to prepare their financial statements in U.S. dollars and pursuant to U.S. accounting principles, while highlighting the differences between the Israeli and the U.S. principles in the notes to the financial statements.

***Tax Returns.*** Foreign corporations (corporations not organized under the laws of Israel) are subject to income tax on all income generated from the conducting of trade or business in Israel and on income "effectively connected" with such income.

## Partnerships

A partnership may be "general" or "limited." In a general partnership, the liability of each partner is unlimited, all of the partners are "general" partners, and all are responsible for all of the partnership's liabilities. In a limited partnership, there must be at least one "general" partner who is responsible for all of the partnership's liabilities; the limited partner is responsible only for his or her share of the partnership capital and does not participate in the management of the partnership.

Partnerships are governed by the Partnerships Ordinance, 1975, pursuant to which they must be registered with the Partnerships Registrar. The registration is only of a declarative nature. There is no difference between a nonregistered partnership and a registered partnership because each one has the status of a legal entity, and, therefore, each has the same rights and obligations.

## Audit Requirements

***Independence.*** The auditor is to be independent of the reporting entity. The terms of independence are stipulated in the Auditors' Law and its regulations and in the Institute's Code of Ethics, which is binding on all of its members. Publicly traded companies are also bound by special instructions issued by the Israel Securities Authority.

***Auditors' Reports.*** The auditor is appointed by the shareholders and reports to them in a standard format (auditors' report), which first identifies the financial statements being audited in an opening (introductory) paragraph, then describes the nature of the audit in a scope paragraph, and finally expresses the auditor's opinion in a separate opinion paragraph.

***Authoritative Sources.*** The Institute of Certified Public Accountants in Israel regularly publishes guidelines for the recommended audit procedures to be applied by auditors, so that the audit examines, inter alia, the risk centers in the companies and focuses the audit on these risk centers.

In addition, there are specific laws covering audits, such as the requirements from the State Comptroller; from accountants in municipalities and local authorities; and even Auditor's Regulations, which were published under the Accountant's Law.

These various pronouncements anchor the rules of conduct of auditors and their mode of operations during the audit of financial statements in Israel.

The Institute is affiliated with the International Federation of Accountants (IFAC), which publishes International Standards on Auditing. The standards are, on the whole, compatible with generally accepted auditing standards in Israel, but they are not enforceable under the Institute's rules of conduct.

## Saudi Arabia

The Kingdom of Saudi Arabia is among the foremost in the Middle East where the process of a modern renaissance has been successfully instituted and is continuing. All laws for governance of the Kingdom, designed to promote the harmony dictated by the canonical law of Islam—the Shari'ah—are promulgated by Royal Decree.

*Statutory Reports.* The form and the content of the financial statements of a corporation, which are specified in the Regulations for Companies, must, at a minimum, comprise a balance sheet, a financial report on its operations reflected in a profit-and-loss statement, and the financial position for the most recent financial year setting out the proposed method for allocating net profits.

The Regulations for Companies further stipulate that in preparing the accounts, the classifications used in the previous year must be used and the basis for valuing assets and liabilities must also remain unchanged. The auditor may recommend altering classifications or evaluation bases, in which case alterations are allowed if they are approved by the stockholders in a general meeting. No official determination has been made regarding the format of financial statements. Therefore, each business entity and its auditor are free to select a format of their own.

It is a requirement of the Ministry of Commerce that all books of account—journal, general ledger, and inventory book, including a comprehensive trial balance of all assets and liabilities as well as constituent elements of the operating results—be maintained in Arabic and kept within the Kingdom.

*Tax Returns.* Entities, including individuals, that are required to file tax declaration with the Zakat and Income Tax Department (ZITD), namely resident corporations, limited liability partnerships (companies), partnerships, contractors and practicing professionals, must prepare audited financial statements for the purpose of assessments by the ZITD of taxes and the Zakat levy. The tax filing requirements as well as the submission deadlines apply, notwithstanding the fact that the foreign shareholders in a limited liability partnership (company) are entitled to a tax holiday.

The directors of a company are responsible for the submission of the annual tax declaration, which should be supported by audited financial statements, irrespective of who actually prepares the documentation. The generally accepted basis for validating information in the tax declaration is by reference to the audited financial statements.

Limited liability partnerships (companies) with foreign participation as well as branches of foreign companies are required to file the final tax returns and to pay the tax and/or Zakat dues within two-and-a-half months of the end of the year. Filing extensions are permissible if requested from and approved by the ZITD before the due date and on payment of tax due on an estimated basis. For companies wholly owned by Saudi nationals, the final Zakat returns must be filed within six months from the financial year-end. For foreign sole practitioners, the filing deadline is 15 days from the year-end and extensions are allowed for six months if application is made within this period to the ZITD. Late payment of taxes is subject to penalties of up to 25 percent of the tax due.

The Tax Regulations require each entity in a group to file a separate tax return directly with the tax authorities, which must be accompanied by its own individual audited accounts.

### Other Requirements

In the case of a corporation, the board of directors must prepare, at least 60 days before the annual general meeting, the corporation's balance sheet, profit-and-loss statement, and reports on the corporation's operations and its financial position. The board must also make proposals for the distribution of the corporation's net profits. These documents together with the auditor's report on the financial statements must be filed with the General Administration for Companies division of the Ministry of Commerce at least 25 days prior to the general meeting.

In the case of a limited liability partnership, the managers must, within four months after the end of each financial year, prepare a balance sheet of the partnership, a profit-and-loss statement, and a report on its operations and financial position and on their proposals for the appropriation of net profits. These documents together with a copy of both the directors' and the auditors' reports must be filed with the General Administration for Companies division of the Ministry of Commerce within two months of their preparation and not later than six months after the end of the financial year.

In the case of companies with variable capital and of cooperative companies, the requirements for the preparation of financial statements are the same as those for either corporations or limited liability partnerships. A cooperative partnership with limited liability is permitted under the Regulations for Companies.

Consolidated financial statements are prepared, usually in accordance with International Accounting Standards IAS27 and IAS28, for the parent company shareholders to reflect the financial position and the results of operations of the group of enterprises as a whole. Further, the financial statements for business combinations are generally prepared and presented in accordance with International Accounting Standard IAS22.

Foreign companies operating in the Kingdom are subject to the provisions of the Regulations for Companies (other than those relating to incorporation). Therefore, they are subject to the same requirements for the preparation and the filing of financial statements as for Saudi corporations.

The directors of a corporation must, within 30 days from the date of their approval at the members' general meeting, file copies of the balance sheet, the profit-and-loss statement, the board of directors' report and the auditors' report with the Commercial Register Office as well as with the General Administration for Companies division of the Ministry of Commerce.

The managers, or those deemed to be the principal officers, of the aforementioned corporate entities, except for general partnerships, limited partnerships, and joint ventures, are required to publish in a newspaper distributed in the locality of the head office of the corporate entity the balance sheet, the profit-and-loss statement, a comprehensive summary of the board of principal officers' (chief executive officer's) report, and the full text of the auditors' report. A copy of each of these documents must also be sent to the General Administration for Companies division of the Ministry of Commerce at least 25 days prior to the date set for the members' general meeting.

At the discretion of the Authorities, late filing of returns with the Ministry of Commerce may give rise to penalties.

## Audit Requirements

The auditing standards used in practice are Saudi Auditing Standards and, in case Saudi Auditing Standards are silent, International Auditing Standards.

The constituent general meeting of shareholders appoints the first auditor of a corporation. The shareholders' general meeting shall appoint one or more auditors (from among those licensed to practice in the Kingdom) and determine their remuneration and term of office. A retiring auditor may be reappointed.

The auditor is required to:

- Submit a report to the annual general meeting indicating whether he has obtained all the information and explanations requested from the corporation and, in his opinion, the extent to which the company's accounts are in conformity with reality. The auditor is also required to report on any violations of the Regulations for Companies or of the company's bylaws.

- Prepare a special report to accompany the statement of the chairman of the board to the general meeting relating to transactions and contracts in which any director has a personal interest. The chairman's statement must be made available to the auditor at least 55 days prior to the date fixed for the general meeting.

- Report any violations of the requirement that, within 30 days of his or her appointment, a director must own shares in the Company's stock to a value of not less than SR 100,000.

Any auditor who knowingly includes false information in the balance sheet or the profit-and-loss statement or in reports prepared by him or her for the partners or general meeting or who conceals essential facts from his or her reports with the intention of concealing the financial position of the company from the partners or third parties, without prejudice to the requirements of the Islamic Shari'ah, shall be liable to imprisonment of not less than three months and not more than one year or to a fine of not less than SR 5,000 and not more than SR 25,000.

# Checklist: Evaluating the Target

I. History/background.
  A. Objective: Gain a general understanding of the target's history and structure.
  B. Recommended information to request.
    1. Organizational structure.
    2. Geographical regions of business.
    3. Major events in target's history including significant acquisitions and divested/discontinued operations and changes in business strategy.
    4. Fiscal year-end.
    5. Subsidiaries/divisions, including structure, reporting method, and measurement of performance.
    6. Minutes of directors' and shareholders' meetings.
    7. List of related parties and transactions.

II. Industry.
  A. Objective: Gain a general understanding of the industry and any opportunities and threats therein.
  B. Recommended information to request.
    1. Industry magazines and other publicly available information.
    2. List of principal competitors, including location and market share.

III. Transaction overview.
  A. Objective: Gain an understanding of the proposed transaction, including its structure, current position, and intermediaries involved.
  B. Recommended information to request.
    1. Offering document.
    2. Letter of intent.
    3. Purchase agreement draft.
    4. Other documentation related to transactions (e.g., financing arrangements).

IV. Management.
  A. Objective: Consider management's strengths and weaknesses.
  B. Recommended information to request.
    1. Organization chart.

    2. Directors and senior executives, including age, length of service, experience, duties, compensation, employment agreements, golden parachutes, pension arrangements, and other benefits.

    3. Resumes of senior management.

    4. Employee benefit plans.

    5. Recently departed directors and senior executives.

    6. Management's stock holdings.

    7. Postretirement plans and policies.

    8. Publicly available information about management.

V. Workforce.
    A. Objective: Consider workforce's strengths and weaknesses.
    B. Recommended information to request.
      1. Head count by department.
      2. Hours in standard work week and overtime by department.
      3. Methods used to select, train, supervise, and evaluate personnel.
      4. Compensation system.
      5. Trade union, including number of unionized employees and details of significant agreements, disputes, and work stoppages.
      6. Severance policy.
      7. Average wage rates by job classification and anticipated increases.
      8. Employee stock ownership plans (ESOPs).
      9. Employee benefit plans.
      10. Performance evaluation system.

VI. Products and services.
    A. Objective: Gain an understanding of the target's past, current, and future products and services.
    B. Recommended information to request.
      1. Product and marketing brochures.
      2. List of products and services.
      3. Proposed new products and product or service withdrawals.
      4. Details of product protection devices (e.g., patents, trademarks, copyrights, license agreements) or other proprietary characteristics.
      5. Substitute products.
      6. Market share by product.

VII. Research and development (R&D).
   A. Objective: Gain an understanding of the extent of R&D resources and success or failure of prior R&D efforts.
      (Note: In many manufacturing businesses, R&D is defined as *Product Development,* or *Engineering*, or a similar term.)
   B. Recommended information to request.
      1. Description of R&D facilities, staff, and strategy.
      2. R&D expenditures and budget.
      3. List of products developed or in development.
      4. Contracted R&D services.

VIII. Accounting policies and procedures.
   A. Objective: Consider the nature of accounting policies and procedures.
   B. Recommended information to request.
      1. Target's significant accounting policies and procedures, including revenue recognition, costing of work-in-process, and basis for cost allocations.
      2. Details of management reporting system.
      3. External and internal auditors' reports.
      4. Management letters.
      5. Chart of accounts.
      6. Periodic and nonrecurring adjustments.
      7. Monthly financial reporting packages distributed to senior management.
      8. Accounting department organizational chart.

IX. Review of target's auditors' workpapers.
   A. Objective: Gain an overall understanding of the accounting methods and procedures of the target, and consider its internal accounting controls.
   B. Recommended information to request.
      1. Auditors' workpapers.
      2. Permanent files.
      3. Annual reports.
      4. Quarterly reports.
      5. Management letters.

X. Internal control structure.
   A. Objective: Gain a general understanding of the internal control environment, and consider its strengths and weaknesses.

B. Recommended information to request.
   1. Organization chart.
   2. Accounting manual.
   3. Job descriptions and authority limits of accounting personnel.
   4. Internal audit reports.
   5. Management letters.
   6. Officer resumes.

XI. Sales—general.
   A. Objective: Gain an understanding of the target's sales.
   B. Recommended information to request.
      1. Historical revenues.
      2. Nonrecurring revenues.
      3. Royalty and licensing agreements.
      4. Sales budget.
      5. Consignment sales.
      6. Canceled orders.
      7. Refunds, returns, credit memos, and discounts.

XII. Customer base.
   A. Objective: Gain an understanding of the customer base, and consider strengths and weaknesses.
   B. Recommended information to request.
      1. Revenues by customer and geographic region.
      2. Significant customers ranked by sales (dollars and units).
      3. Lost customers.
      4. Special discounts and credit terms offered to significant customers.
      5. Internal marketing reports.
      6. Customer profitability information.
      7. New customers.

XIII. Product mix and pricing.
   A. Objective: Gain an understanding of the composition of revenues.
   B. Recommended information to request.
      1. Market share for major products.
      2. Sales dollars and units by product/product line.
      3. Discontinued and/or obsolete products.
      4. Gross profit by product.
      5. Price list and recent/expected price changes.

XIV. Accounts receivable.
   A. Objective: Consider the quality and existence of accounts receivable.
   B. Recommended information to request.
      1. Schedule of accounts receivable by category (trade, nontrade, other, etc.) as of recent date and comparable date.
      2. Credit policy.
      3. Aging analysis and trends.
      4. Allowance for collectible accounts and write-offs.
      5. Collection procedures.
      6. Discounts, returns, and allowances schedule.

XV. Backlog.
   A. Objective: Gain an understanding of the composition of the target's backlog.
   B. Recommended information to request.
      1. Backlog reports.
      2. Shipping reports.
      3. Backorder reports.

XVI. Marketing channels.
   A. Objective: Understand the selling and the distribution methods used.
   B. Recommended information to request.
      1. Description of sales force, including sales offices and service facilities.
      2. Details of agreements with sales agents and distributors, including name, length of service, products and territories covered, terms of commissions and/or other forms of compensation, and copies of standard agents' agreements.
      3. Marketing plan and budget.
      4. Names and fee arrangement with advertising agency and marketing consultants as well as budgets for these.
      5. Sales agents/distributors ranked by sales.
      6. Customer dependency issues.

XVII. Carve-outs and related-party transactions.
   A. Objective: Gain an understanding of the extent of related-party transactions.
   B. Recommended information to request.
      1. Sales to related parties, including price per unit.

2. Intercompany sales and service arrangements.
3. Transfer pricing policy.
4. Services provided by/to parent or related party.
5. Intercompany receivables.
6. Intercompany payables.
7. Consolidating/combining financial statements.

XVIII. Cost of goods sold.
    A. Objective: Gain an understanding of cost of sales components.
    B. Recommended information to request.
       1. Cost of goods sold by product and component (fixed and variable with sufficient detail of types of expenses in each category).
       2. Description of cost accounting system (job costing, process costing, etc.).
       3. Allocation methods for overhead and indirect labor.
       4. Variance reports.
       5. Scrap/rework reports.

XIX. Inventory.
    A. Objective: Gain an understanding of inventory quantities.
    B. Recommended information to request.
       1. Inventory balances by location and product line.
       2. Assigned inventory/consignments.
       3. Accounting principles and procedures.
       4. Turnover by product.
       5. Obsolete or slow-moving inventory.
       6. Inventory write-offs.
       7. Inventory management and control procedures.
       8. Book to physical adjustments.
       9. Major ingredients and specifications including volumes purchased.
      10. Method of delivery and delivery time.
      11. LIFO reserve calculation, if any.

XX. Operating expenses.
    A. Objective: Consider significant operating expenses, and gain an understanding of the underlying reasons for increases or decreases.
    B. Recommended information to request.
       1. Cost allocations from parent, including policies and procedures.

  2. Operating expenses (as a percentage of revenues) by significant category.
  3. Expense budgets.

XXI. Prepaid expenses and other assets.
   A. Objective: Gain an understanding of prepaid expenses and other assets (including deferred charges, investments, and intangible assets).
   B. Recommended information to request.
      1. List of securities and other investments, showing cost, carrying value, and market value.
      2. Schedule of prepaid expenses and other assets (e.g., deferred charges and intangibles).

XXII. Accounts payable and accrued liabilities.
   A. Objective: Gain an understanding of accounts payable and accrued liabilities.
   B. Recommended information to request.
      1. Detailed schedule of accounts that comprise accounts payable and accrued expenses.
      2. Accounts payable aging schedule.
      3. Schedule of roll-forward of reserves.
      4. Details of reserves held in subsidiaries, associates, and overseas entities.
      5. Identification of other current and noncurrent liabilities.
      6. Significant cash disbursements subsequent to the balance sheet date.
      7. Approved suppliers of raw materials and purchasing policy.
      8. Supplier contracts and outstanding supplier claims.
      9. Allowable trade discounts.

XXIII. Commitments, contingencies, and litigation.
   A. Objective: Consider significant commitments and contingencies.
   B. Recommended information to request.
      1. Existing and potential litigation claims.
      2. Capital commitments, distinguishing between authorized and contracted commitments.
      3. Schedule of contingent liabilities.
      4. Details of insurance coverage for specified contingent liabilities.
      5. Attorney inquiry letters as to litigation, actual or threatened.
      6. Safety/accident reports.
      7. Environmental studies and cleanup reports.

8. Product liability claims.
9. Minutes of directors' meetings.
10. Regulatory reports.
11. Schedule of lease obligations and letters of credit.
12. Insurance coverage.

XXIV. Property, plant, and equipment.
  A. Objective: Identify significant individual assets comprising property, plant, and equipment, and consider depreciation expense.
  B. Recommended information to request.
      1. Schedule of fixed assets, including date acquired, original cost, accumulated depreciation, net book value, and appraised value.
      2. General description of office and production facilities, including use, ownership, age, and square footage.
      3. Depreciation methods used for book and tax purposes.
      4. Capital expenditures (historical, current, planned).
      5. Retirements and disposals.
      6. Capacity.
      7. Maintenance expenses.
      8. Building and equipment leases.
      9. Construction in progress.

XXV. Cash, cash flow, and banking relationships.
  A. Objective: Consider cash balances and banking relationships.
  B. Recommended information to request.
      1. Summary of cash balances by major depository.
      2. Reconciliations.
      3. List of compensating balance arrangements.
      4. Cash flow statements.

XXVI. Debt.
  A. Objective: Gain an understanding of the target's debt financing.
  B. Recommended information to request.
      1. Summary of short- and long-term debt, showing principal holders, interest rates, maturities, and amortization schedules.
      2. Principal features of loan agreements, including convertibility, collateral, restrictions on target's activities, required ratios, events of default, and prepayment premiums.
      3. Details of debenture trust deeds, loan stock agreements, mortgages, and other fixed borrowings, including security held by the bank.
      4. Credit rating agency reports.

XXVII. Prospective financial information.
    A. Objective: Gain an understanding of how prospective financial information and supporting assumptions were developed.
    B. Recommended information to request.
        1. Prospective financial data and supporting assumptions (inquire about worst, best, and most probable scenarios).
        2. Names of management and other parties responsible for the preparation of forecasts or projections.
        3. Description of the process and the methodology used to develop the forecast or projection.

XXVIII. Employee benefits.
    A. Objective: Gain an understanding of the target's benefits program and identify the related risks.
    B. Recommended information to request.
        1. Plan documents.
        2. Actuarial reports.
        3. Employee and dependents census.
        4. Plan financial statements.
        5. Government filings.
        6. Employee communications.
        7. Plan experience reports.
        8. Employee account balances.
        9. 5500 forms.
        10. Labor agreements.
        11. Premium renewal statements.

XXIX. Information systems (IS).
    A. Objective: Analysis of the effectiveness of the IS environment and the potential for future consolidation with the client's environment.
    B. Recommended information to request.
        1. IS organization chart.
        2. Hardware, communication, and peripheral equipment list.
        3. Contracts and leases.
        4. Application software portfolio.
        5. Business and systems planning documentation.
        6. Disaster recovery plans.
        7. Controls documentation.
        8. Historical and budgeted IS investment.
        9. IS approach and methodology documentation.

## Appendix 4.1

# Summary of GAAP (by Country)

## Accounting for Long-Term Investments in Share Capital of Other Entities

### *Consolidation*

**United States.** If there is more than 50 percent control of voting securities of another company, significant intercompany transactions are eliminated in consolidated financial statements.

**Brazil.** Same as United States.

**Canada.** Same as United States.

**Mexico.** Similar Mexican GAAP: B-8 "Consolidated and Combined Financial Statements and Valuation of Long-Term Investments."

> *Differences and Similarities*:
>
> - *Consolidation.* When there is a group, consolidated financial statements must be presented. This will be the case when one company owns, either directly or indirectly, more than one half of the voting power of another company. However, two situations exist when the exclusion of a subsidiary from the consolidation is justified:
>   1. Subsidiaries abroad, in countries where exchange controls, restrictions on the remittances of profits, or uncertainty on monetary stability exist.
>   2. Subsidiaries that have suspended payments to creditors or that are in dissolution and bankruptcy.
> - *Equity method.* Holding companies are required to present individual financial statements in order to comply with legal requirements. For this purpose, investments in shares of subsidiaries and associated companies should be valued by the equity method (acquisition cost and adding or deducting proportional part of profit or loss of the subsidiary, from the date of acquisition).
> - *Fair value method.* The interest of minority shareholders should be shown under a separate heading within stockholders' equity in the balance sheet.

**Denmark.** Same as United States.

**France.** Same as United States.

**Germany.** Same as United States.

**Netherlands.** Same as United States.

**Spain.** Same as United Kingdom.

**United Kingdom.** Same as United States, although consolidation can be required for companies with less than 50 percent control if there is "dominant influence."

**Australia.** Same as United States.

**Japan.** Same as United States.

**Singapore.**   Same as United Kingdom.

## *Equity Method*

**United States.**   For 20 percent to 50 percent control. Investment is stated at net asset value. Equity in investee's earnings or loss is included in investor's income statement.

**Brazil.**   Equity method must be used if book value of controlled company is individually at least 10 percent of net worth of investor or 15 percent collectively; equity pickup is related to changes in investee's equity, not its income.

**Canada.**   Same as United States.

**Mexico.**   Similar Mexican GAAP: B-8 "Consolidated and Combined Financial Statements and Valuation of Long-Term Investments"

   *Differences and Similarities.*   Foreign currency transactions are recorded at the exchange rate prevailing on the date of the transaction. Any resulting exchange gain or loss is dealt with through the income statement. At the balance sheet date, monetary assets and liabilities denominated in a foreign currency are normally translated using the closing exchange rate, and any exchange gain or loss is reported as part of the ordinary profit or loss for the year.

   There are two important exceptions to the foregoing:

1. When the translation differences are required to be capitalized as a part of the cost of a fixed asset.

2. When the exchange-rate fluctuations are the result of the net investment in a foreign entity covered by a foreign currency liability. In such a case, the amount of the translation difference should be included as an item of stockholder's equity.

**Denmark.**   Same as United States.

**France.**   Same as United States.

**Germany.**   Same as United States, for consolidated financial statements.

**Netherlands.**   For interest greater than 20 percent of control and for shares in partnerships.

**Spain.**   Same as United States. The equity method also can be used when the global method is not appropriate.

**United Kingdom.**   Same as United States. Joint ventures are required to be included using the "gross equity" method. Although the principles are the same as the equity method, the presentation of the profit-and-loss account and the balance sheet is different.

**Australia.**   Equity method is not acceptable for statutory purposes. If used, the company must present supplementary equity financial statements.

**Japan.**   Same as United States.

**Singapore.**   Same as United Kingdom.

### Cost Method

**United States.** For less than 20 percent control. Investment is stated at cost. Dividends paid by investee company are included in earnings by investor. Provision is required if there is an impairment of value.

**Brazil.** Rarely used.

**Canada.** Same as United States.

**Mexico.** Same as United States.

**Denmark.** For less than 50 percent control, except for bigger companies where it is only used for less than 20 percent control.

**France.** At year-end, investments may be written down to their underlying net worth if it is felt that there is permanent diminution in value.

**Germany.** Same as United States.

**Netherlands.** Same as United States.

**Spain.** Same as United States. The cost method is mainly used for multigroup companies.

**United Kingdom.** Same as United States.

**Australia.** Cost method is normally used where investment is 50 percent or less.

**Japan.** If market price is as least 50 percent less than cost and if decline does not appear to be temporary, market price is used.

**Singapore.** Same as United Kingdom.

### Translation for Foreign Currency Financial Statements and Accounting for Foreign Currency Transactions

*FASB #52 Translation Adjustments*

**United States.** Certain foreign assets and liabilities are translated into U.S. dollars at current exchange rate; gains and losses reported as separate component of stockholders' equity.

**Brazil.** Many companies use FASB #52; but more commonly used is current-rate translation approach.

**Canada.** Same as United States for self-sustaining operations. For integrated operations, gains and losses are recognized in the period in which they occur.

**Mexico.** Similar Mexican GAAP: B-15 "Foreign Currency Transactions and Conversion of Financial Statements of Foreign Operations"

*Differences and Similarities.* Foreign currency transactions are recorded at the exchange rate prevailing on the date of the transaction. Any resulting exchange gain or loss is dealt with through the income statement. At the balance sheet date, monetary assets and liabilities denominated in a foreign currency are normally translated using the closing exchange rate, and any exchange gain or loss is reported as part of the ordinary profit or loss for the year. Two important exceptions to the foregoing:

1. When the translation differences are required to be capitalized as a part of the cost of a fixed asset.

2. When the exchange-rate fluctuations are the result of the net investment in a foreign entity covered by a foreign currency liability. In such a case, the amount of the translation difference should be included as an item of stockholders' equity.

**Denmark.** Balances in foreign currencies are for the monetary assets and liabilities translated at the exchange rate at year-end. Other items in the balance are translated at the current exchange rate. Translation differences are included in the profit-and-loss account. Translation of independent foreign companies' statements is made to the exchange rate at year-end, and the exchange difference must be taken directly on the equity capital.

**France.** Similar to FASB #52 approach.

**Germany.** No accepted convention; the common approach is to use closing-rate methods, but a wide variety of methods is used in practice.

**Netherlands.** Same as United Kingdom.

**Spain.** Normally, the current exchange rate is used, but in some cases a mixed method is used, which includes current and historic exchange rates.

**United Kingdom.** Balances in foreign currencies are required to be translated at the exchange rate at the period-end. Exchange gains and losses are recognized in the profit-and-loss account. Exchange gains and losses arising from the retranslation of the net investment in foreign subsidiaries are charged directly to shareholders' funds.

**Australia.** Similar to FASB #52 approach.

**Japan.** Similar to FASB #52 approach.

**Singapore.** Same as United Kingdom.

### Transaction Gains and Losses

**United States.** Weighted-average exchange rate used to translate revenues and expenses; gains and losses are recognized in income in the accounting period in which they occur.

**Brazil.** N/A.*

**Canada.** Same as United States, except that gains and losses on a liability with a fixed life are amortized over the remaining life.

**Mexico.** Same as United States.

**Denmark.** Transaction gains and losses are translated at the exchange rates at the transaction date.

**France.** N/A.

**Germany.** Realized gains and losses are recognized in income when they occur. For short-term receivables and payables, unrealized gains are deferred and unrealized losses are not.

**Netherlands.** Same as United States.

---

*Not applicable.

**Spain.**   These are considered as extraordinary gains or losses.

**United Kingdom.**   Either closing rate or weighted-average exchange rate can be used to translate revenues and expenses; gains and losses are recognized in the profit-and-loss account in the accounting period in which they occur.

**Australia.**   Transaction gains and losses are translated at the exchange rates current at the transaction date.

**Japan.**   N/A.

**Singapore.**   Same as United Kingdom.

### Investment in Debt Securities

**United States.**   Under SFAS 115, investments in debt securities that an entity has the positive intent and ability to hold to maturity should be measured at amortized cost. Trading securities and available-for-sale securities should be measured at fair value, and realized gains and losses are included in earnings. For trading securities, the unrealized holding gains and losses are included in earnings; these gains and losses are reported in equity until realized for available-for-sale securities.

**Brazil.**   Debt securities are stated at amortized cost; both the effective interest method and the straight-line method of amortization are acceptable.

**Canada.**   Same as Brazil.

**Mexico.**   Same as United States.

**Denmark.**   Investment in debt securities that the company has the positive intent and ability to hold to maturity should be valued at amortized cost. Trading securities should be valued at market value. All revaluation differences are included in the profit-and-loss account.

**France.**   Same as Brazil.

**Germany.**   Stated at cost, but amortization is not required; write-down at market is required if value is permanently impaired.

**Netherlands.**   Long-term investments in debt securities are valued at cost and realizable value. Changes are charged to the result for the year. These investments can also be valued at current cost (market prices). In that case increases in value are added to a revaluation reserve, whereas decreases are charged to the revaluation reserve. If the revaluation reserve is insufficient to cover these decreases in market price, then the losses should be charged to the result for the period. Trading debt securities (short-term) should be stated at market value, or the lower of cost and net realizable value. Changes in valuation are accounted for in the result for the period.

**Spain.**   Stated at cost. Written-down if market value is lesser than cost.

**United Kingdom.**   Stated at amortized cost, using the interest method.

**Australia.**   Stated at cost, but amortization is not required; write-down to market is required if value is permanently impaired.

**Japan.**   Same as United States.

**Singapore.**   Same as United Kingdom.

## *Inventories*

**United States.**   Reported in financial statements at the lower of cost or market at balance sheet date. The methods used are specific identification, FIFO (first-in, first-out), LIFO (last-in, first-out), and average cost. For manufactured inventories, inventory costs include allocation of labor and overhead.

**Brazil.**   FIFO may be used. LIFO not allowed. Moving average method is most common because it results in lower inventory than FIFO and, therefore, lower taxes.

**Canada.**   Same methods as United States, except LIFO not acceptable for tax and is therefore seldom used. Standard cost method is also used.

**Mexico.**   Same as United States.

**Denmark.**   Same methods as United States except that LIFO is not allowed. Inventories can be revaluated at market value, but the revaluation difference must be booked directly at equity as a separate reserve.

**France.**   Same methods as United States, except LIFO only permitted for consolidated groups.

**Germany.**   Same methods as United States. For manufacturing, inventory costs may include production overhead.

**Netherlands.**   Same as United States. Valuation at current cost is also possible. In case LIFO method is applied, the notes to the accounts should disclose the valuation at FIFO, average cost of current cost.

**Spain.**   Same as United States.

**United Kingdom.**   Same methods as United States, except that LIFO is not allowed. Overhead is allocated to costs of inventory.

**Australia.**   Same methods as United States, except LIFO not allowed.

**Japan.**   Same methods as United States. Other methods include base-stock, retail, and purchase price methods.

**Singapore.**   Same as United Kingdom.

## *Reserve for Unspecified Future Losses*

**United States.**   Contingency reserves or general reserves are not allowed. Required are valuation reserves for anticipated losses, which are established via charges to current earnings (shown as a deduction from related asset account on balance sheet).

**Brazil.**   Same as United States, although rarely are they created because there is no tax benefit.

**Canada.**   Same as United States.

**Mexico.**   Same as United States.

**Denmark.**   Same as United States.

**France.**   Same as United States.

**Germany.**   Same as United States.

**Netherlands.**  Same as United States.

**Spain.**  This is only allowed for future responsibilities or guarantees.

**United Kingdom.**  Provisions are required where a fixed asset (tangible or intangible) is subject to an impairment in value. Provisions for liabilities and charges are permitted only where there is a legal or constructive obligation to incur costs in the future relating to an event that had occurred at the balance sheet date and where the cost is capable of being estimated.

**Australia.**  Same as United States.

**Japan.**  Same as United States.

**Singapore.**  Same as United Kingdom.

### Accounting for Capital Leases

**United States.**  Leases that are, in substance purchases, sales, or financing transactions are accounted for as such. Leased property is recorded as an asset in lessee's accounting records, and liability for future lease payments is also established if lease transfers substantially all rights and risks of asset to lessee.

**Brazil.**  Generally accepted practice treats operating and capital leases as rentals.

**Canada.**  Same as United States.

**Mexico.**  Same as United States.

**Denmark.**  Same as United States.

**France.**  All leases are recorded as operating leases, but consolidated companies have option to treat them the same as in the United States.

**Germany.**  Same as United States.

**Netherlands.**  Same as United States.

**Spain.**  Same as United States.

**United Kingdom.**  Same as United States.

**Australia.**  Same as United States.

**Japan.**  Same as United States.

**Singapore.**  Same as United Kingdom.

### Deferred Income Taxes

**United States.**  Required income taxes are provided against current period income as reflected in financial statements even though all or some of such income will not be reported for tax purposes in current period and taxes will not be payable currently (deferral method).

**Brazil.**  This is recommended, but most companies still record and recognize income tax strictly as computed for tax purposes.

**Canada.**  Same as United States.

**Mexico.**  Similar Mexican GAAP: D-4 "Accounting Treatment of Income Tax, Asset Tax, and Statutory Employees' Profit Sharing."

*Differences and Similarities.*  According to D-4, a deferred-tax asset must be created for all temporary deductible differences, for fiscal losses, and for unused tax credits (such as the Asset Tax, in some cases). Also, a deferred-tax liability must be created for all temporary taxable differences.

Notwithstanding, paragraph 28 of D-4 states that deferred-tax assets must be created to the extent that temporary taxable differences exist and under certain conditions. It also states that any remaining temporary deductible difference plus fiscal losses plus unused tax credits must be created only when there is a high probability that all this will be offset against future profit.

**Denmark.** Deferred income taxes must be booked on all timing differences. Deferred income taxes are not calculated/booked on permanent differences.

**France.** Both liability and deferral methods are permitted only in the consolidated statements. Liability method is most frequently used.

**Germany.** The liability method, the deferred method, and the net-of-tax method are allowed.

**Netherlands.** Deferred tax should only refer to timing differences. Deferred-tax receivables should be accounted for fiscal losses to be carried forward. The deferral method is used.

**Spain.** Deferred taxes are normally only considered for temporary differences.

**United Kingdom.** Deferred tax is recognized on all timing differences, but not on permanent differences. Except for very specific circumstances, deferred tax is not provided for on revaluation gains or the unremitted earnings of overseas entities.

**Australia.** The liability method is used; otherwise, same as United States.

**Japan.** The liability method is used.

**Singapore.** Same as United Kingdom.

### Fixed Assets and Depreciation

**United States.** Generally, furniture, equipment, and leasehold improvements are recorded at historical cost and are depreciated on a systematic basis over the remaining useful life of the asset (or terms of lease for leasehold improvements). SFAS 121 requires entities to perform separate calculations for long-lived assets to determine whether recognition of an impairment loss is required.

**Brazil.** Same as United States. Machinery, furniture, and fixtures must be monetarily corrected at least annually.

**Canada.** Same as United States. Write-ups to appraisal value are no longer permitted.

**Mexico.** Similar Mexican GAAP: C-6 "Land, Machinery, and Equipment."

*Differences and Similarities.* In Mexico, it is not only accepted but required to register all fixed assets at historical cost and then restated by inflation using the methodology in B-10. Depreciation is the same as in United States.

**Denmark.** Same as United States. For own manufactured fixed assets, overheads must be included in the value. Fixed assets can be revaluated to market value. The amount occurring from revaluation must be booked as separate reserve equity.

**France.** Same as United States.

**Germany.**   Same as United States.

**Netherlands.**   Same as United States, although fixed assets may be stated at current cost.

**Spain.**   Same as United States.

**United Kingdom.**   Same as United States, although fixed assets may be revalued.

**Australia.**   Same as United States.

**Japan.**   Same as United States.

**Singapore.**   Same as United Kingdom.

### Research and Development Costs

**United States.**   These costs are generally expensed in period incurred.

**Brazil.**   Same as United States.

**Canada.**   Research costs are expensed in the year incurred. Development costs are deferred and amortized if specific criteria are satisfied.

**Mexico.**   Similar Mexican GAAP: No particular GAAP.

*Differences and Similarities.*   Accounting principles require that all research and development costs must be expensed when incurred. The amount of the charge must be disclosed within the accounts.

**Denmark.**   Research costs shall be expensed in the period in which they incurred. Development costs must be considered an asset if the entity, without doubt, will lead to production. Development cost shall be depreciated over the expected operational life.

**France.**   Usually same as United States, but they may also be included as an intangible asset and amortized over five years or less.

**Germany.**   Same as United States.

**Netherlands.**   Same as United States, although capitalization and amortization is permitted under certain criteria.

**Spain.**   Same as France.

**United Kingdom.**   Same as United States. Capitalization and amortization is permitted only under strict criteria.

**Australia.**   Same as United States.

**Japan.**   Usually same as United States.

**Singapore.**   Same as United Kingdom.

### Capitalization of Interest Expense

**United States.**   In certain circumstances, interest expense can be capitalized as part of historical cost.

**Brazil.**   Not allowed, but in preoperation period, interest expense is deferred until normal operations achieved. Interest expense must be disclosed in financial statements.

**Canada.**   Interest expense may be capitalized if amount is recoverable. Amount must be disclosed.

**Mexico.**   Same as United States.

**Denmark.**   Same as United States.

**France.**   Most interest is expense, although interest expense related to finance cost of internal manufacturing or construction may be capitalized.

**Germany.**   Interest is generally expensed, but capitalization is permitted for long-term construction projects.

**Netherlands.**   Same as United States.

**Spain.**   Interest expense on assets acquisitions only can be capitalized during the period that these assets have not been started up.

**United Kingdom.**   Normal practice is same as United States, but must be applied consistently across a class of fixed assets.

**Australia.**   No standards, but normal practice is same as United States.

**Japan.**   Not mandatory, but common practice is similar to United States.

**Singapore.**   Same as United Kingdom.

## Accounting Changes

**United States.**   Change in accounting principles or methods is reported in income statement in the period in which the change occurs. The effect of accounting changes on prior periods is presented as a cumulative amount, net of tax, below income from continuing operations.

**Brazil.**   N/A.

**Canada.**   Same as United States.

**Mexico.**   Similar Mexican GAAP: No particular GAAP, but included in bulletin A-7 "Comparability."

*Differences and Similarities.*   Same as in the United States, except that information should be disclosed in footnotes explaining why this change is better than the prior one and the effect of the change in the income tax, the financial position, and the stockholders' equity during the year in which change occurred.

**Denmark.**   Change in the accounting principles and method is reported in the income statement of the period in which the change occurs. The effect of accounting changes in prior periods is presented as a cumulative amount under equity.

**France.**   Change in accounting principles and method is reported in the shareholders' equity section in the consolidated statements and in the profit-and-loss account in the individual accounts. The effect on prior periods is not specifically identified in the accounts, but it is reported in the notes to the financial statements.

**Germany.**   N/A.

**Netherlands.**   The (net of tax) effect of accounting changes on the opening equity can be presented as a movement in the shareholders' equity (this is the preferred method) or accounted for as an extraordinary result for the period in which the change occurs.

**Spain.**   Changes in accounting principles or methods must be disclosed in the consolidated and individual annual accounts. Their effects must be quantified and qualified.

**Australia.** Same as United States.

**United Kingdom.** Same as United States.

**Japan.** N/A.

**Singapore.** Same as United Kingdom

### Debt Issue Expense

**United States.** Debt issue costs are recorded as a deferred charge and amortized to income over the life of the debt issue.

**Brazil.** Same as United States; amortized over 5 to 10 years.

**Canada.** Optional, but common practice is same as United States.

**Mexico.** Same as United States.

**Denmark.** Debt issue expenses are expensed.

**France.** Same as United States.

**Germany.** Bond issue costs are expensed.

**Netherlands.** Debt issue costs should be expensed.

**Spain.** Same as United States.

**United Kingdom.** Same as United States.

**Australia.** Same as United States, except amortization must be generally completed in 5 years or less.

**Japan.** Same as United States; amortized over 3 years or less.

**Singapore.** Same as United Kingdom

## Business Combinations

### Purchase Methods as Described under United States

**United States.** Purchase methods with acquisition recorded at cost; acquired assets and liabilities are recorded at fair value.

**Brazil.** Usually used.

**Canada.** Acquiring company's interest is recorded at cost; identifiable assets and liabilities at fair value. Any excess is recorded as goodwill.

**Mexico.** Same as United States.

**Denmark.** When establishing a new concern, the assets and the liabilities in the new company shall be revaluated to market value; this also includes items that have not earlier been taken into account of the new company. The difference between value and cost is booked as goodwill.

**France.** The purchase method only is used.

**Germany.** Usually used.

**Netherlands.** The purchase method is normally applied. Identifiable assets and liabilities are stated at fair value. Any excess is recorded as goodwill.

**Spain.**  The purchase method is normally used.

**United Kingdom.**  Same as United States.

**Australia.**  Required.

**Japan.**  The purchase method is used because goodwill is tax deductible.

**Singapore.**  Same as United Kingdom.

### Pooling-of-Interests Method

**United States.**  No longer permitted, effective June 30, 2001.

**Brazil.**  Rarely used.

**Canada.**  Same as United States.

**Mexico.**  Same as United States.

**Denmark.**  The method is allowed.

**France.**  N/A.

**Germany.**  N/A.

**Netherlands.**  Same as United Kingdom, and it is required when certain criteria are met. Due to the impact of the criteria, the pooling-of-interest method is only rarely used.

**Spain.**  N/A.

**United Kingdom.**  This method referred to as "merger accounting" in the United Kingdom and is required when certain criteria are met.

**Australia.**  N/A.

**Japan.**  N/A.

**Singapore.**  Same as United Kingdom

### Goodwill

**United States.**  Goodwill is recognized but not amortized. Impairment tests must be made of goodwill on an ongoing basis (on adoption of SFAS 142, then annually, plus whenever certain factors exist).

**Brazil.**  Same as United States, usually, although amortization is optional.

**Canada.**  Same as United States.

**Mexico.**  Same as United States.

**Denmark.**  Goodwill must be booked at cost and is depreciated over a maximum of 20 years.

**France.**  Capitalized with amortization periods of about 10 to 20 years.

**Germany.**  This method permitted, but seldom used. It may be written off against reserves. If capitalized, the amortization period must not exceed 20 years.

**Netherlands.**  It is not allowed to charge goodwill directly to the reserves or to the result for the year of acquisition. Goodwill should be capitalized and amortized over the period of its useful life, which should not exceed 20 years.

**Spain.**  Goodwill is capitalized and amortized usually in a period of 5 years (a maximum of 10 years is allowed in some circumstances).

**United Kingdom.**   Goodwill is capitalized and amortized. When the period of amortization exceeds 20 years, an annual review for impairment is required. Negative goodwill is also required to be recognized on the balance sheet and amortized.

**Australia.**   Same as United States.

**Japan.**   Same as Germany, except amortization period may not exceed 5 years.

**Singapore.**   Same as United Kingdom.

### Inflation Accounting

**United States.**   SFAS 89 applies only to public U.S. companies. Foreign issuers must comply if currencies' cumulative inflationary effect is 100 percent over the most recent three-year period. SFAS 89 encourages but does not require income adjusted for impact of changing prices for specific goods and services used by the company and for purchasing power gain (loss) on net monetary items for public companies with assets of $1 billion or more or inventories and property, plant, and equipment of $125 million or more.

**Brazil.**   Corporation law requires that financial statements be monetarily corrected (constant currency rather than constant cost information).

**Canada.**   Not required. Disclosure is encouraged if informative.

**Mexico.**   Similar Mexican GAAP: B-10 "Inflation Affects Recognition in the Financial Information."

*Differences and Similarities.*   Bulletin B-10, obligatory for all companies since 1984, establishes rules for adjusting financial statements to reflect the inflation changes.

Only one method is accepted: adjustment for changes in the general price level, which consists of correcting the "measuring" unit utilized for traditional accounting, using constant pesos instead of nominal pesos.

Amounts in the financial statements that should be restated are in the balance sheet (all the nonmonetary items, including those comprising the shareholders' equity) and in the income statement (the cost or expenses associated with non-monetary liabilities).

Public companies must use the B-10 standard; but for adjusting cost of sales, LIFO is the only permitted method.

The effect of inflation accounting and currency exchange is shown within cost of financing in the income statement.

**Denmark.**   There is no specified practice, but the balance must be adjusted to the market value if market is less than cost.

**France.**   Accounting for inflation is required in the consolidated statements if currencies' cumulative inflationary effect is 100 percent over the most recent three-year period; if interest rates, wages, and prices are linked to a consumer price index; and if the prices are usually stated in a foreign currency.

**Germany.**   Accounting for inflation is recommended but not required, and it is not widely used.

**Netherlands.**   Accounting for inflation is required if currencies' cumulative effect is 100 percent or more over the most recent three-year period.

**Spain.**   Inflation adjustments in consolidated accounts are only allowed when the consolidated foreign company is subjected to high inflation rates. Adjustments must be done according to the country's own national rules of the consolidated company.

**United Kingdom.**   Similar to SFAS 89. When distortions caused by hyperinflation are such that they affect the true and fair view given by the group financial statements (guideline levels are as for United States), either the accounts should be adjusted to reflect current prices, or a relatively stable currency should be used.

**Australia.**   No requirements. Statement of accounting practice in current cost accounting is not widely used.

**Japan.**   No legal requirements address accounting for inflation.

**Singapore.**   Same as United Kingdom.

# 5

# Tax Aspects of Inbound Merger and Acquisition and Joint Venture Transactions

*David R. Tillinghast*

**W**hile in principle the tax issues arising in both "inbound" and "outbound" mergers, acquisitions, and joint ventures may be similar, in practice U.S. tax considerations play a much more central role in inbound transactions. In the merger or acquisition context, the target company is a U.S. corporation that will seek to avoid recognizing taxable gain, and the shareholders of the target are also likely to be U.S. people or entities potentially subject to U.S. tax on the transaction. Similarly, in an inbound joint venture, the U.S. participant or participants will have particular U.S. tax concerns that, as discussed later, will affect the way in which the venture will be structured.

## INBOUND MERGERS AND ACQUISITIONS

### Structuring Inbound Merger and Acquisition Transactions

#### *Types of Transactions to Be Considered*

From a tax point of view, there are three basic patterns of structuring an inbound merger or acquisition. The first type of transaction is a *tax-free reorganization*, what is traditionally thought of as a merger, that is, the acquisition by one company of all of the assets or shares of another in a transaction in which the shareholders of the merged company receive shares in the acquiring company. Transactions of this kind are called tax-free because generally neither the merged company nor its shareholders recognize taxable gain or loss as a result, although the shareholders carry over the tax cost, or basis, in their merged company shares to the shares they receive in the exchange, so that they may later recognize the inherent gain. Moreover, the acquiring company succeeds to the tax attributes of the merged company under a type of pooling rule.

The second general type of transaction is a *taxable purchase*, that is, an acquisition by one company of shares or assets of another in exchange for some consideration, usually cash or debt obligations but in some cases shares or warrants to buy shares in combination with cash or debt. Such a transaction is called taxable because the target company, its shareholders, or possibly both recognize taxable gain or loss on the exchange; the acquiring company also accounts for the transaction as a purchase, taking a new cost basis in the shares or assets acquired.

Over the years, a third kind of transaction, referred to here as a *hybrid transaction*, has evolved. It has been designed to afford the U. S. target corporation and its shareholders (or some of them) the tax-free treatment that they would get in a tax-free reorganization, while avoiding the issuance of shares of the foreign acquirer, which may be undesirable for reasons discussed later.

In the 1990s, a technique that was popular with many U.S. investors was to participate in a tax-free share-for-share transaction but then effectively to rea-lize on the shares received by entering into an equity swap or other derivative contract with a financial institution. Under a 1997 law, such a transaction is deemed to be a taxable disposition of the shares if it substantially eliminates the holder's risk of gain or loss on the shares. Under liberalized regulations issued by the Internal Revenue Service (IRS) in 2000, dispositions of shares received in a tax-free reorganization to third parties does not affect the tax-free treatment of the transaction, so that, subject to securities law restrictions, participating shareholders can cash in their interests without jeopardizing the tax treatment of the participating corporations or the other shareholders. This has markedly reduced, although it has not eliminated, the incentive to design hybrid transactions.

## Factors Influencing the Choice of Transactional Form

***Tax-Free Reorganization.*** A tax-free reorganization may be selected for either one of two basic reasons. The first is that shares are the preferred consideration. This may be because the purpose of the transaction is to merge the businesses of the target and the acquirer, giving the holders of both an equity stake in the combined business. In other cases, the acquirer may simply wish to utilize its own shares as the medium of payment.

The second principal reason for choosing a tax-free reorganization is the desire of the shareholders of the selling corporation to avoid recognizing currently taxable gain. In the case of a publicly held corporation, management may be reluctant to propose a taxable transaction unless its shareholders will receive a very substantial premium. In the case of closely held companies (including publicly traded companies where management or a family group holds a large interest), there may be a similar reluctance; and the aversion to recognizing gain may be particularly intense because of estate-planning considerations.

Often, the shareholders of the target company will include one or more older individuals whose basis in their shares is low. Unlike younger shareholders, these older individuals often intend to hold any shares they own until their death. At that time the tax basis of the shares in their estates will step up to fair market value, so that on a sale by the heirs the gain accruing in the decedent's lifetime escapes the gains tax. For shareholders in this position, a taxable sale of their shares is not satisfactory because it requires recognition of the current gain.

A striking example of this was provided in the case of National Starch. Even though this was a publicly traded company, a substantial block of its stock was owned or controlled by its chairman and his wife, both of whom were over 80 years of age. After a tax-free merger of National Starch into Merck fell through, the company was sought by Unilever, which was stymied in its attempts to purchase it by the chairman's refusal to go along with a transaction that would result in a taxable gain. The impasse was finally resolved when Unilever designed a hybrid transaction of the kind discussed later.

***Taxable Purchase.*** There are several reasons why a taxable transaction may be chosen. If the acquirer's medium of payment in the transaction will consist principally of cash or debt, it will not normally be possible to structure a tax-free reorganization. The first step in a hostile takeover is almost always a cash tender offer in some form. In a "friendly" transaction, the selling shareholders may not want to acquire shares of the foreign acquirer, even briefly. The foreign acquirer may be unwilling to issue shares for a number of reasons. It may not wish to dilute its existing shareholders. In the case of the acquisition of a public company, it may not be able or willing to comply with requirements of the U.S. securities laws. The acquirer may, as a matter of financial planning, wish to leverage the acquisition, for example, by borrowing the purchase price in U.S.

dollars to be repaid out of the target company's earnings. (As discussed later, it is not normally tax-efficient for the acquirer to choose a taxable acquisition for the purpose of acquiring a current value or "stepped-up" basis in the assets of the target.)

Some foreign countries, although a decreasing number, have tax systems featuring an integration of corporate-level and shareholder taxation of corporate earnings. Companies resident in such countries may particularly prefer a nonstock acquisition. When such a company pays a dividend to a resident shareholder (and, under some treaty provisions, to a nonresident shareholder), the shareholder receives a credit or a refund of part or all of the corporate tax paid on the earnings distributed. But this rule does not apply to earnings on which that country's corporate tax is not paid. Thus, earnings that are subject to U.S. tax but not to tax in the country concerned do not carry the refund or credit and are therefore anathema to the shareholder. The difference in tax cost can be substantial.

There are ways to minimize this disadvantage (as in the case of the SmithKline Beecham transaction discussed later); but overall, an acquirer resident in a country with an integrated tax system would prefer to lend money to a U.S. acquisition vehicle company, have that company buy the target shares for cash, and repatriate as much of the target's earnings as possible in the form of interest (which, within limits, is deductible in the United States and is subject to tax in the acquirer's country) or repayment of principal (which is tax free).

*Hybrid Transaction.*   The hybrid transaction is, of course, designed to bridge the gap between the potentially different objectives of the parties, allowing the acquirer to avoid issuance of its own shares but affording tax-free treatment to the target and its stockholders, or some of them.

*Virtual Merger.*   A technique that has been used successfully in Europe is to structure what is called a "virtual merger." In such a transaction, there is no actual exchange of shares; the shareholders of the target and the shareholders of the acquirer continue to hold the shares they held before. However, the two corporations enter into equalization and other agreements that ensure that the same management runs the two corporations and that dividends paid by and amounts distributable in liquidation of both corporations will be determined by the combined results of both businesses. Many tax advisers believe that such transactions can be successfully structured in the United States. However, the IRS has informally indicated that it might regard such arrangements as creating a partnership between the target and the acquirer, with the fatal result that the foreign acquirer would be considered to be engaged in business and, therefore, taxable in the United States.

## Issues in Structuring Particular Transactions

### *Tax-Free Reorganizations*

***Definitional Rules.*** A transaction constitutes a tax-free reorganization only if it falls within one of the several statutory definitions outlined in Appendix 5.1. The various types of reorganizations described in the appendix all require that the bulk of the consideration received by the target corporation's shareholders consist of stock. In general, either common or preferred stock, other than "debt-like" preferred, which is redeemable or has an indexed coupon, can be used; and American Depository Receipts (ADRs) may also be used. Some of the reorganization provisions require that the *only* consideration (or in one instance that at least 80 percent of the consideration) paid to the shareholders of the target company be voting shares of the foreign acquirer. A more commonly used transaction form is a "forward triangular merger," in which the target company is merged into a newly created shell U.S. subsidiary of the foreign acquirer under state corporate merger statutes. This form requires only that shares constitute the majority of the consideration delivered, and these may be nonvoting shares. To the extent that a target company shareholder receives cash or other nonshare consideration, however, the shareholder will recognize taxable income or gain.

***Section 367.*** When shares of a foreign acquirer are received by target company shareholders, certain special requirements imposed by section 367 of the Internal Revenue Code apply; but in practice this is infrequently a problem. The normal tax-free rules apply unless after the transaction an individual target company shareholder owns 5 percent or more of the shares of the foreign acquirer. In most cases a shareholder who exceeds this level of ownership, which is rare, can still procure tax-free treatment by signing an agreement with the IRS to recognize any gain later if the foreign acquirer disposes of the target company or substantial portions of its assets. In exceptional cases, when after the transaction the U.S. shareholders of the target company would collectively own 50 percent or more of the total outstanding stock of the foreign acquirer, the transaction will not be tax free.

***The Step Transaction Doctrine.*** In determining whether a transaction qualifies as a tax-free reorganization, all related transactions that form part of the acquisition plan will be taken into account. The effect may be to disqualify a transaction as a tax-free reorganization or, in some cases, to construct a qualifying transaction out of two transactions that would not by themselves qualify. For example, to the extent that an acquirer by prearrangement redeems shares issued in the transaction, it will be deemed to have delivered cash rather than shares. (The IRS has ruled, however, that purchases made in the market by a publicly traded acquirer that operates a share repurchase program will not be counted because there is no way to tell whether target shareholders are sellers.) Even pretransaction redemptions by the target may be taken into account. Moreover, as a famous series of cases involving ITT's acquisition of the Hartford Fire Insurance Company established, "toehold" cash purchases of target stock may disqualify a reorganization that requires all or 80 percent of the consideration to consist of shares of the acquirer. In this connection, the forward subsidiary merger format offers the greatest flexibility, because it requires only 50 percent or more of the total consideration to consist of shares.

***Second-Tier Subsidiary Prohibited.*** A particular annoyance for the foreign acquirer is the fact that a tax-free reorganization can be accomplished only if the surviving company (whether the target company or a U.S. subsidiary) is directly owned by the foreign acquirer itself. The Internal Revenue Code definitions mandate that the shares to be delivered in a tax-free reorganization be shares of the company that ends up with the target company's business and assets or shares of that company's immediate parent. This is inconsistent with the corporate structure that many foreign acquirers already have in place. For example, it is not generally possible to have a U.S. target company merged into a U.S. corporation owned by a tax-haven holding-company subsidiary in exchange for foreign parent company shares and still have the acquisition qualify as a tax-free reorganization. What can be done, however, is to have the target company assets dropped down into a second-tier subsidiary following the acquisition. Alternatively, the foreign acquirer can drop the shares of the target company or the acquiring U.S. subsidiary down into another subsidiary.

***Disposition of Unwanted Business of the Target.*** In general, a tax-free reorganization contemplates the acquisition of all or substantially all of a target company's assets or shares. It does not readily lend itself to the acquisition of divisional assets. In prior years, if an acquirer wanted only one of two or more businesses of a target, the unwanted businesses could be spun off, tax free, prior to a tax-free merger of the target—a so-called *Morris Trust* transaction. Legislation adopted in 1997 has severely restricted the availability of this technique. However, the unwanted assets can be sold for cash or other consideration prior to or after the tax-free reorganization. Of course, taxable gain or loss will be recognized on the sale; but the disposition will not prevent a tax-free transaction, although in those cases where the reorganization definition requires acquisition of substantially all of the target's assets, the proceeds of the sale must be retained.

***Structural Problems Arising from Cross-Border Mergers.*** A merger of two companies located in different countries raises particular problems with respect to postmerger income flows. If dividends are paid from a subsidiary in one country to a parent in another and then paid by the parent back to a shareholder in the subsidiary's country, a pyramiding of withholding taxes may result. More important, in many countries there are rules that make it more advantageous for a shareholder to receive dividends from a company resident in the same country, rather than abroad. In the earlier section Factors Influencing the Choice of Transactional Form, the situation encountered in countries that integrate corporate and shareholder taxation was described. In the United States there may be a similar problem because a U.S. corporation that receives a dividend from another U.S corporation is generally entitled to a "dividends received deduction" that reduces the rate of tax on the dividend, generally to 30 percent of the regular corporate rate (at the present 35 percent rate, to 10.5 percent), whereas no such allowance applies to a dividend received from a foreign corporation.

In the merger of SmithKline, a U.S. pharmaceutical company, with Beecham, a U.K. pharmaceutical, an ingenious way was found to deal with these problems. In essence, the surviving company was a U.K. company that could pay dividends to its U.K. shareholders. At the same time, the shares issued to U.S. holders of SmithKline consisted of a unit of preferred shares of the U.S. company (now a subsidiary of the U.K. parent) and a special class of ordinary (common) shares of the U.K. parent. These units were "stapled" or "twinned," so that neither type of share could be transferred without a transfer of the other. The objective was to permit the lion's share, at least, of the dividends to former holders of SmithKline shares to be paid in the United States, thus avoiding an outbound withholding tax and making the dividends received deduction available to U.S. corporate holders.

### Taxable Purchases

If the foreign acquirer decides on a taxable purchase, there are several important additional decisions that must be made.

*Identity of the Purchaser.* The first is the identity of the purchaser—whether it will be the foreign acquirer itself, a U.S. subsidiary (either existing or created for the purpose), or an offshore holding company. The choice may depend in large part on whether and where debt financing will be raised for the purchase. This is discussed in the later section Funding a Cash Purchase.

*Purchase of Stock or Assets.* A second basic decision is whether to buy stock or assets. Buying assets has the virtue of allowing a U.S. subsidiary of the acquirer to take a current value, or stepped-up basis, in the assets for purposes of tax depreciation or amortization; this objective has become more important since 1993, when legislation was adopted allowing a purchaser to amortize acquired intangible assets, including goodwill (represented by purchase premium over market value of tangible assets) over a 15-year period (even when amortization is not required for financial statement purposes).

In practice, however, the purchase will almost always be a purchase of stock. The reason is that a purchase of assets will cause the target company to recognize taxable gain. If the target is then liquidated to route the sale proceeds to the target's shareholders, the shareholders will recognize a second taxable gain with respect to their shares. The present value to the acquirer of a stepped-up basis in assets is almost never as great as the immediate tax detriment to the target and its shareholders. One exception might be a case in which the target has a large net operating loss for tax purposes, which can be used to offset the gain on the asset sale, and the target shareholders are content to leave the target in existence, rather than to liquidate it. Another exception might be a case in which a U.S. parent corporation is selling a subsidiary and the gain inherent in the subsidiary's assets is about the same as the gain that the parent corporation would recognize on a sale of the subsidiary's stock. Because the parent corporation can liquidate the subsidiary on a tax-free basis, only one level of tax will be paid in either event. Even if the gain on the sale of assets is slightly greater, the benefit of basis step-up to the acquirer may be great enough to justify its paying a higher price to compensate the seller for the increased tax.

*Stock Purchase Treated as Asset Purchase.* Asset purchases are sometimes thought to be unworkable for nontax reasons, such as the need to procure consents or the difficulty or expense of making individual transfers of a large number of properties. In the United States, this is not necessarily a problem. An all-cash statutory merger of the target into a U.S. subsidiary of the acquirer will transfer assets (and liabilities) by operation of law. Moreover, under a provision known as section 338, a purchaser of 80 percent or more of the stock of a target corporation may elect to treat the acquisition as if it were an acquisition of the target's assets. This may solve the mechanical difficulties of an asset purchase, but it does not avoid the double-level tax described earlier. The difference is that, under a section 338 election, the tax on the corporate-level gain is borne by the acquirer, rather than shareholders of the target; and this difference in the incidence of tax burden must be taken into account in setting the purchase price.

*Installment Sale Treatment.* Under the Internal Revenue Code, the gain recognized on a taxable sale of shares can be deferred to the extent that the purchase price is evidenced by promissory notes of the purchaser. In such a case, gain is recognized ratably as the notes are paid off. The shareholders must wait for their cash, of course. In the interim, however, the promissory notes bear interest, normally at market rates, and this represents a return on the pretax value of the shareholder's position.

　　If, moreover, the shareholders of the target company want "upside" participation or if they are more optimistic than the foreign acquirer about the prospects of the target company, a contingent pay format can be adopted. Under this approach, the foreign acquirer agrees to pay a base price in cash or in promissory notes and then agrees to pay more if specified benchmarks are reached, for example, earnings or sales targets or the failure of potential claims to be asserted. Although the contingent-payment feature complicates the computation of the shareholder's taxable gain, proceeds may nevertheless be reported on the installment method so that tax is imposed on the shareholder only as cash is received.

　　Unfortunately, the installment-sale format is not a viable solution in many cases. Installment reporting of target company shareholders' gain is not allowable if either the target company shares are traded in an established securities market or the promissory notes delivered to the shareholders are in registered form or otherwise readily marketable. Installment reporting is disadvantageous where a selling shareholder would receive more than $5,000,000 in installment obligations, because in such a case an interest charge is imposed on the deferred tax.

*Separate Purchase of Overseas Subsidiaries.*   While the actual implementation of the concept may require some complication and possible tax cost, a foreign acquirer purchasing a U.S. corporation that itself has overseas subsidiaries should consider separately purchasing those subsidiaries before purchasing the target. The United States has restrictive rules relating to *controlled foreign corporations* (CFCs) and *passive foreign investment companies* that may be avoided if overseas subsidiaries are not owned through the U.S. target. In addition, the acquirer may find that its own country or a third country has more favorable tax treaties with the countries in which the subsidiaries are located.

### Hybrid Transactions

In cases in which some of the shareholders of the target want a tax-free transaction while others want cash, it may be possible for the acquirer to offer shares and to allow those target shareholders who want to sell to do so in the market. In other cases, however, there may not be a ready market for the shares, or securities law restrictions may be a problem. In addition, there are cases in which target shareholders want tax-free treatment but the foreign acquirer does not want to issue shares.

A number of transactions have been devised to deal with these situations. They basically center on allowing target shareholders who do not want to recognize gain to retain preferred stock in the target or a new U.S. subsidiary of the foreign acquirer. Various forms of such transactions are summarized in Appendix 5.1.

One shadow over preferred stock transactions of the kind just described is created by 1997 legislation under which "debt-like" nonparticipating preferred stock that is redeemable at the option of the issuer or that has a coupon that is indexed to interest rates (directly or through auction techniques) is not treated as stock. In addition, "perfect preferred," having extraordinary protections, such as take-out commitments by the foreign acquirer or highly restrictive covenants limiting the business of the subsidiary issuing the preferred stock, may be treated as debt. Nevertheless, there are cases in which preferred stock will be treated as just that and some in which the tax-free requirements can be met.

## Other Issues

### Covenants Not to Compete

It has been usual, particularly in connection with the acquisition of privately held companies, for the acquirer to seek to allocate some of the consideration paid to covenants not to compete entered into by the principal selling shareholders. This was advantageous to the acquirer because the amounts paid for such covenants could generally be amortized and deducted over the period for which the covenant was in effect. It was disadvantageous to individual shareholders because the payments were ordinary income, rather than capital gains taxable at preferential rates; but it was often possible to increase the payment to the shareholders to compensate them for the tax-rate differential while still preserving a net tax benefit to the acquirer.

The 1993 legislation referred to in the earlier section Taxable Purchases dramatically altered this practice, however. Covenants not to compete entered into in connection with the acquisition of a business are now treated as intangible assets, the cost of which must be amortized over 15 years—a much longer period than the duration of most covenants. This substantially reduces the present value of the tax benefit to the acquirer. It is still possible, however, to obtain covenants not to compete in connection with employment contracts for executives, even if they are also selling shareholders, and to amortize such payments over the not-to-compete period.

### Funding a Cash Purchase

To the extent that a foreign acquirer uses shares to acquire a U.S. company, it obviously does not require funding. When the acquisition will be made for cash, however, the foreign acquirer will often borrow to fund the purchase. While non-tax factors may play the most important role in determining the place and the terms of the borrowing, there are important tax considerations to be taken into account as well.

With some exceptions, interest incurred by a U.S. company is deductible for tax purposes, even when the debt is used to fund a share or an asset acquisition. Often a foreign acquirer will form a U.S. holding company subsidiary to acquire the target company, and the U.S. holding company will borrow dollars in the U.S. market. This will generally permit the interest to be written off against the ongoing profits of the target company or other U.S. operating subsidiaries held by the U.S. holding company through the filing of a consolidated U.S. tax return. In some transactions, the target company itself will also borrow, before or after the acquisition.

In recent years a popular method of funding a U.S. acquisition was the creation of a "reverse hybrid" holding company in the United States. A reverse hybrid is an entity, such as a partnership, that elects to be taxed in the United States as a corporation. The foreign acquirer lends money to this entity, which acquires the target's shares. In the United States, dividends received by the entity from the target are nontaxable under the consolidated return rules, while interest it pays to the foreign acquirer is deductible in the consolidated return. If the entity is treated as a "pass-through" in the foreign acquirer's country, the foreign acquirer may be treated as both receiving the dividend and paying the interest, for a wash. The IRS has now proposed regulations that would eliminate this technique, but at this writing, they have not come into effect.

One funding mechanism that has been used with advantageous U.S. tax consequences is the issue by a U.S. holding company subsidiary of deep discount debt. Generally speaking, original issue discount is accrued as an interest expense over the life of the obligation, thus creating deductions without cash outflows. In principle, equivalent amounts are includable in the taxable income of the lender, but this effect may be of limited significance. Many lenders in the U.S. capital markets are tax-exempt (pension funds and charitable organizations). Moreover, discount income earned by non–U.S. lenders not engaged in business in the United States, although taxable in principle, is subject to withholding tax only to the extent of payments actually made by the borrower. Thus, a zero-coupon obligation is subject to no withholding tax until maturity. Even then, no tax will be withheld if the foreign lender has disposed of the obligation to a U.S. person. Note, however, that the foreign lender must be unrelated to the borrower; discount on debt to related foreign parties is deductible only when withholding tax is imposed on the lender.

In deciding on the most tax-advantageous funding arrangements, the foreign acquirer must take account of two features of U.S. tax law that may affect the decision. As stated earlier, interest is generally deductible in the United States. However, there are three limitations:

1. The United States applies common law "thin capitalization" concepts under which what is nominally debt may be treated as equity for tax purposes. Because the origin of these concepts is in judicial decisions, rather than in statutory law, they are extremely fact-specific. In general, however, the thin capitalization problem will arise when the ratio of the borrower's debt to its equity is high and the borrowings are from related persons. If debt is treated as equity under the thin capitalization doctrine, the result is to deny the borrower interest deductions and also to treat payments (including payments of principal) as dividend distributions subject to withholding tax.

2. Under statutory provisions called the "earnings stripping" rules, interest deductions may be denied under specified circumstances. In broad outline, this can occur when the borrower's debt-to-equity ratio exceeds 1.5 to 1 and when its aggregate interest payable exceeds 50 percent of a figure approximating its net cash flow. The interest disallowed is interest paid to any foreign person who is exempt from tax on the interest, normally by reason of an applicable treaty, or, more important, interest paid to anyone, including fully taxable unrelated U.S. lenders, if the indebtedness is guaranteed by a foreign related person who would be exempt from tax on interest paid to it. Thus, under the earnings stripping rules, if debt or interest-payment levels are excessive, interest deductions can be denied with respect not only to related-party debt but also to unrelated-lender debt guaranteed by the foreign acquirer or an affiliate.

The earnings stripping rules affect only the deductibility of interest paid; they do not affect the application of the withholding tax rules.

3. The Treasury Department has exercised its authority to issue so-called conduit-financing regulations. Under these regulations, if a U.S. company pays interest to a lender located in a country that has a treaty with the United States

exempting that interest from U.S. withholding tax, but in a related ("back-to-back") transaction the lender has been funded in specified ways by a party that is related to the U.S. borrower and would be subject to U.S. withholding tax if it directly received the interest, then the intermediate party may be disregarded and the withholding tax imposed as if the related party had directly made the loan. These rules apply only to impose withholding tax; in contrast to the earnings stripping rules, they do not affect the deductibility of the interest paid. Moreover, the rules apply only if there is found to be a purpose to avoiding the withholding tax; and there are provisions designed to make the rules inapplicable to bona fide group financing subsidiaries that actively manage and control a portfolio of debt or other instruments and accept substantial financial risk in the course of their dealings.

## Summary

The foregoing is only the simplest summary of the sometimes daunting complexities that a foreign acquirer may encounter in planning the tax aspects of a U.S. merger or acquisition. Experience shows, however, that tax problems seldom stand in the way of deals that otherwise make sense. It is the task of the U.S. tax adviser not only to originate ideas that will permit the merger or acquisition to proceed on a tax-efficient basis, but also to shape these ideas to the policies and objectives of the foreign acquirer. It is essential that the way in which the deal is structured satisfy *all* of the foreign acquirer's legal and business requirements. Taxes should never be the tail that wags the dog.

## INBOUND JOINT VENTURES

### Structuring Joint Ventures

When U.S. and foreign corporations enter into "inbound" joint ventures, that is, ventures that will operate principally in the United States, U.S. tax issues will predominate, as they do in "inbound" mergers and acquisitions. The creation of a joint venture will usually resemble a merger, in the sense that it will involve a "pooling" of assets of the venturers, which in exchange receive equity interests in the venture. The difference of course is that in forming a joint venture, the parties "pool" only a part of their respective businesses. In addition, a joint venture these days often involves a number of participants.

As in the case of a merger, the principal tax concerns of the joint venture parties will be to avoid the recognition of taxable gain on the formation of the venture and to minimize taxes imposed on the distribution of its earnings. A U.S. participant will want to ensure that its share of any losses of the venture can be used to offset its U.S. tax on other income.

As a general rule, the U.S. tax burden on a foreign participant in a U.S. joint venture will not be materially impacted by the particular structure adopted; therefore, the structure will usually be determined by the U.S. tax concerns of the U.S. participant(s), as well as by the tax problems encountered by each foreign participant in its home country.

Perhaps the simplest way to organize a U.S. joint venture is to form a U.S. corporation jointly owned by the participants. In the joint venture context, assets can generally be transferred to such a corporation by both U.S. and foreign participants without recognition of U.S. taxable gain. (A U.S. participant will resist forming a foreign corporation because it would recognize gain on a transfer of assets to it if those assets will be used in the United States; and a U.S.–organized vehicle is usually dictated by business considerations in any event.) From a U.S. tax point of view, this should be satisfactory to a foreign participant. The corporation will, of course, be subject to U.S. corporate-level tax, and dividends will be subject to U.S. withholding tax when distributed to the foreign participant; but it is generally difficult to avoid this level of tax on earnings generated in the United States.

From the point of view of a U.S. participant, however, this structure is not optimal. Assuming that the U.S. participant's interest in the venture is less than 80 percent, its share of the venture's results cannot be included in its consolidated income tax return. This has two effects: (1) when earnings are distributed, they will be subject to an intercorporate dividend tax (7 percent if the participant's interest in the venture is 20 percent or more; otherwise 10.5 percent); (2) losses of the venture corporation cannot be used to offset other income of the participant.

The preferred alternative is to utilize a "pass-through" or "fiscally transparent" entity; such an entity is not subject to tax; rather, each participant is treated as directly receiving its share of the entity's revenue and incurring its share of the entity's expenses. Each U.S. participant in the joint venture will thus report its share of the joint venture's income or loss in its own consolidated return, and no intercorporate dividend tax will be imposed. Each foreign participant will bear the U.S. corporate tax on its share of the joint venture's income and, as discussed later, either a dividend withholding tax or an equivalent "branch profits" tax. In sum, a foreign participant will bear essentially the same tax burden that it would bear if a jointly owned corporation were utilized; but a U.S. participant will bear less tax.

It is typical for a joint venture participant to form a special purpose subsidiary to hold its interest. This not only limits liability but also may facilitate disposition of the joint venture interest in the future. In the case of a foreign participant, this may in principle be either an offshore subsidiary or a U.S. subsidiary. If a U.S. subsidiary is employed, this may be owned offshore or by a U.S. holding company subsidiary. From a tax point of view, the choice depends on the balancing of a number of factors.

On the one hand, if the foreign venturer has other businesses in the United States, it may form a U.S. subsidiary held by an existing U.S. holding company subsidiary; this offers the benefits of U.S. tax consolidation—the ability to distribute its share of the joint venture's earnings to the holding company, without withholding tax or intercorporate dividend tax, for use in other U.S. operations, and the ability to offset losses against other U.S.–taxable earnings. On the other hand, a disposition of the shares of the joint venture subsidiary by a U.S. holding company subsidiary will almost always result in the recognition of gain taxable in the United States.

By contrast, if the U.S. joint venture interest is held offshore, the foreign participant may be able to exit the venture by selling the interest without incurring U.S. tax (and in many cases, without tax in the home country as well). In this case, there are also two alternatives: (1) to form a foreign subsidiary that itself becomes the joint venture participant or (2) to form a U.S. subsidiary owned offshore. If the first alternative is chosen, the foreign subsidiary will directly be subject to U.S. corporate income tax and will also be subject to a branch profits tax on earnings that are not reinvested in a U.S. business; the latter is essentially a proxy for a dividend withholding tax but is somewhat more difficult to plan for. If a U.S. subsidiary is used, it will be subject to corporate income tax; and any dividends it pays will be subject to withholding tax. The choice between these two alternatives may depend on a judgment as to which type of interest will be easier to dispose of.

To achieve pass-through tax treatment, the joint venture vehicle must be treated as a partnership for U.S. tax purposes. This is not difficult to accomplish. Under the law in effect for many years, an entity was treated as a partnership if it lacked two or more of four corporate characteristics: (1) limited liability, (2) centralization of management, (3) free transferability of interests, and (4) continuity of life. In late 1996, however, the IRS adopted a new set of rules—the so-called check-the-box system, under which those forming a noncorporate entity can freely elect to have it treated as a partnership for U.S. tax purposes regardless of its characteristics. Under this rule, there is essentially unlimited flexibility to structure U.S. joint ventures as partnerships for tax purposes.

For many years, pass-through entities were formed as either general or limited partnerships. In recent years, the creation of an entity taxable as a partnership has been made easier by the development of a new type of entity known as a limited liability company. This kind of entity offers limited liability to all of its members (equity owners) and otherwise closely resembles a corporation. Nevertheless, it can be structured so that it will be treated as a partnership for U.S. tax purposes.

The use of partnerships and limited liability companies to implement joint ventures is also stimulated by the flexibility with which those entities permit the allocation to each joint venturer of particular classes of revenue, income, gain, loss, or expense. So-called special allocations of any of these items can be made in the documents governing the venture, with the result that the joint venturers need not share the results of the venture on a wholly pro rata basis. To be effective for U.S. tax purposes, however, special allocations must have real economic effect. For example, it is not possible to allocate tax losses to a U.S. participant that can use them in its consolidated return without requiring that the participant actually bear the loss by suffering a reduction in the amount it will receive on dissolution of the venture. These rules are extremely complex and must be carefully applied, but they afford a high degree of flexibility in determining the interest of each participant in the venture.

In many cases, a U.S. limited liability company constitutes what is known as a "hybrid" entity—one treated as a partnership and therefore a pass-through for U.S. tax purposes, but treated as a company and therefore a separate taxable entity under the tax law of the foreign participant's home country. This may permit U.S. participants to achieve their tax objectives while permitting foreign participants to avoid a current tax in their home countries on the entity's income. Under regulations issued by the IRS, however, it is not possible for foreign participants to claim treaty benefits, such as reduction in withholding taxes on dividends, interest, or royalties received by the joint venture, unless those items of income are taxed currently in the home country.

# Checklist: Mergers and Acquisitions

I.  Selection of basic tax pattern (for further details, see Appendix 5.1).
    A.  A tax-free transaction: a merger or an acquisition of the target company's assets or shares for shares of the foreign acquirer.
        1.  No currently taxable gain or loss is recognized by target company or its shareholders.
        2.  Shareholders carry over the tax basis in their target company shares to the shares received, so that inherent gain or loss may be recognized later.
        3.  Foreign acquirer (or a U.S. subsidiary) inherits the tax attributes of the target company.
    B.  A taxable transaction: a purchase of the shares or assets of the target company for cash or cash and debt.
        1.  The target company or its shareholders recognize taxable gain or loss.
        2.  The acquirer gets current cost basis.
    C.  A hybrid transaction, embodying some elements of the taxable and the tax-free.
        1.  A transaction may be taxable to some shareholders and tax-free to others.
        2.  Each shareholder may be partially taxable.
    D.  Use of equity derivative instruments to alter economic consequences of the receipt of share consideration; caveat: constructive disposition.

II. Factors influencing the choice of transactional form.
    A.  Tax-free reorganization.
        1.  Shares as desired consideration.
        2.  Desire of selling corporation and shareholders to avoid recognition of taxable gains.
            a.  Typical in a closely held company, where shares have been owned a long time and the tax basis is low.
            b.  Of critical importance where there are older individual shareholders (if they defer recognition until death, they never pay tax on gain because of step-up in basis of shares to date-of-death value).
    B.  Taxable purchase.
        1.  Target corporation's shareholders may be unwilling to accept shares

2. Foreign acquirers may be unwilling to issue shares.
3. Foreign acquirers may desire to leverage acquisition.
4. Hostile purchase may require cash tender offer.
5. Tax-free format is not readily adaptable to partial acquisitions (e.g., divisional assets or partial share interests).
6. Integrated tax systems in some foreign countries give impetus to pay cash or debt.

III. How to structure a deal when the foreign acquirer does not want to deliver its shares but target company's shareholders want to defer tax.
   A. Buy assets of target company.
      1. Features.
         a. No current taxable gain or loss is recognized by shareholders. Gain is eventually recognized on or sale or liquidation of shares, but postponed.
         b. Gain or loss is recognized by target company.
      2. Disadvantages.
         a. It is usually disadvantageous for target company to recognize taxable gain, which can be avoided in sale of shares.
         b. Exceptions:
            (1) Target company's basis in assets is higher than shareholders' basis in shares, so that there is a loss, no gain, or little gain at the corporate level, although substantial gain at shareholder level.
            (2) Target company's taxable gain is offset by net operating loss carryover, which will otherwise be unusable (see V).
   B. Use an installment sale format.
      1. Features.
         a. Shares are purchased in exchange for promissory notes.
         b. Shareholders can individually elect to defer taxable gain and to recognize it only ratably as notes are paid off.
            (1) Timing of recognition is flexible because a shareholder can trigger gain by disposing of the notes.
            (2) The tax result can be sold as being as good as in a tax-free deal, because even if sellers got shares in exchange at some point they would sell them. Interest paid on notes (see III.B.2.a) gives shareholders return on pretax principal amount.
            (3) If sellers want upside participation or if foreign acquirer is unsure of the value of the target company, a contingent pay format can be used: the foreign acquirer pays a base price in cash or notes and agrees to pay more if specified

benchmarks (earnings, sales, or absence of claims) are met.

    (4) Sellers still can report gain as received, although the contingency complicates the computations.

2. Disadvantages.

    a. Interest must be paid on the notes, or else it will be imputed. This would produce a tax to shareholder on accrual basis when he or she has no cash on hand.

    b. The notes cannot be in registered form or readily marketable.

    c. If selling shareholder receives $5 million or more in notes, he or she must pay interest charge on deferred tax.

    d. Does not work in all cases:

        (1) Installment treatment is not available if the shares of the target company are traded on an established securities market.

        (2) It does not preserve the benefit of the step-up in basis at death (see II.A.2). Gain is fixed at the time of the sale, although time for recognition is postponed.

C. Structure a hybrid transaction.

1. Features.

    a. There are various forms (see Appendix 5.1), but one basic idea is to allow target company shareholders to exchange target company shares for a nonvoting preferred interest, while the foreign acquirer or its U.S. subsidiary buys target company common stock for cash. This is:

        (1) A tax-free transaction to target company shareholders that take preferred stock.

        (2) A taxable transaction to those that sell for cash.

        (3) A taxable transaction to the foreign acquirer.

2. Disadvantages.

    a. Preferred stock cannot be the nonparticipating "debt-like" preferred, which is redeemable or interest-rate indexed.

    b. Foreign acquirer invests cash but does not get a step-up in basis of target company assets.

IV. Consider tax alternatives in funding the purchase price.

A. Basic issues.

1. If foreign acquirer will borrow to fund the purchase, in what country will it be most advantageous to deduct the resulting interest expense?

2. Can deductions be generated in two countries for the same interest expense?

B. Factors to consider.
1. Interest deductible in the United States reduces U.S. tax (currently 35 percent), and this may produce a smaller tax benefit than a deduction allowable in the foreign acquirer's home country.
2. Home country may not allow deduction for interest incurred in acquiring a U.S. company.
3. If debt is to be serviced out of earnings of target company in the United States, withholding taxes on dividends paid by target company must be considered.
4. Lending may be preferred by company in a country with an integrated tax system.

C. Possible solutions.
1. Foreign acquirer borrows in its own country and lends to U.S. subsidiary making acquisition.
Caveat: U.S. earnings stripping rules may disallow deduction by U.S subsidiary of interest paid to foreign acquirer if total interest paid to both related and unrelated lenders exceeds 50 percent of adjusted cash flow.
2. Foreign acquirer borrows in its home country, contributes the funds to a tax haven group finance subsidiary, and that subsidiary lends the funds to a U.S. subsidiary making the acquisition. If allowable under the home country's tax law, this can create a double deduction for interest.
Caveat: Must confirm that arrangements do not violate IRS conduit financing regulations.
3. U.S. subsidiary formed to make the acquisition borrows from unrelated lenders.
a. If U.S. subsidiary acquires at least 80 percent of shares of the target company (or its assets), there is no U.S. tax cost in making the target company's earnings available to service the debt.
Caveat: Earnings stripping rules apply if debt guaranteed by foreign acquirer or affiliate.
b. Consider issuing deep discount debt to unrelated foreign lenders.
(1) Original issue discount is treated as interest over the life of obligation, thus potentially creating deductions without cash outflow.
(2) Discount earned by U.S. lenders is taxable as accrued, but many are tax-exempt (e.g., pension funds).
(3) Discount earned by non–U.S. lenders is in principle subject to U.S. withholding tax, but withholding is made only

out of interest actually paid. A zero-coupon obligation gives rise to no withholding tax until maturity, and a foreign lender can dispose of the obligations before that time.

D. Caveat: If U.S. subsidiary borrows in a currency other than U.S. dollars, foreign currency gain or loss may result, and, unless fully hedged, this may produce U.S.–taxable gain or loss.

V. Take account of limitations on use of net operating loss carryovers.
  A. The basic problem.
    1. Generally net operating loss (NOL) of a U.S. company can be carried forward to offset taxable income for a period of 15 years.
    2. When a company is acquired, the use of NOLs may be restricted.
  B. The limitations.
    1. The NOL is disallowed altogether if the principal purpose of the acquisition is to secure the loss. This limitation will seldom apply in a normal business transaction.
    2. The NOL is also disallowed altogether unless the business of target company is continued for at least two years.
    3. The so-called separate return year limitation (SRYL) and the built-in loss limitation prevent use of preacquisition NOLs of target company (or losses built in as of acquisition date) to offset income of other U.S. companies in U.S. group of the foreign acquirer.
    4. A stringent metering rule limits the extent to which any remaining NOL can be used. This limitation applies regardless of whether the acquisition is tax-free, taxable, or hybrid.
    5. Basic limitation.
      a. Each year the amount of the otherwise allowable NOL that can be used is limited to the value of the shares of the target company at the acquisition date, multiplied by the long-term tax-exempt rate (an interest rate published by the Treasury Department and based on rates of interest on long-term U.S. government obligations).
      b. This is a very complex provision with a large number of special rules.
        (1) Allowable NOL may be adjusted to take account of built-in gains or losses as of the acquisition date.
        (2) Capital contributions to target company to pump up value of its shares may be disregarded.
        (3) Special rules apply in Chapter 11 (insolvent reorganization) cases.
      c. If a loss company acquires a profitable company (other than in a taxable acquisition of assets), it cannot offset its losses by built-in gains inherent in acquired company's assets.

# Checklist: Joint Ventures

I. Basic tax objectives
   A. Avoid taxable gain on formation.
   B. Minimize tax on venture earnings.
   C. Permit U.S. participants to utilize their shares of venture losses in consolidated tax returns.
   D. Consider strategy for exit—avoidance of tax on gain versus other tax objectives.

II. Structure of the venture: jointly owned corporation versus pass-through (partnership) entity.
   A. Corporation.
      1. Intercorporate dividend tax (7 percent or 10.5 percent).
      2. Losses not available on consolidated returns of U.S. participant
   B. Pass-through avoids these problems.

III. Choices for holding foreign participant's interest in the venture.
   A. Special-purpose foreign subsidiary.
      1. Subsidiary subject to corporate tax plus branch profits tax on earnings not reinvested.
      2. Disposition of shares of subsidiary not subject to U.S. tax.
   B. U.S. subsidiary owned outside United States.
      1. Subsidiary subject to corporate tax, and dividends subject to withholding tax.
      2. Disposition of shares of subsidiary not subject to U.S. tax.
   C. U.S. subsidiary owned by U.S. holding company
      1. Share of venture earnings available for use in other U.S. businesses without withholding tax or branch profits tax.
      2. Share of losses available in consolidated return.
      3. However, gain on sale of shares by holding company subject to U.S. tax.

IV. Types of pass-through entities.
   A. General or limited partnership.
   B. Limited liability company.

V. Special allocations of revenue, income, gains, losses, or deductions to particular participants.

     A. Flexibility is accompanied by complexity.

     B. Special allocations must have substantial economic effect.

VI. Possible use of hybrid entities.

     A. Pass-through treatment applies for U.S. tax purposes, but hybrids are separate entities for foreign tax purposes.

     B. IRS regulations restrict treaty benefits to foreign participant unless income of hybrid entity is currently taxable in the home country.

## APPENDIX 5.1

# Tax-Free, Taxable, and Hybrid Transactions

I.   The tax-free transaction.
    A.   General characteristics of this form of transaction.
        1.   It must meet one of the specific statutory definitions of reorganization (discussed in D and F).
        2.   It must be entered into for a valid business purpose and must contemplate a continuity of the business enterprise in modified form.
        3.   There must be a continuity of interest; shareholders of the target company must continue to hold a substantial equity interest in the foreign acquirer.
            a.   IRS view: shares must be at least 50 percent of total price.
            b.   Some reorganization definitions require that *only* stock be used.
            c.   For the types of equity interests that can be used and the form in which they may be delivered, see I.G.
            d.   Dispositions of shares before or after transaction in market or to third parties does not disqualify.
            e.   Caveat: Use of financial derivative instruments to limit equity risk following reorganization.
    B.   Under the integration or step-transaction doctrine, if the overall acquisition plan contemplates more than one step, all of them will be viewed together in determining whether a transaction qualifies. Suppose, for example, the foreign acquirer wants to make a cash tender offer for shares of the target company, followed by a statutory merger of the target into a U.S. subsidiary in which the target company shareholders get shares of the acquirer. The merger and the tender offer will be viewed together in determining whether there is a tax-free reorganization.
    C.   Tax consequences of tax-free reorganization.
        1.   To target company shareholders.
            a.   No taxable gain or loss is recognized.
            b.   Basis in shares surrendered carries over to shares received.
            c.   If a shareholder receives nonshare consideration in addition to shares, this constitutes "boot," which is taxable either as a dividend (generally, if all shareholders receive it pro rata) or as capital gain to the extent it does not exceed the shareholder's overall gain.
            d.   Caveat: Shareholders could recognize fully taxable gain in some limited circumstances described in I.I.1.
        2.   To the target company: no taxable gain or loss.

3. To the foreign acquirer.
    a. It (or a subsidiary) takes a basis in assets equal to their basis in the hands of the target company (no step-up).
    b. It inherits the tax attributes of the target company (e.g., accounting methods), although net operating loss carry-forwards will be restricted.

D. The most commonly used forms of tax-free asset acquisitions.
  1. Forward triangular merger: the target company is merged into a U.S. subsidiary of the foreign acquirer in a statutory merger under state law; shareholders of the target company receive stock of the foreign acquirer in exchange for their stock in the target company.
    a. The stock of the foreign acquirer may be voting or nonvoting.
    b. The U.S. subsidiary must acquire substantially all of the assets of the target company.
  2. The C reorganization: a U.S. subsidiary of the foreign acquirer acquires substantially all of the assets of the target company *solely* in exchange for voting stock of the foreign acquirer, as well as for an assumption of specified liabilities. As part of the plan of reorganization:
    a. The target company is liquidated.
    b. The stock of the foreign acquirer is distributed to its shareholders.
    c. Caveat: even one dollar of consideration other than voting stock disqualifies the transaction. This bars a toehold purchase for cash, but cash can be given in lieu of issuing fractional shares.

E. Considerations in choosing the form of a tax-free asset acquisition
  1. The statutory merger route is usually easier to follow.
    a. Its main disadvantage is that *all* liabilities of the target company, disclosed or undisclosed, are inherited.
    b. For the possibility of a "holdback" or escrow of shares to meet undisclosed liabilities, see H.
  2. The C reorganization is normally used only when it is essential that the foreign acquirer not assume undisclosed liabilities.
    a. It is mechanically a more difficult transaction than a merger (every asset must be conveyed, whereas in a merger all assets pass by operation of law).
    b. The solely voting stock requirement is a disadvantage.

F. The most commonly used forms of tax-free share acquisitions.
  1. The reverse triangular merger: the foreign acquirer forms a new shell U.S. subsidiary, and this is merged into the target company in a state law statutory merger. In the merger, the foreign acquirer

receives shares of the merged company, and the shareholders of the target company receive shares of the foreign acquirer.

    a.  The surviving company must end up with substantially all of the assets of both the target company and the shell subsidiary:

    b.  At least 80 percent of the consideration delivered to the shareholders of the target company must be voting shares of the foreign acquirer.

2.  The B reorganization: a U.S. subsidiary of the foreign acquirer acquires at least 80 percent of the shares of the target company *solely* in exchange for voting shares of the foreign acquirer.

    a.  It must acquire 80 percent of voting power of the target company's voting shares, plus 80 percent of the total number of nonvoting shares.

    b.  Here, as in the C reorganization, only voting shares may be used; one dollar of cash or debt (other than in lieu of fractional shares) totally disqualifies the deal.

3.  A tax-free share-for-share exchange can be framed in the context of a hybrid transaction (see II).

4.  The B reorganization is seldom used.

    a.  The "solely for voting stock" requirement is onerous.

    b.  A share-for-share tender, unlike a merger transaction, is not a freeze-out transaction.

    c.  But a forcing transaction may be structured under the "share exchange" statutes of some states.

G.  What constitutes stock for purposes of a tax-free transaction.

1.  *Almost any form* of stock may be used.

    a.  ADRs are treated as representing the underlying deposited shares.

    b.  Unless voting shares are expressly required, nonvoting may be used.

    c.  Straight or convertible preferred stock may be used, although nonparticipating "debt-like" preferred is not treated as stock. Also, section 306 may require recognition of ordinary income on disposition of preferred stock.

    d.  Warrants and convertible debt are not stock, however.

2.  When delivery of voting stock is required:

    a.  ADRs representing *voting stock* are treated as voting stock.

    b.  IRS has approved issuing voting stock into a voting trust and delivering voting trust certificates to target company shareholders. But voting trusts normally exist only for a period of years (often, a maximum of 10).

H.  Use of contingent consideration in tax-free transactions.
   1.  Holdback and deferred issuance of contingent shares.
      a.  In general, the IRS will not rule favorably on the tax-free nature of the transaction unless at least 50 percent of the maximum amount of stock that may be issued is issued at the outset.
      b.  Deferred issuance of shares is treated as an installment transaction subject to imputed interest rules so that some of the shares later received will give rise to ordinary income inclusion to the target company shareholder even though the underlying transactions remain tax free.
   2.  Issuance of shares in escrow.
      a.  IRS ruling policy here again requires that at least 50 percent of the maximum number of shares be issued unconditionally.
      b.  Because the shares are issued as of closing date (and exchanging shareholders are entitled to dividends), no interest is imputed on the shares issued into escrow.
         (1)  Exchanging shareholders will recognize gain or loss on later forfeiture and cancellation of shares if the shares are recaptured to satisfy a shareholder obligation (e.g., breach of representation) and appreciation in the shares is applied to satisfy the obligation.
         (2)  No gain or loss will be recognized if the forfeiture is only an adjustment to the purchase price (e.g., failure to attain specified earnings level).
I.  Two particular problems for the foreign acquirer.
   1.  Section 367 of the Internal Revenue Code and the regulations thereunder provide that some transactions normally tax free to the shareholders of the target company may be taxable to some or all of them when the shares they receive are shares of a foreign company. This problem arises only in relatively limited circumstances, however. The section 367 rule is inoperative, and the general tax-free rules apply to the transactions described in I if, after the transactions, either:
      a.  The individual shareholder owns less than 5 percent of the voting power and value of the shares of the foreign acquirer. OR
      b.  The individual shareholder owns 5 percent or more, and the shareholder files with the IRS an agreement to recognize gain if, within a five-year period, the foreign acquirer disposes of the target company's shares or substantial portions of its assets.
      c.  However, section 367 may apply to make a transaction taxable to all target company shareholders if, after the transaction,

those shareholders own 50 percent or more of the total out-standing shares of the foreign acquirer.

2. In each of the transactions described in I, the U.S. subsidiary involved must be *directly* owned by the foreign acquirer.

    a. If, for example, the foreign acquirer owns shares of a foreign holding company and the foreign holding company owns shares of a U.S. subsidiary, none of the transactions described in I works. It will be necessary to establish a directly owned U.S. subsidiary to participate in the transaction.

    b. But it may be possible to rationalize the structure after the transaction.

        (1) Assets, for example, received by the directly owned U.S subsidiary can be dropped down into a second-tier U.S. subsidiary without affecting the tax-free nature of the transaction.

        (2) The shares of the directly held U.S. subsidiary can be dropped down into another (new or existing) subsidiary so that the acquisition vehicle ends up as a second-tier (or lower-tier) subsidiary.

II. Forms of taxable and hybrid transactions.

    A. The cash option merger.

        1. Nature of transaction: target company is merged into a U.S. sub-sidiary of the foreign acquirer in a forward triangular merger, under the terms of which shareholders of the target company receive shares of the foreign acquirer or, to the extent they so elect, cash.

            a. Aggregate cash payable is limited to less than 50 percent of total consideration payable to assure compliance with the continuity of interest test. This requires provision for proration of cash if honoring all elections would require more than specified maximum.

            b. Sometimes the foreign acquirer will want to insist on paying cash for minimum percentage of shares (e.g., to prevent exces-sive dilution or to limit added dividend requirement).

        2. Useful where the foreign acquirer is willing to issue some shares and some target company shareholders want shares, while others want cash.

        3. Tax effects.

            a. For all parties other than shareholders of target company who receive cash, tax consequences are identical with those of an all-shares forward triangular merger.

            b. For a shareholder of the target company who receives cash:

(1) If only cash is received (no shares), this is simply a taxable transaction.

(2) If shares plus cash are received, the cash is treated as "boot."

B. Cash tender offer followed by forward triangular merger.

1. Nature of transaction: the foreign acquirer or a U.S. subsidiary makes a cash tender offer for shares of the target company, and this is followed by a forward triangular merger in which the remaining target company shares are exchanged for shares of the foreign acquirer.

2. Useful where the acquisition is hostile or where the foreign acquirer wants to establish a toehold position to place potential competitive bidders at a disadvantage.

3. Tax effects are the same as in the cash option merger: the tender and the merger will be integrated for tax purposes.

4. Aggregate cash again limited to 50 percent of total consideration.

C. The funded subsidiary preferred stock merger.

1. Nature of transaction: target company is merged into a U.S. subsidiary of the foreign acquirer in a statutory merger (not a triangular merger) in which shareholders of target company receive nonconvertible preferred stock of the subsidiary.

a. Preferred stock normally has rights to optional redemption at some future date; but the 1997 rules restricting the use of "debt-like" preferred may limit redemption rights.

b. The foreign acquirer may fund the dividend and redemption obligations of the subsidiary (which of course will own operating assets of the target company or put them in subsidiary whose stock it owns) by contributing cash to its capital, allowing the subsidiary to hold liquid, income-producing assets. Alternatively, these obligations may be funded by the subsidiary itself, in effect accomplishing a "bootstrap" acquisition of the target company.

c. The acquiring corporation can guarantee dividend and redemption obligations.

(1) Caveat: care must be taken not to make the preferred stock so secure that the IRS treats it as debt.

(2) Caveat: under section 305(c) of the Internal Revenue Code, redemption premium can give rise to imputed income inclusions similar to original issue discount.

2. Useful where the foreign acquirer wishes to purchase for cash or to accomplish a bootstrap acquisition and does not wish to issue

its own securities but shareholders of the target company insist on a tax-free transaction (e.g., to preserve prospect of step-up in basis at death). Redemption features may be tied to death and need of estate for cash to pay death taxes.

3. Tax effects.

    a. The statutory merger is a tax-free reorganization.

    b. There are special considerations for shareholders of the target company.

        (1) Preferred is not section 306 stock because they acquire no other shares.

        (2) Ultimate redemption can produce capital gain.

D. The funded subsidiary preferred stock with a cash option merger.

1. Nature of transaction: this is like the transaction discussed in II.C but with the cash option feature discussed in II.B.

2. Useful where the considerations referred to in II.C are present but some shareholders of the target company prefer a taxable transaction for cash. Note, however, that 50 percent of shares must be acquired for shares to satisfy the continuity of interest requirement.

3. Tax effects: As described in II.B and II.C.

E. Recapitalization of target company followed by cash purchase of shares.

1. Nature of transaction: pursuant to agreement, target company adopts plan of recapitalization calling for (possibly disproportionate) exchange of a new preferred stock (which, except in the case of certain family-owned corporations, may not be "debt-like" preferred) for shares of its common stock; then the foreign acquirer purchases the remaining common shares for cash (or debt) in a taxable transaction.

2. Useful where considerations referred to in II.B apply, but 50 percent or more of the shareholders of the target company want cash, so the continuity of interest test cannot be met. It is difficult to assure acquiring company that it will acquire 100 percent of common stock.

3. Tax effects.

    a. The recapitalization exchange of preferred for common stock is a tax-free transaction; the continuity of interest requirement is not applicable, so the exchange itself is tax-free, even though remaining common shares are thereafter sold as part of same plan.

        If preferred stock is undervalued, shareholders who take it may be deemed to have made a gift or paid compensation to shareholders who sell for cash.

      b.  Preferred stock is section 306 stock to a shareholder who retains preferred and common stock but not to a shareholder who exchanges all common for preferred stock.

      c.  Shareholders who sell common stock recognize taxable gain.

      d.  To the foreign acquirer, the transaction is a taxable purchase of common shares.

F.  Exchange offer by U.S. subsidiary followed by freeze-out cash merger.

   1.  Nature of transaction.

      a.  The foreign acquirer forms a U.S. subsidiary, agreeing to contribute cash in return for all common shares.

      b.  Simultaneously, U.S. subsidiary offers to exchange shares of its preferred stock for shares of the target company.

      c.  Upon completion of the preceding a and b, U.S. subsidiary forms a second-tier subsidiary, which is merged into the target company in a cash merger, eliminating remaining minority shareholders of the target company.

   2.  Useful in that this achieves the effect of II.D, without requiring 50 percent of target company's shares to be acquired for stock; improves on II.E because nonexchanging shareholders can be forced out in the merger.

   3.  Tax effects.

      a.  Steps a and b under F.1 constitute a tax-free incorporation transaction.

        (1)  Dispositions of stock received in the incorporation transaction can disqualify it, but this rule looks only to those participating in the incorporation.

        (2)  Effect is that participating shareholders exchange shares of the target company for preferred stock of the U.S. subsidiary without recognition of taxable gain.

      b.  Shareholders frozen out in succeeding cash merger will recognize taxable gain or loss.

      c.  No gain or loss recognized by any of the participating corporations.

# 6

# Tax Considerations in Acquiring Non–U.S. Enterprises

*Robert T. Bossart*
*Jane W. Meisel*

I f U.S. mergers and acquisitions may be viewed as a two-dimensional chess game, international mergers and acquisitions are surely multidimensional. With minor modifications, virtually all of the domestic U.S. tax rules about mergers and acquisitions will apply to international mergers. However, additional U.S. tax rules apply only in the context of international mergers and acquisitions in order to implement certain broad U.S. tax policy objectives. Moreover, the tax rules of one or more non–U.S. jurisdictions and, where appropriate, the income tax treaties between non–U.S. jurisdictions and the United States must be considered as well.

As a result, the acquisition of foreign operations by a U.S. taxpayer presents a variety of tax concerns that either do not exist or exist to a substantially lesser degree in a domestic acquisition. These concerns may ultimately affect the form of the transaction and the financing alternatives.

The authors gratefully acknowledge William L. Burke, Esq., a member of the firm of Pillsbury Winthrop LLP and the author of this chapter in an earlier incarnation of this work, for allowing them to use portions of his original chapter.

## U.S. TAX ACCESSIBILITY AND TAX DEFERRAL

At the heart of the U.S. side of the matter are three broad objectives embodied in U.S. tax rules. First, an entity incorporated in the United States should be subject to U.S. tax without regard to where it earns its income. Next, an entity incorporated in a non–U.S. jurisdiction normally should not have its income earned outside of the United States subject to U.S. tax. Finally, the United States should avoid or mitigate, where possible, the double taxation of non–U.S. income that has been taxed in a non–U.S. jurisdiction when that income finally becomes subject to tax by the United States. These objectives may be referred to as the *accessibility, deferral*, and *foreign tax credit* rules.

### Tax Accessibility

The United States believes that every U.S. corporation should pay tax on its entire income after making appropriate expense deductions. Thus, U.S. corporations pay tax on their worldwide taxable income. Where the corporation earns the income and whether it has been subjected to one or more non–U.S. taxes may be relevant for the U.S. foreign tax credit calculations; but the income is, nonetheless, subject to U.S. tax.

U.S. corporations can earn business income from non–U.S. sources through a variety of means, including by selling products to third parties with title passing overseas, by licensing intangible technology to a third party for use abroad, and by establishing business operations in a non–U.S. jurisdiction through a branch rather than by incorporating a non–U.S. entity. Income and deductions of a non–U.S. branch of a U.S. corporation are added to the other items of income and deductions of the corporation in calculating its net taxable income or loss under U.S. tax accounting rules, just as if the income were earned or the expenses were incurred in the United States. The non–U.S. jurisdiction of the branch may also tax the branch's earnings under its own tax regime, which probably computes earnings under rules that differ from the U.S. tax accounting rules.

When a non–U.S. branch remits profits to the U.S. home office, no additional U.S. tax is incurred. However, the country of the branch may subject the net after-tax branch earnings to a host country withholding tax, which may be payable either when the income is earned or when the branch makes distributions. As discussed in the section on a taxable asset acquisition later in this chapter, other consequences arise both from operating a non–U.S. branch and from subsequently incorporating a non–U.S. branch.

### Tax Deferral

The second broad U.S. tax objective is that an entity incorporated outside the United States should not normally have income earned by it outside the United

States subject to U.S. taxation until it remits a dividend to its U.S. shareholders. However, as more and more U.S. companies expanded their overseas operations through foreign subsidiaries, Congress modified this deferral concept by enacting special rules in order to correct perceived abuses. The most important of these rules in the context of acquisitions of non–U.S. enterprises are the controlled foreign corporation (CFC) rules, which apply to "U.S. shareholders" of "controlled foreign corporations." A "U.S. shareholder" is a U.S. person who owns, directly or indirectly, under certain attribution rules, shares of stock possessing 10 percent or more of the voting power of a foreign corporation. If one or more "U.S. shareholders," individually or collectively, own shares of stock possessing more than 50 percent of the voting power or value of a foreign corporation, it will be a controlled foreign corporation, and the special CFC rules apply.

Examples of the abuses perceived by Congress include:

- Interposing tax haven resale subsidiaries between U.S. manufacturing exporters and non–U.S. local marketing subsidiaries to capture profits offshore and away from U.S. taxing authorities.
- Reinvesting aftertax offshore profits of non–U.S. subsidiaries in nonoperating (passive) non–U.S. assets or repatriating the profits in the form of loans to U.S. affiliates instead of dividending the profits to the U.S. parent and, thereby, postponing or avoiding U.S. tax.
- Establishing offshore holding companies to own non–U.S. subsidiaries, thus facilitating local entity distributions and intermediate reinvestment or redeployment of the funds without subjecting them to U.S. tax.
- Contributing valuable U.S.–funded and developed intangibles, such as patents and trademarks, to related tax haven subsidiaries for use in manufacturing or licensing activities such that both the operating and reinvested profits would not be subject to U.S. tax until dividended to the U.S. parent.
- Converting potential dividends of a non–U.S. subsidiary into capital gains by retaining earnings in the subsidiary in order to enhance the stock's value and then selling the stock.

The modifications to the deferral principle enacted by Congress constitute a large body of U.S. tax rules designed to make U.S. taxpayers include in their U.S. tax returns earnings of their non–U.S. corporations from tainted activities (the abuses described in the preceding paragraph). Inclusion is required irrespective of whether cash is actually distributed to the U.S. shareholders, except in certain instances if the earnings were subject to an effective non–U.S. tax rate greater than 90 percent of the U.S. tax rate. In addition, what might have been capital gains are transformed, in whole or in part, into dividends with appropriate U.S. tax consequences through related taint conversion rules. Thus, while the United States still recognizes tax deferral as a valid concept for overseas activities of U.S. multinationals conducted through non–U.S. subsidiaries, the rules permitting such deferral have narrowed.

## U.S. FOREIGN TAX CREDIT RULES

### Overview

The employment by the United States of the accessibility and modified deferral concepts has meant that foreign source income earned by a U.S. corporation either directly or through a foreign subsidiary would be taxed in the United States either as the income was earned or as dividends were received.

As a result, the United States developed a foreign tax credit system whose goal was to avoid or to mitigate double taxation of income earned and taxed abroad by permitting U.S. taxpayers to credit certain non–U.S. taxes against their U.S. tax liability. Over the years, taxpayers have seen the U.S. foreign tax credit rules proliferate in ways that present serious restrictions on their use. Taxpayers must deal with limitations, baskets, and creditability, among other issues. Each concept is defined extensively in the tax law and regulations with terms that themselves require further lengthy definitions. To optimize utilization of credits, it is critical to understand and to manage the "effective foreign tax rate" associated with items of foreign source income individually and in the aggregate. In connection with the acquisition of a foreign enterprise, the U.S. taxpayer may take steps, some of which are described in the section on a taxable share acquisition a little later in this chapter, to lower the effective foreign tax rate of the enterprise or generate lightly taxed foreign source income so that, going forward, this income can be blended with other income subject to a higher effective foreign tax rate for the purpose of better utilizing foreign tax credits. This allows the U.S. taxpayer to plan for the direct or the deemed repatriation of foreign source income in the most globally tax efficient manner.

Alternatively, the U.S. business may deduct the foreign taxes it pays. The taxpayer decides annually whether to claim foreign income taxes as a credit against its U.S. tax liability or as a deduction in determining U.S. taxable income. The taxpayer's decision applies to all foreign income taxes it paid or is deemed to have paid that year. Since a potential dollar-for-dollar tax credit has a higher economic value to the taxpayer than the 35 percent tax benefit per dollar of deduction, most corporate taxpayers elect to credit foreign taxes. It should be noted that the foreign tax credit rules operate at the federal income tax level only. Even states that tax a corporation's foreign source income do not reduce the state tax liability on those earnings by the non–U.S. taxes paid. However, if the taxpayer deducts foreign taxes on its federal income tax return, sometimes it will be able to do so for state income tax purposes as well.

### Creditability

Only certain types of non–U.S. taxes are creditable in the United States. Ordinarily, where a country bases its general tax levy on gross receipts minus deductions similar to ones allowable for U.S. tax purposes, that general tax will be creditable. The income and deductions need not be identical to those in the U.S. system; but the more dissimilar a system is to the U.S. system, the more likely it is that the Internal Revenue Service (IRS) will challenge the creditability of the tax. In particular, the creditability of a tax may be questioned when there is an alternative basis of assessment other than net income, when special rates or additional taxes apply only to specific industries or sectors, or when the tax rate rises to the highest amount for which the U.S. taxpayer can receive a tax credit (a so-called soak-up tax). Foreign taxes that are not creditable may be deductible.

## Limitations, Baskets, and Blending

To attempt to prevent U.S. taxpayers from using foreign tax credits to offset the U.S. tax liability on their U.S. source earnings, Congress first introduced the notion of a limitation. Initially the limitation provided that a U.S. taxpayer could not offset its U.S. tax liability with foreign tax credits by an amount in excess of the U.S. tax computed on its net foreign source taxable income included in its U.S. tax return. Later, the concept of limitation was expanded to separate limitations for each of several enumerated categories of foreign source income referred to as "baskets." One of many separate baskets currently in existence is the overall basket. This basket is for active, foreign source operating income of a U.S. taxpayer as well as for dividends, interest, and royalties received (and constructive dividends deemed received) from controlled foreign corporations to the extent attributable to active operating income of the controlled foreign corporation. Other baskets include the passive income basket, the financial services income basket, the foreign oil and gas income basket, and the separate baskets for dividends from noncontrolled foreign corporations (the "10/50 baskets"). By establishing the baskets and separate limitations, Congress attempted to minimize opportunities for blending substantially different types of foreign source income that attracted very different effective foreign tax rates in order to offset U.S. tax on lightly taxed foreign income with foreign taxes paid on other income.

In essence, the U.S. taxpayer will not be able to take credits against its U.S. tax liability for foreign taxes paid with respect to a particular category of income in excess of the U.S. tax computed on its net foreign source taxable income in that category. Thus, the U.S. taxpayer first determines its net foreign source taxable income per basket by separating all of its foreign source income by basket and then reducing the income in each basket by the deductions in its U.S. tax return properly allocated or appropriately apportioned to that basket. Next, the taxpayer determines the amount of its foreign taxes per basket based on the income to which the tax relates. The taxpayer then computes a tentative U.S. tax liability on the net foreign-source taxable income in each basket. That computed amount becomes the limitation for the basket—the maximum amount of foreign tax credits in that basket that can offset the U.S. tax liability of the taxpayer. If the computed amount for a specific basket is greater than the taxpayer's credits in the basket, the taxpayer is in an excess limitation position. In such a case, it will be advantageous for the taxpayer to generate income in that basket subject to a high effective foreign tax rate. Conversely, if that computed amount is less than the taxpayer's foreign taxes in the specific basket, the taxpayer is in an excess credit position, in which case the taxpayer will wish to generate additional income in that basket subject to a low effective foreign tax rate.

For example, assume USB, a hypothetical corporation, has two types of foreign-source income. First, it earns $100 in a Canadian branch operation and pays $55 of foreign tax on the branch earnings. In addition, it earns $100 of foreign source interest from cash put into Eurodollar deposits in Bermuda but pays no foreign tax on the interest. If the United States allowed all foreign source income and credits to be blended, the $70 of U.S. tax on the entire income ($200 x 35 percent) would be offset by the full $55 of foreign taxes paid on just the branch income, resulting in only $15 of net U.S. tax (for an aggregate 35 percent effective tax rate). However, because the branch income (and related $55 of foreign taxes) are in the overall basket while the interest income is in the passive basket, USB can only use the foreign taxes to offset the $35 of U.S. tax on the branch income ($100 x 35 percent). USB would pay $35 in taxes on the interest income, resulting in a total U.S. and non–U.S. tax liability of $90 for the year (a 45 percent aggregate effective tax rate) and $20 in excess overall basket foreign taxes. The excess foreign taxes could be carried back for two years or forward for five years to offset U.S. taxes on overall basket income earned in those years. USB has $35 ($100 x 35 percent) of excess limitation in the passive basket.

Blending of high- and low-taxed income may occur only within the confines of a particular basket rather than across all foreign source income. Blending usually occurs within the overall basket because operations outside the United States may be subject to foreign tax rates ranging from zero to over 50 percent. Blending of high- and low-taxed passive income is not possible, however, because passive income subject to an effective foreign tax rate in excess of the maximum applicable U.S. tax rate and the foreign taxes on such heavily taxed passive income are "kicked out" into the overall basket. As a result, the U.S. business that plans to acquire overseas operations will need to consider how the United States taxes foreign source income in order to appropriately structure the acquisition effort.

So, for example, if USB also had a Hong Kong branch operation that earned $100 and paid $16 of non–U.S. taxes, USB's overall basket limitation would be $70 ($200 x 35 percent). In that case, USB could use the $16 in taxes paid with respect to the Hong Kong branch plus $54 of Canadian taxes to offset its U.S. tax liability on the Hong Kong and Canadian branch income, leaving it with only $1 in excess foreign tax credits. USB would have a total U.S. and non–U.S. tax liability of $106, for an aggregate effective tax rate of 35 percent.

## The Direct Foreign Tax Credit

Individuals and U.S. "C corporations" (i.e., corporations that do not elect S corporation status—to be treated as pass-through entities for U.S. tax purposes) may claim credits for foreign income taxes imposed directly on their net income, such as taxes on foreign branch income, as well as for foreign withholding taxes imposed on gross payments like dividends, interest, and royalties received by them. When a pass-through entity like a partnership or certain limited liability companies (LLCs) or an S corporation earns such income, the income and the related direct foreign taxes pass through to the entity's owners for them to report and claim as credits in their U.S. tax returns.

## The Indirect Foreign Tax Credit

A U.S. C corporation may also claim indirect foreign tax credits that arise through the corporation's direct ownership of a foreign corporation that paid the tax (a first-tier foreign corporation) or its indirect ownership through one or more foreign corporations of a lower-tier foreign corporation that paid the tax. In order to claim an indirect credit, the U.S. corporation must own shares having at least 10 percent of the voting power of the first-tier foreign corporation, and each foreign corporation in a chain must own shares having at least 10 percent of the voting power of the foreign corporation below it. Moreover, the U.S. corporation's indirect ownership of second- and third-tier corporations must amount to at least 5 percent of the voting power of such corporations. U.S. corporations can claim indirect credits as low as the third foreign tier when the minimum ownership tests are met and as low as the sixth tier under additional tests.

## Taxpayer Status

The status of the U.S. taxpayer and the foreign entities owned by it affect the utilization of foreign tax credits. For example, as explained in the preceding section on indirect foreign tax credits, only a C corporation may claim indirect tax credits against its U.S. tax liability. However, it may not claim credits for taxes of foreign corporations below the sixth-tier corporation.

As a result, whether an entity would qualify as a partnership or as a corporation for U.S. tax purposes has created significant opportunities for U.S. taxpayers as well as, in prior years, some problems. For example, suppose the buyer is an investment fund structured as a limited partnership, none of whose partners is a C corporation having a 10 percent interest in the foreign target. If the fund uses a non–U.S. entity treated as a partnership for U.S. tax purposes to acquire foreign operating assets of the target, the foreign taxes on that business will be direct credits of the investors, not indirect credits, because pass-through entities like partnerships and limited liability companies treated under U.S. tax rules as partnerships have income, distributions, and related foreign taxes taken into account at the owner (not entity) level. Moreover, using as the acquisition vehicle a non–U.S. entity treated as a partnership may be helpful even for a corporate buyer if the target is a chain of foreign corporations. Such an acquisition vehicle could prevent lower-tier members of the chain from being treated as below the sixth tier for foreign tax credit purposes and, therefore, as incapable of generating creditable foreign taxes.


## FORMS OF TRANSACTIONS

### Modified Symmetry

In U.S. domestic tax applications, the goal of U.S. tax policy is to create symmetry of result between the seller and the buyer, which may be expressed in three rules:

1. When the seller converts the substance of its investment to cash or a cash equivalent, the seller recognizes gain or loss and the buyer gets a fair market value tax basis in what is acquired, which could be shares of stock of a company or the company's assets. Gain, if any, is recognized by the target company when it sells assets or by the target shareholders when they sell their target shares. In the United States, the taxable acquisition of target shares does not normally allow the buyer to step up the tax basis of the target's assets. However, an election can be made to treat a taxable share acquisition as a taxable asset acquisition if certain conditions are met.

2. When the seller merely converts the form of its investment from target shares to buyer shares and the target's business continues, the transaction should normally qualify as a tax-free exchange. In that event, the seller keeps its old stock basis in the new shares. Because the target corporation recognized no gain, the tax basis of its assets continues without any step-up.

3. The United States has virtually unique tax rules involving state-law mergers, using as little as 50 percent equity and the balance of the consideration in cash, to achieve part taxable/part tax-free treatment, and involving tax-free triangular reorganizations using shares of stock of the parent of the acquirer to make the acquisition rather than shares of the acquiring company. In the standard use of these techniques involving only stock, the symmetry continues in that the tax-free reorganization results in neither gain recognition by the seller nor basis step-up for the buyer. In the 50/50 situation, the seller's receipt of cash is treated as a taxable conversion, and the seller recognizes gain on only that part of the transaction. However, there is no step-up in the tax basis of the target's assets because the target did not sell them.

### Taxable Share Acquisition

One of the principal tax objectives of the buyer of a business, whether domestic or foreign, is to get a step-up in the basis of the assets of the acquired business. The step-up will reduce the buyer's future tax costs by increasing future depreciation and amortization deductions and reducing taxable gain on any future asset sales. Accordingly, the buyer may prefer to make a cash acquisition or to use its equity to acquire the business in a way that will not be tax-free to the seller.

The U.S. buyer of a foreign business ordinarily will be able to obtain the desired step-up for U.S. and foreign tax purposes by purchasing the assets of the business rather than by purchasing the company. However, if the entire company is being sold, the seller may not wish to sell assets because the tax cost of an asset sale may be greater than the tax cost of a sale of shares. In addition to non–U.S. taxes on the asset sale, there may be substantial non–U.S. registration, sales, or value-added taxes on the asset transfer. In contrast, a number of countries exempt from taxation the gain on the sale of shares of a subsidiary. Moreover, if the seller of the foreign target is a U.S. taxpayer, the gain on the sale of shares may be treated under the CFC rules like a dividend for U.S. tax purposes, to the extent of the target's undistributed earnings computed under U.S. tax accounting rules. If the U.S. seller is also entitled to indirect foreign credits as a result of the sale of shares or otherwise has excess foreign tax credits that can be used to offset the U.S. tax on the deemed dividend, the U.S. seller is likely to prefer to sell target shares rather than to sell target assets and incur a non–U.S. tax on the sale. There may be nontax reasons as well that make an asset sale undesirable, such as the need for third-party consents or labor laws that treat asset sales as constructive terminations entitling employees to termination payments.

If, instead of buying assets, a U.S. company buys the shares of a foreign target, the buyer gets a tax basis in the shares equal to the purchase price; but ordinarily the target will keep its historical basis in its assets for both non–U.S. and U.S. tax purposes. The acquirer may therefore wish to allocate some of the purchase price to other assets that will produce future tax benefits. For example, it may be possible to enter into a noncompetition agreement with the seller and to allocate some of the purchase price to this agreement, which would be amortizable for U.S. tax purposes. In addition, if the transaction involves the acquisition or the licensing of intangibles such as patents or trademarks from the seller, the U.S. acquirer may wish to acquire them directly, separate from the acquisition of the shares. The U.S. acquirer could then license the intangibles to the foreign business for a royalty; or, if U.S.–made products incorporating the intangibles are sold to the foreign business, the acquirer could reflect the value of the intangibles in an increased transfer price for goods. Either approach would reduce the target's non–U.S. taxable income. The acquirer's amortization deductions for the portion of the purchase price allocated to the intangibles could offset its increased income. An additional benefit is that the royalties or increased sales income will be foreign source and probably low-taxed overall basket income, which will be useful to a U.S. taxpayer with excess overall basket credits.

When target shares are acquired, under the modified tax deferral principle discussed in the earlier section on tax deferrals, U.S. taxation of the profits of the non–U.S. business is deferred until dividends are paid, except to the extent of any tainted income taxable under the CFC rules. The target will pay taxes in the non–U.S. jurisdiction; and the U.S. buyer, if it is a C corporation, ordinarily will get indirect credits for the foreign taxes paid with respect to the foreign business only when dividends are paid (or tainted income is includable in its income).

The mechanism works as follows. The "post-1986" unrepatriated earnings of a foreign corporation (computed in accordance with U.S. tax accounting rules) are pooled, with separate pools for each foreign tax credit limitation basket. The foreign corporation's own creditable taxes are similarly pooled by basket. The target's unrepatriated earnings and taxes for years prior to the year of acquisition will be in a separate 10/50 basket. When a foreign corporation pays a dividend, the dividend carries with it an amount of taxes from the post-1986 creditable taxes pool having the same ratio to the total taxes in the pool, basket by basket, as the portion of the dividend attributable to earnings in a particular basket bears to the total post-1986 undistributed earnings in the pool attributable to earnings in that basket. For "pre-1987 years," pools of unrepatriated earnings and related taxes for each foreign subsidiary are computed on a year-by-year basis. After dividends exceed the amount of the post-1986 unrepatriated earnings pool of a subsidiary, they are sourced, on a last-in, first-out (LIFO) basis, to pre-1987 years. The post-1986 unrepatriated earnings and creditable taxes pools begin in the first year after 1986 in which the foreign corporation has a U.S. shareholder that owns 10 percent of the voting shares. Thus, if a U.S. buyer acquires a corporation that was always foreign owned, the post-1986 pooling will begin in the year of acquisition.

Accordingly, when the target pays a postacquisition dividend to the buyer in excess of postacquisition earnings, some portion of the dividend will be treated as paid from preacquisition undistributed earnings, that is, from a 10/50 basket, and will bring with it credits in the 10/50 basket. If the effective tax rate on the earnings in the target's 10/50 basket is less than the U.S. tax rate on those earnings, the buyer will not be able to use excess foreign tax credits from other baskets to offset the incremental U.S. tax. An exception applies when the foreign target was a CFC acquired from an unrelated U.S. shareholder to the extent of the seller's gain treated as a dividend under the taint conversion rules. In that case, the U.S. buyer may receive such preacquisition earnings tax free in the United States upon distribution by the foreign target. For this reason, if the foreign target is directly or indirectly controlled by a U.S. shareholder before the acquisition, it is critical to gain access to the unrepatriated earnings ("earnings and profits") history and to related foreign tax paid history of the target and every other non–U.S. entity being acquired so as to provide a basis for subsequent planning even though the change of ownership can almost (but not quite) create a fresh start for postacquisition operations.

If the target is the parent of a chain of non–U.S. corporations, as each higher-tier corporation receives dividends from lower tiers, it has both its own creditable taxes and the indirect lower-tier creditable taxes related to the dividends received by it from lower tiers. As a result, based solely on the foreign corporate legal structure, a dividend to the U.S. buyer may bring with it foreign tax credits representing a foreign effective tax rate that differs significantly from the target's statutory tax rate.

Moreover, as noted in the section on tax deferrals, the U.S. buyer may need to include on its U.S. tax return its share of unrepatriated foreign earnings of the target or a target subsidiary if the earnings meet certain "tainted income" tests, irrespective of whether cash is received or the U.S. shareholder owns the foreign company only indirectly. Two common examples of tainted income are (1) dividends received by the target if the company paying the dividend is incorporated in a different country and (2) income of the target from sales of goods purchased from a related company if the goods are manufactured in and the sales are for use in a country different from the one in which the target is incorporated. If a second- or third-tier subsidiary has tainted income, the pro rata share belonging to the U.S. shareholder "hopscotches" the intermediate entities and is directly included in the U.S. shareholder's income, bringing with it indirect tax credits from the tainted income entity but not from the higher tiers. When the subsidiary subsequently distributes the tainted income, the U.S. shareholder is allowed to exclude it from that year's taxable income as previously taxed earnings because it was previously included in U.S. taxable income. As a result, planning opportunities exist for U.S. taxpayers depending on whether direct inclusion of tainted income of a lower-tier company or actual dividends generate a better long-term foreign tax credit utilization strategy because of the different amounts of indirect credits produced in a given instance.

As noted, the indirect credit rules operate so that a calculated percentage of the foreign taxes paid by a foreign entity accompanies a dividend distributed by it to its U.S. shareholder. A key element of the calculation is the ratio of the amount of the dividend to the foreign entity's unrepatriated earnings. This ratio is potentially subject to significant variation based on a variety of differences between the foreign jurisdiction's tax accounting rules and U.S. tax accounting rules, which affect the computation of unrepatriated earnings. Differences in timing for inclusion or deduction can create short- or long-term differences in the amount of unrepatriated earnings and the effective rate of foreign taxes related to those earnings. For example, suppose a foreign jurisdiction (Country X) allows 100 percent of new plant equipment to be written off in year 1, but the United States requires five-year straight-line amortization. The U.S. tax accounting concept of unrepatriated earnings would only reflect a deduction of 20 percent of the equipment cost each year. Therefore, under U.S. principles, the earnings of the Country X subsidiary are higher in year 1 than its taxable income for foreign tax purposes and lower in years 2 through 5 than its foreign taxable income. Thus, even if the statutory tax rate in Country X were the same as the statutory rate in the United States and all other elements were equal, the effective foreign tax rate for U.S. tax credit purposes would be lower in year 1 and higher in years 2 through 5 than the U.S. and foreign statutory rates.

Although, as noted earlier, a purchase of target shares ordinarily will not result in a step-up in the tax basis of the target's assets, the buyer may obtain a basis step-up for U.S. tax purposes (but not for non–U.S. tax purposes) by making an election to treat the share purchase like an asset purchase under section 338 of the U.S. Internal Revenue Code (IRC). This election is available only to a corporate buyer that, within a 12-month period, purchases shares of the target's stock having at least 80 percent of the vote and value. For purposes of the vote and value test, nonvoting shares that are preferred as to dividends and liquidation rights are ordinarily disregarded. As long as the target has no direct or subsidiary U.S. operations, the election is likely to be advantageous for the buyer because its effect is to generate a fair market value U.S. tax basis for all of the target's assets. This should create a higher foreign effective tax rate on future foreign earnings computed under U.S. tax accounting rules, provided the local tax basis of the target's assets did not get stepped up for local tax purposes as a result of the acquisition. For example, if the buyer paid a substantial premium for the target's goodwill, this premium will be amortizable over 15 years for purposes of computing unrepatriated earnings under U.S. tax rules. This would likely produce unrepatriated earnings that are substantially less than the target's distributable reserves for non–U.S. purposes. Thus, the same cash dividend out of postacquisition earnings will bring with it more indirect tax credits.

Furthermore, the deemed-sale election will wipe out the target's prior tax attributes, such as its preacquisition earnings pool and credits, which as discussed earlier would have been separate basket income and credits. The elimination of the preacquisition tax attributes is particularly important if the target has a substantial amount of lightly taxed preacquisition undistributed earnings. All of these considerations will affect the subsequent U.S. indirect foreign tax credit calculations. A section 338 election may not be desirable if the seller was a U.S. person and the target has a substantial amount of unrepatriated previously taxed earnings, which, as previously mentioned, could be distributed to the buyer free of U.S. tax. The election would wipe out the previously taxed earnings account along with the target's other tax attributes.

## Taxable Asset Acquisition

If the acquisition can be structured as an asset purchase, either because the target business is only a division of a foreign company or because the seller agrees to sell assets, the U.S. buyer of the assets must decide whether to acquire them directly or to use a new or existing foreign company to do so. The choice will affect future U.S. and non–U.S. tax consequences.

When a U.S. company, either directly or through a U.S. subsidiary, acquires foreign assets of the target, the result will be a non–U.S. branch with a fair-market-value tax basis in the acquired assets for U.S. and, presumably, foreign tax purposes. The branch will compute its earnings and pay local tax under that country's income tax rules. Under the accessibility rules described in the earlier section on tax accessibility, branch earnings will also be determined under U.S. tax accounting principles for inclusion in the U.S. tax return, on which a direct paid credit may be claimed for the foreign taxes paid by the branch. Operating as a branch allows the U.S. acquirer direct access in its U.S. tax return to the branch's profits, losses, and foreign tax credits.

Should the U.S. buyer later decide to convert the branch into a non–U.S. corporate subsidiary, a number of potential U.S. tax problems arise because of the shift from U.S. tax accessibility to deferral. Ordinarily, many of the assets of a non–U.S. branch can be contributed tax free to a foreign subsidiary, provided the assets meet certain active trade or business tests and the taxpayer complies with reporting requirements contained in the U.S. Treasury regulations. Problems may arise, however, in certain areas, including contributions of inventory, accumulated tax losses, and intangibles. While inventory normally can be contributed to a new corporation tax free, contribution of inventory to a foreign subsidiary might itself be treated as a taxable sale because the future sale of the inventory to third parties by the subsidiary may escape U.S. taxation.

Accumulated branch tax losses pose another problem. Even if the business was profitable for local financial and tax accounting purposes, the branch may have generated a loss under U.S. tax accounting rules that could be used currently to offset income from other operations of the U.S. company or of its U.S. consolidated affiliates. If the branch has appreciated assets, the U.S. company may be subject to U.S. tax on the gain in the year the branch is converted into a subsidiary to the extent of all or a portion of the previously deducted branch losses. Another issue in converting a branch with losses is whether the foreign jurisdiction will allow previously unused branch losses to carry over to the new foreign corporation.

Perhaps the knottiest problem in converting a non–U.S. branch into a non–U.S. subsidiary is the transfer of intangibles. If a U.S. taxpayer transfers intangibles (e.g., patents, trademarks, know-how) to a foreign subsidiary as a capital contribution, U.S. tax rules characterize the transaction as a license to the foreign subsidiary in exchange for deemed annual arm's-length royalty payments, the amount of which must be periodically revised to reflect the value of the intangible. This deems the U.S. transferor to have taxable income without cash, but it also characterizes the phantom income as foreign source so that U.S. tax on it can be offset with foreign tax credits. Clearly, the aim of the IRS was to force U.S. companies to license their intangibles to foreign parties in order to tax the income stream generated by U.S. research and experimentation, the costs of which had been deducted for U.S. tax purposes. However, licensing foreign intangibles may lead to disputes with foreign tax authorities over the appropriateness of the royalty streams paid to the U.S. parent, may trigger foreign withholding taxes on the royalties, or may create tax losses in the foreign jurisdiction that cannot be used by the new subsidiary.

Apart from the U.S. and non–U.S. tax issues that could arise on a later incorporation of a branch, it will probably be preferable for nontax reasons to operate the acquired business from the outset as an entity formed under the law of the country in which it operates. However, if the business is anticipated to have tax losses under U.S. tax accounting principles and the buyer wishes to deduct those losses on its U.S. tax return, or if the buyer is not eligible to use indirect foreign tax credits and wants to be able to treat the foreign taxes of the non–U.S.

operation as direct paid credits, the U.S. buyer may choose to use a foreign entity that receives partnership status for U.S. tax purposes to make the acquisition. For U.S. tax purposes, the result will be similar to operating as a branch because partnerships (and entities treated for U.S. tax purposes like partnerships) have income, losses, distributions, and related foreign taxes taken into account at the partner (or owner) level, not at the entity level.

The lack of a clear definition of what makes an entity a "partnership" rather than an "association taxable as a corporation," in particular in the case of a non–U.S. entity, inhibited creative tax planning for many years, particularly where "hybrid" entities like foreign limited liability companies were involved. Viewed from a cross-border perspective, a hybrid entity is one treated by foreign law as a corporation but by U.S. tax law as a partnership. If a foreign entity is treated by the U.S. tax authorities as a partnership, U.S. individuals and S corporations, as well as C corporations, may use the foreign taxes paid by the non–U.S. entity as credits against their U.S. tax liability. This occurs because the foreign entity's taxes are treated as direct foreign tax credits rather than as indirect foreign tax credits, which only C corporations can claim as credits (and only after numerous calculations). "Partners" simply include in their U.S. tax returns their share of income and claim the foreign taxes paid as each year occurs. The foreign treatment of a hybrid entity as a corporation may be useful because such entity can function as the parent of a foreign country consolidated tax return group, thereby potentially reducing local country taxes, without adding another corporate tier for U.S. tax purposes. However, where a foreign hybrid serves as the parent of a foreign consolidated tax return group, careful planning will be required to generate income in the hybrid itself under the U.S. tax accounting rules in light of limitations on the ability to use the hybrid's losses contained in the U.S. dual consolidated loss rules. Alternatively, a reverse hybrid is an entity treated as a corporation for U.S. tax purposes but as a partnership under foreign tax law. Other planning possibilities arise with reverse hybrids.

Treasury regulations effective January 1, 1997, have essentially eliminated the old uncertainty about whether a non–U.S. entity would be treated as a partnership for U.S. tax purposes by implementing a check-the-box system of entity classification. This system makes status as a partnership or corporation elective, except for specific entities such as corporations formed under U.S. law and certain foreign entities listed by the IRS, which will be treated as corporations. In addition, a wholly owned foreign entity can be treated as a branch of the owner under the new rules. The check-the-box approach has created considerable opportunities for U.S. taxpayers to achieve more tax-efficient offshore expansion.

If the buyer is a C corporation and the target business is expected to be profitable, it will be preferable generally for the buyer to use a newly formed or existing entity treated as a corporation for U.S. tax purposes to acquire the assets. In that case, the modified deferral and indirect foreign tax credit rules discussed in preceding sections on tax deferrals, indirect foreign tax credits, and taxable share acquisitions will apply.

## Tax-Free Exchanges

As a practical matter, tax-free acquisitions of foreign targets seldom occur for at least three reasons. First, because the simpler state-law merger type of reorganization is usually not available, the only practical options are the more difficult to implement acquisition of target shares or target assets, in either case for voting stock.

Second, the rules for tax-free acquisitions under non–U.S. tax systems are often more restrictive than the U.S. rules. In particular, it may not be possible to use shares of the parent of the acquirer rather than shares of the acquiring company or to use cash or notes to buy out substantial shareholder interests and still achieve tax-free exchange status. Thus, a transaction could have the undesirable outcome of being taxable to the foreign seller and satisfying U.S. tax-free exchange requirements. This can create interesting effective-tax-rate considerations for U.S. foreign tax credit purposes. For example, under such circumstances in an asset acquisition, the U.S. tax basis of the target's assets would normally carry over in the reorganization. However, local tax law might allow a basis step-up to fair market value for those same assets. As a result, even if the local statutory tax rate is higher than the U.S. statutory tax rate, the new foreign affiliate could generate a lower foreign effective tax rate than the U.S. tax rate because the U.S. tax accounting rules would generate fewer deductions (and hence higher earnings) than those generated under the local country tax rules.

Third, there is a tendency of foreign tax jurisdictions to apply high transaction taxes to acquisitions. Non–U.S. acquisitions can involve capital taxes for setting up an acquisition vehicle, hefty title recording charges, and transfer taxes, such as sales taxes and/or value-added taxes. In addition, a foreign jurisdiction may apply transfer taxes to intangibles such as goodwill as well as to inventory, plant, and equipment. Thus, the ability to achieve a totally tax free foreign acquisition is usually quite limited.

A U.S. company's acquisition of the shares of an unrelated non–U.S. target in a tax-free share swap under U.S. rules normally results in an affiliate with a pool of undistributed preacquisition earnings and foreign taxes in a separate basket, as is the case for a taxable share purchase. When the U.S. shareholder ultimately receives a dividend from those earnings, it must place the dividend and any related deemed-paid foreign tax credits into a separate basket for foreign tax credit limitation purposes. Consequently, even though the preacquisition earnings may have been generated by active business operations, the U.S. shareholder will not be able to blend those earnings and related foreign taxes with postacquisition earnings and taxes of the target or other non–U.S. subsidiaries to achieve more effective foreign tax credit utilization. Moreover, if the acquisition is a tax-free asset acquisition, the acquirer will succeed to the undistributed preacquisition earnings and foreign taxes, which will also likely be in a separate basket. In contrast, an asset purchase in a taxable transaction does not bring with it preacquisition earnings and credits.

## FINANCING CONSIDERATIONS

If the foreign acquisition involves the use of debt, additional issues arise concerning which entity should borrow the funds. Certain U.S. rules need to be considered if the borrower is a U.S. corporation, whereas other U.S. and foreign rules demand consideration if the borrower is a foreign subsidiary.

The ability to deduct the interest expense fully is a key consideration. The United States currently places restrictions on certain convertible subordinated acquisition indebtedness. The rules of the country in which a foreign borrower operates need to be checked for any restrictions like caps on permissible debt-to-equity ratios (referred to as *thin capitalization rules*) or partial or complete prohibitions on deducting interest expense on acquisition debt. The rules may vary depending on whether the lender is related to the borrower or, if unrelated, whether the debt is guaranteed by a related company. Thin capitalization rules can result in a denial of interest deductions to the borrower and, in some instances, the imposition of withholding taxes if interest payments are treated as deemed dividends because the lender is an affiliate or there is an affiliate guarantee.

Assuming full interest deductibility and sufficient cash flow to service the debt, the effective foreign and U.S. tax rates on taxable income must be considered. Merely noting a country's nominal tax rate on taxable income may not always adequately answer the question of whether the interest deduction is more valuable in that country than in the United States. For example, if the debt is placed on a foreign corporation that acquires the target, but the acquirer is not expected to generate sufficient profits to absorb the interest deduction, it is critical that the foreign country permit tax consolidation or tax-free mergers so that the excess interest expense can be absorbed by the target's profits.

Moreover, even if the nominal U.S. tax rate is higher than the tax rate in the jurisdiction of the target company, "overleveraging" in the United States will ordinarily be inefficient because it will make it difficult for the U.S. acquirer to claim credits against its tax liability for substantial amounts of the taxes paid by its foreign subsidiaries. The reason is that the U.S. foreign tax credit limitation rules require an apportionment of the U.S. affiliated group's interest expense between U.S. and foreign source income (by basket) using an asset method of apportionment. These complex rules inevitably result in a lower foreign tax credit limitation for the U.S. group than if no interest expense existed. Therefore, U.S. groups that are already limited in their ability to utilize all of their foreign tax credits should consider the potential additional limitation cost to the group of a U.S. borrowing as well as the difference between interest rates on a foreign versus U.S. borrowing. Even groups not currently limited in foreign tax credit utilization should consider the impact of a U.S. borrowing on their projected future repatriation plans.

When a U.S. parent considers using funds initially borrowed by it or by a U.S. affiliate and then loaned to a foreign subsidiary to make the acquisition, the problems just described are compounded by three factors: (1) further complexity in the U.S. foreign tax credit limitation calculations under certain "interest netting" rules, (2) the possibility of foreign withholding taxes on the interest paid to the U.S. affiliate, and (3) the intercompany pricing issue of whether the interest rate charged to the foreign subsidiary is too low (under U.S. tax rules) or too high (under foreign rules).

Certain loan covenants in a U.S. borrowing may create a U.S. tax trap for the unwary. One of the rules referred to in the earlier section on tax deferrals, enacted by the U.S. Congress to prevent what it viewed as artificial deferral of U.S. taxation, provides for the potential inclusion by the U.S. group of the earnings of a controlled foreign corporation that provides credit support to the U.S. group. The rule applies if a sufficient amount of that subsidiary's voting shares is pledged or if its assets are pledged or otherwise used as security for a debt incurred by the U.S. group and certain other tests are met. The result is similar if the subsidiary guarantees the debt.

A final factor to consider is the potential natural economic hedge that may arise from a non–U.S. currency borrowing by a foreign subsidiary making the acquisition. Borrowing in the local currency permits matching of the currency of the interest expense with that of operating revenues, thereby avoiding the risk of currency fluctuations. Such benefits, however, must be considered in the context of the overall tax, legal, and business considerations in the acquisition.

# ✓ Checklist: Tax Considerations in Acquiring Non–U.S. Enterprises

I. Initial structural decisions.
  A. Foreign versus U.S. business entity.
    1. Possible foreign law restrictions on use of U.S. entities.
    2. Form of transaction effects on available options. Virutally restricted to existing entity if transaction is to be an acquisition of stock (see IV).
    3. Tax residence rules.
      a. Consider residency rules in each country: The United States determines corporate tax residence by place of incorporation, whereas other countries frequently use another test (such as place of management and control). May be possibility of dual-resident or stateless entity. Generally desirable to avoid both.
        (1) Can have an adverse effect (including loss of treaty relief) on withholding taxes on interest, dividends, and other payments.
        (2) Restrictions on use of dual resident company tax losses and other benefits in U.S. consolidated tax returns.
      b. Change of residence can result in substantial tax liabilities.
      c. Analyze distinctions between taxation on branch versus residence basis by the foreign country.
        (1) Possible exclusion of passive income.
        (2) Possible differences in expense deductions allowable.
        (3) Possible differences in withholding rates on items of income paid or received from another country.
    4. U.S. deferral/credit rules (see V).
    5. Tax planning needs of other equity participants for less than wholly owned businesses.
  B. Foreign entity.
    1. Classification of entity for U.S. tax purposes.
    2. Choice of direct U.S. ownership or ownership through intervening foreign entity.
      a. Utility of multicountry holding companies or chains of ownership limited by potential loss of deferral of U.S. taxation when lightly taxed dividends and passive income are paid by foreign subsidiary in one country to foreign subsidiary in another country.
      b. United States will not recognize foreign tax consolidations.

II.  Financing of the acquisition and ongoing business entity.
   A.  Debt, especially intercompany debt.
      1.  Tax planning factors to consider.
         a.  Potential benefits from reducing foreign taxes.
            (1)  Is foreign marginal tax rate above U.S. marginal tax rate?
            (2)  Does U.S. parent face excess foreign tax credits?
            (3)  Does foreign tax law deduction for interest coupled with reduced withholding rate when treaty applies permit earnings stripping at reduced foreign tax burden?
            (4)  Does use of debt eliminate foreign withholding tax on recovery of original principal?
         b.  Intercompany loans from U.S. affiliates may affect apportionment of U.S. interest expense among the domestic and foreign-source income foreign tax credit limitation baskets.
         c.  On intercompany loans to foreign subsidiary, will the subsidiary have and use additional current foreign tax law deduction equal to interest currently includable in U.S. income? If not, result can be a net increase in total current taxes.
         d  Generally possible to convert debt into equity without tax but not to substitute debt for equity, so initial capitalization with debt tends to provide more flexibility.
         e.  Special tax considerations on intercompany debt.
            (1)  Interest paid to foreign sister companies generally taxed by United States when paid.
            (2)  Arm's-length interest rules apply. Is the interest charge within any safe harbor for intercompany interest under each country's tax laws, and, if not, can the rate be sustained against attack in both jurisdictions?
            (3)  Determine whether interest expense on any borrowings by U.S. entities can be offset against the interest deducted by the foreign subsidiary for U.S. foreign tax credit calculations.
         f.  Amount of allowable debt restrictions on total debt and related company debt, both generally and on borrowings to finance acquisitions.
         g.  Minimum and maximum restrictions (both tax and nontax) on interest rates.
         h.  Currency: foreign versus U.S. tax law treatment of exchange gains and losses.
         i.  Timing: foreign versus U.S. tax law treatment of:
            (1)  Installment and contingent payment purchases—when interest will be deductible and when amounts will be added to basis for depreciation allowances.

        (2) Interest deductions for debt issued at a discount or premium.

B. Equity.

1. Issuance of parent company stock.

    a. Will transaction be tax-free exchange for either U.S. or foreign tax purposes?

    b. U.S. taxation of foreign recipient on dividends and on subsequent sale of stock.

       (1) U.S. withholding tax rate on dividends? (30 percent without treaty reduced to no more than 5 percent by any applicable treaty).

       (2) Benefit of sale of stock by nonresident alien, even on U.S. stock exchange, generally not taxed by United States?

2. Possible inapplicability of U.S. securities law restrictions, but possible local securities law regulations.

C. Hybrid securities.

1. Foreign tax law treatment of convertible debt or warrants to acquire shares of stock of the U.S. buyer.

2. U.S. treatment of local country hybrids without direct U.S, correspondence.

III. Expected ongoing intercompany dealings.

A. Funding transactions.

B. Home office management services and other intercompany services.

1. Consider interplay of U.S. arm's-length and safe harbor rules with foreign tax law rules.

    a. Consider establishing a reasonable and systematic policy for allocating corporate overhead charges.

    b. Take steps to identify, to segregate for retrieval, and to document for foreign tax return examination any costs on which management charge is to be based.

2. Consider whether services will raise risk of service provider being taxed in other country and steps to avoid such taxation (such as transferring employees or making them dual employees).

C. Purchases of goods.

1. Unless there are comparable uncontrolled sales to unrelated third parties as a reference point, intercompany sales are likely to be a point of potential dispute with tax authorities in at least one of the countries.

2. If a problem, consider feasibility of a marketing agency arrangement, but transfer pricing issues remain in a different form.

3. If transaction involves sale by U.S. affiliate, consider having sale

terms with title passing on delivery abroad to maximize amount of foreign-source income.

IV. Form of transaction.
  A. Tax-free versus taxable.
    1. Generally undesirable for transaction to be structured as tax-free under U.S. laws and taxable under other country's laws.
    2. Some restrictions on U.S. rules are applicable to foreign transactions.
        a. More generous statutory merger forms of tax-free reorganizations not available.
        b. Check whether U.S. rules applicable to exchanges involving foreign corporation preclude tax-free characteristics (see IRC section 367).
    3. Foreign tax laws are generally not as generous as U.S. system in allowing tax-free corporate restructuring and ownership changes.
        a. Income tax issues.
            (1) Frequently less developed or less generous rules for use of parent company shares and types and amounts of other consideration that can be used.
            (2) Possible differences in continuity of business and continuity of shareholder interest required.
        b. Check foreign transfer taxes, even if transaction is a share purchase (rates typically are substantial if they apply).
            (1) If sale of shares is treated as sale of assets, then transfer tax could apply to goodwill involved as well as to tangible assets and other intangible assets. May be possible to avoid by purchasing shares in two tranches.
            (2) Stamp duties or other title recording charges may be imposed on registration or consummation of share transfers.
  B. Taxable exchanges.
    1. Use of debt versus cash.
    2. Foreign and U.S. law implications of allocation of purchase price
        a. Treatment of intangibles, including in particular goodwill and covenants not to compete.
        b. Permissible inventory practices.
    3. Foreign law limitations on foreign tax benefit carryforwards (e.g., provisions like U.S. limitations on net operating loss carryforwards).
  C. Hybrid transactions.
    1. Possibilities of combining taxable redemption and tax-free purchase to avoid more restrictive foreign income tax law provisions and maintain parity between U.S. and foreign tax law calculations.

2.  Typically, foreign tax laws have no equivalent to IRC section 338's deemed election provisions and treat distribution of assets (other than to a local parent owning all or substantially all of the shares of the distributing company) as a taxable sale by the distributing company.

3.  Some foreign countries have equivalent of mandatory IRC section 338 for at least transfer tax purposes if all the shares are acquired within a certain time frame.

V.  U.S. deferral and credit rules.
    A.  Consider the differences between U.S. tax law calculation of taxable income (income inclusion measure for a U.S. subsidiary) and earnings and profits (income inclusion measure for foreign subsidiary).
    B.  If foreign subsidiary is used, net income can be taxed under deferral limitation rules before actual cash dividends are paid to the United States.
        1.  Generally no deferral for Subpart F income where recipient does not bear effective foreign tax rate greater than 90 percent of the maximum U.S. corporate tax rate.
            a.  Will the foreign subsidiary earn investment income, provide services to, or purchase goods from or sell goods to related parties in other countries? If so, there is possible Subpart F income.
            b.  Will foreign subsidiary invest in shares or debt obligations of related U.S. corporations or residents, property to be used in the United States, or accounts receivable from related U.S. persons? If so, there is possible Subpart F income.
        2.  If a foreign subsidiary is at least majority owned directly or indirectly by a few individuals or families, then it can possibly be a Foreign Personal Holding Company.
        3.  Deferral can also terminate in connection with arm's-length pricing adjustments.
    C.  Check differences between computations of taxable income under foreign income tax law and U.S. computations of taxable income (if U.S. subsidiary used) or earnings and profits (if a foreign subsidiary is used).
        1.  Absolute differences may arise from:
            a.  Different characterization of form of acquisition.
                (1)  Tax-free or partially tax-free transaction under only one of the tax systems (typically U.S.).
                (2)  Hybrid transaction (particularly where IRC section 338 election made for U.S. tax purposes).
            b.  Treatment of intangibles (e.g., foreign systems that permit goodwill or covenants not to compete to be written off as a

balance sheet equity adjustment instead of deduction on income statement).

    c.  Adjustments to asset basis for foreign government subsidies or tax credits.

    d.  Interest allowances.

        (1)  Restrictions on acquisition debt or related-party borrowings.

        (2)  Imputed interest on interest-free or low-interest loans.

        (3)  Treatment of accrued but unpaid interest.

  2.  Timing differences.

    a.  Depreciation and amortization allowances.

    b.  Inventory calculations.

    c.  Treatment of installment and contingent payment sales.

  3.  Foreign exchange gain or loss exposures.

    a.  Prognosis for inflation and changes in foreign currency exchange rates.

    b.  Election to compute earnings in dollars for subsidiaries operating in hyperinflationary currencies.

D.  Check credits carried with amounts included in U.S. taxable income.

  1.  Foreign taxes that constitute creditable taxes.

    a.  Corporate taxes measured by net income and withholding taxes deducted from payments and distributions qualify.

    b.  Taxes not seeking to reach net income and taxes imposed for specific government services do not qualify and must be deducted as an expense or capitalized.

    c.  Tax does not qualify to the extent it is not compulsory (e.g., constitutes a penalty imposed for noncompliance) or is imposed only to the extent a tax credit is available in another country for the assessment.

  2.  Additional restrictions on credits for income taxes imposed on foreign subsidiary.

    a.  Foreign subsidiary cannot be lower than sixth foreign tier of corporate chain.

    b.  Must be at least 10 percent direct ownership of voting stock of the foreign entity by immediate shareholder and at least a 5 percent flow-through voting stock interest by U.S. shareholder of the chain through third tier and additional rules through sixth tier.

VI.  Always consider availability of resources in personnel, data, and time to perform planning prior to acquisition, and implement or modify strategy after acquisition.

# PART FOUR

# Financial Aspects

In Chapters 7, 8, and 9, our discussion turns to various aspects of the financing of cross-border deals.

In Chapter 7, Roy C. Smith, professor of finance and international business at the Stern School of Business of New York University, and Yonghong Mao of Standard and Poor's describe the history and operation of the Eurobond market and how corporations contemplating cross-border deals can utilize the full range of alternatives. They then cover the rapidly growing international equity securities market, including the important role of pension funds, underwriting methods, and the listing of shares on foreign exchanges.

In Chapter 8, Kenneth D. Brody of Taconic Capital Advisors LLC and Winslow Partners and Roberta J. Waxman-Lenz provide an analysis of government assistance from the developed countries to help finance acquisitions, joint ventures, existing subsidiaries or affiliates, and start-up projects in developing countries. A useful discussion of how to deal with government financial institutions is included, and an extensive list of such institutions, on a country-by-country basis, is provided in the appendixes to the chapter.

In Chapter 9, Scott L. Hoffman of Evans, Evans & Hoffman defines and describes international project finance; treats risk identification and allocation of responsibility; gives an analysis of credit-enhancement opportunities; and, in general, offers guidelines for lenders, government agencies, project sponsors, equity investors, and other transaction participants in structuring and negotiating project finance.

# 7

# International Financing for Cross-Border M&A Transactions

*Roy C. Smith*
*Yonghong Mao*

**D**uring the 10 years ended in 2000, more than 15,000 cross-border merger and acquisition (M&A) transactions, aggregating $2.8 *trillion* in value, took place around the world. This total exceeded by far the level of cross-border merger and acquisition volume of any decade in history. All indications are that the intensity of the activity is continuing and that the next decade will exceed these totals.

However, of the total value of transactions for the 10-year period ended in 2000, only 50 percent was represented by U.S. cross-border deals; the rest were transactions involving mainly European companies, not the United States. Further, for the 10-year period, 64 percent of the U.S. cross-border transactions involved U.S. sellers and non–U.S. buyers.

Cross-border investments need to be financed, just as domestic transactions do. Companies always seek to accomplish such financing in the most efficient

This chapter relies heavily on *Global Banking*, by Roy C. Smith and Ingo Walter (New York: Oxford University Press, 1996, 2000).

way possible, one that involves a combination of low cost, flexibility, and other favorable terms and conditions. Cross-border transactions, however, involve parties from two or more different countries and, on average, tend to be more sizable than purely domestic transactions. Accordingly, financing for many of these deals may involve using the international capital markets, in addition to or instead of domestic capital market or banking sources.

Domestic capital sources will be well known to cross-border "buyers" of other companies. They include banks willing to provide bridge finance and term lines of credit, bond markets, and, of course, the home-country equity market. Generally such transactions are financed with debt—either to pay for cash deals or to repurchase shares that might have been issued to stockholders of the selling company. Sometimes, the debt may be arranged by banks in the country of the seller, sometimes in nondollar currencies; but today large banks in all countries can extend loans in virtually any convertible currency. This chapter, is mainly concerned with "international" financing for the acquiring party. By this is meant that the financing is *nondomestic*, so as to include foreign financing for U.S. acquisitions and euro issues and issues in the United States for non–U.S. buyers seeking to finance transactions in the United States.

The chapter describes the international bond and equity capital markets and how they work so companies might have a better understanding of them to put to use when asking both their domestic and their international bankers for a full range of financing ideas from which to choose. Before proceeding, however, it is worth first reviewing some basic steps to be taken by all corporations seeking to secure financing for overseas acquisitions or direct investments.

## FIRST STEPS

At an early stage in the decision to proceed with the contemplated investment, a banker well known to the company should be contacted, on a confidential basis, to give advice on the financing for the transaction. The banker, or investment banker, may or may not be involved in representing the company in negotiating the deal with the target. But, one way or the other, financing advice should be sought at an early stage. The investing company needs to ask the following questions:

- Approximately how much financing will be required?
- How much of this will be in the form of debt?
- How much of the debt will be in the form of bridge financing, to be replaced by permanent financing, and how long will it take for the permanent financing to be put in place?
- How much of the permanent financing will be in the form of long-term debt, and how much in other forms, especially equity?
- What effect will the transaction have on the company's debt ratings, existing debt covenants, and operating cash flow?

Just as important, the company needs to know how much its lead bank is prepared to commit to lend or syndicate and what the cost and other terms of such financing will be. The company will also want to discuss with its bank, and perhaps with other experts, the tax and foreign exchange considerations of the deal and to examine a wide range of possibilities of permanent financing alternatives. Most transactions are financed first by bank facilities from a lead bank, with enough time-leeway to allow the company the opportunity to deliberate over its permanent financing possibilities before committing to anything. It is probably more important to get the commitment of an eager and willing bank for the full amount sought, often on fairly short notice, than it is to worry about obtaining the best possible terms. The permanent financing that comes later is the place for the fine tuning. Often a company's first-stage, or bridge financing, bank will propose permanent financing either from a syndicated bank term loan or from a capital market transaction. For companies with limited access to capital markets, usually because of their size, complexity, or credit rating, bank financing may be the most appropriate choice. But almost all companies with investment-grade debt ratings (BBB- or better) will have access to international capital markets. Those with below-investment-grade ratings may still use the "junk bond" markets in the United States.

This chapter is concerned with permanent financing for cross-border investments obtainable from international capital markets, mainly fixed-rate, long-term, investment-grade debt and equity markets for common stock.

## THE INTERNATIONAL BOND MARKET

The relative levels of activity in U.S. and international capital markets can be observed in Exhibit 7.1.

During the five years represented in the exhibit, it is clear that capital market finance from debt and equity markets has exceeded global syndicated bank loan volume, in some years by as much as two to one. Capital markets have grown and developed enormously during the time under review as a result of market deregulation, improved technology, and much greater competition across borders. It is also interesting to note that in many years, the volume of new issues in the Eurobond market exceeded that of new issues in the investment-grade U.S. bond market. The rapid rate of growth of new issues in the international markets signifies a coming of age of non–U.S. capital markets and a much greater utilization of these markets by non–U.S. corporations, many of which use them to finance non–U.S. investments.

Foreign bonds have existed for more than a hundred years. These are bonds issued in another country's domestic bond market, denominated in its currency, and subject to its terms and regulations. Bonds of a non–U.S. issuer registered with the Securities and Exchange Commission (SEC) for sale in the U.S. public bond markets are called "Yankee bonds." Bonds of a U.S. company issued in the Japanese domestic market would be called "Samurai bonds. The fees, expenses,

EXHIBIT 7.1

## Capital Market Activity 1996–2000 (US$ billions)

|  | 2000 | 1999 | 1998 | 1997 | 1996 |
|---|---|---|---|---|---|
| **U.S. Domestic New Issues** | | | | | |
| U.S. MTNs | 384.5 | 475.5 | 393.6 | 338.0 | 303.6 |
| Investment-grade debt | 1,211.0 | 1,228.3 | 1,099.5 | 738.4 | 527.6 |
| Collateralized securities | 393.4 | 487.1 | 566.8 | 385.6 | 252.9 |
| Junk and convertibles | 42.2 | 52.7 | 49.2 | 39.9 | 46.6 |
| Municipal debt | 194.0 | 219.0 | 279.8 | 214.6 | 180.2 |
| Total debt | 2,225.1 | 2,462.6 | 2,388.9 | 1,716.5 | 1,310.9 |
| | | | | | |
| Preferred stock | 15.4 | 27.5 | 37.8 | 33.3 | 36.5 |
| Common stock | 189.1 | 164.3 | 115.0 | 120.2 | 115.5 |
| Total equity | 204.5 | 191.7 | 152.7 | 153.4 | 151.9 |
| Total domestic | 2,429.6 | 2,654.4 | 2,541.7 | 1,869.9 | 1,462.8 |
| **International Issues** | | | | | |
| Euro MTNs | 449.8 | 635.3 | 571.8 | 375.1 | 328.9 |
| Euro and foreign bonds | 865.6 | 1,393.9 | 986.9 | 644.6 | 537.4 |
| International equity | 216.7 | 103.0 | 69.0 | 63.7 | 45.1 |
| | | | | | |
| Total international | 1,532.1 | 2,132.2 | 1,627.7 | 1,083.4 | 911.4 |
| | | | | | |
| Worldwide total | 3,961.7 | 4,786.6 | 4,169.4 | 2,953.3 | 2,374.2 |
| **Global Syndicated Bank** | | | | | |
| Loan and note issuance facilities | 1,789.2 | 1,750.0 | 1,223.0 | 1,265.8 | 1,400.0 |

*Source: Investment Dealers' Digest; SIA 2001 Fact Book.*

and interest rates in many non–U.S. countries often make such deals expensive. Foreign bonds are usually quite expensive to issue because of the fees and expenses involved, but also because of the interest-rate structure of the country involved. Also, in recent years, bonds have increasingly been issued in Euro currencies other than the Eurodollar, offering issuers the opportunity, for example, to float a yen-denominated bond in the unregulated Euromarket at a cost of funds that would be lower than that for a Samurai bond issue in Japan. As a result of these two factors, foreign bonds are not frequently issued by corporations (government borrowers use these markets); and consequently this chapter will examine mainly the Eurobond market.

## Eurobonds

Originally, Eurobonds were fixed-rate, unsecured promissory notes denominated in U.S. dollars that were issued by a corporation or a government entity. They were issued outside the United States and therefore were not required to be registered with the SEC or any other national securities authority. Not being registered with the SEC, however, these bonds could not be sold in the United States or to U.S. citizens. Instead, they were sold to non–U.S. residents, principally wealthy individuals and international institutions that wished to invest in high-grade U.S. dollar-denominated securities. Investors paid for the bonds by charging a Eurodollar deposit account in a European bank or a European branch of a U.S. bank. The dollar deposits in banks had accumulated outside the United States (because of the growing U.S. balance-of-payments deficit and regulatory factors); and as most of these were in Europe, they became known as Eurodollar deposit accounts, or "Eurodollars." Once Eurodollars came into existence, they had to be invested in loans or other instruments. Banks sought Eurodollar borrowers, and soon the Eurodollar certificate of deposit appeared. It was only a matter of time before a fixed-rate, medium-term, high-grade instrument denominated in Eurodollars would appear.[1]

### The First Eurobond

The first Eurobond was a $15 million issue for Autostrade, an Italian toll road authority guaranteed by an Italian government agency. The issue was managed in June 1963 by the London firm of S. G. Warburg and comanaged by banks in Belgium, Germany, the Netherlands, and Luxembourg. It was underwritten according to the U.S. underwriting system, in which the issue is announced, syndicated, and marketed for about two weeks before it is priced (as opposed to the British "front end" system, in which the issue is priced, syndicated, and then offered to subscribers, in that order, with the underwriters liable for the unsubscribed portion of the issue). The banks could not offer the bonds to the general public (they were not registered in any of the European countries), but they made them available "privately" to their investment clients, many of whom had granted discretion over their investments to their banks. The bonds were listed on the Luxembourg Stock Exchange, where the banks and their investors could check secondary market prices from time to time.

The Autostrade issue became the prototype for many other issues by various European entities, almost entirely government-related credits. U.S. investment banks with sales offices throughout Europe became active participants in the market, having sharpened their selling skills by distributing foreign bonds issued in the United States by European governments and agencies to investors elsewhere in Europe.

---

[1]Another reason Eurodollars came to be was that certain holders of dollars did not wish to deposit them in the United States or invest them in U.S. securities because they feared the funds might be blocked for political reasons. The Moscow Narodny Bank in London, for example, was an early investor in Eurodollar deposits and Eurobonds.

### Investor Anonymity

U.S. corporates were held in high regard by investors; and when U.S. issuers and their bankers volunteered responsible standards of disclosure and investor protection, these were accepted without question. However, most of the early investors were wealthy families or privately owned businesses, whose financial affairs were managed by banks in Switzerland, Luxembourg, Belgium, France, and, to some extent, the United Kingdom. Many such investors were unwilling to purchase U.S. corporate securities, despite their high regard for the corporation issuing the paper. Their reluctance came partly from the fact that in the United States, issuers were required to withhold part of the required interest payment due to foreigner investors (to ensure that any U.S. taxes due would be paid). The amount withheld could often be reclaimed by filing a tax return in the United States, but few European investors were willing to do that. They were also reluctant to purchase "registered bonds," which required them to disclose their name and address to the issuer, preferring instead bonds payable "to the bearer," which did not require such disclosure. In the United States only registered bonds were available. Eurobond buyers, however, were concerned that the Internal Revenue Service (IRS), the issuer, or some other entity might someday pass information on file about them to the tax officials of their country and reveal wealth or other transactions that the investor was trying to conceal. To attract these investors, there could be no withholding tax and no registered bonds, which meant that U.S. companies would have to issue parent company guaranteed bonds in bearer form through subsidiaries in various tax-haven jurisdictions, usually the Netherlands Antilles. The United States repealed the withholding tax on interest paid to foreigners in 1984, thus ending the requirement for issuing Eurobonds through tax-haven subsidiaries.

***The Eurobond Boom, 1981–1985.*** By 1980 institutional participation in the market was at such a high level that an infrastructure began to develop to support it. Purveyors of such services as bond brokerage (arranging for the sale and the purchase of bonds between dealers), "when issued" trading (or "grey market trading"—buying and selling of primary securities prior to the actual offer date), and bond market research began to arrive in London like waves of an assault force. More capital was committed; more traders and salespeople were hired; and it became important to many banks to be "seen" in the right issues. Some of this was nonsense, but it expanded the market nevertheless as the dollar turned (after tighter monetary policies were introduced in 1979 and Ronald Reagan was elected president in 1980) from a scorned and underappreciated currency to a much admired and overvalued one. In this climate, the Eurobond market soared. The dollar became one of the world's strongest currencies and, unlike strong currencies in the past, yielded very high rates of interest; so the demand for Eurobonds rose to a point where European investors would pay more for a U.S. corporate obligation than U.S. investors would.

***Lower Rates Offered to Issuers.*** This enthusiasm for Eurobonds was spurred by competition; by the expectation that total investment profits would include attractive foreign exchange gains; and by the fact that investors could buy Eurobonds of top-grade U.S. companies free of withholding taxes on interest when they could not buy U.S. Treasury securities on the same basis. So, high-grade corporates became the substitutes for U.S. government securities in the eyes of Euro investors. In the end, a kind of competitive bidding developed between investors to get the top names; and the retail investors, as might be expected, won out—they bid the highest prices or the lowest interest yields for the bonds. Thus, during the 1981-to-1985 period, it was quite common for U.S. companies rated AA and better to borrow 5- to 10-year money in Europe more cheaply than they could in the United States and, in some cases, more cheaply than the U.S. Treasury could. This condition resulted in a surge of Euro issues. In 1982, for example, several U.S. investment banks found that they had sold more corporate bonds at new issue in London than they had in New York—a fact many firms found hard to believe, and few would duplicate after 1983.

*Participation by Institutions.* This feeding frenzy, however, occurred at a time when U.S. nominal interest rates were declining and the dollar was rising. Treasury securities were certainly not unavailable in the United States, as the growing fiscal deficit brought the government to market more and more often. Corporate issuers, forced to compete for investor dollars with government issuers, were nudged toward Europe. It was not important whether an issuer was known as a multinational corporation—many companies that were entirely domestic, including some U.S. public utilities and even savings and loan associations, came in. And the investors began to include insurance companies in Birmingham, bond funds in Lyon, pension fund managers in Melbourne, and agricultural cooperatives in Osaka. Some of these investors had only recently been allowed to invest overseas by their home governments, which, following patterns elsewhere, were dismantling overseas investment restrictions. These institutions were increasingly interested in secondary market liquidity and sophisticated trading ideas, neither of which had been especially important to retail customers, who wanted simple issues of well-known companies that they could hold to maturity.

During the 1980s, the effort to involve the institutions resulted in much emphasis on new investment ideas and market making. Bonds with warrants to purchase additional bonds, zero-coupon bonds, and floating-rate notes appeared at this time. New-issue volume increased, and so did the size of individual issues, from an average below $100 million in 1983, to over $200 million by the end of 1992. Market making, however, was difficult, in part because of the high volume of aggressively priced new issues that often were out of line with secondary-market price levels and because the float in Eurobonds was thin. Though no precise data exist as to the extent of this participation, certain Swiss banks have estimated that during the 1980s, 40 percent to 60 percent of all Eurobonds ultimately found their way into Swiss-managed accounts of individuals, where, for the most part, they were held until maturity. By contrast, less than 5 percent of U.S. corporate bonds are bought by individuals. During this period, opportunities for hedging and borrowing bonds for short-selling by market makers were limited.

## The World's Only Unregulated Capital Market

The Eurobond market is virtually unregulated, but it is subject to self-imposed standards of practice. Eurobonds are typically listed on the London or the Luxembourg stock exchanges to attract investors, and each stock exchange has its own specific disclosure requirements. The issues themselves are typically made subject to U.K. law; and the Association of International Bond Dealers (AIBD), a nongovernmental industry association, sets minimum trading standards.

These standards differ from legal requirements. Whereas individual firms may be regulated by their national authorities, there are no legal requirements on the part of the issuer or bankers to provide for investor protection, orderly markets, or courts of law in which to deal with disputes or abuses. Until 1987, there were no financial regulations that applied to the market, such as queuing, capital requirements for underwriters, or margin rules. However, the Financial Services Act, passed by the British Parliament in 1987, provides for certain capital and other requirements for all Eurobond market participants using London as a base. There is also a draft European Commission (EC) directive proposing minimum capital requirements for securities dealers that would parallel the capital adequacy standards adopted for banks, especially in the area of swaps and other derivative securities.

Market conduct has been self-regulated and, as such, has performed remarkably well. As distinct from normal domestic securities markets, however, the Euromarket is substantially a wholesale market in which sophisticated issuers and investors participate and in which offenders can be punished only by rejection. The market is easy to enter, and competition between dealers has always been sharp. Risk taking, new product innovation, and quick copying are as common in the Euromarket as anywhere in the world. It has never been an easy market in which to make money, due to the need for a substantial commitment of talent and capital. Thus it has tended to be dominated by 25 or so primary players who have set the rules and the procedures that the market must follow. Deals are structured on the basis of what works and what can be replicated in future deals. Recently, large U.S. institutional investors have found the Eurobond market attractive as a source of nondollar investments and arbitrage opportunities to buy securities at larger yield spreads over Treasuries than what is available in the U.S. market for comparable securities (or vice versa).

The absence of regulation and of barriers to competition and the variety of players have made the Eurobond market a hothouse for innovation. Many of the best ideas to influence the U.S. bond markets had their origin in the Eurobond market: the "bought deal," the zero-coupon bond, the floating-rate note, currency option bonds, bonds with swaps, and convertible put bonds are just some of the successful innovations in Europe that have been copied in New York. The section 415 underwriting rules introduced by the SEC in 1984, as part of a general pattern of deregulation, provide virtually immediate access by companies to the U.S. bond market and thus permit the bought deal to be imported to the United

States. Similar rule revisions have occurred elsewhere, especially in Japan, which has imported almost all of its new capital market products during the past 15 years or so.

### The Market Matures

These new Eurobond investors included European pension and insurance funds of U.S. and other companies; bank trust departments; investment companies; supranational financial institutions, such as the World Bank; central banks of various countries; and more frequently, after 1973, Middle East funds managed by Western financial institutions. After the election of Margaret Thatcher in 1979 and the removal of British foreign exchange controls soon thereafter, U.K. investors also began to enter the market, although modestly at first.

Although Eurodollar bond issues have been floated throughout the past 30 years during times of both a strong and a weak dollar, the bulk of market activity has remained in dollars even during times when the dollar has been weak. In contrast to the U.S. bond market, the foreign exchange situation has always had a significant effect on the Eurobond market.

The Eurobond market began to broaden during the latter 1990s, as globally oriented institutions began to participate more actively, especially in the nondollar sector. These institutions were capable of bond arbitrage, using options and futures to hedge positions, and of managing portfolios according to the latest techniques. In addition, they were offered an increasing supply of interesting and relatively liquid investment opportunities euros, yen, and other nondollar instruments.

### Eurobond Issuers

Eurobond issuers represent a vast variety of different governmental and corporate organizations from allover the world, which find capital-raising opportunities in this market to be superior, or supplementary, to markets at home. Supranational institutions (like the World Bank and the European Union [EU]) are frequent borrowers, as are agencies of European, Asian, Australian, Latin American, and other governments. Large banks have used the floating-rate-note (FRN) market, which accounts for about 40 percent of all new issues, to fund their own lending books or for swaps. FRNs pay a rate tied to the London interbank offering rate (LIBOR) and are repriced every three months or so, so as to allow the notes to trade at par. Industrial corporations and their captive finance subsidiaries are also active borrowers.

Bonds are issued in fixed- and floating-rate form, in a variety of currencies, often accompanied by interest-rate or currency swaps. Maturities tend to be less than 10 years, averaging around 5 to 6 years. Most bonds are offered in *plain vanilla* form, that is, with no early call provisions and no sinking funds. Bonds with special features, called *bells and whistles*, are less frequent but appear in force when market conditions are ripe. Most bonds, even those issued by non–U.S. companies and governments, are rated by Moody's and Standard & Poor's. Clearance and settlement of Eurobond trades is generally done on a book entry basis by one of two efficient private companies: Euroclear and Cedel.

The *Financial Times* of London on August 13, 2001, listed 43 bonds in its daily "New International Bond Issues" table, including issues in 6 different currencies (or currency units like the euro).

### Eurobonds with Swaps

It is clear that the United States and the international markets are already very closely linked, not just in terms of the relationship between domestic and Eurodollar interest rates, but also through the newer forms of linkage that the interest-rate and currency-swap markets provide. During the 1980s, a system for swapping interest-rate and foreign currency obligations among debt obligors around the world developed. There is a large market for a company that owes floating-rate debt to swap the interest portion of the debt with another company that has a fixed-rate obligation. Thus, without actually doing a financing, a company can switch its future interest-rate exposure from fixed to floating or vice versa. This is a very useful tool for managing financial liabilities. It is also a useful tool for managing assets—a pension fund investor can swap fixed-interest payments from a bond for a contract to receive a floating rate of interest. Some use swaps more aggressively than that; for example, a AA rated German bank may issue a Eurobond at a very low fixed-interest rate and swap it with a Baa rated issuer like Boston Edison Power Company, a lesser quality credit but one that can still borrow from a bank at a small spread over LIBOR. The Germans want to generate floating-rate funding at a rate *below* LIBOR, which they do by offering an attractively priced fixed-rate obligation to Boston Edison at a premium. Boston Edison can afford this because it cannot, at the time, borrow at a fixed rate in the United States or in Europe on quite as good terms as those offered by the German bank. (See Exhibit 7.2.) A sizable market for swaps of all kinds now exists, and arranging the transactions is not difficult. With such techniques, companies can alter the whole structure of their liabilities on very short notice, or they can use them to lower their costs of funds. It is easy to see how an aggressive banker might line up Boston Edison to do the swap, then immediately offer the sub-LIBOR package to the German bank, the execution of which would provide the banker with an attractive Eurobond issue to lead manage. (The lead managing underwriter, by reason of being the lead, collects the largest fees.)

One can now create "synthetic" dollar assets or liabilities through nondollar bond issues combined with an appropriate currency swap or synthetic fixed-rate securities by combining a floating-rate note with an interest-rate swap. The search for lower-cost liabilities and higher-yielding assets by corporations and financial institutions is extensive, and the spreads between true and synthetic paper are narrowing through arbitrage of these varied and numerous transactions. It is generally believed that around 60 percent of all Eurobond transactions since about 1986 involved swaps of one sort or another.

EXHIBIT 7.2

**An Early Interest-Rate Swap**

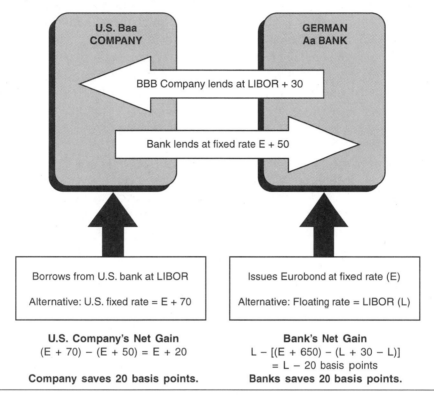

| **U.S. Baa COMPANY** | **GERMAN Aa BANK** |

BBB Company lends at LIBOR + 30

Bank lends at fixed rate E + 50

| Borrows from U.S. bank at LIBOR | Issues Eurobond at fixed rate (E) |
|---|---|
| Alternative: U.S. fixed rate = E + 70 | Alternative: Floating rate = LIBOR (L) |

| **U.S. Company's Net Gain** | **Bank's Net Gain** |
|---|---|
| $(E + 70) - (E + 50) = E + 20$ | $L - [(E + 650) - (L + 30 - L)]$ |
| | $= L - 20$ basis points |
| **Company saves 20 basis points.** | **Banks saves 20 basis points.** |

## New Issue Procedures

In the United States, securities issues must be filed with the SEC, which must declare issues "effective" before they can be sold to the public. To be declared effective, issues must meet disclosure and procedural requirements. In the past, the SEC would routinely take a few weeks to review filings. Today, as a consequence of Rule 415, many companies can file "shelf" registration statements that, when effective, will provide an issuer with the means by which to come to market at any time on very short notice. Issuers must distribute securities through investment bankers acting as underwriters who usually (but not always) will syndicate issues with others. When the issue is ready to be launched, it will be priced and a "fixed" (i.e., nondiscountable by the other underwriters) gross underwriting spread will be established by negotiation between the issuer and the lead underwriter.

Thereafter, the issue will be allocated among underwriters by the lead underwriter. The underwriters will then commence to sell the issue to investors, virtually all of which are experienced institutions that know the secondary market trading levels. All sales to investors must, by terms of the agreements between underwriters, be at the fixed offering price until the lead underwriter "releases" the issue for free trading at whatever price the market may then command.

Issues may be brought as "bought deals," in which one or a few underwriters purchase the entire issue (which may or may not subsequently be syndicated) or through the more traditional practice in which the issue is purchased from the company by the entire syndicate following pricing negotiations. Bought deals may be awarded to the lowest bidder following a competitive process, or they may be awarded without competition if the issuer likes the proposal made to it and wants to avoid taking any risk that the market may move against it before the issue is priced.

In the Eurobond market, there are a number of different practices. There are no requirements for filing an issue with any regulatory bodies except for the listing requirements of the London or the Luxembourg stock exchanges. In earlier years most issues were "mandated" by a corporation to a particular lead manager who would form a syndicate, test the market for a week or two with "road show" visits to principal European cities featuring senior officers of the issuer, and then agree on price and gross spread with the issuer. Today, most issues are bought deals that are mandated to the underwriter offering the best net cost of funds in the currency that is ultimately desired by the issuer.

## Eurobond Pricing

In the Euromarket, "traditional" (but now rapidly fading) practices mandate a gross spread of $1^7/8$ percent to a seven-year issue such as the example given in Exhibit 7.2. However, this extremely high gross spread is largely fictional to all but the continental European bankers participating as underwriters in the deal. Only these banks can hope to retain the full spread because they simply put the bonds into their clients' accounts at a price of 100 percent, with the $1^7/8$ percent difference between the price at which the banks were able to acquire the bonds, that is, representing the bank's profit. But to maintain a $1^7/8$ percent spread and still provide a competitive cost of funds to the issuer (7.31 percent), the bank must lower the coupon to 6.85 percent (which at 98.125 percent yields 7.31 percent over five years). This is so because while private clients or retail investors might accept a yield of 6.85 percent on the bonds, institutions, which focus on secondary market trading levels and required spreads over Treasury securities, would not. This difference in pricing results in a two-tiered pricing structure.

The fixed-price offer method essentially takes the pricing structure for the sale of Eurobonds to institutional investors and locks it into an agreement among underwriters not to sell at any other price so as to preserve the spread. However, it also eliminates the 0.125 percent "praecipium," or special portion of the management fee due to the lead manager, and the practice of charging all the aftermarket stabilization expenses to the other underwriters, practices of the Eurobond market that came to be much disliked. The far more transparent fixed-price method is virtually identical to the method used to price issues in the U.S. market. But to win the mandate, the lead underwriter probably has to come up with a rate to the issuer below 7.30 percent. There are several ways this can be done.

First, an investor somewhere in the world—in Japan or the Middle East, for example—might be found that was prepared to purchase the bonds at a lower yield, thereby allowing the underwriter room to lower the cost of funds to the company. Sometimes before bidding, an underwriter will spend the preceding night scouring investors in different time zones to see if demand can be found at the better price levels. Often, it can.

Second, the underwriter may find a way to create a synthetic dollar bond, using swaps that cost the company less than 7.30 percent. Again, the underwriter scans the world for an opportunity to issue bonds in, say, Australian dollars and simultaneously to enter into a US$/Australian$ currency swap to obtain a lower cost of funds. There are many possibilities on any given day, and many must be checked out in detail. The underwriter could also decide to purchase the bond from the company at an aggressive rate, say at break-even, or 7.25 percent, because it is convinced that interest rates will decline and that its profit will be "bailed out" by the rising market, an event that is not always assured.

Third, the underwriter may decide to offer to purchase the bonds at an even lower rate, say below 7.25 percent, because of an opportunity to use it in connection with a favorably priced swap transaction or simply as a means to buy market share.

Because bond markets around the world have been subject to extensive integration through arbitrage trading and institutional participation, the bonds can be sold at the same yield in all the markets, though demand will vary from place to place for a variety of reasons, including currency, rating, and maturity preferences.

## Using the Eurobond Market

The Eurobond market is accustomed to operating on a competitive-bidding, bought-deal basis with relatively little, if any, prepricing delays for market building. When an issuer is a company that is not very well known to major European institutional investors or private bankers, some reluctance can be encountered to proceeding on this basis. Instead a more conventional underwriting syndicate may be required, with time allowed for "road shows" and market development efforts. For this reason, especially if the company is a first-time user of the market or a borderline credit, it is a good idea to get to know some of the major U.S. or European Eurobond underwriters well before the time for an issue arises. After a deal has been announced, it is time enough to solicit interest and ideas from these underwriters in all or a part of the permanent financing. When the time arrives, the following steps, when appropriate, can make the process of using the Eurobond market more useful and simple.

• Establish the amount and the maturity of the issue needed to provide optimal permanent financing. The Eurobond market is most active in the five-to-seven-year maturity area, with longer-term issues more difficult to place, especially for less well known names. Think of each issue size as being limited to $100 million to $250 million. So for large transactions it may be necessary to sell more than one issue.

• Find out what a fair price would be for such bonds in the United States (or other home-country market). Calculate this in terms of "all-in" cost of funds to the issuer, in terms of the number of basis points over the comparable maturity of U.S. Treasuries. This spread over Treasuries becomes the benchmark on which the company hopes to be able to improve in using the Eurobond market.

• Ask the bankers if they can match or beat the benchmark. Be sure to ask at least one European bank with high Euromarket standing but comparatively less standing in the company's domestic market. Encourage the bankers to come up with their best ideas, and be prepared not to shop those ideas that the bankers declare to be "proprietary."

• Ask also for floating-rate to fixed-rate swap quotes—it may be cheapest of all to finance the transaction in the U.S. commercial paper or medium-term notes market accompanied by such a swap.

• Ask for suggestions for nondollar Eurobond issues with simultaneous currency swaps to return the obligation to U.S. dollars.

## The 144a Private Placement Market

In April 1990 the U.S. SEC approved its Rule 144a, through which it permitted sales of securities not registered with the SEC to qualified institutional investors. Such sales are made through "private placements," are exempt from registration with the SEC and, therefore, do not involve the full disclosure requirements. This rule was developed on the theory that large, sophisticated investors can look out for themselves and because the United States wanted to attract more international issuers to its capital markets. In practice the rule was helpful to non–U.S. governments and corporations that were seeking to use the U.S. debt markets but did not want to incur the accounting and legal expenses required of a public company issuer and did not want to be committed to U.S. disclosure requirements. Now such issuers can arrange a private placement, often on an underwritten basis, to sell to U.S. institutions unregistered securities that may be traded in the market.

## Some Creative Cross-Border Financing Ideas

Over the years a number of creative financing ideas have been applied to cross-border acquisitions and other investments. Often, it is most desirable to hedge the foreign exchange exposure inherent in the transaction, or to take advantage of a strong positive cash flow in a particular currency, by denominating the debt in the currency of the target company's country. Such debt can be obtained by issuing a Eurobond in the desired currency or by swapping dollar financing obligations into the other currency. Such decisions, however, are very sensitive to tax issues—sometimes it is possible to structure an acquisition so as to be able to deduct interest expense in two different tax jurisdictions at the same time ("double dipping"). Before new permanent borrowing programs are undertaken, the plans should be scrutinized from a tax perspective.

The borrowing can be made with traditional banks, local banks, or new international banks, depending on whose rates are the most attractive. Some banks offer multicurrency lines, or swap facilities, to facilitate below-market rates (e.g., borrowing in dollars, swapping into Deutsche marks, and gaining a rate advantage over local Deutsche mark borrowing rates). Most banks will require parent company guarantees, or comfort letters, depending on the creditworthiness of the affiliate.

For companies with access to capital markets, the range of options for securing debt financing is considerably increased. Such firms can issue securities in the U.S. public bond or private placement markets under Rule 144a (enabling foreign companies to avoid U.S. SEC accounting and reporting requirements) or in the Eurobond market. Bond market issues can also be combined with swaps to offer "synthetic" securities that may be more attractive than the real thing.

One example of this is an issue in euros undertaken by the Disney Corporation, which was swapped with a French government entity that had financed in the domestic Japanese bond market (Samurai bonds) to raise yen. The French borrower did not need the yen, which it got cheaply, and instead wanted euros. Disney needed yen to build Tokyo Disneyland, from which it would generate a sizable yen cash flow in the future. The solution was to have Disney borrow euros though a Eurobond and swap the repayment obligation with the French entities for its obligation to repay yen. If Disney had issued Euroyen, which it could have done at the time, its net borrowing rate would have been higher than the swapped rate. As a result, Disney was able to borrow yen cheaper than the Japanese government could have done at the time.

There are many variations of this theme—one needs to check all the markets and pick the best deal, but sometimes companies overlook markets they might be able to use. In 1991, Harsco Corporation, a midsized U.S. manufacturing company, acquired Multiserve S.A. from a U.S. leveraged buyout (LBO) group. Multiserve operated a large number of metal recovery plants outside the United States. The purchase price was in dollars and was fully financed with bank loans. After the acquisition, Harsco identified a number of ways to reduce costs, including refinancing some debt and transferring it to a different tax jurisdiction, and utilizing nondollar cash flows wherever possible to take advantage of lower nondollar borrowing costs. After a year or so, the bank financing (a multicurrency revolver and term loan structure) was replaced by U.S. commercial paper and medium-term bonds issued in the U.S. market through a competitive bidding under a shelf registration. The company considered Eurobond financing, but on that occasion the U.S. market was more attractive.

A number of large non–U.S. companies have financed U.S. acquisitions in the U.S. public bond markets, but many others have done so in the U.S. private placements market (l44a), where bankers underwrite a transaction as if it were a public issue, domestically and in the Eurobond markets. The 144a market is perfect for non–U.S. companies that are not well equipped to file registration statements with the SEC or that are not well known in Europe.

In the United States, many such foreign companies have financed direct investments (including acquisitions) through municipal revenue bonds, leveraged leasing transactions, limited partnerships, and other such special arrangements and procedures. Some companies have also tapped the public and the private markets for junk bonds, medium-term notes, and asset-backed securities.

## International Equity Securities

International equity securities transactions have expanded enormously since the mid-1980s, as reflected in the substantial increase of cross-exchange transactions in secondary markets, cross-border mergers and acquisitions, and new issues offered to investors through one of several different "globalized" distribution techniques. Total such foreign share trading exceeded $16 trillion in 2000, up from less than $1.8 trillion in 1986—a growth rate of 17 percent. The United States has been prominently involved in these developments: total worldwide purchases by foreigners of U.S. shares also expanded at a compound growth rate of 25.5% for the 20-year period 1980 to 2000; however, U.S. purchases of foreign equity securities grew at a 30.4 percent compound rate.[2] Global equity market capitalization has also grown during the past several years, from $7.8 trillion in 1987 to more than $32.2 trillion in 2000 (see Exhibit 7.3).

## Behind the Growth

This extraordinary growth in the appetite for international stocks has not been limited to issues from the United States, Japan, and the major European countries. Shares from other European countries, both West and East, and from a variety of new emerging markets, from Argentina to the People's Republic of China, are in demand. These developments reflect the many factors that have led toward the integration of capital markets around the world: powerful forces such as the opening up of national markets through various deregulatory processes; substantial improvements in financial reporting, information gathering, and dissemination

---

[2]Derived by the Federal Reserve Bank of Atlanta from U.S. Department of the Treasury, *U.S. Treasury Bulletin* (Winter 1991), Table CM-V-5; (Winter 1981), Table CM-VI-10; *SIA Fact Book 2001.*

EXHIBIT 7.3

## Global Equity Markets Capitalization
### (Market value in US$ billions)

| | Australia | Canada | France | Germany | Hong Kong | Italy | Japan | Netherlands | Singapore | Switzerland | United Kingdom | United States | Developed Markets | Emerging Markets | World |
|---|---|---|---|---|---|---|---|---|---|---|---|---|---|---|---|
| 1980 | 60 | 118 | 55 | 72 | 39 | 25 | 380 | 29 | 24 | 38 | 205 | 1,448 | 2,552 | 186 | 2,738 |
| 1981 | 54 | 106 | 38 | 63 | 39 | 24 | 418 | 23 | 35 | 35 | 181 | 1,333 | 2,413 | 163 | 2,576 |
| 1982 | 42 | 104 | 28 | 69 | 19 | 20 | 417 | 26 | 31 | 37 | 196 | 1,520 | 2,579 | 149 | 2,728 |
| 1983 | 55 | 141 | 38 | 83 | 17 | 21 | 565 | 34 | 16 | 43 | 226 | 1,898 | 3,218 | 166 | 3,384 |
| 1984 | 49 | 135 | 41 | 78 | 24 | 26 | 667 | 31 | 12 | 39 | 243 | 1,863 | 3,296 | 146 | 3,442 |
| 1985 | 60 | 147 | 79 | 184 | 35 | 59 | 979 | 59 | 11 | 90 | 328 | 2,325 | 4,497 | 171 | 4,667 |
| 1986 | 95 | 166 | 150 | 258 | 54 | 140 | 1,842 | 84 | 17 | 132 | 440 | 2,637 | 6,276 | 238 | 6,513 |
| 1987 | 106 | 219 | 172 | 213 | 54 | 120 | 2,803 | 86 | 18 | 129 | 681 | 2,589 | 7,499 | 332 | 7,831 |
| 1988 | 138 | 242 | 245 | 252 | 74 | 135 | 3,907 | 114 | 24 | 141 | 771 | 2,794 | 9,228 | 500 | 9,728 |
| 1989 | 141 | 291 | 365 | 365 | 77 | 169 | 4,393 | 158 | 36 | 171 | 827 | 3,506 | 10,967 | 745 | 11,713 |
| 1990 | 109 | 242 | 314 | 355 | 83 | 149 | 2,918 | 120 | 34 | 160 | 849 | 3,059 | 8,795 | 604 | 9,400 |
| 1991 | 149 | 267 | 348 | 393 | 122 | 159 | 3,131 | 136 | 48 | 174 | 988 | 4,088 | 10,447 | 898 | 11,346 |
| 1992 | 145 | 243 | 351 | 348 | 172 | 129 | 2,399 | 135 | 49 | 195 | 927 | 4,485 | 9,941 | 991 | 10,933 |
| 1993 | 205 | 327 | 456 | 463 | 385 | 136 | 3,000 | 182 | 133 | 272 | 1,152 | 5,136 | 12,341 | 1,676 | 14,017 |
| 1994 | 219 | 315 | 451 | 471 | 270 | 180 | 3,720 | 283 | 135 | 284 | 1,210 | 5,067 | 13,218 | 1,897 | 15,115 |
| 1995 | 245 | 366 | 522 | 577 | 304 | 210 | 3,667 | 356 | 148 | 434 | 1,408 | 6,858 | 15,877 | 1,911 | 17,788 |
| 1996 | 312 | 486 | 591 | 671 | 449 | 258 | 3,089 | 379 | 150 | 402 | 1,740 | 8,484 | 18,005 | 2,248 | 20,253 |
| 1997 | 296 | 568 | 674 | 825 | 413 | 345 | 2,217 | 469 | 106 | 575 | 1,996 | 11,309 | 20,949 | 2,167 | 23,116 |
| 1998 | 329 | 543 | 991 | 1,094 | 343 | 570 | 2,496 | 603 | 94 | 689 | 2,374 | 13,451 | 25,093 | 1,855 | 26,948 |
| 1999 | 428 | 801 | 1,475 | 1,432 | 609 | 728 | 4,547 | 695 | 198 | 693 | 2,933 | 16,635 | 32,997 | 3,152 | 36,149 |
| 2000 | 373 | 841 | 1,447 | 1,270 | 623 | 768 | 3,157 | 640 | 153 | 792 | 2,577 | 15,104 | 29,521 | 2,740 | 32,260 |

*Source: SIA 2001 Fact Book.*

technology; and greatly improved trading environments. The growing involvement of major financial institutions, especially those from the United States and Japan, as investors and providers of services to the markets reflects a substantial change in the behavior of these institutions from the more conservative practices prior to 1980, during which investment horizons were mostly limited to domestic markets.

### Market Liberalization and Deregulation

The much-resisted abolition of fixed commission rates by the New York Stock Exchange (NYSE) in May 1975—an event then called "Mayday"—generated a number of fundamental changes in the way equity markets operate all over the world. The basic principle was that a stock exchange could not operate as a private club with rules that prevented market access by nonmembers and required fixed minimum, nonnegotiable per-share commission rates, irrespective of trading volume.

As institutional trading grew during the 1960s, many large investors began to complain about the high cost of commissions and about their inability to recover these commissions by becoming members of the exchange. The SEC and the Antitrust Division of the U.S. Justice Department took an interest in the issue and ultimately forced the NYSE to rescind its minimum commission rules, to allow foreign brokerage firms to become members, and to include nonmembers on its board of directors. Immediately after these rule changes, institutional commission rates plummeted (they are now down to less than 5 percent of pre-Mayday levels on large institutional transactions), and many firms were required to reorganize and to improve their competitive capabilities. In response to such pressures, NYSE member firms introduced many innovations and provided much more extensive and valuable services to customers, thereby considerably improving the quality and the efficiency of the markets. In 1975, the daily trading volume on the NYSE, which accounted for 85 percent of all shares traded in the United States, was 18.6 million shares, annual market turnover was valued at $127 billion, and the market capitalization of listed companies was $134 billion. By 2000, daily trading volume averaged 1 billion shares, annual market turnover was $8.8 trillion, and market capitalization was $12.4 trillion. On the other hand, the development of electronic, screen-based markets like the National Association of Securities Dealers Automated Quotation Service (Nasdaq) increased regional exchange trading; and off-market trading arrangements had reduced the NYSE share of total U.S. equity trading to about 50 percent.[3]

The Mayday effect was not lost on other countries. In the late 1970s, the Labour Government in Britain instituted a lawsuit against the London Stock Exchange (LSE), alleging that its clublike operations were in restraint of trade. The Conservative Government of Margaret Thatcher inherited this lawsuit and settled it with the exchange in 1983. Under the terms of the settlement, the LSE

[3]*New York Stock Exchange Yearbook* (New York: New York Stock Exchange, 1975, 2000); *SIA Fact Book 2001.*

agreed by October 27, 1986, to abolish membership restrictions and the requirement that members act only in a "single capacity," that is, either as dealers or as
brokers, but not as both. This settlement changed the economics of the U.K.
securities business fundamentally and led to what the British press called the "Big
Bang" in London, a total transformation of the equity market in the United
Kingdom. Under the new system that replaced the old rules, any qualified firm
(including commercial and merchant banks and foreign securities firms) could join
the LSE, firms could act as both brokers and dealers (as in New York), and
commission rates were fully negotiable.

The Bank of England, wishing to take advantage of the coming changes to
improve the efficiency of capital markets in the United Kingdom (especially for
government securities and in anticipation of large privatization issues to come) and
to firm up London's position as Europe's most active financial center, also contributed to the reregulation of London financial markets by revising the capital
requirements for market making in government and corporate debt securities and
in equities. And the British Parliament passed a landmark, omnibus securities
regulation bill, the Financial Securities Act of 1986, to set up an institutional
framework for securities market regulation.

In consequence, trading volume in the United Kingdom more than doubled;
commissions were slashed; many of the British brokers and dealers merged into
other, stronger groups; competition increased greatly; and large integrated securities firms, such as S. G. Warburg, Merrill Lynch, and Goldman Sachs, increased
their market share. The benefits of the reforms, as in the early days after Mayday
in New York, were seen to flow mainly to the users of securities market services
at the expense of the providers of such services. The competitive difficulties caused
by the Big Bang were heightened after the worldwide stock market crash of
October 17, 1987.

The rest of Europe was very mindful of the market changes in London. By
this time, preparations were underway for the implementation by the EU of the
Single Market Act by the end of 1992; and the Commission was in the process
of promulgating directives for the future conduct of banking and other financial
services. Liberalization to accommodate greater competition was the key to the
EU reforms, and in all countries some form of financial market deregulation
occurred. Extensive changes, though far less comprehensive than had occurred in
Britain, were made in France, Germany, Italy, and Switzerland. Similar changes
were adopted in Canada, Australia, and New Zealand, and ultimately in Japan,
where regulatory changes were more difficult to enact because of a competitive
impasse between banks and securities firms that had been separated by Article 65
of the Securities and Exchange Law of 1947.

In general, a decade after the Big Bang settlement was reached, the principles
of open access and negotiated commissions were adopted (at least in significant
measure) by almost all countries in which important stock exchanges existed. In
Japan, fixed commissions still existed, but a system of progressively increasing
discounts for large trades in effect did away with minimum rates by 1992. This
wide acceptance of competitive and regulatory practices reflects a degree of global

convergence that had not occurred before, one that has become increasingly difficult for individual countries to oppose. This is because market forces can now create alternative trading venues to one that is blocked by local regulation. If Britain should impose a stamp tax on stock trading, much of the LSE trading business would be conducted somewhere else, for example, in New York, where over-the-counter market makers can quote tax-free prices to U.K. investors. Rather than lose its stock market business to New York, the British would be more likely to drop the stamp tax. Countries now lobby other countries to offer reciprocal access to financial services markets or otherwise suffer denial of such access to financial services by nationals of their country. For example, if the Japanese should deny access to the Tokyo Stock Exchange (TSE) to brokers from the United Kingdom, the Japanese would run the risk of having access to the various London markets denied to Japanese banks and brokers. Between market forces and political pressures, it has become extremely difficult for any country to drag its feet indefinitely in opposition to the emerging global standard of stock market reforms.

### Improved Information Flows

Advances in information and communications technology have been essential to the growth in the international equities markets. Market information of all types is now available internationally, through newspapers, screens, and contact with brokers. Securities can also be traded internationally in most Organization for Economic Cooperation and Development (OECD) countries with a high degree of reliance on trouble-free payment and delivery, which was rarely the case before 1980 when dealing outside the United States, the United Kingdom, and Canada. It is now possible to receive by telephone, from just about anywhere, a reliable quote on virtually any stock whose home market is one of the major financial centers. Quotes are also available for securities from many other countries on very short notice.

The computerization of various national markets, such as in Britain, France, Switzerland, and Germany, has introduced a variety of new technological capabilities for screen trading, futures and options transactions, and paperless trading that did not exist before the Big Bang. These developments have had the effect of linking international marketplaces, making possible a level of expansion that probably could not otherwise have occurred.

With these developments has come a large increase in the number of trained professionals who provide the many services needed to sustain a growing market. These services include such front office activities as providing investment research information (about an increasing number of different companies and securities from an increasing number of countries); block and program trading and portfolio insurance services offered to institutional clients; indexing and other services offered to investment companies and mutual funds; and an increasing use of derivative securities for customer risk-management programs. Internal and back office capabilities include various firmwide exposure-risk-management and hedging functions; optimal financing of trading positions; improved payment and settlement activities; and more efficient record keeping, management control, and information services.

### Better Trading Markets

Trading markets in international equity securities have improved steadily since the early 1980s. Before then, secondary trading in international stocks was limited. The level of trading activity in the home markets, especially in continental Europe, was often low and liquidity was limited. The American Depository Receipt (ADR) market was useful for some stocks, mainly British, Japanese, and Canadian; but prices were still set in the home market, and gradually U.S. investors shifted their business there. A few multinational companies were listed on the New York, Toronto, or London exchanges; but trading volumes in foreign markets were rarely significant compared to the home market. Frequently, foreign companies chose not to list on the NYSE because of the expense and the awkward disclosure requirements associated with becoming an SEC "reporting company." Many of such companies instead passively allowed their shares to be traded in the Nasdaq system or in over-the-counter markets by firms specializing in international stocks.

For years, the principal international trading activity was foreign stock arbitrage, in which one would buy an ADR[4] of, say, a Dutch stock and simultaneously sell the number of underlying shares represented by the ADR in Amsterdam. To do this profitably, one needed to be a master of the details involved. The purchase in dollars after commissions must cost less than the proceeds of the sale of the shares, after commissions and transfer expenses and after the foreign exchange costs of converting back into dollars. Such arbitrage activities have kept prices of international shares around the world in line with their home-market values.

The next development was to provide improved market-making services to customers interested in buying foreign securities that were not available on exchanges. For example, a U.S. pension fund might want to buy shares in Fujitsu Ltd., which was not listed on any U.S. exchange or on the Nasdaq, but for which ADRs were available. The pension fund might call a Japanese broker based in New York, who could say, "We will take your order and purchase Fujitsu shares in Japan overnight. We will confirm tomorrow and tell you at what dollar price the order was executed. We will then deposit the shares with the agent bank in Japan and have ADRs put into your account in New York." Alternatively, the pension fund might call a U.S. market maker in Fujitsu and be told, "We will sell you Fujitsu-dollar ADRs right now for \$x." If the U.S. broker does not have Fujitsu ADRs in inventory, it will try to buy them in the New York market or to trade with a Japanese broker overnight to get the shares to deliver to the pension fund. The market maker's price will reflect the various uncertainties with which it must

---

[4]ADRs are issued by a U.S. bank reflecting a deposit with the bank abroad of shares of a foreign stock. The ADRs are quoted and traded in the United States, and transactions are settled and dividends are paid in dollars as a convenience to U.S. investors. However, many institutions today prefer to own the underlying shares directly so as to have access to the home-country trading markets.

contend. Such international block-trading services are popular with major U.S. and European institutional investors. Certain stocks have become international favorites, and the U.S. and British firms offer research coverage of them. These services are offered to investors all over Europe and in Japan. Over time the trading volume in international equities has built up considerably and pricing tightened up accordingly.

With foreign membership now available on exchanges in Europe and the Far East, as well as in North America, it is possible for participating firms to be active market makers in U.S., European, and Asian stocks around the clock. Such firms are able to balance orders from around the world, not just from their home market. They are also able to limit their market-making activities to stocks for which they see international demand, without finding themselves in the position of being a market maker for all comers, as some national dealers feel they must do. The commitment to dealing in international equities by major firms is now very substantial and is reflected in the number of personnel that have been added in research, trading, sales coverage, systems, back office, and foreign exchange by major U.S., British, Japanese, and other firms. A very large increase in market infrastructure has occurred, which not only makes improved services possible but also provides competitive energy in the market as all of these new employees seek to advance their careers. The result of these developments has been a substantial increase in the value of worldwide equity trading activities, which jumped more than eightfold from $5.8 trillion in 1987 to $47.9 trillion in 2000.

### In Europe

The improvement in access to market making for international shares is also very important. In London, increasing interest in continental European stocks on the part of British, U.S., and Japanese institutional investors has caused many London-based market makers to offer French, German, Dutch, Italian, and Swiss shares through the LSE's Stock Exchange Automated Quotation (SEAQ) system. Many European shares are now listed in London, where reportedly more than 50 percent of all European cross-exchange share trading now occurs. SEAQ, which is similar to the Nasdaq in the United States, claims to handle as much as three-quarters of all trading in blue-chip shares based in Holland, half those in France and Italy, and a quarter of those based in Germany, though these figures are subject to some double counting due to interdealer purchases and sales.[5] Approximately half of the total trading volume in SEAQ, however, is now provided by trading in non–U.K. shares.

The diversion of this business to London has encouraged continental European markets to accelerate long overdue internal reforms, to consolidate local and regional exchanges into a single national market (this has recently been completed in Germany and Switzerland), to optimize efficiencies, and to encourage innovations and competition to recapture market share. Futures and options exchanges

---

[5] "Too Many Trading Places," *The Economist*, June 19, 1993, 21–23.

have also been opened in Paris, Frankfurt, and Zurich and recently in Madrid and Milan; and the use of equity-based derivatives is rapidly increasing. New market developments and innovations in New York or London are often copied quickly in these other markets, and trading volumes are rising.

The SEAQ system benefits from being the first European electronic trading system in place and from being located at the hub of European institutional trading activity, where U.S. presence is greatly felt. It has some disadvantages, though: it still depends on local market prices for its activities; it is subject to certain nontransparent LSE market-making practices for large blocks of securities that detract from market efficiency; and its settlement practices are considerably less modern than some of the newer continental exchanges.

Market capitalization of the various European stock markets has grown steadily since 1983. It is not inconceivable that some trading in European stocks could migrate to other, more competitive marketplaces; but for the moment the massive English-speaking trading infrastructure, the regulatory environment, and the relative size of the London market compared to other European markets indicate a continuing advantage for market makers to remain in London. While competition between London and the other markets continues, the ultimate EU goal is a single, integrated European market, at least for professional investors.

## Growth of Pension Funds

Much of the new money flowing into the international equity market has been from pension funds. These have continued to enjoy a substantial inflow of funds each year, especially in Europe and Japan, where the practice of providing for retirement benefits through market returns is more recent than in the United States. Not only have total pension assets grown, but (for reasons discussed later) there has also been a substantial increase in the percentage of total assets invested in foreign securities. As depicted in Exhibit 7.4, this has been true for pension funds in countries all over the world.

Japanese pension funds especially have been growing very rapidly as the country adjusts to an aging population that has not had sufficient pension programs in the past. An increasing amount of this money, which is managed by insurance companies and trust banks (and recently opened to foreign money managers), is invested in international equities. As Japanese money managers become more familiar with international portfolio management practices (which vary considerably from portfolio management practices in Japan), the Japanese are expected to become increasingly important in the international investment field.

## New Issues and Distribution Methods

Shares offered to the market for the first time are called *new issues*. Generally the term refers to shares newly issued by a corporation that are sold to the public

EXHIBIT 7.4

**World's Pension Assets**

Cross-Border Investment—1990/1995/2000 (US$ billions)

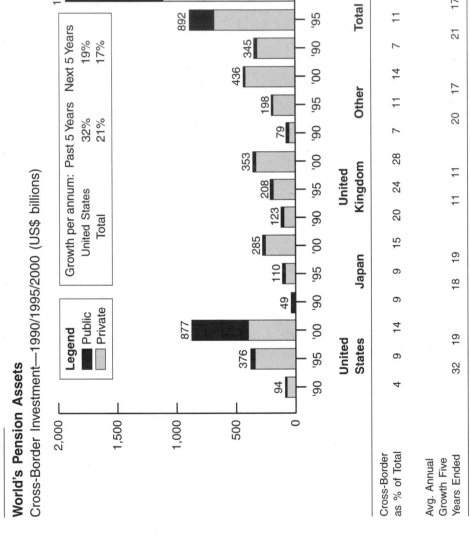

|  | Growth per annum: | Past 5 Years | Next 5 Years |
|---|---|---|---|
|  | United States | 32% | 19% |
|  | Total | 21% | 17% |

Legend
■ Public
▨ Private

|  | United States | | | Japan | | | United Kingdom | | | Other | | | Total | | |
|---|---|---|---|---|---|---|---|---|---|---|---|---|---|---|---|
|  | '90 | '95 | '00 | '90 | '95 | '00 | '90 | '95 | '00 | '90 | '95 | '00 | '90 | '95 | '00 |
| Cross-Border as % of Total | 4 | 9 | 14 | 9 | 9 | 15 | 20 | 24 | 28 | 7 | 11 | 14 | 7 | 11 | 15 |
| Avg. Annual Growth Five Years Ended |  | 32 | 19 |  | 18 | 19 |  | 11 | 11 |  | 20 | 17 |  | 21 | 17 |

*Source:* InterSec Research Corp.

through an underwritten distribution and that are subject to applicable disclosure, registration, and other regulations pertaining to new issues. When these shares are sold, they are said to constitute a *primary offering*, because they are being sold for the first time. Shares offered for sale by an existing shareholder are done so in the *secondary market*, which is where ordinary brokerage transactions occur. However, when a large existing shareholder sells shares through a public distribution (as in the case of a privatization issue by a government shareholder), the process is called a *secondary offering*, and it too is usually subject to the same regulations as a new issue. International equity issues have been a growing and continually active part of international capital markets since the mid-1980s.

Most distributions are made by a group of underwriters; that is, the underwriters guarantee the sale of a specified number of shares at a specified price and commission; that is all the underwriters do. The distribution (or sale) of the securities to investors is the responsibility of brokers, who may or may not be among the underwriters. Some distributions, especially smaller private placements that are usually exempt from national disclosure and registration requirements, are made directly with institutional investors on a "best efforts" basis and do not have to be underwritten, although private placements often are. Underwriting methods are discussed in the next section.

There are several methods for achieving international distribution of new issues of equity securities:

### International Tranches

Issuers may tap equity markets in other countries through an international tranche to supplement domestic market liquidity. U.S. companies are common users of international tranches, in which the underwriters set aside 15 percent to 25 percent of the shares to be offered simultaneously with the U.S. distribution in the Euro-equity market by a separate group of international underwriters. The international underwriters are usually led by the international affiliate of the lead U.S. underwriter to ensure tight control over the allocation of shares. Shares allocated to the international underwriters may not, by agreement, be sold in the United States, and vice versa. International underwriters, except for the U.S. lead manager(s), are not included among the underwriters of the domestic U.S. offering.

### Euro-Equity Issues

There is an equity equivalent of the Eurobond market, called the *Euro-equity* market, that can be used when an issuer wishes to tap a different and larger investor base because its domestic market is insufficient to meet the requirements of domestic participants or as a way to avoid domestic market regulations and expenses. As in the case of the Eurobond market, the lack of regulation, the relatively low cost of issuance, and the presence of a large, highly diversified and very liquid pool of international investment funds has attracted many issuers from all over the world.

The Euro-equity market evolved to provide a source of equity finance for European issuers whose domestic market was too small or too inactive to accommodate large institutionally oriented distributions. Equity issues might be indigestible if offered only in the home country of the companies. Government privatization issues almost always fall into this category because of their large size and the need to attract institutional investors with adequate market liquidity. Almost all of the countries in Western Europe have taken advantage of the opportunity on privatization issues of large industrial companies owned by the governments. Privatization issues by non-European governments, such as the sale of shares in the Argentine national oil company, YPF, or the Shanghai Petrochemical Company, rarely are attempted without heavy reliance on the Euro-equity market.

### Rule 144a Placements

Rule 144a applies to both debt and equity securities, though in the beginning very few 144a equity issuers appeared because the Euro-equity market was an effective competitor for issuers seeking foreign investors and because the U.S. investors had not yet fully warmed up to international equities. As they did, they became especially interested in issuers from *emerging markets*, for example, third world countries with promising economic potential, the growth-stock markets of the future. Soon U.S. institutions were eager investors in debt and equity issues from Mexico, Chile, Argentina, and, in early 1993, Brazil and Peru. Other countries of interest at this time included Indonesia, Philippines, Portugal, Greece, Turkey, and Poland. Few (if any) companies from these countries could meet U.S. SEC registration requirements. During 1992, more than $5.5 billion of 144a equity issues occurred, approximately 48 percent of which were international issues.[6] The 144a total was only a small percentage (7.3 percent) of total U.S. equity issues, but a somewhat more significant percentage (24.3 percent) of total international equity new issues.

Today most Euro-equity issues, have a provision for sale of the securities to U.S. investors through Rule 144a tranches.

## Underwriting Methods

Underwriting is the process of assuring an issuer that an offering will occur for a specified number of shares at a specified price per share. It is in effect an insurance policy (hence the term *underwriter*). But what is being insured can vary greatly depending on which underwriting method is employed. The methods differ between the U.S. market, the Euro-equity market, and the traditional British market. Virtually all national markets utilize one or the other (or a combination) of these methods.

### Underwriting in the United States

In the United States, underwriting procedures are designed to obtain the highest price for the seller of the securities being offered. This is done by forming a

---

[6]Securities Data Corporation, July 1993.

syndicate of securities firms that will agree to purchase the shares from the issuer and resell the shares immediately to investors. The price is not fixed until just before the offering is made to the public, after a period during which well-briefed sales personnel from the underwriters have marketed the issue to their customers. The customers are not committed to purchase shares until they accept the final price, but salespeople talk to them about probable price levels to make judgments as to where and how much they will buy. This process is called "building a book" and is essential to precise pricing efforts. A successfully priced issue is one in which the entire issue is sold out at the agreed offering price and the issue opens for trading at a premium of no more than about 10 percent. The underwriting syndicate in such an issue is exposed only to a minimal holding period between the purchase and the confirmation of sales with customers. Of course if the issue is mispriced or if the market changes before the distribution is complete, underwriters can suffer losses.

To minimize these risks and to provide strong potential support in the aftermarket, underwriters generally overallot shares and companies usually agree to provide the underwriters with a "Green Shoe option." Under such an option (named for the company first employing it, the underwriters may call on the company to increase the size of the issue by an additional 10 percent to 15 percent. The lead underwriter will allocate to the selling brokers (based on their reported orders for shares) 10 percent to 15 percent more shares than are actually being issued. Thus the lead manager, on behalf of the underwriting syndicate, has gone "short" shares, having sold shares it did not own but is still required to deliver. Almost all underwritings involve some degree of short position that the lead manager covers by purchasing shares in the aftermarket to stabilize the offering price. If demand for the shares is weak, it will purchase unsold or unwanted shares in the market (from the other underwriters or its customers) to support the offering at the original offering price. If the demand is strong, the underwriters will exercise the Green Shoe option to create the shares to cover the short position; otherwise they would have to buy them in the market at a premium price because of the strong demand for the shares. Paying a premium for the shares substantially increases the cost to the underwriters of covering their short position. In exchange for granting the Green Shoe option, the issuer expects tighter and more aggressive pricing for the issue.

From the issuer's point of view, there are some negatives associated with the U.S. underwriting procedures. First, the market risk stays with the issuer while the issue is being prepared for the market; the seller must register the shares with the SEC and wait a few weeks for authorization to proceed with the offering. Nothing can be done about this delay; but under the U.S. underwriting method, any market decline during the SEC review period is the issuer's risk, not the underwriter's. (It is possible to issue new equity securities under the shelf registration procedures established by SEC Rule 415, but very few companies wish to announce new share issues that might or might not occur over the next two years for fear of the effect of the "overhang" such an announcement might have on the market price.)

All the underwriter in a U.S. transaction ensures is the price agreed with the registrant the night before the offering is made, not a great risk under ordinary market conditions. The underwriter provides a more useful service acting as a broker/distributor for the issue by providing the sales effort needed to achieve the highest possible price for the offering. Ideally this would be reflected by stimulating widespread interest in the offering and in the company's future so as to generate a higher stock price than would have existed if no offering were made at all. In other words, the new issue would not have resulted in a lowering of the share price to reflect the greater number of shares to be outstanding after the offering. When such is the case, the only cost to the registrant is the gross spread (commission) paid to the underwriters and the out-of-pocket expenses associated with the issue. This result of an underwriting, however, is not guaranteed: the issuer must rely on the underwriter's best efforts in distributing the shares. These efforts may be frustrated by a variety of factors at the issuer's expense.

### Underwriting Euro-Equities

The U.S. book-building method of underwriting is used in the Euromarket, but there are several significant differences. Perhaps most important is the fact that the Euromarket does not require any waiting period while registration procedures are processed. Issuers may enter the market on virtually no notice; thus sellers need not be exposed to market risk while waiting for the offering to proceed. As a practical matter, however, for all but the best-known companies, some sort of marketing period to generate demand is essential if a steep discount in the underwriting price is to be avoided.

Because most of the European underwriters on which the lead manager must rely are banks with limited securities distribution capabilities (except when distributing to customer accounts within the bank) and an unwillingness to admit that they cannot place all the shares they have agreed to underwrite, the lead manager is unable to rely on those banks' prepricing order book as much as it would be able to do in the United States. It may also be more difficult to maintain a fixed offering price during the underwriting period, as some underwriters will sell their unsold shares in the interdealer market or back in the home-country market. This significantly inhibits the stabilization efforts of the lead manager. Thus, precise pricing is more difficult to achieve and stabilization is more erratic and unreliable than in the United States.

### British Underwriting

In the United Kingdom and in many other parts of Europe, an older system of underwriting is used, which many people refer to as the British, or "front-end" underwriting method. In this system, the announcements of the transaction, the offering price, and an agreement with a group of underwriters (usually merchants or investment bankers) to insure, or "backstop," the issue are made simultaneously, two or three weeks before the issue will be available for trading. That day the underwriters arrange a "subunderwriting group" to reinsure their commitment. Subunderwriters are usually institutional investors that are prepared to take down their share of any portion of the issue unsold after its completion. The bulk of the total commission paid by the issuer is made available to the subunderwriters as an insurance premium. Subunderwriters may reduce their risk to the extent that they subscribe to purchase shares in the offering. Most of the subunderwriters expect to be invited into all underwritings during the year and, therefore, see the risks as being spread over a pool of many underwritings, for which significant fees, in the aggregate, can be earned.

British and many other European companies provide their shareholders with *preemptive rights*—the right to purchase new shares of the company before any nonshareholder. As an inducement to shareholders, the preemptive rights are offered at a discount to market. This discount may vary from 5 percent to about 25 percent. The share price will be reduced by the market to reflect the dilution in the number of shares to be outstanding, and the rights will have value equal to the difference between the new share price and the subscription price. The rights can be sold if the shareholder decides not to subscribe.

Because it takes about two weeks to notify shareholders of the offer and to receive their subscriptions, there is a waiting risk for U.K. issues, too. In the United Kingdom, however, this risk is assumed by the underwriters and the subunderwriters. Their risk is tied to market movements as well as to mispricing by the underwriters. Until the subscription period ends, it is impossible to know to what extent the issue has been "taken up" by shareholders or by purchasers of rights.

Apart from arranging the subunderwriting syndicate, brokers have little to do in the process. The underwriters, including the lead merchant bank handling the issue, have little to do with marketing. This system recognizes that the main institutional investors in the market will be the likely buyers. So they are used as subunderwriters—paid a fee for using their capital to prop up the issue while individual and other investors go through the subscription process. The definition of a *successful* issue is one that is fully subscribed, not fully priced; in fact, some believe the more oversubscribed the issue is, the more successful it is. Unfortunately, such oversubscription tends to result in a sharp rise in the stock price when it is free to trade (or put another way, the subscription price tends to be set sufficiently low to be sure that oversubscription occurs). On the other hand, if the issue is undersubscribed, the subunderwriters can sustain substantial losses. Clearly in the U.K. system, priority is given to getting the deal done (with existing shareholders if possible) with less regard to price.

The British method was once in use in the United States and in Japan, when preemptive rights were popular with many large companies and their principal investors. The last such "rights issue" occurred in the United States in the late 1960s, and a bit later in Japan. They went out of style because companies wanted to broaden their shareholder bases to include new investors. They wanted more competition for their newly offered shares, more flexibility to take advantage of market opportunities abroad, and more opportunities to influence the market price by prepricing sales efforts; and they wanted to avoid large dilution in the earnings and book value per share as a result of the discounts required for rights issues. Investors were agreeable, so companies began to vote out their preemptive rights.

The British method is still in use in the United Kingdom, where the large institutional investors are unwilling to surrender preemptive rights. Privatization and other secondary new issues, however, can be made directly to the market, as in the United States, though for the most part the British underwriting method continues to be used. Recent privatization issues have involved a considerable amount of prepricing sales and marketing efforts and other innovations so as to obtain the best from both the U.S. and the U.K. systems.

## Listing Shares on Foreign Exchanges

As may be seen in Exhibit 7.5 for the past 20 years companies have considered listing their shares on foreign exchanges to promote local investment, to provide a quotation in the shares for the benefit of local employees, and to gain appropriate recognition as a multinational firm. Frequently, however, such listings proved to be expensive, and very little trading on the local exchanges occurred. As foreign investors, especially in Europe, became more sophisticated, they preferred to trade in U.S. shares on U.S. markets, where they believed they could obtain better executions. The same came to be true for Japanese and U.S. investors who found trading in overseas shares more efficiently accomplished in the home-country

EXHIBIT 7.5

**Foreign Companies Listed on Major Foreign Exchanges and on U.S. Markets as of July 31, 2001**

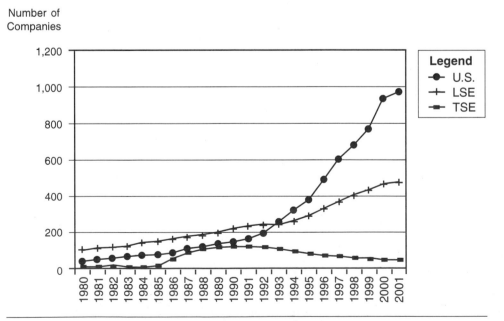

*Sources:* NYSE, Nasdaq, London Stock Exchange, Tokyo Stock Exchange.

markets. These developments diminished to some extent the need for U.S. and Japanese companies to list their shares abroad.

In the United States, however, listings by foreign companies increased significantly during the 1990s. In the United States, *Listings* is a term that includes all foreign companies that report annually to the SEC and, therefore, can be freely traded on stock exchanges or in over-the-counter markets. The companies listing in the United States want to tap the large equity markets in the country, especially at a time when U.S. investors are increasing investments abroad and purchasing new issues of foreign debt and equity. In 2000 the volume of such new issues was at record levels, and of course many foreign issuers wanted to be close to the action.

To qualify as a "reporting" company in the United States, a foreign corporation must provide most of the information required of U.S. companies by the SEC. It must, for example, supply financial statements prepared according to U.S. generally accepted accounting principles (GAAP) or at least show and reconcile the differences between the company's home country accounts and U.S. GAAP. This undertaking alone is expensive, time-consuming, and more illuminating of the issues than most European and Japanese reporting standards require. Many prospective issuers balk at these requirements and forgo the opportunity to be listed in the United States as a result. However, in the early 1990s, market forces drew many foreign companies to the U.S. equity market for new issues. Some issued private placements of equity securities under Rule 144a; but in increasing numbers, others preferred to undertake the burdens of becoming a reporting company in order to have access to the broader market and listing on the NYSE. During 1992, 13 foreign companies listed for the first time on the NYSE; during 1993 approximately three times that number listed, including about 12 from Latin America. By the end of 2000, a total of 472 foreign companies were listed on the NYSE, and 454 more were traded on the Nasdaq and other exchanges. More foreign companies were listed on such exchanges and reported annually to the SEC than there were foreign companies listed on the exchanges of any other country in the world, including the LSE.

## Cross-Border Equity Finance

In theory a company seeking to acquire another company could offer shares for shares of the target company. Sometimes this occurs, but often the target's shareholders are reluctant to accept shares of a less well known company that are traded in a foreign market.

This may mean that the buyer has to sell shares in its home market or possibly in the international equities market and use the proceeds to acquire the target company for cash, though such a step would preclude pooling-of-interest accounting treatment in the United States. Or a deal could be worked out with those target shareholders who did not want to hold the buyer's shares by having a market provided for them by an investment banker in their home country. Non–U.S.

companies can offer shares to U.S. investors only when they are registered or issued under a 144a private placement exemption. If the U.S. target company is widely held, the private placement exemption will not apply, and the issuer will be required to register the shares with the SEC. Such shares could then be publicly traded on the NYSE or the Nasdaq or other exchanges.

It may also be possible to offer shares of the buyer's subsidiary, either in exchange for target company shares or to raise the cash to accomplish the transaction. This has been done in Japan, where price/earnings ratios were high and the parent company benefited by selling the shares at a value higher than the one they would have been accorded in the United States.

Other possibilities exist, including *convertible debentures*—debt securities convertible into or accompanied by warrants to purchase stock in subsidiary companies, or commodities, or other investments.

Working out a plan for an equity issuance and then carrying it out can take a year or more for companies not already experienced in using international equity markets. The long planning and preparation period means that market conditions may be substantially different when the time comes to do the issue from what they were at the time of planning. A close association with an investment bank willing to work over a long period of time with an uncertain result is essential. Not all investment banks wish to have such engagements; but in these competitive markets, there are always several who do.

## SUMMARY

Over the past several years, international capital markets have grown substantially and developed along U.S. lines. Overseas financial markets may be used to finance U.S. acquisitions of non–U.S. corporations, and foreign companies may tap the U.S. markets in a variety of ways to do likewise. Using the markets in the country of the target company may be desirable if it creates a trading market in the buyer's shares in the local market, especially if that market has higher investor appraisal ratios than does the home market. Every year, the range of possibilities of achieving global market penetration increases, making the arranging of acquisition finance more and more a question of selecting the "highest bidder."

# Checklist: International Financing for Cross-Border M&A Transactions

I. First steps in seeking international financing. Consider:
   A. How much financing will be required?
   B. How much of debt?
      1. Long term.
      2. Short term.
   C. How much of equity?
   D. Will bridge financing be required?
   E. Accessibility of domestic and overseas capital markets.
   F. Effect of the transaction on the company's:
      1. Debt ratings.
      2. Existing covenants.
      3. Operating cash flow.
   G. Cost of each tranche of:
      1. Debt.
      2. Equity.
   H. How much of the debt will be commuted by the company's lead bank?

II. Foreign bond financing.
   A. Historically expensive.
      1. High fees and expenses.
      2. Interest rates that are often higher outside the United States.
   B. What to consider respecting Eurobonds and their market.
      1. Traditionally sold principally to non–U.S. residents but more recently accessed by U.S. institutional investors.
      2. Not highly regulated but subject to self-imposed standards of practice.
      3. Usually listed on London and Luxembourg stock exchanges.
      4. Typically subject to U.K. law (especially the Financial Services Act) and trading standards set by the Association of International Bond Dealers.
      5. Customarily denominated in dollars.
      6. Issuers may be governmental or corporate entities.
      7. Issued in fixed or floating form with maturities usually less than 10 years (5 to 7 years typical).

      8. Most Eurobonds rated by Standard & Poor's and Moody's (even with non–U.S. issuers).

      9. Clearance and settlement by Euroclear and Cedel.

    10. Eurobonds with swap features increasingly popular to better manage financial liabilities.

C. Eurobond new-issue procedures. Consider:

    1. In the United States, use of Rule 415, which (subject to the rule's eligibility requirements) permits shelf registrations, thus allowing the ability to come to market on short notice.

    2. Typically these are "bought" deals, mandated to the underwriter offering the best net cost of funds in the currency desired by the issuer.

D. Eurobonds pricing.

    1. Fixed-price method.

    2. Same yield in all markets due to arbitrage and institutional participation.

E. Using the Eurobond market.

    1. Establish amount to be raised and maturity (often $100 million to $250 million with 5-to-7-year maturity).

    2. Consider all-in cost of funds versus U.S. financing using U.S. Treasuries as a benchmark.

    3. See if bankers can match or beat the benchmark.

    4. Consider floating-rate to fixed-rate financings.

    5. Ask for suggestions for nondollar Eurobond issues with simultaneous currency swaps into U.S. dollars.

III. Some cross-border financing ideas previously used:

A. Through a buyer's usual bank, a bank in the target's country, or via international banks, issuing Eurobonds to finance the deal in the currency of the target company.

B. Swapping deal debt into such currency (subject to tax considerations).

C. Public offering in the United States or elsewhere.

D. The U.S. private placement market through the use of a Rule 144a transaction (subject to the ability of the issuer to comply with its terms)

E. Consider less typical debt financing strategies.

    1. Municipal revenue bonds.

    2. Leveraged leases.

    3. Limited partnerships.

    4. High-yield bond offerings.

F. In all instances, compare and contrast the pluses and minuses of utilizing U.S. versus overseas capital markets.

IV. International equity securities.

   A. Consider the use of international tranches to supplement domestic market liquidity in U.S. public equity offerings used to fund cross-border M&A transactions.

   B. Investigate the use of Euro-equities (the equity equivalents of Euro-bonds) to tap into a new investor base or to minimize domestic regulation and expense.

   C. Review the possibility of an equity 144a private placement.

   D. Consider hybrid debt-equity securities such as convertible debentures or debt with detachable equity purchase warrants.

   E. Understand the pluses and minuses of U.S. public equity underwritings.

   F. Compare and contrast the pluses (e.g., high liquidity) and minuses (e.g., risk stays with issuer until deal goes effective) of a U.S. public equity offering with those of a Euro-equity transaction or an underwritten equity offering in an overseas market. Note differences in legal requirements in each market (e.g., preemptive rights in the United Kingdom resulting in many rights offerings there).

   G. Note that the issuer of any of the securities described (A–F) may be the acquirer or an affiliate, typically a subsidiary.

   H. Consider listing U.S. publicly traded shares on non–U.S. exchanges via tradable securities such as ADRs and EDRs.

# 8

# Government Assistance in Financing Cross-Border Transactions

*Kenneth D. Brody*
*Roberta J. Waxman-Lenz*

**G**overnment assistance can spell the difference between success and failure in cross-border transactions and often makes the difference between good and mediocre financing. This chapter explores the availability of government assistance from the developed countries to help finance acquisitions, joint ventures, existing subsidiaries or affiliates, or start-up projects in developing countries.

Developing countries significantly differ from each other. Brazil is not Botswana, China is not Chile, and India is not Israel. There are about 170 developing countries in Asia, Latin America, Central and Eastern Europe and the former Soviet Union (generally labeled *countries in transition*), the Middle East, and Africa. They are diverse—as big as China and India, with 1.3 billion and 1.0 billion people, respectively, and as small as Tanzania, with almost 1 million people. Some are fully democratic, some are still in a transition from Communism, and some are under the rule of dictators. Some have a well-developed rule of law, many do not. Most have enormous infrastructure needs. Most have large agrarian populations that are moving toward more industrialized ones. Some have climbed the technology curve, and some have yet to begin the process. These and other characteristics underline the need for dealing with each developing country individually, based on its unique characteristics.

The very term *developing countries* is considered by some specialists to be almost passé. Not too long ago, the focus for potential growth in economies was on the "third world." The fall of the iron curtain and the dissolution of the Soviet Union produced countries in transition. With recognized high growth and significant global integration, many third world countries are now referred to as "emerging markets," an appellation that speaks volumes about the widespread optimism for the prospects of the populations of these countries. The developing world encompasses approximately 170 countries with over 4 billion people, or roughly 75 percent of the world's population.

Optimism about the prospects of these countries is well supported by the facts. Forty years ago, today's emerging markets barely appeared on the world's economic radar screen. Today, these markets constitute almost half of total world production. Furthermore, they are growing at least twice as fast as the markets in the industrialized world. Virtually all observers of this phenomenon expect the trends to continue, which means that the majority of the growth in the world will come from today's emerging markets.

With the fall of the Berlin Wall and the collapse of Soviet power, hundreds of millions of people have entered the free market system for the first time. The pace of change has been staggering. The experience of the Export-Import (Ex-Im) Bank of the United States over the past three years is illustrative. Ex-Im Bank's mission is to finance U.S.–produced exports to emerging markets. In 1992, approximately three-fourths of Ex-Im Bank's financings were with foreign government and foreign government–owned buyers. In 1995, approximately two-thirds of its financings were with private sector buyers. This change in three years emphasizes the transition from government to private sector activity in the emerging markets, changes that have created an environment in which fierce battles for initial market shares are being waged around the world.

This enormous growth and change comes with substantial barriers to entry and with significant risks. Financing in many of the emerging markets is proving to be quite difficult. The key reasons are concerns about political stability, inchoate domestic capital markets, and governments overwhelmed with the speed of change. Despite the risks (of which only some have been enumerated), private sector capital from developed to developing countries has now significantly surpassed the public-sector capital from governments and multilaterals.

Equipped with a general understanding of financing in emerging markets and a specific understanding of the country in which business is to be done, the financier needs to address certain issues that do not arise in developed countries, such as political risk, weak legal/regulatory structures, lack of a well-developed domestic capital market, and a general lack of availability of long-term debt. *Political risk* refers to transfer risk (the risk that local currency cannot be converted or transferred from the country), expropriation, and political violence. *Expropria-*

*tion* is government confiscation of property without reasonable compensation. *Political violence* typically refers to riots or war. In general, political risk is due to political instability, a feature of many developing country governments over the past 30 years, but one that has decreased over the past 5 years.

Weak legal/regulatory structures and underdeveloped domestic capital markets are facts of life in most emerging markets. The relative scarcity of long-term debt is another fact of life. These realities, in part exacerbated by the risk of political instability, cause the financier to think about financing cross-border transactions differently from domestic developed-country ones and cause the financier to look toward government assistance in financing. Government assistance can help solve or mitigate the problems of political risk, absence of a well-developed domestic capital market, and the scarcity of long-term debt.

The financier needs to know what government assistance is available to complete the transaction and to fund the company's ongoing business after the transaction is completed. The initial capital structure is just the starting point; the subsequent capital structures are often the key to successful long-term financing. To help develop this understanding, the assistance available from the most significant government sources will be examined, namely the governments of the United States (e.g., the Overseas Private Investment Corporation, or OPIC), Japan, Germany, England, France, and Canada; and from several multilateral financial institutions, such as the International Finance Corporation (IFC), the European Bank for Reconstruction and Development (EBRD), and the Inter-American Investment Corporation (IIC). These institutions are undergoing substantial change as they attempt to cope with a new world of emerging markets, a world dominated by private sector initiatives. In addition to the traditional government financing institutions, others are created to fill existing voids. For example, the U.S. Department of Defense created a division for export financing for defense applications, which would otherwise not be available. The astute transactor will need to develop mechanisms to keep abreast of these changes in order to know what kinds of financings are available in a particular situation. International banks with broad and deep experience in financing cross-border transactions are typically good sources of up-to-date information.

OPIC (and its foreign counterparts) and the multilateral financial institutions are among the first to consider for financing assistance in an emerging market. The Export-Import Bank of the United States (and its foreign Ex-Im Bank counterparts) come into play afterward. We first review the institutions most useful to doing the deal and follow with those useful after the deal is done.

## OPIC

OPIC, a U.S. government agency, provides political risk insurance and financing to U.S. companies investing in emerging market economies. Established in 1971 as a self-sustaining agency, OPIC operates in 140 countries and had an exposure as of 2000 of more than $8.0 billion. Its mandate is to facilitate private sector investment in the economic development of emerging nations in order to advance U.S. foreign policy goals. OPlC's mission is to encourage U.S. businesses to invest in emerging market countries, and its programs are intended to help generate U.S. exports and jobs.

OPIC places particular emphasis on those geographic areas where it can best promote U.S. foreign policy goals, including the support of economic reform and democratization in developing and formerly Communist societies. OPIC has established well-defined requirements regarding investors, the kinds of projects and investments it will support, and the countries eligible for such support. It will not support investments in countries with poor human rights records or in countries that do not implement internationally recognized worker rights. It reviews potential projects to ensure that they will not cause job loss in the United States. OPIC is also required to consider the environmental effects of proposed projects, and it will not provide financing for projects that pose significant hazards to public health, safety, and the environment. It gives special consideration to projects that enhance the environment and that benefit worker health and safety in host countries. OPIC's finance program provides medium- to long-term project finance in the form of loan guarantees and, to a lesser extent, direct loans. Guarantees permit the funding of large projects, including infrastructure and energy projects, whereas direct loans support smaller projects across many industries. Guarantees and loans generally have terms of 5 to 15 years, and interest rates vary based on the risk assessed by OPIC.

OPlC's finance program often provides the long-term, limited-recourse leverage needed to attract debt or equity from the private sector. OPIC may provide political risk insurance to projects it supports through the finance program. Eligible projects must be commercially viable. OPIC provides loan guarantees for up to 50 percent of project costs to a limit of $200 million, although guarantees generally range in size from $10 million to $100 million. Guarantees may cover up to 75 percent of costs for expansion of existing projects.

OPIC also supports investment funds, mobilizing new sources of private capital to invest in overseas projects sponsored by U.S. companies in developing markets. It provides a significant part of each fund's capitalization through loan guarantees, while institutional investors provide the remaining capital. The funds are managed by private sector firms with appropriate investment experience. OPIC representatives have a seat on each fund's advisory board. At the end of fiscal year 2000, OPlC's commitments to roughly 25 funds totaled $2.2 billion.

Appendix 8.1 outlines the programs similar to those offered by OPIC that are available from Canada, France, Germany, Japan, and the United Kingdom.

## IFC

The IFC, a member of the World Bank Group, was founded in 1956 to promote economic development in its member countries by encouraging the growth of private sector projects. The IFC provides debt or equity financing for a project, mobilizes resources from other financial institutions, and provides advisory services and technical assistance to businesses and governments on investment-related matters. The IFC's project finance activities include long-term loans, guarantees, standby financing, and equity investments. Investments range from $1 million to $100 million and generally do not exceed 25 percent of a project's estimated cost. The IFC may provide up to 35 percent of a project's equity capital provided that the IFC is not the largest shareholder in the project. The addition of private sector institutional lending under the IFC umbrella can significantly increase the funding for an IFC-sponsored project. The IFC charges market rates for its products and shares all project risks with its partners; it does not accept government guarantees for its loans.

The IFC analyzes each project for profitability, for beneficial effect on the host country's economy, and for the project's environmental impact. For fiscal year 2000, the IFC approved over 259 projects in more than 65 countries, providing $3.5 billion in financing for its own account and approximately $5.8 billion in syndications.

## EBRD

EBRD was founded in 1991 to focus on developing the economies of countries in central and eastern Europe and the former Soviet Union. The institution's mandate is to assist these countries in their transition to market economies and to promote private sector activities. The founding agreement states that "at least 60 percent of the Bank's committed loans, guarantees, and equity investments must be provided to the private sector." The EBRD views itself as a catalyst for mobilizing additional capital to finance projects in this region, and it seeks to attract foreign direct investment to benefit projects in these emerging markets. By December 2000, the EBRD made commitments of 12.2 billion euros ($11.0 billion). It was expecting to mobilize an additional 41.9 billion euros ($37.8 billion) for project commitments.

The EBRD offers a wide range of financial instruments and is flexible in structuring its financial products. As a guideline, the standard minimum involvement of the EBRD is 5 million euros ($4.5 million), though this can vary if the project has fundamental benefits for the country. In practice, the average amount of the EBRD's involvement is around 22 million euros ($19.9 million). The EBRD also provides direct financing and support for small and medium-size private sector companies through a number of loan and equity facilities.

Joint ventures have been targeted by the EBRD to receive financing, particularly if they have sophisticated experienced sponsors. The primary financing instruments utilized by the EBRD include loans, guarantees, and equity. In all cases, the commercial viability of a project determines whether the EBRD will participate. Its staff will also consider the environmental impact on the host country and whether the project will benefit the host country's economy.

Repayment terms for EBRD loans typically range from 5 to 10 years, though

15-year terms may be granted for infrastructure projects. Rates are set on a commercial basis and reflect project-specific risks. Loans are expected to be repaid from project cash flows; thus, the decision to make a loan is based on the project's commercial feasibility. Terms and conditions on equity investments depend on the risks involved, the expected returns on the invested capital, and the entity receiving the financing.

The EBRD finances up to 35 percent of a new project's cost and up to 35 percent of the long-term capitalization of an existing company. The EBRD requires that other investors provide significant equity participation, with a particular emphasis on contributions from industrial sponsors for greenfield projects. It also seeks additional funding from other financial institutions, such as multilateral agencies, commercial banks, and export credit agencies.

## IIC

The IIC is a multilateral institution formed in 1989 that facilitates investments in Latin America and the Caribbean. Though the IIC is a part of the Inter-American Development Bank Group, its resources and management are independent. The IIC provides direct loans and direct equity investments primarily to small and medium-size private sector companies without requiring government guarantees. It had a total exposure as of year-end 2000 of $1.3 billion.

A capital increase of $500 million was approved in 1999, bringing the IIC's total capital to $700 million. In addition, as a result of the capital increase negotiations, five new members were admitted in 2000 (Belgium, Finland, Norway, Portugal, and Sweden).

The IIC has clearly defined criteria for lending and investing. To be considered eligible, projects must be commercially viable and must advance economic development in any or all of the following respects: creating jobs; facilitating foreign currency income or savings; enabling transfer of technology, resources, and management skills; promoting public participation in company ownership; or contributing to the economic integration of Latin America and the Caribbean. Projects must also comply with the IIC's environmental protection guidelines.

## EX-IM BANK

Ex-Im Bank, founded in 1934, has the mission of financing exports to assist the private sector in creating and maintaining U.S. jobs. This government agency provides loans, guarantees, and insurance to facilitate export of U.S. products; and since its inception it has provided financing of approximately $300 billion. The Executive Order that established Ex-Im Bank stated that it was "to aid in financing and to facilitate exports and imports and the exchange of commodities and services" between the United States and other nations. Although the approach and the specific goals have been modified to address shifts in the international economic and financial marketplace and national priorities, Ex-Im Bank's basic functions remain the same today as in 1934, with the exception that the focus is exclusively on U.S. exports.

Ex-Im Bank guarantees the repayment of loans or makes loans to foreign purchasers of U.S. goods and services. In a relatively small program, it also guarantees working capital loans for small U.S. company exporters. Its programs address the needs of commercial lenders that require additional security on their loans and exporters that are not able to obtain private sector financing. It also provides insurance against political and commercial risks of nonpayment by foreign buyers. For fiscal year 2000, it had authorized expenditures of almost $12.6 billion.

Ex-Im Bank seeks to provide a level playing field for U.S. exporters by countering export credit subsidies of other governments. To take advantage of current economic trends, the Bank focuses on assisting exports to developing countries. Its project finance activities enable it to play a role in infrastructure development. In addition, the Bank has a mandate to facilitate the export of goods and services beneficial to the environment, and it has made a special effort to assist small business exporters.

Four significant underlying principles of Ex-Im Bank are: (1) it supports the export of goods and services from the United States; (2) it will not compete with commercial lenders, but it provides financing for transactions that the private sector is not able to support; (3) it requires a reasonable assurance of repayment; and (4) it can support only transactions that do not have an adverse effect on the U.S. economy. Ex-Im Bank direct loans or guarantees may support up to 85 percent of the export contract. Local costs may be financed up to 15 percent of the U.S. contract amount, and interest costs during the construction phase may be covered by loans or guarantees. To determine maximum repayment terms, the Bank follows the guidelines of the Organization for Economic Cooperation and Development (OECD). Thus, depending on the country and the type of project, the maximum repayment term is 12 years. OECD directives state that for a contract value of $75,000, a repayment term of 2 years is available; for a $150,000 contract value, 3 years; for a $300,000 contract value, 4 years; and for a contract value exceeding $300,000, 5 to 12 years. Short-term policies under the insurance program generally cover 100 percent of the principal for political risk and 90 to 95 percent of the contract amount for commercial risk. Fees and interest rates are based on risk and are usually similar to the pricing of the principal Ex-Im Bank foreign counterparts.

Project financing enables equity investors to participate in larger or more risky projects than would be possible without the participation of a government agency. To obtain Ex-Im Bank support, the transactions must be creditworthy, and the equity investor must assume some of the risk. Fees and interest rates reflect the risk involved and are roughly at market rates.

Appendix 8.2 outlines the programs similar to those offered by Ex-Im Bank that are available from agencies in Canada, France, Germany, Japan, and the United Kingdom.

## DEALING WITH GOVERNMENT FINANCIAL INSTITUTIONS

Government financial institutions are fundamentally different from private sector financial institutions; government institutions exist to promote policy, whereas private institutions attempt to maximize profits. This fundamental difference, along with the nature of government, means that dealing with a government financial institution is very different from dealing with a private sector financial institution, such as a bank.

The good news is that government institutions, in many instances, are willing to take greater risks and to extend longer debt terms then private institutions are. Government institutions are also often more flexible in deal structure and covenants. On the other hand, rigidities abound in the public sector because of a need (sometimes real, sometimes perceived) to adhere strictly to governing laws, regulations, rules, and customs. For example, export credit agencies have debt terms that must conform to OECD rules; the amount and definition of allowable foreign content is typically established by country law; and the amount of debt financing is limited by OECD rules to 85 percent of the total project cost. These examples are only the beginning of a very long list that varies significantly from agency to agency. In addition to the prescribed rigidities, and to a large extent because of them, government agencies tend to be process orientated and relatively slow moving.

What are the implications for the financier? It is our belief that the key to successful dealings with government agencies is for the financier to develop a deep understanding of the requirements and processes of each of the agencies with which he or she deals. Financiers should also develop real relationships with midlevel managers so that they can understand how these managers think and act. It is the midlevel managers in most of these agencies who make the critical calls, although they are almost always subject to review by a body that is the equivalent of a loan committee or board of directors.

How to develop the understanding and relationship is very much dependent on the volume of financing with the particular institution. Some who do a substantial number of financings have a company representative designated to do this job on close to a full-time basis. Most companies will find this approach impractical and too costly. As a start, it is useful to review the publicly available information published by the agency and to attend training sessions sponsored by the agency. However, this start will leave one quite far away from being a sophisticated user of any particular agency. Because government agencies act so differently from the commercial banks with which financiers customarily deal, it is usually not enough to proceed based on publicly available information.

In order to become a sophisticated user of government agency programs, financiers must first identify the commercial banks that do significant business with their particular agency and choose one to act as their agent. Armed with a team of experienced professionals, the financier will know what material to present, the appropriate format to use, what is negotiable, the likelihood of the deal being approved, how long it will take, and the critical issues involved.

Appendix 8.3 sets forth relevant addresses and phone numbers for the institutions discussed in this chapter or for those listed in Appendixes 8.1 or 8.2.

Privatization's fast pace is causing institutions not described in this chapter to change their programs. Thus, companies seeking funding should also review the offerings of the World Bank and the regional multilateral financial institutions. In addition, a company needs to be familiar with each developing country's assistance programs.

The increasing level of private sector cross-border activity has taken lenders from the relatively easy task of assessing country credit to the much more complex task of determining individual company or project creditworthiness. Fortunately, the credit rating agencies have rapidly expanded internationally to help deal with this issue. Although governments and multilateral financial institutions talk about credit risk in very different ways, they tend to come to similar conclusions, with the U.S. institutions having a slightly larger appetite for assuming greater credit risk (down to a single B credit).

Financing cross-border transactions in developing countries is complex, time-consuming, and often frustrating. With 80 percent of the world's population poised to join the developing world, the results of obtaining government assistance for financing in developing markets will surely be worth the effort.

## APPENDIX 8.1

# Financing Investments

### Eligible Investors

*Canada: EDC.*   Canadian exporters.

*France: COFACE.*   Domestic French entities.

*Germany: C & L Deutsche Revision.*   Domestic German entities.

*Japan: EID/MITI.*   Domestic Japanese interests.

*United Kingdom: ECGD.*   Persons and companies conducting business in the United Kingdom, also certain foreign subsidiaries of U.K. companies.

*United States: OPIC.*   U.S. citizens and entities beneficially owned by U.S. citizens and foreign entities 95 percent owned by U.S. citizens.

### Eligible Investments

*Canada: EDC.*   Insurance, loans, guarantees to Canadian exporters.

*France: COFACE.*   Equity, some loans. New investments only. No portfolio investments.

*Germany: C & L Deutsche Revision.*   Equity, loans, endowment capital. New investments only.

*Japan: EID/MITI.*   Equity, loans, loan guarantees. New investments only. No portfolio investments.

*United Kingdom: ECGD.*   Equity, loans, loan guarantees provided by equity shareholder. New investments and existing investments only to extent they are matched by new investment. No portfolio investments.

*United States: OPIC.*   Investments in new ventures or expansion of existing enterprises. Equity, loans, loan guarantees. Technical assistance agreements, cross-border leases, assigned inventory or equipment, other forms of investment. No portfolio investments. No projects that would have negative impact on U.S. jobs.

### Eligible Foreign Enterprises

*Canada: EDC.*   Host country must carry an acceptable level of risk. A foreign buyer is eligible if EDC is open for business in the market in question and has some remaining appetite. The creditworthiness of the borrower/guarantor must be determined in commercial lending situations. Transactions must be assessed according to EDC's risk management practices prior to approval.

*France: COFACE.*   No restriction as to host country, although attitude to human rights may be considered. Bilateral investments are a prerequisite in principle but may be waived.

*Germany: C & L Deutsche Revision.* No formal restriction. Bilateral agreement usually required.

*Japan: EID/MITI.* No restriction to host country. Bilateral agreements not required.

*United Kingdom: ECGD.* No restriction on host country. Bilateral agreements not required. No projects that conflict with U.K. national interests or that are not developmental in nature.

*United States: OPIC.* Developing countries and most post-Communist countries. Bilateral agreement required. Host government attitude toward human rights and worker rights considered.

## Risks Covered

*Canada: EDC.* Political coverage and a combination of commercial/political coverage offered. Political coverage includes transfer/inconvertibility, memorandum on external debt, expropriation, nationalization, war, revolution, insurrection, cancellation or nonrenewal of import or export permits. Political/commercial coverage includes insolvency of foreign buyer, nonpayment by foreign buyer, contract termination, refusal of goods by foreign customer, memorandum on external debt, nationalization, cancellation or nonrenewal of import or export permits.

*France: COFACE.* Expropriation, war, inconvertibility, breach of government commitment vital to project. Cover only issued as a package.

*Germany: C & L Deutsche Revision.* Expropriation, war, breach of commitment, inconvertibility, blockade of payments, or moratorium. Cover only available as a package.

*Japan: EID/MITI.* Expropriation, war, inconvertibility, bankruptcy after two years of operation.

*United Kingdom: ECGD.* Expropriation, war, inconvertibility, breach of contract by host government in certain cases.

*United States: OPIC.* Expropriation, political violence, inconvertibility, breach of contract by host government in certain cases.

## Amount of Insurance

*Canada: EDC.* Most types of insurance carry 90 percent coverage. Bulk agriculture credits can carry up to 100 percent coverage.

*France: COFACE.* Equity: initial investment plus reinvested earnings up to 100 percent. Loans: principal plus up to 70 percent of interest.

*Germany: C & L Deutsche Revision.* Initial investment plus earnings up to 10 percent per annum and up to overall limit of 50 percent in case of equity and 100 percent in case of loans.

*Japan: EID/MITI.* No formal limit on amount of investment of earnings eligible for cover. In practice, some country limits may apply.

*United Kingdom: ECGD.*   Equity: initial investment plus retained earnings up to 300 percent per annum of that amount plus distributed earnings. Loans and loan guarantees: loan amount plus interest.

*United States: OPIC.*   Insurance commitments available for up to 270 percent of the initial investment, 90 percent representing the initial investment and 180 percent to cover future earnings.

## Duration of Insurance

*Canada: EDC.*   Maximum 15 years, depending on type of insurance, though most types carry 180 to 360 days coverage.

*France: COFACE.*   Maximum 15 years, minimum 5 years.

*Germany: C & L Deutsche Revision.*   Maximum 15 years, but 20 years if project involves long construction period.

*Japan: EID/MITI:*   Political risk: maximum 15 years, with longer periods for projects with long construction periods. Commercial risk: maximum 10 years, with longer periods possible.

*United Kingdom: ECGD.*   Maximum 15 years, extendable to 20 years. Minimum 3 years for equity. "Three years" means repayment period for loans.

*United States: OPIC.*   Maximum 20 years. Normal minimum 3 years.

## Cost of Insurance

*Canada: EDC.*   For most types of insurance, one-time processing fee; premium payments made on pay-as-you-go basis with premium rates set as percentage of total declared volume. For some types of insurance, rates are based on a rate table and a case-by-case analysis; premium paid in advance.

*France: COFACE.*   Rate varies according to host country and nature of project. Normal range 0.7 to 1.1 percent on amount invested.

*Germany: C & L Deutsche Revision.*   Premium: 0.5 percent per annum on the amount of coverage at the beginning of the contract year.

*Japan: EID/MITI.*   Political risks: base 0.55 percent per annum variable, depending on country and investment type. Commercial risk: base rate 1 percent per annum variable 0.7 to 1.8 percent.

*United Kingdom: ECGD.*   0.7 to 1.8 percent, depending on country. Standby cover 0.175 to 0.45 percent.

*United States: OPIC.*   Varies according to industry and risks covered.

## APPENDIX 8.2
# Financing Trade

### Eligible Exporters

*Canada: EDC.*   A person or organization operating a business in Canada.

*France: COFACE.*   French exporters and banks financing exports.

*Germany: Hermes.*   German exporters or banks.

*Japan: Ex-Im Bank.*   Japanese exporters or banks involved in export transactions. May also be foreign company exporting to Japan natural resources, manufactured goods, or technology. (*Note*: Japan Ex-Im is also involved in overseas investment financing.)

*United Kingdom: ECGD.*   U.K. exporters or banks involved in export transactions.

*United States: Ex-Im Bank.*   Any company or bank involved in exporting goods having at least 50 percent U.S. content.

### Eligible Exports

*Canada: EDC.*   Canadian exports must have an acceptable level of Canadian content, usually 50 percent, to meet the benefits criteria, or the transaction must generate other significant benefits to Canada.

*France: COFACE.*   Medium- and long-term guaranteed exports must have at least 30 percent French content. Medium- and long-term policies cover projects and large capital goods business, nonrepetitive, mostly more than three years. Short-term comprehensive covers consumer goods, light equipment, services payable on cash terms or on credit terms less than three years.

*Germany: Hermes.*   Most goods and services. Foreign content generally limited to 10 percent; within the European Union (EU), 40 percent. Under comprehensive cover scheme (maximum two years), foreign content may be up to 100 percent.

*Japan: Ex-Im Bank.*   Focus on export of ships and equipment for factories. Technical service loans available for export of technical services. Also provides financing for some imports, particularly natural resources, manufactured goods, and technology.

*United Kingdom: ECGD.*   Typically U.K. products; however, foreign content allowable: up to 40 percent for EU; up to 30 percent for Japan; up to 15 percent for other countries.

*United States: Ex-Im Bank.*   Product or service must have at least 50 percent U.S. content. Export must not affect the U.S. economy adversely. Particular focus on increasing export of environmental goods and services. Short-term: consumer goods, raw materials, spare parts, bulk agricultural commodities, consumer durables, capital goods. Medium-term guarantees: capital goods. Long-term guarantees: large projects, capital goods, and project-related services.

## Eligible Foreign Enterprises (Importers)

*Canada: EDC.*   A foreign buyer is eligible to receive support if EDC is open for business in the market in question and has some remaining appetite. The creditworthiness of the borrower/guarantor must be determined in commercial lending situations. Transactions are assessed according to EDC's risk management practices prior to approval. The country must carry an acceptable level of risk.

*France: COFACE.*   Availability of guarantees depends on risk classification of destination country.

*Germany: Hermes.*   Non-German buyers/importers and banks.

*Japan: Ex-Im Bank.*   Foreign importers and financial institutions. Financing may be used by these institutions, among other things, to extend loans to joint venture companies with Japanese firms. Import loans also to Japanese companies importing natural resources, manufactured goods, and technologies.

*United Kingdom: ECGD.*   Non–U.K. buyers.

*United States: Ex-Im Bank.*   Export to any country where there is "reasonable assurance of repayment," depends on risk classification of destination country. Focus on developing economies.

## Risks Covered

*Canada: EDC.*   Commercial risks, including those due to buyer insolvency, default, refusal to accept shipped goods, and unilateral termination of contract. Political risks, such as transfer difficulties, expropriation and war, or insurrection.

*France: COFACE.*   Precredit risk: prior to policyholder's delivery of goods. Credit risk: postdelivery of goods—insolvency or protracted default of buyer; political risks.

*Germany: Hermes.*   Commercial risks, including those due to insolvency of foreign buyer or protracted default. Political risks, including legislative and administrative measures, war, inconvertibility.

*Japan: Ex-Im Bank.*   Political risks, including war and internal disorder. Commercial risks, including bankruptcy.

*United Kingdom: ECGD.*   Insurance for exporters: commercial risks, such as buyer default. Political risks, such as war and lack of foreign exchange. Finance guarantees: all risks.

*United States: Ex-Im Bank.*   Commercial and political risks, including political violence, expropriation, and inconvertibility.

## Amount of Financing

*Canada: EDC.*   Credit insurance: most of EDC's programs offer 90 percent coverage. Documentary Credits Insurance offers 100 percent coverage for bulk agriculture with a sovereign, foreign bank; 95 percent commercial and 100 percent political coverage for bulk agriculture with a nonsovereign bank. Medium Term Bulk Agriculture offers up to 100 percent coverage. The percentage of the contract amount eligible for financing may vary. Financing: exporter coverage for financing programs ranges from 85 percent to 100 percent, depending on the program. The exporter's financial institution is eligible for 60 percent to 90 percent, depending on the program. Contract bonding: coverage ranges from 90 percent to 100 percent, or as per contract, or as negotiated; rates vary per program.

*France: COFACE.* Supplier credits—Commercial risks: maximum 85 percent, 90 percent when under bank guarantee. Political risks: maximum 90 percent. Buyer credit policy: 95 percent for any cause of loss. Exchange risk insurance: 100 percent of exchange loss.

*Germany: Hermes.* Export guarantees for private buyers—Political risks: 90 percent; insolvency risks: 85 percent; protracted default: 85 percent; protracted default with comprehensive policy: 85 percent. Buyer credit guarantees for private buyers—Political risks: 90 percent; commercial risks: 85 percent; special applications including protracted default: 95 percent.

*Japan: Ex-Im Bank.* Typical loans are up to $1 million equivalent. Generally coverage is up to 85 percent of contract amount for machinery and factory exports, up to 80 percent of the contract amount for ship exports.

*United Kingdom: ECGD.* Insurance: 90 percent. Finance guarantees: 100 percent (for loan of 85 percent of contract price).

*United States: Ex-Im Bank.* Loans, guarantees, medium-term insurance: 85 percent of contract price; 100 percent of financed portion. Foreign buyer required to make 15 percent cash payment. Short-term policies: 100 percent of principal for political risks; 90 to 95 percent for commercial risks. Guarantees of commercial loans for political and commercial risks: 100 percent of principal and interest.

## Duration of Financing

*Canada: EDC.* Short-term: 180 days up to one year. Medium-term: up to five years. Long-term: five years or more.

*France: COFACE.* Short-term credit insurance: less than three years. Duration of medium- and long-term follows OECD Consensus guidelines: maximum duration 8.5 or 10 years, depending on country category. Longer than 10 years for specific exports as specified by OECD guidelines.

*Germany: Hermes.* Short-term for consumer goods: up to 180 days, though may be extended to 360 days. Medium-term for investment goods: typically maximum of 5 years. Long-term: 8.5 or 10 years, based on OECD guidelines.

*Japan: Ex-Im Bank.* Duration of financing based on OECD Consensus guidelines for machinery and factory exports and on OECD Understanding for transactions involving ships. Factors considered include export item, destination country, and contract amount. Financing typically 3 to 10 years, but may be up to 15 years, depending on the specific program utilized.

*United Kingdom: ECGD.* Insurance: Usually payments soon after delivery. Finance guarantees: Typically 2 to 10 years. Duration follows OECD Consensus guidelines; medium duration 8.5 or 10 years, depending on country category.

*United States: Ex-Im Bank.* Short-term: up to 180 days, exception of 360 days. Medium-term: up to 5 years, exception of 7 years. Long-term: generally maximum of 12 years.

## Cost of Financing

*Canada: EDC.* Interest can be charged on the basis of a fixed rate, a floating rate, or a combination thereof. The rate is comprised of an appropriate benchmark (i.e., before U.S. Treasuries or U.S. LIBOR [London interbank offering rate]) plus a margin for credit risk. The appropriate rate is determined as a combined view on length of term, consensus rule minimums, and underlying commercial principles.

*France: COFACE.* Premium depends on destination of goods, type of risk, and duration of the risk. Exchange risk insurance: premium depends on currency, duration of cover, and percent of participation in exchange profits for certain types of cover.

*Germany: Hermes.* Premium depends on country, type, amount, and duration of cover. Also depends on destination of products.

*Japan: Ex-Im Bank.* Financing priced according to OECD Consensus guidelines for machinery and factory exports and for OECD Understanding for transactions involving ships.

*United Kingdom: ECGD.* Premium largely depends on the destination country and duration of cover. Interest rates follow OECD Consensus guidelines on fixed interest rates. Can also guarantee loans in wider range of currencies.

*United States: Ex-Im Bank.* Premium depends on duration of financing, risk of buyer, and country risk rating. Commitment fee 0.125 percent to 0.75 percent per annum. Short-term private sector buyer minimum premium: $10,000.

## APPENDIX 8.3

# Contact Information

**The Overseas Private Investment Corporation (OPIC)**
Mailing address: 1100 New York Avenue, NW
Washington, DC 20527
Tel: (OPIC InfoLine): 202-336-8799
Fax: 202-408-9859
E-mail: info@opic.gov

Information on federal export assistance programs—Trade Information Center:
Tel: 1-800-USA-TRADE (1-800-872-8723)
Fax: 202-482-4473
TDD: 1-800-833-8723

**The International Finance Corporation (IFC)**
Mailing address: 2121 Pennsylvania Avenue, NW
Washington, DC 20433
Tel: 202-473-3800
202-477-1234
Fax: 202-974-4384

**The European Bank for Reconstruction and Development (EBRD)**
Mailing address: One Exchange Square
London EC2A 2EH
United Kingdom
Tel: 44-171-338-6000
Fax: 44-171-338-6100
Telex: 8812161 EBRD LESSOR G
Swift: EBRD GB2L

Project inquiries and proposals:
Tel: 44-171-338-6282/6252
Fax: 44-171-338-6102

**The Inter-American Investment Corporation (IIC)**
Mailing address: 1300 New York Avenue, NW
Washington, DC 20577
Tel: 202-623-3900
202-623-3902
Fax: 202-623-3815

Project inquiries and proposals:
Tel: 202-623-3987; 202-623-3920
      202-623-3948; 202-623-3977
E-mail: alejandrav@iadb.org; iicmail@iadb.org

**The Export-Import Bank of the United States (Ex-Im Bank)**
Mailing address:  811 Vermont Avenue, NW
                  Washington, DC 20571
Tel:  202-565-3946
      1-800-565-EXIM (U.S. toll-free number)
Fax: 202-565-3380
Internet: http://www.exim.gov

**The World Bank**, aka The International Bank for Reconstruction and
Development (IBRD)
Mailing address:  1818 H Street, NW
                  Washington, DC 20433
Tel:  202-477-1234
Fax: 202-477-6391
Telex:  MCI 64145 WORLDBANK
        MCI 248423 WORLDBANK
Cable address:    INTBAFRAD
                  WASHINGTONDC
Internet: http://www.worldbank.org
E-mail: feedback@worldbank.org

**The Inter-American Development Bank (IDB)**
Mailing address:  1300 New York Avenue, NW
                  Washington, DC 20577
Tel:  202-623-1000
Fax: 202-312-4123
Internet: http://www.iadb.org
          gopher://www.iadb.org

Private Sector Department:
Tel:  202-623-1501
Fax: 202-623-3639

**Canada—EDC**, The Export Development Corporation
Mailing address:  151 O'Connor Street
                  Ottawa K1A 1K3
                  Canada
Tel:  613-598-2500
Fax: 613-237-2690
E-mail: export@edc4.edc.ca
Internet: http://www.edc.ca

**France—COFACE**, Compagnie Francaise d'Assurance pour le Commerce Exterieur
Mailing address:   Cedex 51
                   92065 Paris La Defense
                   France
Tel:  49-02-20-00
Fax: 47-73-77-36
Telex: 614 884 F
Minitel: 3614 COFACE

Information Office:
Tel:  49-02-10-03
      49-02-17-70
      49-02-17-32

Information on Project Financing:
Tel:  49-02-14-10
      49-02-18-13

Office in the United States:
Tel:  609-395-2196
Fax: 609-395-5717


**Germany—Hermes**
Mailing address:   Hermes
                   Kreditversicherungs-AG
                   Friedensallee 254
                   22763 Hamburg
                   Germany
Tel:  49-40-88-340
Fax: 49-40-88-347744


**Japan—The Export-Import Bank of Japan**
Mailing address:   4-1, Ohtemachi 1-chome
                   Chiyoda-ku
                   Tokyo 100
                   Japan
Tel (information): Tokyo 03-3287-9106
Tel (loan consultation): Tokyo 03-3287-9500
Fax (information): Tokyo 03-3287-9539
Fax (loan consultation): Tokyo 03-3287-9579
Telex: 2223728 (AAB) 2223728 YUGIN J
Cable address: EXPORTBANK TOKYO
Internet: http://www.japanexim.go.jp

Representative Office in Washington, DC:
2000 Pennsylvania Avenue, NW
Suite 3350
Washington, DC 20006
Tel: 202-331-8547
Fax: 202-775-1990


**United Kingdom—ECGD, The Export Credits Guarantee Department**
Mailing address:    P.O. Box 2200
                    2 Exchange Tower
                    Harbour Exchange Square
                    London El4 9GS
                    United Kingdom
Tel (switchboard): 0171-512-7000
Tel (helpdesk): 0171-512-7887
Fax: 0171-512-7649
Telex: 290350 ECGD HQ G

# 9

# Overview of International Project Finance

*Scott L. Hoffman*

International project finance is an emerging solution for financing infrastructure needs in many parts of the globe. Because it must respond to changes in economic conditions, political risks, market risks, and other factors, it is a financing technique under constant development.

In emerging markets, where the demand for infrastructure far outstrips the economic resources available, international project finance provides a financing scheme for important development. In countries moving from centralized to market-based economies, it provides needed upgrades or replacement of existing infrastructure assets that have not been adequately maintained. The need for enormous debt and capital, coupled with the risks involved in large project development, often makes a project financing one of the few available financing alternatives in the energy, transportation, and other infrastructure industries.

Other potential sources of capital, like governments and multilateral institutions, are increasingly unavailable for infrastructure finance. Governments in developing countries do not have the economic resources to finance infrastructure needs. Multilateral agencies, such as the World Bank, are attempting to promote privatization of infrastructure facilities, making project financing an important financing tool; but their resources are not sufficient to address existing and future capital needs.

For two reasons, project finance tends to involve large projects, requiring substantial sums. First, economies of scale can be enjoyed in development and operation. Second, the large-scale, immediate needs of developing countries for the cornerstones of modern economies (safe water, electricity, transportation, communications) require that larger projects be developed to provide as much needed infrastructure as possible, as soon as possible.

The purpose of this chapter is to offer practical guidelines for lenders, government agencies, project sponsors, equity investors, and other project finance participants in structuring and negotiating an international project financing. This chapter is organized into four parts: (1) an introduction to project finance; (2) an overview of financing sources, including multilateral and bilateral programs; (3) risk identification and risk allocation considerations; and (4) risk improvement and credit enhancement.

## INTRODUCTION TO INTERNATIONAL PROJECT FINANCE

### Definition of Project Finance

The term *project finance* generally refers to the arrangement of debt, equity, and credit enhancement for the construction or the refinancing of a particular facility in a capital-intensive industry. Project lenders base credit appraisals on the projected revenues from the operation of the facility (rather than on the general assets or the credit of the promoter of the facility) and rely on the assets of the facility, including the revenue-producing contracts and cash flow, as collateral for the debt.

### Nonrecourse Project Finance

Project finance is nonrecourse or limited-recourse financing predicated on the financial and the technical merits of a project rather than on the credit of the project sponsor. The credit appraisal of the project finance lender is therefore based on the underlying cash flow from the revenue-producing contracts of the project. The project sponsor has no direct obligation to repay the project debt or to make interest payments if the cash flows prove inadequate to service debt.

The project sponsor's ability to produce revenue from project operation is the foundation of a project financing. The contracts constitute the framework for project viability and control the allocation of risks. Contracts that represent obligations to pay the project owner on the delivery of some product or service are of particular importance because these contracts define the details of cash flow. Each of the contracts needed to construct and operate a project, such as the revenue-producing contract, the construction contract, and the operating agreement, must be consistent with the expectation for debt repayment from project revenues. Project risks must be allocated in an acceptable way. To the extent that project risks do not provide sufficient comfort for the project lender, credit enhancement from a creditworthy third party is needed. Examples of credit enhancement include letters of credit, capital contribution commitments, guarantees, and currency and credit insurance. Also, the project finance contracts must be enforceable and must be realizable to the lender as collateral.

A project financing is also based on predictable regulatory and political environments and stable markets, which combine to permit dependable cash flow. To the extent that predictability is absent or the risks of dependability are allocated unacceptably, credit enhancement is necessary to protect the lender from external uncertainties, such as commercial and political risks. In many instances, however, the project exists in an uncertain environment that subjects the project lender to unallocated risks.

## Advantages of Project Finance

Project financing is used by companies to meet several objectives. Established, well-capitalized corporations often select a project finance structure to assist in undertaking large debt commitments with a minimum of risk. Entrepreneurial developers rely on project financing to permit development of several projects in different geographic areas, each based on the merits of the project, independent of the financial obligations of the other projects, and with minimal equity requirements.

### Nonrecourse Debt Financing

Classic nonrecourse project financing does not impose on the project sponsor any obligation to guarantee the repayment of the project debt if the cash flows are insufficient to cover principal and interest payments. Each project is financially independent from each other project. The independence of each project provides protection of the sponsor's general assets from most difficulties in any particular project. The lender relies solely on the individual project's collateral in enforcing rights and obligations in connection with the particular project finance loan.

### High Leveraged Debt

A second objective of project finance sponsors is to finance a project using high leverage. The amount of leverage acceptable to a lender varies from project to project. Often the loan-to-value ratio is between 75 and 80 percent, but transactions are sometimes structured with higher ratios. The amount of equity required of the project sponsor is influenced by many factors, including the project economics and whether any other project participants, such as the contractor or the equipment supplier, invest equity in the project. The amount of equity required also depends on the risk perceived by the lender, including country risk, and the amount of debt that can be serviced by the project.

A lender's belief that a high level of equity will translate into a high commitment by the project sponsor may influence the amount of equity the lender requires. This view holds that there is a direct correlation between the percentage of equity invested in a project and the project sponsor's dedication to the project's success. This is particularly true in project financings of facilities located in developing countries. A large equity investment, coupled with a reasonably high rate of return, will help ensure the involvement of the project sponsors if problems arise.

Subordinated debt can serve as an equity substitute in project financings. There are sometimes advantages to a project sponsor that lends money on a subordinated basis, such as deductibility of interest payments. However, lenders will want the subordinated debt to be junior in payment priority and lien priority to the senior loans.

### Avoidance of Restrictive Covenants in Other Transactions
A project financing permits a project sponsor to avoid restrictive covenants, such as debt coverage ratios, in corporate loan agreements and indentures or restrictive covenants relating to other projects, because the project financed is separate from other projects of the sponsor. Thus, existing restrictive covenants do not typically affect the project financing.

### Favorable Financing Terms
Lower interest rates and lower credit enhancement costs are often available to the project than might be available to the project sponsor. This occurs where a credit appraisal of an individual project is more favorable than a credit appraisal of the project sponsor.

### Political Risk Diversification
The project finance structure allows a project sponsor to protect its other assets from political risks of any individual project. This occurs because of the non-recourse nature of the underlying project debt and of the customary willingness of the lender to segregate the other assets of the sponsor from the project collateral.

## Disadvantages of Project Finance

### Complexity
Project financings are complex transactions involving many participants with diverse interests. Documentation for a typical project financing will include agreements with the host-country government, construction contracts, operating agreements, fuel supply agreements, offtake agreements, loan documentation, guaran-

tees, political risk agreements, and a number of others. Each of these agreements is interrelated with the others, making a clause in one contract affect the outcome of a clause in another.

Tensions respecting risk allocation exist between the lender and the project sponsor on the degree of recourse for the loan and, among others, between the contractor and the sponsor concerning the nature of guarantees, resulting in protracted negotiations and increased costs to compensate project participants for accepting risks.

The complexity of this risk allocation process has slowed the pace of project financing in developing countries. Many countries often do not have sufficient credit support to accept an allocation of project risk and back it up with credible assets or payment promises. Bilateral and multilateral financial institutions, such as the International Finance Corporation (IFC) and export-import banks, frequently accept some of the risks in a way to make individual projects financeable (see Chapter 8).

### Host-Country Financial Strength

The financial health of the host-country government for the project adds to the complexity. The International Monetary Fund (IMF), a sister organization to the World Bank, monitors economic policies of member countries, assisting in debt problems, inflation, unemployment, and balance-of-payments deficits. Although the IMF is not directly involved in project finance transactions, its policy interventions affect a country's debt load and can thereby affect project finance credit decisions and the underlying projects. The interventions can extend to tax, tariff, and pricing issues. For example, in countries where energy prices are maintained at artificially low levels, the IMF can set conditions for currency support that can pressure a member country to adopt a market-based approach to energy pricing. That approach would strengthen an energy infrastructure project based on the higher prices for energy that could be charged by the project.

A position taken by a country that is contrary to IMF policy recommendations can also affect a project financing. Because IMF currency support can be important, the failure of a country to address IMF concerns will affect the willingness of the private financial community to participate in the proposed project.

### Increased Lender Risk

The degree of lender risk in a project financing is material. Many project financing risks cannot be effectively allocated or the resulting credit risk enhanced. This high-risk scenario results in rates and fees charged by lenders for the transaction that are higher than those charged in other types of transactions, and it results in an expensive due diligence review by the lender's counsel.

### Lender Supervision

Another disadvantage of a project financing is the degree of supervision a lender will impose on the project's management and operation. This obligation is incorporated into the project loan agreements, which require the sponsor to satisfy certain tests, such as debt service and operating budget, and to comply with covenants, such as restrictions on transfer of ownership and management continuity.

Lender supervision during construction, start-up, and operations results in higher costs, which are typically borne by the sponsor. This includes costs for the continuing review by independent engineers and consultants required to monitor construction progress and performance during project operations.

## Examples of Facilities Developed with Project Finance

### Electrical Energy
Project finance is most commonly used as a technique for financing construction of new energy infrastructure. It is used in industrialized countries, such as the United States, and in emerging countries, such as in Eastern Europe and the Pacific Rim, or in countries with tremendous new infrastructure demands, such as in Latin America.

In emerging countries, project finance presents an alternative to the traditional, non-market-based development of electricity resources. Historically, in these countries, electrical resources were owned by vertically integrated public monopolies that generated, transmitted, and distributed electric power; financed by the utility or official borrowings; and subsidized by the local government or cross-subsidized by industrial and residential customer groups. Project finance permits the traditional structure to move from these monopolies to private generation of electricity. Project finance is possible when a creditworthy purchaser of power enters into a long-term contract to purchase the electricity generated by the facility.

Private power projects financed on a project finance basis are developed by special-purpose companies formed for the specific purpose of developing, owning, and operating the facility. The special-purpose company has no other assets or operations, although the contracting parties are expected to be knowledgeable and experienced. Lenders rely on the cash flow of the project for debt repayment and collateralize the loan with all of the project's assets. A power sales agreement, a type of offtake contract, is the linchpin of the project. This contract creates a long-term obligation by a creditworthy power purchaser to purchase the energy produced at the project for a set price.

### Pipelines and Refineries
Development of new large pipelines and refineries is also facilitated by project finance. Before the use of project finance as a financing technique, these facilities were financed either by the internal cash generation of oil companies or by governments.

### Mining
Project finance is also used as a financing technique for development of copper, iron ore, and bauxite mining in countries like Chile, Peru, and Australia.

### Toll Roads

Development of new roads is sometimes financed with project finance. Project financing is particularly attractive for financing toll roads, because of the capital-intensive nature of roads in a time of limited governmental resources. The financeability of toll roads, which is based on toll revenues, depends on the certainty of traffic and toll revenue projections. It is obviously easier to finance a toll road in a highly traveled corridor than in a location with no demonstrated traffic demand.

### Waste Disposal

Similarly, project finance is an attractive financing vehicle for household, industrial, and hazardous waste disposal facilities. The revenue generated by so-called tipping fees (the term has its genesis in the physical act of a garbage truck "tipping" its contents at a landfill) can be the revenue flow necessary to support a project financing.

### Water

The water industry (impounding and treating raw water, distributing water, collecting sewage, and treating sewage) is the last utility business to open itself to privatization and project finance. The industry is generally monopolistic in nature (water is important to society; water systems are typically local in nature; multiple wastewater treatment vendors usually do not coexist in a service area). As such, although marketplace risk is greatly reduced, government regulation is often assured. Apart from the risks inherent in ongoing governmental rate regulation, a combination of factors, including weak local government credit, competition between agricultural irrigation and urban needs, small facility size, and high transaction costs, can make project financing a challenging solution. Further, because water is highly subsidized in many emerging economy countries, successful commercial pricing is difficult unless meaningful tariff reform is implemented successfully. Yet each of these issues must be addressed by emerging countries in some manner. The private sector has sometimes found that increased operational efficiencies possible in many water systems can produce reasonable equity returns and can justify privatization and project financing.

### Other Projects

The use of project financing is limited only by the necessity of a predictable revenue stream and the creativity of financiers and counsel. Other uses include telecommunications, airports, and oceangoing vessels.

## FINANCING THE PROJECT

### Generally

For several decades, multilateral development banks and bilateral aid provided financing for most large-scale public-sector infrastructure projects. Often, the host country's sovereign credit formed the underlying credit for the project. On the one hand, providers of private debt and equity did not take large positions in individual countries because of sovereign, political, or other risks—real or perceived. Public or governmental development banks, on the other hand, were viewed as more able to assess and to control risks in countries with infrastructure needs, primarily because of their existing financing role for these countries. Multilateral development banks and bilateral aid are not now the only source of financing for this infrastructure growth. Funds are available from various sources and in most project financings are provided by a combination of debt and equity. Commercial banks and consortia of commercial banks, leasing companies, insurance companies, pension funds, mutual funds, captive finance companies, and customers of the project sponsor are all among the potential financing sources.

Other potential sources of project financing debt include the project finance participants: contractors, equipment vendors, raw material and fuel suppliers, and output and service purchasers. The motivation for each participant to provide financing to the project varies. The contractor, equipment vendors, and raw material and fuel suppliers may be motivated by a declining market for their goods and services. By contributing to the financing of a project, the project participants can assist in the creation of a new market for their goods or services. Similarly, the entity that will use the product produced or service offered by the project can ensure that a scarce product or needed service is available.

## Financing Sources

At the writing of this chapter, the potential sources of financing and equity investment in infrastructure project financings seem both limitless and limited. A vast pool of money is eagerly awaiting the returns associated with infrastructure development around the globe. However, the risks associated with international project financings limit the willingness of potential lenders and equity investors to participate.

Close attention to the financing and investment sources is also necessary because of the frequent changes in the goals and the capacities of lenders and investors. A risk that materializes within an individual project in the same country as a project in development could temporarily delay all other financings in the same country. Debt crises (like the Mexican peso crisis and the financial crises of the 1980s), attitudinal changes at multilateral institutions (such as increased attention to the effect of projects on the environment), and other factors can also influence loan and investment fund availability. It is sometimes prudent for the project sponsor to pursue alternate financing schemes for the same project.

Financing sources are also affected by the goals of host governments and of project sponsors. Host governments are increasingly unwilling to support infrastructure projects with unlimited financial guarantees. Project sponsors are reluctant to undertake large-scale projects in a way that requires long-term project debt to be recourse to them. For income-reporting purposes, project sponsors desire to limit the presence of long-term debt on their balance sheets over an extended period of time. These goals limit the flexibility for financial structures.

### Banks and Institutional Lenders

Commercial banks and institutional lenders are obvious choices for certain kinds of financing needs: for intermediate-term project debt or for certain kinds of construction funds. Commercial funds are available from banks located in the host country or in other countries. Local banks are typically less able to provide financing for projects because they have less capital and less ability to assess project risks as compared to banks that do business worldwide. Interest of domestic banks sometimes increases, however, if international banks are involved in the financing.

Generally, funds come either from independent loans from a number of lenders or from syndicated loans, in which several banks provide debt on a pro rata basis under identical terms. As lenders, these participants tend to be risk averse. Risk identification and management for commercial and institutional lenders often results in relatively expensive credit enhancement.

### The Equity Markets

Equity is often raised in the stock markets and from specialized funds. The price associated with capital is reflective of the risks assumed by the investor and fluctuates as the risks fluctuate. Local capital markets provide access to significant amounts of funds for infrastructure projects. Although capital markets in developing countries are only now beginning to emerge, the growth and success of these markets suggest that they will provide an important amount of funds for infrastructure development. Potential sources of domestic capital include issuance and sale of equity interests on a stock market; sale of equity interests to institutional investors, such as insurance companies and pension funds; and sale of equity to individual investors.

International capital markets provide access to significant amounts of funds for infrastructure projects. This is generally limited to large, multinational companies, however. Access to international equity markets by companies in developing countries is limited because of legal limitation on investments and a lack of reliable, accurate financial information.

### The Capital Markets

Bond purchasers are usually the most risk averse of all sources of potential financing for a project. Although international bond offerings have been closed under a project finance structure, the bond component has been only a portion of the total debt. The risks inherent in a project finance transaction and the conservatism of the bond markets have combined to block the international capital markets from providing all the required debt in an unenhanced, nonrecourse project financing. Established bond markets are found in Germany, Japan, the

United Kingdom, and the United States. Other bond markets in Europe and Asia are emerging. In the United States, bonds are sold to individual and institutional investors.

The failure of the bond market to emerge as a large source of project finance funds is due, in part, to the difficulty in rating bonds for an international project financing. Bonds issued to the public receive a rating by a recognized rating agency, such as Standard & Poor's, Moody's, and Duff & Phelps. Rating of projects is a new, emerging area. In general, the rating of a project reflects the prospects for timely debt repayment. Among the factors that are considered in applying a rating to the debt for a project are sovereign risk, currency risk, political risk, legal (contract) risk, and market for output.

The credit rating process is time-consuming. Issuers are most successful when the process begins early. In emerging markets, the strength of the project, from a credit rating perspective, depends on the solidity of the project's important contracts and on whether all the project elements are appropriately covered by the contracts.

Project sponsors, lenders, and governmental agencies constantly monitor the availability of financing sources and develop structures to address shortfalls in access to debt and capital. For example, one recent solution to the failure of the public debt markets to provide sufficient project debt is a mini-perm structure, an abbreviation for a "short-term, permanent" financing. Under this financing structure, construction and term debt is loaned by private institutions, with a contemplated refinancing by a public bond issuance at the end of the term. The term of the institution debt is typically 5 to 7 years, repaid under a long-term amortization schedule (12 to 25 years), with the remaining balance maturing at the end of the term. This balance due is often referred to as a *bullet maturity*. At maturity, proceeds from the bond issuance are used to repay the institutional debt.

Another alternative is the amortizing mini-perm structure. This structure eliminates the risk that the project will be unable, for whatever reason, to successfully access the public debt markets on attractive terms at the time of the maturity of the institutional debt. Under this structure, financing is provided by both the public debt market and institutional lenders, with the public debt market providing the most significant percentage (i.e., 85 percent). The debt is amortized so that all institutional debt is repaid within the initial short-term maturity schedule (5 to 7 years). During this time, the public debtholders defer to the default, consent, and waiver decisions of the private institutions. An exception occurs when a default exists that is of fundamental significance to the public debtholders, such as when the interests of the private institutions conflict significantly with the interests of the public debtholders.

There are two important advantages of the amortizing mini-perm structure to project finance. First, there is no refinancing risk, and the institutional lenders can charge lower rates and fees in the absence of that risk. Second, the public debtholders enjoy the project expertise of the institutional lenders, which monitor the project construction and performance, thus minimizing structuring costs and allowing for greater project flexibility.

### Investment Funds

Investment funds mobilize private sector funds for investment in infrastructure projects. These specialized funds are sponsored by governments or by the private sector.

## PROJECT RISK IDENTIFICATION AND ALLOCATION OF RESPONSIBILITY

### Generally

Because a project financing is nonrecourse to the project sponsor, financial responsibility for project risks must be allocated to parties willing to assume recourse liability and possessing adequate credit to accept the risks. The allocation of risk varies from transaction to transaction and is largely dependent on the bargaining position of the participants and on the ability of the project to cover risk contingencies from underlying cash flow and reserves. There are three categories of risk in a typical, project financing: (1) design engineering and construction risks, (2) start-up risks, and (3) operating risks.

An analysis of a project financing by each participant, and the negotiation approach for the project documents, typically begins with a compilation of risk and a determination of the party best capable of bearing each through credit support. The allocation of risk is determined on the basis of control over the risk, the reward associated with that control, and creditworthiness. It is generally true that the participant that is best able to exercise control over a risk or that will realize the greatest reward if the risk does not materialize is allocated the risk.

For example, a risk identified in a project may be that a key contract will terminate if a change in law occurs. No party can control the occurrence of that risk, but all parties in the project will benefit if the project is completed. The party selected to bear the change of law risk, however, may be the project sponsor because the change of law risk is a risk sometimes allocated to equity. If the project sponsor lacks the financial resources to address this risk, other participants must examine the risk, determine the likelihood of the risk materializing and the value of participation in the project, and establish the terms on which allocation of the risk is acceptable. The allocation accepted often results in the transfer of some project reward to the participant accepting the risk through a higher contract price or an additional role, such as from purely contractor to the dual role of contractor and equity participant.

### Transnational Project Risks

Some of the risks in an international project financing are identical to risks found in a domestic project. Others arise from the transnational nature of the project.

This section identifies the major categories of transnational project risks. A later section identifies mechanisms for addressing these risks.

## Inconvertibility of Currency

A foreign exchange shortage in the host country may result in an inability to convert local currency into the foreign currency with which loan or other payments must be made. To determine the seriousness of this risk, the project's lenders and other project participants must examine the foreign exchange position. Currency inconvertibility comes in two forms, active and passive. Active inconvertibility results from exchange controls or moratoriums. Passive inconvertibility occurs when the central bank lacks the foreign exchange properly requested by a project sponsor.

## Currency Transfer Risk

Currency transfer risk arises in situations where the central bank of the country in which the project is notionally located converts the local currency into foreign exchange on its books and acknowledges the obligation but refuses to make transfers out of the country. This type of activity sometimes precedes a rescheduling of foreign exchange obligations.

## Currency Devaluation Risk

Currency devaluation risks arise in situations where, for example, a loan is made in one currency and repayment is in another. The risk is that the borrower's currency depreciates in value to a point where the borrower is unable to generate sufficient amounts of its local currency for the conversion necessary for debt service. Although protection against this risk is limited, its mitigation is possible through synthetic and natural hedging. For example, a turnkey construction contract with a foreign equipment supplier may provide for an automatic price adjustment on the occurrence of a currency rate fluctuation.

   In some projects, where fixed-price contracts govern cash flow, revenue streams cannot be adjusted to offset a detrimental change in exchange rates. However, this risk can be improved by matching the revenue currency with the debt currency.

## Expropriation Risk

Nationalization of project assets or the equity ownership of the project by the host country in an arbitrary, discriminatory way or without just compensation is called the expropriation risk. It can be accomplished in a single governmental act or in a series of "creeping" acts. Failure to pay "just compensation" for such a taking is considered a violation of international law. The determination of what is just compensation is an evolving one. The U.S. view has been that compensation is just when it is "prompt, adequate, and effective," a standard that is becoming the international standard. Under this standard the equity holders are entitled to a payment equivalent to the "value of the expropriated property as a 'going concern,'" payable in hard currency, not in the soft currency of the developing country.

Often, debt outstanding on the expropriated property is assumed or kept current by the expropriating government to maintain good lending relationships.

### Change of Law

The change of law risk is the risk that a governmental body (legislative, judicial, or executive) will change the legal, regulatory, or judicial framework in which a project was developed. The risk is that a lawful governmental action will affect the ability of the project to service debt or will otherwise make the project unprofitable. Examples of a change in law that may affect a project include import and export restrictions, increased taxation, and changes to environmental standards requiring capital improvements.

If such governmental action is lawful, political risk insurers will not typically insure the risk. However, the host country may be willing to contract with the project sponsor that certain regulatory actions will not be taken. If so, such political risk insurance providers may be able to insure against the risk that the contract is repudiated or abrogated.

### Political Violence

The risk of political violence, whether manifested in civil war or revolution, regional or world war, insurrection or civil strife, sabotage, or terrorism, can affect a project's construction or operation or even the very existence of the project.

### Sovereign Risk

*Sovereign risk* is the term applied by credit rating agencies to the actions of states respecting certain kinds of debt payment risks. In a project issuing debt in cross-border capital markets, one such risk is that a country may impose exchange controls or put other restrictions on the ability of a project to pay foreign debtholders. Another risk is the inability of a project to service debt denominated in the currency of the project's location.

### Political Environment

The political climate of the host country must be analyzed carefully to ascertain the receptivity to host-country investments. The risk of and the consequences resulting from a change in the political environment where a project is located is best exemplified by the experience of project finance lenders in Iran. The risk of expropriation by developing countries is obvious. Less obvious is the negative effect of indirect governmental action in the form of tax increases or demands for equity participation on project economics.

## Construction Risks in a Project Financing

### Increase in Construction Costs

The risk that construction of the project will cost more than the amount of funds available from the construction loan, from other debt sources, and from equity is perhaps the most important risk for participants in a project financing. Construction costs exceed estimates for reasons that include inaccurate engineering and plans, inflation, and problems with project start-up. This cost-overrun risk may result in increased debt service costs during construction and unavailability of sufficient funds to complete construction. Even if the overrun costs are funded, there may be an inability of the project owner to pay increased interest and principal that result from the additional debt required to complete construction.

Amelioration of the cost-overrun risk is possible even where the contractor has not assumed that risk in a fixed-price turnkey contract. Thus, in the event of a cost overrun, contractual undertakings can require the project sponsor, other equity participants, or standby equity participants to invest additional equity. Similarly, standby funding agreements for additional financing from the construction lender, from subordinated debt loaned by project participants, or from third parties can be used. Another alternative is to establish an escrow fund or a contingency account under which the project sponsor provides funds to complete the project in the event of a cost overrun.

### Delay in Completion

A delay in project completion may result in an increase in project construction costs and a concomitant increase in debt service costs. The delay may also impact the scheduled flow of project revenues necessary to cover debt service and operations and maintenance expenses. In addition, a delay in project completion may result in damages under, or termination of project contracts, such as fuel supply and output contracts.

### Experience and Resources of Contractor

The experience and the reputation of the contractor, subcontractors, and suppliers for a project should ensure the timely completion of the project at the stated price. Similarly, the contractor, subcontractors, and suppliers must possess the financial resources necessary to support contractual provisions relating to liquidated damage payments, workmanship guarantees, indemnities, and self-insurance obligations.

The contractor must possess sufficient human and technical resources necessary to satisfy contractual requirements. The potential risk is that the contractor or a major subcontractor or equipment supplier will be unable to perform a contractual obligation because of a low commitment to the industry, insufficient resources, or lack of knowledge or experience.

In an international project, the contractor should be particularly adept at working with the local labor force. Experienced, local, construction-site managers are especially useful in reducing the risk of local labor problems.

### Building Materials

A project finance risk often overlooked in industrialized countries is the risk of unavailability of building materials necessary for project construction. Although in theory any material is available at a price, the price and the time necessary to manufacture or to transport the material can impact project economics in a manner similar to cost overruns and delays. Of particular concern is the impact of import and export laws either when the project is located abroad or where imported materials are contemplated for construction.

### Facility Site

Preexisting conditions on the project site can affect construction and long-term operations, especially if the site has hazardous waste problems. Site condition problems that can impact the project's cost, construction schedule, and operations include geological formations and ongoing mining and other underground site conditions.

### Technology

Project finance participants cannot ignore new technologies because such technologies can result in profitable project financings. Nevertheless, without credit enhancement to cover the risk that the new technology will not perform as expected, project financings do not often involve these technologies. Cash flows from unproven technologies are not sufficiently predictable and therefore form an unstable basis for a project financing. An example of this risk is exemplified by the early technology difficulties in resource recovery projects. However, new technology can be used in a project financing if the obligation to repay project debt is supported by a guarantee of technological performance from the participant that owns or licenses the technology, such as the equipment supplier or contractor.

### Construction of Related Facilities

International projects, particularly in developing countries, often require the simultaneous construction of facilities related to the project. Large gas pipelines, docks, railways, manufacturing facilities, electrical interconnections, and transportation facilities may be required. Each of these facilities will affect the project's success and must be examined to determine the risks. Construction synchronization is perhaps the most important initial concern to the project's promoters.

Of equal concern is compatibility of systems. For example, rail beds, roads, and docks must be adequately designed to conform with the project's requirements. Existing infrastructure must be examined to determine whether these can satisfy project requirements.

### Permits and Licenses

The risk that a project does not have or might not obtain permits necessary for the construction or the operation of the project is a significant concern to all project participants. Generally, permits for the project must be obtained before closing or at least be obtainable without unreasonable delay or expense. At the time of construction funding, permits are classifiable in three categories: (1) permits already obtained and in full force and effect, which are not subject to appeal, further proceedings, or any unsatisfied condition that might result in a material modification or revocation; (2) permits routinely granted on application that would not normally be obtained before construction; and (3) permits other than those in full force and effect and those routinely granted on application. The last category is a source of concern for project participants. The application and approval process for this category must be carefully examined to determine the likelihood of issuance, the cost associated with possible conditions attached to permit approval, and similar issues.

Necessary permits vary depending on the state, site, technology, process, and other variables. In any financing, the governmental agencies having jurisdiction can range from the local authorities to the central government. The process of determining which permits are required is typically the responsibility of the project sponsor in conjunction with the contractor and the operator.

## Operating Risks in a Project Financing

### Creditworthiness of Offtake Purchaser

Lenders base credit appraisals on the projected revenues from the facility's operation. Because the ability of the project sponsor to produce revenue from project operation is the foundation of a project financing, the contracts constitute the framework for project viability and control the allocation of risks. Revenue-producing contracts, like purchase agreements, are critical.

The purchaser of the project's product or service must be creditworthy, with sufficient cash to pay its bills, as proven by past, present, and expected future, financial performance. If this is not present, credit enhancement, such as a guarantee by a creditworthy central government or multilateral support, is needed.

### Market for Product or Service

Many project financings are based on long-term, take-and-pay contracts, in which one or more purchasers agree to accept the production of the project at a fixed or a predictable price. Thus, if the purchaser's credit is adequate and the project operates, a market for the product exists and the cash flow to the project is assured. But product risk does not disappear simply because a long-term take-and-pay contract is executed. Competition with other producers, new technologies, changing demand, increased operating or production costs, changes in the purchaser's needs, and other events can combine to render the take-and-pay contract less valuable to the project than had been contemplated. In some projects, such as solid waste resource recovery projects, long-term agreements are used to ensure that project cash flow is sufficient to service debt. Such contracts (also referred to as service agreements) provide for the processing of waste through a project for an agreed-upon price. The purchaser agrees to pay for the service whether or not it is used.

### Raw Material Supply and Utilities

The project must be assured a supply of raw materials and utilities at a cost within the range of the projections. The formality of the commitments for the supply depends on the availability of the materials in the project area. In addition, costs of import or export fees, transportation charges, storage costs, product stability, supplier market monopoly, and finance costs are all potential risks in determining whether an adequate supply exists.

To reduce these risks, long-term requirements contracts are developed to provide the necessary raw materials at a predictable price. Less frequent are supply-or-pay contracts, in which a supplier agrees to purchase the output of the project and to provide some or all of the raw materials needed by the project. With both contracts, the supplier's credit must be sufficient to ensure performance of the contract.

### Operator Experience

The project's efficient, reliable operation is essential to its long-term success. The entity operating the project, typically under a long-term operating agreement, must have sufficient experience and reputation to do so at the levels necessary to generate the projected cash flow. Similarly, the operator must have the financial ability to support operating guarantees and other obligations under the operating agreement.

### General Operating Expenses

Operating expenses in excess of estimates is another project risk. These excesses arise, among other elements, from errors in design engineering, excessive equipment replacement and unscheduled maintenance, poor labor productivity, and incorrect assumptions concerning the labor force required to operate the project.

### Management Experience

Similarly, the project sponsor must have the requisite experience to manage the project in areas other than actual project operation. Day-to-day decisions about the project are essential to the project's success and the repayment of project debt.

### Interest Rate

Where interest rates vary over the term of the financing, the risk of unrealistic interest rate projections can impact the project's ability to generate cash flow to service debt. The interest rate projections are typically a component of the feasibility study.

### Acts of God and Force Majeure

The terms Acts of God and *Force Majeure* refer to events beyond the control of a party claiming that the event has occurred (fire, flood, earthquakes). Which party will bear the risk is always a subject of negotiation, but it typically rests with the party best able to control the costs associated with each risk.

### Economic Projection and Feasibility Report Inaccuracy

The risk that economic projections and feasibility reports are inaccurate affects each of the risks discussed in this section. An inaccuracy in the appraisal of equipment, for example, relates to the amount of insurance coverage necessary, which in turn relates to ability to operate the project and to achieve projected cash flows.

### Legal Risks

Because the contract's usefulness to the project sponsor and the lender depends on enforceability by law, the fundamentals of contract law must be examined for each important project contract.

From the project sponsor's perspective, the project contracts are the basis for the project's revenue and expenses. From the lender's perspective, the principal collateral in a project financing are the contracts entered into by the project sponsor to develop, construct, and operate the project. The contractual rights of the project sponsor are, of course, subject to the contract's terms and a number of defenses, claims, and other offsets. These defenses and claims subject the project finance lender to a variety of risks relating to the project sponsor's performance and the enforceability of the contract.

In some countries, particularly the developing ones, a project financing, based on the underlying cash flow from the revenue-producing contracts of the project, is a new concept. Thus, key project finance contract provisions that are standard in the United States and elsewhere are not yet developed in these countries. Examples of these standard provisions include obligations to purchase a project's output at a defined price and defaults and remedies for aggrieved parties.

In a developing country that lacks this experience and laws to support project financings, it is not uncommon for project sponsors to enter into an implementation agreement with the country. An implementation agreement is designed to provide a legal and regulatory framework that supports project finance. In other situations, project sponsors must await legal reforms.

### Enforcement Risks

Reliable methods for enforcing a revenue-producing contract on which a project financing is based must be carefully considered. These include ease of access to the relevant judicial system, length and cost of the judicial process, and the ability to enforce arbitration provisions.

Even if contract enforcement is lengthy, costly, or otherwise unpredictable, the project might still be creditworthy. For a project to be successful without a firm output agreement, however, the market for the project's output and the price payable for that output must be assured based on demand and other economic conditions.

## CREDIT ENHANCEMENT

### Introduction to Credit Enhancement in Project Financings

The risks listed in the preceding discussion demonstrate that mere reliance on contracts is often insufficient to protect the lender from risk. Credit support from a creditworthy source is often necessary.

Credit support can take the form of direct guarantees by the project sponsor or the project participants, guarantees by third parties not directly participating in the project, or contingent guarantees.

Commercial risks must generally be covered by credit support of the project sponsor or by a responsible third party. Although the project sponsor, in theory, is the fundamental risk taker, the nonrecourse nature of a project financing limits its willingness to accept risks. While a sponsor may be asked to directly accept some risks, it will most likely also be asked to provide additional equity contributions on the occurrence of certain specified events and to provide credit enhancement in the form of insurance, third-party guarantees, or letters of credit.

In evaluating the usefulness or a particular form of credit enhancement, several factors need to be considered. These include the term of the device selected, the cost, and the difficulty of and time necessary for enforcement. For example, in determining whether to use insurance or a third-party guarantee to decrease the risk of a force majeure to the project, the premium, term, and time necessary to enforce insurance claims must be compared to the cost, term, and enforcement issues of a guarantee.

Risk allocation in a project financing is designed to combine credit enhancement mechanisms to distribute the risks among the participants. This combination must produce a bankable project without burdening any single participant to the point that the project financing is converted into a recourse financing. Credit enhancement is not limited to third-party guarantees, although these are an important component of many financings. Other credit enhancement mechanisms include limited, indirect, implied, and deficiency guarantees; comfort undertakings; insurance; letters of credit; surety obligations; liquidated damages; take-or-pay, through-put, and put-or-pay contracts; indemnification obligations; and additional equity commitments.

### Guarantees

A guarantee shifts risks to entities that prefer little direct involvement in the operation of a project. A guarantee is a mechanism that permits parties to put capital at risk for a fee without becoming directly involved in the project's operation. By assuming the construction and the operating risks of a project financing through a guarantee (versus a loan or an equity contribution), a third-party guarantor might characterize the guarantee as an off–balance sheet liability, although it may have to be footnoted.

There are two types of guarantors in a project financing: sponsor guarantors and third-party guarantors. The most typical guarantor is the sponsor itself. In most project financings, the sponsor establishes a special-purpose subsidiary to construct, own, and operate the project. The subsidiary, however, lacks sufficient capital or credit rating to support risks associated with the underlying loan obligation. To effect a loan, the sponsor must arrange some form of credit enhancement to cover the risks. Often this is provided in the form of a guarantee by the project sponsor of the obligations of the project owner.

The sponsor guarantee can be variously structured to satisfy the sponsor's objectives and the enhancement needs of the project. For example, a completion agreement is sometimes used in which the project sponsor is required to complete construction of the project. Once the project is completed to agreed-on performance levels, the agreement terminates, at which time the liability is also terminated and the project sponsor is able to guarantee other projects.

The value of a guarantee to the project depends on the guarantor's creditworthiness. It is also influenced by the guarantee language. Unless the guarantee provides a waiver of defenses and is an absolute and unconditional obligation, it may not provide the credit enhancement necessary to comfort a lender that creditworthy support is in place.

## Sovereign Guarantees

Often, certain political, legal, regulatory, and financial risks within the host government's control must be addressed through a sovereign guarantee. Such risks include an uncreditworthy local governmental entity or an unfavorable political or economic climate.

In a sovereign guarantee, the host government guarantees to the project owner that if certain events do or do not occur, the government will compensate the project owner. The scope of a sovereign guarantee depends on the risks of a particular project.

The sovereign guarantee may take various forms, including: (1) the host government's guarantee of agency obligations under the revenue-producing agreement; (2) "comfort" language, indicating the host government's support for the project; (3) a commitment by the host government to reform its law and regulations to support private infrastructure development; (4) setting tariffs that permit recovery of costs and a favorable equity return; and (5) a commitment to guarantee private debt needed for project development. The sovereign guarantee is often contained in a separate instrument that is not a part of the implementation agreement. In some projects, private-sector entities could be sufficiently creditworthy to guarantee the public entity's purchase obligations.

In countries where the infrastructure will be privatized in the future, the host government may be unwilling to provide a sovereign guarantee that extends over the term of the revenue-producing agreement. In such instances, the terms and the scope of the guarantee must be tailored to fit the possibility of privatization. One possible compromise is a reduction in the coverage of the guarantee based on the creditworthiness of the privatized entity.

## Limited Guarantees

Traditional guarantees are direct, unconditional commitments by a guarantor to perform all the obligations of a third party. Guarantees limited in amount or in time can be used to provide minimum enhancement necessary to finance the project. Examples of limited guarantees include those that are effective only during the construction phase of a project or that are limited in amount. An example of the latter is a cost-overrun guarantee in which the guarantor agrees to finance construction of a project to the extent design changes or changes in law require additional funds for project completion.

## Indirect "Guarantees"

In contrast to these direct but scope-limited guarantees are indirect "guarantees," which are based on the underlying credit of one of the project participants. Indirect guarantees are not subject to defenses available to a guarantor under a guarantee agreement. The most common indirect guarantee in a project financing is an offtake agreement. This obligation is typically in the form of a take-or-pay contract, in the case of goods, or of a through-put contract, in the case of services.

Other examples of indirect guarantees include agreements to provide additional funds, note-purchase agreements that require the purchase of notes held by a lender on the occurrence of certain specified events, and agreements to purchase project assets. They have in common the purpose of paying or reducing the project indebtedness if the project is not completed as required or if some other problem arises that affects the ability of the project to produce sufficient revenues to satisfy the obligations incurred.

## Surety Obligations

The risk that the project will not be completed to a point that permits operations consistent with projections is typically covered by a completion guarantee, which states that the project will be completed and will operate at a specified level of production and efficiency. This guarantee is provided by the contractor, but the risk is often assumed by a surety that issues performance and payment bonds.

## Commercial Insurance

There are several types of insurance policies available to cover risks in project financings. Changes in the insurance industry's desire to cover certain risks make it very difficult to predict what coverages may be available at the time a project is actually in operation. For example, presently available coverages for change in law and force majeure risks are limited. The only viable market is currently in London, and the cost seldom justifies the limited coverage provided.

## Political Risk Insurance

### Generally

Various national and multilateral agencies establish programs for political minimization in so-called political risk insurance programs. The use of the term *insurance* is somewhat misleading. The risk coverage is narrow in scope, and the claims procedure is cumbersome. Also, these programs do not completely substitute for a project management program that is sensitive to local customs and procedures.

### Multilateral Investment Guarantee Agency

The Multilateral Investment Guarantee Agency (MIGA), an affiliate of the World Bank, is organized to encourage foreign investment in developing member countries by providing limited insurance against currency inconvertibility and transfer, expropriation, war, revolution and civil disturbances, and breach of undertakings by the host government.

MIGA provides coverage of up to 20 years for debt and equity investments. The coverage extends to 90 percent of the principal and interest risk for debt and up to 90 percent of the equity plus 180 percent additional, to cover investment earnings.

To be eligible for the insurance, the lender or investor must be organized and have its principal place of business in a member country, or it must be majority owned by nationals of member countries.

MIGA provides coverage against currency inconvertibility risk (losses due to the inability to convert local currency due to excessive delays, changes in laws or regulations, and a lack of foreign exchange); currency transfer risk; expropriation coverage (against the risk of a total or partial investment loss caused by a taking by the host government of the project assets or investor control over a project, whether by expropriation, creeping expropriation, nationalization, or confiscation); war risks (coverages against losses associated with physical damage to tangible assets or a substantial interruption of business due to war, revolution, terrorism, or sabotage); and the risk of breach of an undertaking by the host government.

### *Commercial Insurance*

Complementary and alternative political risk insurance is offered by a small community of insurers. These include Lloyd's, American International Underwriters, Chubb Group of Insurance Companies, and Citicorp International Trade Indemnity, Inc. In general, these coverages are of a limited term and do not typically match the term of the project debt. However, private insurance companies are generally more flexible than are the Overseas Private Investment Corporation (OPIC), MIGA, or the export-import agencies because they are not constrained by public policy considerations. In addition, they provide benefits of confidentiality and possible cost savings associated with negotiation of complete, single-source insurance protection for a project, including casualty, liability, and other insurance.

## Liquidated Damages

Even if construction of a project is not complete to a point necessary to begin commercial operation or if the project does not operate after completion at guaranteed levels, the project sponsor still needs to pay debt service and to satisfy other contractual obligations. One solution to this risk is a liquidated damages payment by the project contractor. A liquidated damage payment constitutes an estimate by the contractor and the project sponsor of the ramifications of late or deficient performance by the contractor on the project. However, the enforceability of a liquidated damage clause must be carefully considered, particularly in the international context. Not all jurisdictions recognize the concept of liquidated damages.

# Checklist: Structuring the International Project Financing

I. Initial considerations in selecting project finance as the finance structure.

  A. Form of organization of project entity, tax implications (home and host country), expatriation, and so on.

    1. Corporation.

    2. Partnership.

    3. Limited liability company.

    4. Other form permitted by local law.

  B. Advantages of project finance that may be applicable to the project.

    1. Highly leveraged debt.

    2. Rate of return goals.

    3. Avoidance of restrictive covenants in other transactions.

    4. Favorable financing terms.

    5. Political risk diversification.

  C. Disadvantages of project finance that may be applicable to the project.

    1. Complexity.

    2. Increased lender risk.

    3. Lender supervision.

    4. Insurance costs.

  D. Identification of transnational risks.

    1. Inconvertibility of currency: Examine the foreign exchange position of the host country.

    2. Currency transfer: Analyze previous reschedulings of foreign exchange obligations.

    3. Currency devaluation risk: Consider synthetic and natural hedging.

      a. Automatic price adjustment on the occurrence of a currency-rate fluctuation.

      b. Matching revenue currency with the debt currency.

    4. Expropriation risk: Consider any prior nationalization experience.

    5. Change of law.

      a. Import and export restrictions.

      b. Taxation.

      c. Changes to environmental standards requiring capital improvements.

      d. Consider contract with the host country that certain regulatory actions will not be taken and obtain political risk insurance.

    6. Political violence.

      a. Civil war or revolution.

    b.  Regional war or world war.

    c.  Insurrection or civil strife.

    d.  Sabotage or terrorism.

  7.  Sovereign risk: Restrictions on the ability of a project to pay foreign debtholders.

E.  Identification of construction risks.

  1. Increase in construction costs (cost overrun).

    a.  Sufficiency of insurance.

    b.  Sufficiency of delay liquidated damages.

    c.  Availability of standby financing.

  2. Delay in completion.

    a.  Sufficiency of business interruption insurance.

    b.  Sufficiency of delay liquidated damages.

    c.  Availability of standby financing.

  3. Failure of project to meet performance standards at completion.

    a.  Sufficiency of business interruption insurance.

    b.  Sufficiency of delay liquidated damages.

    c.  Sufficiency of performance penalties to "buy down" debt.

    d.  Availability of standby financing.

  4. Experience and resources of contractor.

    a.  Experience with this type of project.

    b.  Reputation.

    c.  Dedication of personnel.

  5. Availability of building materials.

    a.  Export/import restrictions.

    b.  Transportation to site.

  6. Facility site.

    a.  Acceptability.

    b.  Environmental condition.

    c.  Utilities.

    d.  Access.

  7. Technology: New technology or proven technology.

  8. Construction of related facilities.

    a.  Transportation equipment.

    b.  Facilities (docks, railways, etc.).

  9. Raw material supply and utilities.

    a.  Fixed (or predictable) cost of raw materials and utilities.

    b.  Transportation infrastructure availability and cost.

 10. Market for product or service: Realistic projections (current or future).

 11. Operator experience.

    a.  Experience with this type of project.

      b.  Reputation.

      c.  Dedication of personnel.

12. General operating expenses (operating-cost overrun).

      a.  Inflation.

      b.  Changes in cost of finance, exchange, or interest rates.

13. Management experience of project sponsor in this type of project.

14. Permits and licenses: Status of permits.

      a.  Final.

      b.  Nonappealable.

      c.  Not subject to judicial review.

15. Political environment: Country and sovereign risks addressed.

16. Increased financing costs.

      a.  Availability of standby debt or capital.

      b.  Interest-rate hedging.

17. Acts of god and force majeure: Are force majeure provisions in the project contracts consistent?

18. Economic projection and feasibility report inaccuracy.

      a.  Consider recommendations.

      b.  Review assumptions.

      c.  Match projections to underlying documents.

19. Contract enforcement risks.

      a.  Sanctity of contract.

      b.  Experience of country with revenue-producing contracts as financing support.

      c.  Length of judicial process.

F.  What credit enhancement can be structured to enhance the identified risks?

1. Guarantees.

2. Limited guarantees.

3. Indirect guarantees.

4. Letters of credit.

5. Surety obligations.

6. Insurance.

      a.  Business interruption.

      b.  Political risk.

      c.  Casualty.

      d.  Liability.

7. Liquidated damages.

8. Indemnification obligations.

9. Sovereign guarantees.

10. Implementation agreements.

      a.  Authorization to do business.

        b.  Governmental cooperation on permits and other governmental approvals.

        c.  Currency concerns.

        d.  Tax benefits and incentives.

        e.  Legislative protection.

        f.  War, insurrection, and general strikes.

        g.  General cooperation.

II.  Financing the project.
  - A.  Bank financing.
    1. Construction financing or permanent financing.
    2. Senior or subordinated.
  - B.  Bond financing.
    1. Construction financing or permanent financing.
    2. Senior or subordinated.
    3. Credit rating for bonds.
       - a.  Sovereign risk.
       - b.  Currency risk.
       - c.  Political risk.
       - d.  Legal risk.
       - e.  Market for output/project.
  - C.  Export/import financing agencies.
  - D.  World Bank.
  - E.  Governmental agencies.

III.  Collateral for debt.
  - A.  Project contracts.
    1. Construction contract.
    2. Site lease.
    3. Output or other revenue-producing contract.
    4. Fuel contract.
    5. Operating agreement.
    6. Other contracts.
  - B.  Other assets.
    1. Real estate.
    2. Equipment.
    3. Miscellaneous.

## APPENDIX 9.1

# Case Study 1: Rockfort Power Project Financing— Example of Financing Structure

Participation by bond investors, multilateral agencies, and commercial banks can be combined to maximize financing sources and to reduce borrowing and equity costs for a project. An excellent example of this is the project financing of the Rockfort Power Project in Jamaica, West Indies. The project is a $120 million, 60 megawatt, diesel-fired power plant in Rockfort, Jamaica. The state-owned power utility agreed to purchase the project's power output over a 20-year period. The utility's obligations were guaranteed by the Jamaican government. A 20-year fuel supply agreement is in place with the state-owned refinery.

Project sponsors are CMS Energy (a subsidiary of a Michigan utility), U.S. Energy Corporation, Precursors Systems Incorporated, and International Energy Finance, each of which is an owner of the project company, a special-purpose entity.

The financing structure required a slightly higher percentage of equity than is typical of a highly leveraged project financing. Thirty percent of the project costs is paid by equity. The equity was contributed by the project sponsors and by third-party investors.

Construction debt costs are financed from several sources. Commonwealth Development Corporation (CDC) financed $20 million of the costs. Bonds issued by the Caribbean Basin Projects Financing Authority (CARIFA) issued five-year bonds, backed by an $83 million letter of credit issued by a German bank.

On project completion and at the maturity of the CARIFA bonds, permanent project financing is provided by the Jamaica Private Sector Energy Fund (JPSEF), a government-owned financing entity. JPSEF is financed by the World Bank and the Inter-American Development Bank.

Political risk is addressed through a guarantee by MIGA. The guarantee covers both debt and equity, up to $50 million.

The Rockfort project is also an excellent example of leverage and credit support. With one exception (the CDC), none of these entities, including the project sponsors, contributed cash to the financing. The other funds were raised when CARIFA sold bonds, underwritten by First Boston. The portion of the CARIFA bond issuance used to fund the debt is backed by the letter of credit from a German bank mentioned earlier. The bonds issued to finance the equity were supported by another bank's letter-of-credit. Thus the credit rating for the bonds reflected the credit rating of the letter of credit banks, not the project.

## APPENDIX 9.2

# Case Study 2: Tribasa Toll Road Project Financing—Example of Financing Structure

Mexico has relied on the private sector for infrastructure development. Under a highway concessions program, the government grants to private entities the right (concession) to develop, finance, operate, and maintain a road for an agreed-on period. The private entity is given the right to collect tolls, which revenue stream can form the basis of a project financing. The government is involved in approval of design plans, the monitoring of construction, regulations regarding the road, and similar governmental functions. On termination of the concession, the road reverts to the government.

The concession term is based on projected road use. If there is a short-fall in toll revenues, the term can be extended. If toll revenues and road use are greater than expected, either the term can be shortened, or the excess revenues can be transferred to the government. Concessions can also be terminated for certain defaults, such as nonpayment by the private entity or failure of it to maintain the road.

Grupo Tribasa, S.A. de C.V., obtained concessions to construct, operate, and maintain two toll roads, one north of Mexico City (Ecatepec-Pirmides) and one on the west coast (Armari-Manzanillo).

Tribasa decided to access the international capital markets for financing the projects only after several years of reliable operating data were available. Before that time, the financing costs were derived from the contractor, from Mexican banks, and from the local Mexican capital markets.

The resultant $110 million bond offering was structured to include both a Eurobond offering and a U.S.–based Rule 144A offering. The bonds represent U.S. dollar–denominated securities supported by Mexican peso-denominated revenue.

The Tribasa offering is an excellent example of revenue-supported project financing, despite unpredictability in revenue flow. It is very difficult to determine with any certainty whether a road once built will be used. The project sponsors needed to await reliable historical data on that use before accessing the debt markets. An important element of project finance—predictability of revenue—is sometimes absent at the beginning of a project; but predictability can develop over time and thus form the basis for a take-out financing of other debt.

## Appendix 9.3

## Case Study 3: When a Financial Crisis Challenges Project Finance—the East Asian Financial Crisis

The 1997 East Asian financial crisis is particularly instructive about the effects of such a crisis on project financings. The four most severely affected economies—Indonesia, Malaysia, the Philippines, and Thailand—all have private power projects financed using the project finance model. The full effects of the financial crisis will not be known for years, but this much is certain: the private power projects experienced an increased cost of power, attempts to renegotiate power contracts surfaced, and the region experienced a decrease in market demand for private power.

*Increased Cost of Power.* The currency depreciation that East Asian countries experienced caused an increase in the cost of goods and services and in the cost of power. Although the magnitude of the increase varied by country, they all experienced pressure to increase power rates. At the same time, the cost of capital and interest rates increased sharply as a result of new financial risks—real and perceived—associated with the crisis. These effects were magnified by a general underlying decline in the credit quality of the governmentally owned utilities that purchased project power. These utilities, with high levels of foreign debt, experienced associated foreign exchange losses in servicing that debt.

Also, the cost of fuel supply for some of the projects was severely increased, particularly in countries where fuel is imported for power projects. Typically, fuel costs are a pass-through for power purchasers in emerging country project finance. Thus, the cost of wholesale power must increase to offset the increased fuel costs.

The selection of currency for power purchases from private power projects also caused an increase in power costs in some countries. Where the wholesale power price was tied to a hard currency, the power cost increase was severe. In other countries, where the wholesale power price was tied to local currency, the effect was less severe.

Similarly, the currency for project debt affected the degree of power cost increase. Those projects with high levels of host-country debt experienced less exchange rate volatility, while those with high levels of hard currency debt were more exposed to a mismatch between wholesale power prices tied to local currency and borrowing tied to hard currency.

Finally, the extent of progress in power tariff reform had a direct effect on the utilities that purchased the power. The ideal, postreform, average wholesale price for power is generally thought to be two-thirds of the retail price charged to end-users. The other one-third is the amount available to the purchasing utility for costs of transmission, distribution, and administration. Those countries with advanced tariff reform have sufficient price spreads between wholesale and retail prices to allow some absorption of higher power costs without a challenge to the financial health of the purchasing utility. Where this was not the case, these utilities needed additional capital or government subsidies to ensure financial stability.

*Power Purchase Contract Renegotiation.* Demands for renegotiation of power purchase contracts are a tempting host-country solution to an underlying financial crisis. A contract renegotiation, threatened or actual, can cause negative long-term uncertainty about a host government's commitment to contract performance and sector reform. This effect is perhaps most pronounced on lenders and investors. Nonetheless, some form of contract renegotiation may be in the long-term best interests of a private power project located in a country with a severe financial crisis. Although a great deal of effort is employed in the risk allocation and mitigation process, it is in no one's interest to have a failed project.

Renegotiation may be less likely in a project financing where the host government and the purchasing utility analyze, in advance, the potential financial implications of the power contracts and limit governmental credit support. However, in some countries, such as the Philippines, governmental guarantees and other support were determined as necessary to attract development and financing of early private power projects.

The East Asian financial crisis reveals the implications of government risk sharing in a project. Where the host government accepts certain financial risks, such as through governmental guarantees of purchasing utility obligations, the implications of that risk absorption can be particularly severe in a financial crisis.

Also, the financial crisis suggests that renegotiation will take place less frequently for projects that are selected for development through a competitive bidding process rather than through direct negotiation with a developer. Competitive bidding should produce lower wholesale power costs, thereby improving a project's chance for success in a financial crisis.

*Decrease in Market Demand for Private Power.* Finally, the crisis caused an immediate reduction in demand for private power in the region, as the economies slowed. The decline made clear that market projections for power are, in the end, a function of economic health of a host country and the region and of the financial assumptions made about that health.

*Conclusions.* Obviously, the East Asian financial crisis will result in greater scrutiny of projects by lenders and investors. More important, it reveals that contractual risk allocation among the host country, its state-owned utilities, and the project company have financial implications that can be experienced in the real world. The ultimate lesson of the financial crisis may be that domestic financing, local currency purchases of output, competitive bidding, tariff reform, and reduced levels of governmental credit support will be important components of future project development discussions. Perhaps its greatest lesson is that sovereign guarantees and other forms of host-country credit support do not necessarily remove risk in a financial crisis.

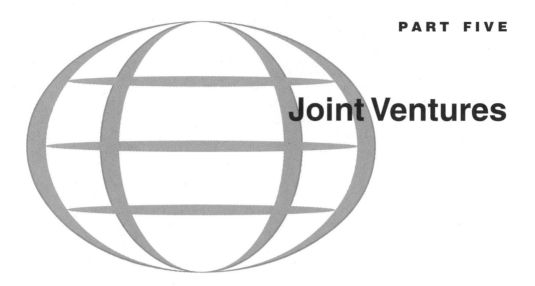

# PART FIVE

# Joint Ventures

In the next two chapters, Vladimir L. Kvint, a professor at Fordham University's Graduate School of Business and an expert on Eastern Europe, and Robert F. Ebin of the law firm of Sussman Sollis Ebin Tweedy & Wood, LLP, discuss international joint ventures and strategic alliances.

In Chapter 10, Kvint first analyzes the business and legal nature of the international joint ventures (IJVs), including such relevant topics as the strategy for creating IJVs and key issues involved in their creation. He then addresses the operating aspects of IJVs and the relationships with multinational financial institutions and national government agencies. The differences and the similarities of IJVs in emerging markets compared to those in developed countries are discussed. A checklist is included to consider risk factors in choosing locations for IJVs.

In Chapter 11, Ebin presents the legal aspects of joint ventures and strategic alliances. He covers organizational forms, regulatory framework in the United States and abroad, important legal restrictions abroad, and the structuring of joint ventures and/or strategic alliances. A special section on problems associated with technology joint ventures is offered. Finally, a checklist is included for the principal issues to be considered for international joint ventures and strategic alliances, with sample agreements for a manufacturing joint venture and for a cross-border research alliance.

# 10

# Nature of International Joint Ventures and Their Role in Global Business

*Vladimir L. Kvint*

## INTRODUCTION

International politics during the 1980s were marked by the collapse of Communism; the end of the Cold War; breakdowns of dictatorships in Latin America, Pacific Asia, and the Indian subcontinent; and the end of apartheid in South Africa. These changes and those from the technological revolution, especially in telecommunications, have enhanced the globalization of business. The increase in the gross domestic product of leading countries during the 1980s and 1990s was largely the result of the globalization of business (more than 50 percent of industrial products in developed countries are the result of international cooperation with each other and especially with emerging market countries). One of the major forms for implementing the globalization of business is the international joint venture (IJV). As the markets of developed countries have become saturated, companies have been driven to enter the global marketplace.

Formation of an IJV can decrease risk for both local and foreign partners. These risks include product risk (raw materials/part risk, human resources risk, credit risk, operating risk, regulatory risk, legal risk, aftermarket risk, and liability risk) and financial risk (currency risk, interest-rate risk, liquidity risk, settlement risk, derivative risk, and fraud risk). Also, IJVs maximize equity-risk transfer.

A joint venture (JV) may take the form of either a partnership or some other form of business cooperation. Whether a partnership or a corporate form is chosen, the resulting entity is a joint venture if it represents the collaborative efforts of two or more existing companies united for short- or long-term economic purposes. A JV is an IJV when the parties are from different countries.

The underlying nature of IJVs is the mutual interest of domestic and foreign companies in cooperating on business deals. Typically, foreigners contribute know-how, brand names, and managerial skills. Locals contribute production facilities, established marketing networks, cheap natural resources, and efficient labor resources.

Project financing, which was also an increasing trend in the 1990s, allows companies with limited resources to participate in deals through the use of mutual resources. IJVs also have opportunities to receive project assistance from multilateral and national agencies. Companies from different countries involved in project financing, focusing on managing risks and profits, are likely to create an IJV. Because of that, new forms of IJVs (accommodative and conventional) appeared. An *accommodative* IJV helps partners to reallocate risks associated with the project and to build more efficient ties between suppliers and consumers. A *conventional* IJV usually has limited contract support between partners, who share full market risk. This form may cause the IJV to be less leveraged.

A study conducted by the United Nations Commission on Sustainable Development, covering the years from 1985 to 2000, revealed that three out of four joint ventures between international and domestic partners in emerging markets and developing countries have been successful. However, the IJVs in which all the partners are from developed countries are more successful (e.g., Japanese and Swedish car manufacturers have created successful joint ventures in the United States with leading U.S. car manufacturers, using experienced, less expensive U.S. labor resources and energy).

Other contributors to the establishment of IJVs have been multilateral institutions like the World Bank, the International Monetary Fund (IMF), the World Trade Organization (WTO), and others (see the section in this chapter on IJVs and their relationships with financial institutions). *Globalization* of business and involvement of multilateral institutions (e.g., setting regulations on economic and business activities, offering financial aid and loans, etc.) create a favorable climate for establishing and operating IJVs. As an example, the objective of the WTO is to eliminate trade barriers. By breaking down such barriers, the WTO enhances expansion of international business and the creation of IJVs capable of producing goods and services abroad for import-export purposes. Product standards set by the WTO make products more desirable for other organizations.

*Regionalization*, another global trend, also enhances the climate for the formation of IJVs. Regionalization in this context means the establishment of favorable conditions for countries that are members of any regional organization or union. For instance, the North American Free Trade Agreement (NAFTA) creates a favorable climate for U.S. companies in dealing with Mexican and Canadian companies, but challenging conditions nonetheless remain for companies outside these regions. Thus, although companies in the European Union (EU) enjoy the benefits of regionalization, countries that do not belong to the EU often face greater constraints due to regionalization. Regional agreements may not directly benefit companies outside the region; but such agreements loosen restrictions on international business activities and create a favorable climate, and hence a greater opportunity for international partnerships within the region. Companies in nonmember countries can take advantage of regionalization by forming IJVs with companies from EU member countries, as Japanese companies do in dealing with members of the Association of South and East Asian Nations (ASEAN). If Japanese companies were simply to export to the ASEAN member countries, they would confront tariffs and other barriers that are mitigated by creating IJVs with companies from ASEAN member countries.

Consequently, foreign companies have increasingly used IJVs as a vehicle for direct investment in new markets. The formation of JVs between U.S. and international companies has increased at an annual rate of 27 percent since 1985. Usually, IJVs are not a form of full integration of the constituent companies, but rather a form of partial cooperation for particular activities in a new market. Analysis has demonstrated that the benefit resulting from joint efforts (net of the transaction costs arising from the formation and operation of the IJV) is often greater than the net benefit from separate efforts. The synergies created by the IJV result in risk reduction, economies of scale, production rationalization, convergence of technologies, and better local acceptance.

This chapter provides guidance for companies interested in taking advantage of the expanding potential of IJVs. Because countries and regional markets have very different regulations and opportunities, the chapter attempts to provide the reader with general rather than specific guidance.

## Business and Legal Nature of IJVs

Typically, IJVs involve international investment in existing local operations of domestic companies or domestic operations owned by entities from a third country. IJVs provide a vehicle for decreasing the investment required by companies when entering new markets in foreign countries. In emerging and developed countries, IJVs provide an ideal vehicle from business and legal perspectives for doing business in highly competitive markets. IJVs often provide the best opportunity for competing in domestic markets within foreign countries.

My studies have shown that nearly 20 percent of all IJVs are created to implement in practice proactive business policy with the primary purpose of gaining share in foreign markets, as U.S. and Western European companies have done in Latin America, Eastern Europe, China, and Russia. In places like China and Russia, the IJV may protect companies where laws and business practices create risk levels dramatically higher than those in the West. But many companies from well-developed countries take on themselves those risks to materialize reactive business policy under pressure of their competitors and of newcomers on their original markets.

## IJVs as a Business Approach

Before IJVs are formed as legal entities, companies generally enter *business cooperation agreements*. These agreements allow companies to "test the water" before entering into IJV partnerships. During this phase, the highest priority remains the independence of each company. These contractual agreements serve as feasibility studies and are often a critical phase in the development of IJVs. Business cooperation agreements that do not result in IJVs are also quite common in international trade. In practice, either such agreements develop into IJVs, or cooperation ends when the purpose intended by the business cooperation agreement is achieved.

Another legal relationship between companies that does not lead to the creation of a new legal entity is formation of a strategic alliance. Although it is seldom that an IJV in a new market does not include domestic partners, in theory, the venture could be between two experienced foreign companies whose only need is to combine capital resources and technology.

## IJVs as a Legal Form

IJVs are comprised of two or more entities from two or more countries. The first step is the choice of legal form. A JV typically will be either a partnership or an agreement for cooperation, depending on the desires of the constituent companies Whether a partnership or a cooperative relationship is chosen, the resulting form is a JV if it represents the collaborative efforts of two or more existing entities united for short- or long-term purposes. The JV partners have two choices. They can sign an Agreement of Mutual Activity, describing how they will coordinate their activities and listing their mutual rights and responsibilities. However, under this scenario each company will separately incur its own expenses. Each can pursue its own profit, or the JV can share expenses and profits. To decrease expenses, the companies agree not to compete with each other. Often they share office space and production facilities and combine marketing efforts. They share the costs of purchasing materials to lower overall costs. Alternatively, they can create a new entity. In many countries, an entity created in such a manner is referred to as a JV. Hence, this term refers to a new legal entity, not an Agreement of Mutual Activity.

As an example of an international joint venture, consider the relationship among McDonnell Douglas, Boeing, Rockwell Corporation, and Tupolev Construction Bureau, a Russian company. The parties are engaged in an international joint project to develop a supersonic passenger aircraft, for which they are using the Russian supersonic Tupolev 144, with McDonnell Douglas, Boeing, and Rockwell Corporation providing additional technology.

Some countries specifically regulate IJVs. These IJVs may be in a legal form for which the country of activity has special regulations, or they may simply represent a form of business cooperation between a domestic and a foreign partner in a country where there is no such regulation. Other than as described in this chapter, most countries do not have regulations concerning IJVs. Without such regulations, the laws that apply to the domestic partner apply to the IJV as a whole. If a government wishes to encourage IJVs, it will establish favorable IJV regulations, as was the case in the 1980s with the internationalization of Chile, South Africa, the Soviet Union, Czechoslovakia, and Hungary.

## Political and Economic Factors

International business, political, and economic strategies are strongly interrelated. Depending on the influence of modern political processes on the region, international business may influence a country's foreign policy, and vice versa. When considering potential IJVs, priority must be given to the evaluation of political and economic factors. Unlike investing in the United States or Western Europe, when investing in a foreign market, investors must often evaluate and consider political risks separately.

*Government instability* presents many problems. Among these are economic risk, as well as the uncertainty of volatile change in government regulation, legal authority, and the potential nationalization of the IJV's assets. For example, companies thinking about Russian or Argentinian IJVs have concerns about government stability. Investing in China, however, is quite different. Companies are not as concerned about the potential changes in the dictatorship as they are about the uncertainty of the Chinese political hierarchy toward foreign investment. Knowledge of the functions and activities of government bodies, state companies, and private companies is critical. It is also very important to know when, for what reason, and to whom in the government one must go for information and approval. In fact, bureaucratic issues are reported to have caused 16 percent of all IJV failures in emerging market countries between the years 1988 and 1992.

The August 1998 Russian currency turmoil followed by a payment crisis literally forced several IJVs into bankruptcy. The Turkish government's currency float in 2001 and economic problems in Argentina in the same year dramatically squeezed profit margins of several IJVs. In the example of Turkey, the decline of the U.S. dollar exchange rate by 30 percent diminished the U.S. dollar–denominated income of several IJVs, including Bulgarian and Albanian ventures.

In addition to bureaucratic issues, legal issues cause problems for IJVs. The government of the jurisdiction in which an IJV is located may continue to change laws in favor of the formation of IJVs. However, the legal issues causing 10 percent of all IJV failures in emerging markets between the years 1988 and 1992 were as a result of the form, not the substance, of legal documents. IJV agreements are often not approved if written in a format other than that embraced by the government. To avoid this problem, local counsel should be consulted.

*Internal political instability* or *regional conflicts between countries* create uncertainty and increase political risk. Such instability in the country in which an IJV is located negatively affects international trade balances in that country. Often, as a result, the government begins to place restrictions on international transactions and especially on the repatriation of profits and assets. Although some economic risks are inseparable from political risks, there are other economic risks that are quite independent of such risks. The economic risks that affect foreign investments in general, but especially emerging markets, relate, in part, to the presence or the absence of membership in international economic organizations (World Bank, IMF, European Bank for Reconstruction and Development [EBRD] and WTO, regional trade blocs, etc.).

*Currency fluctuation and inconvertibility* are common risks in IJVs, because the value of the dollar relative to the currencies of the partner's country determines the value of the IJV's overseas assets and earnings. An increase in the value of the U.S. dollar reduces the value of assets and earnings of U.S. multinational companies with substantial investments abroad. In addition, currency swings can affect competitiveness in global markets because of the impact on the prices of goods manufactured in different countries. Problems of inconvertibility and currency fluctuations were reported to have been the cause of 20 percent of the IJVs that failed between the years 1988 and 1992 in emerging markets.

*Inflation rate differences,* which are related to currency values, are yet another economic risk to consider for companies involved in IJVs. The United States and many Western industrialized countries have benefited from relatively low inflation rates over the past several years. However, many countries, including those in South America, the Pacific Rim, and Eastern Europe, have experienced inflation rates of several hundred percent.

*Democratization* of the former Communist and military dictatorship countries appeared to offer major business opportunities for Western companies. But these countries often initiated privatization before they demonopolized, demilitarized, and decentralized their economies. The consequences of failing to demonopolize were price increases initiated by those holding monopoly power, causing the majority of the population to fall below the poverty line. As a result, a lessened desire for privatization and an impetus toward renationalization began to take hold.

Depending on the industry in question, foreign companies involved in IJVs in some former Communist countries may face the risk of tremendous loss. In Russia and Belarus, the defense industry has been the target of renationalization. A Moscow court canceled the privatization of several defense aviation plants acquired by a foreign company, ruling that the foreign company did not have the appropriate government approvals at the time of the auction in 1994, even though initial approval had been granted by the government. This ruling suggests that almost any privatization deal made during the first stage of the privatization can subsequently be held to have been illegal.

If renationalization results from the kind of political changes that do not recognize prior domestic or international statutory or case law, the political and economic risks of a potential IJV are increased to a level that makes its creation economically disadvantageous.

## Strategy for Creation of IJVs

The first step for a foreign investor contemplating an IJV is to make a series of strategic decisions as to what kind of industry, in which country, and in what par-ticular region it seeks to invest. During the past 10 years, reasons for foreign investment have substantially changed. While traditional reasons, such as lower production costs and potential new markets, still exist, new and quite important factors have appeared. Today's consumer demands quality products at reasonable prices. Thus, companies must produce at high-quality levels and modest costs or lose their competitive advantage. This means that it is practically impossible to succeed with a reactive business strategy for entering an emerging market to pro-duce high-quality low-cost products while substantially reducing operational costs.

### Choosing a Location

Whether the IJV prospers depends in part on the resources available in the place where it is located. For example, the initiator of an IJV may enter a new market with a chemical technology that consumes large amounts of water; but if the IJV's location has a water shortage or a pollution problem, the expenses required to address the problem will make it extremely difficult to profitably implement the technology. The same holds true with an investor entering a new market with an energy-consuming technology when there is a significant shortage of energy or high energy costs. A frequently made mistake of electrotechnical companies or clothing manufacturers is to select a new market and to simply assume that they can readily acquire a cheap labor force. In reality, many less developed countries have limited numbers of skilled workers and relatively low unemployment levels, which cause the required salaries to be much higher than the investor had assumed.

Rapid changes in emerging markets easily confuse initiators of IJVs. For example, in the beginning of the 1990s, with the disintegration of the former Communist Yugoslavia, one British fashion factory decided to use cheap labor resources in Slovenia by establishing an IJV. But soon, living standards and employment compensation substantially increased, and that company was eco-nomically forced to leave Slovenia and to reestablish its production in Ukraine.

There are several important factors to consider when deciding on the location of a new IJV, such as development of the region, presence or absence of capitalist institutions (commercial and investment banks, insurance companies, accounting and law firms), and the availability of these services. Also important are the level of development of the region's capital and financial infrastructures; of the host nation's trade and distribution systems; and of its telecommunications, transportation, and energy services. A second priority is the level of development of the social infrastructure in and around the region of the new IJV. Thus, although China is one of the world's richest countries in labor and natural resources, the low cost of such resources has often been offset by costs resulting from its poor and unreliable transportation systems, which make it difficult to obtain such resources. Because most foreign companies are located in free economic zones in coastal cities, they find it cheaper to import resources from nearby countries than to transport them from inland China.

## Decision-Making Process

Strategic decisions regarding establishment of new IJVs must be consistent with the internal policy of the company considering an IJV. It is possible to use computer models to make a decision regarding the IJV, in a process guided by experience, common sense, and logic. Modeling allows one to choose from a variety of potential scenarios and from an infinite number of possible outcomes. An alternative to an IJV is a wholly owned structure. Sometimes, transactions are best facilitated by using wholly owned structures rather than IJVs. This is particularly true when it is anticipated that the goals of IJV partners may diverge after time or where a company seeks unadulterated control to better integrate the subsidiary into the parent company's production, sales, and marketing plans.

The establishment of an investment by a new wholly owned subsidiary is often a complex and costly process, but the advantages described earlier may make the problems worth addressing. In the decision-making process, one must consider how difficult or easy it will be to acquire the knowledge typically supplied by IJV partners to operate alone in foreign markets.

## Choosing a Partner

A major problem for many investors intending to enter a new market is finding a suitable partner. History demonstrates that a company less experienced in a new market has a higher risk of failure without a partner. In emerging market countries, for example, this factor, as my study shows, has caused 28 percent of the failures during the first four years (1988 to 1992) of international business activity in the emerging market; but in the fifth year it caused only 15 percent of the failures. The major reason for the decline appears to be that domestic and foreign parties gain experience over time and therefore learn how to find better partners.

In addition, my study shows that more-experienced foreign entrepreneurs know there is a higher risk of market failure when there have been unfavorable negotiations; language barriers; and conflicts of attitudes, cultures, and business approaches. During the first four years, 10 percent of the IJV failures in the former Soviet Bloc were alleged to be due to unfavorable negotiations; and in the fifth year the failure rate increased to 13 percent. One of the explanations for the 3 percent increase is the retention of Western lawyers in the IJV negotiating process. Hiring a lawyer or an international business consultant sometimes complicates the issue at hand if such a person lacks specific knowledge of the local market. This lack of knowledge handicaps the foreign partner and heavily favors the domestic firm.

Without a proper partner or vast experience of its own, a company is ill-advised to form an IJV, even if the business reasons are solid. It is necessary for each partner to bring complementary strengths to the partnership. Moreover, partners must be compatible and willing to trust one another. It is important that no partner seeks to acquire another's strength, for this undermines any mutual trust that has been developed. For example, Dow Chemical Company, which is involved in many IJVs, uses the early negotiation process to evaluate the other side's corporate culture and to assess the likelihood of compatibility and mutual trust.

It is necessary to formulate a business strategy consistent with the goals of the partners. Each partner must be willing to share strategic information—an early test of the parties' trust and commitment. Operational responsibilities of each party must also be clearly defined up front to reduce role ambiguity. Details regarding objectives and resource commitments should be clearly stated and documented in the IJV Agreement. Flexibility should be built into the agreement to allow for restructuring the IJV if the need arises.

Because trust is an essential element of an IJV and cannot be written into a contract, it may make sense to phase in the relationship between the partners to allow them to get to know each other better and to develop trust. Philip Benton, Jr., former president of Ford Motor Company (which has been involved in several IJVs over the past decade, most notably with Mazda), has said that the first time two companies work together, many opportunities arise. Working together on relatively small projects initially helps to develop trust and determine compatibility, while minimizing economic risk. Each partner can gauge the skills and the likely contribution of the other; and as trust and confidence build, further investment can be considered. Obviously, the best way to build these vital elements is by working together in a new marketplace.

The degree of trust relates in part to the question of interdependence. The higher the degree of interdependence, the more incentives there are for each party to behave in a trustworthy manner. Failure to meet expectations of trustworthiness may dry up the resources on which the disappointing party depends. This dynamic encourages self-policing behavior, which in turn increases trust. Trust, versus combativeness in resolving disagreements or tendencies to engage in opportunistic behavior, is partly cultural. In cultures where contractual trust is high, the contract language of the IJV need not be very specific. Conflict is avoided rather than encouraged and is resolved amicably rather than adversarially. In low-trust cultures, conflict is common and acceptable and is resolved adversarially, sometimes through litigation. Although cultural tendencies may provide a rough approximation of expected levels of trust between parties from different cultures, variation within these stereotypes must be accounted for as well. In fact, 10 percent of all

IJV failures between the years of 1988 and 1992 in emerging markets were a result of cultural differences.

The most recent study of IJVs conducted under my supervision was made in the year 2000, based on the statistical data of 1998. Ten years of internationalization of the economy and the experience gained through the creation of IJVs substantially changed the level of success and the reasons for IJVs' failures in emerging market countries. In 1992 only 10 percent of inexperienced entrepreneurs and executives were able to create successful IJVs; in 1998 the level of success reached 52 percent. The reasons for failure also were substantially transformed. The incidence of "no partner found" being reported as a reason for failure decreased from 28 percent to 7.5 percent. With the new data it was found that financing problems became the major reason why the venture was not created. Nine percent of all failures in 1998 resulted from bureaucratic obstacles, a quarter of which were related to licensing. A critical role in the creation of IJVs in 1998 was played by taxation. Thirty-eight percent of all failed IJVs were due to unfavorable feasibility and market studies: this revealed considerable complications resulting from existing tax structures. Fifteen percent of legal problems were due to taxation. It is also interesting that 75 percent of the financial disagreements were related to auditing, due diligence, and tax issues (see Exhibit 10.1).

## EXHIBIT 10.1

**Reasons for International Joint Venture Failures (1998)**

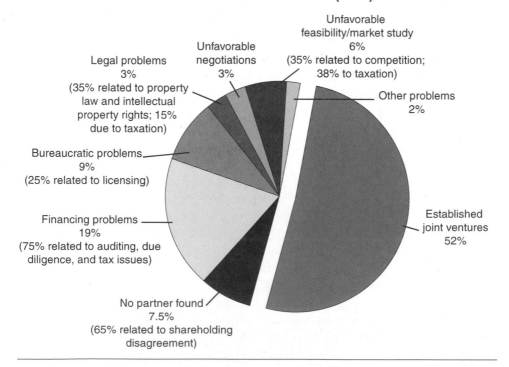

## Specific Legal and Business Issues In the Creation of IJVs

### *The Negotiating Process*

The IJV negotiating process frequently unravels. Some of the reasons are: (1) When two parties have equal knowledge of the market, negotiations can become overwhelmed with detail, and the process becomes unreasonably prolonged; (2) the inability to resolve the question of how much each participant will invest; and (3) lack of candor between partners. Too often, U.S. companies spend considerable money on trips and negotiations only to discover that their partners have lied to them. Many companies claim to be significantly profitable when they have earned absolutely nothing. Prospective IJV partners should request documentation supporting claims of historic profitability. This documentation should be audited in accordance with internationally accepted standards. Both partners should agree on an auditor and should decide which party will pay for the service. One needs to be aware of the poor quality of some financial information. The accounting systems in emerging markets, for example, do not allow for a realistic appraisal of products or assets. Concepts like "current market value" barely exist. The difficulty of obtaining accurate financial data makes the case for independent auditors that much more compelling. On other informational issues, the prospective IJV investor is likely to receive more reliable data from lower- rather than senior-level executives. Such data should, where possible, be supplemented by data from the central and the regional governments.

While defrauded foreigners can hazard the application of foreign law and litigate, the amount of the settlement or judgment will probably not justify the costs and the injury to the plaintiff's reputation in the foreign business community. A better approach is a rigorous, up-front due diligence process.

### *Drafting the Letter of Intent*

The principal document resulting from successful initiation of discussions between potential IJV partners is an IJV Agreement. The best way to create the document is to start with a letter of intent (LOI) instead of negotiating the IJV Agreement immediately. With some exceptions, the LOI is a nonbinding, legally unenforceable document. A useful tactic is to put all the points that have been discussed from the beginning of the negotiation into memorandum form and to have the memorandum in hand before creating an LOI. Points of mutual understanding are the basis of the LOI. The LOI is an extremely important element in creating a successful IJV.

What kinds of issues should be covered in the LOI? Surely one is the exact names of the potential partners of the IJV. The company names of the partners must match the names under which they are legally registered. One Swiss company signed an LOI with a Russian counterpart, which later became the basis for an IJV Agreement. Both documents were signed and the IJV was registered. Before the IJV started its activity, a U.S. company showed interest in partnering with the Russian company. The Russian partner was very attracted to the U.S. company, which offered the Russian company better terms than the Swiss did. The

Russian company, however, was presumably bound by its agreement with the Swiss partner. The U.S. company showed its U.S. and Russian lawyers the IJV Agreement between the Russian and Swiss companies. The lawyers discovered that at the moment the LOI and the IJV Agreement were signed, the Swiss company did not exist and, in consequence, was not registered, a process that was completed only after the LOI and IJV agreements were signed. The applicable law governing the Russian partner did not permit a company not registered as a legal entity to be a partner in an IJV. As a result, the agreement between the Russian and Swiss partners was void. The name under which the IJV acts and its legal address must be exactly as it is registered. Furthermore, as the preceding example clearly illustrates, the company must be registered before the deal documents are signed.

A very important part of the LOI is a clear description of the IJV's activities. Absent this, should the partners decide to diversify the IJV later, they will have to reregister the IJV Agreement. Accordingly, prudence dictates a laundry list of potential IJV activities.

In both the LOI and the IJV Agreement, the role of each party must be clearly set forth—briefly in the LOI and extensively in the IJV Agreement. In the LOI, there is a schedule of steps to be taken in executing the IJV, which is unique to the LOI and not found in the IJV Agreement. Apart from the requirement to bargain in good faith, the LOI, in anticipation of an IJV Agreement (as are most such documents), is not legally binding.

### Structure of an International Joint Venture Agreement

An IJV Agreement is a legal document binding parties to specific obligations and proportionate shares in the venture. As a written agreement, it clarifies party obligations as well as the purpose of the venture in order to document the agreements made and to mitigate conflicts between parties. The following major sections should be included in the written agreement:

- *Legal Status, Official Name, and Seat of Activity.* Statement of legal status of contracting parties and the country under whose legislation the combined venture will operate. The legal name of the venture shall be defined in the languages of all participants in the venture. The official seat of activity as well as the company seal and logo are included in this section.

- *Statement of Purpose.* Description of the venture's purpose of formation and business activities. This shall be a thorough description of all venture operations, including descriptions of all establishments required to be formed in order to perform this venture's activities.

- *Assets, Funds, and Business Activities of the Venture.* Definition of the venture's assets, their composition, and the contributions of which they will be composed are included in this section. It is important that the written agreement clearly state the participants' contributions and their proportionate shares in the venture. The amount of assets required to cover obligations shall be included. The agreement shall also state that the venture is liable for obligations against its assets. However, it is not liable for obligations of participants, and the participants are not liable for obligations of the new joint venture.

- *Management Bodies.*   Definition of the organizational structure of an IJV is required. This section states the members of the Joint Venture Board as well as their objectives, obligations, and rights in controlling the operations of the venture. The president in charge of venture operations and his or her obligations and rights must also be defined. In addition, the creation of other bodies required to complete the objectives and the functions of the venture must be clearly stated.

- *Auditing Commission.*   Defines the establishment and activities of an Auditing Commission. The Auditing Commission shall consist of members appointed by the Board. The term and the number of members shall also be mentioned in this section.

- *Accounting Requirements.*   The venture shall keep business records, books of account, and statistical records according to the procedures established by the Board in compliance with the legislation of the country of IJV registration. Accounting records shall be in the language of the country of the IJV registration. Cost accounting shall be used in the currency of the country of IJV registration. Typically auditing opinion for the IJV has to be issued in two accounting standards: (1) an international standard and (2) the host country's domestic standard, if there is any difference.

- *Rights and Duties of the Participants.*   The legal rights and responsibilities of all parties involved in the venture must be clearly stated.

- *Liquidation and Preemption.*   Requirements for approval and procedures for liquidation and preemption must be clearly stated. Usually, the venture may be liquidated by mutual agreement between the participants. The money received from realization of the venture's property as well as financial funds left after settlement of accounts with creditors shall be distributed among participants in proportion to their paid-up shared. The venture shall lose the status of a legal entity and be considered as terminated from the moment its liquidation is registered in the established order. A notification of liquidation shall be published in the press.

### Cultural Challenge in IJVs

This chapter has been at pains to emphasize that cultural differences often spell the difference between the success and the failure of IJVs. This is certainly true at the contract stage, where parties should be aware of cultural differences that affect the outcome. Subject to the limitation of all generalizations, German negotiators tend to approach the process in a thorough, systematic, but sometimes rigid manner, resulting in the need for a high degree of preparation, as well as for clarity and precision in communications. French and Belgian negotiators are observed to engage in "lateral" negotiations, preferring to discuss general principles before considering the specifics. The British have been observed to be informal in style, flexible, and open to suggestions. Potential partners from Russia and Ukraine, during the initial stages of negotiations, may appear very tough and taciturn. This may especially be the case if the meeting is early in the morning and follows a late night spent out with friends. However, do not be surprised if these negotiations become friendly toward the end of the negotiations, especially after the first shared dinner. Albanian negotiators can create considerable mistrust during negotiations by presenting facts and documents regarding the ownership of potential assets for investment that do not represent reality. However, Albanians will maintain all obligations that they will take upon themselves. This includes old contracts. One may also become very confused by negotiations with Bulgarians and Albanians simply through gestural communication. In these countries nodding the head means no, while shaking it means yes—the exact inverse of everywhere else. For representatives of Georgia, any result of negotiation in writing does not mean much. Georgian friendliness does not necessarily suggest that they subscribe to the obligations set forth for them, and the most serious issue is not the written contract but the friendship between negotiators. Negotiators from Korea, during the majority of negotiations will assent out of politeness; however, in the final moment will reserve the right to say no. Those from Asian cultures may appear tediously slow to U.S. businesspeople, who may, at their peril, become impatient and press their partners too aggressively toward closure. Japanese negotiators often demand a close interpersonal relationship characterized by mutual trust. U.S. partners often view the development of empathy as needless and even harmful in light of the U.S.–style goal of relatively depersonalized negotiations. On entering negotiations, U.S. partners must be aware of nuances in differing approaches to bargaining and should try to understand the other party's expectations.

Reliance on trust as a substitute for a formal agreement requires either strong cultural norms, under which trust is so institutionalized as to be a viable proxy for a contract, or a history of ongoing relations between the parties to the IJV. In such instances, mutual confidence compensates for a cultural environment of mistrust. Therefore, where the partner's culture is resistant to a formal contract, it may be advisable to replace the formal contract process with a negotiation-and-planning process.

The first years of an IJV typically involve the need to mesh what may be conflicting cultural attitudes by board members, executives, and managers from different countries. With goodwill on the part of all, this process can conclude satisfactorily, provided the participants are prepared to be flexible in learning how to work with one another.

### Determining Shares of Initial Capital

In some countries, a minimum amount of foreign capital must be invested for the joint activity to be considered an IJV. Although this amount varies from country to country, a minimum ownership of 30 percent of the outstanding shares and a capital investment of $100,000 to $1,000,000 is typically required for a foreign partner. For example, Ukraine requires foreign partners to invest 20 percent of the initial IJV capital, and the Russian government requires foreign partners to invest 30 percent of the initial capital. Initial investments can be limited in other cases. The government of Indonesia requires a minimum of 5 percent of the initial capital to come from within the country, thus allowing the local government to have at least minimum control over the activities of the foreign partner. In international practice there are also examples of countries allowing 100 percent of initial capital to be of foreign origin. In this case, regulations typically require that partners of the IJV be from different countries.

Parties quite often invest assets other than cash. For example, one party can contribute production facilities and know-how, and the other can contribute cash and/or marketing skills. It is very difficult to quantify the value of intangible assets contributed to the IJV. Given this fact, it may be better to start negotiations with defined shares of initial capital rather than with a finite investment figure. Usually, parties come to a mutual understanding through this approach because they share an interest in determining the value of the initial investment of all parties.

Mistakenly, many U.S. businesses consider the problem of convertibility of foreign currencies as the most important aspect of their negotiations. Lately, inconvertibility has become less of a problem. Through banks and financial companies, U.S. businesses can buy dollars with domestic currency at auctions and invest domestic currency in a dollar-producing business, or they can opt for a barter or collateral deal instead. In addition, bartering is common in emerging markets. This is due to lack of hard currency, the limited number of financial institutions whose guarantees can be accepted in developed countries, and the scarcity of cash. Few banks in emerging markets accept Western letters of credit because such banks lack working capital. Even if banks accept letters of credit, some lend on only half the required amount. A common practice for addressing this problem is for Western firms to buy raw materials from companies in emerging markets and to pay for them with equipment instead of cash, pursuant to a predetermined agreement.

Another form of international lending has the local manufacturer pledge a title documenting interest in a precious metal or other commodity to a bank in a third country, a practice that permits the non–U.S. borrower to acquire foreign-made machinery and equipment. As the business begins to generate profits, the borrower repays the loan and is returned the pledged title on full payment.

The most important point during the negotiations is determining the share of initial capital investment that each party contributes to the IJV, an element that may last the life of the IJV and govern the division of profits. Western companies should calculate the purchasing power of currencies from emerging markets during the negotiations and recognize the value of any contributed property.

## OPERATIONAL ISSUES

### Export-Import Activities and Special Privileges of IJVs

In many countries, IJVs have the temporary privilege of importing parts and materials necessary to produce and to export finished goods. In many emerging market countries, export-import operations are the only legally permissible way to open IJV accounts abroad and keep money in them. This is very important for IJV operations in countries with inconvertible or partially convertible currencies. Quite often, IJVs in emerging markets report higher annual imports than exports because they repatriate only a portion of their export revenues. A major part of the profit is kept in foreign accounts to fund imports and to avoid excessive home-country taxation or currency devaluation.

Inconvertible currency makes it difficult to finance imports of equipment, components, and services unless the IJV is involved in import-export operations. The IJV must export enough to offset any imports needed for the production process and to generate foreign currency for remittance to the parent.

Some countries isolate IJVs from the rest of the economy, through either special regulations or outright zoning. Countries do so hoping that such an arrangement will attract advanced technology and generate hard-currency inflow. Most countries impose a special tax on repatriation of profits of foreign investors. Some countries, especially those trying to attract foreign investors, offer tax holidays that avoid such repatriation.

Many countries create free economic zones (FEZ). Foreign companies and IJVs registered in the zone usually have privileges of tax exemption on profit, on repatriation of profits or capital, on export-import incentives, and on other tax holidays. In some FEZs, there is a regulation giving an IJV the right to use any currency or to enjoy special privileges in investment activities. For example, China has five FEZs and fourteen Special Technology and Economic Development Zones. Uruguay, Bulgaria, and Albania are now trying to create special zones as well.

### Hiring and Compensating Employees

The governments of some countries apply regulations to IJVs that differ from the ones applied to domestic companies. IJVs have greater flexibility in employee compensation than domestic companies do. Often, IJVs can pay their employees either in the domestic currency or in U.S. dollars and euros. Such an option is viewed favorably by most employees, therefore the IJV is more preferred by international investors.

Cultural, economic, and social differences must be considered when setting salary levels for local employees. For example, the average Russian or Ukrainian worker is often better educated than his or her U.S. counterpart and can be an excellent employee given the proper conditions. But the average salary of a

Ukrainian employee is only about $120 per month. Some of the gap is filled by employers who supply amenities, such as apartments, food, and household and medical products, that are in short supply in many transitional and emerging market countries. Such amenities represent excellent ways to motivate workers and to strengthen relationships between employer and employee.

## Restriction of Activities

Companies engaged in IJVs are typically driven by a consistent set of goals. Some ventures are created to provide entry into a host country that otherwise restricts direct foreign investment. Contrary to popular belief, postsocialist countries are not the only ones to impose such restrictions. For example, foreign investment in Japan was relatively restricted until the 1960s but was gradually liberalized through the 1970s and 1980s. Likewise, Mexico has traditionally prevented foreign corporations from operating wholly owned subsidiaries within its borders. Indonesia does not allow foreign companies to directly participate (even in an IJV) in building bridges, roads, or housing projects.

### *China*
Chinese industrial policy encourages foreign investors to purchase from local vendors new equipment or materials that address local needs, particularly in the energy, transportation, and telecommunications industries. Producers that fail to comply with these priorities may be ordered to cease production and may have their business license revoked and their sales proceeds confiscated. At a minimum, all products must meet product quality standards, which are determined either by the State Council Quality Supervision and Control departments or by industry custom and practice. Typically, however, IJVs do not produce the type of goods that are rigorously controlled by the Chinese government.

### *Eastern Europe and the Former Soviet Union*
Before the demise of Communism, foreign direct investment (FDI) was generally prohibited or suffered from overregulation. Around 1989, most countries in Eastern Europe and the former Soviet Union removed restrictions. Since 1992, most have enacted or amended foreign investment laws, often in advance of legislation, to support the new market environment.

As markets have liberalized, most organizational forms and economic activities have been opened to foreign capital. It is now common for governments to ensure that foreigners are not less favorably treated than their domestic counterparts. Complete foreign ownership is permitted in most former Soviet Bloc countries and in Albania. But there are some industries and regions where FDI is restricted. Special registration procedures for IJVs are still required in some former Soviet Bloc countries; and depending on the business segment, authorization and licensing are frequently required. Not unlike the practice in the United States and elsewhere, limits on FDI generally apply to certain military products and in the financial, insurance, banking, and mass media industries. Foreign participation in voucher privatization programs is increasingly permitted but is often subject to approval by different levels of authorities. But normally, in cash privatizations, foreigners are allowed to participate in both the primary and the secondary markets, as is the case in Bulgaria and Russia. In most countries with a transition economy, foreign investors are permitted unrestricted after-tax repatriation of profits, but many countries permit capital reparations only when the IJV's operations cease. In addition, capital control rules in Slovenia, the Czech Republic, Hungary, and the Slovak Republic restrict the transfer of salaries to expatriates. Romania, Slovenia, the Slovak Republic, Ukraine, and Uzbekistan charge withholding taxes of 10 percent to 15 percent on such remittances. Conversion of revenue derived from local currency by means of foreign exchange may be subject to prior approval. Furthermore, in some of the republics of the former Soviet Union, profits in local currency must be exchanged at less favorable rates than those applicable to other current account transactions. In some countries, governments extend guarantees to foreign investors against losses due to restrictions on property use by such investors. In the majority of countries, subject to some restrictions, foreign enterprises may own buildings and other assets, though land ownership is either prohibited or remains the subject of debate. Thus, in many countries like Poland, some argue that were it not for restrictions, nations like Germany could easily acquire considerable amounts of Polish land. This issue has raised painful political as well as economic questions. Restrictions on property ownership may be ameliorated by government-granted leases of up to 99 years.

### Latin America

Latin American countries have also shown increasing interest in attracting foreign investment to develop their economies, though much progress still needs to be made. New legislation and economic programs involving privatization and elimination of tariffs have facilitated access to these markets through free trade agreements in the region. For example, prior approval for foreign investment is not required nor is capital or dividend repatriation restricted in Venezuela and Argentina. New legislation and economic programs in Peru give foreigners the right to acquire up to 100 percent of Peruvian enterprises. Privatization of state-owned companies, as part of a government effort to attract foreign investment, has also helped increase private investment in Peru by 30 percent.

Another benefit of investment in Latin America is access to natural resources and the ports from which to ship them. Ecuador's location, for example, allows easy passage to North America, Japan, and Europe; but the privatization of telecommunications systems, roads, airports, and highways has only recently begun. Many of these countries offer great potential for mining. Chile, being such a country, is the world's largest producer of copper. The state-owned petroleum producer provides the Venezuelan government with 80 percent of its revenue. Yet the drawbacks of political and economic instability, demonstrated by high inflation rates, recessions, and high levels of poverty and unemployment, require foreign investors to carefully evaluate each opportunity. Countries with a high level of government debt are likely to reduce spending, which includes the funding of economic development programs.

### *Africa*

In South Africa, Egypt, Morocco, and Tunesia, the situation is similar to that in Latin America. All require external investment to alleviate low savings rates and deficits. Egypt and South Africa have loosened their restraints on investment by not restricting repatriation of investment capital and by permitting the transfer of dividends and branch profits if the income is derived from trading. South African development has and will promote regional cooperation among southern African countries, including the development of telecommunications and energy systems. Yet South Africa still has protective tariffs that diminish its attractiveness as a good passageway to the sub-Sahara. Liquidity problems and high levels of government debt result in minimal tax incentives. On the positive side, South Africa has good communication networks (albeit government-controlled), efficient port facilities and a highly developed financial infrastructure, including the world's tenth largest stock exchange. The elimination of apartheid has drawn foreign investors despite risks of political instability, racial polarization, and violence, factors worth assessing when considering the merits of a South African IJV.

## IJVs AND THEIR RELATIONSHIPS WITH MULTILATERAL FINANCIAL INSTITUTIONS AND NATIONAL GOVERNMENTAL AGENCIES

The past 30 years have seen the development of international rules and standards covering IJVs, among them the International Chamber of Commerce Guidelines (1972), the International Labor Organization Tripartite Declaration Concerning Multinational Enterprises and Social Policy (1977), and Principles and Equitable Rules of the United Nations Conference on Trade and Development (1982). The development of these rules and standards may reduce the application of conflicting laws in IJV contracts.

IJV activities are not restricted to the private sector. Many multilateral institutions, like the World Bank Group and the IMF, consider IJVs to be a useful vehicle for implementing global strategy in the developing world economy. Of course, these institutions mainly fund governments and their agencies, but their expertise and participation are crucial in many cases. IJVs are arguably the most efficient foreign investment mechanism used by these institutions. After 50 years of operation, the World Bank experimented with three private projects in 1995. The Philippines, Indonesia, and Pakistan were selected to receive World Bank loans for the energy sector. Because of the participation of domestic companies and well-known international companies, such as Enron Corporation (still successful at that time) and others, all three projects took the form of IJVs.

In addition, IJVs have gained strong support from national institutions of many countries, such as the Export-Import Bank of Japan, the U.S. Export-Import Bank, and the U.S. Overseas Private Investment Corporation (OPIC). OPIC is a semigovernmental agency that offers financial support and insurance to protect private U.S. companies from political risks when investing abroad. When OPIC or any of the export-import banks offer loans, they become important partners of the private investors. The involvement of these institutions assists companies monetarily and helps address bureaucratic problems too difficult to solve for companies entering new markets.

## DIFFERENCES AND SIMILARITIES IN IJVs IN EMERGING MARKETS COMPARED TO THOSE IN DEVELOPED COUNTRIES

Purposes for establishing IJVs vary depending on whether the IJVs are to be established in an emerging or a developed market. When companies decide to establish IJVs in emerging markets, one of their purposes is to reduce costs because by so doing, companies often gain access to cheaper labor, raw materials, natural resources, and energy sources. As a result of low production costs, a company may obtain the competitive advantage of low prices in the market in which it intends to sell. Most frequently, an IJV located in an emerging market targets the market of developed nations, rather than the emerging market in which the IJV operates. One reason for locating IJVs in emerging markets is that there are fewer environmental regulations—a phenomenon not likely to continue indefinitely.

Conversely, IJVs in developed countries are often formed to acquire high technology that may be employed to reduce overhead costs. Establishing and registering IJVs in developed countries can reduce the political, legal, and financial risks associated with foreign investment in emerging markets. For example, PLD Telekom Inc. is a company registered in Canada (1993) that operates exclusively in former Soviet Union republics like Russia and Kazakhstan. The firm was listed on both the Toronto Stock Exchange and the Nasdaq (from year 2000 it is part of Metromedia), from which it can access capital. A recent example of IJVs among companies from developed nations is the IJV of the Royal Dutch/Shell Group and Exxon Corporation.

## SPECIAL ROLE OF IJVs IN THE INTERNATIONALIZATION OF THE WORLD ECONOMY

The IJV is a rapidly developing form of global business organization. The advantages of different IJV forms of business organization may reasonably be expected to result in their proliferation. In the process, they will help bring the businesses of developed and emerging market countries together and, by so doing, become a vehicle to assist in the continuing development of a global marketplace. Creation of IJVs can bring together strengths such as inexpensive labor force, rich raw materials, cheap energy, high technology, and managerial skills from parent companies of different countries. IJVs where people from different cultures work together help create and develop new standards of business management and are thus a vehicle for unifying management systems. We confidently predict that (1) they are models from which new international standards will be developed and applied; (2) IJVs will be one of the forms for implementing project finance systems; and (3) multilateral financial institutions will increase their role beyond that of providing project finance and will become partners of IJVs. An IJV is one of the most effective ways of attracting foreign investors to the primary markets in the emerging market economies' privatization process. As the potential IJV partners negotiate the IJV and its location, each party will have different priorities, although there will be certain common concerns requiring mutual attention. These issues will help both parties evaluate political, economic, business, and technological risks of investing in the IJV. The following checklist of risk factors, while not all-inclusive, provides a fairly clear understanding from which prospective partners can make the critical choices.

**Checklist: Risk Factors to Consider When Choosing the Location for an IJV**

I.   Political factors.
  A.  Enforceability of constitutional and other rights; stability of constitutional and political structures.
  B.  Risk of expropriation and nationalization of invested assets.
  C.  Risk of civil disobedience and property vandalism.
  D.  Risk of currency inconvertibility.
  E.  Political relationships with neighboring countries and bilateral agreements.
  F.  Membership in international political and military organizations (UN, NATO, etc.); willingness to abide by nuclear nonproliferation treaties and agreements concerning export restrictions on weapons or dual-use high-tech products.

II.  Economic factors.
  A.  Membership in international economic organizations (World Bank, WTO, IMF, EBRD, regional trade blocs).
  B.  Business laws to protect private property, foreign investment, foreign trade transactions.
  C.  Tax laws (profit tax, export tax, tax on repatriation of profits, double taxation treaties).
  D.  Trade barriers (duties, quotas, export-import licenses, nontariff barriers).
  E.  Trade relations (such as most-favored-nation status).
  F.  Existence of free trade zones or special economic zones.
  G.  Relations with Paris and London Clubs.
  H.  Competition (difficulty of gaining and maintaining market share when confronted by both foreign and domestic competition).
  I.  Confidentiality of purchase and sale agreements, trade secrets and technology, operational information.
  J.  Patent, trademark, and copyright protection.
  K.  Nepotism/corruption.
  L.  Nationalism and its effect on legal and commercial areas.

III. Infrastructural factors.
  A.  Availability of business services.

1. Legal services.
2. Insurance services.
3. Accounting and auditing services.
4. Investment and commercial banks.
5. Trust services.
6. Stock exchanges.
7. Commodity exchanges.
8. Foreign exchange services.
9. Trade settlement and clearinghouses.
B. Development of capital and financial markets.
C. Level of activity of institutional investors.
D. Existence of established trade and distribution systems (whether there are established channels of distribution, such as import/export firms, distributors' agents, brokers, wholesalers, warehousing facilities, retail outlets, and aftermarket service and support).
E. Adequacy, quality, and cost of telecommunications, including local, long distance, and international telecommunications channels; telephone penetration access to fax, cellular, or satellite communications; data communications links; packet switching abilities; LAN (local access network) capacity.
F. Transportation.
1. Quality and extent of highways and secondary roads.
2. Access to air, rail, or water transportation.
3. Freight-forwarding and customs-clearing services.
4. Quality and cost of transportation services.
G. Energy (availability, reliability, and cost of energy for industrial and residential use).
H. Medical services, education, housing, and nutrition for local and foreign personnel.
I. Hotel and hospitality services (availability, quality, and price of hotels, restaurants, and other hospitality services).
J. Level of development and growth potential for:
1. Heavy industries (mining, metallurgy, machinery building, etc.).
2. Light industries (textiles, clothing, food processing, etc.).
K. Agriculture.

IV. Types of business risks requiring evaluation in the process of preparing feasibility studies for IJVs.
A. Product risk.
1. Raw material/parts risk.
2. Human resources risk.

          3.   Credit risk (financial services).

          4.   Operating risk.

          5.   Regulatory risk.

          6.   Legal risk.

          7.   Product risk.

  B.  Financial risk.

          1.   Currency risk.

          2.   Interest-rate risk.

          3.   Liquidity risk.

          4.   Settlement risk.

          5.   Derivative risk.

          6.   Fraud risk.

V.   Specific legal and business problems for the creation of IJVs.

  A.  Unequal treatment by the law in the jurisdiction of the foreign partner.

  B.  Regulations limiting the rights of the two parties of IJVs (almost always the foreign partner).

  C.  Disagreements in the negotiation stage between the partners on issues such as the division of shares of initial capital each partner will contribute.

# 11

# Legal Aspects of International Joint Ventures and Strategic Alliances

*Robert F. Ebin*

The era of the multinational corporation, extending its hegemony throughout the world, has given way to the era of joint ventures and strategic alliances. It is no longer possible or wise for even the largest corporation to expand internationally by the sole strategy of planting wholly owned subsidiaries around the globe. This chapter will focus on the principal legal issues to be addressed in choosing to do business in other countries in a close relationship with enterprises that in prior times would have been viewed as competitors or targets. Although the principal focus of this discussion will be on the legal aspects of establishing a venture sited in the United States, many similar issues are applicable to ventures established abroad and, where appropriate, will be noted. Besides a checklist for joint ventures and strategic alliances, included as appendixes to this chapter are two forms of agreement: (1) the formation of a traditional manufacturing joint venture partnership and (2) a strategic alliance for the discovery, development, and commercial exploitation of novel pharmaceuticals.

## FORMS OF TRADITIONAL JOINT VENTURES

Cross-border cooperation between companies is, of course, not a new idea. International joint ventures have a long history and have assumed several well-defined forms. A preliminary distinction can be made between those alliances that involve the creation of a separate entity through which the business of the controlling parties will be transacted and those that are organized as purely contractual arrangements between the venturers. The former constitutes the traditional joint venture; the latter includes joint ventures and, in recent years, sophisticated arrangements encompassing all manner of strategic alliances, sometimes also referred to as "copartnering" arrangements.

A separate entity is the logical choice when the parties intend a long-term or an indefinite-term alliance where there is needed a high degree of flexibility in managing for changing conditions and, most important, where the business can operate as an entity independent from the venturers. There are several forms the separate entity can take, the best known of which are the corporation and the partnership. Less commonly used forms in the United States include the limited partnership, the limited liability company (an increasingly popular vehicle), and the business trust (now rarely used). In each of these entities the participants will hold various combinations of ownership, control, and rights to earnings and will assume various degrees of liability in contract, tort, and taxation.

### Corporations

The corporation offers the greatest degree of uniformity and predictability in the package of rights it affords its shareholders (the joint venturers). Strictly a creature of law, the corporation brings with it a well-defined bundle of statutory rights, including the rights of the owners (shareholders). In addition, some U.S. states (California, for example) have adopted special provisions applicable to closely held corporations. The Internal Revenue Service (IRS) recognizes four major characteristics in a corporation: (1) continuity of life, (2) free transferability of interests, (3) centralization of management, and (4) limited liability. When joint venturers choose the corporate form, it is likely to be for the sake of continuity of life, centralization of management, and limited liability (meaning that only the corporation and not its shareholders is legally responsible for the liabilities of the entity). The transferability of interests will generally be strictly limited by a shareholder agreement because international joint ventures require a high degree of trust and familiarity between the co-owners.

As joint venture vehicles, corporations have the additional benefit of offering substantial financing opportunities, including the ability to sell interests in the form of shares and the issuance of corporate debentures and mortgage bonds. The benefits of the corporate form are offset, to a greater or lesser extent, by the fact that corporate earnings are subject to taxation at the corporate entity level and again as dividends respecting distributions made to the joint venturers as shareholders. Relief from these adverse tax consequences is obtainable through use of Subchapter S corporations and, with increasing frequency, the limited liability company described later.

U.S. corporations are creatures of state law. In the United States each of the 50 states has its own corporation statute governing such matters as creation, governance, personnel, and finances. Although the Model Business Corporation Act forms the basis for the corporate statutes of 35 states and influences the provisions of many of the others, reference to the laws of the particular state of incorporation is essential for a complete analysis of all issues relating to a corporation's creation, powers, limitations, and governance. Delaware corporate law is highly developed and provides certainty in business transactions, as well as substantial flexibility in corporate organization and operation. Hence, unless there are other countervailing considerations, the Delaware corporation is often used as a vehicle of choice for new business ventures.

## Partnerships

The partnership form requires fewer formalities in its creation than does the corporation and presents a correspondingly less structured entity. Essential to the partnership is the legal concept of *agency*, which is the power of each partner to act for and bind the partnership as a whole. The degree of confidence that each partner must have in the others is so great that if one partner abandons the enterprise or is removed by the others, the partnership itself dissolves as a matter of law. In partnerships with many partners, this rule may be attenuated by an agreement that the partnership will immediately reconstitute after a change in membership, but such an agreement is likely to be contrary to the needs of an international joint venture having few members.

The second basic concept underlying the partnership is that partners share profits and losses, with all the partnership's revenues and expenses flowing through to the individual partners. This leads to the substantial tax advantage that the partnership has over the corporation: profits of the partnership are taxed only once at the level of the individual partner.

Partnerships are created not by statutory formalities, but by private agreement among the partners. However, the Uniform Partnership Act, adopted in either its original or revised form in each state in the United States except Louisiana, establishes the legal relationship between partners and governs their liabilities and rights as against third parties.

## Limited Partnerships

The limited partnership is an entity midway between the corporation and the partnership. It is formed by a general partner (often a corporation) that manages the business and assumes all liabilities. The limited partners purchase partnership interests and receive shares of the earnings, losses, or tax benefits flowing from the limited partnership's business. The limited partners normally have no control over (and only the most limited voice in) the management of the limited partnership and no liability for its debts. (In fact, limited partners who participate in management run the risk of general liability as if they were general partners.)

The limited partnership, if created in accordance with IRS regulations, is treated as an ordinary partnership for tax purposes and does not pay income taxes at the entity level. Instead, all income, gains, losses, deductions, and credits are passed through to the partners, both general and limited. Interests in limited partnerships can be designated to be transferable (usually upon the consent of the general partner), and in recent years public limited partnerships have been listed on U.S. stock exchanges.

Every state except Louisiana has adopted the Uniform Limited Partnership Act in either its original or revised version. In the formalities required to create a limited partnership and the statutory restrictions on the partners' relationship with each other and with third parties, the limited partnership more closely resembles a corporation than a general partnership.

## Limited Liability Companies

Limited liability companies (LLCs) are relatively new to the United States, having been first recognized for tax purposes in 1988. Most states have adopted limited liability company statutes, and interest in this new form of business entity is growing rapidly. The limited liability company combines features of the corporation and the limited partnership and offers both tax and nontax benefits.

Like a corporation, the limited liability company protects all its owners (generally referred to as members) from liability, whether or not they participate in the management of the company. Like a limited partnership, the limited liability company passes through all the profits and losses of the entity to its members without income taxation at the entity level.

To obtain favorable "pass-through" tax treatment, IRS regulations require the LLC to adopt an organization agreement that destroys at least three of the four characteristics of a corporation; continuity of life, centralization of management, and free transferability of shares. Usually LLCs provide for dissolution in case of the death, insanity, bankruptcy, retirement, resignation, or expulsion of any member, thereby negating continuity of life. Centralization of management can be avoided by expressly placing the management of the LLC in the hands of all members; free transferability can be restricted by conditioning any change in membership on consent of all members. The IRS has recently enacted "check-the-box" regulations that permit entities to simply elect whether to be treated for tax purposes as corporations or as pass-through entities. These regulations will eliminate the necessity of meeting the hitherto formalistic IRS requirements.

A major drawback to the use of LLCs in international joint ventures is their relative newness. Many important issues of governance, taxation, accounting, and liability have not yet been clearly determined in actual practice. However, the use of LLCs is growing rapidly, and it seems likely that the principal LLC benefits of flexibility in structure among the members and pass-through taxation will often outweigh these uncertainties.

## Business Trusts

The essential characteristic of a trust is the conveyance to trustees of the legal title to property that is to be managed, operated, or invested for the benefit of nonmanaging beneficiaries. Trusts are normally created by agreement between joint venture participants (the grantors) and trustees without requiring governmental authorization. Although rarely used today, a number of states have statutes governing the creation and the operation of business trusts. Reference must be made to the laws of the particular state in which the trust is organized for analysis of the formalities of creation and operation of the trust entity.

## Limited Life Joint Ventures (International Construction Projects)

When the purpose of the joint venture is limited in scope and duration, such as a large public works project, the parties may decide that it is unnecessary to create a separate entity. This will occur most frequently in situations in which it is possible to anticipate the contributions and the duties of each partner, to agree in detail on the sharing of revenues and expenses, and to clearly define the length of the project. The benefits of a joint venture between contractors intending to bid on a project include the ability to qualify for a contract restricted to nationals of the project's country, the sharing of risks, and increased bonding capacity.

Reinventing the wheel is not part of the agenda of these ad hoc joint ventures. On the contrary, there will be a broad area of preexisting agreement as to the subject matter and scope of the joint enterprise. For this reason, major construction projects are especially well suited to the contract-based, as opposed to the separate entity-based, joint venture. The roles of the owner, architect, engineer, general contractor, and subcontractors in the various trades are clearly delineated by established practice. Standard forms of contract exist in most countries (e.g., the American Institute of Architects Standard Forms of Agreement, the Model Form of Contract for Process Plants of the Engineering Advancement Association of Japan, and the Conditions of Contract of the Institution of Civil Engineers in England).

In the international construction joint venture there is often the additional factor of governmental participation. Either the owner is a national government or a local authority, or the financing is provided in whole or in part by a governmental or multigovernmental agency such as the World Bank or the European Development Fund.

A joint venture between contractors intending to bid together on a contract is a specialized type of partnership. Because the act of one coventurer binds the venture vis-à-vis third parties and creates liability in contract or in tort against the other coventurers, the joint venture agreement will provide for adjustment of contract payments made by one of the venturers and for indemnification in case of tort liability caused by one of them. These internal arrangements do not affect the rights of third parties to proceed against any of the coventurers with respect to the project.

Management of the joint venture in international construction involves recognizing the stages through which the particular project will progress. Thus, one venturer may be authorized to prepare the bid, subject to the approval of the others, and another delegated the task of supervising the on-site work or dealing with the owner regarding changes and modifications.

In addition to ordinary construction contracts, joint ventures are frequently involved in bidding for design-build contracts, in which the contractor does not simply execute prepared plans for the owner but actually provides the architectural and engineering documents on which the construction is based. This can involve contractors who have architects and engineers on their staffs or independent architects or engineers who are themselves members of the joint venture.

A third type of project in which contractual joint ventures are used is in BOT (build-operate-transfer) projects. In these projects it is anticipated that the completed plant or public work will generate revenue by, for example, the sale of electric power from a generating plant or the collection of tolls from a bridge or a tunnel. The joint venturers will look to this revenue for a portion of their payment and will own the project until it is transferred to its ultimate owner.

## Strategic Alliances

The term *strategic alliance* broadly refers to a wide assortment of arrangements for intercorporate cooperation, including the types of joint ventures just described and many looser arrangements. It may consist of contractual agreements for technology licensing or cross-licensing, distribution, research and development, and favored supplier and cooperative marketing programs. The terms of the strategic alliance are driven by the objectives and needs of the participants.

## WHEN TO USE THE JOINT VENTURE OR THE STRATEGIC ALLIANCE

The decision to create an international joint venture or a strategic alliance arises out of the recognition that the strengths of one party can complement the weaknesses of the other. When a foreign manufacturer seeks to introduce its products into a local market, the alliance offers benefits that include the use of an existing distribution system, guidance in adapting the goods to local customer demands, and a broader product line for the local distributor.

When the participants intend to develop and exploit technology created by one of them or complementary technologies created by each, the benefits of an alliance include access to financing and manufacturing capacity for the smaller partner, faster development time through joint research, and flexibility in meeting changing market demands. If the purpose is a joint bid for a major construction project, the anticipated benefits include avoidance of protectionist (e.g., nationals only) legal restrictions, wider financing options, availability of specialized personnel and equipment, and expertise in accommodating the requirements of in-country labor organizations, zoning authorities, and other agencies whose approvals are required.

The first consideration in assessing the viability of a potential alliance must be the parties themselves, their viewpoints, and their separate interests. For a successful alliance, the parties must first examine their internal objectives, and communicate them in detail to each other and to their advisers. Unless the parties recognize that a strategic alliance needs a high degree of commitment by all levels of management, it is unlikely to prosper.

Cooperation and collaboration distinguish the strategic alliance from an ordinary intercorporate transaction. Therefore, each party must make an effort to appreciate the objectives of the other. One party may regard the alliance as an opportunity to enlarge its product line with new technology. Another may see it as the source of physical plant and capital. These viewpoints are not incompatible, but they may cause the parties to emphasize different aspects of the transaction. The party with technology to contribute will be most concerned about confidentiality of intellectual property, flexibility of deadlines, product specifications, and avoiding the intrusion of bureaucratic management. The party with capital and existing distribution networks to contribute will be concerned about predictability of costs, reliable deliveries, and continuing rights to obtain product in case of failure of the other party. Effectively dealing with these sometimes conflicting, sometimes complementary objectives requires that each party recognize the concerns of the other and its willingness to address these issues from the outset. Failure to do so will only provide points of friction that may ultimately doom the relationship to failure.

Both parties will be concerned about maintaining the management style and the culture they prefer, and neither may be desirous of making the changes that will prove essential to harmonious relations. Many alliances prove to be the first step toward acquisition of the smaller party by the larger; but unless this possibility is recognized by both at the outset, the parties should be viewed as much as possible as equals and the alliance negotiated on that basis.

## REGULATORY FRAMEWORK—UNITED STATES AND ABROAD

Although there is a wide range of regulation among nations, some industries are heavily regulated in almost all countries. A foreign party planning to enter a regulated industry abroad must find experienced and reliable local counsel to identify local laws and regulations restricting entry because the type of local partner needed and the form the venture will take will depend largely on provisions of domestic law. Closely regulated industries typically include defense contracting and government intelligence work, securities and finance, telecommunications and media, air and marine transportation, energy and natural resources, and public works.

Even outside those industries that attract the attention of government regulators, the foreign entrant should anticipate across-the-board restrictions dealing with currency movement, investment approvals, antitrust rules, intellectual property, labor and tax matters, and, in some places, condemnation or expropriation. Here as well, experienced local counsel is essential to prevent unexpected prohibitions and expenses from destroying the viability of the venture.

## Legal Restrictions in the United States

A foreign entrant into the U.S. market benefits from an absence of many of the foreign investment restrictions found elsewhere. There is no restriction on bringing foreign funds into the country or on repatriating capital and earnings, nor is there any general requirement of governmental approval of investment by foreign interests in U.S. entities. Essentially, the foreign party contemplating an alliance with a U.S. company faces only the same restrictions applicable to alliances between U.S. companies. There are, however, certain industries in which U.S. federal or state laws and regulations prohibit or restrict participation by non–U.S. parties; these industries include defense contractors, airlines, communications (radio and television broadcasting), banking, insurance, land ownership, mineral exploration, and marine transportation.

### U.S. Antitrust Considerations

Generally, U.S. antitrust law applies to activities of international strategic alliances in the same way that it does to domestic entities. Whether structured as a traditional joint venture or as a strategic alliance, any joint activity by actual or potential competitors, or those involving arrangements between vertical enterprises (e.g., manufacturer/distributor), may involve anticompetitive aspects and should be reviewed with experienced and knowledgeable antitrust legal counsel early in the process. Note that if the alliance deals solely with exports of goods or services from the United States, a certificate of exemption under the Export Trading Company Act of 1982 may be available from the Secretary of Commerce.

Acquisitions of U.S. companies by foreign enterprises are subject to provisions of the Clayton Antitrust Act, especially Section 7, which prohibits any combination causing anticompetitive effects in the United States. In 1992 the U.S. Department of Justice promulgated Horizontal Merger Guidelines, containing a five-point test of anticompetitive effect. The factors in the guidelines are: (1) increased concentration resulting in a concentrated market; (2) adverse competitive effects in the market; (3) possibility of additional entrants into the market;

(4) efficiency gains achieved by merger; and (5) likelihood of failure of either party absent a merger. Violators of the Clayton Act can incur civil and criminal penalties, including treble damages. Section 7 applies equally to acquisitions, mergers, and joint ventures.

### Hart-Scott-Rodino Act Filings

The mechanism by which the regulatory agencies, the Federal Trade Commission (FTC), and the Department of Justice identify possible violations of the Clayton Act is the Hart-Scott-Rodino (HSR) filing described in the chapter on inbound merger and acquisition transactions. It suffices for these purposes to observe that HSR may also implicate joint ventures. In determining whether a proposed corporate joint venture is subject to HSR filing requirements, the joint venturers are all considered buyers and the joint venture itself is considered the target.

### Antitrust Considerations in Technology Ventures

Technology joint ventures, which are specifically provided for in European Union (EU) antitrust regulation, do not receive special treatment under U.S. law, with the exception of research-and-development (R&D) joint ventures. Such joint ventures can be registered with the Federal Trade Commission under the National Competitive Research Act of 1984, which provides a shield against treble-damage suits for antitrust violations. In addition, the act creates a presumption that where there are at least four comparable R&D efforts underway in a particular area of technology, a new R&D joint venture is unlikely to be deemed anticompetitive.

Strategic alliances involving technology licensing can run afoul of the antitrust laws. Although the U.S. Department of Justice has retreated from a previous position that viewed intellectual property licensing as dangerously close to monopoly practice, it still scrutinizes such contracts under its rule of reason. The department weighs the perceived anticompetitive effects of terms such as exclusive territories and fields of use against the procompetitive effects of efficiency and the dissemination of new technology. Because strategic alliances usually involve more than basic licensing and typically create continuing obligations and restrictions on the parties, the antitrust analysis of such arrangements is necessarily highly complex. Vertical arrangements in strategic alliances such as exclusive dealing and exclusive sourcing agreements are subject to a "rule of reason" analysis. Generally speaking, this means that if the arrangements are entered into for valid as opposed to anticompetitive purposes, they will generally be permitted. However, resale price maintenance agreements are more strictly analyzed and may be considered per se violations of the antitrust laws.

Antitrust issues affecting joint ventures and strategic alliances can arise at the state level as well as at the federal level. Each U.S. state has its own form of antitrust legislation that must be taken into account in any joint venture or strategic alliance. Although not usually a matter for concern, if the proposed arrangements involve considerations of particular importance to state officials (for example, adversely affecting consumers or employment within a particular state), it is not uncommon for a consumer advocacy group or a competitor to persuade state officials to open an investigation or to commence legal action to prevent a proposed joint venture from proceeding. Needless to say, this can be a very delicate area, and prospective coventurers are well advised to seek guidance from knowledgeable and experienced legal counsel early in the planning stages.

### CFIUS Notification

The president of the United States has the authority, under the Exon-Florio amendment, to prohibit or reverse any acquisition of control of a U.S. company by a foreign entity if it is found that the acquisition threatens national security. This very broad grant of power has been to some extent limited by provision in the amendment for notice to the Committee on Foreign Investment in the United States (CFIUS). Parties contemplating international acquisitions or certain joint ventures can file voluntary notices with CFIUS. If notice is properly given and CFIUS approves the transaction, further review under Exon-Florio is foreclosed.

### Reporting Requirements of Foreign Persons

Under the Direct Foreign Investment Survey Act all transactions that result in ownership or control by a foreign entity of 10 percent or more of the control of a U.S. company must be reported to the U.S. Department of Commerce within 45 days after consummation of the transaction. In addition, under the Foreign Investment in Real Property Act, investments that result in direct or indirect foreign ownership of a controlling interest in U.S. farming, ranching, forestry, or timberland must be reported to the U.S. Department of Agriculture within 90 days of completion of the transaction. These are reporting requirements only, and neither of these laws restricts such acquisitions.

### State Law Restrictions on Real Property Ownership by Foreign Persons

Many states have restrictions on the ownership, and sometimes on the leasing, of real property by foreign individuals or entities. These restrictions fall into several general categories. Some states prohibit non–U.S. controlled corporations from owning or leasing state lands; some prohibit non–U.S. entities from acquiring land from the state; some require non–U.S. land ownership to be registered with state agencies; some limit the acreage that foreign corporations can own; some allow only reciprocal rights. State restrictions are, in all cases, subject to bilateral treaty rights because treaties made by the federal government preempt contrary state legislation. If a venture involves the acquisition or leasing of any form of real estate, even indirectly, this element needs to be reviewed with knowledgeable legal counsel.

### U.S. Corporate Law Considerations

U.S. corporate law is highly developed and has a number of mechanisms for protecting shareholder interests against management and in controlling shareholder abuses. In most cases, these protections are substantially more stringent than those encountered outside the United States. Accordingly, a foreign enterprise planning to establish a strategic alliance in the United States under the corporate form should anticipate the degree to which directors, officers, and controlling shareholders can incur liability to shareholders generally and to the corporation itself.

The fiduciary responsibilities of directors and officers include the duties of care and of fair dealing. The duty of care obliges directors and officers to use the care of an ordinarily prudent person in performing such functions. This obligation is tempered by the business judgment rule, a presumption that directors and officers are acting with care after they make reasonable inquiry and when they are not personally interested in the subject of their actions.

The duty of fair dealing applies not only to directors and officers but also to controlling shareholders. It requires that, in transactions with the corporation, each disclose any conflict of interest and seek ratification by disinterested directors or by the shareholders generally. In addition, under the doctrine of "corporate opportunity," directors and officers may not benefit by business opportunities learned in the course of discharging their duties unless they first offer the opportunity to the corporation. In addition, material nonpublic information known only to directors, officers, or controlling shareholders may not be used in a way that injures the corporation. All of the foregoing is subject to the ability of directors to be indemnified by the corporation and to certain statutory good faith presumptions in their favor.

Allegations of breach of fiduciary duties are most frequently asserted in derivative actions (suits by one or more shareholders in the name and right of the corporation) or in class actions where individual shareholders purport to act on behalf of all shareholders. In addition to the fiduciary responsibilities of directors and officers, most corporation statutes impose specific duties to prevent waste of corporate assets or the declaration of illegal dividends and to protect the wage claims of corporate employees. These statutory duties are frequently enforceable by governmental action, and their breach may also entail criminal penalties. This area can be a legal trap for the unknowledgeable and unadvised non–U.S. participant (officer, director, manager, partner, or stockholder) in a U.S.–based venture.

## Legal Restrictions Abroad

When a U.S. firm plans to enter a strategic alliance with a foreign partner abroad. it will face a wide range of governmental regulation. Some of these restrictions are analogous to those that foreign companies face in entering the United States, but most are dissimilar in nature and scope to anything U.S. companies normally encounter at home. The following discussion focuses on some of the more common areas of concern. However, for a complete analysis, the U.S. enterprise must conduct an in-depth review of the local laws and regulations applicable to the particular proposed venture abroad.

### *Investment Approvals*

The necessity of requesting government approval in order to invest in a non–U.S. business appears both as a general requirement for all types of industries and as a prerequisite to entering a specially regulated field. Most countries have some sort of restriction on foreign investment. The simpler types of regulation require no more than a notification to the foreign investment agency of the country or to the central bank that a foreign investment has been made. In other countries, prospective shareholders must first obtain a license before holding any interest in a domestic corporation. Although some licenses are granted as a matter of course, others are difficult to obtain and may contain onerous conditions dictated by the investment authority.

Restrictions sometimes apply only if a substantial or controlling interest in a domestic firm is acquired by a foreign investor. Countries belonging to a regional economic organization may restrict investment from countries outside the organization. In addition to the EU, these organizations include the French Franc Zone in Africa and the Andean Common Market in South America. Some countries provide for the creation of a special type of exempt entity in which foreigners can invest without restriction or for special industrial zones or bonded factories having similar characteristics.

Other countries have additional restrictions, or complete prohibitions, on foreign investment in protected industries. Shipping, mining, transportation, banking, insurance, utilities, telecommunication, and real property are the most common such industries. Aircraft and defense manufacturing, leather products, commercial fishing, smelting, refining, cultural affairs, motion pictures, cement production, home construction, and alcohol are among other protected industries.

### *Foreign Exchange Authorization*

Before any investment is made in an international alliance, the parties will need to determine whether their capital can be repatriated and whether the venture's profits will be available for distribution to the partners. Inbound and outbound foreign currency control regulations must be consulted because in many countries an investment that has not been properly reported to the central bank cannot later be repatriated. Thus, the same rules as those discussed in the chapters on mergers and acquisitions (M&A) also apply to joint ventures and strategic alliances.

If the venture intends to rely on foreign borrowing for any important part of its needs, foreign currency controls may limit the amount of the loans or their terms. Other contracts that may be subject to currency controls are royalty agreements on intellectual property and fees for technical assistance. Such contracts may need to be registered with the currency authorities before any foreign remittance can be made.

Failure to comply with currency exchange regulations can result in blocked funds, which can be used only for domestic payments and which cannot be repatriated. In many countries, exporters must deposit all payments in foreign currency with the central bank and have such payments converted into local currency. In addition, there are frequently limits on credit terms that exporters may extend to their overseas customers.

### Competition Law Approvals

Some countries have antimonopoly authorities with the power to prohibit entirely or to regulate proposed combinations (including joint ventures) of foreign firms with domestic companies. In addition there are merger controls administered by the EU. The EU Merger Control Regulation is roughly parallel to the U.S. Hart-Scott-Rodino Premerger Notification Rules. Those, too, apply to cross-border joint ventures and strategic alliances.

It is impossible to generalize on the variety of competition law approvals necessary in other countries. Any party contemplating a joint venture or other strategic alliance must obtain competent local counsel to avoid the pitfalls of failing to meet requirements of notification and compliance with domestic anticompetition law.

### Tax Clearances

It is sometimes necessary to seek advance rulings on the tax status of proposed international joint ventures. In France, for example, the corporate income tax status of a regional headquarters can be settled by negotiation with the tax authorities. In Germany informal clearance can be obtained on certain questions, but it is not always available. In Hong Kong advance clearance is rarely available under any circumstances. In Mexico it is available, but the procedure is very lengthy. Canada provides for advance clearance on many tax questions.

In India advance clearance is necessary when a proposed combination is intended to utilize tax benefits belonging to one of the merged companies. In the Netherlands a tax-exempt merger or a consolidated filing is available only if advance clearance has been obtained. If foreign personnel are to be stationed in the country, some countries require tax clearance when an expatriate seeks to leave the country. Given these wide variations in outcome, it makes good sense to seek the advice of local tax advisers on clearance issues.

### Employment Law Considerations

U.S. employers are subject to legislation on wages and hours, safe working conditions, equal employment opportunity, and social security benefits and anticipate that negotiations with labor unions or individual employees will cover most other matters. But the labor law of most European countries is much more extensive. Companies intending to operate through joint ventures need to determine their obligations to their prospective employees abroad with great care.

The areas in which to expect employment legislation abroad typically include required benefits and job protection. Required benefits cover matters such as mandatory annual vacations and paid holidays, sometimes including a thirteenth month of pay, subsidized canteens and transportation, paid training time, and sick pay. Job protection legislation may require a notice period of up to seven months, governmental agency approval of dismissal of an employee, a transfer allowance if the employee is transferred to another location, and consultation with workers' councils before making employment decisions. In addition, local rules may restrict the ability to downsize an enterprise by discharging workers.

Some countries require the employment of a specified percentage of apprentices, and almost all require some form of work permit for the employment of foreign nationals. In addition, employing expatriates may be subject to numerical or percentage limitations.

## STRUCTURING THE JOINT VENTURE

Assuming the parties have determined that their arrangement requires the creation of a separate entity, either because they anticipate cooperating for an indefinite period or because they need the flexibility of an independent jointly owned firm, the negotiations will likely be lengthy and the final agreement extensive.

The first agreement usually signed is a letter of intent. This preliminary document should state clearly whether, and to what extent, it is binding on the parties. Normally the letter of intent is brief, covering only the parties' obligation to negotiate with one another, their obligation not to commence negotiations with other prospective joint venturers for a limited period of time, and any confidentiality of disclosure agreements. Attached to the letter of intent may be a much longer term sheet, setting out the details of the venture as initially proposed. It is often said that the devil hides in the details; and it is not uncommon to find that as the parties turn to documenting and implementing the venture, adjustments may have to be made that vary from the parties' original intentions.

### Form of the Joint Venture

As described earlier, the most common forms of joint venture are the corporation and the partnership. Tax considerations are likely to favor the partnership because only one level of taxation will be encountered in distributing profits. However, this benefit can be secondary to the advantages available only through the corporate form. For example, if the industry in which the joint venture is intended to operate is protected by domestic law, a local corporation may be the only workable structure. If the venturers plan a large, multilevel organization requiring clearly drawn lines of authority, the corporation is the logical choice. If the corporate form is chosen, the related question of place of incorporation must be decided, both for the main entity and for any corporate subsidiaries that are to be created.

### Contributions of the Venturers

It is the rare international joint venture that brings together two parties with identical contributions. Negotiation of the agreement normally requires reaching a fair evaluation of very different assets, including capital, physical plant and equipment, goodwill, and intellectual property. The shares or partnership interests of the joint venture will be distributed in accordance with the value contributed by each party as negotiated by the parties, although separate classes of shares may be needed for control purposes.

The parties providing the joint venture's assets may have very different intentions about the protection, use, and eventual recovery of their contributions. The party providing capital has the usual concerns of an investor—rate of return and safety of principal. However, because the joint venture is not merely a passive investment, this partner generally expects a substantial voice in managing the entity. In technology-driven ventures, it is often the case that a share in the intangible benefits of the enterprise, such as rights to future developments in intellectual property, is more important to the capital contributor than its share in the profits.

The contributor of physical plant and equipment will likely require that the enterprise value this contribution in terms of increased production and ease of distribution, not in the mere replacement or rental value of the assets. At the same time, especially in high-technology industries, the contributed plant and equipment may rapidly lose value through obsolescence.

A contributor of goodwill (frequently a domestic distributor of imported goods and services) offers the joint venture assured entry into valuable new markets. In return for providing a known reputation for quality, valuable customer lists, and familiarity with local market conditions, this contributor will expect the joint venture to provide a reliable and, if possible, exclusive supply of the venture's products. Guarantees of price stability are also important to this type of contributor.

## Management and Control

In joint ventures, the parties seek as much control as possible over the enterprise. If the joint venture is a small one and if it is structured as a partnership, this demand for control can be easily satisfied. Normally, however, an international joint venture will be managed indirectly, and the negotiators of the agreement will be faced with the need to adjust the parties' demands for control to the exigencies of efficient and responsible management.

Usually, control is clearly distinguished from ownership by the use of shareholder agreements or voting trusts or by issuing different classes of shares. Generally the determining factor in control questions is not the size of the parties' contributions but the absolute size of the parties themselves. On the other hand, this is less often the case when a very large corporation in need of new technology allies itself with a much smaller but highly innovative firm.

Control issues should be negotiated with an eye to differentiating between day-to-day management and major strategic decisions. The most successful joint ventures are those in which one party is responsible for most routine management decisions, with the other parties joining in deliberations only when the issue is fundamental to the venture itself. The venture agreement must define these make-or-break issues and address how they are to be resolved, either by majority vote or by veto rights given to one or more of the parties.

An important issue is whether to draw management personnel of the joint venture from the staff of the venturers. Personal liability of officers and directors must be considered, as well as any restrictions on the employment of foreign managers.

## Allocations of Profits and Losses and Subsequent Adjustments

Allocation of profits and losses will normally follow directly from the allocation of shares or partnership interests. However, in an international joint venture, the parties may wish to provide by agreement that profits and losses in a particular national market should be attributed largely to one or another of the venturers. This may be done by creating a subsidiary to operate in that market. Likewise, profits and losses attributable to one product or product line out of many may be allocated to a particular venturer.

When the profits flow from intellectual property rights contributed by one of the parties, royalties or payments for know-how may be used for profit allocation purposes. When the profits are due to distribution or marketing efforts of a venturer, fees and commissions can be used for the same purpose. Likewise, rental payments can be used to allocate profits attributable to specific equipment. Because all these payments are between related parties, it is important that there be a rational business basis for profit allocations. Such allocations must be supported as valid expenses of the venture so that tax deductions are not lost by excessive or questionable payments.

## Provision for Additional Financing

Because flexibility is one of the main purposes for creating a separate entity to operate the joint venture, the parties should anticipate that, in time, the venture will require additional financing. Which parties are empowered to decide upon the need for additional financing and the form such financing may take must be clearly exposed in the joint venture or strategic alliance agreement.

The venture agreement should contain a clear statement of the powers of the entity to issue additional ownership interests or to incur debt. The amount of additional equity interests to be permitted should be agreed on by the parties, as should their proportionate rights to subscribe for such additional interests.

If the joint venture requires debt financing, the agreement must provide that the parties consent to the pledge or the mortgage of the venture's assets. In addition, if assets of the parties allocated to the use of the venture are needed as collateral, the agreement must require such parties to execute any necessary pledge or security documents. Finally, if the guarantees of the parties are needed to obtain financing on favorable terms, the agreement should provide for such guarantees.

These provisions are certain to be undesirable to those parties who risk loss of their assets if the venture cannot repay its debts. In negotiating the agreement, it may be necessary to increase the economic benefits to such parties to compensate them for assuming this risk.

## Dispute Resolution

It can be anticipated that disputes between the parties to a joint venture will arise. Three clauses in a well-drafted joint venture agreement can provide the procedure for dispute resolution.

1. One clause is a *choice of law* provision, stating the jurisdiction whose law governs the interpretation of the agreement. This provision should be drafted with an eye to the likely outcome of litigation in any of the parties' home countries and to the attitude of those countries' courts in enforcing choice of law provisions in the joint venture agreement.

2. A second important clause is a definition of *deadlock* and a clear statement of what events trigger various types of dispute-resolution procedures. It is important not to draft this clause so narrowly that minor disagreements lead to drastic resolution.

3. An *arbitration* clause is usually employed to address major disagreements. Such a clause should define the type of dispute subject to arbitration, the place of arbitration, the rules under which arbitration will proceed, and the arbitral institution that will have jurisdiction. Each of these elements is subject to negotiation and agreement.

## Termination

Parties to a joint venture may choose to set a definite term in the agreement itself or to state that the venture will continue until completion of a project or projects. However, in most cases the agreement does not contain a predetermined termination date. Nevertheless the question of termination must be dealt with in the agreement. Most international joint ventures remain in existence for longer than five years.

The events leading to termination are essentially the same as those described in the deadlock clause. In addition, the parties will normally be entitled to terminate their venture by mutual consent. But whether in a consensual or a hostile environment in which dispute resolution has failed or has not been invoked, there must be detailed provisions for terminating the joint venture. This may include buy-sell provisions or a complete unwinding of the parties' rights and obligations.

When the joint venture depends to a large extent on technology provided by one of the parties, termination is especially complex. Disputes about the ownership of property invented during the venture should be anticipated and provided for. Confidentiality agreements and agreements not to compete will normally be needed to place the parties, as far as possible, in the same position as they were in before they entered the venture.

## Transfers of Joint Venture or Strategic Alliance Interests

Often, parties to a joint venture or a strategic alliance will place limits on the parties' ability to convey their interests to third parties, on the commonsense theory that each party entered the arrangement contemplating a relationship with the other and not with a stranger. In agreements that permit transfers under certain circumstances, the joint venture partners or the venture itself may have rights of first refusal. It is usually the case that the agreement will permit the parties to transfer their interests to corporate affiliates without restriction. In addition, the joint venture or similar agreement will usually contain provisions permitting admission of additional parties with the consent of the original parties to the transaction.

In addition, the parties may have the right to "put" their interests to the venture, and the venture may have "call" rights on such interests. In situations permitting transfer, there may be drag-along or tag-along provisions whose effect may result in a third-party purchaser acquiring not only the interest of the joint venture party whose interest it seeks to acquire, but also the interests of other parties to the joint ventures. A *drag-along* provision requires a party not otherwise interested in conveying its interest to the third party to do so. A *tag-along* provision allows a joint venture party—not the original target of the third party—to join its venture partner in conveying its interest to the third party.

## STRUCTURING THE STRATEGIC ALLIANCE

The strategic alliance that does not involve a separate entity is nevertheless a complex one that will require planning and careful negotiation to provide both parties with the benefits they expect. Many of the same problems involved in setting up a joint venture are found in starting a strategic alliance.

## Choice of Partner

Because of the less formal nature of the strategic alliance, the parties must cultivate a much stronger degree of confidence in the good faith of the other members of the alliance. Differences in corporate or national culture that could be minor inconveniences if the parties were co-owners of a corporation may be completely destructive of the harmony needed to successfully operate a strategic alliance.

## Delineation of Strategic Objectives

The most critical issue in a strategic alliance is defining the scope of the relationship. The parties need to be aware that alliance partners often have divergent goals to achieve through the alliance and should recognize the need to proceed with an express understanding of the purpose of the alliance. The agreement between the parties should clearly set forth the areas in which the alliance will operate and those in which the parties may operate independently.

## Mechanisms for Change over the Life of the Alliance

The strategic alliance agreement should contain provisions for modifications to take advantage of opportunities, and to avoid difficulties, not initially anticipated by the parties. For instance, if the alliance develops a product outside the scope of the alliance as originally conceived, the rights to the product should be subject to an agreed right of purchase by one of the parties. If one of several strategic allies is unable to continue in the alliance, the other parties should have agreed in advance how the share of the discontinuing ally is to be divided.

## Support and Control by Venturers

In a strategic alliance where no separate entity is created, the contributions of the parties are not actually transferred but are simply used for the alliance's purposes while remaining in the hands of their owners. This may cause problems in financing because the alliance does not have the ability to borrow for its own account. The parties' agreement must therefore expressly state the obligations of each to provide capital not only at the commencement of the alliance, but also whenever specified events occur that increase the alliance's need for funds.

Because the strategic alliance, as distinguished from the joint venture, does not have its own management personnel, the question of control is especially acute. Delegating certain areas of activity to particular parties is usually necessary and should be clearly set out in the agreement.

## SPECIAL PROBLEMS RELATING TO TECHNOLOGY VENTURES AND ALLIANCES

Strategic alliances and joint ventures are especially attractive to high-technology firms and their customers and suppliers. The opportunity to obtain necessary capital and manufacturing capacity draws firms that have few assets other than their intellectual property. The benefits of immediate access to fast-changing technical products and services and to markets for specialized equipment and services lead larger companies to seek out smaller and more technologically advanced partners.

A preliminary question facing parties planning such ventures is how to handle questions of ownership. Many technological assets exist only as know-how, not as patents or patentable inventions. Disclosure except under strictly controlled circumstances destroys their value entirely. In addition, patentable developments may be treated as trade secrets to protect them from reverse engineering.

Disclosure of sufficient information about such technology to satisfy the other parties without unduly exposing the proprietary rights of its owners is a difficult balance to strike. Carefully worded confidentiality agreements are essential, as are provisions for liquidated damages and/or specific performance in case of breach of these agreements.

Other issues to be addressed include cross-licensing of technology between the venturers or, in the case where a separate venture entity is created, between the venturers and the entity. In addition the agreement should focus on the ownership of technology developed by the venture during the life of the venture and on termination. Disclosure issues in technology ventures are particularly difficult in the case of partnerships because of the fiduciary disclosure obligations imposed on partners under the laws of many jurisdictions. A full discussion of this subject is beyond the scope of this chapter; however, these issues and their solutions can be quite complex and need to be closely examined and dealt with in the basic venture documents.

# Checklist: International Joint Ventures and Strategic Alliances

Following is a list of principal issues to be considered in joint ventures and strategic alliances. For specific issues to be addressed in the principal contractual arrangements between the coventurers, refer to the forms of agreement included as Appendixes 11.1 (for a manufacturing joint venture partnership) and 11.2 (for a strategic alliance for the discovery, development, and exploitation of novel pharmaceuticals).

I.  General understandings of the parties.
    A.  Objectives of each coventurer.
    B.  Purpose of venture.
        1.  Definition of field of venture.
        2.  Scope of venture within field.
        3.  Territory of venture.
        4.  Field/territory reserved to each coventurer.
        5.  Noncompetition within field and territory by coventurers.
    C.  Mission and strategy of venture.
    D.  Duration of venture.
    E.  Form of venture.
        1.  Stand-alone entity (corporation, partnership, LLC, trust).
        2.  Contracted ventures (co-dependent, co-marketing, favored supplier, etc.).
    F.  Special issues.
        1.  Governmental licenses, restrictions, and notifications.
        2.  Antitrust or competition notifications or approvals.
        3.  Currency authorizations.
        4.  Business or cultural issues.
        5.  Political instability/expropriation issues.
        6.  Other.

II.  Formation.
    A.  Contributions of venturers.
        1.  Cash.
        2.  Assets.
        3.  Guarantees/credit facilities.
        4.  Technology (patents, trademarks, copyrights, and know-how).
        5.  Liabilities to be assumed by venture.
        6.  Excluded businesses and assets of each venturer.

      7.   Valuation of contributions.

      8.   Subsequent capital requirements.

  B.  Contractual arrangements between co-venturers.

      1.   Management services.

      2.   Accounting or other services.

      3.   Co-marketing agreements.

      4.   Technology arrangements (cross-licensing; rights of first refusal; ownership and mandatory licensing of improvements; etc.).

      5.   Confidentiality, nonsolicitation of employees and customers.

      6.   Other.

  C.  Management of the venture.

      1.   Management/staffing of stand-alone entities.

      2.   Joint management committees for contractual ventures.

      3.   Matters requiring unanimous/majority consent of venturers.

      4.   Subsequent amendments to arrangements.

  D.  Operation of the venture.

      1. Responsibilities of co-venturers.

      2. Allocations of profits and loss, and so forth.

      3. Reports to co-venturers.

      4. Dividend policies.

      5. Force majeure provisions.

      6. Term and termination.

      7. Dispute resolution (applicable laws, arbitration, and venue).

      8. Termination.

      9. Ownership of assets on termination.

     10. Rights of venturers to continue in business after termination.

  E.  Transfers of interests.

      1.   Restrictions on transfer; permitted assignments to affiliates.

      2.   Admission of additional parties.

      3.   Rights of first refusal among venturers/call by venture.

      4.   Drag-along provisions.

      5.   Tag-along provisions.

      6.   Redemption by (or put to) venture.

# APPENDIX 11.1
# Manufacturing Joint Venture Partnership Agreement

PARTNERSHIP AGREEMENT
by and between

U.S. PRODUCTS CORPORATION

and

JAPAN PRODUCTS CORPORATION

This Agreement is made as of this _____ day of [month/year], by and between U.S. PRODUCTS CORPORATION, a New York corporation with its principal office at XXX Fifth Avenue, New York, NY (hereinafter referred to as "U.S. Co."), and JAPAN PRODUCTS CORPORATION, a Delaware corporation with its principal office at XXX Avenue of the Americas, New York, NY (hereinafter referred to as "Japan Co.").

### ARTICLE I
### FORMATION OF PARTNERSHIP

U.S. Co. and Japan Co. hereby enter into a partnership under the provisions of the Uniform Partnership Act of the State of Delaware. The rights and liabilities of U.S. Co. and Japan Co. in connection with such partnership shall be as provided in that Act, except as otherwise expressly provided herein.

### ARTICLE II
### DEFINITIONS

The following terms when used in this Agreement with initial capital letters shall have the meanings set forth below unless the context clearly requires otherwise:

2.01    Period. Each of the four (4) periods of account, which comprise the Partnership's Fiscal Year.

2.02    Affiliate. An Affiliate of a Partner is any corporation, company, or other corporate entity controlling, controlled by, or under common control with such a Partner.

2.03    Japan Co. License. Shall have the meaning ascribed to it in Section 5.03 hereof.

2.04    Closing. The completion of the transactions contemplated by this Agreement shall take place at U.S. Co.'s offices at XXX Fifth Avenue, New York, NY at 10:00 A.M. on March 1, 2002 (or at such other place or time as the Partners may mutually agree), all such transactions being effective as of the Effective Date.

2.05    Code. United States Internal Revenue Code of 1986 as amended; provided that references to a particular provision of the Code or the Treasury Regulations thereunder shall also refer to any successor provisions or regulations.

2.06    CPM. Company Productos de Mexico, S.A. de C.V.

2.07    U.S. Co. License. Shall have the meaning ascribed to it in Section 5.03 hereof.

2.08    Effective Date. This Agreement shall come into full force and effect on January 1, 2002, or on such other date as the Partners may mutually agree.

2.09    Executive Committee. The Executive Committee to be established under Section 8.03 hereunder.

2.10    Field of the Agreement. The development, manufacture, and sale of Products as well as the other products presently being produced by CPM, and the development, manufacture, and sale of such other goods and products, ancillary to the foregoing, as the Partnership may decide.

2.11    North America. Canada, Mexico, and the United States of America.

2.12    NouvelleCo. The new French company being formed to hold the Products business of U.S. Co. France S.A.

2.13    Partner. U.S. Co. or Japan Co., as the case may be, and U.S. Co. and Japan Co., when used in the plural.

2.14    Partnership. The partnership formed pursuant to Article I hereof.

2.15    Partnership Interest. A Partner's respective interest in the profits and losses and in the assets and liabilities of the Partnership.

2.16    Partnership Fiscal Year. For purposes of Partnership accounting and income tax reporting, the Partnership fiscal year shall end on the Sunday closest to December 31 each year.

2.17    Products. All parts used in the fabrication of _____ used for _____.

2.18    Term of the Partnership. The Partnership shall commence Operations on the Effective Date and shall continue in existence until [Date], subject to the provisions of Article XIII hereunder.

2.19    Western Europe. Those countries that are presently members of either the EU or the European Free Trade Association.

## ARTICLE III
### GENERAL PROVISIONS

3.01    Name of the Partnership. The name of the Partnership shall be _____ Products Company (acronym "XPC") or such other name as the Partners may agree, and such name or acronym shall be used at all times in connection with the business and affairs of the Partnership.

3.02    Principal Office. The principal office of the Partnership shall be located at XXX Fifth Avenue, New York, NY or at such other location as the Partners may from time to time designate.

3.03    Partnership Business. The business and purpose of the Partnership shall be commercial activities in the Field of the Agreement. In this connection, the Partnership may seek to obtain by purchase and license the right to practice both patented and unpatented technology owned by third parties or to develop such technology on its own behalf, and to undertake such other related business activities as may be agreed upon by the Partners. This Agreement does not and shall not be construed to create any partnership relationship between U.S. Co. and Japan Co., or any of them or their respective Subsidiaries or Affiliates with respect to any activities other than those conducted in the name of the Partnership created hereby and except as otherwise expressly provided herein.

3.04    Assumed Name Certificates. The Partners shall execute all assumed or fictitious name certificates required by law to be filed in connection with the formation of the Partnership or the conduct of its business, and shall cause any such certificates to be filed in appropriate governmental offices as required by law.

3.05    Activities in the Field. The Partners (including their Affiliates) will use the Partnership as their exclusive vehicle in the manufacture and sale of Products in North America and Western Europe (except that Japan Co. and its Affiliates shall retain the right to sell directly in Western Europe to existing European customers of Japan Co. and its Affiliates).

3.06    Staffing. U.S. Co. shall be responsible for staffing the Partnership, and on the Effective Date U.S. Co. will make available to the Partnership all those personnel who immediately prior to [Date] were engaged in U.S. Co.'s U.S. Products business.

## ARTICLE IV
### PARTNERSHIP CAPITAL CONTRIBUTION

4.01    Capital Accounts. Capital accounts shall be established for each Partner that shall consist of the amount of each Partner's initial capital contribution to the Partnership and set forth in Section 4.02, increased by the fair market value of any additional capital contribution made by such Partner to the Partnership, decreased by the amount of any distribution from the Partnership to such Partners and adjusted to reflect all items of profit and loss allocated to such Partner pursuant to this agreement. Each capital account shall be maintained in accordance with the rules set forth in the Code and the Treasury Regulations thereunder, including Treasury Regulation Section 1.704-1 (b).

4.02    Initial Capital Contributions. At the Closing, the Partners shall contribute the following property to the Partnership:

(a)    U.S. Co. shall contribute: (i) the net assets more fully described and set forth in the Transfer of Assets and Assumption of Liabilities Agreement to be signed between the Partnership and U.S. Co. (the "Transfer Agreement"), which shall be in the form of Appendix A attached hereto; (ii) the shares of CPM together with the representations and warranties pertaining thereto all and more fully described and set forth in the schedule attached hereto as Appendix B; and (iii) the U.S. Co. License. In exchange for such contribution, U.S. Co. shall receive a XX percent interest in the Partnership; and the Partnership shall (i) assume the liabilities more fully described and set forth in the Transfer Agreement and (ii) distribute $XXX million in cash to U.S. Co. at the Closing. The Partners agree that the net amount of U.S. Co.'s initial capital contribution to be credited to its capital account pursuant to Section 4.01 (after taking into account the assumption of liabilities and the $XXX million cash distribution) is $XXX million, of which $XXX million is attributable to the shares of CPM.

(b)    Japan Co. shall contribute cash in the amount of $XXX million. In exchange for such contribution, Japan Co. shall receive a XX percent interest in the Partnership. The Partners agree that the net amount of Japan Co.'s initial capital contribution to be credited to its capital account pursuant to Section 4.01 is $XXX million, of which $XXX million is attributable to the shares of CPM.

(c)    The Partners agree that for U.S. federal income tax purposes, the transactions described in paragraphs (a) and (b) of this Section 4.02 are to be treated pursuant to Section 707(a)(2)(B) of the Code as a sale from U.S. Co. to Japan Co. of a percentage undivided interest in all of the assets contributed by U.S. Co. pursuant to paragraph (a) of this Section 4.02 for a consideration of $XXX million. The percentage undivided interest is equal to a fraction, the numerator of which is $XXX million and the denominator of which is the agreed fair market value of $XXX million (which value is substantially confirmed in the appraiser's summary attached hereto as Appendix C).

(d)    The Partners agree to file Form 8594 with the U.S. Internal Revenue Service based on the agreed fair market value of $XXX million.

4.03 License Agreements. In addition to the foregoing contributions to the Partnership, at the Closing U.S. Co. shall enter into a Technology Transfer and License Agreement with the Partnership, and Japan Co. shall enter into a Technology Transfer and License Agreement with the Partnership as well, both being referred to in Section 5.03 below. It is intended that both such technology Transfer and License Agreements are to be a part of the establishment of the Partnership and to be effective currently with the formation thereof.

4.04 Initial Partnership Interest. At the commencement of the Partnership following the contributions referred to in Section 4.02 above, U.S. Co.'s Partnership Interest shall be XX percent and Japan Co.'s Partnership interest shall be XX percent.

4.05 Increase in Japan Co. Partnership Interest. On the first business day of each calendar year starting in 2003, Japan Co. shall acquire a further XX percent Partnership interest so that following its acquisition of XX percent at the beginning of 2007, Japan Co. shall have a Partnership Interest of XX percent. The price (if by direct purchase from U.S. Co.) for each XX percent shall be $XXX million, of which $XXX million shall be attributable to CPM.

4.06 Additional Capital Contributions. If at any time or times hereafter the Partners agree that the capital of the Partnership should be increased, then the Partners shall determine the total amount of additional capital required and when such additional contributions to the capital shall be made by the Partners. Capital contributions shall be in cash unless the Partners agree to allow the contribution of property and agree upon the fair market value of said property. At the request of either Partner, the Partners shall make scheduled capital contributions or authorized Partnership borrowings earlier than scheduled, if necessary for a Partner to utilize its portion of the Partnership's federal tax loss under the Code in the year such loss was incurred by the Partnership.

4.07 Partnership Capital: Interest and Withdrawals. The Partners shall receive no interest on their contributions to the capital of the Partnership. The Partners shall make no withdrawals from the capital of the Partnership except as otherwise agreed to by the Partners.

## ARTICLE V
## PARTNERSHIP PROPERTY

5.01 Property to Be in Partnership Name. The title to all Partnership property, real and personal, shall be taken and held only in the name of the Partnership, and each Partner shall be a co-owner with its Partner of specific Partnership property holding as a tenant in Partnership.

5.02 Inventions, Patents, Licenses, and Technology. Any invention, patent, license, or technology that is acquired, conceived, or developed by the Partnership or by a Partner expressly acting on behalf of the Partnership pursuant to a written agreement shall be an asset and the property of the Partnership. Any such invention, patent, license, or technology that is not directly or indirectly related to the business purposes of the Partnership or that, although related to such business purposes, the Partnership does not wish to pursue or exploit directly or through the licensing of a third party shall be made available to both U.S. Co. and Japan Co. on reasonable terms and conditions to be mutually agreed between the Partnership and the partner concerned.

5.03 Parent Licenses to the Partnership. U.S. Co. shall grant to the Partnership a royalty free license, which shall be non-exclusive (except for North America and Western Europe where the license shall be exclusive), worldwide, in the existing technology and patents belonging to U.S. Co. in Products, with the right to sublicense. Such license shall be substantially in the form set forth as Appendix C hereto (the "U.S. Co. License"). Japan Co. shall grant to the Partnership a royalty bearing license, which shall be non-exclusive (except for North America and Western Europe where the license shall be exclusive), worldwide (except for Japan) in the technology and patents belonging to Japan Co. in Products, with the right to sublicense. Such license shall be substantially in the form set forth herein as Appendix C (the "Japan Co. License").

5.04 Sublicenses. The Partnership shall sublicense

    (a)    CPM and

    (b)    NouvelleCo.

to make, use, and sell Products under the technology (including patents and know-how) licensed to the Partnership pursuant to the U.S. Co. and Japan Co. Licenses.

5.05 Sublicenses to Third Parties. In the event that the Partnership wishes to sublicense a third party (other than the sublicensees referred to in section 5.04 above), then the Partnership shall first obtain a written consent to such sublicense from the Partners, which consent shall not be unreasonably withheld by either Partner.

## ARTICLE VI
## PROFITS AND LOSSES

6.01 Partner's Share of Profits and Losses. The profits and losses of the Partnership (including items of income, gain, loss, deduction, or credit for U.S. federal income tax purposes) shall be allocated to each Partner in accordance with their respective Partnership Interests. For U.S. federal income tax purposes, items of income, gain, loss, or deduction resulting from property contributed to the capital of the Partnership shall be allocated as required by section 704( c) of the Code and the Treasury Regulations thereunder. If under the provisions of Section 482 of the Code or other provisions of applicable federal income tax law or corresponding provisions of applicable state law, there is deemed to arise any deduction or income to the Partnership, then the deduction shall be allocated to the Partner to which (or to the Affiliate of which) the deduction is deemed paid, and the income shall be allocated to the Partner from which (or from the Affiliate of which) the income is deemed received.

6.02   Reports of Profits and Losses. During the Term of the Partnership, the Partners shall each be provided with a report for each Accounting Period of the profits and losses of the Partnership within twenty (20) business days after the end of each fiscal quarter. Within sixty (60) days after the close of each Partnership Fiscal Year, a consolidated financial statement shall be prepared showing the Partnership's unusual profits and losses. Each Partner shall receive a copy of such financial statement certified by the person responsible for the financial affairs of the Partnership and shall have thirty (30) days to request in writing any desired corrections or clarifications thereto. Either Partner may request that the auditors selected pursuant to Section 7.06 below prepare audited consolidated financial statements showing the Partnership profits and losses and assets and liabilities for the preceding Partnership Fiscal Year. Upon such request and at the expense of the Partnership, such statements shall be promptly completed, certified by the auditors, and delivered to both Partners.

6.03   Tax Returns. The Partners shall each be provided with copies of all federal, state, and local income tax returns and reports proposed to be filed by the Partnership at least thirty (30) days prior to their filing date. To the extent permissible under applicable law, charges and expenditures shall be treated for income tax purposes as current expenses unless otherwise agreed by the Partners. A decision whether to exercise or revoke any election available to the Partnership under the Code shall be made by mutual agreement of the Partners, provided that the Partnership shall be required to make an election to adjust basis under Section 754 of the Code upon the request of either Partner, and in such event each Partner shall supply the Partnership the information necessary properly to give effect to any such election.

6.04   Tax Matters Partner. U.S. Co. is designated the "Tax Matters Partner" as provided in Section 6231 (a)(7) of the Code and any corresponding provision of applicable state law. U.S. Co. shall be entitled to reimbursement by the Partnership of its reasonable expenses for activities conducted as Tax Matters Partner.

6.05   Distribution of Partnership Profits and Royalties. The Partnership shall have a distribution policy involving a planned annual payout of forty (40) percent or more of the Partnership's profits. With respect to profits of the Partnership that are not distributed to the Partners in the Partnership Fiscal Year in which they were earned, such profits must be distributed to the Partners pro rata based on the Partners' interests in the Partnership for the Partnership Fiscal Year in which such profits were earned before the profit for any subsequent Partnership Fiscal Year may be distributed to the Partners. Profits of the Partnership shall be available to the Partnership for use in the business of the Partnership until distributed, except that profits not required to be retained in order to finance the business of the Partnership or its planned expansion shall be distributed to the Partners. Royalties received by the Partnership pursuant to sublicenses shall be paid to the Partner or Partners (as the case may be) within thirty (30) days of receipt by the Partnership.

## ARTICLE VII
## ACCOUNTING ORGANIZATION

7.01   Method of Partnership Accounting. All accounts of the Partnership shall be kept on the accrual basis. All matters of accounting for which there are no provision in this Agreement are to be governed by United States generally accepted accounting principles.

7.02   Books of Account and Records and Accounting Controls. Books of account and records of the Partnership shall be kept in reasonable detail and accurately and fairly reflect all Partnership transactions, and the Partnership shall maintain appropriate systems of internal accounting control sufficient to provide reasonable assurances that: (a) transactions are executed in accordance with the Partners' general or specific authorizations; (b) transactions are recorded as necessary to permit preparation of financial statements in conformity with United States generally accepted accounting principles or any other criteria applicable to such statements and to maintain accountability for assets; (c) assets of the Partnership are treated only in accordance with Partners' general or specific authorization; and (d) the recorded accountability for assets is compared with the existing assets at reasonable intervals with appropriate procedures being established to take appropriate action with respect to any differences that may be determined.

7.03   Place Where Books and Records to Be Kept. The Partnership books of account and all records, securities, papers, and writings of the Partnership shall be kept at the principal office of the Partnership referred to in Section 3.02 above or in such other place as may be mutually agreed by the Partners.

7.04   Access to Books and Records. Each Partner shall have free access at all times to examine and copy the books, papers, and other written records of the Partnership.

7.05   Partnership Bank Accounts. The Partnership shall establish and maintain checking and other accounts in such bank or banks as may be determined by the Executive Committee. All funds received by the Partnership shall be deposited in such accounts. Withdrawals from such accounts shall be in accordance with the instructions, policies, and procedures authorized by the Executive Committee.

7.06   Appointment of Auditors. The Partners agree that XYZ AUDITORS will act initially as auditors of the Partnership books and records. The appointment of auditors shall be reviewed on a yearly basis.

ARTICLE VIII
PARTNERSHIP MANAGEMENT

8.01    Responsibility of Partners. The Partners shall devote such time and effort to the business of the Partnership as may be necessary to ensure orderly operations. The Partners shall regularly consult with each other and keep each other advised of all developments affecting the Partnership; and whenever any Partnership act with tax consequences might lie accomplished in alternate ways, the Partners agree to make every effort to accommodate the interests of both Partners.

8.02    Delegation of Powers. The Partners hereby delegate to the Executive Committee the right to subscribe the Partnership name, to open bank accounts, to withdraw and deposit sums in connection therewith, and to make contracts, purchase goods, and otherwise trade, buy, sell, and manage on behalf of the Partnership within the Field of the Agreement, all subject to the express limitations set forth in this Agreement; and the Executive Committee, subject to such express limitations, may further delegate such rights to the appropriate officials of the Partnership. All decisions and agreements of the Executive Committee shall be considered decisions and agreements of the Partners.

8.03    Executive Committee. The Executive Committee shall consist of five members, three of whom shall be appointed by U.S. Co. and two of whom shall be appointed by Japan Co. Each member shall serve until replaced by the appointing Partner. Each such member of the Executive Committee shall have one vote.

8.04    Members of the Executive Committee. Any member of the Executive Committee may appoint by a signed instrument delivered to the Executive Committee an alternate (not otherwise a member) to attend any meeting in his stead with full power to vote and otherwise participate in the meeting.

8.05    Quorum. During the period in which the Executive Committee consists of five members, the presence of three or more members (or their alternates) shall constitute a quorum at any meeting of the Executive Committee provided that at least one representative of each Partner is present. A minimum of three votes shall be required to take any action.

8.06    Meetings of Executive Committee. Each Partner has the right to call a meeting of the Executive Committee. The Executive Committee shall normally meet upon the call of the Chief Executive or at such times and at such locations as a majority of the members shall decide. Meetings may also be held using any communications equipment, if all parties' participating members can hear each other. Participation in a meeting pursuant to the foregoing sentence shall constitute presence at such a meeting. Meetings shall take place at least semiannually. The first such meeting each year will approve the annual distribution of profits in accordance with Section 6.05 hereof, and the second semiannual meeting shall approve the annual operating budget for the succeeding year.

8.07    Notice of Meetings. At least fourteen (14) days before the date set for any such meeting, written notice from the Chief Executive or the Partner calling the meeting stating the place, day, and time of the meeting of the Executive Committee along with a general statement of the purposes for which the meeting is being held shall be given to each member personally or by fax confirmed by ordinary mail. Notice of any meeting may be waived in writing by any member.

8.08    Chief Executive. At the first meeting of the Executive Committee in each Partnership fiscal year, U.S. Co. shall appoint the Chief Executive of the Executive Committee from among its three Committee Members. The Chief Executive shall preside as chairman over all meetings of the Executive Committee and shall cause a written record of the meetings of the Executive Committee to be prepared and forwarded to all members within twenty-one (21) days after each meeting. In the absence of the Chief Executive from any Executive Committee meeting, another U.S. Co. member shall act in his stead.

8.09    Matters Requiring Unanimity of Executive Committee or Written Agreement of the Partners. A unanimous vote of all of the members present including at least one member (or his alternate) appointed by each Partner at a meeting of the Executive Committee at which a quorum is present or the written agreement of the Partners shall be required to decide to: (a) increase or decrease the Partnership capital; (b) other than as provided in the approved operating budget of the Partnership, acquire, mortgage, pledge, sell, lease, assign, transfer, exchange, waive, or forgive or make other disposition of any Partnership property (other than sales of Products), real or personal (including without limitation any debt owed the Partnership or any claim of the Partnership), with a value in excess of $1,000,000 or of any interest (regardless of value) in the legal or beneficial ownership of any corporation or enterprise; (c) major investments (exceeding $5,000,000) for capital programs such as plant expansion and cost reduction; (d) an increase in the level of borrowing of the Partnership by more than twenty (20) percent above the approved operating budget of the Partnership; (e) any license of technology to or by the Partnership with a third party other than the sublicensees referred to in Section 5.04 above; (f) agreements between the Partnership and a Partner or an Affiliate of a Partner other than at arm's length; (g) change in the Partnership name or Field of this Agreement; (h) any material change to significant accounting policies of the Partnership (other than those brought about by operation of law or by pronouncements of the Financial Accounting Standards Board or other accounting regulatory authority having jurisdiction over the Partnership or an Affiliate of the Partnership; (i) change the independent auditors of the Partnership; (j) make a distribution to Partners otherwise than in accordance with Section 6.05 above; or (k) add any additional Partners to the Partnership.

8.10    Additional Matters Requiring Majority Approval of Executive Committee. The following matters must be approved at meetings of the Executive Committee at which a quorum is present (unless a Partner waives in writing his right to have any such matter so approved):

(a)    The Annual operating budget of the Partnership;

(b)    The Annual financial statement and closing balance sheet of the Partnership;

(c)    Agreements with third parties having a value in excess of $[1,000,000] per annum other than sales contracts and raw materials, components, or services agreements in the normal course of business;

(d)    Agreements between the Partnership and a Partner or an Affiliate of a Partner (other than those covered by Section 8.09(f) above).

## ARTICLE IX
## PARTNERSHIP FINANCING

9.01    Partners to Seek Financing. Whenever the Partners agree that any investment, project, or purchase by the Partnership should be financed by the credit of the Partnership, each Partner shall use its best efforts to arrange such financing on the best terms available.

9.02    Partners Share of Financial Obligations. Unless otherwise agreed by the Partners in writing, U.S. Co. and Japan Co. shall be liable as guarantor or surety under any guaranty or surety required in connection with any financing on behalf of the Partnership or as a Partner as a result of any such financing only in proportion to their respective Partnership Interests.

## ARTICLE X
## RELATIONS BETWEEN PARTNERSHIP AND PARTNERS

10.01    Partnership to Be Independent Enterprise. The Partners agree that the Partnership will be managed as an independent enterprise.

10.02    Services Agreement. The Partnership shall enter into a one-year renewable management Services Agreement with U.S. Co. in the form of Appendix E hereto with respect to those services presently supplied to U.S. Co.'s Product business.

10.03    Manufacturing Services Agreements. The Partnership shall enter into a multiyear contract with U.S. Co. in the form of Appendix F hereto with respect to the manufacture of those Product components manufactured at U.S. Co.'s XXX manufacturing facility.

## ARTICLE XI
## TRANSFER OF INTERESTS

11.01    Partner Restrictions. Except as specifically permitted by Sections 11.02 and 13.03, neither Partner shall assign, mortgage, pledge, or sell, in whole or in part, its Partnership Interest or enter into any agreement as a result of which any other person, firm, company, or corporation shall become interested with such Partner in the Partnership or do any act that makes it impossible to carry on the business of the Partnership.

11.02    Assignment to an Affiliate. Either Partner may assign its Partnership interest to an Affiliate reasonably acceptable to the other Partner. Unless the Partners otherwise agree in writing, in the event of such an assignment, all of the provisions of this Partnership Agreement shall continue in full force and effect, and the assigning Partner shall guarantee both the total performance of its Affiliate and its liability for all of the obligations of the Partnership. The assigning Partner shall have the responsibility for filing any amendments to Partnership certificates as required by law.

## ARTICLE XII
## LIABILITIES AND INDEMNIFICATION

12.01    Liabilities of Partnership. The liabilities of the Partnership are to be borne by the Partners proportionate to each Partner's Partnership Interest, except that where the liability was caused by a Partner's act or omission that was performed or omitted fraudulently, or in breach of this Agreement or in bad faith, or constituted gross negligence or willful misconduct, such liability shall be borne solely and made good by the Partner so causing the liability.

12.02    Cross-indemnification by Partners. Each Partner shall indemnify and hold harmless the other Partner and officers of the Partner from and against any loss, expense, damage, or injury suffered or sustained by the other Partner disproportionately to its Partnership Interest by reason of any acts, omissions, or alleged acts or omissions arising out of the Partner's activities on behalf of the Partnership, or in furtherance of the interests of the Partnership including, but not limited to, any judgment, settlement, reasonable attorney's fees, and other costs and expenses incurred in connection with the defense of any actual or threatened action, proceeding or claim and including any payments made by the Partner to any of its officers or employees pursuant to an indemnification agreement no broader than this Section, if the acts, omission, or alleged acts or omissions upon which such actual or threatened action, proceedings, or claims are based were for a purpose reasonably believed to be in the best interests of the Partnership and were not performed or omitted fraudulently in breach of this Agreement or in bad faith or as a result of gross negligence or willful misconduct by such Partner or its officers and were not in violation of the Partner's fiduciary obligation to the Partnership.

ARTICLE XIII
DISSOLUTION, WINDING UP, LIQUIDATION

13.01    Events of Dissolution. In addition to those events giving rise to the rights of dissolution under the Uniform Partnership Act of the State of Delaware, the occurrence of any one of the following events shall cause a dissolution of the Partnership: (a) upon the option of the nondefaulting Partner exercisable upon written notice to the defaulting Partner, if either Partner materially breaches this Agreement and such breach remains uncured for thirty (30) days after receipt of written notice thereof; (b) upon the bankruptcy of either Partner unless the other Partner elects not to dissolve the Partnership by written notice to the bankrupt Partner delivered within thirty (30) days of such bankruptcy; (c) at the other Partner's option exercisable by written notice to the affected Partner upon the merger or consolidation of the affected Partnership into another corporation other than an Affiliate or the acquisition of more than fifty (50) percent of the voting securities of such affected Partner by another corporation or entity other than an Affiliate or the sale by the affected Partner of all or substantially all of its assets; (d) immediately upon the dissolution of either Partner unless its obligations hereunder are assumed in whole by an Affiliate reasonably acceptable to the other Partner; or (e) immediately upon the mutual agreement of the Partners.

13.02    No Action for Dissolution. Except as expressly allowed in this Agreement, neither Partner shall intentionally cause a dissolution of the Partnership before January 1, 2010; and the Partners recognize that subject to the provisions of this Agreement allowing dissolution, each Partner is relying on the continued existence of the Partnership at least until January 1, 2010.

13.03    Transfers in Lieu of Dissolution. In the event that (a) a Partner materially breaches this Agreement and such breach remains uncured for thirty (30) days after receipt of written notice thereof or (b) a Partner wishes to sell its Partnership Interest after January 1, 2010 (other than pursuant to Section 11.02 above), then the other Partner shall have the right to acquire the Partnership Interest of the defaulting Partner or the Partner wishing to sell. In such circumstances, the Partners shall negotiate in good faith for the transfer of such Partnership Interest from one to the other, provided that either Partner may by written notice to the other Partner require the following appraisal procedure (the "Appraisal Procedure"): (i) Within thirty (30) days of receipt of the foregoing notice each partner shall select an appraiser, which shall be a U.S.–based investment banking firm of nationally recognized standing, to value the entire Partnership and shall instruct such an appraiser that in reaching such a value it shall consider, among other things, companies engaged in the same or similar businesses, age, and commercial development, as well as tangible and intangible factors such as sales, sales growth earnings, liquidation value, new products, new product development, recent inventions, competition, and price trends, as well as other factors that a reasonable, sophisticated investor would deem relevant to an investment decision, and that such appraisal shall be completed within thirty (30) days from the selection of such appraisers and submitted in writing to both Partners. If the value of the Partnership in such appraisals does not vary by more than five (5) percent, the appraised value of the Partnership (the "Appraised Partnership Value") shall be determined by the numerical average of the value in each appraisal. (ii) If the appraisals of the value of the Partnership vary by more than five (5) percent and the Partners cannot otherwise agree on the value of the Partnership, a third appraiser shall be selected by agreement of the Partners, or failing such agreement, by the Partners within thirty (30) days after the submission of the appraisals described in subsection (i), then such appraiser shall be selected by the two appraisers described in subsection (i). Any such third appraiser shall also be a U.S.–based investment banking firm of nationally recognized standing and shall be given the same instructions as are required to be given the appraiser described in subsection (i) above. (iii) After receipt of the third appraisal described in subsection (ii), the Appraised Partnership Value shall be determined by the numerical average of the two highest appraisals. Each Partner shall be solely responsible for paying the fees and expenses of the appraiser it selects, and the fees and expenses of the third appraiser shall be paid by the defaulting Partner or the Partner wishing to sell for a period of sixty (60) days after the Appraised Partnership Value is established under the Appraisal Procedure. The Partner shall have the option to purchase the Partnership Interest of the defaulting Partner or the Partner wishing to sell at the price for such Partnership interest derived from the Appraised Partnership Value. If the foregoing option is not exercised within the period specified, the Partner wishing to sell (but not the defaulting Partner) shall, for an additional period of six (6) months. have the option to sell the Partnership Interest to a third party reasonably acceptable to the other Partner at a price equal to or greater than the price offered to such other Partner. The rights of the nondefaulting Partner contained in this Section shall be in addition to and not in lieu of any other rights or remedies open to the nondefaulting Partner as a result of a material breach of this Agreement.

13.04    Liquidation. If the Partnership shall be dissolved, no further business shall be conducted except for the taking of such action as shall be necessary for the winding up of the affairs of the Partnership and the distribution of its assets to the Partners pursuant to the provisions hereof. On such dissolution, the Partners may mutually agree that one of the Partners may act as liquidator, or the Partners may appoint in writing one or more liquidators, unless the dissolution was caused by the bankruptcy, merger, consolidation, or dissolution of one of the Partners, in which case the other Partner may appoint one or more liquidators. The liquidator shall have full authority to wind up the affairs of the Partnership and make final distribution as provided herein. Upon any dissolution of the Partnership, the following steps shall be accomplished by the liquidator: (a) subject to the restrictions set forth in this Article XIII, the liquidator shall make such sales of Partnership assets as it, in its sole discretion, deems advisable or necessary, whether or not such sales are necessary for the payment of debts or other obligations or expenses; (b) the liquidator shall pay all Partnership debts and expenses, valid and existing claims of third persons, and indebtedness against such assets, both real and personal, or otherwise make adequate provisions therefor, including, but not limited to, establishing cash reserves it deems necessary for any reasonable contingent or unforeseen liabilities or obligations of the Partnership; and (c) the liquidator shall apply the remaining assets (including cash resulting from any sales of assets) and distribute them to the Partners in the following manner: (i) if after paying the Partnership debts, claims, and expenses as provided above, there remain any Partnership assets, the liquidator shall convey and assign to each Partner assets of a value that will effect a repayment to the respective Partner of its capital account, provided that in the event there are insufficient assets to effect such a repayment, the liquidator shall convey and assign to the Partners the remaining Partnership assets pro rata in accordance with their capital accounts; and (ii) if any assets remain after the foregoing steps have been accomplished, the liquidator shall distribute such assets, including cash, to the partners in accordance with their respective Partnership Interests. Any gain or loss realized by the Partnership upon the sale of its property and assets shall be allocated to the Partners in the manner set forth in Section 6.01 above. To the extent that an asset is distributed in kind, the amount of the distribution shall be decided to be the fair market value of the asset on the date of distribution; and the gain or loss thereon shall be allocated in accordance with Section 6.01 above. If, at the time of dissolution, a Partner has a negative capital account after taking into account the allocations required by Section 6.01, such Partner shall contribute to the Partnership, in immediately available funds, such additional capital as is required to bring its capital account to zero.

13.05    Accounting. Within a reasonable time following the completion of the liquidation of the Partnership, the liquidator appointed pursuant to Section 13.04 shall supply to each Partner a statement audited by the Partnership's auditor that shall set forth the assets and the liabilities of the Partnership as of the date of complete liquidation and the Partner's portion of distribution pursuant to Section 13.04.

13.06    Licenses between Partners.

(a)    In the event of a dissolution of the Partnership pursuant to Section 13.04 above, other than pursuant to Section 13.01(a) of this Agreement, then each Partner shall, upon written notice from the other Partner made within sixty (60) days of the commencement of such dissolution, negotiate in good faith with the other Partner a nonexclusive license to such other Partner to make, use, and sell products in the Field, subject to a reasonable royalty not to exceed X percent (X) of the net sales value of the products subject to such a license in any technology (including know-how and patents) that a Partner had previously licensed to the Partnership and that absent such a license would be infringed by use of technology including know-how and patents owned by the Partnership.

(b)    In the event of a dissolution of the Partnership pursuant to Section 13.04 above, where a Partner is in breach of its obligations hereunder, the nonbreaching Partner shall, upon written notice to the Partner in breach, receive a nonexclusive, royalty-free, worldwide permanent license (to the extent permitted by law) from the Partner in breach to use for any purpose, technology, know-how, or patents owned by the Partnership.

13.07    Termination. Upon the completion of the liquidation of the Partnership and the distribution of all Partnership assets and funds, the Partnership shall terminate, and the liquidator appointed pursuant to Section 13.04 shall have the authority to execute and record a Certificate of Cancellation of the Partnership as well as any and all other documents required to effect the dissolution and termination of the Partnership.

## ARTICLE XIV
## NOTICES

All notices and demands required or permitted under this Agreement shall be in writing and shall be sent by certified or registered mail, fax, or telex to each Partner at its address as shown from time to time on the records of the Partnership with a copy to the principal of the Partnership. All such notices shall be sent to the following addresses:

If to U.S. Co.: _____

If to Japan Co.: _____

or to such other address as either Partner from time to time by written notice shall designate as its address for the purpose hereof.

## ARTICLE XV
## APPLICABLE LAWS

This Agreement and the rights and obligations of the Partners hereunder shall be governed by and interpreted in accordance with the substantive laws of the State of New York without regard to law provisions thereof except to the extent that partnership affairs are subject to the provisions of the Uniform Partnership Act of the State of Delaware.

## ARTICLE XVI
## AMENDMENT OF PARTNERSHIP AGREEMENT

16.01    Amendments by Mutual Agreement. Except as otherwise permitted or prohibited by law, all provisions of this Agreement may be amended in any respect only, by the agreement of the Partners, evidenced by the execution of a written amendment.

16.02    Amendment of Certificate of Partnership. In the event this Agreement shall be amended pursuant to Section 16.01, the Partners shall execute and record an amended Certificate of Partnership to reflect such change, if such recording is deemed necessary or appropriate.

ARTICLE XVII
MISCELLANEOUS

17.01    Right of Partition. The Partners agree that the Partnership properties are not and will not be suitable to partition. Accordingly, each of the Partners hereby irrevocably waives any and all rights that it may have to maintain any action for partition of any of the Partnership properties.

17.02    Severability. If any provision of this Agreement or the application of such provision to any person or circumstance shall be held invalid, the remainder of this Agreement, or the application of such provision to persons or circumstances other than those to which it was held invalid, shall not be affected thereby.

17.03    Further Acts. The Partners agree to perform such further acts and to execute such additional instruments as may be necessary to put this Agreement into full effect.

17.04    Trademarks and Trade Names. The Partners agree to seek by copyright or registration protection for any trademarks, trade names, or service marks developed by the Partnership and to guard against loss of such rights by cancellation. All such trademarks, trade names, and service marks shall be the property of the Partnership.

17.05    Counterparts. This Agreement may be executed in three counterparts, each of which shall be deemed an original, but all of which shall constitute one and the same instrument.

17.06    Headings. The headings in this Agreement are inserted for convenience and identification only and are in no way intended to describe, interpret, define, or limit the scope, extent, or intent of this Agreement or any provision hereof.

17.07    Application of Agreement. This Agreement applies to, inures to the benefit of, and binds the parties hereto and their respective successors and assigns.

17.08    Scope. This Agreement together with the Appendices attached hereto constitutes the entire agreement between the Parties. It supersedes any prior agreement or understandings between them as to the subject matter, and it may not be modified or amended in any manner other than as set forth herein.

17.09    No Transfer or Assignment. Except as otherwise expressly provided herein, this Agreement and the rights and obligations hereunder may not be assigned or transferred by either Partner.

17.10    No Brokers. Each Partner represents to the other that, except as otherwise previously disclosed to the other Partner in writing, no agent, broker, person, or firm acting on behalf of the representing party is or will be entitled to a financial advisory fee, broker's commission, or like payment in connection with any of the transactions contemplated hereby.

17.11    Insurance. The Partnership shall maintain in full force and effect insurance coverage as determined by the Executive Committee from time to time. All policies and insurance shall name the Partnership and each of the Partners as named insureds, as their respective interests may appear.

IN WITNESS WHEREOF, the undersigned have executed this Agreement as of this _____ day of [month/year].

U.S. PRODUCTS CORPORATION


By: _____

ATTEST:


By: _____


JAPAN PRODUCTS CORPORATION


By: _____

ATTEST:


By: _____

## APPENDIX 11.2

# Strategic Alliance Agreement

RESEARCH AND LICENSING AGREEMENT
by and between
U.S. PHARMACEUTICALS CORPORATION
("U.S. Co.")
and
SWISS PHARMACEUTICALS LIMITED
("Swiss Co.")

Swiss Co. has recognized the importance and the potential of ABC Technology as hereinafter defined for future products of its biological Business Units and desires to enter into a cooperation with U.S. Co. on its ABC Technology project.

As a future senior partner, as expressed by this Agreement, Swiss Co. intends, subject to the terms and conditions of a Stock Purchase Agreement of even date herewith, to make an equity investment in U.S. Co.

1. Definitions.

 1.1. License Period shall mean with respect to any license the period of time commencing on the date of grant of such license and extending on a country-by-country basis until (unless terminated as provided for herein) the later of

 (a) the last to expire in each country of the patents of licensor covering the manufacture, use, or sale of the Products (as defined in Paragraph 1.7) or the other products dealt with in this Agreement, or Generic Inventions, as the case may be; or

 (b) the expiry of seven (7) years from the day of the first commercial sale by licensee of the respective Product, or other product dealt with in this Agreement, as the case may be, the manufacture, use, or sale of which is covered by the patents or know-how that are the subject of such license, in each country.

 The term *patents*, as used above, shall mean issued, valid, and unexpired patents.

 1.2 Agreement Period shall mean the period of time commencing January 1, 2002, and extending until the last to expire in all countries of all patents issued with respect to Patent Rights that constitute U.S. Co., Swiss Co., or Joint Technology or, if no such patents are issued, extending for a period of twenty (20) years from the date hereof, unless terminated as provided for herein.

 1.3 Research Cooperation Term shall have the meaning set forth in Paragraph 14.2(a) hereof.

 1.4 Research Collaboration shall mean U.S. Co.'s and Swiss Co.'s research efforts in the field, described in Paragraph 14.2(a).

 1.5 ABC Technology, in the context of this Agreement, shall mean [SPECIFICALLY DEFINE], including but not limited to the technology covered by the potential applications listed on Annex I annexed hereto.

 1.6 The Field shall mean ABC Technology as a basis for the development of therapeutics, primarily for humans, but also feasible for animals and plants, and as diagnostics. The Field will be limited to the following biochemical targets (the "Targets"): [LIST TARGETS].

 The Field may be amended from time to time by mutual written agreement between U.S. Co. and Swiss Co. An extension of the scope of the cooperation (e.g., to other Targets), upon the same conditions, shall be discussed by the parties in good faith including, without limitation, when research results have been obtained in the Targets listed above.

 1.7 Product(s) shall mean the finished form of chemical specialities for biological uses having activity against the Targets in humans, animals, and plants resulting from the Research Collaboration or otherwise falling within or derived from Patent Rights or Know-How that are developed during the course of the Research Collaboration.

 1.8 Use shall mean all indications for any of: (a) a therapeutic or (b) a diagnostic or (c) other use for (i) humans, (ii) animals, or (iii) plants.

 1.9 Patent Rights shall mean any patent applications or patents, now or hereafter made or issued, including, but not limited to, those relating to a method of use or to process, and any substitutions, continuations, continuations-in-part, divisions, reissues, reexaminations, renewals, or extensions of the terms thereof.

 1.10 Know-How shall mean any and all unpatented and/or nonpatentable technical data, information, materials, biological materials, samples, and other information that

(a)     relate to products or tools to investigate, create, or manufacture products, including, without limitation, chemical, biological, pharmacological, toxicological, nonclinical and clinical data, formulations, specifications, and/or usage, or

(b)     relate to processes, techniques, and specifications for the manufacture of products, including, without limitation, preparation, synthesis, recovery and purification, and quality control processes, techniques, and specifications.

Know-how shall not include (i) Patent Rights, or (ii) information that relates to nonclassical, nonconventional, high technology delivery systems for products.

1.11    Generic Invention(s) shall mean all Patent Rights with respect to entities (molecular entities, processes, uses), inventions or otherwise, based on discoveries in ABC Technology made by a party during the course of the Research Collaboration that due to their generic character can be applied and/or incorporated to ABC Targets inside and/or outside the Field, including but not limited to for purposes of providing superior properties (potency, affinity, absorption, stability, ease of manufacturing, cost, etc.) to such ABC Targets inside and/or outside the Field.

1.12    Generic Know-How shall mean all Know-How (including Excluded Generic Know-How) with respect to entities (molecular entities, processes, uses), inventions or otherwise, based on discoveries in ABC Technology made by a party during the course of the Research Collaboration, that due to their generic character can be applied and/or incorporated to ABC Targets inside and/or outside the Field, including but not limited to for purposes of providing superior properties (potency, affinity, absorption, stability, ease of manufacturing, cost, etc.) to such ABC Targets inside and/or outside the Field.

1.13    U.S. Co. Technology shall mean all Know-How and Patent Rights including without limitation Generic Inventions and Generic Know-How, but not including Joint Technology, that U.S. Co. has on the date hereof or may develop or acquire during the Research Cooperation Term, whether in the course of or outside of the Research Collaboration, necessary or useful for the manufacture, use, or sale of Products. Notwithstanding the foregoing, U.S. Co. Technology shall not include any technology developed by U.S. Co. in connection with a Third Party or acquired from any Third Party, in each case under any agreement that restricts U.S. Co. from making the technology available as provided for herein and in the event that any such agreement provides for a royalty or other payment associated with making such technology available, such technology will only be available if Swiss Co. agrees to pay any such royalty or other payment.

1.14    Swiss Co. Technology shall mean all Know-How and Patent Rights including without limitation Generic Inventions and Generic Know-How, but not including Joint Technology, that Swiss Co. has on the date hereof or may develop or acquire during the Research Cooperation Term, whether in the course of or outside of the Research Collaboration, necessary or useful for the manufacture, use, or sale of Products. Notwithstanding the foregoing, Swiss Co. Technology shall not include any technology developed by Swiss Co. in connection with a Third Party or acquired from any Third Party, in each case under any agreement that restricts Swiss Co. from making the technology available as provided for herein and in the event that any such agreement provides for a royalty or other payment associated with making such technology available, such technology will only be available if U.S. Co. agrees to pay any such royalty or other payment. However, Swiss Co. Technology shall not include the Know-How and Patent Rights of Swiss Co. that is generated by Swiss Co.'s Business Units, unless developed while engaged in the Research Collaboration or otherwise agreed.

1.15    Joint Technology shall mean any Know-How and Patent Rights including without limitation Generic Inventions and Generic Know-How that is developed jointly by U.S. Co. and Swiss Co. during the course of the Research Collaboration pursuant to Paragraph 9.4.

1.16    Affiliate(s) shall mean all corporations or business entities that, directly or indirectly, are controlled by, control, or are under common control with Swiss Co. or U.S. Co., respectively.

1.17    Third Party shall mean any person or entity other than a party to this Agreement, its Affiliates, and/or its respective employees.

1.18    Net Sales shall mean the amount billed by a selling party to this Agreement, such party's Affiliates or sublicensees to Third Parties for the sale of products (or intermediates thereof), including license fees paid by a Third Party who is also purchasing products, less cash discounts and/or quantity allowances actually allowed, credits for customers, returns and allowances, charges for freight, handling and transportation separately billed, and sales and use taxes and other similar taxes incurred, as reasonably and fairly determined in accordance with Swiss Co.'s standard accounting method. For purposes of determining the amount of royalty payable on Net Sales of a product,

(a)     a product (or intermediate thereof) shall not be deemed to have been sold until it shall have been sold to a purchaser that is not an Affiliate of the seller (unless the Affiliate is the ultimate end user of the finished product), and

(b)    royalties payable to a licensor shall accrue only once with respect to the same unit of product (or intermediate thereof).

For example, if a party to this Agreement sells the active ingredient for a Product to a Third Party, for formulation and resale of the finished Product by the Third Party, then Net Sales of such Product shall be based on the amount billed to such Third Party by the party to this Agreement.

1.19    U.S. Co. Research Cost shall mean the cost incurred by U.S. Co. for the work in the Field conducted in accordance with this Agreement, necessary for the decision whether or not to recommend an [Bio-element] for development into a Product, including but not limited to the cost for the scientists (university-trained personnel) to be assigned to the Field and all other Target specific costs incurred, such as operating, leases, rents, equipment, supplies, outside services and contracts, travel, seminars, depreciation, and related company overhead.

1.20    Development Cost shall mean the cost incurred by U.S. Co. and Swiss Co. for the work starting with Phase 0 and ending with the submission of the registration dossier to the registration authorities in all Major Countries (including NDA filing with FDA and the registration authority of the European Union), including the cost for additional data eventually requested by such registration authorities for obtaining registration.

1.21    Phase 0 shall mean Phase 0 according to the definition set forth in Annex 1 hereto.

1.22    Co-Promotion shall mean the promotion in the United States in accordance with this Agreement by both parties of Products under the same trademark owned by Swiss Co. Products subject to Co-Promotion shall be sold solely by Swiss Co. and/or its sublicensee using field force of both U.S. Co. and Swiss Co. and/or its sublicensee and shall be identified by a trademark chosen by Swiss Co. with due consideration to trademark suggestions, if any, from U.S. Co.

1.23    Abandoned Product(s) shall mean Products with respect to which a party does not exercise its option under this Agreement or subsequently to such exercise relinquishes at any time its rights under this Agreement, whether worldwide or with respect to a particular country or countries, by written notice of such relinquishment, or Products that otherwise become Abandoned Products pursuant to Paragraph 5.3.

1.24    Major Country shall mean and include the following countries: Japan, the United Kingdom, Germany, Italy, France, and the United States of America ("USA").

1.25    Exclusive Territories shall mean all countries of the world except the USA.

1.26    Excluded Generic Know-how shall have the meanings set forth in Paragraphs 3.1 and 4.1 hereof.

1.27    Swiss Co.'s Business Units shall mean all Swiss Co. businesses (e.g., Pharmaceuticals Division, Agricultural Division) outside of Swiss Co.'s Central Research Laboratories in _____, Switzerland.

2.    Research Activities.

2.1.    During the Research Cooperation Term, U.S. Co. and Swiss Co. shall deal exclusively with each other in conducting research in the Field, and all research conducted by either party in the Field during the Research Cooperation Term shall be subject to this Agreement, excluding the research conducted by Swiss Co.'s Business Units, unless otherwise agreed.

2.2    The provisions of this Paragraph 2.2 and Paragraphs 2.3 through 2.7 shall apply during the Research Cooperation Term.

Upon execution of this Agreement, the parties hereto shall set up (i) an Executive Committee, to be composed of U.S. Co.'s CEO and the Head of Swiss Co.'s Central Research Laboratories, and to be chaired by the latter, and (ii) a Research Management Committee, to be composed of representatives of the responsible research line functions from both U.S. Co.'s, and Swiss Co.'s Central Research Laboratories, as well as, when needed and appropriate, of Swiss Co.'s Business Units, to be chaired by a representative of Swiss Co.

2.3    Both Committees shall hold meetings as necessary or required at intervals and locations to be mutually agreed upon, but at least twice a year. The minutes to the meetings shall be marked as "confidential" and shall be subject to the secrecy obligations and restrictions on use as per Paragraph 11 hereinafter.

2.4    The Executive Committee shall decide on strategic issues pertaining to the Field, including Targets and major changes within Targets, on overall resource allocations, including manpower and financial funding, and the membership on the Research Management Committee. It shall further decide on matters brought to the Executive Committee by the Research Management Committee, particularly on proposals made by the Research Management Committee of [Bio-elements] to propose to Swiss Co. for development and any other matter for which no decision can be found by the Research Management Committee. The Executive Committee's proposal for development of an [Bio-element] will be made separately for every use. Decisions of the Executive Committee shall be taken by unanimous vote, except that the chairman shall have a deciding vote on allocation of resources among Targets within the Field. All other matters shall be submitted, if no decision can be reached, to pre-Arbitration according to Paragraph 25.

2.5    The Research Management Committee's functions shall be the following, unless otherwise decided by the Executive Committee:

(a)    assignments of financial resources and personnel to specific Targets,

(b)    assignment of Targets to Project Teams to be composed of scientists of one or of both parties,

(c)    appointment of Project Team leaders and members,

(d)    approval of Target specific research plans, including operational objectives, proposed by the Project Teams,

(e)    review and evaluation of progress in specific Targets,

(f)    developing of specific performance criteria for Phase 0 for each [Bio-element] for each Use, based on recommendations by the Project Teams, and taking into consideration the requirements of Swiss Co.'s Business Units,

(g)    proposal of [Bio-elements] for development, based on recommendations by the Project Teams,

(h)    scientific evaluation of necessary operational changes (e.g., scientific approach) within specific Targets.

Both U.S. Co. and Swiss Co. shall have one vote each. Decisions of the Research Management Committee shall be taken, if possible, by unanimous vote. If no decision is reached, the matter shall be put to the Executive Committee's final decision.

2.6    Each party shall periodically submit to the other party progress reports with respect to its activities under the Research Collaboration. The Project Teams shall periodically submit research plans and progress reports to the Research Management Committee and shall propose research results [Bio-elements] for development. After approval of the research plans by the Research Management Committee, which must occur in a timely way so as not to impede the progress of the Project Teams, the Project Teams shall coordinate and implement all day-to-day activities of the parties, respectively, under this Agreement. The Project Teams shall work openly and cooperatively and shall meet periodically, as the parties reasonably determine may be necessary, to coordinate the research activities. The results of such meeting shall be recorded in writing. The minutes shall be approved and signed by both parties' project leaders. The minutes shall be marked as "confidential" and shall be subject to the secrecy obligations and restrictions on use as per Paragraph 11 hereinafter. The research activities shall be carried out by each party at its own locations.

2.7    Unless otherwise agreed, U.S. Co. shall assign, during the Research Cooperation Term, the full-time equivalent of _____ to _____ scientists (of varying levels of university training acceptable to Research Management Committee).

2.8    Each party warrants to the other party that it is free to enter into this Agreement and carry out its obligations hereunder and that its execution and delivery of this Agreement and performance of its obligations hereunder will not violate, be in conflict with, or constitute a default (or an event that, with notice or lapse of time or both, would constitute a default) under any agreement to which it is party or by which it is bound.

2.9    Each party warrants to the other that to the best of its knowledge, its use (or use by the other party under this Agreement) of its existing ABC Technology in the Field does not infringe any issued patent of any Third Party of which it is aware, and it has not received any communication alleging that it has infringed on or acted in conflict with or by conducting its business as proposed would infringe on or act in conflict with the rights of any Third Party. U.S. Co. further warrants that the inventors listed in the patent applications listed in Annex 1 hereto have assigned to U.S. Co. such patent applications and any Patent Rights issuing therefrom. In addition, each party warrants that it has not entered into any license or other agreement with any Third Party in the Field.

3.    Rights of and Licenses Granted to Swiss Co.

Swiss Co. will have the following rights:

3.1.    Unlimited and royalty-free access during the Research Cooperation Term to and right to use and (subject to Paragraph 11) disclose, free of charge, perpetually and worldwide U.S. Co.'s Generic Know-How inside and outside the Field, subject to the terms and conditions of this Agreement, provided however that in the event that U.S. Co. informs Swiss Co. prior to or contemporaneously with the disclosure of an item of Generic Know-How owned by U.S. Co. that U.S. Co. has reasonably determined that such item could have significant commercial value, then such item (the "U.S. Co. Excluded Generic Know-How") shall be excluded from the provisions of this Paragraph 3.1.

3.2.  The right to receive during the Research Cooperation Term, as a U.S. Co. senior partner, through attendance to the meetings of U.S. Co.'s scientific board, full information on U.S. Co.'s research activities in other fields not covered by agreements with Third Parties, and the possibility to extend the Research Collaboration in the same spirit to such other fields, provided however that U.S. Co. may exclude from such disclosure information with respect to a collaboration with a Third Party that U.S. Co. has obligations to maintain in confidence. U.S. Co. acknowledges that Swiss Co., in the course of its business, conducts research and development resulting in and also has access from Third Parties to confidential and proprietary information, which may be disclosed by U.S. Co. during such meetings, U.S. Co. agrees that prior to such meetings it will inform Swiss Co. of the general nature of the information to be discussed at such meetings so as to allow Swiss Co. the opportunity to determine whether it wishes to attend those portions of the meetings at which such information will be discussed and have access thereto.

3.3  (a)  The option to be granted a worldwide license during the License Period under U.S. Co. Technology and Joint Technology to develop, manufacture, use, and market the Products, with the right to grant sublicenses. If Swiss Co. wishes to exercise the option, it shall do so within ninety (90) days from the decision of the Executive Committee to propose an [Bio-element] for development for any Use.

(i)  Said license shall be exclusive in the Exclusive Territories, against payments of royalties as set out in Paragraph 6.2.

(ii)  Said license shall be co-exclusive with U.S. Co., at U.S. Co.'s option, in the USA, to the extent of XX percent of the Development Costs and of minimally XX percent of the contribution/losses of the Co-Promotion, as set out in greater detail in Paragraphs 7.2 and 7.12, royalty free. Specific agreements dealing with co-development, co-manufacturing and Co-Promotion in the USA are to be negotiated in good faith between U.S. Co. and Swiss Co. In case U.S. Co. fails to exercise the option set forth in Paragraph 4.3, the license to Swiss Co. shall be exclusive and Swiss Co. shall pay to U.S. Co. a royalty according to Paragraph 6.2.

(b)  At the end of the License Period (unless the License Period is terminated pursuant to Paragraph 14.4) for any Product in each respective country, each party shall have the unrestricted right to use any of the other party's Technology or the Joint Technology that was the subject of the license, free of charge, in the development, manufacture, use, or marketing of such Product in such country.

(c)  During the Agreement Period the option to reconsider within thirty (30) days from U.S. Co.'s proposal to Swiss Co. of previously Abandoned Products for development, manufacturing, use, and marketing after an initial rejection or relinquishment of rights by Swiss Co., U.S. Co. shall make such proposal in each of the following cases:

(i)  at the time when U.S. Co. has an offer by a Third Party to license or acquire an Abandoned Product, and

(ii)  in the case of U.S. Co. developing the Abandoned Product(s) without a Third Party, at the beginning of phase III clinical trials, the terms for a license to develop, manufacture, use, and market such Product shall be negotiated in the spirit of this Agreement. In case of a Third-Party offer, Swiss Co. shall at least meet such offer if it exercises this option to reconsider.

3.4  During the Research Cooperation Term the option to be granted a worldwide license during the License Period under U.S. Co.'s Know-How and Patent Rights to develop, manufacture, use, and market U.S. Co.'s products committed to a Third Party, if this Third Party has declined its rights to the product, and if U.S. Co. is free to develop and market such product through a licensee, and if U.S. Co. determines to develop or market the products with a partner, under conditions to be negotiated in the spirit of this Agreement, particularly with regard to the business in the USA. In such case, U.S. Co. shall so inform Swiss Co.; and U.S. Co. shall offer to grant the license to any other Third Party and U.S. Co. shall provide all information in U.S. Co.'s possession and control, including but not limited to a summary of the terms, which is reasonably necessary to enable Swiss Co. to evaluate whether it wishes to accept U.S. Co.'s offer. Swiss Co. shall accept or reject such offer within ninety (90) days from receipt of U.S. Co.'s offer and information. If Swiss Co. accepts the offer, Swiss Co. and U.S. Co. shall enter into a written agreement with respect to grant of such license. In the event Swiss Co. rejects any such offer, U.S. Co. shall be free to grant such license to any Third Party on terms no more favorable to such Third Party than those rejected by Swiss Co.

3.5  U.S. Co. shall be free to offer to grant a license to any Third Party regarding U.S. Co.'s products not covered by any cooperation with Swiss Co. or a Third Party, under such terms as it may agree upon. If U.S. Co. is unable to reach agreement with the aforesaid Third Party, then Swiss Co. shall, during the Research Cooperation Term, have the option to be granted a worldwide license during the License Period under U.S. Co.'s Know-How and Patent Rights to develop, manufacture, use, and market such products, under conditions to be negotiated in the spirit of this Agreement, particularly with regard to the business in the USA. In such case, U.S. Co. shall so inform Swiss Co. and U.S. Co. shall offer to grant the license to Swiss Co. before offering to grant the license to any other Third Party and U.S. Co. shall provide all information in U.S. Co.'s possession and control, including but not limited to a summary of the terms, which is reasonably necessary to enable Swiss Co. to evaluate whether it wishes to accept U.S. Co.'s offer. Swiss Co. shall accept or reject such offer within ninety (90) days from receipt of U.S. Co.'s offer and information. If Swiss Co. accepts the offer, Swiss Co. and U.S. Co. shall enter into a written agreement with respect to grant of such license. In the event Swiss Co. rejects any such offer, U.S. Co. shall be free to grant such license to any Third Party on terms no more favorable to such Third Party than those rejected by Swiss Co.

3.6   The right to discontinue the Research Collaboration in (a) specific Target(s) within the Field after a Target review taking place twenty-four (24) months after initiation of Research Collaboration relating to such Target, or thereafter at such other time requested by Swiss Co., by giving twelve (12) months' prior written notice. In this case, U.S. Co. shall be free to continue research and to develop, manufacture, use, and market the resulting products (except that U.S. Co. shall have no license under Swiss Co.'s Patent Rights or Know-How to develop, manufacture, use, or market such resulting products, unless and until such license is granted by Swiss Co.), subject to the terms of Paragraph 3.3(c) hereinbefore.

3.7   The option to be granted at any time during the life of any Patent Rights that are based on a Generic Invention owned by U.S. Co. or any U.S. Co. Excluded Generic Know-How (or, if there are no Patent Rights based on a particular item of U.S. Co. Excluded Generic Know-How with respect to such item of U.S. Co. Excluded Generic Know-How, at any time during the Agreement Period), a worldwide, nonexclusive license to make, use, and sell products not falling within the definition of Products herein, inside and outside the Field during the License Period, with the right to sublicense, against payment of a royalty to be negotiated in good faith, and if the parties fail to agree, such royalty rate shall be determined pursuant to Paragraph 25. In addition, U.S. Co. will grant to Swiss Co. a nonexclusive license under any U.S. Co.'s Patent Rights relating to U.S. Co.'s inventions existing on the date of this Agreement, solely to the extent that such license is necessary and solely to enable Swiss Co. to efficiently practice such Generic Invention, or a Generic Invention that is jointly owned by the parties.

At the end of the License Period (unless the License Period is terminated pursuant to Paragraph 14.4) in each respective country, each party shall have the unrestricted right to use any of the other party's Technology that was the subject of the license free of charge.

3.8   The parties agree that, subject to Paragraphs 3.3, 4.2, and 4.3, each party shall have the unrestricted right to use and disclose (subject only to Paragraph 11), free of charge, perpetually and worldwide, inside and outside the Field, the Joint Technology, with no obligation of accounting.

4.   Rights of and Licenses Granted to U.S. Co.

U.S. Co. will have the following rights:

4.1.   Unlimited and royalty-free access during the Research Cooperation Term to and right to use and (subject to Paragraph 11) disclose, free of charge, perpetually and worldwide Swiss Co.'s Generic Know-How inside and outside the Field, subject to the terms and conditions of this Agreement, provided however that in the event that Swiss Co. informs U.S. Co. prior to or contemporaneously with the disclosure of an item of Generic Know-How owned by Swiss Co. that Swiss Co. has reasonably determined that such item could have significant commercial value, then such item (the "Swiss Co. Excluded Generic Know-How") shall be excluded from the provisions of this Paragraph 4.1. It is understood that Know-How and Patent Rights of Swiss Co.'s Business Units are also excluded from the provisions of this Paragraph 4.1 unless arising during the course of the Research Collaboration.

4.2   The option to be granted a license during the License Period under Swiss Co. Technology and Joint Technology, subject to Paragraph 5.4, to develop, manufacture, use, and market the Abandoned Products for the territories for which such Products are abandoned by Swiss Co., subject to Paragraph 3.3(c) hereabove, exclusively, against payment of royalties, with the right to grant sublicenses. In case such option is exercised, the royalties payable thereunder are set forth in Paragraph 7.1. If U.S. Co. wishes to exercise such option, it shall do so within ninety (90) days after receipt of notice from Swiss Co.

At the end of the License Period (unless the License Period is terminated pursuant to Paragraph 14.4) for any Abandoned Product in each respective country, each party shall have the unrestricted right to use any of the other party's Technology or the Joint Technology that was the subject of the license, free of charge, in the development, manufacture, use, or marketing of such Abandoned Product in such country.

4.3    The option to be granted a co-exclusive license, with no right to sublicense, during the License Period, under Swiss Co. Technology and Joint Technology to co-develop, co-manufacture, and Co-Promote with Swiss Co. or Swiss Co.'s sublicensees, the Products in the USA to the extent of XX percent of the Development Costs and of up to XX percent of the contribution/losses of the Co-Promotion, as set out in greater detail in Paragraphs 7.2 and 12, royalty free. Specific agreements dealing with co-development, co-manufacturing, and Co-Promotion in the USA are to be negotiated in good faith between U.S. Co. and Swiss Co. If U.S. Co. wishes to exercise such option, it shall do so within one hundred (100) days from the decision of the Executive Committee to propose a [Bio-element] for development, but no later than ten (10) days from Swiss Co.'s decision to accept such [Bio-element] for development.

In case all or substantially all of the assets of U.S. Co. are transferred to a Third Party, or in case the control of U.S. Co. changes, in addition to having rights and obligations under any co-exclusive license in the USA in accordance with the foregoing, U.S. Co. shall pay royalties to Swiss Co. according to article 7.1 hereinafter, such royalties to be based on the proportion of Swiss Co.'s Net Sales for such Product in the USA corresponding to the proportion of U.S. Co.'s compensation/loss sharing as described in Paragraph 12.4. For purposes of this Agreement, "control" of U.S. Co. shall mean the ownership of fifty (50) percent or more of the voting or income interest of U.S. Co., or such other relationship as, in fact, constitutes actual control.

At the end of the License Period (unless the License Period is terminated pursuant to Paragraph 14.4) in each respective country, each party shall have the unrestricted right to use any of the other party's Technology or the Joint Technology that was the subject of the license, free of charge.

4.4    The option to be granted at any time during the life of any Patent Rights that are based on a Generic Invention owned by Swiss Co. or any Swiss Co. Excluded Generic Know-How (or, if there are no Patent Rights based on a particular item of Swiss Co. Excluded Generic Know-How, with respect to such item of Swiss Co. Excluded Generic Know-How, at any time during the Agreement Period) a worldwide, nonexclusive license to make, use, and sell products not falling within the definition of Products herein, inside and outside the Field during the License Period, with the right to sublicense, against payment of a royalty to be negotiated in good faith; and if the parties fail to agree, such royalty rate shall be determined pursuant to Paragraph 25. In addition, Swiss Co. will grant to U.S. Co. a nonexclusive license under any Swiss Co.'s Corporate Unit Research's Patent Rights relating to Swiss Co.'s Corporate United Research's inventions existing on the date of this Agreement, solely to the extent that such license is necessary and solely to enable U.S. Co. to practice such Generic Invention, or a Generic Invention that is jointly owned by the parties.

At the end of the License Period (unless the License Period is terminated pursuant to Paragraph 14.4) in each respective country, each party shall have the unrestricted right to use any of the other party's Technology that was the subject of the license, free of charge.

4.5    The parties agree that, subject to Paragraphs 3.3, 4.2, and 4.3, each party shall have the unrestricted right to use and disclose (subject only to Paragraph 11), free of charge, perpetually and worldwide, inside and outside the Field, the Joint Technology, with no obligation of accounting.

5.    Responsibilities of the Parties.

5.1.    The overall responsibility for IND Application and Clinical Development of the Products for which Swiss Co. has exercised its option according to Paragraph 3.3, whether or not U.S. Co. has exercised its option to Co-Promote in the USA according to Paragraph 4.3, along with the overall regulatory strategy during clinical development, NDA approval, and post-NDA approval phases, is agreed to be with Swiss Co. However, if U.S. Co. and Swiss Co. have entered into a specific agreement covering co-development of Products, then U.S. Co. may jointly participate in all of such development activities for said Products, subject to Paragraph 12.5. Both parties will have full access to all submissions to, including clinical studies and other supporting information, and communications with the FDA related to the Products subject to Co-Promotion. Swiss Co., or its Affiliates and/or their sublicensees, shall file and hold title to all regulatory applications, approvals, and supplements thereto in the USA and all other countries worldwide, except, with respect to any Product, for countries in which Swiss Co. has relinquished its rights under this Agreement for such Product. With respect to a Product subject to Co-Promotion in the USA for which U.S. Co. is in compliance with Paragraph 7.2, U.S. Co. shall have the irrevocable right, (i) for purposes of Co-Promoting such Product in the USA, in conformance with Swiss Co.'s direction as set out in Paragraph 12.5, to use all U.S. clinical data for such Product, and (ii) for purposes of obtaining or maintaining registration for such Product in another country where it has the right to market such Product hereunder, to refer to and cross-reference all U.S. clinical data for such Product, subject to the terms of this Agreement, and U.S. Co. shall have no right to use any such U.S. clinical data for any other purpose.

5.2 For any product Swiss Co. and U.S. Co. are Co-Promoting in the USA or both marketing in different territories, they shall have continuing obligations to timely advise each other of all adverse drug reactions and other similar matters relevant to maintaining approvals and registrations of such product. Swiss Co. and U.S. Co. shall have the continuing obligation to timely advise each other of any governmental regulatory problems, notices, actions, or communications relating to such product.

5.3 The party being granted a license pursuant to Paragraphs 3 and 4, respectively, shall use commercially reasonable efforts consistent with good business judgment to develop, commercialize, and sell the respective products with the care and in the manner reasonably required (hereinafter, such standard of care to be referred to as "Commercially Reasonable Efforts"). In the event that either party shall fail to use Commercially Reasonable Efforts with respect to any product for any Use in any territory, at the option of the other party and after written notice from the other party and opportunity to cure in accordance with Paragraph 14.4, any license granted by the other party hereunder for such product for such Use in such territory shall terminate and all rights to such product for such Use in such territory that were granted by the other party under such license shall revert to the other party; and if such product was a Product marketed by Swiss Co., it shall become an Abandoned Product for purposes of Paragraphs 3.3(c) and 4.2. In any such event, at the other party's request, the party who failed to use Commercially Reasonable Efforts agrees to negotiate in good faith with the other party the terms upon which additional Patent Rights and Know-How (including, without limitation, preclinical and clinical data, rights to the registration file, and rights under the PLA, NDA, or equivalent regulatory approval) will be made available to such party for use in connection with such product for such Use in such territory.

5.4 Notwithstanding anything in this Agreement to the contrary, the parties agree that if U.S. Co. wishes to have the right to use with respect to any Abandoned Product for any Use in any territory, any Patent Rights or Know-How (including, without limitation, preclinical and clinical data, rights to the registration file, and rights under the PLA, NDA, or equivalent regulatory approval) other than as specifically provided for in Paragraph 5.1 hereof, resulting from Swiss Co.'s or its consultants' activities during Phase 0 and thereafter, then U.S. Co. shall so inform Swiss Co. and the parties shall negotiate in good faith the terms upon which such Patent Rights or Know-how will be made available to U.S. Co. with respect to such Abandoned Product for such Use in such territory.

6. Financial Commitments of Swiss Co.

6.1 It is agreed that no up-front and/or milestone payments are to be made.

6.2 In consideration of the licenses to develop, manufacture, use, and market the Products agreed in Paragraph 3.3 hereabove, Swiss Co. agrees to pay to U.S. Co. during the License Period a royalty for human therapeutic uses of XX percent of the Net Sales of such Product in countries where U.S. Co.'s or jointly owned Patent Rights relating to such Product exist in the form of issued, valid, and unexpired patent(s); of XX percent of the Net Sales of such Product (falling with U.S. Co. or Joint Technology) in countries where no U.S. Co.'s or jointly owned Patent Rights relating to such Product exist in the form of issued, valid, and unexpired patent(s).

For every other Use the parties will negotiate the royalties in good faith.

In the event that the Research Cooperation Term or any Target is terminated prior to the proposal of any [Bio-element] for development, the royalty with respect to a Product containing such [Bio-element] shall be reduced by fifty (50) percent; provided, however, that in the event that the Research Cooperation Term or any Target is terminated prior to three (3) years from the date hereof due to the acquisition of either party, the royalty rate for any such product shall be further reduced by multiplying the royalty rate (as already reduced by fifty (50) percent by a fraction equal to the actual term of the Research Collaboration, divided by three (3) years.

Should the parties agree on a Co-Promotion of a Product in the USA, Swiss Co. shall not be obliged to pay royalties to U.S. Co. on Net Sales of such Product in the USA. The parties will renegotiate in good faith a reduction in the royalty due by Swiss Co. to U.S. Co. in case a Product contains in its finished form, [besides [Bio-element] resulting from the Research Collaboration (and) other active substance(s)].

The royalties to be paid by Swiss Co. to U.S. Co. in consideration of the licenses agreed in Paragraphs 3.4, 3.5, and 3.7 hereabove shall be negotiated in good faith.

6.3 Swiss Co. agrees to make an equity investment in U.S. Co. of XX million United States Dollars

(US $XX,XXX,XXX) not later than March 31, 2002, as agreed in the Stock Purchase Agreement of even date herewith.

The parties agree that U.S. Co. is granting to Swiss Co. certain rights to have a seat on U.S. Co.'s board, in case a Third Party cooperating with U.S. Co. has a seat on U.S. Co.'s board, pursuant to the terms of a Swiss Co. Investor Rights Agreement between the parties referred to in such Stock Purchase Agreement. The parties further agree that such rights shall remain in full force and effect to the extent and as provided in said Swiss Co. Investor Rights Agreement, independent of whether this Agreement, the Research Cooperation Term, or any license granted pursuant hereto is terminated or remains in effect.

6.4 Swiss Co. agrees to pay U.S. Co. for the U.S. Co. Research Costs incurred by U.S. Co. during the Research Cooperation Term, by making payments of up to US $XX,XXX,XXX per year in quarterly installments in advance, which sum is calculated by multiplying the number of U.S. Co. scientists dedicated to the Research Collaboration by a maximum average total cost per year per the equivalent of a full-time scientist of US $XXX,XXX as adjusted herein for inflation. This sum shall depend on the number of scientists (university-trained personnel) assigned by U.S. Co. to the Research Collaboration, assuming up to the full-time equivalent of XX scientists (university-trained personnel), subject to reduction following the termination of (a) research Target(s) pursuant to Paragraphs 3.6 and 14.2 and also subject to reduction during the extended portion of the Research Cooperation Term that may be extended by Swiss Co. pursuant to the last sentence of Paragraph 14.2(a), at a maximum average total cost of US $XXX,XXX per full-time scientist per year. This average total cost is adjusted annually to the U.S. inflation rate of the previous year.

Swiss Co. shall not have the obligation to pay any research cost, exceeding the above payments, to U.S. Co., unless decided otherwise by the Executive Committee.

7. Financial Commitments of U.S. Co.

7.1. In consideration of the licenses to develop, manufacture, use, and market the Products agreed in Paragraph 4.2 hereabove, U.S. Co. agrees to pay to Swiss Co. during the License Period a royalty for human therapeutic use of XX percent of the Net Sales of such Product in countries where Swiss Co.'s or jointly owned Patent Rights relating to such Product exist in the form of issued, valid, and unexpired patent(s); of XX percent of the Net Sales of such Product (falling within Swiss Co. or Joint Technology) in countries where no Swiss Co.'s or jointly owned Patent Rights relating to such Product exist in the form of issued, valid, and unexpired patent(s).

For every other Use the parties will negotiate the royalties in good faith.

In the event that the Research Cooperation Term or any Target is terminated prior to the proposal of any [Bio-element] for development, the royalty with respect to a Product containing such [Bio-element] shall be reduced by fifty (50) percent; provided, however, that in the event that the Research Cooperation Term or any Target is terminated prior to three (3) years from the date hereof due to the acquisition of either party, the royalty rate for any such Product shall be further reduced by multiplying the royalty rate (as already reduced by fifty [50] percent) by a fraction equal to the actual term of the Research Collaboration, divided by three (3) years.

Should the parties agree on a Co-Promotion of a Product in the USA, U.S. Co. shall not be obliged to pay royalties to Swiss Co. on Net Sales of such Product in the USA, subject to the provisions of Paragraph 4.3 in case all or substantially all of the assets of U.S. Co. are transferred or sold or the control of U.S. Co. changes.

The parties will renegotiate in good faith the royalty due by U.S. Co. to Swiss Co. in case a Product contains in its finished form besides the [Bio-element] any other active substance(s). The royalties to be paid by U.S. Co. to Swiss Co. in consideration of the licenses agreed in Paragraph 4.4 hereabove shall be negotiated in good faith.

7.2 In case Swiss Co. has exercised its option according to Paragraph 3.3 and U.S. Co. has exercised its option to Co-Promote a Product in the USA according to Paragraph 4.3, U.S. Co. agrees to bear XX percent of the Development Costs incurred by the parties while generating data specifically directed at obtaining registration of that Product in the USA. Furthermore, since substantial parts of the data necessary to obtain worldwide registration can also be used to obtain registration in the USA, U.S. Co. agrees to reimburse to Swiss Co. up to XX percent of the worldwide Development Cost, the exact percentage to be agreed from case to case. U.S. Co.'s sharing of Development Costs not previously borne by U.S. Co. shall become due with the introduction of a Product in the USA and shall be deducted from royalties due to U.S. Co. from Swiss Co. under any license granted to Swiss Co. pursuant hereto or from U.S. Co.'s share of Swiss Co. Contribution for such Product pursuant to Paragraph 12. Swiss Co. shall reimburse U.S. Co. for any Development Costs borne by U.S. Co. in excess of its obligation.

8. Settlement of Financial Obligations.

8.1. All royalty payment shall be made in [Swiss Francs] for each calendar half year (ending on June 30 and December 31, respectively) within ninety (90) days after the end of such calendar half year. Such royalty payments shall be accompanied by a written statement indicating Net Sales of each product, as applicable, by country and by Use.

8.2 Each party shall have the right to have, at its own expense, an independent certified accountant, to which the other party has no reasonable objection, inspect the books and records of account of the other party or such other party's Affiliates and sublicensees to determine and communicate to the requesting party only whether appropriate payments have been made and the amount of any discrepancy. The parties agree that such records are maintained or will be maintained in sufficient detail to permit such determination for a period of at least three (3) years from the date of their origin. If any review by the independent accountant of such books and records should indicate that the amounts paid have not been correct, the parties shall seek to mutually agree to settle any discrepancies raised by the accountant.

8.3 The provisions set out in Paragraph 8.2 hereabove shall apply analogously to U.S. Co.'s invoices and Swiss Co.'s payments of U.S. Co. Research Cost agreed in Paragraph 6.4 hereabove, as well as to Swiss Co.'s and U.S. Co.'s bearing of Development Cost agreed in Paragraph 7.2.

9. Patents and Know-How.

9.1. Subject to Paragraph 9.4 below, all inventions (whether patentable or not and whether resulting in Patent Rights or Know-How) and Patent Rights with respect thereto made during the course of the Research Collaboration by a party's employees or consultants shall be owned by and held in the name of such party ("A") and the other party ("B") shall cooperate concerning all matters related to patent filings and prosecution for such items and shall have the right to make comments and suggestions with regard to the content and scope of any such applications, including the claims thereof, and the countries in which the applications are to be filed. Reasonable consideration should be given by A to the comments and suggestions of B. In the event that A declines to file a patent application in a country or countries desired by B, B may file at its own cost in any such country or countries in the name of A.

9.2 A agrees that during the Research Cooperation Term and during the License Period for a license relating to such patents, it shall be responsible for, and timely pay, all fees or other payments that may be required to maintain the patent applications and patents, in full force and effect. If A decides to abandon any patent application or patent and relinquish its rights thereunder in any particular country, it shall promptly notify B in writing, and B shall have the right to assume responsibility for maintaining such patent application or patent at its own expense. A agrees to cooperate with B so as to enable B to undertake such maintenance without loss of patent rights. B shall have complete responsibility for such continued maintenance and may, in its sole discretion, allow any such patent application or patent to lapse at any time.

9.3 A agrees to diligently prosecute all pending patent applications that constitute a part of its Technology, Generic Inventions, or Excluded Generic Know-How; to promptly transmit to B copies of all official communications relating to obtaining or maintaining Patent Rights in said Technology, Generic Inventions, or Excluded Generic Know-How within thirty (30) business days after receipt thereof by A from the various patent offices around the world (or from attorneys or foreign associates who forward such official communications to A) or to have counsel concurrently transmit to B copies of all papers filed or received in such pending patent applications; and to give due consideration to the advice of B with respect to the further prosecution of such pending patent applications.

9.4 Inventions (whether patentable or not and whether resulting in Patent Rights or Know-How) made jointly by the parties pursuant to the laws of inventorship shall be jointly owned, with no obligation of accounting or limitations on use except as set forth herein.

9.5 Unless otherwise agreed, the filing and maintenance of patent applications and patents based on jointly owned inventions shall be subject to the provisions of Sections 9.1 through 9.3 with Swiss Co. acting as party A.

10. Exchange of Know-How.

10.1. Subject to the confidentiality provisions of Paragraph 11 and without limiting the obligations of each party to disclose information to the other party as provided elsewhere in this Agreement, U.S. Co. and Swiss Co. shall share their Generic Know-How with each other. If necessary, each party also will provide such information to the other, to the extent reasonable, in suitable form for regulatory approval and registrations purposes.

10.2 The Research Management Committee and Project Teams, as described in Paragraphs 2.5 and 2.6, shall be responsible for the exchange of Generic Know-How between U.S. Co. and Swiss

Co. (As appropriate, written reports shall be prepared for the meetings of the Research Management Committee and Project Teams.)

10.3 During the Research Cooperation Term, the parties shall share all Know-How derived from the Research Collaboration, subject to the provisions of Paragraphs 3.1, 3.2, and 4.1 hereof.

11. Confidentiality and Publications.

11.1 Unless otherwise provided for in this Agreement, both parties shall treat the Generic Know-How, any other Know-How disclosed hereunder by the other party, and any and all information and data derived under this Agreement as strictly confidential and shall not disclose the same to any Third Party during the Agreement Period and for five (5) years thereafter, except for information that:

(a) is or shall have been known to the receiving party prior to the disclosure by the other party as evidenced by written record or other proof;

(b) is or shall have been public knowledge through no fault of the receiving party;

(c) has been received from a Third Party who did not acquire it directly or indirectly from the disclosing party;

(d) needs to be disclosed to government officials for purposes of obtaining registration of the products; or

(e) is compelled to be disclosed in the course of litigation by a Third Party, provided that the party compelled to make such disclosure provides the other party to this Agreement with notice of such compulsion sufficiently in advance of disclosure so as to provide such other party a reasonable time period to seek a protective order.

Notwithstanding the above, both parties may disclose such information to their legal representatives and employees, to Affiliates, licensees and sublicensees, to legal representatives and employees of Affiliates, licensees and sublicensees, and to consultants to the extent such disclosure is necessary to achieve the purposes of this Agreement and provided such legal representatives, employees, consultants, licensees, and sublicensees are covered by obligations of confidentiality with respect to such information not less stringent than those set forth herein; and as required by law.

11.2 The parties acknowledge the legitimate interest of their respective employees in publishing findings under this Agreement to the scientific community. On the other hand, the parties recognize their mutual interest that publications be made and lectures, seminars, or other presentations be given only to the extent that both parties' commercial interests have been reasonably safeguarded through patent protection or otherwise so that Third Parties cannot make commercial and/or industrial use of the information contained in such disclosures. For this purpose, each party shall ensure that the other shall have XX days after receipt for the opportunity to comment in advance on any publication or oral presentation in public involving disclosure of any information under this Agreement that may constitute confidential information and that no such publication or presentation relating to such confidential information under this Agreement shall be made without such other party's prior written consent. The party from which such consent is requested shall not unreasonably withhold or delay such consent. A request from the nondisclosing party that any such publication or presentation be delayed until a patent application is filed thereon shall be a reasonable request to delay, provided that such delay lasts no more than XX days from the date of such request.

12. Co-Promotion in the USA.

12.1. In the USA, Swiss Co. and U.S. Co. will have co-exclusive, Co-Promotion rights to the Products for which Swiss Co. has exercised its option according to Paragraph 3.3 and U.S. Co. has exercised its option to Co-Promote according to Paragraph 4.3, subject, as applicable, to the following:

12.2 Subject to the provisions of Paragraph 12.7 below, U.S. Co. and Swiss Co. agree to negotiate in good faith the details of their Co-Promotion agreement at mutually agreeable time and in accordance with the terms and conditions described in this Paragraph 12 and elsewhere in this Agreement as applicable. Such negotiation, however, shall commence not later than the end of clinical phase III in the USA or at such other earlier time as U.S. Co. and Swiss Co. determine is commercially reasonable.

12.3 U.S. Co.'s and Swiss Co.'s or Swiss Co.'s sublicensee's compensation/loss sharing shall be fairly determined based on the contribution/losses from such Co-Promotion computed in a mutually agreeable manner based on Swiss Co.'s standard accounting procedures ("Swiss Co. Contribution/Losses"), which Swiss Co. Contribution/Losses are defined as the difference between Net Sales of the Products in the USA and Swiss Co.'s "Total Marketing Expense" in the USA. Swiss Co.'s "Total Marketing Expense" shall include but not necessarily be limited to the following costs incurred by Swiss Co. and by U.S. Co. (which U.S. Co. costs not exceeding

XX percent of such Total Marketing Expense, unless otherwise agreed, shall have been reimbursed by Swiss Co.), if any, as may be reasonable:

(a) cost of goods to Swiss Co., as appropriately determined in accordance with Swiss Co.'s standard accounting procedures;

(b) product-specific marketing expenses (PSME), which include but are not limited to costs for direct advertising, films, samples, exhibits, clinical conference aids, peer promotion activities, marketing research, and such other costs as are normally included in PSME according to Swiss Co.'s standard accounting procedures;

(c) field force costs (FF), which are the direct and indirect costs of the combined U.S. Co. and Swiss Co. field forces, such costs to be borne by U.S. Co. and Swiss Co., respectively, properly allocated to the sale of the Products and in accordance with Swiss Co.'s (and U.S. Co.'s) standard accounting procedures;

(d) other marketing expenses according to Swiss Co.'s standard accounting procedures; and

(e) overhead costs and cost of services as determined in accordance with Swiss Co.'s standard accounting procedures.

12.4 U.S. Co.'s compensation/loss sharing shall be a percentage of Swiss Co. Contribution/Losses. Such percentage shall not exceed XX percent of Swiss Co. Contribution/Losses. Such percentage shall be determined by the multiplication of RFFT and RFFP, as those two factors are described below:

(a) Relative field force time (RFFT) is that amount of U.S. Co.'s field force time spent in direct promotion of the Products to the Products target audience, divided by that time spent by the combined Swiss Co. and U.S. Co. field forces.

(b) Relative field force productivity (RFFP) is that amount of the U.S. Co. field force experience, in terms of years, in promoting Products in the indication(s) for which the Products are approved divided by that quantity for the Swiss Co. field force. RFFP shall at no time be less than three-quarters of one (0.75) or greater than one (1.0).

12.5 U.S. Co. acknowledges that it shall permit Swiss Co. to design and implement the overall development, manufacture, marketing, and sales programs as Swiss Co. determines is commercially reasonable for the Products, with consideration of such input as U.S. Co. representatives may from time to time provide.

12.6 Swiss Co. acknowledges that, in accordance with its sole right to determine the overall development, manufacture, marketing, and sales strategy for the Products, and in consideration of the input to same that, from time to time may be provided by U.S. Co., it shall provide U.S. Co. with a commercially reasonable opportunity to achieve its compensation/loss sharing of up to XX percent of Swiss Co. Contribution/Losses defined above.

12.7 In case Swiss Co. decides to sublicense its co-development, co-manufacturing, or Co-Promotion rights in the USA and does not wish to develop, manufacture, or market and sell a Product itself, U.S. Co. shall negotiate in good faith with Swiss Co.'s sublicensee for such co-development, co-manufacture, or Co-Promotion, respectively, the details of such arrangement in accordance with this Agreement.

13. Indemnification; Liability; Infringement.

13.1. Swiss Co. shall indemnify and hold U.S. Co. harmless from and against any and all claims, damages, costs, expenses, and other liabilities, with respect to the Products sold by Swiss Co., its Affiliates and sublicensees, except those with respect to Products subject to Co-Promotion and except as provided in Paragraph 13.4 provided that

(a) not later than ten (10) days after receipt of notice by U.S. Co. of such claim, U.S. Co. shall notify Swiss Co. thereof;

(b) U.S. Co. fully cooperates with Swiss Co. in the defense of such claim without out-of-pocket cost to U.S. Co.; and

(c) Swiss Co. shall control the defense and/or settlement thereof.

Swiss Co. also agrees to add U.S. Co. as an additional named insured on any product liability insurance policy that Swiss Co. may have inside and/or outside the USA that covers such Products and to furnish satisfactory evidence of same upon request from time to time.

13.2 U.S. Co. shall indemnify and hold Swiss Co. harmless from and against any and all claims, damages, costs, expenses, and other liabilities, with respect to the Products sold by U.S. Co., its Affiliates and sublicensees, except those with respect to its Co-Promotion and except as provided in Paragraph 13.4; provided that

(a) not later than ten (10) days after receipt of notice by Swiss Co. of such claim, Swiss Co. shall notify U.S. Co. thereof;

(b)     Swiss Co. fully cooperates with U.S. Co. in the defense of such claim without out-of-pocket cost to Swiss Co.; and

(c)     U.S. Co. shall control the defense and/or settlement thereof.

U.S. Co. also agrees to add Swiss Co. as an additional named insured on any product liability insurance policy that U.S. Co. may have inside and/or outside the USA that covers such Product and to furnish satisfactory evidence of same upon request from time to time.

13.3     With respect to any Products that are subject to Co-Promotion, the parties shall negotiate in good faith indemnification provisions, if any, in the agreements relating to Co-Promotion.

13.4     The parties agree, however, that neither party nor their officers, directors, and employees shall be liable to the other party pursuant to Paragraph 13.1 or 13.2 for any claims, damages, costs, expenses, or other liabilities arising out of the negligence, willful misconduct, or illegal acts of the other party.

13.5     If U.S. Co., Swiss Co., or its respective Affiliates or sublicensees becomes aware of any actual or threatened infringement of any Patent Rights constituting U.S. Co., CB or Joint Technology under which either party is or has the option to become licensed, such party shall promptly notify the other party in writing and in any event with respect to patent infringements in the USA, within ten (10) business days. Swiss Co. and its Affiliates or sublicensees, shall have the first right to bring, at Swiss Co.'s own expense, an infringement action against any Third Party in its own name, or if necessary in the name of U.S. Co. If Swiss Co. or its Affiliates or sublicensees do not bring a particular patent infringement action within six (6) months from the date of notification, or within two (2) months prior to expiration, whichever is earlier, of any applicable statute of limitations on such action, U.S. Co., after notifying Swiss Co. in writing, shall be entitled to bring such infringement action at U.S. Co.'s own expense. The party not conducting such suit shall assist the other party and cooperate in any such litigation at the other's reasonable request without out-of-pocket expense to the party providing such assistance. The award or settlement in such litigation shall first be used to pay the legal costs and expenses of such suit and any remaining amount shall be divided between the parties in proportion to each party's respective injury caused by the infringer.

14.     Term and Termination.

14.1.     This Agreement comes into force when signed by both parties, retroactively to [Date], and on a country-by-country basis, unless earlier terminated as permitted hereunder, shall remain in effect for the Agreement Period.

14.2     (a)     The Research Collaboration agreed hereunder beginning on [Date] can be terminated by either party by giving nine (9) months' written notice to the other party, but not before a duration of the Research Collaboration of five (5) years (the duration of Research Collaboration is referred to herein as the "Research Cooperation Term," which term shall include any extension of the Research Cooperation Term made pursuant to the following sentence). However, Swiss Co. shall have the unilateral right to extend the Research Cooperation Term, on the terms of this Agreement, within the Field existing at the time of receipt of such notice of termination.

(b)     Notwithstanding the above, either party shall have the right to immediately terminate the Research Collaboration hereunder in one or more specific Target(s) within the Field in the event the other party is acquired (whether by way of a sale of stock or assets or merger or otherwise) or the control of the other party changes.

14.3     A termination of the Research Collaboration according to Paragraph 14.2 (a) or (b) hereabove or 14.4 (b) below has no effect on licenses granted by one party to the other or, if licenses have not yet been granted, on the parties' option to be granted licenses, according to Paragraphs 3 or 4 hereabove, respectively, or on the parties' other rights or obligations under this Agreement (whether set forth in Paragraphs 3 and 4 or elsewhere), except to the extent they are specifically stated to apply during the Research Cooperation Term.

14.4     (a)     Either party may terminate (i) any license for any product for any Use in any territory granted to the other party pursuant to this Agreement, in the event of a material breach by the other party of such respective license, and (ii) this Agreement, in the event of a material breach of this Agreement by the other party that is not related to a particular license, in each case provided that the breaching party is given written notice of such claimed breach from the nonbreaching party and a reasonable time, not to exceed sixty (60) days after receipt of such notice, in which to cure such claimed breach or submit same to prearbitration or arbitration hereunder. Such period to cure may be extended for up to one hundred twenty (120) days, upon written request, if such additional time is reasonably necessary to effect such cure, provided that such breaching party is using its reasonable efforts to diligently pursue such cure.

(b)    In the event U.S. Co. institutes or there is instituted against it any proceeding under any bankruptcy, insolvency, or similar law, or a receiver is appointed for the benefit of its creditors, and such proceeding or such appointment is not dismissed or discharged within a period of ninety (90) days, or in the event U.S. Co. is adjudged bankrupt, then Swiss Co. shall have the right to terminate (i) the Research Collaboration hereunder and/or (ii) any co-exclusive license granted to U.S. Co. pursuant to Paragraph 4.3 with respect to the co-development, co-manufacturing, and Co-Promotion of any Product in the USA, in which case any such termination can be made effective the date notice of termination is given.

If Swiss Co. elects pursuant to the preceding sentence to terminate any co-exclusive license granted to U.S. Co. pursuant to Paragraph 4.3 with respect to any Product in the USA, the provisions of this paragraph shall apply. Swiss Co. shall reimburse U.S. Co. for Development Costs with respect to such Product incurred by U.S. Co. in accordance with this Agreement that were not previously reimbursed by Swiss Co., or paid by U.S. Co. to Swiss Co. in accordance with Paragraph 7.2, minus the aggregate amount of any share of Swiss Co. Contribution previously paid by Swiss Co. to U.S. Co. with respect to such Product, plus the aggregate amount of royalties that would have been payable by Swiss Co. to U.S. Co. under Paragraph 6.2 if the co-exclusive license granted to Swiss Co. with respect to such Product in the USA referred to in Paragraph 3.3(a) had been an exclusive license to Swiss Co. instead. In addition any right of U.S. Co., to use or disclose in the USA any information or data arising from the development of such Product pursuant to this Agreement during Phase 0 and thereafter by Swiss Co., U.S. Co., or their respective consultants shall terminate, and (without limiting any other provisions of this Agreement) Swiss Co. shall own and have the full, unrestricted right, exclusive of U.S. Co., to use and disclose all of such information and data. Furthermore, from and after the effective date of the aforesaid termination of U.S. Co.'s co-exclusive license, the license to Swiss Co. with respect to such Product in the USA referred to in Paragraph 3.3(a) shall become exclusive, and Swiss Co. shall pay to U.S. Co. royalties according to Paragraph 6.2 with respect thereto.

(c)    Termination of this Agreement pursuant to Paragraph 14.4 shall not relieve the parties from any amounts owing between them and shall not terminate any rights or obligations arising and existing prior to or upon termination of this Agreement.

15.  Force Majeure.

Neither party shall be liable to the other for failure or delay in the performance of any of its obligations under this Agreement (except of the obligation to pay money to the other party as provided for herein, in which case for a period of one year such money is to be paid into escrow) for the time and to the extent such failure or delay is caused by riots, civil commotions, wars, hostilities between nations, embargoes, acts of God, storms, fires, accidents, labor disputes or strikes, sabotage, explosions, or other similar or different contingencies that affect its performance and are beyond its reasonable control. If the performance of any obligation under this Agreement is delayed owing to a force majeure for any continuous period of more than six (6) months, the parties hereto shall consult with respect to an equitable solution, including the possible termination of this Agreement.

16.  Nondisclosure.

The existence and terms of this Agreement shall not be disclosed by U.S. Co. or Swiss Co. to any Third Party or be published unless both parties expressly agree otherwise in writing. However, this restriction shall not apply to disclosure of information set forth in the form of an agreed press release, which will be prepared in mutually agreeable format and substance following the closing of this Agreement, and to announcements required by law or regulation except that in such event the parties shall coordinate to the extent possible with respect to the wording of any such announcement. Also, this restriction shall not apply to disclosure of this Agreement by either party to certain private Third Parties, such as the shareholders of such party, its investment bankers and other financial consultants, and prospective investors in such party or its technology under development, but excluding Third Parties who are competitors of the other party, if such disclosure is made under confidentiality obligations extending for at least three (3) years and otherwise similar in substance to the provisions of Paragraph 11. Except for disclosure pursuant to the press release to be mutually agreed following closing, U.S. Co. expressly agrees that subsequent press releases or other disclosure for press publication will be subject to the obligations of nondisclosure under this paragraph, unless such disclosure includes, in substance, only the information set forth in such agreed press release. The disclosing party shall submit for the other party's review in advance any description of this Agreement in any document it proposes to give to prospective investors. The other party shall promptly, within five (5) working days after receipt, provide its comments on such description, and the disclosing party shall give reasonable consideration to such comments.

17. Notices.

   All notices or communications sent or delivered hereunder by one party to the other party shall be in writing and shall be deemed duly given when delivered after having been mailed by registered or certified mail to the other party at the address set forth below or immediately when sent by electronic facsimile transmission (Fax), with receipt evidenced by Fax transmission acknowledgment, to the Fax number set forth below. A party's address or Fax number may be changed upon notice of such change given to the other party as provided herein. Notice to the parties shall be delivered to their respective addresses or Fax number, as follows:

   If to U.S. Co.: _____

   If to Swiss Co.: _____

18. Relationship of Parties.

   Both parties are independent contractors under this Agreement. Nothing contained in this Agreement is intended nor is to be construed so as to constitute U.S. Co. or Swiss Co. as partners or joint venturers with respect to this Agreement. Neither party shall have any express or implied right or authority to assume or create any obligations on behalf of or in the name of the other party or to bind the other party to any other contract, agreement, or undertaking with any Third Party.

19. Assignment.

   The rights and obligations of the parties hereunder shall not be transferred or assigned by either party, except to a buyer of all or substantially all of the stock or assets of a party, or as otherwise permitted in compliance with the requirements of this Agreement, without the prior written consent of the other party. This Agreement shall be binding upon and inure to the benefit of any such permitted assigns or successors.

20. Severability.

   If any part of this Agreement shall be held unenforceable, the remainder of the Agreement shall nevertheless remain in full force and effect.

21. Entire Agreement and Amendment.

   As of the date hereof, this Agreement constitutes the entire understanding between the parties with respect to the subject matter hereof and supersedes any previous understandings or agreement between the parties. No modification or amendment of this Agreement shall be valid or binding upon the parties unless made in writing and duly executed on behalf of both of the parties. The parties also acknowledge execution of that certain Stock Purchase Agreement of even date herewith.

22. Waiver.

   No failure or delay by any party to insist upon the performance of any term or condition of this Agreement or to exercise any right, power, or remedy hereunder consequent upon a breach hereof shall constitute a waiver of any such term, condition, right, power, or remedy or of any such breach or shall preclude such party from exercising any such right, power, or remedy at any later time or times.

23. Agreement to Perform Necessary Acts.

   Each party agrees to perform any further acts and to execute and deliver any and all further documents, agreements, and/or instruments that may be reasonably necessary or desirable to carry out or effect the provisions of this Agreement.

24. Compliance with Applicable Laws.

   The parties hereby agree to comply with all laws, rules, regulations, ordinances, and other governmental requirements in connection with the performance of their respective rights, responsibilities, and obligations hereunder, including without limitation, laws governing export, import, or other shipment of the Product, regulating approvals and registrations of the Product, and requiring identification of Patent Rights on labels and containers for the Product.

25. Dispute Resolution.

   25.1    In case of disputes between the parties arising from this Agreement and in case this Agreement does not provide a solution for how to resolve such disputes, the parties shall discuss and negotiate in good faith a solution acceptable to both parties and in the spirit of this Agreement.

   25.2    If after negotiating in good faith pursuant to Paragraph 3.7 or 4.4, the parties fail to reach agreement on a royalty rate referred to in such Paragraphs, then such royalty rate shall be determined as follows: The parties shall submit the dispute to the decision of a neutral and agreed upon expert in the field of such dispute, who shall give his decision within sixty (60) days from being approached by the parties. If the parties fail to agree on such expert or if such expert fails to find a solution, the parties shall submit to arbitration.

26.    Applicable Law, Arbitration, and Venue.

26.1    This Agreement shall be construed in accordance with the laws of [Switzerland].

26.2    Except where otherwise expressly provided, the parties hereby agree to submit to arbitration any and all disputes, controversies, differences, or claims that may arise between them in relation to or out of this Agreement, or the breach thereof, if parties fail to reach an amicable settlement or earlier resolution by mutual agreement.

26.3    Any controversy or claim relating to this Agreement shall be submitted to final and binding arbitration pursuant to the Rules of the London Court of International Arbitration then in effect by three arbitrators knowledgeable as to industry standards, sitting in a location in [the United Kingdom] designated by the nonfiling party. One arbitrator will be appointed by each of the members of the Executive Committee within ten (10) days of the filing of the arbitration claim, and the two arbitrators shall appoint a third arbitrator within thirty (30) days. None of the arbitrators shall be related to or have any interest in Swiss Co. or U.S. Co. The arbitrators will be instructed to consider, in making any determination, the customary practices in the industry to the extent such practices exist.

26.4    The arbitration proceeding shall commence within thirty (30) days of the selection of the arbitrators. Discovery shall be limited so as to allow the taking of a maximum of five (5) depositions by each party.

26.5    The arbitrators shall be authorized to provide for interim and final injunctive relief. The parties acknowledge and agree that such arbitration shall be the sole forum for such interim and final injunctive relief, and the parties agree to accept and abide by such injunctive relief. The arbitrators shall have the right but not the obligation to award to the prevailing party the cost of resolving any dispute regarding this Agreement or the formation, breach, enforcement, or performance hereof, including any reasonable fees of attorneys, accountants, and expert witnesses incurred by the prevailing party. Punitive damages shall not be recoverable in any arbitration initiated pursuant to this Agreement. Judgment upon the award rendered by the arbitrators may be entered in any court having jurisdiction thereof. Notwithstanding anything to the contrary contained herein, if, at any time an initiating party can show that it would suffer irreparable harm by following the above procedures solely because of the time that it would take to engage the arbitrators and the nonfiling party will not agree to immediately appoint the arbitrators and that money damages would not be adequate to compensate it for the harm so suffered, the initiating party may apply to any court of competent jurisdiction for an order or judgment granting that party a provisional remedy, including, but not limited to, a temporary restraining order, a preliminary injunction, or an attachment.

IN WITNESS WHEREOF, this Agreement has been executed on [Date].

U.S. PHARMACEUTICALS CORPORATION

By: _____

SWISS PHARMACEUTICALS LIMITED

By: _____

# PART SIX

# Valuing Companies and Negotiating Transactions

In Chapter 12, Arthur H. Rosenbloom, managing director of CFC Capital LLC, discusses the related topics of pricing of companies and negotiation of cross-border mergers and acquisitions. In his comprehensive treatment of valuation of companies, Rosenbloom covers comparative company analysis, asset-based valuations, and discounted cash flow analysis. In the discussion of negotiations, he takes the reader through the six stages of the deal: (1) finding, (2) qualification, (3) preliminary investigation, (4) serious negotiation (including practical suggestions for both buyers and sellers), (5) contract, and (6) closing. Extensive checklists on both pricing and negotiation are included.

# 12

# Pricing and Negotiations

*Arthur H. Rosenbloom*

## PRICING

Pricing cross-border merger and acquisition (M&A) or other transactions employs many of the traditional valuation yardsticks used to price purely domestic transactions, with variations required to give recognition to the international character of such deals. *Valuation* means the process by which, through the use of objective yardsticks and informed judgment, the target's fair market value can be determined. Fair market value, however, may or may not equate to purchase price in any given context. The fair market value concept takes into account only those elements that would be considered by theoretically arm's-length parties, both reasonably well informed and equally interested in and capable of doing the deal. In the real world, different buyers will pay higher or lower than fair market value prices given variables like additional business synergy, the need to shore up a sinking business, or, in the case of a cross-border deal, the desire (by buyer or target) to diversify out of a politically unstable environment. Targets may demand a premium price, for example, when management is reluctant to convey control or may sell for a reduced price when selling shareholders (even with good successor management) are old, sick, or just tired.

Nevertheless, pricing indexes set objective price ranges for discussion. Desire to close, bargaining power, and bargaining strength move a price within and sometimes above or below the range of fair market value. In market economy countries with modern, well-developed accounting systems (like the United States, Canada, Japan, France, and England) and with local stock exchanges that contain companies in many industries, practitioners tend to use the same sorts of comparative company, discounted cash flow, asset analysis, and control premium data. Although multiples and market–book value ratios will vary from country to country creating special complexities for the cross-border transaction, the ground rules are much the same. Such is not the case in countries not having these characteristics.

The following discussion describes pricing and negotiation in negotiated transactions. Analyses of offensive and defensive measures in hostile transactions are beyond the scope of this chapter.

Assume in an inbound transaction, that a non–U.S. buyer (Luxor) seeks to acquire for cash a minority or controlling interest in Jones Widget Manufacturing Co. Inc. (JonesCo), a closely held automotive parts manufacturer. What criteria will Luxor use in its pricing process?

## Criteria for Pricing

1. The percentage ownership to be acquired (ultimately to be reflected in discounts for minority interests in closely held companies and control premiums in instances of a sale of control) and attendant voting rights of each class of shares to be acquired.
2. Voting and other rights of the shares to be acquired by Luxor (assuming a purchase of shares rather than assets) and any past transactions in JonesCo securities that may be probative of their value.
3. JonesCo's history and management, the nature of its businesses, its strengths and weaknesses, and factors affecting those businesses.
4. JonesCo's financial condition—historical, at the valuation date, and as projected; and an analysis of the company's assets, liabilities, invested capital, and net worth.
5. Historical operating results, particularly earnings generated and factors affecting these.
6. JonesCo's outlook at the valuation date; the outlook for the overall economy of the United States; the structure of and outlook for the automotive parts industry in which JonesCo is engaged.
7. Bases of investor appraisals of publicly traded shares of companies that can be employed for comparative purposes in this case, together with comparisons between the financial performance of JonesCo and the comparatives, discounted cash flow, asset valuation, payback analysis, and other elements. The closest competitors may not be public, and so

data may not be available. A comparative company may not be a direct competitor but may be close enough in business type to be usable for comparative purposes.

8. If an M&A transaction, recently completed M&A transactions in industries usable for comparative purposes.
9. The marketability of the subject securities.
10. If an M&A transaction, premium for control elements.
11. The strategic importance of JonesCo to Luxor.

The 11 criteria listed are typically considered as part of an informed pricing analysis. All such elements need to be considered, but different fact patterns will make some elements more important in one case and less so in another. In a pricing analysis for a producer of phosphate rock a number of years ago, value turned largely on the industry element of criterion 6, in that case, prices of imported Moroccan phosphate. A pricing analysis arising out of the need to sell an apparel business on the death of its founder and chief executive officer (CEO) made the management portion of criterion 3 a critical element. A chemical industry transaction considered by the author involved two classes of stock, one with superior voting power, thus making criterion 1 of key importance. The high multiples paid by companies like Cisco Systems have been justified partly because of Cisco's own soaring multiples and the red hot multiples of companies in the wireless technology space but also because of the perceived strategic importance of the targets to it (criterion 11). Time will tell whether the high compound-growth-rate forecasts implicit in these multiples or the ability to integrate a large number of small acquisitions represented by deals of this sort will produce successful results. All of the 11 criteria need to be considered, even if some ultimately play little or no part in the ultimate pricing process.

After setting forth the pricing criteria but before the pricing analysis takes place, it is important for the buyer to do a thorough due diligence investigation of the target. If the target is taking the buyer's shares or notes, it will be foolish not to do the same with the buyer. The rudiments of this will be covered in the discussion later about the target's descriptive memorandum. It suffices for present purposes to note that among other elements, the process should include a consideration of these 10 items: (1) details surrounding the target company's founding; (2) the principal milestones during its corporate history; (3) a description of the process by which new products or services are created; (4) if the target is a manufacturing company, details respecting raw material procurement, production, plant, and equipment; (5) the target company's labor situation; (6) details related to the target company's sales and marketing efforts; (7) the target company's current and projected competitive position; (8) information respecting the target company's senior management; (9) a thorough consideration of the target company's historic and projected financial statements; and (10) data respecting the target company's future plans.

The importance of the due diligence process cannot be overstressed. Soon after Bridgestone Corporation of Japan acquired Firestone Tire & Rubber Co. for

$2.6 billion, General Motors, who reportedly accounted for 25 percent of Firestone's original equipment manufacturing (OEM) business, announced it was dropping Firestone as a supplier. Putting aside Firestone's woes resulting from the massive tire recalls of 2000 and 2001, the transaction offers a cautionary tale as do the much discussed problems associated with the acquisition of Chrysler by Daimler-Benz—a case study of due diligence gone awry. Due diligence is critical in all deals; it is imperative in international transactions where it is usually the case that the buyer is exposed to greater informational gaps.

Similarly, one should scrutinize with particular care elements purportedly resulting from conservative accounting treatment whose purpose is to minimize taxable income. Areas in which such practices are likely to be present include understated inventories, whose income statement consequence is an increase in cost of goods sold and a corresponding decrease in taxable income; travel and entertainment expenses and charitable gifts at levels exceeding those reasonably required for business purposes; redundant personnel (often family members) on the target company's books; and unreported sales, particularly in countries in which value-added taxes or other sales taxes are high. Many prospective targets will attempt to reconstruct current or historic earnings and assets by adding back the difference between the earnings reductions resulting from the four practices just described and normal expenses for such items. An earnings multiple attached to that difference can frequently result in a dramatic increase in sale price. Thus, the parties should recognize that reasonable persons may differ on the extent to which earnings in these or other categories are properly reconstructable. In addition, the quality of reconstructed earnings or assets is usually less persuasive concerning the target's future earning power than historically generated earnings and assets. Given this presumption, it may be appropriate to attach lower earnings or cash flow multiples and lower market–book value ratios to reconstructed earnings and assets versus their historical counterparts. Moreover, projections of the "hockey stick" variety (curving dramatically upward from historical levels) need to be viewed with a healthy dose of skepticism. A rigorous testing of the assumptions on which such projections are made is strongly advised. Clearly, the ability of projected cash flows to support the interest charges and the amortization of purchase price debt should be given close scrutiny.

Thus, due diligence turns the pricing analysis from an exercise in number crunching to a tool from which, based on the facts revealed to the due diligence process, a realistic price range can be determined. Note that the pricing exercise is a necessary tool for each side; it is most assuredly not the exclusive preserve of the buyer.

### Comparative Company Analysis

This form of analysis compares the target's financial performance to that of other companies, usable for comparative purposes. Factors considered include growth in revenues and profits, profit margins, returns on assets, returns on equity, working capital and leverage ratios, and inventory and asset turnover ratios. It is often useful to consider industry-specific kinds of ratios, such as revenues per passenger mile and passenger load factor for the airline industry or sales per square foot in the retail industry.

The kind of comparative company analysis just described determines the value of a freely traded minority interest in the target. A control premium is added to this result. An alternative form of comparative company analysis is considering the price-revenues ratios, the price-earnings ratios, and market–book values paid in recent acquisitions of companies in the same industry as that of the target. While this kind of data is very useful when available, it may be difficult to find recent transactions of companies sufficiently close in business to that of the target. Older transactions reflecting investor appraisal ratios at times removed from the valuation date may reflect stock market realities not relevant to pricing at a later date. In addition, comparative transaction pricing is made more difficult where transactions used for comparative purposes have noncash components (the need to value bonds or preferred stock that may be worth other than face or par). The size of the premium may also vary depending on whether cash or the buyer's equity securities are the form of consideration. Experience suggests higher premiums in cash deals and lower ones in share deals, presumably because of the extinction of target shareholders' speculative opportunity in the former case.

### Single-Company Analysis

This technique attempts to measure the target by itself in terms of discounted cash flow and asset valuation.

### Affordability

The ability to pay what may be a fair price is a real-world constraint on price; for even if the target measures up under both comparative and single-company analyses, the transaction may not be cash affordable by the buyer or may be excessively dilutive or have some other incurable impediment to "doability."

Let us now look more closely at comparative analysis and single-company analysis.

## Comparative Analysis

The basis of this analysis is to compare the financial performance of the target against that of a group of companies offering a comparable product or service in order to infer a value for the target as a result of how well or how poorly its financial performance compares to that of the array chosen for such purposes. That is sometimes more easily said than done. For one thing, the closest comparisons may be from closely held companies for which little or no public data are available or from subsidiaries or divisions of publicly held companies primarily engaged in other business. Even when companies report on a separate product line basis, the price-earnings multiple is a function of the total company.

These problems notwithstanding, it is usually possible to develop a defensible array of companies usable for comparative purposes. Assuming a non–U.S.

buyer and a U.S. target, probably the best way to start the search is by determining the target's SIC Code (the U.S. Commerce Department Standard Industrial Classification Code) and then through Standard & Poor's Corporation Records, the *Directory of Companies Filing Annual Reports with the SEC,* or Standard & Poor's Compustat data base, determining the potential universe of publicly held comparative companies having the same or a similar SIC Code. In the future it may be the case that SIC Codes will be supplemented or replaced by the North American Industrial Classification Systems (NAICS). This system, developed jointly by the United States, Canada, and Mexico, more precisely identifies companies in twenty-first-century industries like online services, wireless communications, and health maintenance organizations (HMOs). In addition, the NAICS system restructures and redefines the classification of traditional industries. NAICS codes are organized in 6-, 7-, and 10-digit codes compared to the 4-, 5-, and 7-digit SIC codes, thereby creating greater precision than before in the choice of comparatives. Evidence of the likely use of NAICS codes in the future may be derived from the fact that in 2001, the U.S. Federal Trade Commission adopted the NAICS codes for Hart-Scott-Rodino antitrust compliance filings.

Directories similar to the ones just mentioned exist in most countries having well-developed stock markets. After determining the potential universe, it is necessary to weed out companies that do not make sense as comparatives. These include material differences between the target and the potential comparative in product line; profitability (if the seller has been generally profitable, exclusion of consistently unprofitable potential comparatives may be warranted); and facts affecting market price, such as merger announcements. After selection of the comparatives, accounting adjustments may be required to put the comparative companies on a similar footing with the target and with each other. For example, reconciliation in alternative accounting methods for inventory or for depreciation practices will result in greater comparability, as will be the need to reconcile different accounting practices of parties in cross-border deals as a result of differences in accounting practices, country to country. (For a further discussion of this subject, readers are directed to the accounting chapter in this book, Chapter 4.)

We can consider how a defensible array of comparatives can be picked in the hypothetical JonesCo situation. The comparatives should share with each other and with JonesCo a series of common characteristics. If the comparative company selection process has been correctly performed, there should be, other than the array chosen, no other publicly held companies that meet all of the criteria. Thus, the only sustainable attack would be on the rationality of the manner in which the array was developed.

### Comparative Array

The automotive parts manufacturers to be used for comparative purposes with JonesCo were selected on the basis of the following criteria.

    1. Each was a U.S. corporation operating principally as a manufacturer of automotive or truck parts for both the OEM and replacement parts markets,

found in SIC Code 3714, with at least two-thirds of total revenues generated by such sources.

2. Companies that met the first criterion but that were distinguished from JonesCo because their primary products were body parts, bumpers, wheels, or other nonconsumable parts were excluded, as were those that produced parts primarily for stationary or other non-over-the-road engines. Likewise, those companies that were primarily producers of speed or custom parts were excluded, as they operate in different markets from those served by JonesCo.

3. The company could not primarily be a wholesale or a distribution company, nor a nonproducing importer of foreign car parts.

4. Like JonesCo, each company had most recent total revenues of less than $1 billion and was profitable for at least four of the past five fiscal years.

5. No company was the subject of an ancillary transaction, such as a merger, tender offer, or going-private offer.

Companies meeting these criteria, and the principal trading market of the common stocks of each, are:

| | |
|---|---|
| Atlantic Auto Parts | NYSE |
| Edison Spark Plug Company | NYSE |
| E-Z Air Filter Company | NYSE |
| Hercules Gasket Mfg. Co. | AMEX |
| Miracle Muffler Company | NYSE |
| Winning Motor Products, Inc. | AMEX |

The characteristics of the listed companies make clear that in order to be within the comparative company array, each comparative company, like JonesCo, had to be (1) principally an OEM producer of automotive or truck parts; (2) one that specialized in consumable parts for nonstationary over-the-road engines; (3) a manufacturer and not a distributor or an importer; (4) one having shares that were publicly traded in quantity; (5) within specific revenue and profit constraints; and (6) one whose freely traded value was not affected by an ancillary transaction, the effect of which would be to raise the company's stock market price over the levels of a freely traded minority interest because of the addition of speculative elements concerning a possible "premium for control," "going private" premium, or otherwise.

For U.S. companies seeking to acquire abroad ("outbound" transactions), the process is much the same. One should attempt to identify a universe of companies usable for comparative purposes in the target company's country of origin, although the supply of companies usable for such purposes outside the United States may be more limited due to less-developed public markets and less-stringent disclosure requirements. Caveat: It is frequently the case that investor appraisal (price-earnings or market–book value) ratios for companies in a given industry in the public markets of one country may be quite different from those in another country at the same date. As an example, at the time of the 2000 acquisition of International Filler Corporation by Safeguard International Fund, there was a 10 percent to 20 percent disparity between U.S. comparatives' price-earnings multiples and price-earnings multiples for such companies in Europe or elsewhere. Given this, it is desirable wherever possible to develop comparatives in the same country as that of the target company.

Once the comparatives have been selected, the process of comparison begins. The measuring period is typically either five years or an average business cycle (whichever is longer) for each principal industry in which the target company operates. The author recognizes that a five-year measuring cycle is far more extensive than the conventional one-year and latest-12-months measuring cycles typically found in pricing studies. But it may prove invaluable in the analysis of target companies in cyclical industries because the shorter measuring period is likely to capture the company's performance at one extreme of the cycle or another. This is an exercise as important for the target as it is for the buyer to prepare for subsequent price discussions.

Exhibits 12.1, 12.2, and 12.3 compare JonesCo's growth trend in revenues, operating income, and net income versus that of the comparatives. Using year 1 as the 100 percent or base year, the exhibits demonstrate that in all three categories JonesCo compares poorly to the median of the comparatives.

Measuring growth trends in operating income and net income allow one to determine, in the former instance, how well the target's base business, uncomplicated by other elements, compares with the comparatives; and in the latter instance, the impact of interest income and expense, taxes, and other items on its financial performance. Note that there is no reason to slavishly compare the target company against a median. Although a median irons out statistical highs and lows

## EXHIBIT 12.1

### Revenue Comparison

|  | Year | | | | |
|---|---|---|---|---|---|
|  | 1 | 2 | 3 | 4 | 5 |
| *Revenues* | | | | | |
| Atlantic Auto Parts | 100 | 115 | 120 | 140 | 182 |
| Edison Spark Plug Co. | 100 | 102 | 98 | 96 | 102 |
| E-Z Air Filter Co. | 100 | 138 | 163 | 187 | 229 |
| Hercules Gasket Mfg. Co. | 100 | 109 | 111 | 118 | 131 |
| Miracle Muffler Co. | 100 | 118 | 142 | 165 | 194 |
| Winning Motor Products, Inc. | 100 | 125 | 142 | 164 | 188 |
| Median | 100 | 117 | 131 | 152 | 185 |
| Jones Widget Mfg. Co. | 100 | 120 | 127 | 143 | 168 |

*Sources:* Company financial reports; computations by CFC Capital LLC.

EXHIBIT 12.2

**Operating Income Comparison**

| | Year | | | | |
|---|---|---|---|---|---|
| | 1 | 2 | 3 | 4 | 5 |
| *Operating Income* | | | | | |
| Atlantic Auto Parts | 100 | 130 | 120 | 192 | 329 |
| Edison Spark Plug Co. | 100 | 85 | 98 | 75 | 81 |
| E-Z Air Filter Co. | 100 | 182 | 263 | 291 | 394 |
| Hercules Gasket Mfg. Co. | 100 | 138 | 157 | 201 | 268 |
| Miracle Muffler Co. | 100 | 158 | 190 | 242 | 290 |
| Winning Motor Products, Inc. | 100 | 344 | 420 | 577 | 635 |
| Median | 100 | 148 | 174 | 222 | 310 |
| Jones Widget Mfg. Co. | 100 | 114 | 148 | 173 | 158 |

*Sources:* Company financial reports; computations by CFC Capital LLC.

better than an average, if one or more comparatives are strikingly more similar to the target company than the others are, recognition of that fact should be given in the analytical process and ultimately be reflected in the choice of investor appraisal ratios.

The next three exhibits compare JonesCo's profit margins to those of the comparatives in terms of the relationship of gross profit, operating income, and net income, respectively, to sales. While JonesCo has turned in superior gross margins and operating margins (Exhibits 12.4 and 12.5), its after-tax profit margin

EXHIBIT 12.3

**Net Income Comparison**

| | Year | | | | |
|---|---|---|---|---|---|
| | 1 | 2 | 3 | 4 | 5 |
| *Net Income* | | | | | |
| Atlantic Auto Parts | 100 | 164 | 143 | 242 | 398 |
| Edison Spark Plug Co. | 100 | 85 | 72 | 72 | 76 |
| E-Z Air Filter Co. | 100 | 145 | 303 | 350 | 500 |
| Hercules Gasket Mfg. Co. | 100 | 119 | 121 | 149 | 193 |
| Miracle Muffler Co. | 100 | 135 | 194 | 247 | 351 |
| Winning Motor Products, Inc. | 100 | 342 | 457 | 640 | 693 |
| Median | 100 | 140 | 168 | 245 | 375 |
| Jones Widget Mfg. Co. | 100 | 125 | 164 | 192 | 132 |

*Sources:* Company financial reports; computations by CFC Capital LLC.

## EXHIBIT 12.4

## Gross Margin Comparison

| | Year | | | | |
|---|---|---|---|---|---|
| | 1 | 2 | 3 | 4 | 5 |
| *Gross Income* | | | | | |
| Atlantic Auto Parts | 18.3% | 17.5% | 18.1% | 17.9% | 17.4% |
| Edison Spark Plug Co. | 35.3 | 32.6 | 33.5 | 33.0 | 32.1 |
| E-Z Air Filter Co. | 33.0 | 31.6 | 33.1 | 32.7 | 32.5 |
| Hercules Gasket Mfg. Co. | 38.5 | 38.1 | 40.7 | 41.5 | 42.1 |
| Miracle Muffler Co. | 29.5 | 31.1 | 32.9 | 33.1 | 32.3 |
| Winning Motor Products, Inc. | 38.4 | 43.9 | 44.7 | 47.4 | 47.3 |
| Median | 32.4% | 32.1% | 33.3% | 33.1% | 32.4% |
| Jones Widget Mfg. Co. | 40.6% | 46.4% | 46.8% | 48.4% | 46.8% |

*Sources:* Company financial reports; computations by CFC Capital LLC.

in year 5 (Exhibit 12.6), while still exceeding the median, is relatively less attractive than its gross margin or operating profit and sharply less than its after-tax profit margin in years 3 and 4. This suggests some care in analyzing elements such as JonesCo's other Income and Expense category and the company's historic tax rates. In the real world company from which JonesCo was drawn, the answer was to be found in high social costs (a day-care center) adversely affecting pretax income and a higher than normal tax rate (few tax credits), both of which ultimately and adversely affected net income.

## EXHIBIT 12.5

## Operating Profit Comparison

| | Year | | | | |
|---|---|---|---|---|---|
| | 1 | 2 | 3 | 4 | 5 |
| *Operating Profit* | | | | | |
| Atlantic Auto Parts | 4.0% | 4.5% | 4.0% | 5.5% | 7.2% |
| Edison Spark Plug Co. | 9.1 | 7.5 | 9.0 | 7.1 | 7.2 |
| E-Z Air Filter Co. | 6.4 | 8.5 | 10.4 | 10.0 | 11.1 |
| Hercules Gasket Mfg. Co. | 4.5 | 5.7 | 6.4 | 7.7 | 9.2 |
| Miracle Muffler Co. | 8.5 | 11.5 | 11.6 | 12.7 | 12.9 |
| Winning Motor Products, Inc. | 5.3 | 14.6 | 15.6 | 18.7 | 17.9 |
| Median | 5.9% | 8.0% | 9.7% | 8.9 | 10.2% |
| Jones Widget Mfg. Co. | 13.5% | 12.8% | 15.7% | 16.3% | 12.7% |

*Sources:* Company financial reports; computations by CFC Capital LLC.

## EXHIBIT 12.6

**Profit after Taxes Comparison**

| | Year | | | | |
|---|---|---|---|---|---|
| | **1** | **2** | **3** | **4** | **5** |
| *Profit after Taxes* | | | | | |
| Atlantic Auto Parts | 1.8% | 2.5% | 2.1% | 3.1% | 3.9% |
| Edison Spark Plug Co. | 4.9 | 4.0 | 3.6 | 3.7 | 3.6 |
| E-Z Air Filter Co. | 2.9 | 3.1 | 5.4 | 5.4 | 6.4 |
| Hercules Gasket Mfg. Co. | 3.0 | 3.3 | 3.3 | 3.8 | 4.5 |
| Miracle Muffler Co. | 4.6 | 5.2 | 6.2 | 6.8 | 8.3 |
| Winning Motor Products, Inc. | 2.6 | 7.2 | 8.4 | 10.2 | 9.7 |
| Median | 3.0% | 3.7% | 4.5% | 4.6% | 5.5% |
| Jones Widget Mfg. Co. | 7.4% | 7.7% | 9.6% | 10.0% | 5.9% |

*Sources:* Company financial reports; computations by CFC Capital LLC.

A consideration of return on average total assets or net income divided by average total assets (Exhibit 12.7) demonstrates JonesCo's performance, evidence of its relatively unleveraged state. Its return on average common equity (Exhibit 12.8) is likewise attractive. These ratios test the extent to which a company's asset and equity bases are effective engines for the development of profits.

JonesCo's working capital ratio (Exhibit 12.9) (current assets divided by current liabilities) is also attractive, as is its quick asset ratio (Exhibit 12.10) (cash, marketable securities, and accounts receivable divided by current liabilities).

## EXHIBIT 12.7

**Return on Average Assets Comparison**

| | Year | | | |
|---|---|---|---|---|
| | **1** | **2** | **3** | **4** |
| *Return on Average Total Assets* | | | | |
| Atlantic Auto Parts | 4.2% | 3.6% | 5.7% | 8.9% |
| Edison Spark Plug Co. | 5.2 | 4.6 | 4.8 | 5.1 |
| E-Z Air Filter Co. | 4.4 | 7.3 | 7.8 | 10.1 |
| Hercules Gasket Mfg. Co. | 6.1 | 6.0 | 6.9 | 17.5 |
| Miracle Muffler Co. | 6.4 | 7.9 | 9.1 | 24.3 |
| Winning Motor Products, Inc. | 9.6 | 10.9 | 12.9 | 26.1 |
| Median | 6.6% | 6.7% | 7.4% | 13.8% |
| Jones Widget Mfg. Co. | 12.4% | 14.9% | 16.5% | 16.8% |

*Sources:* Company financial reports; computations by CFC Capital LLC.

EXHIBIT 12.8

## Return on Average Total Equity Comparison

| | Year | | | |
|---|---|---|---|---|
| | **1** | **2** | **3** | **4** |
| *Return on Average Total Equity* | | | | |
| Atlantic Auto Parts | 7.9% | 6.7% | 10.6% | 15.7% |
| Edison Spark Plug Co. | 8.3 | 7.5 | 7.8 | 8.2 |
| E-Z Air Filter Co. | 7.4 | 12.9 | 13.8 | 17.8 |
| Hercules Gasket Mfg. Co. | 9.2 | 9.6 | 13.2 | 35.9 |
| Miracle Muffler Co. | 9.6 | 11.5 | 13.1 | 34.9 |
| Winning Motor Products, Inc. | 16.7 | 17.0 | 20.1 | 40.9 |
| Median | 8.8% | 9.5% | 13.1% | 26.3% |
| Jones Widget Mfg. Co. | 36.3% | 34.1% | 32.5% | 32.0% |

*Sources:* Company financial reports; computations by CFC Capital LLC.

Exhibit 12.11 displays JonesCo's ratio of total debt-equity with that of the comparatives. This ratio is only one of many ways of testing leverage or debt-bearing capacity. Other ratios by which to measure leverage include common stock equity to total invested capital (the sum of all the long-term debt and equity accounts), total debt to common or total equity, and the like. Which leverage ratio to choose depends on the capital structure of the target and on patterns of analysis common to a particular industry or a specific country, among other factors. Exhibit 12.11 demonstrates that JonesCo was far more leveraged than the median of the comparatives in years 1 through 3; its reduced leverage in years 4 and 5 made

EXHIBIT 12.9

## Working Capital Ratio Comparison

| | Year | | | | |
|---|---|---|---|---|---|
| | **1** | **2** | **3** | **4** | **5** |
| *Working Capital Ratio* | | | | | |
| Atlantic Auto Parts | 3.5 | 4.1 | 3.5 | 3.0 | 2.8 |
| Edison Spark Plug Co. | 2.6 | 2.3 | 2.2 | 2.4 | 2.4 |
| E-Z Air Filter Co. | 4.0 | 2.8 | 2.5 | 2.7 | 2.4 |
| Hercules Gasket Mfg. Co. | 3.3 | 2.8 | 3.4 | 3.0 | 3.2 |
| Miracle Muffler Co. | 2.4 | 2.7 | 2.7 | 2.7 | 2.9 |
| Winning Motor Products, Inc. | 2.7 | 2.7 | 4.1 | 3.8 | 3.5 |
| Median | 3.0 | 2.8 | 3.1 | 2.9 | 2.9 |
| Jones Widget Mfg. Co. | 4.6 | 4.9 | 6.0 | 6.3 | 4.1 |

*Sources:* Company financial reports; computations by CFC Capital LLC.

EXHIBIT 12.10

**Quick Asset Ratio Comparison**

| | Year | | | | |
|---|---|---|---|---|---|
| | 1 | 2 | 3 | 4 | 5 |
| ***Quick Asset Ratio*** | | | | | |
| Atlantic Auto Parts | 2.0 | 2.2 | 1.8 | 1.7 | 1.5 |
| Edison Spark Plug Co. | 1.0 | 0.8 | 0.9 | 1.1 | 1.0 |
| E-Z Air Filter Co. | 1.1 | 0.9 | 0.8 | 1.1 | 0.9 |
| Hercules Gasket Mfg. Co. | 1.2 | 1.0 | 1.4 | 1.3 | 1.5 |
| Miracle Muffler Co. | 1.0 | 1.0 | 1.0 | 1.1 | 1.0 |
| Winning Motor Products, Inc. | 1.2 | 1.1 | 2.0 | 1.7 | 1.4 |
| Median | 1.2 | 1.0 | 1.2 | 1.2 | 1.2 |
| Jones Widget Mfg. Co. | 2.7 | 2.6 | 3.6 | 3.6 | 2.3 |

*Sources:* Company financial reports; computations by CFC Capital LLC.

it more desirable as a leveraged buyout vehicle and hence more attractive. (In the real world, the company from which this case was drawn was slowly working down the nonrecurring debt from an industrial revenue bond.) Note that a proper understanding of debt-equity ratios may require one to differentiate between what the author calls *deal debt* and *operating debt*. Deal debt, exemplified by debt created incident to a transaction (e.g., a buy-in of company shares or an M&A transaction) is ultimately paid off and may or may not be renewed. Operating debt, exemplified by debt required to sustain ongoing operations, is likely to persist as part of the company's permanent capital structures, and is thus a more onerous

EXHIBIT 12.11

**Debt-Equity Ratio Comparison**

| | Year | | | | |
|---|---|---|---|---|---|
| | 1 | 2 | 3 | 4 | 5 |
| ***Debt-Equity Ratio*** | | | | | |
| Atlantic Auto Parts | 1.0 | 0.8 | 0.9 | 0.8 | 0.8 |
| Edison Spark Plug Co. | 0.6 | 0.6 | 0.6 | 0.6 | 0.6 |
| E-Z Air Filter Co. | 0.6 | 0.7 | 0.8 | 0.7 | 0.8 |
| Hercules Gasket Mfg. Co. | 0.5 | 0.6 | 0.6 | 0.8 | 1.1 |
| Miracle Muffler Co. | 0.6 | 0.5 | 0.5 | 0.5 | 0.4 |
| Winning Motor Products, Inc. | 1.1 | 1.0 | 0.6 | 0.5 | 0.6 |
| Median | 0.6 | 0.7 | 0.6 | 0.8 | 0.7 |
| Jones Widget Mfg. Co. | 2.4 | 1.5 | 1.1 | 0.9 | 0.9 |

*Sources:* Company financial reports; computations by CFC Capital LLC.

burden than deal debt. Operating debt, like all of the analytical tools described in this chapter, should be judgmentally considered in arriving at value.

Exhibits 12.12 and 12.13 demonstrate JonesCo's turnover ratios (revenues divided by assets and revenues divided by inventory). These ratios demonstrate how effectively a company has converted its assets and inventories into revenues. The data illustrate that JonesCo has, in both instances, exceeded the median of the comparatives.

Note that all of the ratios described in the exhibits must be understood as attractive or unattractive relative to the same ratio for other companies used for

## EXHIBIT 12.12

### Asset Turnover Ratio Comparison

| | Year | | | | |
|---|---|---|---|---|---|
| | 1 | 2 | 3 | 4 | 5 |
| *Asset Turnover Ratio* | | | | | |
| Atlantic Auto Parts | 1.4 | 1.7 | 1.7 | 1.8 | 2.2 |
| Edison Spark Plug Co. | 1.3 | 1.3 | 1.3 | 1.3 | 1.4 |
| E-Z Air Filter Co. | 1.3 | 1.2 | 1.3 | 1.4 | 1.5 |
| Hercules Gasket Mfg. Co. | 1.8 | 1.8 | 1.9 | 1.9 | 2.0 |
| Miracle Muffler Co. | 1.3 | 1.4 | 1.3 | 1.4 | 1.5 |
| Winning Motor Products, Inc. | 1.3 | 1.4 | 1.4 | 1.4 | 1.4 |
| Median | 1.3 | 1.4 | 1.4 | 1.4 | 1.5 |
| Jones Widget Mfg. Co. | 1.6 | 2.1 | 1.9 | 1.8 | 1.9 |

*Sources:* Company financial reports; computations by CFC Capital LLC.

## EXHIBIT 12.13

### Inventory Turnover Ratio Comparison

| | Year | | | | |
|---|---|---|---|---|---|
| | 1 | 2 | 3 | 4 | 5 |
| *Inventory Turnover Ratio* | | | | | |
| Atlantic Auto Parts | 6.0 | 7.7 | 7.9 | 9.0 | 9.6 |
| Edison Spark Plug Co. | 3.1 | 3.2 | 3.5 | 3.8 | 3.8 |
| E-Z Air Filter Co. | 2.9 | 2.8 | 3.1 | 4.0 | 3.9 |
| Hercules Gasket Mfg. Co. | 4.0 | 3.9 | 4.1 | 4.1 | 4.8 |
| Miracle Muffler Co. | 4.1 | 4.9 | 4.4 | 4.8 | 4.3 |
| Winning Motor Products, Inc. | 3.2 | 3.0 | 3.5 | 3.1 | 2.7 |
| Median | 3.6 | 3.6 | 3.8 | 4.1 | 4.1 |
| Jones Widget Mfg. Co. | 6.7 | 6.2 | 6.9 | 6.2 | 6.3 |

*Sources:* Company financial reports; computations by CFC Capital LLC.

comparative purposes. There is never an absolutely correct ratio at any given time. Industry norms, the accounting and regulatory environment of a specific country, and stock market conditions at a particular valuation date are the relevant factors.

The preceding exhibits represent a limited array of ratios usable in comparative company analysis. Other general ratios, including dividend yield (per share dividends to common stock price), dividend payout ratio (percentage of net income to dividends), or inventory turnover (revenues or cost of sales divided by inventory), may be used. Industry-specific kinds of ratios described earlier are often extremely helpful.

## Income and Cash Flow–Based Approaches to Equity Value

From the analysis of JonesCo's performance versus that of the comparatives, a comparative company *earnings* approach to value can be developed.

Exhibit 12.14 considers price-earnings multiples for the comparatives based on average five-year, three-year, latest-year, latest-12-months, and latest-current fiscal-year projected earnings. While such analysis is contrary to the prevailing wisdom of pricing only off of most recent or projected earnings, given the often disastrous future financial performance of companies priced this way, perhaps a rethinking of current practice is warranted. However, in high-tech, biotech, and

### EXHIBIT 12.14

**Jones Widget Mfg. Co. versus Comparative Companies Investor Appraisal Ratios**

| Company | Price-Earnings Multiples | | | | | Ratio of Market Price to Tangible Book Value |
|---|---|---|---|---|---|---|
| | Latest 5 Years | Latest 3 Years | Latest Year | Latest 12 Months | Year Projected | |
| Atlantic Auto Parts | 15.6 | 12.5 | 8.3 | 7.9 | 7.6 | 114% |
| Edison Spark Plug Co. | 10.8 | 11.9 | 11.8 | 11.8 | 10.5 | 89 |
| E-Z Air Filter Co. | 21.6 | 16.3 | 12.6 | 12.0 | 13.0 | 213 |
| Hercules Gasket Mfg. Co. | 10.4 | 8.2 | 5.5 | 6.3 | 5.9 | 98 |
| Miracle Muffler Co. | 12.2 | 10.6 | 8.0 | 8.0 | 7.8 | 139 |
| Winning Motor Products, Inc. | 10.6 | 8.2 | 7.1 | 8.2 | 8.5 | 146 |
| Median | 11.5 | 11.3 | 8.2 | 8.1 | 7.0 | 127 |

*Sources:* Company annual and interim reports; projected earnings from Standard & Poor's Earnings Forecaster; stock prices from *Barron's*; computations by CFC Capital LLC.

other industries where prior performance is often less indicative of current value than projected performance, a multiple of projected revenues and earnings for the company's next fiscal year and the one succeeding it should be considered.

The multiple for each such period results from dividing the company's current price (typically an average price over a week or a month prior to the valuation date to avoid possible atypicalities from single-day prices) by the earnings per share for the period in question. Multiples of earnings before interest, taxes, depreciation, and amortization (EBITDA), of earnings before interest and taxes (EBIT), and of net operating income after taxes (NOPAT) are, for a variety of reasons, also in wide use. When pricing off of earnings per share, practitioners vary on whether to use primary or fully diluted earnings per share and on how to calculate earnings per share when, in a given year, earnings have been affected by an atypical event that nonetheless falls short of being an extraordinary item for accounting purposes. In this instance as in many others in the pricing process, the decision should be based on an examination of the facts of a particular case (the extent to which dilution is reasonably foreseeable or the earnings enhancing or depressing events are isolated ones).

Which of the five earnings periods should be used as the basis for comparison? The answer is a resounding "It depends." Where the target is involved in a cyclical industry (ranching, oil and gas, and the like), a pricing analysis that fails to consider price-earnings multiples based on longer periods (average *five-* or *three-*year earnings) may well be incomplete. In industries characteristically priced on recent results (like microelectronics and biotechnology) or where a company has recently changed the nature of its business, *latest-year, latest-12-months,* or *projected* results as suggested earlier are generally more pertinent. Whether to consider latest-year or latest-12-months results involves a balancing of the equities between the greater certainty of audited versus unaudited numbers and picking a date closest to the valuation date. The ability to price based on *projected* earnings often depends on the availability of earnings projections for the comparatives and the target or of brokerage firm research reports and the extent to which projections made by or for the comparatives or the target have been on the mark in the past.

Quite often, when pricing a company for which both cyclical and current elements are relevant, more than one earnings period is used. Moreover, pricing a company with operations in a number of industries or countries may result in one pricing period for one company subsidiary and another for other subsidiaries. In pricing Hyatt Corporation a number of years ago, the investment banker used longer pricing periods for its hotel business and then-existing medical business and, due to the then-existing stock market, a shorter period for its gaming operations. In companies having a number of unrelated businesses (a common phenomenon in many countries), the whole is usually worth less than the sum of its parts. This is true because it is unlikely that any given investor will be equally interested in buying a variety of totally disparate businesses.

The illustrations displayed in Exhibit 12.14 are based on multiples of net income. In some industries (publishing, for example), companies are sometimes priced on multiples of pretax income. This proved to be the case in the acquisition by VNU (a Dutch publisher) of Hayden Publishing, a U.S. publisher of technical magazines. (In some high-tech industries where constant earnings patterns have not developed, companies are priced by reference to *revenues*.)

In industries characterized by high levels of depreciation (e.g., real estate, equipment leasing, steel manufacture), conventional pricing practice uses a market capitalization–EBITDA multiple. *Market capitalization* is defined as the company's total common shares, multiplied by its share price plus its debt (including capitalized leases) and preferred stock, minus its cash and marketable securities. From the total *enterprise value* thus derived, one must subtract the target's total debt (net of cash) to arrive at the value of the *equity*. One may perform a similar analysis using a market capitalization–EBIT multiple. Both the EBITDA and the EBIT multiple processes have the virtue of determining value without the sometimes distorting elements of capital structures that necessarily vary from company to company.

A second way to value earnings is through the analysis of the target's future earnings or cash flows. A conventional tool for doing this, particularly in leveraged buyout scenarios, is the use of payback analysis.

Exhibit 12.15 considers the period over which a 100 percent common stock equity investment of $100,000 will be fully paid back. Projected pretax profits are reduced by 40 percent (the presumed sum of then applicable federal, state, and local taxes) to yield an after-tax profit. Depreciation (a kind of shorthand for the sum of depreciation and amortization and other noncash charges), minus capital expenditures (CAPEX) yields a net cash flow number. This number, added to subsequent years' cash flows, produces a cumulative cash flow. Exhibit 12.15 demonstrates that under the facts presented the investment will be returned in three years. Comparing the payback periods of a series of alternative investment opportunities and judging the payback period of each offers a means by which to decide whether to invest in one company versus others. As in the case of any projections,

**EXHIBIT 12.15**

**Payback Period on $100,000 Investment**

|  | Year | | |
|---|---|---|---|
|  | 1 | 2 | 3 |
| Pretax profit | $25,000 | $41,667 | $ 50,000 |
| Income taxes (40% total rate) | 10,000 | 16,667 | 20,000 |
| After-tax profit | 15,000 | 25,000 | 30,000 |
| Depreciation | 20,000 | 20,000 | 20,000 |
| Cash flow before CAPEX | 35,000 | 45,000 | 50,000 |
| CAPEX | 10,000 | 10,000 | 10,000 |
| Net cash flow | 25,000 | 35,000 | 40,000 |
| Cumulative cash flow | $25,000 | $60,000 | $100,000 |

to make this analysis a practical tool for decision making, one must be thoughtful in the assumptions going into the process. Thus, careful scrutiny needs to be given to the likely levels of pretax earnings and the effect on such earnings of investments in property, plant, equipment, people, research and development (R&D), and the like, over the period studied required to realize them. Current and foreseeable changes in tax rates and depreciation practices must also be considered in order to produce "real world" results.

It is also true in the real world that very few deals are financed with 100 percent equity. Thus, in a leveraged transaction, the cash flow will be reduced by interest and amortization payments on borrowed funds. Payback analysis, like discounted cash flow analysis, is one way to measure the relative attractiveness of alternative investment opportunities. All other things being equal (as they seldom are), one would opt for the transaction with the fastest payback period. Payback analysis is useful in cross-border transactions involving targets in countries in which it is difficult or impossible to find comparative publicly traded companies and in which historical accounting records make it difficult to determine the target's true historic earnings on which to place an earnings multiple.

Discounted cash flow (dcf) analysis proceeds on the assumption that dollars, pounds, francs, marks, liras, yen, and so on, received today are more valuable than those to be received in the future because today's currency in hand can be invested to yield a return. The higher the return, the lower the present value. If the current market return on $1.00 is 5 percent, the value to be received in a year is $.95; but if the current market return is 8 percent, that value is only $.92. There are four components to dcf in mergers and acquisitions: The first is the *net free cash flows* projected for the target (net profits plus depreciation, amortization, and other noncash charges less cash required for reinvestment, retirement of debt or otherwise, dividends, and working capital changes) or some other evidence of cash flow such as NOPAT.

A second dcf component is the *period over which the cash flows are to be measured.* That period is typically 5 to 10 years. Discounting over shorter periods tends to produce more reliable cash flow projections but higher sensitivity to the terminal value calculation because the earlier the time for measuring terminal value, the higher the present value decimal. The converse is true when discounting over longer periods. The dcf exercise should consider the results based on both shorter- and longer-term discounting.

A third element in the dcf process is the *discount rate.* The discount rate is generally chosen after performing a capital asset pricing model (CAPM) and a weighted average cost of capital (WACC) analysis. Exhibit 12.16 develops a typical model of one client—a closely held, Subchapter C corporation real estate and hotel company.

The CAPM analysis, sometimes called the "buildup method," is one from which the required return on equity is obtained. The required return on equity is added to the target company's cost of debt to arrive at the WACC.

To perform the CAPM analysis, first consider the appropriate unlevered beta for the target. (Betas are measurements of a share's price volatility versus a broad

EXHIBIT 12.16

## Calculation of Weighted Average Cost of Capital

| WACC | Rate | Source of Data |
|---|---|---|
| % of debt to total capital | 60.0% | Based on estimated market values |
| Cost of debt | 8.2 | Weighted cost of existing debt |
| Marginal tax rate | 40.0 | C corporation—federal and state |
| % of equity to total capital | 40.0 | Based on estimated market values |
| Cost of equity | 15.4 | Derived via CAPM below |
| **WACC** | **9.1%** | |

| CAPM | Rate | Source of Data |
|---|---|---|
| Beta (unlevered) | 0.30 | Review of comparative companies |
| Beta (levered) | 0.57 | Based on capital structure |
| Risk-free return | 6.5% | U.S. Treasury, 10-year note |
| Beta-adjusted market risk premium | 4.8 | Unadjusted premium per Ibbotson at 8.4% |
| Small-stock adjustment | 2.6 | Ibbotson Associates |
| Specific company adjustment | 1.5 | Due diligence of the target company |
| Required return on equity | 15.4 | |

| Comparative Company | Debt/ Total Capital | Levered Beta | Unlevered Beta |
|---|---|---|---|
| **Hotels** | | | |
| Boca Resorts | 60% | 1.06 | 0.56 |
| Cavanaugh Hospitality | 63 | 0.99 | 0.49 |
| Janus Hotels & Resorts | 82 | 0.77 | 0.21 |
| John Q. Hammons | 97 | 0.81 | 0.04 |
| Lodgian | 86 | 1.51 | 0.32 |
| Prime Hospitality | 56 | 1.25 | 0.71 |
| Sunburst Hospitality | 78 | 0.57 | 0.18 |
| | | | |
| **Real Estate** | | | |
| Castle & Cooke | 56% | 0.72 | 0.41 |
| Echelon International | 49 | 0.42 | 0.27 |
| Forest City | 77 | 0.94 | 0.31 |
| Hallwood Realty | 65 | 0.42 | 0.15 |
| National Realty | 70 | 0.27 | 0.08 |
| Newhall Land & Farming | 23 | 0.61 | 0.47 |
| Pacific Gateway | 51 | 0.48 | 0.30 |
| St. Joe Company | −10 | 0.86 | 0.91 |
| | | | |
| Median—Hotel | 78% | 0.99 | 0.32 |
| Median—Real Estate | 54% | 0.55 | 0.30 |

*Sources:* Company; annual and interim reports; and Bloomberg News Service.

index. A beta exceeding 1.0 evidences higher than normal volatility, and vice versa.) An unlevered beta gives no recognition to the debt ("gearing") on the target's balance sheet; the converse is true for the levered beta. Here it would make sense to pick an unlevered beta of .30, which was the median for the real estate comparatives. (In this case, the company's real estate operations accounted for a dramatically higher portion of its cash flow than did its hotel operations.) Leveraged beta was calculated by multiplying .30 by the following formula: $1 + (1 - \text{tax rate}) \times (\% \text{ debt}/\% \text{ equity})$. The resulting leveraged beta of .57 was then multiplied by the unadjusted beta risk premium (derived from the classic Ibbotson Associates studies, which measure annually premiums over risk-free rates for companies having a variety of investment risk profiles) of 8.4 percent. The result was a 4.8 percent beta-adjusted market risk premium. Then add the 4.8 percent beta-adjusted risk premium to the 6.5 percent risk-free return based on the return of 10-year Treasury notes at the time of the analysis. As the target company was small, one must also add the Ibbotson-based 2.6 percent small-stock premium. Finally, given the geographic restriction of the company's holdings, one should judgmentally add a specific-company risk premium (here 1.5 percent) to arrive at a total required return on equity of 15.4 percent—the sum of 6.5 percent, 4.8 percent, 2.6 percent, and 1.5 percent. Returning to the WACC, note that the company's pretax cost of debt was 8.2 percent, which, at a 40 percent marginal tax rate, equated to a 4.9 percent after-tax cost of debt. The 15.4 percent cost of equity derived as just set forth, was multiplied by .40, the percentage of equity to the company's total capital, to yield 6.2 percent, while the 4.9 percent after-tax cost of debt was multiplied by 60 percent, the percentage of debt to total capital, to yield 2.9 percent. The 2.9 percent cost of debt plus the 6.2 percent cost of equity yielded a 9.1 percent WACC.

But outbound cross-border transactions contain risk elements not found in purely U.S. transactions. These are typically of two types: (1) political risk (expropriation, currency blockage, etc.) and (2) sovereign risk (the sum of political risk plus default risk). In practice, the adjustment to be made for sovereign risk is added to the WACC and is calculated as a percent representing the difference between the dollar-denominated yields on the country's sovereign bonds (such as Brady bonds, Yankee bonds, or Eurobonds) and the yield on U.S. Treasury bonds of the same maturity. The difference in spread between the dollar-denominated yield on the sovereign bonds and the Treasuries is added to or subtracted from the outbound target's WACC.

At whose discount rate should the target's net free cash flows be discounted: its own discount rate or that of the buyer? This question is a particularly vexing one in international transactions where costs of capital, betas, and risk premiums may vary dramatically from country to country at the same valuation date. Discounting at the *target's* cost of capital provides the most realistic means by which to measure the risk of its projected cash flows not materializing. Discounting at the *buyer's* cost of capital best measures the buyer's opportunity cost. (The benefit from choosing the first alternative is the opportunity cost of not having chosen the second.) Because persuasive arguments are available for discounting at both target and buyer cost of capital, it pays to run models using both such approaches. By doing so, one will be best armed for the price discussions to come.

The fourth element in dcf analysis is *terminal value*. Terminal value expresses the theoretically perpetual value capable of being generated by the target's cash flow. One can arrive at terminal value by a variety of means, seven of which are: (1) a perpetual cash flow stream; (2) a price-earnings ratio that assumes the target will be sold at the end of the discounting period for a price that may be an industry-appropriate price–cash flow ratio (most often used where industry price–cash flows have been fairly constant over the years); (3) a price–cash flow ratio (over whatever period measured) equal to that paid by the buyer at the closing; (4) a figure equal to the sum of the target's cash flows generated during the measuring period (which has the merit of not requiring the use of a second independent variable); (5) target's projected net asset value at the end of the period (a methodology generally providing the most conservative result without the use of an independent variable); (6) a price–cash flow multiple representing the reciprocal of the discount rate (an approach that is most useful when the risk factors at the end of the discounting period are presumed to be the same as those present at the beginning of the period, because the risk factors reflected in the choice of discount rate are mirrored in the reciprocal price–cash flow multiple); and (7) as a perpetuity by multiplying the cash flow in the year following the projection period by a number representing the reciprocal of the discount rate plus-or-minus the projected growth rate, discounted to present value at the applicable discount rate.

Exhibit 12.17 assumes a target with $24 million in most-recent-year net profits seeking a purchase price of $240 million. From the comparative company pricing analysis, one can determine whether the resulting price-earnings ratio of 10 times the latest-year profits is reasonable (assuming the appropriateness of a price-earnings ratio based on latest-year net profits). Exhibit 12.17 attempts to answer the same question from the perspective of dcf analysis.

Exhibit 12.17 discounts 10 years' worth of projected net free cash flows at 18 percent (as a result of the methodology just described) to yield a discounted cash flow of $179,939,435. Terminal value was determined by using the reciprocal of the discount rate as a price–cash flow multiplier applied to 10-year net free cash flow to yield a terminal value figure of $56,104,899. Adding the sum of 10 years of discounted cash flows and terminal values results in a value of $236,044,334, thus suggesting that a $240,000,000 price is a bit tight. Real-world considerations, such as the difficulties projecting long-term cash flows and the sensitivity of the result to minor adjustments in discount rate or terminal value, make clear that pricing exercises like this cannot be expected to produce results with micrometer-like precision. Thus, an eclectic approach that makes use of a number of pricing methodologies, no one of which is the Rosetta stone to value, is, wherever possible, highly recommended.

Given the element of "art" in all financial analysis and the fact that the value determined is within 3 percent of the targeted sum, a "buy" decision by the buyer at $240 million and a persuasive "sell" case by the target might each be support-

## EXHIBIT 12.17

**Discounted Cash Flow Analysis of Jones Widget Mfg. Co.**

| Year | Cash Flow | 18% Present Value | Discounted Cash Flow |
|------|-----------|-------------------|----------------------|
| 1 | $34,680,000 | .84746 | $ 29,394,768 |
| 2 | 35,547,000 | .71818 | 25,529,114 |
| 3 | 36,457,350 | .60863 | 22,189,037 |
| 4 | 40,303,218 | .51579 | 20,787,997 |
| 5 | 41,306,886 | .43710 | 18,055,653 |
| 6 | 42,360,724 | .37043 | 15,061,683 |
| 7 | 46,357,247 | .31392 | 14,551,467 |
| 8 | 47,519,114 | .26604 | 12,641,985 |
| 9 | 48,739,070 | .22546 | 10,088,710 |
| 10 | 52,910,033 | .19106 | 10,108,991 |
| | | | $179,939,435 |
| | | Terminal Value | 56,104,899 |
| | | Total | $236,044,334 |

Terminal value, or 52,910,033 x 5.55 (Reciprocal of 18% = 293,650,683 x .19106 = Terminal value of 56,104,899).
*Sources:* Company projections; computations by CFC Capital LLC.

able. Discounted cash flow analyses should be made for the target on a "stand-alone" basis and should be combined with the buyer to determine the effects (if any) of synergy.

## Asset-Based Approaches to Value

Thus far, only the valuation of earnings or cash flows has been discussed. What about *asset* valuation? There are at least two basic methods of asset valuation: (1) a return on equity–market–tangible book value approach and (2) an asset-by-asset approach. We shall take them up one by one.

The comparative company methodology offers a useful means by which to measure the way the investor community values assets by measuring the relationship between a company's return on average common equity and its market price to tangible book value. It is often the case that the higher the return on equity, the higher the market price to tangible book value. This is true because investors will often bid up or bid down a company's shares in relation to its equity base, depending on how well or how poorly that equity base serves as an engine by which to generate earnings or cash flow. Consider the illustration of this methodology in Exhibit 12.18.

Note in Exhibit 12.18 that companies (like Edison and Atlantic) with a low return on equity (ROE) sell at low market–tangible book value ratios, whereas high ROE companies (like Hercules and Winning) sell at higher market–tangible book

EXHIBIT 12.18

## Jones Widget Mfg. Co. versus Comparative Companies

|  | Return on Average Common Equity | Ratio of Market Price to Tangible Book Value |
|---|---|---|
| Edison Spark Plug Co. | 8.2% | 89% |
| Atlantic Auto Parts | 15.7 | 98 |
| E-Z Air Filter Co. | 17.8 | 213 |
| Miracle Muffler Co. | 34.9 | 125 |
| Hercules Gasket Mfg. Co. | 35.9 | 139 |
| Winning Motor Products, Inc. | 40.9 | 146 |
| Jones Widget Mfg. Co. | 36.0 | — |

*Sources:* Company statements; stock prices from Standard & Poor's; computations by CFC Capital LLC.

value ratios. This relationship is almost never a perfect one. Note that E-Z, with a 17.8 percent ROE, one exceeded by three of the comparatives, has the highest market–tangible book ratio. Still, the relationship generally holds true. If such is the case with an array of comparatives in a manner demonstrable through a linear regression analysis (plotting ROE on one axis and market–tangible book value on the other to determine whether the plot results in a reasonably straight-line relationship among the companies plotted), the technique may be useful. Here, we can *infer* a market–tangible book value relationship for JonesCo, given its 36.0 percent ROE of about 140 percent (a bit greater than Hercules's market–tangible book, but clearly lower than that of Winning). Among the variants on the same approach is comparing the relationship of return on average total assets to the ratio of market price to tangible book value or EBITDA/Total Assets and Enterprise Value/Total Assets. If none of these (or similar) relationships provide anything like a straight line, one may reasonably conclude that the securities markets are simply not pricing the kinds of companies in the array on a market–book value basis. In such cases, this methodology should be rejected.

A second method for determining asset value derives from single company methodology. It is an asset-by-asset approach, under which each asset and liability is written up or down from the historical cost manner in which it appears on the target's balance sheet to its fair market value. Assume a hypothetical balance sheet that includes these assets: cash, marketable securities, accounts receivable, inventory, and depreciation.

## Assets

### *Cash*

This is the first balance sheet item on U.S. balance sheets. Note that cash may not always be equal to its stated balance sheet value. Thus, $10,000,000 cash on the balance sheet, some portion of which is the subject of a compensating balance at the company's bank or is spoken for as part of a "carve-out" pursuant to a restriction in a prior placement agreement, is worth less than $10,000,000. How much less depends on the nature and the length of the restriction.

## Marketable Securities

The next U.S. balance sheet item requires some scrutiny. Not only must share or bond prices current to the valuation date for the securities held by the target be checked, but care should be taken to see that what purport to be marketable securities are in fact freely tradable under applicable law and not subject to contractual restrictions or restrictions by operation of law. Finally, trading volume for each security on the balance sheet should be examined to determine whether, given the size of the holding compared to then-current trading levels, that security could be sold at once without depressing its market price. Sometimes (albeit rarely) a common shareholding on a target's balance sheet may be worth a premium if it represents a control block or a swing block that, while minority in nature, can shift control to a party holding an almost controlling block. What percentage constitutes control depends on the law of the jurisdiction that governs the transaction.

## Accounts Receivable

This also requires careful scrutiny. Their quality, and hence their value, depends on the answers to several questions.

*Are They Really Receivables?*   Has more than order taking occurred? Have the goods actually been shipped? What is the purchaser's obligation? Is it perhaps only a conditional sale with a right of refusal by the customer? What are the practices of the trade in this regard?

*How Collectible Are They?*   Old receivables are less valuable than current ones because they are less likely to be collected. The process of attributing value to receivables based on dates on which payment is due is called *aging*. An aging schedule should be prepared.

*How Fast Are They Collectible?*   A simple measuring rod to determine the speed of collection is to divide the ratio of receivables to sales into 365 days. The resulting answer must be judiciously applied. Assume the following example:

- $10 million in annual revenues.
- $2 million in annual accounts receivable.
- $10 million divided by $2 million results in a revenue-receivables ratio of 5 to 1; 365 days in a year divided by 5 equals 73 days on average from billing to collection.

Whether this 5 to 1 ratio is a good one or a bad one depends to a large degree on how it compares to the company's historic experience and to the experiences of other companies in the same industry in the same country at the same time. Consideration should therefore be given to how the target compares to the comparatives used in the pricing analysis or to general industry norms (data contained in the Robert Morris Annual Statement Surveys, which, organized by SIC codes, contains this and many other ratios). The business under review may be subject to seasonal variations; therefore, balance sheets for different periods in the year should be examined. The ability to collect receivables may be slowed by local political, social, and economic factors. These should be carefully reviewed as part of the due diligence in all transactions, but especially in those that cross borders.

### Inventory ("Stocks")

Inventory consists of raw materials, work in process, and finished goods. The value of the inventory includes the cost of labor and the manufacturing expense necessary to transform the inventory into the finished product. Buyers should look for and target companies should be prepared to answer a series of inventory-related questions including the following.

***Is This Really Inventory?*** Similar to the need to verify the quality of receivables, the buyer must examine the target's inventory to make sure that it contains only materials and goods pertaining to the target's business. Inventories of other people's goods that are held for sale on consignment or that include goods of the target sold on consignment are obviously not as valuable as inventories that are the subject of unconditional sales. In cross-border deals, it is necessary to ask this characterization question loudly and clearly.

***What Is the Accounting Procedure?*** Material variations can result from differences in inventory accounting within a given country or procedures that vary country to country. The buyer and the target must reconcile the method used by the target with the buyer's method of inventory accounting and make adjustments up or down as required. This too must be examined with special care in the cross-border transaction.

***How Fast Is the Inventory Turning?*** Here it is necessary to go back to one of the basic ratios, revenue divided by inventory, to determine how fast the goods move out. As in the case of receivables, use of comparative company methodology and industrywide statistics provide useful measuring rods by which to gauge target company financial performance. Poor inventory turns are a warning to the buyer of the possibility of significant amounts of obsolete inventory. Targets having low inventory turns will need to explain why such is the case. Stories of obsolete inventory in Central and Eastern European transactions still exist, but in reduced amounts from the levels immediately following the opening up of the region following the demise of Communism in that part of the world.

***To What Extent Is There an "Inventory Cushion"?*** To what extent have inventories been stated ultraconservatively with tax avoidance in mind? In places like

Italy and Latin America where tax-avoidance schemes have made it difficult to evaluate inventory, care in inventory pricing is urged. As previously indicated, targets frequently seek to be paid on the basis of reconstructed income, which, among other elements, adds back the amount of the cushion. Buyers are usually less than fully accommodating on this score. Milestone payments, or installment and other payments with a right of set-off often found in venture transactions, resulting in payments to the target conditioned upon reaching preagreed goals, may be useful in bridging gaps between the target's price demand and the buyer's offer. Alternatively, an *earnout* consisting of additional postclosing purchase price contingent on future years' financial performance during which the target reduces or eliminates the cushion, may be the only viable way of addressing the problem (earnouts are discussed later in this chapter). Even then, the solution is less than perfect. Several years before making their companies available for sale, thoughtful targets should consider the reduction of inventory cushions because reconstructed earnings are generally capitalized at lower multiples than historical ones and there are many variables that may hinder or make impossible the full realization of contingent earnouts.

## Fixed Assets

Thus far, the discussion has been devoted exclusively to the valuation of current assets. What of *fixed assets* like property, plant, and equipment?

The most commonly used approach to valuing these is to determine the cost required to buy the target's facility new, less physical deterioration and functional obsolescence of each major asset. Although each appraisal of physical assets stands alone, there are certain measuring rods that should be used.

### Depreciation

The buyer should examine the target's plant and equipment and get a feel for real values by independent appraisal, especially if the industry being examined is unfamiliar to the buyer. Comparing these results to the way in which such items are booked may reveal a very different picture (often more favorable) of the target company than that emerging from a reading of the financials alone.

### Value in Use to the Buyer

In all asset valuations, it is important to consider opportunity cost elements. If, for an equivalent price, the same facility can be built in one year, what is the value of the one-year lead time? (This may be especially true in cross-border deals where delays in building a facility can result from shortage of materials to hassles with local bureaucracies.)

The value thus derived may vary considerably from the value recorded on the target's books. For transactional purposes, "value in use" is probably more a useful pricing arbiter than "replacement value" or "liquidation value" (either the orderly or the "fire sale" kind) because it most nearly approximates the going-concern character of such assets.

## Intangible Assets

In many service businesses (like advertising and public relations) or in businesses with uniquely proprietary features covered by nominally booked patents, copyrights, or trademarks (computer software or biotechnology) or by mandatorily booked development expenses, *intangible asset* values may represent substantially all of the company's fair market value. In the new and increasingly technological millennium, it appears that such assets will warrant particularly careful review. Thus, such intangible assets as favorable leases (leases at less than market rate), trained workforces, customer lists, brand names, and business goodwill, which may not appear on the balance sheet at all, require close scrutiny. Separate analysis of these intangibles is a must.

## Liabilities

Not only the asset side but also the liability side of the balance sheet must be measured. Usually, however, measuring the liability side involves less difficulty because the accounts payable, notes payable (if any), and income tax payable are described in the target's books and records. The same is true with respect to the target's long-term obligations, on which the fixed payment schedules make analysis fairly simple. Be certain, however, especially where footnotes are scanty, to fully understand the terms of such debt.

In analyzing the liability side of the balance sheet, *caution must be taken* in at least three areas.

1. See that current earnings and cash flows are not puffed by the delay of payments of accounts payable beyond the accounting period under scrutiny. Vigorous short-term collection of receivables, while delaying the payment of accounts payable, can create a picture of current profits or cash flow that is largely illusory.
2. Look carefully at the terms and conditions of loan agreements and particularly at items such as floating-rate interest provisions and repayment schedules. Consider the affirmative and the negative covenants in bank loan agreements, trust indentures, and elsewhere that can, given an unwaived breach, turn long-term debt into debt due immediately by reason of acceleration clauses in such agreements.
3. Scrutinize off–balance sheet liabilities. In our Enron age of special-purpose vehicles, credit derivatives, gain-on-sale treatment features, and 21st-century forms of off–balance sheet financing, caution is the watch-

word. More conventional risks include actual or impending product liability, tax disputes, and the costs associated with compliance with governmental regulation over issues such as environmental pollution, workplace safety, and employee pension and termination rights. In cross-border transactions in countries without well-developed environmental, consumer, or similar laws, part of the legal due diligence is to consider the impact of legislation in these areas that is pending or foreseeable.

## Deriving Conclusions on Price

Thus far, the values derived under comparative company analysis have been considered from two points of view: (1) a price-earnings or price–cash flow multiple approach and (2) an asset-based relationship between return on equity and market price to tangible book value. We have also considered an asset-by-asset approach. Usually, a weighting (by a formal weighting process or by "eyeball") of the conclusions derived under the earnings approach and the asset approach is made with the result under the earnings approach weighted more heavily, because investors tend to value companies more nearly on the basis of their earnings than on their assets.

Values derived from the comparative company approach are of minority interests and do not give effect to a premium for control.

However, sale of control of a profitable company carries with it a bundle of rights that are not enjoyed by minority shareholders. A control block carries with it the right to determine day-to-day corporate policy and to increase, decrease, or withhold dividends. If the block is sufficiently large in size, it carries the right to sell, merge, or liquidate the company. In the case of the closely held company, some of this premium otherwise applicable may be eroded by a discount that gives recognition to the lack of marketability of the company's closely held shares. Although many practitioners believe that a premium for control is inherent in the terminal value calculation in discounted cash flow analysis, comparative company analysis demands that it be separately determined. One objective yardstick by which to determine the amount of the premium for control is consideration of the range of premiums paid for control in transactions involving companies usable for comparative purposes with the target. This is called the comparative transaction approach. In the United States and elsewhere, databases organized by SIC code, such as those provided by Standard & Poor's (S&P), and others may be used. If these are unavailable, a general range may be established by looking at a number of sale-of-control situations by merger or tender offer close to the valuation date. Exhibit 12.19 illustrates typical ranges measured on the basis of premium over unaffected market price and relationship of price to tangible book value in a particular industry group. Frequently, such data is supplemented by total enterprise value, total equity value, latest-12-months revenue growth, EBITDA, EBIT, and net income for each target company and the resulting multiples of revenues, EBITDA, EBIT, and net income.

EXHIBIT 12.19

**Successful Cash Offers for Common Stock Control[1]—January 1 through December 31, 20XX[2]**
(Market Price of Stock 30 Days Prior Announcement)

| Company | Where Traded | Date of Initial Offer | Price per Share | Price per Share[3] | Indicated Premium | Latest Available Tangible Book Value | Price to Tangible Book Value |
|---|---|---|---|---|---|---|---|
| Arkansas-Smith, Inc. | PSE | 5/27/XX | 24.00 | 15.75 | 52.4 | 18.60 | 129.0 |
| Bullet Templates | ASE | 4/8/XX | 6.25 | 5.00 | 25.0 | 4.92 | 127.0 |
| Carroll Industries, Inc. | OTC | 2/16/XX | 6.50 | 5.75 | 13.0 | 6.14 | 105.9 |
| Deca Amp Corporation | ASE | 4/30/XX | 6.30 | 4.00 | 57.5 | 6.16 | 102.3 |
| Elliott Supreme, Inc. | OTC | 4/14/XX | 7.80 | 6.00 | 30.0 | 13.57 | 57.5 |
| Famous Industries, Inc. | ASE | 2/24/XX | 12.00 | 7.50 | 60.0 | 9.45 | 127.0 |
| Georgette & Sons, Inc. | OTC | 2/1/XX | 5.00 | 3.25 | 53.8 | 8.38 | 59.7 |
| Median | | | | | 52.4 | | 105.9 |

[1]In cash tender offers or in merger proposals.
[2]Period within which transaction was completed.
[3]Closing price of stocks.
Sources: *Wall Street Journal*; Standard & Poor's Corporation Records; Daily Stock Price Index; Stock Guide and Stock Reports; SEC forms 10-K, 10-Q; interim and annual reports to stockholders; proxy statements; offer to purchase documents; computations by CFC Capital LLC.

Note that in all instances, price is determined by a premium over a market price presumably unaffected by news of the transaction. Thus, it is conventional to consider a price from which the premium is derived that dates back at least 30 days from the date of the announcement of the proposed transaction. To avoid questions of valuation of noncash consideration in the form of securities or other noncash consideration, it may be best to confine the premium analysis to all cash offers.

These statistical measurements offer some general insight on ranges of premiums (the median premium over market price has been in the 40 percent to 50 percent range for a number of years), but the ultimate premium will depend on the facts of a given case. Here, several elements need to be considered, including these eight items: (1) the target's historic and current results; (2) its future prospects, on a stand-alone basis and within the framework of the buyer company giving effect to such synergies as may exist; (3) the strategic importance of the target to the buyer;[1] (4) the willingness (rational or otherwise) of buyer or target management to complete the transaction (the "ego factor"); (5) the presence or absence of other bidders; (6) in public transactions, the influence of arbitrageurs; (7) the nature of the consideration, as previously suggested, where the buyer's shares represent the consideration, little or no premium may result [e.g., the Reed/Elsevier or Blockbuster/Viacom mergers] because the target's shareholders will continue to hold speculative opportunities in what may be a stronger company versus an end to such opportunities if they are simply cashed out; and (8) in international transactions, the opportunity to buy at investor appraisal ratios lower than those payable in one's home country or when currency exchange relationships effectively lower the price for overseas buyers (a cheap dollar attracts buyers with marks, pounds, francs, or yen).

All of the preceding elements assume a playing field in which each side comes to the table with different aspirations (i.e., to buy for a bargain or to sell for a windfall) but with a common frame of reference on how to approach the question of purchase price (i.e., a comparison of the company's historic performance versus that of a group of comparative companies and, from this comparison, drawing appropriate inferences of value based on earnings multiples, discounted cash flow analysis, or the fair market value of the target's assets and liabilities).

This model works well for international transactions involving companies in countries where Western-style deal pricing based on comprehensible and consistent financial statements is the norm. But what about deal pricing in other countries (notably in the former Soviet Union or in Central or Eastern Europe) where the transition from command to market economies has been anything but easy? Consider for a moment at least five sets of problems that are quite typical in Central and Eastern European deals. *First*, how does one get a handle on price in countries that regard "Anglo Saxon" due diligence (comprehensive disclosures and extensive

---

[1] One of the reasons generally assumed to account for why non–U.S. buyers generally pay higher premiums for U.S. targets than do U.S. buyers is the strategic importance for some such buyers of obtaining a toehold in the United States.

documentation) as somewhere between countercultural and intrusive? *Second,* how are deals to be done there when, despite the recent adoption of common European accounting standards, historical and current financials may be notoriously unreliable due to volatile price swings, arbitrary assignments of asset values, uncertainties about inflation, translation errors, and the absence of independence by former state-owned companies? *Third,* how does one have a price negotiation with a former Iron Curtain apparatchik who equates *fair market value with net asset value* and who has never had to worry about the amount of bottom-line earnings or of the size of returns on assets and equity? *Fourth,* how does a pricing analysis proceed in the absence of local comparatives? *Fifth,* how does one price a company with an extraordinary supply of redundant assets, like the pattern in Hungary where such assets were bought to avoid having to dividend retained earnings to the State?

There are no magic-bullet answers to any of these questions. On the issue of conflicting styles of due diligence, Anglo Saxon practitioners may need to accommodate to a style that involves more modest early due diligence, which, if mutual trust is built, leads to provisional agreements. These agreements are followed by more intense due diligence and more extensive documentation. As to the notorious (but diminishing) unreliability of historic accounting statements, present practice calls for an audit team using current-day practices (i.e., relatively short asset-depreciation periods versus the 30- to 40-year periods frequently seen in command economy financials) to reconstruct historical numbers in light of contemporary Western standards. In the real world, however, no amount of reconstruction will entirely erase the problems associated with self-serving subjectivity with which some of these financials were created (i.e., looking good to one's political boss). Thus, dcf that does not depend on historical numbers may be a better pricing tool than comparative company analysis in situations where historic accounting will always be, to some degree, less than totally reliable.

The third issue—historically the most currently intractable of the lot, but now in the process of change—is getting across the notion that increasing earnings and cash flow rather than the size of one's asset base is the means by which corporate value is determined. In command economies, where the name of the game is to fill quotas rather than increase shareholder wealth, value is measured by one's asset base even if the business perennially loses money. That fundamental difference in belief, wholly apart from the political and social implications, is what makes corporate downsizing so painful in the former Eastern Bloc. As the "triumphant" ideology, the methodology of Western-style countries will ultimately prevail, and the new cadre of corporate managers in the bloc are beginning to embrace modern corporate pricing theory, but the reeducation process will be slow and painful.

Assuming a universe of discourse on pricing, how does one price a deal, say, in a country whose exchange currently trades relatively few stocks and in which trading is quite light? In the absence of comparatives in the country in question, one may use Western comparatives with multiples adjusted against a relevant index. Such a technique was used in testimony on behalf of OPIC (the Overseas

Private Investment Corporation) before the U.S./Iranian Claims Tribunal. OPIC had insured Hyatt Hotels and Motorola in Iran and was seeking recompense for the money it had paid out when the local affiliates of those comparatives were seized. In that situation, price-earnings (P-E) multiples for U.S. hotel and electronics companies at the time of the expropriation were used, adjusting those multiples for the difference between the multiples of the S&P index against a broad index of stocks on the Teheran Stock Exchange. In the case of the thin trading market example previously cited, one might adjust the S&P index against a similar index on the closest large exchange, say the Vienna exchange.

Conglomerate corporate holdings are quite common outside the United States. In other countries they may have been formed without any central business strategy. Take for example an Eastern European auto parts distributor sought to be acquired by a German company in the same business. The target company, in addition to its automotive parts distribution operation, owned commercial office buildings in the heart of the capital city and resort properties in the countryside. In determining the value of the business, a conventional pricing analysis on the main business was performed, supplemented by local appraisals on the real estate whose immediate sale would produce proceeds by which to pay down the installment sale price in the deal.

Given the difficulties just described, perhaps the safest way to price a transaction in a country whose pricing institutions are other than those employed in Western deals is to approach the situation as a venture capitalist would approach a greenfield investment, where historic earnings don't exist and projections are often hopelessly optimistic. In such a situation, price is determined after a critical examination of at least seven facts: (1) the product or service offered by the company; (2) the market for that product or service; (3) its defensibility against competitive threat; (4) competence of existing management; (5) adequacy of workforce; (6) required capital investment (typically for new equipment, marketing, and addressing regulatory issues like pollution); and (7) the potential business synergies between the parties (in technology, production, marketing, and distribution). A dcf analysis that takes these facts into account and adjusts them for risk elements, like political and economic instability, currency fluctuation, ability to repatriate profits, and other variables, is often the most reliable pricing mechanism. That sort of analysis, together with escrows, milestone payments, and earnouts (described later) can help mitigate financial risk.

## Preferred Stock and Debt Security Valuations

Sometimes preferred shares or debt securities are issued as part of the purchase price consideration. In such instances, a variant of common share valuation methodology is required. Unlike common shares, both preferred shares and debt securities derive their value principally from their internal characteristics (dividends or interest rate, seniority versus other classes of the target company's securities, liquidation preference, coverage ratios, and the like). Thus, the form of comparative company methodology employed here compares the subject securities to securities having like characteristics irrespective of the industry of the issuer.

Assume that if XYZ Corporation was offering $10 par value 8 percent cumulative nonvoting preferred shares to acquire ABC Limited, XYZ's preferred stock might be valued as follows:

1. Determine XYZ's ability to cover preferred dividends (pretax income divided by total annual dividends required to be paid on the preferred stock).
2. Compare XYZ's preferred dividend coverage with the dividend coverage of an array of preferred shares with similar internal characteristics (see Exhibit 12.20).
3. Determine the current yield of the comparative company preferred stocks.
4. Divide XYZ's proposed dividend by the current yield or yields of companies having similar preferred dividend coverage to arrive at a percentage of par value.

Thus, if XYZ's coverage were around 3.18 times (the median of the comparatives in Exhibit 12.20), its current yield might be appropriately 9.6 percent of the median current yield: $0.08 \div 0.096 = 83.3\%$ of par.

Thus, XYZ's preferred would be worth 83.3 percent of $10.00, or $8.33, assuming a freely traded preferred stock. Lacking a freely traded market, a discount of 10 percent to 15 percent would be typical. This discount is smaller than the typical common stock discount because of the fixed dividend and greater seniority of the preferred stock.

A debt security analysis is very similar to a preferred stock analysis, except that interest rather than dividend coverage is sought and comparative bonds rather than comparatives preferred are used.

## The Contingent Earnout

The contingent earnout is a device by which to bridge the target's characteristic optimism about the future of its business and the buyer's customary unwillingness to pay for earnings materially higher than those historically recorded by the target company. In this circumstance, assume a target whose company has the following characteristics.

| | |
|---|---|
| Sales | £10,000,000 |
| Net profits | £500,000 |
| Net worth | £3,000,000 |

Further assume that the target seeks £6,000,000 for the business (12x earnings) and that the buyer is willing to pay only £5,000,000 (10x earnings).

"But," says the target's CEO, "my company's financial statements do not

EXHIBIT 12.20

## Publicly Traded Preferred Stocks

| Company | Description | Exchange | S&P Rating | Cumulative | Voting | Annual Dividend | Coverage Year 1 | Coverage Year 2 | Current Price | Average Coverage | Current Yield |
|---|---|---|---|---|---|---|---|---|---|---|---|
| Arthur Industries, Inc. | $4.50 Pref. | NYSE | AA | Y | N | $4.50 | 2.88 | 3.47 | $47.00 | 3.18 | 9.6% |
| Beechwood Corp. | $3.50 Pref. | NYSE | AA | Y | N | 3.50 | 2.88 | 3.47 | 36.75 | 3.18 | 9.5 |
| Casual Time, Inc. | $3.75 Cum. Pref. | NYSE | AA+ | Y | N | 3.75 | 3.00 | 5.00 | 39.50 | 4.00 | 9.5 |
| Dismore Development Corp. | $5.00 Cum. Pref. | NYSE | AA+ | Y | N | 5.00 | 3.00 | 5.00 | 52.25 | 4.00 | 9.6 |
| Edwards & Co. | $3.75 Pref. | NYSE | AA– | Y | N | 3.75 | 6.10 | 10.05 | 35.00 | 8.08 | 10.7 |
| Furrey Bros., Inc. | 4.25% Pref. A | NYSE | AA– | Y | Y | 4.25 | 3.07 | 3.20 | 42.50 | 3.14 | 10.0 |
| Gowanus Rubbish Corp. | $5.45 Cum. Pref. | NYSE | AA– | Y | N | 5.45 | 2.77 | 2.06 | 54.63 | 2.42 | 10.0 |
| Median | | | | | | | | | | 3.18 | 9.6% |

*Sources:* Company financial statements; Standard & Poor's Stock Guide; computations by CFC Capital LLC.

truly reflect its value. For years I have been depressing earnings to save on taxes. I have been undervaluing my inventory (the inventory cushion described earlier) so that my inventory is understated by £1,000,000. My salary, instead of being £100,000 (which might be considered normal for a company this size) is £200,000. I charge my car and the mortgage on my house to the business, and several of my relatives are on the payroll to perform jobs that could be filled for much smaller salaries. If I had a financial incentive to uncover my earnings, I could show considerably more—maybe even 50 percent more."

In response, a buyer might propose a transaction with £4,500,000 payable at closing and the opportunity to earn more (typically over a three-to-five-year period), if future earnings warrant it.

What follows is an earnout proposition. While there are limitless variations on the earnout approach, Exhibits 12.21 and 12.22 describe two of the more common ones.

Exhibit 12.21 shows an average earnout. As indicated, the target receives £4,500,000 at closing. To this is added the contingent feature, here an amount equal to 10 times the net after-tax profits in the five years following the acquisition minus base-year earnings. If the target realizes the projected earnings levels, it receives an additional £1,500,000 earnout payment at the end of year 5. Although it is true that the sum of the £4,500,000 payment at closing plus the £1,500,000 earnout payable in year 5 is, on a present-value basis, clearly less than the £6,000,000 sought by the target, it is greater (on any reasonable present-value basis) than the £5,000,000 the buyer was prepared to pay without an earnout.

## EXHIBIT 12.21

### Contingent Earnout/Average Earnout

#### Deal Structure
At closing: £4,500,000
Earnout: 10 × average net after-tax earnings in the five years following the acquisition less base year net after-tax earnings paid at the end of year 5.

#### Net After-Tax Earnings Assumptions

| Base Year | Year 1 | Year 2 | Year 3 | Year 4 | Year 5 |
|-----------|--------|--------|--------|--------|--------|
| £500,000 | £550,000 | £600,000 | £650,000 | £700,000 | £750,000 |

#### Results

| | |
|---|---|
| Total net after-tax earnings: | £3,250,000 |
| Average net after-tax earnings: | £650,000 |
| £650,000 − £500,000 (base year) = | £150,000 |
| £150,000 × 10 (P-E multiplier) = | £1,500,000 |

| | |
|---|---|
| £4,500,000 | At closing |
| 1,500,000 | Contingent |
| £6,000,000 | Total |

## EXHIBIT 12.22

### Contingent Earnout/Percentage of Profit Earnout

*Deal Structure*
At closing: £4,500,000
Earnout: 50% of net after-tax earnings (either annually or at the end of a specific period)

*Net After-Tax Earnings Assumptions*

| Base Year | Year 1 | Year 2 | Year 3 | Year 4 | Year 5 |
|---|---|---|---|---|---|
| £500,000 | £550,000 | £600,000 | £650,000 | £700,000 | £750,000 |

*Results*

Base year not considered
Total net after-tax earnings: £3,250,000
.50 × £3,250,000 = £1,625,000

£4,500,000
1,625,000 (payable at end of year 5)

£6,125,000 Total

*OR*

Payment as follows:

| Year 1 | Year 2 | Year 3 | Year 4 | Year 5 |
|---|---|---|---|---|
| £275,000 | £300,000 | £325,000 | £350,000 | £375,000 |

Exhibit 12.22 illustrates a percentage of profit earnout in which the target shareholders receive a percentage of the profits earned over a period of years, either annually or at the end of the period. On a present-value basis, the annual earnout clearly favors the target. Waiting until the end of the earnout period before paying the earnout clearly favors the buyer, which has the benefit of the use of the earnout funds over the period in question and, in addition, a means to lessen the target's incentive to generate earnings early in the earnout period at the possible expense of future earnings.

There are limitless varieties of earnouts. Some may be revenue based rather than earnings based. To ensure against the development of revenues without profits, the buyer may wish to condition earnout payments on the maintenance of certain profit margins. In an overseas magazine transaction sometime back involving several publications, the earnout was limited to the results generated by one particular magazine. In a leveraged buyout of a non–U.S. motor carrier, the earnout was related to increases in revenues subject to the maintenance of operating margins at agreed-on levels. In the sale of an equipment leasing company, the earnout was based on a sharing between buyer and target of profits after the buyer obtained a designated return on the capital representing that portion of the price paid at the closing. There are also earnouts that require the target, as a condition to receiving earnout payments for a particular year, to have achieved earnings in that year higher than in any previous year.

Some fact patterns are less conducive to earnouts than others: Where the businesses of the parties are to be closely integrated following the transaction (as, for example, in the case of a consolidation of factories or a merger of sales forces), it may be difficult or impossible to determine which of the parties will have been responsible for future results. Earnouts seldom work unless key members of target company management are prepared to continue to operate the business for the length of the earnout period. Earnouts are uncommon where the target is publicly owned, presumably due to the perception that only those shareholders responsible for producing incremental future earnings should receive earnout payments. This perception notwithstanding, General Motors' acquisition of Hughes Aircraft and of Electronic Data Systems illustrates instances of contingent earnout payments being made to public shareholders.

A target's shareholders may find an earnout acceptable if the following conditions are met:

- *Is It Reasonably Attainable?* A target should consider the answer to questions such as these: (1) How much hidden earnings can I uncover? (2) What is the future of my business? (3) Will I have a genuine chance at earning the contingent portion of the purchase price? In that connection, the target may be well advised to negotiate in the purchase contract a kind of "nonmolestation" clause granting target company management control over day-to-day operations, placing limits on buyer's ability to upstream cash from target, and granting target management certain expenditure authority and a say on the sums to be reinvested for research and development (R&D), capital improvements, and the like. (4) Will affiliation with buyer make it harder or easier to earn the earnout?

- *Is It Sizable Enough?* The target should determine whether there is enough of an earnout to induce it to forgo some of the money that might be paid at closing by agreeing to take the earnout. In short, how high a contingent price-earnings ratio or what percentage of profits is the target receiving?

Note that under U.S. tax laws, with no escrow, tax-free exchange rules provide a limit on the number of shares issuable for earnout purposes. To ensure tax-free treatment, the number of earnout shares issuable may not exceed the number of shares issuable at closing, although there is some flexibility on this if the disparity between the two is not great and if there is a genuine hurdle to attain in order to make the earnout.

From the buyer's point of view, the earnout offers the advantage of paying only for earnings actually achieved. Conversely, contingent shares issued for earnouts must be reported by the buyer as part of fully diluted earnings under U.S. accounting principles.

## Securitized Deal Designs

Deal designs featuring asset securitization devices can be hard to implement in countries without modern commercial codes. Consider the following:

A Western European buyer sought to acquire control of a large heavy equipment dealer in Central Europe. In the United States, a considerable portion of the purchase price could be financed by a pledge of the perfectly good equipment to which the target company had clear title. But exactly how does a lending institution perfect a lien on those assets in the absence of a Uniform Commercial Code or its equivalent? Assuming a bonded-warehouse-type solution, in which the lender advances funds as assets leave the warehouse under the lender's control, would a claim of title by the lender in the event of default be enforceable under a local law otherwise silent on the subject? The buyer could get no comfort on this issue from local counsel and was forced to borrow in the West on its local credit lines (the Western lender would not lend on Central European assets), thereby diminishing credit available to its existing operations. To this simple example, one could add dozens more.

## NEGOTIATION

The merger process is like a play in six acts, the scenario of which can generally be described as: (1) the finding stage; (2) the qualification stage; (3) the preliminary investigation stage; (4) the serious negotiation stage; (5) the contract stage; and (6) the closing stage. Some of the stages may take place concurrently (like contract and closing), and there are blurry lines about when one stage becomes the next.

How long each stage takes also depends on the specific transaction, whether there were prior negotiations, whether the companies are in similar or different businesses, the time and distance between the parties, and so on; but in general, the outline suggested here generally holds true. Each stage shall be examined.

## The Finding Stage

This is the point at which *someone* (broker; attorney; accountant; commercial, investment, or merchant banker; company employee; supplier; customer; or someone else) approaches either of the two parties and makes it aware of the possible interest of the other side in initiating a transaction.

## The Qualification Stage

Each party now decides whether it wishes to go forward. If the introducer's role was performed effectively, the buyer should have some idea of the target company, including its basic business, sources of supply, production and selling processes, and management. For the buyer's part, it is usually best to have a set of acquisition criteria against which to measure the target. This includes data such as product line sought, minimum and maximum size of the target, required investment returns, whether target company management will be expected to continue, and so on. Much wasted time and effort can be avoided if the buyer has clearly defined acquisition criteria, for most acquisition prospects are fatally flawed in one or more of the areas just described. For the target, the initial considerations include (1) how good an investment the buyer's shares or debt are (if the transaction involves other than all cash); (2) how financially strong the buyer is, particularly if direct funding from the buyer or parent company guarantees are important reasons for selling; (3) whether the target's organization is culturally similar to that of the buyer (for example, if the target company seeks management autonomy, is it likely to be realized with the particular buyer with whom the transaction is being negotiated?); (4) whether an affiliation with the buyer will provide the target company with benefits otherwise unavailable to it (sales, marketing, R&D, production, or financial synergy); and (5) how badly target company management wants to sell.

The international transaction adds an extra layer of complexity to the qualification stage for both parties. Each must consider the likely impact of: (1) language differences, whose nuances often escape the most skilled interpreter; (2) cultural barriers (e.g., a low tolerance for vodka when attempting to do transactions in Russia); and (3) difference in laws and law enforcement with respect to issues like tax compliance and "sensitive" payments (a legally cognizable commission in one country may constitute a bribe in another) and the impact of local statutory or case law on the conduct of business. The legal litany also includes the impact of local antitrust laws; "social" laws affecting compensation, benefits, and termination of personnel; export control laws; and currency control laws. Indeed, the very definition of what constitutes a cross-border transaction has changed. Who, not long ago, would have imagined that a nominally U.S. transaction (GE's acquisition of Honeywell) might run afoul of European Union antitrust regulators?

To this daunting array of legal issues must be added a consideration of potentially positive legal developments, including the easing of trade barriers among members of the European Union (EU) in 1992, the United Nations Convention on Contracts for the International Sale of Goods (adopted in 1988), and other statutory changes, bilateral and multilateral tax, and other treaties that simplify international transactions and tax "holidays" designed to encourage foreign investment. Other important considerations are the effect of different labor conditions, economic circumstances, exchange rates, and competitive environments in other countries; issues relating to government policy, such as percentage of ownership, if any, allowed to foreign businesses or individuals; and attitudes toward public ownership.

All of this suggests a cautionary tale. Whether as buyer or target, understand as early as possible the extent to which the international character of the transaction adds to its upside potential and downside risk. Assuming a willingness to go forward following this risk assessment, ingenuity will often be required where substantive rules do not exist. For example, where local law is silent on issues likely to affect the deal (i.e., conditions that trigger bankruptcy or the enforcement of title claims to real and personal property), parties are increasingly using long arbitration clauses that, among other elements, stipulate the applicability of the laws of a third country as controlling such issues (i.e., German substantive law in transactions between companies in the West and those in Central and Eastern Europe). Business risk can be further ameliorated by becoming familiar with local decision makers, using preliminary discussions to determine whether cooperation with the other side is possible; resolving tough issues up front; obtaining war, insurrection, and other insurance; and accepting risk in exchange for concessions on price and terms. Caution is advised. Perhaps it makes sense to work on a small "demonstration" project with the prospective overseas partner before undertaking a larger one. Most important, the buyer should try to ensure that the overseas partner has a meaningful financial stake in the project. "Sweat equity" is easily abandoned.

None of the problems previously described (to which one could add considerably more) is intended to suggest that companies should not undertake to do cross-border transactions. But it is important to go in with eyes wide open to some of the stumbling blocks to deals over and above the ones previously enumerated. Many believe that some of the enterprises likely to show the largest internal rates of return (IRRs) are greenfield investments with modest capital input. As is the case in M&A transactions where most deals (many of them extraordinarily successful) are done between small private companies and pass below Wall Street's radar screen because of their small size and the absence of the need for public disclosure, one may never get to hear about a lot of the best deals that are done in remote parts of the world.

If the would-be target is genuinely serious about sale, it ought to be genuinely prepared. This involves having a decent idea of what the business is likely to be worth to a given buyer and preparing a descriptive memorandum that tells the company's story fairly and fully. This memorandum (receipt of which by investors should be preceded by a confidentiality agreement) generally contains these 10 elements.

1. A history of the company and the principal milestones in its business life.
2. If the company is a manufacturer, details about its raw material sources and procurement, the issues of availability of certain critical materials, supplier dependency, a description of the flow of production, and the equipment used in the process including capital expenditure budgets.
3. Data on the company's R&D and product development or the way that new services are conceived.
4. A synopsis of the company's sales and marketing efforts; who sells the company's products (house salespeople, representatives, company prin-

cipals), to whom sales are made (wholesalers, retailers, consumers, governments, and customer dependency), terms of sales, marketing, advertising, and other promotional efforts.

5. A description of the company's principal officers, including name, title, age, educational background, state of health, job function, length of service, and (if not overly sensitive) compensation.

6. Employee data, including the number of nonexecutive personnel, union status, wage scales, fringe benefits, and the basic terms of any existing collective bargaining agreements.

7. Information about governmental regulatory compliance and areas of contingent liability (taxes, product liability, and the like).

8. Full financial statements for the longer of five years or an average business cycle and projections, if available, accompanied by the assumptions on which the projections are made.

9. Details on capital structure and equity ownership.

10. A discussion of the company's plans for the future—Will it be in the same business or a different one? What changes in procurement, production, sales, marketing, and capital expenditures are needed to realize the goals of the plan?

No company's story is one of unadulterated success. It is often best to disclose a company's weaknesses in the descriptive memorandum. If, for example, the target is dependent on a single supplier, it should tell why such is the case, what the target is doing about it, or why no action is needed. The prospective buyer is likely to find out anyway. Targets should spare themselves the buyer's perception that they have been hiding unfavorable facts by disclosing them initially, in a manner that can put them in perspective.

Caution should be taken in the preparation of descriptive memoranda. It is conventional practice for such documents to contain a disclaimer that the buyer is not entitled to characterize the statements in the memorandum as the equivalent of warranties and representations about the business and, rather, must rely solely on its own due diligence.

The descriptive memorandum is especially important in cross-border transactions, where the litany of questions surrounding the target company is expanded by the many political, economic, financial, legal, and social issues that will form a material portion of the body of the buyer's due diligence investigation.

## The Preliminary Investigation Stage

If the negotiations continue, there will often be a face-to-face meeting of principals at the target's office or on neutral ground, such as an investment bank's office, in a private room in a private club, or in an airport hotel away from town.

Discretion is the watchword because premature merger talk can cause concern among employees, customers, and suppliers, thus making the transaction more difficult to close. At the first meeting, the parties will get to know one another, define their businesses, and have a brief discussion of price. Some preliminary understanding of the price range may be necessary if the buyer is to have access to the target company's records. The buyer, of course, will make any statement on its part dealing with price subject to a thorough due diligence investigation of the target's operational and financial affairs.

## The Serious Negotiation Stage

As each party begins to collect data on the other party's business and begins its pricing analyses, the hard bargaining begins. The following are some suggestions on how to get the most out of the negotiation.

### *Understand the Personalities on the Other Side of the Table*
If you are the buyer, judge whether the target is risk averse or a maximizer of upside potential. Offer a fixed price to the former and a contingent deal to the latter. If you are selling, attempt to satisfy the corporate culture of the buyer. If the buyer demands detailed company descriptions and projections, do your best, within reason, to supply them. Protect proprietary data with a confidentiality agreement signed by the buyer.

### *Understand the Constituents of Fit*
The experience of the years is that the transactions that succeed the best are the ones where the fit is best. The company fit analysis, which is part of the due diligence process, is also a subject for discussion at the bargaining table. Each side should stress what it can bring to the postmerger process in terms of financial fit, business synergy, and management fit.

   *Financial fit* involves whether, ideally, the greater financial resources of one party can feed the faster growth potential of the other in a way that gives each investment returns superior to those that would occur were no transaction to take place.

   *Business synergy* involves exploring R&D, production, sales, marketing, or economies of scale, recognizing that incremental costs or less dramatic synergies than were anticipated are frequently the case. In the international arena, access to markets, proprietary technology, lower wage rates, and other factors are elements to consider under the business synergy heading.

   *Management fit* involves considerations such as whether either party has managers to be retained for whom there are limited growth opportunities within the company and the extent to which investment returns of either party could be enhanced by the infusion of new management. These and related matters need to be explored at the bargaining table.

## *Some Suggestions for Prospective Buyers*

As in the case of purely domestic transactions, a series of rules applies in international transactions.

- Do not approach targets with a condescending attitude that says that you are bigger and, hence, probably smarter than they are. Project yourself as ready, willing, and able to complete a fair and reasonable transaction.

- Avoid a long due diligence checklist until the parties get to know each other. Remember that deals are like courtships.

- Have a backup person on your team to field questions by target management in your absence.

- Do not haggle over small differences in the purchase price. You will either lose the deal or create postmerger ill will.

- Do not waste time. If it really is not a worthwhile proceeding, get out quickly. Prescreen carefully to avoid this time-wasting process. Recognize that international transactions often take longer to complete than domestic ones because of time differences and differences in legal, tax, accounting, and other issues.

- Develop with the target a clear plan for postmerger integration, including reporting relationships, plans for integrating the businesses, and details regarding financial accountability of the target to you.

- Remember that no deal is perfect and that you will have to work hard to optimize results in the postmerger period.

## *Some Suggestions for Prospective Targets*

- Do not assume that the buyer will behave badly on price and terms. Assume that the buyer wants the deal and will complete it on reasonable terms if you are fully prepared on price, terms, and fit.

- Do a good due diligence on the buyer. If it is a public company, get its annual reports, summaries of meetings with security analysts, and research reports of brokerage firms.

- Get good legal, tax, and accounting advice early enough in the deal so that you do not make a concession on price and terms that you will later regret. A concession once made is generally retrievable only at a cost. This advice takes on critical importance in international transactions where one may be dealing with a series of legal, tax, and accounting concepts that are very different from what one is accustomed to.

- Do not bargain for every last bit of the purchase price, and do not use price as an excuse for withdrawing from the transaction when, in reality, you never really wanted to sell at all. Make that decision *before* you get into the negotiation.

- Cooperate with the buyer to smooth out the people, financial, and operating problems that will inevitably attend the postmerger process.

## Some Suggestions for Prospective Buyers and Prospective Targets

*Professional Advisers.*   Good professional advisers can make the transaction considerably easier to complete. Use your *lawyer* (and local counsel in cross-border situations) not only as negotiator and drafter for the purchase contract and employment agreement (but only on the legal, not the business, terms of these), but also as someone who can check the legal and regulatory status of the other side, critical elements in cross-border deals. Use your *investment banker* to help you identify the other party to the deal and to assist in pricing and negotiating the business elements of the transaction. Your *accountant* (and local accountants in cross-border deals) can offer valuable advice on the tax and accounting implications of the deal and assist in the business review. Other experts like real estate appraisers, actuaries, and consulting engineers may be needed in specific instances.

*Negotiating Style.*   For both sides, a negotiating style should be calculated to minimize conflict while still getting all or most of what each side wants. To what purports to be a *nonnegotiable demand,* shift the dialogue to items that are easier to resolve. A difficult demand, when there are 30 items to bargain for, can become considerably easier if it is the only one left on the table. If a party must say no to something the other side wants, state why it is unacceptable and try to offer an alternative that it can live with. If a formula for fixing renewal rates on a long-term lease is needed, have one to present (e.g., increases in accordance with an index) and an alternative (e.g., three appraisers) if the first idea is rejected. *Trade off* a provision that will not cost much (additional registration rights on common stock issued) against something one wants very badly (strong indemnification language). Be mindful of cultural differences in negotiating style.

*Agreement in Principle.*   Not everybody likes agreements in principle. They have some usefulness because, even though they are not legally binding (except for a few items like confidentiality), they reflect a general understanding that most parties will honor, and they help avoid convenient loss of recollection by either side on key points. However, agreements in principle probably do not make sense unless the basic structure of the deal, including price and terms, has been worked out or unless the deal is near completion, at which point one might just as well go to the contract stage. In situations involving an agreement in principle in a sizable deal with a publicly held buyer or target, generally applicable disclosure rules will probably necessitate a public announcement. If the parties regard that disclosure as premature, it would be best not to have an agreement in principle.

*Management Contracts.*   Part of the serious negotiations will usually involve a consideration of management employment contracts for key executives. If the people who are going to run the company to be sold are not the recipients of the purchase price (as in a divestment), these contracts can be of critical importance.

They generally include length of term, base and bonus compensation, stock option or other equity participation, scope of responsibilities, and a restrictive covenant. Restrictive covenants in the United States are enforceable only if they are reasonable in nature, balancing the buyer's reasonable need for exclusivity and the executive's right to make a living in the field in which he or she has acquired expertise.

The final stages of the serious due diligence phase generally involve a great deal of time and paperwork. Detailed inspections of physical facilities and analyses of the historic, current, and projected operations and of the financial picture of each party take place. Side by side are lawyers working on things like assignments of proprietary rights from seller to buyer and regulatory clearance. In the United States, many transactions will require Hart-Scott-Rodino antitrust clearance. Cross-border transactions involving U.S. company targets may require regulatory approval under the Exon-Florio statute. Mergers involving U.S. targets in media or other industries may require additional kinds of regulatory scrutiny. In the on-again, off-again confusion typically found at this stage, there are always problems that, if not adequately addressed, threaten to abort the transaction. One such problem is whether the buyer or the target gets the benefit of recent earnings. Another is the selling shareholder who wants either an extremely generous employment contract or a very small one to maximize the earnout. Opposition to the transaction by employees or from the outside (the selling company's local community, suppliers, or customers), by regulatory bodies, or by trade unions or worker's councils may have to be anticipated and dealt with.

## The Contract Stage

Because a discussion of the parties' representations and warranties, covenants, conditions to closing, escrows, indemnifications, and other elements of acquisition agreements is beyond the scope of this chapter (for a brief description of these, see Checklist: Negotiation, IV.A–B), it is sufficient to point out that these are the very stuff of which transactions are made or not made. They form the basis on which the parties make disclosures respecting their businesses, in which prices and terms are set forth and for breach of which claims may be asserted. Thus, they need to be negotiated with care. Full recognition must be given to the unique drafting problems in international transactions, like governing law issues, remedies for breach of agreements that vary from country to country, and cultural differences— among them, the fact that contracts drafted by U.S. lawyers generally tend to be longer and more complex than those drafted by their non–U.S. counterparts.

## The Closing Stage

Contract signing and closing may be simultaneous, but generally they are not. At the closing in share transactions, the target's shareholders surrender their stock certificates, and the buyer issues its own shares or cash or whatever constitutes the consideration. In asset transactions, documents evidencing the title change on the assets and liabilities conveyed are executed. Among the many closing documents are opinions of counsel and/or those of the accountants. In the case of a publicly held target, and sometimes the buyer, a fairness opinion from an independent investment bank may be required or useful. Required approvals from national or regional regulatory bodies are produced, loan agreements are signed, checks for fees are drawn, and the transaction is concluded.

The M&A process frequently is long, complex, and demanding, but it is rather exciting as well. Length, complexity, and excitement tend to be multiplied in international transactions. However, with thoughtful planning, hard work, and some luck, the process can be a rewarding one for both sides.

# Checklist: Pricing

I.  Precede the pricing analysis with the most rigorous due diligence investigation available under the circumstances surrounding the specific transaction.

II. Where required, have the historical and the projected financial statements of either or both the buyer company and the target company restated up or down in accordance with the provisions of the buyer's accounting system. Typical areas of inquiry include the following (pay particular attention to these items in cross-border transactions, where the accounting conventions of the target's domicile vary materially from those in the West).
    A.  Inventories.
    B.  Travel, entertainment, and charitable contribution expenses.
    C.  Personnel.
    D.  Property, plant, equipment.
    E.  Impact of the transaction on projected earnings and cash flows.

III. Elements in a defensible comparative company analysis.
    A.  Pick the array of comparative companies properly.
        1.  Be sure that each comparative shares with the others and with the target company a series of operating and financial characteristics.
        2.  Know whether there is a sufficiently viable public market and financial data available to make these companies appropriate for comparative company purposes.
        3.  Be certain that no companies that might have been used are missing, and have a reason for all those that are excluded.
        4.  If the target is in a country outside the United States, one in which no good comparative companies can be found, come as close as possible in picking the best possible array of comparatives by using comparatives drawn from a country nearby to the target and adjusting investor appraisal ratios or by adjusting U.S. comparatives for differences in broad indexes between U.S. financial markets and those of the target's home country.
    B.  Compare the financial performance of the target company on a historical or reconstructed basis with the financial performance of the comparatives using all of the important ratios.
        1.  Generally applicable ratios (growth in revenues and profits, profit margins, return on equity, return on assets, debt-equity, working capital, and quick ratios).

      2.   Industry-specific ratios and data (sales per square foot, revenues per passenger mile, etc.).

  C.  Pick an appropriate price-earnings or price–cash flow multiple.

      1.   Choose P-Es that reflect a period appropriate to the business under scrutiny (P-Es based on average three- or five-year earnings for businesses in cyclical industries and on latest-year, latest-12-months, or projected earnings for growth companies, new businesses, or companies that have recently and materially changed the nature of their businesses).

      2.   The P-E or the price–cash flow multiple should be reasonably related to the target company's financial performance against that of the comparatives.

  D.  Explore the comparative company methodology to develop an assets approach to value.

      1.   Determine if there is a relationship between ratios (such as return on average common equity or average assets and market price–tangible book value) among the comparatives, on the basis of either the most recent fiscal year or an average over several of the most recent years.

      2.   Determine if a linear regression analysis will support this conclusion.

  E.  Weigh the results under the earnings-and-assets tests properly in light of all the facts in arriving at freely traded minority interest value.

  F.  Pick an appropriate premium for control.

      1.   Try to find relatively recent transfers of control for companies in the same general line of business.

      2.   Consult general data on premiums for control if data on relatively recent transfer of control data is sparse or nonexistent.

      3.   In applying the premium, give due recognition to the nature of the consideration offered (cash versus shares), the shares, and the historic, current, and projected results for the target company.

         a.   On a stand-alone basis.

         b.   Within the corporate framework of the buyer.

         c.   Within the corporate framework of a competitive bidder from inside or outside the target's home country.

IV.  Elements in a defensible single-company analysis.

  A.  Payback analysis.

      1.   The assumptions giving rise to the projections should be realistic in terms of the target company's projected growth or lack of growth.

      2.   Include incremental costs or benefits.

         a.   Factor in debt service from the transaction.

      b.  Include additions to property, plant, equipment, sales force, R&D, and so on, required of the target.

      c.  Give consideration to the ability to dispose of nonessential assets to generate cash.

3.  Identify and calculate potentially beneficial aspects of the transaction.

      a.  Cost reduction through elimination of redundant property, equipment, or personnel.

      b.  The positive effects of business synergy in R&D, procurement, sales, marketing, production, insurance, and so on, often offset by greater costs or smaller savings than had been anticipated.

4.  Consider at least three scenarios (conservative, optimistic, and average).

5.  Consider scenarios of the target company both on a stand-alone basis and within the framework of the buyer company.

6.  Consider characteristics unique to international transactions (including the effect of time and distance on the proposed business relationship between buyer and target).

      a.  Currency fluctuations.

      b.  Exchange controls.

      c.  Export controls.

      d.  Applicability of local laws to the business relationship.

      e.  High "social costs" respecting job terminations in certain countries.

      f.  Reconciliation of non–U.S. accounting concepts to generally accepted accounting principles (GAAP).

      g.  Tax effects of repatriation of earnings from affiliates outside the parent company's country.

      h.  Cultural differences.

      i.  Differences in legal systems.

B.  Discounted cash flow analysis.

1.  In determining the net free cash flows, discount rate, and terminal value elements, consider the items described in IV.A, respecting payback analysis.

2.  In selecting the number of years over which the net free cash flows are to be discounted, consider:

      a.  The relative certainty or variability of the projected cash flows.

      b.  The sensitivity of the ultimate conclusion to the terminal value element.

3.  In selecting the discount rate, consider:

      a.  Both the buyer's and the target's cost of debt and equity capital (which may vary greatly in cross-border deals).

      b. The increment over a risk-free rate that is appropriate for the specific target.

      c. The buyer's or the target's alternative opportunity costs.

   4. In selecting the approach to terminal value, consider:

      a. Whether the perceived risk elements are likely to be the same at the end of the discounting period as at the beginning.

      b. Whether relevant industry price-earnings or price–cash flow multiples have been relatively constant in the past.

      c. The advisability of a perpetual annuity approach.

   5. Use the discounted cash flow methodology to offer an internal rate of return calculation that may be used as a measure against company benchmark IRRs or to elect between alternate investment possibilities.

   6. Perform discounted cash flow analyses for the target on a stand-alone basis and as combined with the buyer.

C. Asset and liability analysis.

   1. Current assets.

      a. Does the cash account represent free cash available to the buyer (less that needed for the target company's working capital needs), or is it encumbered or restricted by compensating balance requirements or other elements?

      b. Are what purport to be marketable securities immediately convertible to cash, or is the holding of such securities so large in relation to the public market for them or trading in them so thin that they need to be discounted for a partial lack of marketability? (This may be especially true for securities traded on the newer non–U.S. exchanges.) Have such securities booked at the lower of cost or market been marked to the current market (allowing in international transactions for the effect of currency translations)?

      c. Are what purport to be receivables really receivables? How collectible are they? Has an aging schedule been prepared? How fast are they collectible? Has a "day's sales" schedule been prepared? What is the industry experience in the target company's home country?

      d. Is what purports to be inventory really inventory? What is the accounting procedure and how are disparities between U.S. GAAP and non–U.S. accounting principles to be reconciled? How fast is the inventory turning? Has an inventory turn schedule been prepared? To what extent have inventories been understated with tax avoidance in mind? What effect does a restatement of these have on asset value and earnings? What civil or criminal liabilities for tax evasion exist under relevant local law?

2. Fixed assets.
   a. Value each principal physical asset, giving recognition to the costs to acquire that asset new less physical deterioration and functional obsolescence.
   b. Consider fixed-asset value in light of the value of such assets on a fully depreciated basis, on a replacement value basis, on a going concern value basis, and on orderly and forced liquidation bases.
   c. Consider fixed-asset values as a part of buyer's opportunity cost (the value of assets in place versus having to build or buy them).
   d. Consider variables affecting asset value associated with the acquisition of overseas assets, including their insurability against loss, expropriation, and so on.

3. Intangible assets.
   a. Value patents, trademarks, copyrights, brand names, capitalized computer software, future publishing rights, back lists, and so on.
   b. Value covenants not to compete.
   c. Value favorable leases.
   d. Value trained workforce and the competence and sophistication of management.
   e. Value customer lists.
   f. Value business goodwill.

4. Current liabilities.
   a. Mark each current liability to market.
   b. Give particular care to the exposure of future earnings to the slow payment of accounts payable.

5. Long-term liabilities.
   a. Mark each long-term liability to market.
   b. Check affirmative and negative covenants in loan agreements to see if the target company is in or near a default status.

6. Off–balance sheet liabilities. Determine how price will be affected by off–balance sheet liabilities, actual or threatened, for items such as:
   a. Environmental liability.
   b. Tax liability.
   c. Product liability.
   d. Pension and retirement plans.
   e. Workplace liability.

         f.   Equal opportunity in employment liability.

         g.  Laws unique to the place in which the buyer or the target company operates.

V.  For transactions that might call for a contingent earnout:

  A.  Are there reasons to believe that historical earnings do not necessarily reflect future financial performance?

     1.  "Hidden" historic earnings.

     2.  Something in the future suggesting greater or lesser earnings than those historically achieved.

  B.  Have a variety of earnout scenarios been considered?

     1.  Cash versus common stock earnouts.

     2.  Average earnout (with or without hurdles).

     3.  Percentage of profit earnout.

     4.  Highest previous year earnout.

     5.  Earnouts based on revenues versus those based on earnings.

  C.  Should an earnout proposal be advanced—target's point of view?

     1.  Is it reasonably attainable?

         a.  How many dollars of "hidden" earnings can be uncovered?

         b.  How attractive does the future of the business appear to be?

         c.  Is the deal structure one that gives the target company a reasonable ability to earn the earnout?

            (1)  Does the acquisition agreement or management contract allow the target company management to control day-to-day affairs (including R&D and capital expenditures)?

            (2)  Are there limits on the buyer company's ability to upstream cash from the target company?

            (3)  Will the target company not be burdened with professional or home office expenses higher than those traditionally borne by it?

     2.  Will the target company's affiliation with the buyer make it harder or easier to attain the earnout?

     3.  Is there enough of an earnout to make it more attractive than a noncontingent deal? (How high a contingent P-E or what percentage of profits can be bargained for?)

     4.  Will the proposed earnout, if sought, bar tax-free reorganization treatment under relevant U.S. tax principles?

  D.  Should an earnout proposal be advanced—buyer's point of view?

     1.  Is the advantage of paying for results only when they are achieved offset by difficulty in attempting to integrate the businesses?

     2.  Will an earnout reduce incentive among buyer company personnel

      in like organizations within the buyer's company that have no such incentive?

    3. What will motivate the recipients of the earnout once the earnout terminates?

VI.   Does the transaction call for an installment sale?
- A. Is more than one payment to be made?
- B. Can it be coupled with an earnout?

VII.  Are there other means by which to mitigate risk?
- A. Milestone payments.
- B. Escrows.
- C. Installment sales with a right of set-off.
- D. Indemnifications.

# Checklist: Negotiation

I.  The finding stage.
A.  As buyer.
    1.  Make known your acquisition goals to those able to identify target companies.
        a.  Employees.
        b.  Investment or merchant bankers.
        c.  Commercial bankers.
        d.  Attorneys.
        e.  Accountants.
        f.  Suppliers.
        g.  Customers
    2.  Determine whether your internal staff is sufficient to find, screen, price, structure, and negotiate M&A transactions and to identify the various sources of financing that may be required to fund the transaction. Are such persons adequate to do cross-border M&A, too?
    3.  Clearly describe the characteristics you deem important in target companies.
        a.  Industry or industries in which you seek to acquire.
        b.  Target company size and price range.
        c.  Required investment returns to buyer.
        d.  Required market position of target.
        e.  Preferred species of payment (shares or cash).
        f.  Whether initial earnings or book value dilution is acceptable should other characteristics of the target company be attractive.
        g.  Whether target company senior management in place is a requirement (usually the case in cross-border transactions).
        h.  If particular kinds of fixed assets are sought, a description of these.
        i.  Characteristics unique to overseas acquisitions, including:
           (1)  Product or markets sought to be attacked.
           (2)  Whether certain characteristics of overseas acquisitions will be difficult to assimilate into the buyer's corporate culture (social costs, sensitive payments, etc.).
B.  As target or divestor.
    1.  Ascertain if your internal personnel are sufficient to do the job or whether you will require help from others.

2. Do the following:
   a. Price the company for sale.
   b. Describe the business in a descriptive memorandum after first receiving a signed confidentiality agreement from prospective investors. Take the time to:
     (1) Describe the founding of the business—when, where, by whom.
     (2) Detail the history and the principal milestones in the life of the business.
     (3) Tell how new products or services are conceived and developed.
     (4) Supply data respecting raw material procurement (historic availability, number of suppliers, supplier dependency, and price fluctuations and the ability to pass these along to customers).
     (5) Develop data respecting shipment of raw materials to the target company facility (by what means, who bears risk of loss in transit).
     (6) Supply information respecting the flow of production that transforms raw materials to finished goods (plant and equipment required, plant and equipment age, when these need to be replaced).
     (7) Offer details on plant, including ownership or lease terms and adequacy of plant and equipment for current and future needs.
     (8) Enumerate data on production and office personnel, including how many, adequacy of local labor pool, terms of existing union agreements or other agreements with labor, current and planned, and number of work shifts.
     (9) Develop sales and marketing data including compensation by whom and to whom, customer dependence issues, and details on marketing and advertising.
     (10) Set forth information on competition, market size, and market share.
     (11) Describe senior management (age, education, title, work history prior to joining the target company, history and current duties at the company, state of health, and compensation and benefits).
     (12) Enumerate share ownership, including number of shareholders and how much each owns.
     (13) Set forth legal and regulatory issues facing the target (pro-

duct or workplace liability, environmental, pension or tax claims, etc.).

(14) Include historical financial statements for five years together with projections and the assumptions on which they are based.

(15) Candidly explain the weak points as well as the strong points of the business.

(16) Generally describe plans for the business (same or new products or services, what the future goals are, and what it will take to get the goals accomplished).

(17) State why the business is for sale or why divestment is being considered.

(18) Explore why the company might be an especially attractive fit for an overseas acquirer.

    (a) Ability of the target company to provide new markets for the buyer, or vice versa.

    (b) Other attractions, such as technology, reduced labor costs, and reduced political risk.

II. The qualification and the preliminary investigation stages.

  A. As buyer.

    1. Carefully analyze the preliminary information on the target company.

    2. Make a preliminary assessment about whether the target company meets your acquisitions requirements.

    3. Make some preliminary judgments about completing an overseas transaction.

      a. Language and cultural barriers (including issues like tax compliance, sensitive payments, etc.).

      b. Legal implications.

        (1) Local antitrust laws.

        (2) "Social" laws.

        (3) Export control laws.

        (4) Currency control laws.

        (5) Laws affecting foreign ownership.

      c. Differences in the market versus conditions in your own market.

        (1) Labor conditions.

        (2) General economic conditions.

        (3) Competition and market share considerations.

      d. Issues relating to government policy.

        (1) Percentage of ownership allowed.

        (2)  Favoring or not favoring overseas ownership.

        (3)  Favoring or not favoring foreign suppliers.

     e.  Issues relating to political stability.

B.  As target.

    1.  Develop all the information you can on the prospective buyer.

    2.  Make a preliminary judgment on whether you really want to sell, assuming a reasonable price and reasonable terms. Consider the following.

     a.  Personal liquidity.

     b.  Management succession.

     c.  Access to:

        (1)  Funds with which to grow the business.

        (2)  A working relationship with the buyer with possibles for synergies in R&D, production, marketing, or otherwise to help grow the business.

     d.  Elements unique to an overseas acquisition.

        (1)  International expansion opportunities.

        (2)  Likelihood of greater autonomy.

C.  Both buyers and targets should enter into preliminary negotiations:

    1.  With a willingness to hear what the other side has to say.

    2.  Without a great number of checklists.

D.  Hold the first meeting at a neutral place.

    1.  Investment banker's office.

    2.  Airport hotel.

    3.  Private office.

    4.  Other site where confidentiality of discussion can be maintained.

III.  The serious negotiation stage.

  A.  In framing your position on price and terms, take into account the personalities of the other side.

    1.  "Downside risk hedgers" versus "upside potential maximizers."

    2.  The "corporate culture" of the other side.

     a.  Entrepreneurial versus structured.

     b.  Centralized versus decentralized.

     c.  Foreign versus domestic.

  B.  In planning for the serious negotiations, fully consider the complexities of an international merger and acquisition transaction.

    1.  Given what may be significant time differences and distances between countries, allow sufficient time for due diligence activities and negotiations.

    2.  Be prepared to investigate and try to design around specific problems in the international M&A.

  a. Cultural issues, like the need for consensus building in certain countries.

  b. The issues described in II.A.3.

C. In the serious negotiation, fully explore the constituents of fit (and especially the international implications of these).

  1. Financial fit.

  2. Business synergy fit.

  3. Management synergy fit.

D. Both sides should begin to discuss how the postmerger period will be handled in terms of:

  1. The kind of information about the deal to be given to executives and workers.

   a. By whom.

   b. In what form.

   c. At what point.

  2. Effecting business synergy by removing redundancies in:

   a. People.

   b. Property, plant, and equipment.

  3. Reporting relationships.

   a. Who from target to whom from buyer.

   b. Nature of written reports.

    (1) Frequency.

    (2) Their form.

    (3) Nature of operational and financial information required.

E. DOs and DON'Ts for buyers.

  1. Avoid buyer hubris. Being the buyer does not make you the superior company in the transaction. Present yourself as ready, willing, and able to complete a transaction that is fair and reasonable to both sides.

  2. Avoid long due diligence checklists until the parties get to know each other. Remember that mergers and acquisitions are like courtships.

  3. Be sufficiently well staffed to conduct a good due diligence investigation from an operational and a financial point of view, but have a clearly defined team leader and a second in command to that person.

  4. Do not negotiate for the last bit of purchase price lest the transaction fail to close over trivial amounts of money or close with a sense of ill will from the other side.

  5. Consider the postmerger integration process (see III.D).

  6. Balance the attractive against the unattractive elements of the transaction, recognizing that no deal is perfect.

F.  DOs and DON'Ts for target companies.
1.  Assume that the buyer will pay a reasonable price for your business, but only if you are thoroughly prepared to defend your asking price and have appropriately described your company.
2.  Perform the best possible due diligence on the buyer.
    a.  If it is publicly held, obtain:
        (1)  Its annual and interim reports.
        (2)  Summaries of its meetings with securities analysts.
        (3)  Research reports of brokerage firms.
    b.  Whether or not it is publicly held:
        (1)  Ask to meet executives in companies previously acquired by the buyer.
        (2)  Make your own evaluation of the transaction from a business point of view.
3.  Get good legal, tax, accounting, and investment banking advice early enough in the transaction so that you do not make concessions whose full implications you have failed to consider.
4.  Do not try to exact the last drop of purchase price or to use price as an excuse when you did not really want to sell in the first place.
5.  Cooperate with the buyer in addressing the people, financial, and operational problems necessarily associated with the postmerger process.
G.  Intelligent use of professional advisers. In planning the international merger or acquisition, consider how you will staff the transaction in your home country and abroad with:
1.  Attorneys to:
    a.  Negotiate legal and tax points and draft agreements.
    b.  Determine the legal and regulatory issues requiring work.
    c.  Issue legal opinions on the legal capacity of the parties to complete the agreement.
2.  Accountants to:
    a.  Perform the audit work with related opinions.
    b.  Offer assistance on tax issues.
    c.  Perform a business review of the financial aspects of the target company's business.
3.  Investment or merchant bankers, finders, and brokers for:
    a.  Introductions to the other party to the transaction.
    b.  Assistance in pricing and negotiation.
    c.  In the case of target companies or divestors, preparing the selling memorandum to be sent to a group of prospective buyers.
4.  Other professionals sometimes used.
    a.  Real estate and property appraisers.

        b. Environmental consultants.

        c. Consulting engineers.

        d. Actuaries.

        e. Marketing consultants.

H. Whether as buyer or target, develop a negotiating style congruent with both cultures and calculated to minimize conflict while getting all or much of what you want.

    1. If there is disagreement over nonnegotiable demands, shift the dialogue to matters easier to resolve, and go back to the difficult ones after the easier ones have been settled.

    2. State why a proposal advanced by the other side is unacceptable to you, and, if possible, try to help solve the other side's problem in a way that will be acceptable to you.

    3. Trade off provisions that do not cost you much against provisions you want very badly.

I. Agreements in principle.

    1. Uses.

        a. To reflect a general understanding between the parties.

        b. To avoid convenient loss of recollection on key business points later in the transaction.

    2. Limitations.

        a. Except as to a limited number of terms, they are not legally binding, although they may impose an obligation to negotiate in good faith.

        b. They are not usable too early in the transaction, if the basic structure has not been worked out, nor too late in the transaction, when one might as well go to contract.

        c. They cannot be used with a publicly owned party if the nature of the transaction requires an unwanted public disclosure.

J. Management contracts for key executives of the target—whether as buyer or as a key executive of the target company, consider with counsel:

    1. The desirability of entering into such agreements.

    2. The terms of such agreements, including differences in compensation and perks for U.S. and non–U.S. citizens in the United States or abroad.

        a. Scope of authority.

        b. Base and incentive compensation.

        c. Fringe benefits.

        d. Equity participation (e.g., stock options).

        e. A reasonable restrictive covenant.

K. Typical issues in the late due diligence stage—whether as buyer or target, be prepared for:

1. Detailed inspections of physical facilities.
2. Negotiation on financial areas giving rise to questions, including all of the areas described in the pricing checklist.
3. Assignment of proprietary rights.
4. Issues dealing with regulatory clearance.
   a. The U.S. Securities and Exchange Commission and comparable bodies outside the United States.
   b. Other regulatory clearance designed to protect certain national interests (Federal Trade Commission, U.S. Justice Department, Interstate Commerce Commission, Federal Reserve Board, Department of Defense, Exon-Florio, Hart-Scott-Rodino clearance, and their overseas counterparts).
   c. Shareholder approval if required.
   d. Clearance required to obtain funding (documents involved in rights offerings and other public filings on securities used as purchase consideration in the transaction).
5. Issues involving target company shareholders.
   a. "Sellers' remorse."
   b. Contractual issues.
      (1) Purchase agreement.
      (2) Selling shareholders.
6. Opposition to the transaction:
   a. From regulatory authorities.
   b. From other would-be buyers.
   c. From local communities.
   d. From workers or their unions.

IV. The contract and the closing stages. Consider the typical acquisition agreement as a series of promises and limitations by buyer and target, bound within specific time frames.
   A. Forms of contractual promises and limitation.
      1. Warranties and representations—a statement that certain facts are true or correct.
      2. Covenants—promises to act or to refrain from acting.
      3. Conditions to closing.
      4. Indemnifications.
      5. Escrows.
   B. Time frames in which promises and limitations are effective.
      1. As of the date of the target company's most recent audited or unaudited financial statements.
      2. In the period between contract and closing.

       3.  At the closing.

       4.  After the closing.

  C.  Closing. Consider the typical characteristics of the closing.

       1.  May be, but is usually not, simultaneous with the contract.

       2.  Typical happenings at the closing.

          a.  Purchase agreements and other agreements conveying title to the target company are signed.

          b.  Opinions of counsel and of the accountants and, with public targets (and sometimes buyers), an investment bank's fairness opinion are delivered.

          c.  Documents providing the financing are executed.

          d.  Regulatory approvals are received.

          e.  Investment banking, legal, and accounting fees are paid.

# PART SEVEN

# Special Topics

In Chapter 13, Alexander E. Fisher of A. Fisher & Co. and Richard M. Inserra of Union Carbide discuss the additional levels of complexity in the risk management associated with cross-border transactions. They cover risk analysis of assets and liabilities, including reserves and off–balance sheet liabilities; existing insurance; safety and loss control; environmental issues; liability of owners, directors, and officers; local government regulations; and political risk. Then the authors present a framework for a risk management due diligence report and provide a checklist for what should be included in that report.

In Chapter 14, Richard F. McClurg provides a detailed analysis of the human resource aspects in outbound acquisitions by U.S. companies, based on his extensive hands-on experience as a human resources consultant. He begins with preacquisition evaluation criteria, including commonly experienced cultural and government issues. Then, staffing strategy and planning; compensation, benefit, and severance policies; training and team building; and transitional support programs are discussed. A checklist is included that provides a framework for the step-by-step identification and management of human resource problems in overseas acquisitions.

In Chapter 15, Cynthia N. Wood, human resources consultant and a professor in the School of Business and Economics, Longwood College, and Richard Porter of Young & Rubicam treat the often-mismanaged area of postmerger integration. The authors concentrate on inbound transactions. This chapter covers the key indicators of postdeal success or failure that should be considered in the due diligence process and then provides a detailed analysis of the important postmerger integration issues. A series of examples and a checklist are provided covering general considerations; communications; overall organizational structure; postmerger implementation of functional areas; people; national and organizational culture; and, finally, mission, values, and common language.

# 13

# Risk Management in Cross-Border Transactions

*Alexander E. Fisher*
*Richard M. Inserra*

Country borders and cultural differences do not change the basic risk management approach to cross-border transactions but rather add an additional level of complexity to such transactions. In *all* deals, local or cross-border, risk management is an integral part of the due diligence process and may materially affect the price and the structure of the transaction.

The topics discussed in this chapter should aid those assessing risk in responding to the challenges presented by cross-border transactions and likewise inform those to whom such people report as to the areas of risk in the deal.

## THE NATURE OF THE TRANSACTION

The first step is to understand the nature and the scope of the transaction; and a careful reading of the entire draft contract, particularly the insurance, indemnification, and operating agreement sections, is a good starting point. Understanding can further be enhanced through discussion with those involved in the negotiations.

Typical transactions (domestic or cross-border) are mergers and acquisitions (M&A) or joint ventures/strategic alliances. However, every deal is unique and the individual characteristics of the transaction must be reviewed. In the case of transactions involving a partial or an entire change of ownership (as distinguished, for example, from a strategic alliance in which no such change takes place), the acquirer may buy shares of the seller. This creates a level of obligation for all of the seller's liabilities. In transactions in which *assets* are acquired, the acquirer (with some exceptions) acquires only those assets and liabilities specifically assumed. Thus, the form of the transaction also sets the boundaries of risk.

In mergers and acquisitions there will usually be a surviving party with responsibility for the liabilities of both parties. Hence, a careful review of the history of both companies is important in identifying the risks assumed by the combined entity. Old, discontinued products, manufacturing procedures, or personnel practices may give rise to future claims, which may be the responsibility of the surviving company or may be left behind in a nonacquired entity. For example, in the United States, manufacturers of heavy machinery that divested these operations years ago have nonetheless been held liable for bodily injury because no company with sufficient assets existed to pay the loss; and noisy workplaces and poor hearing protection programs going back in time as much as 30 years have created increasing numbers of hearing loss claims. There may also be a specific time limit for the retention of certain liabilities (e.g., the period of a statute of limitations) that would need to be addressed in developing future risk management programs. In either event, the new entity's exposure to specific risk clearly needs to be presented to management of that company. Joint ventures may require a different approach. Absent a change in control, it is typical for the parties to collaborate on a program designed to identify and to deal with the risks associated with the venture.

If there is any interdependency between the joint venture and its constituent parties, resulting exposures must be identified, analyzed, and quantified. Responsibility for any loss to the venture as a result of the interdependency must also be clear: does it belong to a constituent party or to the joint venture itself? If the latter, the exposure should be minimized, retained (if within acceptable limits), or transferred via insurance.

Joint venture structures are on the rise for a variety of reasons, such as the need for a local partner; interest in obtaining technology, skills, or knowledge; and, of course, capital. Developing countries, in particular, have a need to expand their economic base, to create jobs, and to improve technical skills while at the same time ensuring a local presence. As more fully set forth in this book, the growth of joint ventures has been particularly strong in the Asia/Pacific region and in China as countries seek access to technology and global markets.

Certain strategic alliances (not formal joint ventures) may not give rise to additional legal liabilities. However, additional risks may be created that parties should recognize. For example, a strategic alliance with a key supplier may create contingent business exposures from the failure of the supplier to meet certain supply requirements or quality standards.

During contract and document review, each party must recognize that the interests of the other members of the same company's due diligence team may not completely align. Thus, a party may retain liability for products manufactured prior to the closing. Operational personnel may regard this as acceptable, but the legal and risk management representatives may seek greater clarification. Can the date of manufacture be clearly identified? Is it clear who has responsibility for injury that occurs after the closing from a product that was manufactured prior to the closing? Does the surviving entity have the financial strength to bear the liability, or are escrow funds or insurance necessary to satisfy the liability? If the target is to retain liability for suits generated from products manufactured or services provided prior to the sale and if there is a continuing relationship with the customer, what mechanism will be used to settle claims amicably so as to retain the customer for the buyer?

## THE OPERATIONS REVIEW

Gathering the necessary documents, data, and reports to produce the risk management due diligence report is critical to doing a thorough job. The checklist provided at the conclusion of this chapter suggests, at a minimum, what should be produced and reviewed during the course of a thoughtful risk management due diligence process.

### Assets

Identifying the property, plant, equipment, and inventories that accompany a transaction may appear to be the easiest part of the risk management due diligence review, but this is usually not the case. Obtaining accurate replacement costs or even historical costs for various assets may be difficult or impossible. The same may be true of location addresses, particularly for off-site storage areas. Contingent exposures will not be evident from documents. Such information is likely to be developed only by asking the right questions of the right people during the due diligence process and having the answers flow into the warranties and representations section of the agreement and the schedules thereto.

### Liabilities

Assessing the liabilities of the new venture or of the seller can be a crucial element in the risk management due diligence review. Accruals for self-insured exposures, such as Workers' Compensation, pension liability, employee benefits, and other liability claims, are key points on which to focus.

Are reserves realistically valued, reflecting adjustments for inflation and for other circumstances requiring a change in the claims estimate? Who set the reserves and what methodology was used? Have specific claims development factors been calculated based on the particular claims history of the target company? Are the claims reserves calculated to show their cost, if they were to be paid out during the current year?

Maturity of the reserves should also be analyzed to determine cash flows and payout patterns. "Cash flow" programs that require minimal up-front cash outlays and monthly reimbursement of *paid* losses only may have reserves that are understated and unreliable. Under such programs, it may take years for the cash flow to reach its normalization level (when the claims payoffs start to level off). The reasons for the implementation of any cash flow plan should also be investigated. If the reserves appear inadequate, the transaction price may have to be renegotiated. On the other hand, conservative, well-established reserves may result in greater value for the acquirer or for the joint venture should the reserves fail to fully develop to projected levels. If time allows, a full, independent actuarial review of the reserves should be initiated. The larger the transaction, the more essential this actuarial work often becomes.

Managers should also be alert for exposures and liabilities that may have been overlooked in the past. This could occur because certain assets or liabilities of a corporate affiliate to be divested may be quite material given the smaller size of the affiliate but not material in the context of the larger divesting parent.

Due diligence visits are important and should provide the following:

- Information on the construction and physical protection of a facility and how it is maintained and operated, as well as local management's response to engineering/loss control recommendations and safety issues.

- Evidence of whether unprotected or poorly protected operations require a capital investment or higher insurance costs.

- An awareness that special equipment or machinery, not available except with long lead times, can indicate the potential for long downtime in the event of a loss involving such equipment.

- Data evidencing supplier or customer dependency.

- Information on the accounting principles employed, which may be helpful in identifying inventory or other asset discrepancies.

- Variance between the cost allocations for insurance and the real risk exposure.

- The presence of any obvious flood or earthquake exposures, such as nearby rivers, streams, or dams, and whether there had been losses from such exposure in the past.

While at the facility whose risk elements are to be assessed, it is necessary to obtain a working understanding of the manufacturing or production process involved. Questions related to planned or foreseeable changes can also provide a better understanding of current and projected risks.

The use of outside contractors to provide security, maintenance, and other services will also need to be ascertained. What liabilities are being assumed or transferred under contracts with these service contractors? Do such contractors have access to sensitive areas of the business? What controls exist as to such access? A review of contracts for outside services is a necessary part of the due diligence process, with particular attention to indemnity provisions of each contract and the potential damage flowing from the contractor's employee's negligence.

A thorough analysis of the operations having been completed, recommendations for a risk management program need to be developed for incorporation into the due diligence report. Most often, in an acquisition, the target's risk management program is incorporated into that of the buyer at the same levels of risk retention and under the same coverage structures. However, the acquisition of a distinctly different business may require different retentions or different coverages. If an acquisition is a smaller business of the same sort as that of the buyer, a reevaluation of retention levels may be appropriate because the larger company would probably have a greater capacity to bear increased risk. A highly leveraged company that makes an acquisition with additional debt may choose to maintain or even to reduce retentions. In fact, lender requirements may be more stringent in a deal involving substantial debt such that the lender, to protect the quality of the insured's financial statement, will not permit substantial deductibles or self-insured retentions.

A joint venture will probably require agreement on coverage limits, deductibles, and so on. However, each party should do its due diligence and develop independent recommendations. Consensus on a program can then be worked out by the venture partners. Establishing such a program can be a difficult exercise if the coventurers have different philosophies regarding risk retention (or aversion) and coverage type and limits. For instance, a Japanese firm that is risk averse and a French company comfortable with large risk retentions would be challenged to develop an insurance program that meets the needs of both.

## SPECIFIC AREAS FOR REVIEW

Are liability policies "claims made," requiring an incident *and* reporting of that incident during the policy term; or are the policies "occurrence," requiring only that the incident occur during the time the coverage was in effect? If the former, are there any coverage gaps due to changing insurers and retroactive dates? If there were prior policies, were claims made and coverage changed? Were there extensions for reporting claims? If so, for how long? If there are gaps in coverage due to gaps in the retroactive dates, the exposure must be carefully analyzed. Consider a form of retroactive cover to "close the gaps," and provide coverage on claims (1) for incidents occurring prior to coverage being in force; (2) where there was coverage in force but the claim was not reported in the required time period of the policy; (3) relating to the bankruptcy of an insurer where there was no prior knowledge of the claim; and (4) where policy limits are insufficient based on the current legal climate.

It is necessary to obtain complete copies of all current policies and all previous general liability (including umbrella and excess) policies. Such policies and workers' compensation policies, or at least a list of the insurers that provided the coverage for all assumed liabilities, should be disclosed in a schedule to the underlying agreement.

Liability policies such as auto liability and general liability and workers' compensation policies should also be reviewed. Retrospective plans dealing with loss-sensitive issues will usually have excess insurance that limits the liability of the policyholder for any one claim and/or an aggregate feature that defines the limit for all claims during the policy period.

The end use of the seller's or the venture's products and the manner in which such products are distributed should be determined as well. Liability could be significant if the buyer is the only "deep pocket" around in the event of injury to an ultimate user. This is especially true for medical and aviation products.

It is always necessary to identify any insurers that are insolvent or in "run-off." A carrier that is in a run-off mode generally has ceased accepting new business. Therefore, there may be a shortfall between its liabilities and its assets available to pay claims. In addition, one must review audit features of current policies being assumed to determine if additional (debit) or return (credit) premiums are likely to appear upon such an audit. In particular, one must be aware of any unusual coverage extensions or restrictions.

Property valuations should be compared for consistency from plant to plant and from building to building. It is not unusual to find discrepancies, especially if the plants are in different areas of the country or the world, if the buildings were built or modified over many years and if valuation methods have changed. Countries with high inflation rates may have property values modified *monthly* to maintain insurance at current values. For example, companies in Argentina and Brazil employed monthly indexing practices in the 1970s and 1980s. The buyer should also compare values of the replacement of *productive* capacity versus current replacement values because new construction methods often result in the replacement of the damaged asset at a lower cost than may be shown on the valuation. Also, physical protection requirements may be different requiring further adjustments to the cost of replacing or restoring a damaged facility.

Have captive insurers been used to assume risks? If so, how were premiums developed? Are reserves adequate, and were they determined or verified by an independent actuarial study? Did or does the captive insure third parties, or has it participated in any reinsurance pools? If it has accepted business from unrelated parties and/or participated in reinsuring pools of unrelated business, there may be no reliable figures available to determine what liabilities may be incurred through these books of business. This is true because there normally is a long lag time, or "tail," for claims to fully develop with little information available to the reinsurer in the interim. If the captive carrier is to be acquired, will it be continued, combined with the acquiring company's insurance subsidiary, or put into a run-off situation? If the captive remains with a divesting company, are there any obligations to pay premiums under retrospective or other programs?

## SAFETY AND LOSS CONTROL

A review of any written safety and loss control programs is necessary to determine the scope of formal programs. The programs should be assessed to determine whether they are generic or specifically adapted to the operations. Do senior officers of the company endorse these programs and take an active role in the safety efforts of the organization?

It is necessary to verify that all written procedures are followed at all the locations to be acquired. This includes production facilities, offices, warehouses, and technical centers. The buyer should ascertain whether there are formal safety training programs for new employees and refresher courses or ongoing training. A good guide as to the quality of the safety program is to compare incident and severity rates against those of comparable companies, which can be obtained through trade associations, publications of the Department of Labor, or from third-party claims administrators.

A company's dedication to loss control and safety may be evidenced by a system that offers rewards for good loss control and safety experiences and penalizes bad ones.

## ENVIRONMENTAL ISSUES

Whether cross-border or not, any acquisition of property requires a particularly careful due diligence effort to assess the extent of air, ground, and ground water pollution. This due diligence effort is important, and it can be a key point in the negotiations. Thus, if unexpected or undisclosed on-site ground contamination is found, the cost of cleanup needs to be determined and an adjustment to the purchase price negotiated. The impact of national and local toxic tort issues is perhaps the most significant contingent liability in any transaction.

The starting point of an environmental review is a complete assessment of all sites to be acquired. Should any contamination be found, the prospect of migration from the affected site into ground water must be considered with an eye to establishing responsibility for injury or damage to third parties. At a site where only a portion of the operation is being acquired and the target has operations that may continue to emit pollutants, the need to defend against future claims may require indemnification from the seller. If the hazard is sufficiently greater, indemnification of the entire purchase price may be insufficient.

Environmental laws in the United States may be the strictest in the world, but other countries are expanding their laws to impose stricter liability on those responsible for pollution. This trend is likely to continue throughout the world for the foreseeable future. In recent years, Germany and Switzerland have increased their environmental standards for manufacturing industries. Competent environmental counsel should be sought for all acquisitions involving property. Environmental assessments should include consideration of all prior uses and operations of the site, particularly in the United States. This is because the strict liability provisions of the Comprehensive Environmental Response Compensation and Liability Act (Superfund) hold the current owner responsible even if it never conducted any type of operation on the site.

## LIABILITY OF OWNERS, DIRECTORS, AND OFFICERS

Liability of officers and directors is typically more of an issue in U.S. transactions because U.S. laws impose greater responsibility on such parties than do laws elsewhere. Often, business combinations are challenged in court in class action lawsuits. Despite recent legislation calculated to limit the impact of such suits, under U.S. securities laws the threat is nonetheless real.

If the acquisition requires the resignation of some or all of the acquired company's board of directors and certain officers, it may be necessary to provide ongoing directors and officers coverage for claims made after the completion of the transaction. Due to typical change of control provisions in the policies that terminate, such policies would leave the directors and officers of the acquired company without any coverage unless the extended claims reporting provision of the policy was activated, an idea that makes sense if there is a reasonable likelihood of claims. The extension of indemnification and director and officer (D&O) coverage for former directors and officers is likely to be an issue for any acquisition involving a U.S. company. However, discussions with U.S. insurance and deal counsel should make clear the nature of the exposure.

Indemnification can be for a specific period, or it can be unspecified in duration. However, *should D&O insurance be canceled or changed, these coverage extensions may be lost*. Because most suits naming officers and directors as defendants are filed within several months of any deal, thus triggering the extended reporting provisions of existing D&O policies, coverage will usually exist.

## GOVERNMENT REGULATIONS

The key point here is to be aware that each locale will have government regulations with which companies must comply. Every country in the world has different insurance regulations and requirements. A company making a cross-border acquisition may find it costly to buy local coverage due to government controlled rates (tariffs) that offer little or no cost savings for increasing the deductible. Many countries in South America and in the Asia/Pacific region have such restrictions. For an organization used to accepting significant risk and to using larger deductibles to reduce insurance costs, this can be quite frustrating. International insurance brokers or advisers should be utilized to provide information on each country's rules and regulations and to suggest strategies to harmonize corporate insurance strategies with local requirements.

In the United States, myriad government organizations, such as the Occupational Safety and Health Administration (OSHA) and the Environmental Protection Agency (EPA), have strict requirements that must be adhered to. Failure to comply may result in substantial fines and penalties. In addition, equal opportunity and antidiscrimination laws, including the Americans with Disabilities Act (ADA) and Employment Practices Liability, may be viewed as unusual by overseas companies seeking to expand into the United States. Local regulations are always changing, and their impact on a deal must be viewed in each transaction. Thus, for example, expanding product liability laws in Europe, Japan, and other parts of Asia may require review.

## POLITICAL RISK

Any cross-border transaction brings with it the possibility of *political risk*, which may be defined as the potential for loss resulting from arbitrary government action. Such risks are most often found in developing countries where uncertainty as to the continuity of governmental policies and programs is genuine. Moreover, events having an adverse impact on businesses can be initiated by other than a foreign government. For example, the national government of a global company's home country could institute a trade embargo against another country. Over the years the U.S. government has imposed embargoes that adversely impacted many U.S. companies. Political risks can be both obvious and subtle, as there are a great many governmental actions that can give rise to a loss. Nevertheless, these risks may be categorized as follows:

- *Confiscation, expropriation, and nationalization.* Coverage for these is often referred to as "CEN" coverage. These risks relate to a company being deprived of its assets by the host government. The assets may be taken outright or over a period of time ("creeping expropriation") and may take a variety of forms, such as discriminatory taxes, restrictive regulations or operating criteria, or other actions that diminish the value of the enterprise.
- *War/political violence.* This is an obvious risk in certain areas of the world, but one for which limited insurance exists. An investment in Kuwait might, in view of the Gulf War, stimulate interest in this type of coverage.
- *Currency inconvertibility.* New currency restrictions may prevent conversion of local currency into a freely traded currency or may delay or block currency transfer. Coverage is generally not provided for exchange rate fluctuation.
- *Contract frustration.* Such risks involve the outright repudiation of a contract as well as governmental interference in the contract's performance that affects the business venture. Examples include the curtailment or restriction of a favorable raw material supply agreement or the revocation of import or export licenses.

Assessing political risks is a challenging exercise for any party. Sources usable to determine political risk include consultants in the jurisdiction that is the source of the risk, the joint venture partner (if there is one), local counsel, or appropriate governmental agencies, such as the U.S. Department of State. There is no substitute for a thorough understanding of the political risks associated with a cross-border business transaction to fully assess the potential for such risks.

Whether to buy political risk coverage is often based on the size of the investment and the perceived level of political risk. If such coverage is elected, the parties will have nontraditional markets from which to choose. For instance, export credit agencies in a variety of countries, such as Export-Import Bank (United States), SACE (Italy), Hermes (Germany), and so on, may offer coverage for companies based there. The Overseas Private Investment Corporation (OPIC) is available to firms based in the United States; and the Multilateral Investment Guarantee Agency (MIGA), part of the World Bank, is available to all companies.

These governmental and quasi-governmental insurers are the only substantial providers of war/political violence coverage and, therefore, can be quite important to any company planning a venture in an area of the world where such an exposure is a threat. Certain restrictions (limits in the amount of coverage) and qualifications apply, and it is appropriate to make application and receive approval prior to making any final investment decision.

Private insurance carriers, such as AIG and Lloyd's, provide most of the other types of political risk insurance and may be more flexible than the public markets. However, there may be capacity limitations for certain risks and for specific countries.

## THE DUE DILIGENCE REPORT

Management should receive a concise summary of major findings and recommendations on risk. At a minimum these should include the following:

- An insurance pro forma outlining the costs of including the target operation within the acquiring company's insurance program. These costs should be compared to the costs currently projected for such coverage. Increases and decreases should be clearly indicated.
- A comparison of current risk retentions and deductibles relative to the company's risk management practices. It should be determined whether different retentions will apply to the newly acquired operation and why.
- An outline of significant coverage improvements or other benefits that the acquirer's program will provide to the newly acquired business.
- A highlighting of any significant exposures presented from the new business (floods, earthquake, or other hazards) and an indication of any coverage sublimits, restrictions, or uninsurable exposures.
- A description of any safety, loss control, or loss trends that are either a negative or a positive to the deal.
- An identification and quantification of any additional cost issues (e.g.,

"loss reserves are understated by $500,000") or potential cost benefits (e.g., "a retrospective refund of $300,000 is expected").

- An indication as to the timing for integrating the acquired assets with the buyer's risk management and insurance program. Usually the best approach is to do this before closing the transaction.
- A discussion of whether there are any limits requiring an increase or whether the acquired assets may require different coverages or sublimits.

## SUMMARY

Risk management in cross-border transactions provides an opportunity to add value and to contribute to the overall success of the deal. Although each transaction is unique, the basic concepts discussed in this chapter provide a solid foundation on which to approach any cross-border transaction.

# Checklist: Risk Management

I. Examine the following:
   A. Copies of all current insurance policies and descriptions, summaries, and lists covering:
      1. Employees, properties, products, or operations (including fire, public liability, and vehicular insurance policies) for as many years as records exist.
      2. Liability, umbrella, workers' compensation, and other policies for as many years as records exist.
      3. Insurance costs for the business to be acquired and exposures for the past three years.
      4. Insurance values for the business (indicating the replacement cost) for buildings, machinery and equipment, inventory, vehicles, and cargo and transportation equipment. These should include worksheets dealing with business interruption. Appraisals if available on physical assets should be reviewed.
      5. Locations with descriptions of their construction and protection and ownership. If leased, responsibility of tenant to insure or to pay additional rent for taxes, insurance, and/or common area charges.
      6. Loss prevention surveys relating to the business for the past three years with all outstanding recommendations identified.
      7. Claim and loss experience relating to the target's business for the past five years with an explanation and identification of all claims over a minimum dollar sum.
      8. Insurance company inspection reports relating to the target's business for the past three years.
      9. Deductibles or self-insured retentions for each coverage listed in items 1–8.
      10. Agreements for all open retrospective ratings, self-insured retentions, and deductible plans, together with the last retrospective adjustment for each year in which a retrospective rating plan was in force. One should use all of the applicable factors to determine potential future liabilities.
      11. Balance sheet accruals for any of the items listed in item 10. Actuarial reports, if any, to support valuations and ultimate payouts or future liabilities.
      12. Open OSHA citations, the current status of compliance, and copies of any similar citations for international operations.

13. Any assumptions of liabilities or waivers of subrogation provided to any third parties.
14. Any special insurance requirements for third parties, such as providing coverage for goods in care, custody, and control; or the agreement to extend a liability policy due to contractual requirements for a third party.
15. Current insurance brokers used by the target and the identity of third-party claims administrators.
16. Leases for all locations and for all equipment.
17. The potential liability impact of operations or products that were discontinued in the past 10 years.

B. Copies of financial data covering:
1. Financial statements including a pro forma for the transaction and a business plan for the next five years; also, annual reports covering the most recent three years for public companies.
2. Losses shown as valued on same date for a policy year (loss triangulation) and actual payment projection of claim payments.

C. Copies of operating data covering:
1. Safety manual and safety award programs, if any, for supervisors, managers, and production staff and a description of training programs for new hires and continuing training for existing employees; also, a corporate organizational chart indicating responsibility for safety issues.
2. Any current offering memorandum or prospectus that describes the products being purchased and their use.
3. Sales by geographic area.
4. Product marketing and distribution/shipping information.
5. Environmental issues and/or site information, including reserve estimates for remedial action and a list of any citations.
6. Biographical information on current officers and directors.
7. Any available written guidelines relative to sexual harassment and age, race, gender, or other discrimination.
8. The presence or absence of security posed with insurers used to collateralize any insurance programs and identification of the amount, the insurer, and the year(s) involved.
9. The names and telephone numbers of:
   a. Chief financial officer.
   b. Risk or insurance manager.
   c. Director of human resources.
   d. Director of safety.
   e. Plant managers.

# 14

# Human Resources Concerns

*Richard F. McClurg*

## IMPACT OF HUMAN RESOURCES

Despite best intentions, human resources issues are largely overlooked until after the deal is done and publicized. The players typically investigate and understand the legal, financial, economic, marketing, and production aspects of the venture. Confidentiality and the vagueness of many of the human resources issues, when compared to the relative certainty of technologies, production capacities, distribution systems, and laws, contribute to this deferral. But failure to consider people issues puts the whole venture in jeopardy. Without the people there may be no business!

If human resources aspects have not been considered before the deal is done, attention must be focused on them immediately upon announcement. Employees know that mergers, acquisitions, and joint ventures usually result in significant reductions in head count and in change. Unless addressed rapidly and professionally, apprehension exists, whether real or perceived, diluting performance, motivation, and commitment. The culture, skills, and experience of the current employees have probably shaped the business. How the organization works internally is a major factor, for better or worse. Resulting employee unrest may be enough to undermine all the successful planning previously done.

Employee goodwill and cooperation could be more important than the company's bricks and mortar.

Clearly, the success of a global venture often depends on the proper management of human resources. In a study of British acquisitions by Egon Zender International, 59 percent of successful acquirers gave their combined organizational structures a clear "people shape," whereas 61 percent of acquirers with subsequent problems focused exclusively on the business.

Human resources professionals offer a unique perspective and an ability to communicate in the field of mergers, acquisitions, and joint ventures because of their obligations to both management and the employees. They are in the best position to gain the trust and respect of the target company employees and to objectively communicate their ideas and represent their interests. As a part of management the human resources team can establish truthful and effective communications with all of the target company employees. This is important because the concern of other management people is often limited to their own functional area, with little responsibility to employees outside of their jurisdiction and usually no time to pursue other causes.

Early involvement of a human resources team allows business enterprises to successfully understand and navigate the myriad laws, practices, cultural traditions, and customs that concern the treatment of personnel during and after a merger or an acquisition. It also encourages the team to take early ownership of a project, which should potentially be very challenging, exciting, and satisfying. Equally important, plans and practices may be developed and initiated that will meet pressing short-term concerns as well as long-term organizational and employee objectives and needs.

Because of the complexity of issues surrounding establishment of overseas businesses, this chapter will focus almost entirely on outgoing ventures from the United States, rather than on internal U.S. deals. Most of the principles and actions required, however, will be the same for ventures initiated from other home countries or for incoming U.S. ventures. Assistance for inbound ventures is well documented and readily available.

The target company's size and sophistication will greatly influence how and if some of the ideas in this chapter are introduced into the new organization. The judgments require objectivity, experience, and a determination to make the new company succeed.

## INITIAL ANALYSIS AND EVALUATION

Prior to introducing any change, it is absolutely necessary to thoroughly understand the objectives of the resulting entity and every detail of the organization that exists at the outset of the planning. This work can best be done by skilled human resources (HR) professionals using extensive interviews with existing employees and available external sources of information, coupled with tediously detailed notes on all of the conversations and readings. The local HR staff, if competent, will be able to help somewhat in this, but primarily it must be done by the controlling company's HR professionals to avoid being influenced by past practice and the sometimes convoluted reasons for it. Although understanding the local situation is paramount, it must be done from the acquirer's viewpoint, assuming that their perspective will largely influence the end venture. Committing to particular courses of action during these interviews must be avoided. The solicitation of information should be strictly nonjudgmental. HR's job is solely to listen and to guide conversations in intelligent directions without setting up unreasonable and unattainable expectations or making promises that would compromise future actions.

## External Considerations

The expectations and the objectives of the new venture will determine many of the personnel policies and practices that should be introduced to the new organization. A limited sales organization requires different human resources than does a more complex manufacturing, sales, and distribution company, for example. Anticipated growth or projected changes in operational requirements will impact the number and the quality of employees needed short term and long term, the employee development programs that are required, the compensation and benefit strategies of the new company, and, perhaps, the organization structure. Focusing on the company end result will help determine whether a relatively permanent, growing workforce is needed, requiring a more sophisticated human resources approach than the alternative will. Training strategies and the need for expatriate workers will be better defined as well.

Once the end objectives are known, the details of the existing HR situation must be studied. A first consideration is the quality of the existing HR staff, if one exists at all. A smart, trustworthy, local staff is worth its weight in gold and should immediately be taken into the evaluation and planning sessions. This policy encourages them to become part of the team. Their knowledge and guidance will help the team to understand internal organizational issues, to approach local competitors for information, and to implement decided strategies. Including the local staff in planning from the outset will help make any necessary changes palatable to other employees as well.

Differences in cultures and the resultant influence on personnel policies must be analyzed and understood. No matter how much control a U.S. corporation retains, the target company's local culture will impact dealings at many levels, including human resources. A culture that is task oriented may have difficulty following time lines. Instituting employee autonomy will be extremely difficult where the culture is hierarchical, accustomed to autocratic leaders or chiefs. In extreme situations culture can dictate the workforce makeup, making it necessary to hire employees in accordance with their tribal heritage by maintaining the same tribal ratio that exists in the country's population. Motivating employees, cooperation between employees, safety considerations, and relations with governments will be affected by culture. Vacation and compensation practice is invariably influenced by local practice or law. For example, whereas Americans tend to schedule vacations throughout the year, Europeans are accustomed to taking their vacations from June through August, which can threaten the continuity of an operation. Another example, a major corporation eliminated the thirteenth-month bonus in its Belgian operations at the request of the employees, incorporating it into base pay, only to be faced with a demand after two years for its reinstatement because it was competitive with local company practice and the culture.

Legal and governmental issues must be investigated carefully at the outset. There may be unexpected restrictions on what is commonly believed to be a management right. Terminating individual employees is almost always a more complex process than anticipated. Laying off significant numbers of employees can present almost insurmountable obstacles. In some countries unions may be a de facto part of the government, a condition that requires some thought in dealing with organized labor. Tradition or law in certain Middle Eastern and Asian countries requires that a national be placed in a management position regardless of qualifications and experience. If expatriates are necessary for your operations, be certain of the requirements for their gaining entry into the country, the duration of their stay, and the red tape and the time likely to be involved in accomplishing the paperwork. It may require reassessing your skilled needs or allowing more time to complete the administrative action.

The political climate, including government stability, civil unrest, and terrorist presence, must be clearly evaluated and understood. Although these are largely beyond company control, their effect is real on the security of employees, particularly key employees and expatriates, and on the facilities. Risk assessment in these areas may require consideration of kidnap insurance or the development of contingency plans for key employees in the event of severe political disruptions. It may also cause evaluation of prospective expatriates in terms of their religious affiliation or ethnic background.

In countries with unstable currencies, it is mandatory to ensure that capabilities exist to assess business results in hard currency, usually dollars, and to transfer currencies across national borders. This requires particular attention to the availability of local financial expertise, both people and institutions, and must be done in conjunction with acquiring company financial experts.

Areas sometimes overlooked would include those local practices that might "not play in Peoria." Obvious violations of decency and fair play, such as child labor usage and underpayment, pollution and other environmental issues, and, a few years ago, apartheid in South Africa, are issues that will rightfully bring down the wrath of stockholders and others. If standards are not high enough, your stockholders and existing employees may become involved to your detriment. Be certain these potentially huge problems are identified and addressed.

## Internal Considerations

Existing compensation and benefit practices within the target company must be thoroughly understood. Determine whether wages paid are fair and reflect a value-added structure or "just happened." It is important to carefully investigate government mandates and local practice regarding base pay, bonuses, paid vacations, retirement, holidays, sick leave, personal service, required government service, and severance pay. The analysis should determine if the wages and plans are fair, not discriminatory, and whether they encourage long- or short-term employment. The use and advisability of incentive pay programs must be understood. Know that the wages and benefits are competitive locally to the extent possible, although this will have to be done definitively later. Analyze employee agreements and union contracts to determine financial, legal, and practical implications of change.

Corporations may enter an overseas transaction with sound intentions of hiring or supplementing the existing workforce with local people, only to discover that certain fundamental skills do not exist. The availability of qualified mechanics, engineers, or computer technicians may range from few to none. With the help of the local management, the presence of these skills and experience internally and in the community should be closely investigated.

The existing organization structure must be understood in terms of how work gets done. Compare the written lines of authority with what actually happens. For example, it would not be unexpected to find, in an organization with strong ethnic overtones, that effective lines of authority and communication followed those ethnic lines rather than the usual organization lines. At times, dominant individuals undermine the existing structure by setting up their own effective means of communicating and producing results. By knowing the real arrangements, it becomes easier to introduce the changed structure, perhaps taking advantage of the existing strengths. At minimum such an analysis will show weaknesses and strengths that must be understood.

In many countries, occupational health and safety practices will not exist or will not be up to adequate standards. Investigation must determine what policies are in place and what services are available to ensure the basic health and safety of the workforce and the security of the facility. This is made more difficult in developing countries by the workers' unfamiliarity with basic tools, let alone high-tech machinery. Success in this area requires innovative thinking to teach workers about hazards, how to avoid unsafe conditions, and how to institute safe work practices. One company in Africa found that the best way to alert workers to danger was to place images of a fierce crocodile on threatening equipment.

The lack of local infrastructure may determine a corporation's ability to do business in an area or may point out the need to provide it. Power, water, and sanitation issues impact manufacturing and other facilities and must be investigated at the outset. Analysis of the local school system (or lack of one) will help determine the effectiveness of the workforce and the requirements for future training. Lack of housing, public transport, and roads in some situations may require the corporation to provide them. These are major undertakings requiring consultation with experts, governments, and employees to set required standards, to monitor construction, to set rules for use, and to manage the whole project. It is virtually impossible to accomplish these undertakings without alienating significant groups of people. The lack of adequate infrastructure also becomes a factor in attracting expatriates to the location.

# DEVELOPING AND IMPLEMENTING HUMAN RESOURCES PLANS FOR THE NEW ORGANIZATION

## Organization and Staffing

Putting a new organizational structure in place is one of the first orders of business. Operational managers will usually make final decisions on this. However, a human resources overview is needed in several areas to guide the decision-making process. Initially HR can help obtain input concerning an optimum form of organization from all levels within the target company. Conveying this information to the acquiring management ensures some consensus and participation in developing a management- and employee-supported staffing plan, which considers local government mandates and the effect on morale. Once the organization structure is understood, HR should assist in implementing the staffing plan and in the evaluation of key managers to fill positions in the new organization. Utilizing the best people from both companies to form an optimal team takes considerable planning, time, and patience, but it makes use of already seasoned people and offers continuity. It is often preferable and cheaper to use local people, providing them with training as necessary. This also tends to mitigate some of the concerns and stresses of the local employees and community engendered by the change. Assuming some of the vacancies will not be filled with immediately qualified local people, decisions must be made concerning how the qualified people will be found and trained if necessary. Adding expatriates to the staff can offer immediate, qualified help. Developing employees is a longer-term option. Both of these issues will be discussed separately.

Be sure that the new organization clearly defines responsibility and accountability and that the people appointed to the new positions understand their own responsibility and accountability. Finally, when the organization is complete, make certain the results are communicated quickly, clearly, and honestly to the employees and the community. The optimum time to do this is when the company change is made to help counter the negative feelings engendered by the merger or acquisition.

## Use of Expatriates

The new venture may require the use of expatriates, usually to provide senior management or technical skills. Ideally these employees should be selected for their experience in the particular business area and their likely success in dealing with the local employees, customers, vendors, and governments. Consideration should be given to overseas experience, facility with local language, and ability to function in a multinational workforce. Length of assignment will usually vary from a few months to several years. Compensation can be expensive and complex, sometimes including incentive and hardship premiums, cost-of-living and housing allowances, and excess income tax reimbursement. Families will not usually accompany expatriates on shorter assignments or in situations involving unusual political unrest or questionable security.

Relocation impacts expatriates and their families both positively and negatively. Depending on the level of sophistication of the new location, there may be considerable real and emotional discomfort. The family must be capable of adjusting to and accepting the new way of living. Frequently the nonemployed spouse bears the primary burden of the relocation: moving into the house, settling children in schools, relearning how to shop for necessities, and making new friends. This often must be done while the employed spouse is totally involved at the new site or traveling out of the country.

Continuity of careers is a real and often legitimate concern of expatriates. "Out of sight, out of mind" can be a real detriment to accepting the new job. The fears revolve around missed promotional opportunities in the home organization, salary, bonus, and just being out of the loop. With this background, career opportunities for expatriates must be carefully planned, often with precommitted reentry to their home country. Some companies address these issues by assigning mentors in the home country to manage the expatriate's career, including reentry.

## Management Development and Contingency Plans for Key Positions

Certain positions are critical to the daily and long-term success of the new operation. With the personnel turmoil inherent in these transactions compounded by merging foreign and corporate cultures and operating methods, these positions are usually at great risk in an international deal. Often employees capable of filling these positions are in great demand, possibly in short supply, making them easy targets to be hired away by local companies. Particular attention must be paid to retaining these key employees in the new enterprise. This may require action such as special personnel policies, unique pay arrangements, one-time incentive bonus payments, and special recognition of their importance.

Cross-training existing employees will eventually build a supply of employees who have the required competencies to perform work in the key areas. This may be sufficient to provide skills needed for a relatively small operation.

For larger companies that expect growth and continued operations, some have had success in implementing detailed programs that provide trained employees for vacancies forecasted over a two- or three-year period. Such a plan must have the total involvement and commitment of top management and must be kept totally confidential among the group executing the plan. It begins with a studied projection of expected vacancies by top operations managers. These same top managers, guided by a top HR professional, select people from within the organization or the parent company organizations who have the interest and the potential to perform the work with additional training or job exposure. The people identified should have indicated interest in the work by providing career aspirations in performance reviews conducted by operating managers. Senior HR people must carefully monitor these reviews for objectivity. Specific plans for the development of the selected individuals, including formal training, position changes, and special projects, are agreed upon among top management and assigned to one individual to monitor and manage. An experienced HR professional must track the whole system in detail. Correctly done this process produces well-trained individuals for the long-term vacancies and is highly motivating to employees who experience their career moving in directions they have chosen.

It is important to remain focused on the interrelated nature of staffing, performance review, compensation, and individual growth and development. Administration of a successful HR program must insist on the successful integration of all these elements with attention to detail, common sense, and a touch of optimism.

## Compensation and Benefits

Merging two companies' compensation and benefit plans or creating a new plan can be a difficult task, yet it has one of the most sensitive and important impacts on the employees. Initial local concerns with regard to the deal can be partially ameliorated by quickly instituting a fair, competitive wage-and-benefit package and clearly communicating it to employees.

Local practice will impact decisions in this area. Therefore steps must be taken immediately to accumulate local data concerning compensation and benefit practices at local competing companies and multinational corporations with a local presence. Primarily, information must be obtained from those who compete to hire similar employees. It will be important to discover whether multinationals are expected to offer premium pay because of the presumed risk and uncertainty involved with such employment or whether they are viewed as preferred employers because they will institute higher employee standards. Both perceptions are possible.

In certain locations, international consulting firms and local governments may be able to supply some of this information. This is a starting point. It is preferable to conduct your own survey of local and multinational companies using qualified international human resources employees. Surveyed companies will usually agree to provide reasonably accurate information because the alternative is for the new entity to upset the applecart and overcompensate employees. The survey should encompass actual pay rates or ranges for all employee levels, bonus plans, incentives, severance, disability, overtime requirements and practice, vacation time, holidays, work practices, adjustment for cost of living, and government-required pay and benefits. Information must also be accumulated concerning subsidy of transport, cafeterias, provision or subsidy of housing, schooling assistance, and provision of medical help to employees and their families. Investigate the effect of seniority, promotions, and pay for performance, if they are factors. Health, medical, and social welfare plans, insurance, and pensions will vary from home-country perceptions and must be surveyed. If unions exist, learn how the company deals with them and what, if any, terms of the company/union relationship are mandated by the government. Different work policies and practices should be explored. The key to this survey is to carry it out with an open mind, trying not to impose home-country solutions on local problems.

Even experienced survey takers are likely to be exposed to unique ideas and procedures in the local environment. Usually after talking with several companies, the differences begin to gel into a tapestry reasonably depicting local practice. Because this information builds on previously collected facts, many surveyors have found it useful to initially estimate the importance of the companies to be surveyed and to then approach companies in order from least to most importance. This ensures obtaining all necessary information from the key companies with whom you compete in the local market.

When you are comfortable with survey results, your own wage-and-benefit structure should be developed, integrating local practice with your own needs. Try to keep the structures simple, bearing in mind that they are then easier to communicate and that the local employees may not be used to any system or, even worse, an illogical or discriminatory system. Consider whether employees are to be encouraged to remain for their entire work career or whether turnover is to be tolerated, even encouraged. Local culture and practice may make it difficult to introduce such concepts as equal pay for equal work, pay for performance, non-discriminatory policies, and bonuses, although they should be part of the short- and long-term objectives. Every aspect of these structures should be developed to enhance the company's overall goals while presenting a fair and attractive package to employees. Because of the complexity and essentially local thrust of benefit plans, it is often necessary to engage outside consultants or specialized people from the acquiring corporation before finalization.

Administering the compensation system requires addressing such concerns as whether performance will be evaluated and communicated to the employee (in most successful companies, this is mandatory) and whether the results of the evaluation will determine pay increases and bonuses, as opposed to them being tied to longevity and past practice. Ideas such as these, customary to many of us, could be illegal locally, unacceptable in the local culture, or acceptable with a lot of explanation. Adding some of these new concepts to a program requires total commitment of the top management and constant, clear communication.

## Severance

When two companies combine, some employees will be terminated or will leave voluntarily. Uneasiness is created for employees of both companies, which lowers productivity and adversely affects morale. When little information is available, speculation is rife. Communicating facts quickly and accurately, even if negative, will undermine rumors. As soon as decisions are made with respect to which employees will leave, change jobs, or be retained, the facts should be communicated to the individuals involved. Forthrightness will begin to build trust and will enhance credibility. Throughout the changes a general communication program should be devised to keep all employees and the local community apprised of what is occurring.

If severance is to be involved when companies combine, a plan must be devised that takes into consideration local practice and laws. Well-intentioned schemes that ignore local law can result in expensive and time-consuming lawsuits while alienating and demoralizing employees who stay. If time permits, a severance strategy should be developed using a multifunctional and multinational planning team. The strategy should focus on long-term business goals but should also take into account skills and resources needed to perform short-term activities. Compromises may have to be made when skills are not available within the company or in the local area. Employees with average performance history or unusually high salaries may prove to be cost effective for a period of time. Increased training, either on the job or formal, should be pursued to help fill out the skills needed as an alternative to severance.

When employees are to lose their job, human resources should oversee all aspects of the severance actions, seeking legal assistance when necessary. Individuals who are to be terminated should meet with someone from their management who will personally convey the message with respect and sensitivity. The discussion should include termination date, base and severance pay, status or expiration dates of any benefit plan, any additional benefits such as outplacement, and any governmental assistance that should be utilized or that is available. Secrecy agreements or concerns should be clearly discussed and written concurrence obtained if appropriate. If in-house assistance with interviews and placement at local companies is provided (usually an excellent idea), procedures should be thoroughly explained and employees should be encouraged to participate. This information should be given to the departing employee in writing.

Actions taken by a company at termination, the perceived fairness of these actions, and the severance benefits will resound through remaining employees and the community. It is a first indication of the new company's values, ethics, and commitment to remaining employees. This is a one-time opportunity that must be done right!

## Training and Team Building

Training programs should begin as soon as the dust settles and should cover such things as needed job knowledge, augmented managerial skills, sharing of production and marketing expertise, cultural exchange, and company strategies and vision. Key training should focus on competencies needed to understand and to operate within the new organization, the reasons for doing the deal, and how the new entity will succeed. In larger mergers and acquisitions involving people of different nationalities, cross-cultural training should be instituted to develop a foundation for teamwork and trust. All of the training performed should be directed to meeting immediate needs but should also address strategic, longer-term requirements. As a part of developing training programs, the claimed background and job skills of candidates should be verified through interviews. One cannot assume that standards of performance between cultures are the same. The value of these efforts will not be lost on the employees, who will begin to develop a sense of security and trust from them.

Before developing courses the existing knowledge base must be confirmed along with literacy levels, preferred language, and the amount of time and money that will be made available for the training. These will obviously affect the scope of the training. Consideration must then be given to delivery. Will outside trainers be brought in, or should trainers be drawn from the ranks of the existing company to transfer information? Available skills, time, and money will determine the best approach; but many companies have found advantage initially in providing in-house training to ensure that the company philosophies and objectives are being promoted.

Training programs, from the outset, should take advantage of employee interests and desired career direction whenever possible. Of course, first concentrations are often to get an operation up and going, so some of the ideals of career development may have to be put aside temporarily. Focus as soon as possible, however, on tying development and training efforts to both the desires of the employee and the strategic needs of the company. The employee's objectives should be discerned from performance appraisals and incorporated into group and selective training. The company must continually assess its specific long-term workforce requirements. In this context, overseas assignments and formal training should be planned for fast-track employees who, on return, are in a superb position to combine and to use the strengths of different cultures and methods of operation.

When businesses are combined, unique and different cultures must function harmoniously, which requires that blending cultural issues be addressed. Management must set the tone, allowing each group to accept the culture of the other, from which a foundation for teamwork arises leading to a more effective organization. Techniques for addressing cultural integration include multicultural training, language instruction, and videos highlighting values and cultural mores of the different groups. Social integration should be encouraged by company-sponsored events and by insisting on a managerial style that helps individuals come together, thereby reinforcing corporate identity.

Studies by noted management experts such as R. M. Fulmer and R. Gilkey prove that continued interaction among cultural groups speeds cultural integration. Initial antagonism, suspicion, and territorialism may be reduced by the development of intergroup structures such as committees and task forces that use people from each company to work toward common goals. Charging departments to develop their own interdepartmental team-building strategies may highlight the effort and produce great results, particularly if this is included in performance reviews.

## Communications

Restructuring causes most employees to shift their focus from work to what is going to happen to them. They want to know whether they have a job and, if so, whether it will be changed. If left to fester, this seriously impacts their morale and work, both quality and quantity. The strategies discussed in this chapter address these negative and destructive attitudes, but none of them will be effective unless communicated clearly, honestly, and regularly. Good news or bad, a unified message allows employees to feel included in the process, minimizes unfounded rumors, confirms the employees' importance, and gradually builds trust in management.

Because of the public relations and informational aspects of the communication effort, it is critical to have top management communicate essential information to both the U.S. and the new operations. In addition, some companies will create a central communications source to answer any questions and to help employees understand their new roles. This must be approached with care though, so that employees do not perceive it as being too impersonal. Employees will be quick to criticize if they believe their collective or individual importance is being minimized.

During critical times, it is important to communicate to employees every week, or even sooner, if there is a major incident that requires it. Direct exchanges, such as scheduled employee forums, are the best way to convey information. Top management can use these forums to outline progress in consolidating the deal, to project what the future will bring, and to address asked and anticipated questions of the employees.

Employee meetings with top management must be a constant, and they must be conducted by upper echelon managers. Substituting lower-level or staff spokespersons must be avoided because it conveys the idea that it is not an important function, particularly in the early, suspicious atmosphere. But there are times when it is impossible to schedule top managers concurrent with publishing critical information. In that event, release should be coordinated to assure employees receive the information at the same time as news media. This information could be directed to employees through their senior managers, through hard copies, or through e-mail or voice mail.

An effective communication program creates acceptance and trust at all organizational levels. People become personally involved in the venture and begin to operate from a common interest and perspective. Of course, communication must be a two-way street. Management, particularly the HR people, must actively listen to employees both formally and informally. They must become aware of the employees' concerns and fears, of what they want to know about, and of the current rumors. This requires all managers, but especially HR managers, to purposefully make themselves available to the employees on a regular basis. This must be proactive, much beyond an open door policy. Employee concerns should be conveyed to top management and utilized where possible. Responses should be given back to employees when appropriate.

## Policies and Procedures

Initial concerns of the employees will involve how the new management will run the operation and how the work environment will change. This area must be addressed to ensure that the initial work experiences are positive and fair. Written policies and procedures should be developed quickly, using any existing in the local company as a base and incorporating information gleaned from the external surveys. Policies should discuss such things as holidays, vacations, seniority, benefits, wages or ranges as applicable, hours of work, grievances, processes for filling positions, and management rights. In developing and publishing a manual, it is advisable to consult with a spectrum of local employees and experts to ensure that it has a local flavor and that all local concerns and legalities are addressed. The presence of a union will probably require that these issues be negotiated or, at minimum, be discussed with them.

## POSTDEAL ASSESSMENT

Transitions rarely have neat beginnings and endings. Because the understanding of successes and failures can facilitate future HR efforts, a posttransition study could be useful.

Several months to a year into the venture, HR staff should discuss the transition with key local and foreign managers as well as with other representative employees. If the venture's size justifies it, a formal written survey might be created. The opinions of all employees should be solicited concerning the success of all the HR endeavors discussed in this chapter. Specific questions could be asked about compensation and benefits, organization structure, staffing, communication, and training. The emphasis should be to find out what, if anything, went wrong and, more important, how these or other processes may be improved for the future. These views should be analyzed and forwarded to top management for action. Results should be communicated back to all employees.

**Checklist: Addressing Human Resources Issues**

I. Preacquisition evaluations.
   A. Internal issues involving the new company.
      1. Structure of the venture.
         a. Autonomy expected.
         b. Expectations and objectives.
         c. Organizational structure and conflict resolution.
      2. Personnel strength of new company.
         a. Business, technical, and functional expertise.
         b. Internal relationships between groups and employees.
         c. Job definition and accountability for action.
         d. Relationships with customers and community.
         e. Anticipated support for new company and operating plan.
         f. Existence and quality of union.
   B. Company and community cultural issues.
      1. Impact of local culture.
         a. Customary seat of decision-making power.
         b. Operating flexibility.
         c. Efficacy of anticipated management style.
         d. Employee motivation.
         e. Appropriateness of ethnic, race, disability, and gender issues.
         f. Work ethic.
         g. Employment standards and policies.
         h. Importance and understanding of safety and health issues.
         i. Outlook concerning foreign ownership.
         j. Usual cooperation between workers, management, government, and unions.
         k. Language usage.
         l. Acceptance of termination and change.
      2. Impact of target company's culture.
         a. All of the concerns listed under "Impact of local culture" (I.B.1).
         b. Financial reward system.
         c. Evaluation of performance.
         d. Relating pay to performance.
         e. Aspirations of employees.
         f. Motivation of employees.
         g. Job evaluation or grading.

       h. Productivity improvement.

       i. Career development.

       j. Long-standing practices and traditions.

C. Government and legal issues.

   1. Staffing restrictions or requirements.

       a. Ability to change existing staff.

       b. Unions and collective bargaining practice and law.

       c. Work hours/overtime.

       d. Termination.

       e. Child labor.

       f. Migrant workers.

       g. Minimum wage and other pay issues.

       h. Employment of expatriates.

       i. Safety and health.

       j. Severance requirements.

       k. Other mandated programs.

   2. Compensation and benefit practice.

       a. Wage rates and required increases.

       b. Bonus structures, including thirteenth month.

       c. Cost-of-living adjustments.

       d. Changes in pay.

       e. Taxation rates.

       f. Vacations and holidays.

       g. Sick leave/personal days.

       h. Required government service.

       i. Social programs such as day care and disability requirements.

       j. Social security.

       k. Medical support programs and health care.

       l. Unemployment and workman's compensation.

       m. Cost to company of mandated social programs, present and anticipated.

       n. Impediments to changing or assimilating existing compensation/benefits.

   3. Miscellaneous issues relating to the target company.

       a. Affirmative action policies and requirements.

       b. Environmental concerns.

       c. Health and safety regulations.

       d. Existing collective bargaining agreements.

       e. Top management severance agreements or commitments.

       f. Outstanding vacation commitments.

       g. Pending lawsuits.

D. Availability of necessary infrastructure.

    1.   Workforce skills and availability.

        a.   Target company's employee population.

        b.   Local labor pool.

        c.   Unemployment rates.

        d.   Target company turnover rates and average employee seniority.

    2.   Health, safety, and security services, both external and internal.

    3.   Local and internal concerns.

        a.   Transport for employees and goods.

        b.   Lockers and showers.

        c.   Cafeteria.

        d.   Medical facilities on site and local.

        e.   Housing.

        f.   School system.

        g.   Training facilities.

        h.   Communications support—telephones, fax, computers.

        i.   Power.

        j.   Water.

        k.   Sanitation.

II.  Staffing strategy.

   A.  Organization.

      1.   Working with top management and departments to develop organization structure; clarifying positions and their accountability

      2.   Creating stepped organizational scheme if appropriate; moving from initial structure through identified checkpoints to future organization.

   B.  Available personnel resources.

      1.   Existing workforce.

        a.   Number of people available from target company.

        b.   Skills and experience compared to projected needs.

        c.   Attitudes toward the new venture.

        d.   Basic personnel records and demographic data.

        e.   Forecasted voluntary and involuntary turnover.

        f.   Estimated potential and trainability of employees.

      2.   Local employee market.

        a.   Unemployment rates if available.

        b.   Estimated skill and experience to match forecasted vacancies.

        c.   Potential plan for reaching prospective employees—ads, networking, word of mouth.

      3.   Expatriate employees.

        a.   Expatriates available and willing to join new venture.

      b.  Assessment of expatriates' potential for successfully working in new organization.

      c.  Requirements for entry into country and length of process time.

      d.  Projected length of stay and plan for replacement.

      e.  Development of compensation package and resolution of career path issues.

      f.  Facilities for accompanying families.

C.  Filling of positions in new organization with best available employees; comparison of staffing needs with skills and experience of existing employees.

  1.  Focus on need for performance.

  2.  Consideration of legal commitments to and impact on current employees.

  3.  Risks and benefits of local or expatriate employees.

  4.  Development of short-term or on-the-job training programs to qualify employees for new responsibilities.

  5.  Involvement of managers in the hiring of people reporting to them.

  6.  Choice of key employees who support the new organization and have the ability to work in a changing environment.

D.  Longer-term personnel plan.

  1.  Positions for which longer-term training is necessary.

      a.  Replacement of expatriates.

      b.  Enhancing skills for key jobs.

      c.  Developing backup support for key positions.

      d.  Anticipated turnover in key skills that are in short supply.

  2.  Creation and implementation of specific developmental programs for key people.

      a.  Focus on longer-term company needs and expressed desires of employees documented in performance reviews.

      b.  Utilization of job transfers internally and abroad along with formal training.

      c.  Assignment of top manager to be responsible for assuring the development occurs.

III.  Compensation, benefits, human resources policies.

A.  Wage structure.

  1.  Comparison of existing programs with survey results and consultant and government information.

      a.  Comparison to local or multinational companies competing for same skills.

      b.  Assessment of likely need to meet or exceed competition.

    2. Need to be competitive for key skills.

    3. Determination of wage structure.

       a. Identification of levels of competence and performance.

       b. Fixed or random rates for each job.

          (1) Union preference for fixed rates.

          (2) Salary growth to encourage retention of employees.

          (3) Fixed rates and restricted benefit plans to encourage turn-over.

    4. Costs assimilated by operations.

    5. Job analysis to fix duties and responsibilities of each position.

    6. Positions fairly included in wage structure; facilitates functioning of the new organization.

B. Determination of benefit structure.

    1. Must supplement statutory programs.

       a. Existing and proposed costs carefully analyzed preferably with external and internal specialists.

       b. Requirements of local law, including discrimination in all forms and disability.

    2. Utilize survey data to determine what benefits to include:

       a. Effect of supportive plans on employee retention.

       b. Consider for inclusion:

          (1) Pension.

          (2) Insurance, life and medical.

          (3) Health care support.

          (4) Social services, such as day care.

          (5) Transportation.

          (6) Cafeteria.

          (7) Educational support for employees and dependents.

          (8) Formal training for employees.

          (9) Housing.

          (10) Disability, permanent and temporary.

C. Wage and salary administration.

    1. Adjustments to base pay.

       a. Method of giving merit increases.

          (1) Performance goals.

          (2) Evaluation of performance.

          (3) Increases tied to attaining objectives.

       b. Promotions.

       c. Use of seniority or time in grade.

       d. Cost of living.

       e. Demotions.

2. Bonuses and stock options.
   a. Efficacy within the culture.
   b. Absolutely clear and communicated standards.
   c. Based on company, unit, and/or individual performance.
   d. Organizational levels to which bonuses apply.
D. Severance.
   1. Competitive and fair package developed using data from the survey.
      a. Integration of local law.
      b. Influence of position, seniority, and salary.
      c. Availability of plan to all people or those selected by company.
         (1) Retention of key people.
         (2) Mass exodus.
         (3) Availability of plan to those offered equal or lower jobs.
      d. Financial and employee relations aspects of golden parachutes.
      e. Impact of prior internal severance packages for consistency.
   2. Need to fill all possible positions in the new organization: work with top management and department managers to select candidates for each position remaining in the new organization.
      a. Offer positions to those selected.
      b. If offer rejected, offer next qualified until all positions filled.
   3. Implement severance plan.
      a. Announce the new organization and its key employees.
         (1) Use group meeting chaired by top management supplemented with written material.
         (2) At group meeting notify all other employees of details of severance plan available and specifically who will talk to them about details concerning themselves.
      b. Communication of details of severance package to each individual employee with written confirmation, including:
         (1) Termination date.
         (2) Base and severance pay.
         (3) Status and expiration dates of benefit plans.
         (4) Additional benefits such as career counseling, help with local employers, job placement, job search training.
         (5) Application of secrecy agreements.
         (6) Waiver of future claims if legal and appropriate.
         (7) Availability of government assistance, such as unemployment compensation, or providing job leads.
E. Policies.
   1. Use of survey results to determine needed policies to enhance operations.

    2.  Short-term fixes with no regard to the longer term results.

    3.  Policies totally supported by management and clearly published.

    4.  Strict adherence of positions to legal requirements.

        a.  Vacation—eligibility and administration.

        b.  Holidays, including pay entitlement.

        c.  Safety and health.

        d.  Overtime.

        e.  Seniority.

        f.  Promotion.

        g.  Sick leave and personal days.

        h.  Employee assistance plans.

        i.  Required government service.

        j.  Work assignment between job classifications as necessary.

        k.  Management rights.

        l.  Unionization.

            (a)  Existing union and collective bargaining agreement.

            (b)  Role of government in union-management relationship.

IV.  Transitional support mechanisms.

    A.  Communications about organization and company change.

        1.  Stabilize the workforce.

            a.  Continuing uneasiness, distrust, and much concern to address for some time.

            b.  Clear, honest, and unified message.

            c.  Consistent message.

            d.  Awareness of language and cultural differences.

        2.  Information communicated.

            a.  Strategies and goals of the new venture.

            b.  Progress in consolidating the deal.

            c.  Understanding the new organization and helping it function smoothly.

            d.  Changes in terms and conditions of employment.

            e.  Correcting rumors and uncertainties.

            f.  Timing of important anticipated events.

        3.  Communication vehicles.

            a.  Weekly employee meetings conducted by top management.

            b.  Simultaneous internal and public news releases.

            c.  Letters to employees.

            d.  E-mail and voice mail.

            e.  Company-sponsored social events.

        4.  Listen to employees.

            a.  Input actively sought from employees.

      b.  Information conveyed to top management.

      c.  Feedback of information where possible to employees.

B.  Training and development.

   1.  Core curriculum for short- and medium-term training needs.

      a.  Company strategies and goals, addressing job security concerns.

      b.  Operating and functional skills.

      c.  Language and cultural differences.

      d.  Safety.

      e.  Personnel policies and practices.

      f.  Response to perceived needs, such as lack of control, change, stress, increased and different workloads.

      g.  Team building and interdepartmental cooperation.

         (1)  Interdepartmental project teams.

         (2)  Intradepartmental team-building projects.

   2.  The programs.

      a.  Base skills of prospective trainees to properly set course levels.

      b.  Cultural and literacy issues.

      c.  Costs and money available.

      d.  Methodology and materials.

      e.  Use of internal or external trainers.

   3.  Evaluation of programs by continual discussion with managers to ensure accomplishment of enhanced performance.

   4.  Implementation of longer-term development programs.

      a.  Anticipation of vacancies over three-year period.

      b.  Determination of employees with potential to fill long-term key vacancies; use of performance reviews to elicit information about individual goals.

      c.  Development of detailed plan to include formal training, job transfer, and overseas assignment to qualify candidate for advancement.

      d.  Assignment of responsibility to accomplish training plan to top operating manager.

      e.  Maintenance of confidentiality of individual plan.

      f.  Assignment of top human resource manager to monitor every step of the program.

IV.  Posttransition assessment—informal or formal attitude survey after dust settles on new venture.

# 15

# Postmerger Integration

*Cynthia N. Wood*
*Richard Porter*

In 1988, the Bridgestone Corporation of Japan attempted to expand tire sales in the United States by purchasing Firestone, an old-line tire manufacturer. Within months, however, the company was embroiled in labor problems that led to a public rebuke of the company's Japanese managers by President Bill Clinton and to large financial losses. Even after slowly winning acceptance of its new work schedules, the company's problems were not over. A massive recall of tires in the United States has led to more financial losses and negative publicity; in February 2001, Bridgestone reported its worst results in a decade, with group net profit for 2000 down by 80 percent from the previous year.

Breaking into the U.S. entertainment industry seemed essential to both Matsushita Electric Industrial and Sony. In the late 1980s, Matsushita purchased MCA and Universal Studios, and Sony acquired Columbia Pictures. Both Matsushita and Sony wanted "entertainment software" to run on their VCRs. Unfortunately, they had great difficulty adapting to Hollywood-style management practices. Matsushita admitted defeat and sold an 80 percent stake in MCA and Universal Studios to the Seagram Company in 1995 (Seagram has been subsequently purchased by Vivendi). After investing billions, ousting highly paid Hollywood executives, and taking a $3.2 billion write-off in 1994, Sony appears to have solved many of its problems.

In 1998, Daimler-Benz and Chrysler announced a "merger of equals" that was trumpeted as a "marriage made in heaven." It was the largest acquisition ever of a U.S. company by a foreign buyer and was supposed to remake the worldwide automobile industry. Employees were assured that there would be no layoffs; indeed, the plan was to increase capacity. Shortly after the announcement, Walter Huizenga, president of the American International Automobile Dealers Association (AIADA), stated that the merger underscored the global nature of the automobile industry and revealed the fallacy of the Big Three manufacturers' position as the only true U.S. automobile manufacturers.

Today, DaimlerChrysler is worth less than Daimler-Benz alone was before the merger. On February 26, 2001, DaimlerChrysler announced that it would show a net loss of $2 billion after taking an even larger charge for restructuring costs. Subsequently, there has been speculation that Chrysler will be sold unless relatively quick improvements can be achieved. Indeed, plans are underway to cut 26,000 jobs in the United States by closing six plants and trimming production at seven others; to reduce the cost of parts and materials by 15 percent; and to renew Chrysler's aging line of minivans, Jeeps, and sports utility vehicles.

This chapter examines the factors that affect the successful postmerger integration of inbound acquisitions. The chapter is divided into three parts. The first part examines critical warning signs of a high potential for failure. The second examines key considerations for postmerger integration and discusses actions that the buyer can take to help ensure the successful integration of the two organizations. The third part provides a checklist of practical considerations for companies making inbound acquisitions.

## KEY INDICATORS OF SUCCESS AND FAILURE

With the increasing globalization of business, cross-border acquisitions seem to make strategic sense, especially in the United States. There is political stability and the regulatory environment is generally favorable. Until recently, there has been double-digit growth in key market areas. Even more important, the United States is the world's largest single market. Consequently, many European firms acquire companies in the United States that will allow them to expand their product lines with strong U.S. brand names that do not yet have widespread global distribution.

In 1999, the United States was the leading country for inbound deals, attracting a total of $293 billion, or 37 percent of the value of all deals (an increase of 450 percent in value since 1990). Of the inbound acquisitions made in the U.S. market since the late 1970s, however, the majority failed to improve the financial performance of the target company. In many of these "failed" acquisitions, the acquiring company did not take into account the importance of:

- A thorough understanding of new markets, including the implications of cultural differences.
- The allocation of adequate resources to the integration process.
- "People" and leadership issues.
- Globalization as a strategic organizational issue.
- Access to different management skills for each stage of the acquisition.
- The size of the merging companies.

## Knowledge of Market

Although all acquisitions are inherently risky, the ones that move companies into new markets are especially difficult. Even after the initial due diligence is complete, there is a tendency to assume that whatever worked in the home market will be appropriate everywhere else. This cultural bias in favor of one's own experience is so strong that it can cause companies to disregard very obvious differences when entering new markets.

For example, when a British-owned spirits company first entered the U.S. market, the company had years of experience distributing alcoholic beverages in the United Kingdom and Europe. Even though it had conducted extensive research prior to completing the acquisition, it still assumed that its European experience would be transferable to the newly acquired U.S. business. The company totally underestimated the impact of the federal government, which has led, in essence, to 50 different and highly regulated state distribution systems. Consequently, the company lost nearly 18 months in consolidating its market share.

When Bridgestone entered the U.S. tire market, it failed to understand the potential difficulties inherent in negotiating with organized labor and subsequently lost millions of dollars and considerable time while trying to implement a more efficient work schedule.

When a British-owned food products company entered the U.S. private-label food industry in the early 1980s, it assumed that private-label brands were as popular here as they were in the United Kingdom. It also assumed that U.S. consumers would be comfortable with the same packaging that was used overseas. Unfortunately, private-label brands were just beginning to gain acceptance in the United States, and the company was unable to compete effectively with established brand names.

## Adequate Resources

Being spread too thin—too many markets, too many products, and too few resources—is another warning sign that an acquisition may fail during the postmerger integration period. In the drive to diversify and increase their presence in the U.S. market, many companies have expanded too rapidly into very diverse markets. For example, when Sony bought Paramount Studios, the company soon discovered that the entertainment industry in the United States is quite different from that in Japan. Sony did not have the appropriate management expertise or industry-specific knowledge to manage its acquisition effectively, and that deficiency put a strain on the rest of the company.

## People Issues

"People" and leadership issues are another potential source of difficulty in the postmerger period. Traditionally, the financial aspects of the acquisition process have often been considered to the detriment of the human element. Mergers and acquisitions are naturally threatening to employees who tend to expect the worst, engage in crisis management, and restrict the flow of information in an attempt to protect themselves. Early in the merger of Daimler-Benz and Chrysler, Thomas Stallkamp, president of Chrysler, commented on the amount of time he was spending trying to ease the anxiety of his 22,000 employees. He routinely held mass meetings, answered e-mailed questions, and used Chrysler's television network and newspaper to disseminate important information. In one month alone, he received over 1,000 e-mail inquiries.[1] In many cases, there are also clashes of national and corporate cultures and a strong sense of "us versus them" or superior versus inferior. If the deal is announced as a merger of equals but is really a stealth takeover, then all of these factors are exacerbated.

In a misguided attempt to reassure employees that nothing has really changed, many buyers do not move quickly enough to resolve important issues, such as which employees will be retained, how the new organization will be structured, who will be in charge, what the new entity will be named, what the expectations will be for employee performance, and whether facilities will be consolidated. For nearly a year, the DaimlerChrysler deal was portrayed as a merger of equals, even though it was not. Partly in deference to American sensibilities, Daimler was slow to integrate the two businesses. Until late 1999, there was still talk of maintaining separate head offices and corporate cultures, even while most key decisions were being made in Germany. Thus, many Americans felt left out of the decision-making process. Many acquiring companies fail to understand the importance of immediately developing a strong, new corporate culture with a clear, new way of doing business. As the chairman of Beecham pointed out after the merger of SmithKline and Beecham, immediate recognition that a new organization has been created is critical.

---

[1]"DaimlerChrysler Merger: Lessons in German, Culture, and Red-Eye Flights," *Naples [Florida] Daily News*, October 17, 1998.

## Globalization

By the 1980s, most large companies realized that to ensure long-term viability, they could no longer confine themselves to just domestic operations, no matter how big their markets. Not until much later, however, did they understand that effective global competition involved more than a series of independent overseas operations. Consequently, after making a series of transnational acquisitions, many companies found their operations fragmented, inefficient, and not truly global. Their international acquisitions did not live up to expectations, in large part because the companies did not have a core management team capable of being effective in cultures other than their own or dealing with the complexities of truly global operations. Many companies also failed to develop the management talent readily available in acquired companies. Recently U.S. companies also have been confronted with the reality that an acquisition is no longer judged in only one country, even if the acquisition involves two U.S. companies. The General Electric/Honeywell deal, for example, collapsed because of the objections of the European Union.

## Different Types of Skills

Perhaps because of the emphasis placed on the need for strong financial skills during the acquisition process, many companies discount the importance of other complementary skills that may be needed after the completion of the initial due diligence. In addition, some companies are not equally proficient at managing all stages of the acquisition process. They excel in one or more areas, such as negotiations, crisis management, cost control, reorganization, or team development. The successful completion of the postmerger integration period, however, requires extensive expertise in a broad range of areas, including strategic thinking and decision making, process design, communications, organizational effectiveness, and team building.

## Size of Merging Companies

"Bigger is better" is today's corporate mantra. The largest mergers in the 1990s and 2000 are four or five times larger than the biggest in the 1980s. Not since the age of the Robber Barons has there been such a rush to the consolidation of corporate resources and industries. In nearly every country, it is becoming increasingly difficult for more than two or three companies in any industry to be profitable. Companies need the synergies that can be achieved by combining distribution channels and by offering broader product lines—not just crackers, for example, but cheese and crackers. The rush toward the creation of ever-larger organizations through mergers, however, creates numerous challenges. Size alone makes integration difficult. If the merging organizations are not a good strategic fit, have very different cultures, and are not financially stable, integration will not achieve the desired results.

## POSTMERGER INTEGRATION ACTIVITIES

The postmerger integration period is critical for the successful completion of *all* deals, but especially those in which there are some warning signs of potential problems. An examination of numerous inbound acquisitions has shown that there are a number of general considerations, as well as six specific areas of concern (communications; people; national and organizational culture; mission/values and common language; overall organizational structure; and functional areas), to which companies should pay careful attention.

### General Considerations

The postmerger integration period requires careful analysis of the newly acquired organization, the reexamination of the strategic reasons for making the acquisition, and the willingness to devote substantial resources to the acquisition. Of primary importance is the buyer's previous experience. Expertise in making acquisitions and in operating in overseas markets is helpful. Knowledge of the specific market involved is also important. There is a natural tendency to focus on the similarities between the United States and other markets, especially English-speaking ones, which can lead to difficulties. For example, because of the increasing emphasis on globalization, there has been considerable speculation that many of the top-tier law firms in New York and London will ultimately merge to create organizations that can provide a continuum of services in both countries. These law firms already advise some of the world's largest companies and banks, and they work in English, the language of international business. Even more important, they understand British and U.S. law, a strategic advantage during a period when international business is increasingly conducted under either U.S. or British law. To date, however, only one such merger has occurred. The differences between New York and London law firms may be too big to bridge. New York firms have close ties to major investment banks, whereas London firms tend not to have such close ties. Firms in both cities operate as partnerships. Even more important, however, they have different compensation schemes. In New York, firms share profits among partners according to how much business each one generates. In London, the top firms share profits according to seniority, thus making successful mergers difficult. Consequently, those firms with little experience should spend considerable time analyzing cultural and market factors that might affect their success and should consider hiring an outside consultant to provide insight into U.S. business practices.

Assuming integration of the businesses as a goal, immediately after the completion of an acquisition, the buyer should put together a multidisciplinary project team whose sole responsibility is the integration of the target company into the overall organization. There are two approaches to assembling the team. Companies that routinely engage in numerous acquisitions may want to consider establishing a permanent corporate office for postmerger integration. As each new deal is completed, this office assumes responsibility for assembling and managing a team of experts to provide company-specific assistance. Companies that do not complete many deals may want to set up a new team each time. In both cases, the objective should be to customize every integration process without having to start all over again. The postmerger integration team should include individuals from both organizations, as well as outside consultants who can provide specialized expertise.

For large integration projects, the team should be organized into an oversight group and a series of highly specialized subteams that can deal with specific issues and then report their findings to the oversight group. In addition, all team members should be assigned to the project for the duration of the integration period because continuity helps build trust and teamwork. To ensure that expatriates' expertise is not lost from the organization after their assignment to the integration management team ends, there should be specific plans for reintegrating the expatriates into other corporate operations. Reintegration plans are especially important in large mergers that require key team members to be removed from their regular operational assignments for several years. Talented individuals may refuse assignments to integration teams unless they are assured that such a long-term assignment will not harm their career.

Cultural sensitivity is also important because there are significant differences in the way various cultures perceive team efforts. Although U.S. managers are beginning to value teamwork, they have traditionally been strong individualists. British managers, on the other hand, generally prefer working within a team or project environment where the group rather than the individual assumes responsibility for critical tasks. The Dutch also value cooperation and trust. They believe that teams are essential for the success of most undertakings. Both the Germans and the French are most comfortable with highly structured teams where roles are clearly defined.

During the early stages of planning for corporate integration, Daimler and Chrysler placed little emphasis on the resolution of cultural problems, even though the deal involved very different national and corporate cultures. Executives made the assumption that the main issues, efficiency and planning, were not affected by cultural differences. They soon discovered, however, that these assumptions were not correct. The Chrysler team resented what they saw as a German invasion of process-driven experts who wanted to change Chrysler's freewheeling, hunch-driven work and design practices. There were difficulties in managing simple things, such as the time difference between Germany and the United States. Both sides had trouble understanding the other's travel policies. Even while emphasizing cost consciousness, for example, the Germans tended to travel first class and to stay in expensive hotels.

As soon as possible, the project team should be given detailed information on the buyer's strategic intent for the acquisition; the critical sources of added value that the acquisition is expected to contribute; the desired time frame for recouping its return on investment; and the resources that it is willing to commit to the effort. All four items will affect the amount of integration that should be undertaken, as well as its potential for success. The availability of human resources is especially important because experience has shown that transactions almost always require more resources than anticipated.

The project team should also be given access to all due diligence that was completed prior to the acquisition. All analyses should be reviewed, and the core competencies of the organization being acquired should be reaffirmed.

### Key Lessons from Previous Experience

- Assemble a strong, credible integration management team.
  - —Members must be free to commit as much time as necessary.
  - —When completing many deals, consider establishing a permanent office of postmerger integration management.
- Establish subteams to deal with specific functional areas or strategic considerations.
- Ensure that the team has a sense of urgency about its work and understands the strategic objectives of the deal.
- Have a plan for moving integration team members back into the organization once their work is completed.
- Remember that the integration process should always be customized for each deal but should also incorporate "lessons learned" from previous deals.
- Make key personnel decisions as soon as possible; do not delay difficult, unpleasant personnel decisions.
- Have a plan for managing consultants.
- Have a methodical procedure for assessing information about the company that was acquired.
- Do not be misled by spurious market similarities, such as language.
- Encourage the integration management team to focus first on opportunities with the lowest risks and the highest potential for success. Early "wins" will give them credibility and will help build momentum.

## Communications

Companies that make successful acquisitions value communications and symbols, such as corporate names and slogans, and are committed to open communications throughout the process. They understand that investors and employees within the company being acquired may be uneasy, and they move quickly to make key announcements, such as what the name of the new organization will be, whether the target's CEO will be retained, and how decisions concerning the integration of the two organizations will be made. They also emphasize that change will occur and do not downplay it in their communications.

Even before the acquisition is made public, the buyer should prepare a comprehensive communication plan. Both the integration management team and the corporate public relations staff should participate in its development. Many companies also hire consultants who specialize in postmerger communication issues. These individuals write press releases, advise on communication strategy, and develop the proper public relations "spin" for the announcement of corporate changes. They also help create targeted messages to ensure customers and employees that a merger will be beneficial.

Some of these consultants assist in the creation of a new name and a related image for the postmerger entity, a skill that has become increasingly important in cross-border mergers. The new corporate names must be distinctive, memorable, and available as domain names; they must pass trademark hurdles; and they must have no undesirable meanings in a foreign language. To satisfy all these needs, there has been a shift toward unique but nondescriptive names that work well across national borders. Initials and hyphenated names are both popular. The British Petroleum-Amoco merger resulted in the formal adoption of BP, while the Daimler-Benz and Chrysler merger resulted in DaimlerChrysler. Classical names are also popular. The merger of Guinness and Grand Metropolitan resulted in Diageo, composed of the Latin prefix *dia* for day and the Greek suffix *geo* for the world.

The completed communication plan should identify specific target audiences and their unique needs, the critical messages for each audience, factors that might affect communications to each audience, and appropriate communications media for each audience and message. The plan should also include guidelines for measuring the outcome of each communication initiative. Many companies find that various combinations of personal letters, "road shows," question-and-answer sessions, newsletters, and videotapes are effective for delivering key information. Web sites that deal solely with merger-related information are a relatively new and effective means of reaching a broad range of stakeholders. DaimlerChrysler used such a web site during the first two years of its merger. Ongoing, interactive briefings and forums provide a means of reinforcing critical values, beliefs, and behaviors. Regular news releases, letters, and briefings are essential for providing information to the local community, to government officials, and to shareholders. In addition, the communication plan should include strategies for dealing with rumors, information leaks, and the need to give out "bad" news. While still president of Chrysler, Thomas Stallkamp reported that much of his time was spent dispelling rumors and correcting "misinformation."

As the communication plan develops, special attention should be paid to the identification of cultural differences that might impact its effectiveness. For example, informal communication is especially valued in the United States. Managers often have an open door policy that invites the informal discussion of business issues, and spoken communications are often preferred to written ones.

Employees are encouraged to ask questions. In France, however, formal written communication is preferred, and particular attention is paid to the selection of precisely the right words. In the United States, people tend to get to the point very quickly in business discussions; whereas in Asian, Arab, and many Latin American countries, the pace is much slower and preliminary social pleasantries are essential.

There are also cultural differences in the treatment of time. In the United States, "time is money" and executives do not want to waste time. Promptness for business meetings is considered essential. In Japan, however, the time of arrival at a meeting is governed by rank; junior people arrive first, followed by more senior individuals. In Asian, Arab, African, and Latin American countries, time is seen as a continuum. Consequently, interrupting business meetings for family matters or arriving several hours past the stated time is not considered rude. In most Western cultures, important matters get immediate attention and are resolved as quickly as possible. In some African countries, only unimportant matters get handled quickly.

When SmithKline and Beecham decided to merge, both were concerned about establishing an intensive communication program for employees. To symbolize the need for the merger, the management team immediately announced a new corporate identity based on the slogan "Simply Better," which incorporated the new company's initials. "Simply Better" was posted at the top of corporate headquarters in both the United States and the United Kingdom, and signs saying "Now We Are One" were prominently displayed. Videotapes, bulletin boards, briefings, and newsletters were all used to disseminate information about the merger. Internal corporate magazines featured monthly articles on key corporate values and the benefits of the merger. Senior managers attended briefings and were encouraged to ask questions about the new organization.

Just as important as the timely dissemination of information concerning corporate integration plans is the establishment of effective communications channels among the new management team. Individual and cultural differences in communication styles must be identified and taken into consideration. Many companies find that the mapping of personal communication styles is an effective means of reducing the initial barriers among senior managers and encouraging them to work together. After several sessions in which they learn about each other's styles, they begin to develop a common language for interpreting their communications.

### Key Lessons from Previous Experience

- Clarify the key message to be communicated and the desired outcomes.
- Understand the needs of each target audience.
- Be prepared to monitor the effectiveness of each communication and to make changes as necessary.
- Communicate, communicate, communicate.
- Be consistent, clear, and honest.
- Avoid corporate speak.

- Use many different forms of communications.
- Make only promises that can be kept.
- Do not play down the level of change; people will be expecting change.
- Never assume that the message was understood; have a plan for dealing with rumors, leaks, and misinformation.
- Use face-to-face communication as often as possible.
- Avoid trendy name changes and logos that people cannot relate to easily.

## People

The employees of an acquired company are a valuable resource for the acquiring organization. In companies that deal primarily with intellectual property, employees *are* the company. They have the unique expertise to provide the company's service or product. They understand the market, customers, government rules and regulations, the culture of the country where the acquired company is headquartered, and, in many cases, the strengths and weaknesses of the company. Yet, within 12 to 18 months, most acquiring companies lose the management teams of their new acquisitions. Senior managers are accustomed to being their own bosses and may not want to work for someone else. Former owners may have made so much money on the sale of the company that they no longer need the aggravation of dealing with a new business situation. Competent technical personnel and professionals can often find employment in a potentially less threatening environment. Chrysler, for example, has experienced a loss of senior executives and designers since the merger was announced.

### Personnel Decisions

Because acquisitions are often troubling to the employees of both the acquiring and the acquired organizations, it is important for personnel decisions to be made as quickly as possible. Many successful acquiring companies have found that it is helpful to name the members of the new senior management team when the acquisition is announced. A quick announcement avoids speculation and uncertainty concerning who is in charge. SmithKline and Beecham used this approach in the merger of the two companies. On the day that the merger was made public, the corporate staffs of both companies resigned and the members of the new merged team were announced. The team included both senior U.S. and U.K. managers, thus sending the message that nationality would not be a key factor in the selection of personnel. Because of the quick, orderly decision, employees, customers, and shareholders were all reassured that business would continue in an efficient manner.

### Review of Human Resources Requirements

As soon as the new senior management team is announced, the integration management team should begin a thorough review of the human resources requirements of the acquisition. The review should involve as many key managers from the acquiring company as possible. Their participation will help allay the fears and the animosity of employees who may feel that they are being unduly scrutinized. It will also help build commitment to the new organization. The review should focus on:

- *Types of human resources required immediately after the acquisition, as well as over the next several years.*   Many companies find that immediately after an acquisition, they require additional personnel who can analyze sales data, design and implement new management information systems, hold briefings and workshops, conduct training, and harmonize different benefits packages. DaimlerChrysler, for example, has spent considerable time trying to harmonize the compensation of German and U.S. executives.

- *Availability of appropriate human resources within the acquired organization.*   One integration management team developed a matrix that showed the positions to be filled in the new organization, the qualifications for each position, the availability of potential internal candidates for each position, the geographic location of each potential candidate, and the willingness of each candidate to relocate.

- *Strengths and weaknesses of available resources.*   As one company identified internal candidates for each position, the candidates were ranked according to their strengths and weaknesses. Both high performers whom the company did not want to lose and individuals whom the company had decided not to retain were also identified.

- *Unique skills and competencies that might be valuable either within the acquisition or elsewhere in the organization.*   One company's organizational review identified several individuals who were especially skilled in sales training and thoroughly understood several unique market segments. The review also identified several young managers who had experience in other international markets and were willing to travel.

### Staffing Plan

As soon as the human resources analysis has been completed, the integration management team should prepare a staffing plan that lists:

- Employees who will receive offers to stay with the new organization. Those with expertise considered unusually critical to the success of the organization should be noted.
- Employees who will be terminated.
- Employees who will be recruited from elsewhere in the organization.
- Positions that must be filled with new hires.
- Information on severance packages.
- Types and amounts of training required for each employee position.

- Information on compensation packages, including how the benefits offered by the acquired company and the acquiring company will be harmonized.

The components of the compensation packages are especially important because they will help bind employees to the organization. Indeed, compensation programs often provide an early warning of cultural incompatibility that may jeopardize a merger. In today's tight labor market, there is a need for considerable flexibility in the development of compensation packages. The same perks do not always motivate younger workers and older ones.

If a substantial number of positions must be filled with new hires, the integration management team should consider hiring an outside consultant to manage the recruiting. Because one company had to fill over a hundred positions with new employees, a two-part strategy was used. First, a consultant was hired to identify and screen potential job candidates. Second, key positions were temporarily filled with employees from elsewhere in the organization; some of these "loaned" employees were retained for as long as two years.

As employees begin to accept offers with the new organization, training becomes critical. All employees should be involved in some form of training to ensure that they know what is expected of them and that they have the requisite job skills to perform satisfactorily. At a minimum, the integration management team should provide training or indoctrination in corporate mission, vision, and values; company benefits; policies and procedures; the new organizational structure; the performance appraisal system; basic computer software; telecommunications systems; and job-specific procedures. One company required all employees to attend an orientation session that provided an overview of the company, its policies and procedures, benefits, products, and strategic goals. All employees were also required to meet with their managers to develop an individual training plan specifying the types of training in which they would need to participate to meet job requirements. In addition, within their first year of employment, all employees participated in a series of workshops on the new company mission and values. On a smaller scale, DaimlerChrysler has developed a cross-cultural executive training program for managers and their families being relocated between the United States and Germany.

### Key Lessons from Previous Experience

- Expect a high level of anxiety among employees.
- Be prepared to repeat key messages concerning organization and staffing.
- Expect that there will be a higher than usual level of employee turnover, even among employees who have accepted offers with the new organization, for at least 18 months after the acquisition.
- Train, train, and then train some more.
- Understand that mistakes will be made in staffing; be prepared to cut losses quickly.

- Sell the corporate culture as a major company benefit.
- Examine compensation packages carefully to ensure that they correctly reflect corporate values and will be effective in retaining employees.

## National and Organizational Culture

Every organization has a culture or a common set of values, traditions, and beliefs that influence behavior. Corporate culture provides the unwritten rules that shape employees' behavior, sets expectations for performance, and determines the types of rewards that will be offered. Consequently, corporate culture can affect an organization's long-term economic performance, and it is likely to become even more important during the next few years as companies continue to globalize.

Large organizations generally have a dominant overall culture, as well as a series of subcultures that reflect unique local differences. Inbound acquisitions in the United States, then, involve not only two potentially strong corporate cultures but also distinctive national cultures as well. Unless the cultural differences are recognized and dealt with, the integration of the two organizations may not succeed.

When a company is acquired, employees find that behavior that was once rewarded may now be unacceptable. Values and traditions change. Even more important, expectations for performance may differ completely. Since Cadbury Schweppes acquired Snapple in September 2000, the Snapple management team has been striving to combine the best of both corporate cultures. Snapple is young, entrepreneurial, and quick to respond to changes in its market. Cadbury Schweppes is very strategy driven. Ongoing management development is an essential activity. The challenge for Snapple is to retain its organizational agility and youthful outlook while learning to think and act strategically, behaviors that are quite different from those that have been rewarded in the past.

If employees become confused about what is considered appropriate behavior, their productivity may decline. In the past, some companies have avoided potential culture clashes by managing their acquisitions as essentially separate entities. With the increasing emphasis on globalization and the accompanying need for economies of scale, however, this approach is rarely feasible today. Unilever, for example, has solved this problem by creating a strong corporate value system while also taking care not to obliterate productive local cultural traits. Clearly, the integration management team must give considerable attention to the creation of an appropriate new culture.

### Culture Profiles

The first step that the integration management team must take is to develop a profile of the organizational culture of both the acquiring and the acquired companies. Information can be gathered through surveys, interviews, and the observation of management styles and practices. Some key questions are:

- What are people rewarded for?
- What are they punished for?
- What is valued?
- How are people rewarded?

Company documents, such as mission and vision statements and lists of corporate values, should also be reviewed. As the profile of each company is completed, the integration management team should develop a matrix that shows how the two cultures are alike, how they are different, and how each culture's characteristics support or detract from the strategic goals of the new organization. The results should be reviewed with the senior management team. Team members should be asked to reach a consensus concerning the analysis and the major characteristics of the new combined culture. For example, when a British spirits company acquired a bourbon distiller, it discovered that one organization valued teamwork, whereas the other emphasized individualism; that one believed in developing people, whereas the other preferred to lure already trained employees from competitors; and that one had few formal systems and only informal business planning, whereas the other emphasized formal systems and conducted extensive planning. Both companies, however, valued financial performance highly. The new culture combined the best qualities of both companies and supported its strategic vision.

### Culture Implementation Plan

After the new culture has been described, the integration management team should develop a plan for implementing it or for at least moving the existing culture in the right direction. The plan should include:

- A detailed description of the new culture, including an explanation of how it builds on the cultures of the two merging companies and how it supports the new company's competitive position.
- A list of policies, procedures, and processes that may need to be changed, for example, if the new culture values teamwork, compensation plans may need to be modified to ensure that teamwork rather than individual performance is rewarded.
- Training programs designed to help employees understand the cultural changes and make appropriate adjustments in their behavior. Employees should feel involved in the cultural realignment.
- A company-wide communication plan designed to keep everyone informed of the value of the new culture and progress in implementing it. Opportunities should be provided, whenever possible, for employees of the merging companies to get to know each other. (See pages 514 to 517.)
- An implementation timetable.

In making cultural change, most companies have found that examples are much more effective than pronouncements. At one British company, for example, senior managers were encouraged to "walk the talk" and to model appropriate behavior for their teams. Training programs were developed to provide managers and staff with a guide to behavior, as well as examples that illustrated what was acceptable and what was not acceptable. Work teams were brought together to discuss these guides and to review how they might put them into practice. Similarly, employees were given information about the new culture—why it would make the organization more competitive and how it would help them be more effective. Employees were also asked what they thought the implications were for daily behavior.

### National Cultural Differences

The integration management team should examine the national cultural differences that might affect the successful integration of the two organizations. Even with the increasing emphasis on globalization, national cultural differences have not disappeared; in fact, they may be intensifying. The integration management team's responsibility, then, is not to eliminate national cultural differences but to make employees aware of the differences and their implications. For example, not long after Marks and Spencer acquired Brooks Brothers, managers from both companies concluded that many of their difficulties were caused by cultural differences in communication styles. Brooks Brothers employees were disturbed that Marks and Spencer managers often closed their office doors and communicated more by memo than by telephone. Through management training sessions designed to increase each group's awareness of the other's cultural preference, they have learned to work together. The Brooks Brothers managers have become much more proficient in communication in writing. Their formal business presentations have also become more effective. Despite all of these improvements, Marks and Spencer decided to put Brooks Brothers back on the market in 2001 in order to concentrate on its core European business.

Some of the most frequently encountered national cultural differences that might conflict with a U.S. view are summarized in Exhibit 15.1. Some implications for management are also suggested.

When integrating U.S. and British managers into a cohesive team, one company held a series of management discussion groups to help senior managers develop a higher degree of cultural self-awareness. The managers discussed differences in management and communication styles, as well as problems they were having relating to each other. A facilitator then pointed out the cultural dimensions of the differences, and team members developed strategies for working around those differences. After they returned to their jobs, the managers discussed their findings with their teams and developed strategies for increasing cultural sensitivity within their own operating areas. One of the most important discoveries to come from these team meetings was the U.S. employees' deep resentment of the use of British English in orientation materials, company brochures, internal memos, and so forth. There was a strong sense that the British managers should comply with local usage and refer to "orientation training," for example, rather than

## EXHIBIT 15.1

**National Cultural Differences**

| U.S. Cultural View | Other Cultures' Possible View | Implication for Management |
|---|---|---|
| We are in charge of our destiny: Where there is a will there is a way. | Fate determines everything. | Planning |
| Hard work is always rewarded. | Luck and family connections are essential for success. | Motivation and reward systems. |
| We promote people according to their merit; the best-qualified person gets the job. | Family and other connections are more important than merit. | Hiring, promoting, and reward systems. |
| Employees should be given both good and bad feedback concerning their performance. It is good to praise employees in public. | Calling attention to individuals is embarrassing and results in loss of face. Feedback should be indirect. | Performance appraisal systems. |
| Corporate communications should generally be open and free. Informality is good. | Information is power. Therefore, it should be guarded carefully. Formal communications are preferred. | Management style, interpersonal and interdivisional communications. |
| Time is valuable and should not be wasted; punctuality is important. | Personal matters are just as important as business. | Planning, meetings, protocol. |

"induction training" and that employees should be "let go" or "terminated" rather than "made redundant." Chrysler employees have expressed similar resentment of the British English used by Daimler-Benz.

### *Key Lessons from Previous Experience*

- The culture of an organization and the values of the people that make up the organization must be compatible; expect to lose some employees because they cannot or will not change.
- Culture is hard to change, even in a global economy.
- Change should not be made just for change's sake; changes should always be explained.
- Culture change programs need a very visible and highly respected champion who will "walk the talk."
- Language difficulties are not always obvious; people do not like to admit that they do not understand.

- Management style is very much a part of culture.
- Expatriates and their families benefit from briefings on cultural differences that help them adjust to their new assignments.

## Mission, Values, and Common Language

Integral to the establishment of a new, cohesive corporate culture is the development of a mission statement that reflects the values, goals, and strategic vision of both the acquiring and the acquired organizations. The mission statement provides employees with a common sense of identity that transcends national boundaries and areas of specialization. It generally includes an explanation of the company's:

- Purpose or reason for existing.
- Unique products, services, or technology.
- Economic goals, such as expansion of market share or profitability.
- Competitive strengths and operating philosophy.
- Values that are most important in a global environment.

After an acquisition, the acquired company is often given the mission of its new owner and is expected to comply. In the case of "mergers of equals" and the combination of very different organizations, however, the creation of a new mission is advisable. The new mission should delineate the purpose of the new organization while also incorporating as many positive traits of the old organizations as possible. When a large organization acquires a very small, unique company, there may be other considerations. When Unilever acquired Ben & Jerry's in 2000, both companies were acutely aware that the ice cream company's strong social mission was vitally important for the company's success. As soon as the acquisition was announced, Unilever's chairmen commented on Ben & Jerry's strong brand name and unique consumer message. They stated that Unilever intended to continue nurturing Ben & Jerry's commitment to community values. The president of Unilever North America further reiterated the chairmen's message. It appears, however, that Unilever's commitment to support Ben & Jerry's social agenda was only for a specific number of years. Analysts are now wondering if the brand will continue to thrive without that support.

To ensure that the corporate mission statement serves as an effective unifying element and a guide for behavior, the integration management team should provide copies for all employees. The mission statement should be discussed in all employee orientation sessions. The integration management team should also hold a series of follow-up briefings to review the mission statement again and to discuss its implications for daily operations and behavior. Discussions should encourage open debate of the meaning of the mission statement and of the way it differs from the organization's previous one. The integration management team should be prepared to resolve any areas of conflict, especially those involving cultural differences. After the conclusion of the follow-up briefings, the integration management team should involve key managers in the development of new mission statements for their operating units. Again, employees within each unit should be encouraged to discuss the implications of the mission statement for their activities.

Many multinational organizations also find that as they make increasing numbers of acquisitions, they need to periodically reconsider their corporate mission statements to make them more all-inclusive. After a series of global acquisitions that rapidly expanded the company, one British company set up an international task force to review its corporate mission statement. The task force concluded that:

- A new corporate culture could not be bought off the shelf.
- New values and approaches could not be implemented by mandate nor could old values be dislodged by decree.
- All employees have a responsibility to operate within the bounds of the agreed-upon values.

To clarify the direction of the organization and to provide guidelines for employees, the task force revised the mission statement and drafted a new list of corporate values. Among the values included were internationalism, respect for people, involvement in local communities, social responsibility, environmental concern, standards for performance, growth and development of brands, and a sense of common purpose. Internationalism and a sense of common purpose were considered especially important because these values recognized that the company was made up of many different personalities, styles, and backgrounds, all unified by a shared mission.

### Key Lessons from Previous Experience

- Values are culturally sensitive.
- Values are best taught through examples.
- Most organizations do not fully understand what their values are until they are challenged by another organization.
- Employee involvement in the development of a mission statement is critical for its acceptance.
- Strong, well-articulated values can be a powerful marketing tool.
- Overly ambitious or idealistic mission statements lead to cynicism.

Sometimes the mission of an acquired company is so unique and so powerfully linked to that company's success that it should not be changed.

## Overall Organizational Structure

When Guinness began to acquire worldwide, the company's slogan was "Think Global; Act Local." By the early 1990s, however, the senior management team realized that it also had to simultaneously think globally and locally while also acting globally and locally. This change in attitude was reflected in modifications to the organizational structure. Early acquisitions were grouped by geographic region. The corporate staff, however, increased in size because most strategic decisions were still made in London. This contributed to the company's Eurocentric focus. Concurrently, there was considerable duplication of services within the various regions. It was difficult to identify and to use specialized expertise that was spread throughout the organization.

Clearly the successful integration of an acquisition requires a new organizational model with emphasis on:

- Local autonomy combined with centralized control and coordination.
- Greater input into corporate decisions from subsidiaries.
- The coordination and transfer of information among subsidiaries.
- The use of cross-functional and cross-divisional teams and informal networks.
- The equal treatment of all subsidiaries, including the domestic ones.
- A strong, unified corporate culture that is flexible enough to allow for unique needs within the subsidiaries.
- The selection of senior managers by qualifications and skills, not just in conformity with the buyer's nationality.
- The re-engineering of work processes to improve efficiency and the transfer of information.

To help develop the new organization and to gain commitment to its new structure, the integration management team should organize smaller teams to assist in conducting analyses and in making recommendations. These should be composed of members of both the buyer and the target companies. The smaller teams should review the existing structure and management practices; select best practices; identify redundant sites, processes, and positions; and make recommendations concerning the centralization and decentralization of various functions. SmithKline and Beecham used this team approach during their merger and found that in some instances dedicated teams actually organized themselves out of their jobs. Even more important, by the end of the process, the remaining teams had established sound working relationships and eliminated the us-versus-them syndrome.

As the final recommendations for the organizational structure are completed, the integration management team should develop a plan for implementing the new structure. The plan should include detailed strategies for communicating the changes to employees and for encouraging them to see the strategic value the changes will offer. The plan should also include strategies for providing training to ensure that employees can perform satisfactorily in their new positions. The best such plans include general information on the strategic advantages offered by the transaction; an overview of the merged companies, the newly created company's mission, and key products; information on changes in the reporting structure;

and technical training in the performance of new job duties and the use of new software programs.

To monitor how well the implementation of the new organizational structure is proceeding, the integration management team should provide for an annual or a biannual employee survey to assess various dimensions of organizational effectiveness. After the survey results have been analyzed, a summary of the findings should be communicated throughout the organization. Details relating to potential problems throughout the new organization should be provided to the appropriate managers and should be used as the basis for organizational interventions designed to encourage discussion of the problem and the development of solutions. The integration management team should also make provisions for a series of post-implementation reviews of the new organization's structure. Most organizations find that a series of organizational corrections are still required 12 to 24 months after the initial reorganization.

### Key Lessons from Previous Experience

- Expect resistance to change; remember that realigning boxes on a chart does not make a new organization come to life.
- Be honest with employees about what has to be done.
- Remember that employee involvement makes changing the organizational structure easier and helps build teamwork.
- Think in terms of processes, not just reporting relationships.
- Do not delay the reorganization.
- Follow-up is critical.
- Expect to continue to make adjustments for several years.

## Functional Areas

When most companies conduct their initial due diligence of a target, they generally spend a lot of time considering top-level strategic issues, financial concerns, and perhaps even the "softer" cultural factors; but they often fail to examine the strengths, weaknesses, and unique characteristics of individual functional areas. Very few examine how or if they should be integrated. Even experienced global companies overlook the implications of combining potentially very different marketing and sales organizations, distribution mechanisms, accounting practices, information systems, and information technologies.

Studies by Booz Allen, by New York University, and by others conclude that as many as 33 percent to 60 percent of all mergers ultimately destroy the value of the acquired company. Just as significant, many targets are later divested. The target's performance often declines immediately after the acquisition is announced. Chrysler is a recent example. There may be some loss of market share as customers consider other suppliers, just in case there is an interruption in service. Sales personnel may also leave and take key accounts with them. In addition, there may be a decline in productivity because of the increased uncertainty in the daily operating environment. Employees have many questions, but there are few answers because little thought has been given to operational details. Consequently, there is a tendency for acquiring companies to go through an initial reorganization immediately after completing an acquisition and to then repeat the process 18 to 24 months later.

To lessen the potential for poor performance immediately after an acquisition and to take advantage of unique skills and capabilities provided by the target company, the integration management team should conduct an audit of the functional areas within both companies. The result of the audit can be invaluable in achieving the overall integration of the two companies and identifying unique competitive advantages. Consider the integration possibilities in the sub sections that follow.

### Information Systems

Although companies are increasingly dependent on computerized information systems (IS) for communications and decision making, this area is one of the most frequently overlooked during the due diligence process. However, it should be one of the most carefully studied because information technology is expensive and often hard to integrate. On the other hand, the correct use of information technology, such as e-mail, web sites, facsimile, centralized order processing, and automated warehousing, are often critical for facilitating the overall integration process. ABB, for example, has a standardized systems base that helps the company operate more innovatively and creatively.

Important questions that the postmerger integration team must address are:

- The extent to which the acquiring and the acquired companies will be integrated.
- The degree of centralization versus decentralization desired.
- The availability of someone to champion IS changes.

If the buyer intends to allow the target organization to function relatively independently, its information systems can be left relatively intact as long as communications linkages between the two organizations are established. For example, when a French company acquired a U.S. manufacturer of surgical instruments, it determined that the two operations were so different that they should continue to operate independently. A review of IS in both organizations revealed that, with minor modifications, they were compatible and that communications could be established. Consequently, both systems were left intact. The French company merely specified the types of information it required, as well as how and when the information should be reported. In those areas where the U.S. company's system could not readily communicate with the French company's system, a stand-alone personal computer (PC)–based system was provided. No immediate attempts were made to standardize software or to make the IS more effective in meeting the overall needs of the new postmerger organization.

But if the buyer intends to integrate the target company, the task is more complex, and the combination of both information systems into a new operation is usually required. Recent studies by Cossey suggest that nearly 70 percent of acquiring companies opt to combine their IS operations immediately after the acquisition is completed, whereas almost 90 percent eventually combine them. The emergence of enterprise resource planning (ERP) software has made system integration and standardization much easier to accomplish.

As soon as the integration management team has determined the extent to which the buyer and the target organizations will be integrated, it should conduct a review of both company's information systems to determine their quality and effectiveness. The team should begin by examining existing due diligence information and, if necessary, should supplement that information with indepth discussions with systems experts and visits to key installations in both organizations.

The review should focus on at least six areas:

1. Hardware.
2. Software.
3. Communications capabilities and networks.
4. Technical support.
5. Business requirements and the systems needed to support them.
6. Compatibility of existing systems.

Because few companies have a clear understanding of all their hardware and software, the integration management team should catalog all the hardware used and specify whether it is owned or leased, where it is located, and how it is used. The age, reliability, and estimated capacity of each item should also be identified because these are especially important if the buyer intends to make additional acquisitions in the same market.

The integration management team should examine all communications technology and networks to determine the types of voice and data communications systems used, whether there are local-area or wide-area networks, and the number and location of all terminals and microcomputers that might permit network access. The current effectiveness of all networks, as well as their ability to meet additional demands, should also be analyzed. The team should also review any web-based services, such as order inquiry and supply chain management, and should make provisions for keeping these services up and running while changes are being made.

As hardware and software are identified, the team should analyze the types of technical support available, including technical documentation; vendor agreements concerning training, troubleshooting, and maintenance; in-house training and support functions; and standards for systems development and operation. The capacities of both the vendor-provided and in-company services should be compared to anticipated demand for the next two to three years. Areas of strengths and weaknesses should be noted. To determine customer satisfaction with technical support services, team members should interview some of their customers.

After an inventory of existing systems and their characteristics has been completed, the integration management team should examine the overall information needs of both companies and define the type of IS needed. During this process, the team should consider whether the existing systems are compatible and have the capacity to handle additional demands. Particular attention should be paid to unique qualities that the target's systems may possess because there is often a tendency for these to be overlooked in favor of the buyer's systems. Potential culture clashes and power struggles between the target and the buyer, however, should not be allowed to impact the development of an appropriate IS.

In a typical postmerger integration of systems, key system users are asked to agree on specific areas of common development and processing. Often such selections will include order processing, traffic, financial processes, market spend, and sales-promotion tracking.

After all data collection and analysis have been completed, the integration management team should develop a plan for systems integration. As information and systems requirements are defined, appropriate staffing levels should be determined. The team should assess whether existing staffing levels are adequate and whether personnel have the right technical skills. A training plan for both technical systems personnel and all systems users should be developed. If new systems are being implemented, the team should also pay particular attention to providing ongoing user support during the period of changeover from the old system to the new. In addition, because of the expense and the time required, the team should try to minimize the amount of customized system design required.

Experience in integrating IS indicates that there is a tendency to underestimate the period of time required to achieve all integration goals. In large cross-border deals, the period may span the tenure of several corporate leaders.

### Key Lessons from Previous Experience

- Position a systems integration project as a business change initiative linked to strategic objectives.
- Ensure that there are several respected, high-level champions of systems integration committed to the project. These individuals must ensure the commitment and involvement of all stakeholders.
- Conduct a thorough IS and technology analysis during the preacquisition due diligence.
- Understand that the standardization of global IS and a decentralized corporate culture are rarely compatible.
- Make sure that newly integrated IS add value and support ongoing changes.
- Establish detailed plans for data management across borders.
- Resist the temptation to operate with fragmented systems.
- Review communications technology to ensure that it is adequate to promote high levels of interaction throughout the organization.
- Expect the integration of IS to be harder and to take more time than planned.

- Communicate, communicate, communicate to ensure that key stakeholders understand the benefits of systems changes and the timetable for completion.
- Conduct a postintegration review to ensure that all systems are operating as expected and to identify the "lessons learned" for the next acquisition.

## Finance

Although considerable financial information is typically collected during the preacquisition due diligence, often little thought is given then to how multiple financial functions can be integrated. The first issue that the integration management team should address is very broad and affects all subsequent ones: How can the finance functions be integrated to capture the most value while also providing the best support for future business operations? The second issue is to determine the buyer's strategy for integrating the target's financial system. If the target is to remain separate, its finance and accounting organizations may remain relatively intact and may operate more or less autonomously so long as they report required information to the buyer's headquarters.

Many companies making acquisitions in the U.S. market prefer to place one of their most trusted employees in charge of the finance function. When a French manufacturer acquired a company in the United States, the French company replaced the chief financial officer in the acquisition with a French employee from headquarters. The French company wanted to ensure that the information it was receiving could be trusted and that it had a uniquely French perspective on the new business. Other companies believe, however, that using an expatriate is too expensive and may lead to charges of cultural imperialism.

The third issue that the integration management team must consider is the degree of centralization versus decentralization desired. Traditionally this decision has been made on the basis of cost and the perceived need for local autonomy. In today's increasingly competitive and globally integrated market place, however, the most important criteria are the selection and execution of strategic focus. As Michael Treacy and Fred Wiersema concluded in *The Value Disciplines*, successful companies focus their strategic intent on a value discipline, such as operational excellence, customer intimacy, or product innovation. If *operational excellence* is selected, then the provision of products and services at the lowest total cost becomes critical, and the implication for the organizational structure is centralization with top-down decision making and highly standardized efficient business processes. If, on the other hand, *customer intimacy* is selected as the company's strategic focus, then the organizational implication is to place key functions as close to the customer as possible. Consequently, the finance and accounting functions would be decentralized to operating units.

This is the approach that a British spirits company evolved for its operations in the United States. Although separate finance functions were initially retained for each U.S. acquisition, when the decision was made to fully integrate them into North American operations, a new regional finance function was established. Its purpose was to provide all routine financial services, as well as specific types of data required by both the London office and local operations. The initial plan called for the development of a common monthly reporting format, the implementation of a standardized annual budgeting and planning process, the consolidation of the purchasing function, and the centralization of cash management and credit and collections. Continued consolidation in the spirits industry is forcing the company to regularly reexamine the issue of centralization versus decentralization.

Once the strategic issues of integration and centralization versus decentralization have been settled, the integration management team should conduct a thorough review of existing financial controls and systems. Particular attention should be paid to budgets, plans, cost systems, operating procedures, reports, and flow charts of key processes. Budgets should be examined to determine whether the company has both capital and operating budgets, as well as the time period covered by each. There should also be an analysis of who gets the budgets and how the information is used. For example, are variances incorporated into the budgets throughout the year? Are the budgets used as a control mechanism or merely generated and then filed until the next budgeting cycle? Similar information should be collected concerning cost systems and plans. When reviewing financial reports, the team should identify not only the types of reports generated but also their frequency, distribution, and use. The team should also determine whether the amount of financial information produced is adequate, inadequate, or too much. Throughout the review process, the team should also consider two overall concerns: (1) whether the acquired organization has any operating procedures or reports that should be adopted by the acquiring company and (2) whether the existing processes and procedures can be easily integrated into those of the acquiring company.

A similar review should be conducted for credit and collection functions, as well as for information systems. Throughout its review, the integration management team should pay particular attention to any unique skills or types of expertise possessed by personnel within the acquired organization. The overall strengths and weaknesses of personnel should also be assessed.

Potential philosophical differences relating to planning, as well as the use and disclosure of financial information, should also be identified because they can have an impact both on the achievement of overall strategic objectives and on how well managers from both organizations work together. For example, Japanese companies tend to have longer planning horizons than their U.S. counterparts. South American companies tend to place less emphasis on long-range planning than either Japanese or U.S. companies do. Many Eastern European and Russian companies have little experience in planning and budgeting because they are accustomed to operating in centrally planned economies. Both Russian and French companies are more reluctant to disclose financial information than those in the United States or England. If the integration management team understands these potential philosophical differences, it can help managers in both the acquiring and the acquired organizations learn to work together more effectively.

The importance of careful due diligence in all of these areas is exemplified by the experience of a British food company in the United States. When the company acquired a New York–based, family-owned pasta company, the due diligence revealed that the acquired company had no planning process and only a very rudimentary budgeting process. Further review revealed that cost systems were inadequate and that operating procedures were rarely followed. Family members were accustomed to just doing whatever they thought was appropriate for a particular situation. In spite of these concerns, the acquiring British company decided to keep family members in key management positions after the acquisition because they were respected members of national trade associations and well connected in the Northeastern food industry. Unfortunately, however, the family members never accepted the need to submit budgets and plans to their new corporate owner, and the British company lost considerable time trying to gain control of the finance functions of its acquisition.

When a British beverage company reviewed the finance and accounting functions of its U.S. acquisitions, it had an entirely different experience. The company discovered that credit and collection procedures were quite different from those used in Great Britain. It also learned that the financial reports generated by the acquisitions were inadequate and that a new reporting structure would be required. Unlike the British food company, the beverage company decided to replace the chief financial officers of its acquisitions with one individual who was a U.S. citizen and who had experience working for them in North America. The result was a much smoother transition because this individual understood both the peculiarities of the U.S. market and the needs of the acquiring British company.

After completing its analysis of existing financial functions and the needs of the new organization, the integration management team should prepare a plan that addresses:

- Development of common reports and reporting intervals.
- Development of common operating procedures for key areas.
- Interfaces required for information systems.
- Need for the adaptation of existing systems or the development of new ones.
- Staffing and training requirements.
- Time and resources required to complete all integration activities.

In all of these areas, the team should consider how to achieve maximum efficiencies while also providing adequate information and controls for future growth. The focus should be on added value.

Throughout the integration period, the team should ensure that financial and accounting services are not interrupted and that staffing transitions take place in an orderly manner. To ensure maximum compliance with new operating and reporting procedures, representatives of both the acquiring and the acquired organizations should participate in their development. The benefits of the new procedures should be clearly stated. In addition, adequate training in the use of new procedures and IS should be provided for all personnel.

### *Key Lessons from Previous Experience*

- Focus on capturing value through cost savings and the provision of better data for decision making.
- Be aware that cultural differences affect planning, budgeting, and the disclosure of financial information.
- Be aware that legal differences also affect the disclosure and the reporting of financial information.
- Make sure that IS are adequate to support financial information needs.
- Ensure that the flow of adequate financial information is not disrupted during the integration period.
- Look for any unique types of expertise resident in the acquired organization that should be retained.
- Conduct a postintegration review approximately 6 to 12 months after the completion of all integration activities to determine what worked really well and what should be improved for the next acquisition.

## *Sales*

The first two issues that the integration management team must consider are strategic in nature and affect all other integration activities. The first issue relates to centralization versus decentralization. Depending on the size of the acquiring and the acquired companies, the acquiring company's experience in the global market place, the markets both companies serve, and the nature of their primary product lines, the acquiring company may choose to manage the new acquisition as a relatively independent entity or to more fully integrate it into overall operations. Companies without extensive international operations often decide to leave a new acquisition's sales function essentially intact because it allows them to extend their operations with little effort.

The second issue focuses on the strategic intent of the acquisition: the value that the sales function of the acquired company is expected to contribute to the new organization. The integration management team should review the premerger analysis, determine if it is still valid, and then use it as a guideline throughout all subsequent postmerger integration activities.

As soon as the overall strategic issues related to the management of the acquired company have been resolved, the integration management team should begin a thorough review of both the acquiring and the acquired company's products and services. The team should compile a detailed inventory of all products and services, including descriptions of their characteristics and typical users. New products and services currently being developed should also be reviewed. The completed inventory should then be compared to the acquiring company's objectives for product-line coverage to determine areas of duplication, potential synergies, continuing gaps in offerings, potential conflicts between the acquiring company's products and those of the acquired company, and the strengths and weaknesses of each item.

In their recent acquisitions, both Cadbury Schweppes and Nestlé have followed current conventional wisdom for success in the food industry: Increase offerings of fully branded products and dominate shelf space. Cadbury Schweppes acquired Snapple Beverages Group to expand its position in the U.S. soft drinks market. For the past several years, colas have not been growing as fast as noncolas. Snapple is the leading brand in the profitable, high-growth premium tea and juice segments of the New Age beverage market. Similarly, Nestlé acquired Ralston Purina to expand its pet food business, especially in the rapidly growing dry-dog-food category. Pet food is one of the few expanding categories in the food industry. Ralston Purina had a 39 percent share of the dry-dog-food market, whereas Nestlé had only 6 percent. Nestlé is now the world's largest producer of pet food.

An additional review should be conducted to determine whether there are legal liabilities related to any of the products or whether there are government regulations affecting the distribution and the use of some items. For example, in the United States the acquisition of a spirits brand name does not necessarily give the acquirer the right to assign it to another distributor. The laws governing the discounting of alcoholic beverages also vary by state. Even companies with extensive global experience in their markets can misunderstand the implications of foreign government regulations. A British spirits company underestimated the differences between British and U.S. laws governing the sale of spirits. The company initially tried to implement the British approach to distribution in the U.S. spirits market. Because each state governs the sale of alcoholic beverages within its borders, however, the United States is essentially composed of 50 different markets. Consequently, distribution systems and sales regulations vary considerably. In some states, alcoholic beverages cannot be sold on Sundays; in other states, all sales are through state-controlled stores. Within some states, there are "dry" areas where alcoholic beverages cannot be sold.

After the product review has been completed, the integration management team should focus on sales forecasting techniques and systems, as well as overall sales systems. The team should consider whether the acquired company has a sophisticated forecasting system based on historical trends and industry-specific information or whether the forecasts are just the sales force's best guesses. The team should review how forecasts are used, how they are analyzed for accuracy, how often they are modified, and how accurate they have been over the past five years. In industries where a long lead time is required for production, such as the production of forest products, accurate forecasts of demand are essential.

In reviewing the sales systems and their effectiveness, the integration management team should analyze all sales processes, including developing and tracking leads, calling on customers, closing sales, placing orders, training staff, resolving complaints, and compensating sales personnel. E-commerce sales processes should also be carefully examined. To determine how all the processes interact, the team should prepare flowcharts of each process and designate the appropriate input and output. The team should also note the type and the effectiveness of all technology used in each process, for example, whether sales personnel have laptop computers or other electronic devices that they can use in the field to input orders and to update their forecasts.

When reviewing the sales-related processes, particular attention should be paid to staff training. Some sales organizations prefer to hire individuals who already have considerable experience and, consequently, who require little additional training. Others prefer to hire inexperienced personnel so they can be trained in the company's unique sales approach. Still others tend to hire inexperienced personnel and to then train them by the sink-or-swim method. These organizations usually have high personnel turnover rates, but they consider them part of the normal cost of doing business.

The team should identify the types of sales approaches used by both the acquiring and the acquired companies—whether sales are made through a catalog, via the Internet, in company-owned stores, by sales representatives who are company employees, or by an external sales force that represents several other companies. The team should also determine whether the sales are made directly to customers or to a distributor. While reviewing sales systems, the integration management team should identify and examine any potential strategic differences, as well as their implications. This review is particularly important because it impacts the acquiring company's ability to obtain maximum value from the acquisition. Sales strategies can be customer driven, revenue driven, or profit driven. When a British beverage company reviewed its acquisition's sales operations, the integration management team discovered that the sales force's overall objective was to maximize revenue, even if that meant minimizing profit. The development of key accounts was not considered a high priority. The acquiring company's objective, however, was twofold: (1) to maximize profit and (2) to increase market share. Consequently, significant changes had to be made in the sales force's overall focus.

The integration management team should also examine the sales function's management and staffing. The initial review should focus on how they can be organized to optimize their effectiveness. The amount of annual personnel turnover should also be carefully reviewed. If the sales forces of the acquiring and the acquired companies are to be combined, then the integration management team should determine the appropriate level of staffing for the new organization. Subsequently, an in-depth examination of the strengths and the weaknesses of individual managers and sales personnel should be conducted. It should include the following areas:

- Knowledge of products, market, and customers.
- Contacts within the industry.
- Accuracy of managers' and sales personnel's forecasts.
- Consistency in achieving sales goals.
- Ability to retain key accounts.
- Ability to work well with others.
- Understanding of other functional areas within the organization and how sales interacts with them.
- Ability to assess sales data and take corrective action.

- Ability to train and develop others.
- Unique skills or areas of expertise.
- Commitment to the goals and values of the new organization.

Key sales personnel and managers whom the acquiring company wants to retain should be notified as soon as possible so that service to their customers will not be disrupted.

After the overall sales approach and personnel issues have been examined, the integration management team should focus on the optimization of distribution channels and systems. In addition to opportunities for synergy, key considerations should be accessibility to domestic and international markets, responsiveness to customers, cost effectiveness, and stability.

Both warehousing and shipping operations should be reviewed to determine if they have adequate information systems support for monitoring inventory levels and tracking shipments. Careful attention should also be paid to potential government regulations or other legal requirements that might impact the acquiring company's ability to standardize distribution systems throughout the acquired company or to make sales via the Internet. For example, some companies are finding that they may have to restrict the Internet sale of some items in other countries, even when their web sites are based in the United States.

After completing its review of the acquired company's sales systems, the integration management team should review all processes for dealing with customer service. Procedures for monitoring and resolving complaints should be identified and examined for effectiveness. Similarly, the average number and the type of customer complaints should be reviewed to determine if there are recurring patterns of problems with specific product lines or sales personnel.

Key accounts should also be identified. For each account the integration management team should develop a profile that describes types and volume of purchases, unique challenges in meeting customer requirements, and price sensitivity. In addition, profiles describing the types and the volume of purchases should be developed for each account. In industries where there has been significant consolidation of major customers, the profile should also include implications for the postmerger organization, particularly its ability to deliver value. Because acquisitions tend to make customers uneasy, members of the integration management team or senior representatives of the acquiring company should contact all key customers to reassure them that service will not be disrupted.

As the review of all critical areas of the sales function is completed, the integration management team should begin preparing a detailed plan for integrating the sales function of the acquired company into the acquiring company. The plan should focus on creating value in six key areas: (1) the structure of the sales function, (2) sales strategies, (3) sales processes, (4) products, (5) personnel issues, and (6) customer retention. The plan should detail any rationalization of product lines and distribution channels that may need to be accomplished. Sales strategies and processes should be described.

Guidelines should be provided for the disposition of all personnel, including roles and responsibilities within the new organization, severance packages for those being terminated, compensation packages, arrangements for relocation to other geographic areas, and training requirements.

With the current emphasis on continuous organizational learning and skills improvement as a means of improving competitive advantage, ongoing sales training becomes particularly important. Provisions should be made for both immediate and long-term training sessions. The initial training should focus on changes in procedures and sales techniques, the use of new technology, and the characteristics of new products. Subsequent sessions should emphasize sales performance, changes in customer requirements, and new product introductions. Many global organizations find that the cost of ongoing training can be prohibitive if training personnel are maintained in all sales units. To solve the problem, these organizations often identify units or individuals throughout their operations who are particularly proficient in conducting specific types of training and use them as resources.

There should be an implementation time line detailing key activities and completion dates. Provisions should be made to review the effectiveness of the integration activities within 12 to 18 months.

### Key Lessons from Previous Experience

- Restructure sales to capture the most value while allowing flexibility for meeting future business objectives.
- Review all products and services from a strategic point of view—how these products can further the strategic-value-building objectives of the company.
- Expect customers to be concerned about the impact of an acquisition; make sure that service does not decline during the integration period.
- Communicate all planned changes as quickly as possible to staff and customers.
- Emphasize the positive aspects of changes in sales portfolios, personal assignments, and so on.
- Have a plan for modifying the culture of the sales organization in the acquired company so that it will be compatible with that of the acquiring organization.
- Conduct training programs to provide all sales personnel in the newly integrated organization with information on unfamiliar products.
- Look for ways to leverage training expertise from one part of the organization to another.

### Marketing

The current emphasis on globalization often means that traditionally centralized support services, such as marketing, are being decentralized or contracted to outside suppliers. Unilever, for example, emphasizes creating brands on a global basis, while also giving regional and country marketing managers considerable autonomy to respond to local conditions. However, it is interesting to note that in 2001 Unilever implemented a significant rationalization program to enhance its focus on key brands. Repositioning some marketing services in operating units increases awareness of unique local needs and shortens the response time to changes in market conditions. Using outside vendors reduces costs and improves flexibility. In beginning a review of the marketing function of a newly acquired company, the integration management team should consider how best to capture the most value in the new organization.

*Market Review*.   Once decisions have been made concerning the location and the overall integration of the marketing function, the integration management team should conduct a detailed review of all markets served by both the acquiring and the acquired companies. The review should focus on the similarities and differences between all markets and should include details, such as:

- Levels of market maturity.
- Potential impact of consolidation or other industry trends.
- Stability versus seasonality of product lines.
- Legal issues and other special circumstances affecting operations.
- Possible areas of conflict in terms of markets served.
- Cultural differences in foreign and domestic markets.
- Marketing strategies for each product line.
- Support services provided by marketing personnel.

Levels of market maturity are especially important if the acquiring company already has numerous products reaching maturity. Similarly, stable demand is very important if the acquiring company has numerous products that are only in demand during specific seasons. For example, a company producing a seasonal confectionary product, such as Easter eggs, might want to balance that product line with another that is consumed year round. Market maturity, as well as changing consumption patterns and industry consolidation, is currently a major concern in the food industry. Cadbury Schweppes was eager to acquire Snapple in order to move more aggressively into the New Age beverage market. Similarly, Unilever recently announced two very dissimilar acquisitions on the same day: Ben & Jerry's and Slim-Fast. These two acquisitions allow Unilever to respond to diverging trends: the growing demand for low-fat diet foods and the steady demand for indulgences, such as super premium ice cream.

*Legal Restrictions*.   Laws regarding advertising and other promotional activities also vary by country. Consequently, the acquiring company should not assume that it can use the same approach in all new markets. The laws governing the sale of tobacco and alcohol, for example, are quite different in the United States from what they are in Europe. The restrictions on what can be claimed in advertising campaigns are also distinctive. In other instances, there are no absolute legal restrictions on particular types of advertising, but there is a "gentleman's agreement" not to use certain types. The spirits industry, until recently, operated under such an agreement in the United States with respect to advertising on television.

Cultural differences are particularly important because it is not always possible to market products the same way everywhere. A British spirits company discovered that bourbon is a complicated product for foreign companies to market to Americans. It failed to understand, for example, that Rebel Yell is a very southern drink and often the first alcoholic beverage, other than beer, that young adults in certain regions of the United States consume. Consequently, when the company tried to introduce Rebel Yell to nontraditional U.S. markets here and overseas, it had difficulty positioning the product correctly.

*Marketing Strategies.* Because marketing strategies are such an integral part of the image and positioning of products, the integration management team should conduct a review of all marketing strategies within the acquired company. For each major product or product line, the team should determine the image associated with it, review related marketing campaigns, and also look at all other supporting promotional activities. The team should consider whether overall marketing strategies are compatible with those of the acquiring company. For example, the team should determine if there are competing strategies for the same market or strategies that would not be effective in other national markets. The acquiring company should also review advertising images associated with individual products for consistency with the image projected. A similar review should be conducted for the acquiring company's strategies and advertising images if they are going to be used in the market of the acquired company.

*Support Services.* The integration management team should also review all support services currently being provided by the marketing function. Typical ones include advertising, public relations, printing, and publications. The team should determine if the services are provided in-company or by outside vendors. If outside agencies are used for advertising or printing, then their contracts and samples of their work should be reviewed. In addition, a cost-benefit analysis should be conducted to help determine whether in-company or contract services would be more effective. If there is a market research function, the team should review the type of research being conducted, verify how it is used, and assess its effectiveness.

When a British company reviewed its U.S. acquisitions, it found that few of these services were provided in a methodical manner. Consequently, the company initially decided to provide public relations and market research services in-house at the U.S. headquarters. All other support services, such as advertising and printing, were contracted to outside agencies. After less than six months, however, the marketing and the sales functions jointly concluded that the public relations service should be eliminated. They also decided that the corporate marketing staff should provide assistance in marketing research and market mapping.

The latter activity was considered especially important because it would help determine how to position specific brands against key consumer groups. All other activities, such as assistance with special promotions, were transferred to the sales function.

***Staffing***.    The integration management team should also examine staffing for the marketing function. The review should include:

- Types of expertise available and their appropriateness for the overall strategy of the organization.
- Overall effectiveness of staff members.
- Areas of duplication between the acquiring and the acquired companies.
- Areas of unique expertise available within the acquiring company.
- Geographic location of staff—in the field or at headquarters.

As with other functional areas, the team should determine which individuals should be retained and where they should be located. Offers should be made as quickly as possible to those individuals whom the acquiring company wishes to retain.

***Implementation Plan***.    After all components of the marketing function have been examined, the integration management team should prepare an implementation plan for all planned integration activities. As for other functional areas, it should include detailed information on:

- Opportunities for synergy and cost savings.
- Centralization or decentralization of marketing activities.
- Personnel decisions, including terminations and relocations.
- Changes in strategies, product positioning, and identifying images, including web site design.
- Types of services to be provided in-company and those to be provided by vendors.
- Any required interfaces with the organization's information system.
- Timetable for completion of all activities.

In all of these areas, the key consideration for the integration management team should be the identification and the capture of value for the new organization.

### Key Lessons from Previous Experience

- Weigh the costs versus the benefits of providing all marketing services in-company.
- Review the marketing strategies of both the acquiring and the acquired companies carefully for areas of conflict.
- Expect to find cultural factors that will impact the implementation of standardized images and marketing campaigns for some products.

- Verify all laws and regulations concerning advertising and promotional activities, including web site content and related e-commerce components.
- Do not confuse the consumer by making drastic changes in the image of a product or a service.
- Identify opportunities for synergy and cost reduction early in the integration process.

### Manufacturing

As in all other functional areas, the first considerations of the integration management team are the extent to which the two organizations are to be integrated and the degree to which operations are to be centralized or decentralized. Objectives for value creation through cost reduction and expansion into new markets should also be reviewed. When Daimler-Benz and Chrysler announced their merger, there were few expectations that eliminating excess factory capacity and laying off workers could achieve quick cost reductions. Indeed, the expectation was that Chrysler would provide Daimler-Benz with much-needed production capacity outside Germany, where worker wages and benefits are some of the highest in the world.

Similarly, the geographic advantages offered by the acquired company's manufacturing facilities should be evaluated. Unilever, for example is reorganizing its worldwide manufacturing network to enhance efficiency. The objective is to invest wherever production costs are lowest rather than to produce all products in each market.

Once these strategic decisions have been made, the team should review the data collected during the preacquisition due diligence. In particular, the team should focus on facilities, manufacturing planning processes, manufacturing operations, purchasing functions and suppliers, and staffing resources.

*Facilities Inventory.* The first step is to revalidate the facilities inventory by discussing it with key personnel, such as plant managers, or by visiting each location. Items to be verified for each manufacturing facility include:

- Overall capacity.
- The percentage to which the facility currently operates over or under capacity.
- The potential for expansion at a reasonable cost.
- The potential for future cost reductions.
- The age and the condition of all equipment and technology.
- The adequacy of maintenance budgets.
- Compliance with environmental regulations.

As the inventory is completed, the team should note manufacturing capabilities that duplicate those of the acquiring company and decide whether the duplicate facilities are more efficient than those of the acquiring company or offer some other competitive advantage. Duplicate facilities that do not offer any particular advantage should be earmarked for elimination. Plans should be made to sell the facilities, to lease them to another company, or to use them for alternative functions. Some companies decide to donate unneeded facilities to local community development projects.

When a British company entered the private-label food market in the United States, it faced a similar situation. Existing manufacturing facilities were antiquated and located in isolated areas that made the distribution of finished products expensive. Because the company had not completed a thorough analysis prior to making its acquisitions, it was forced to spend additional money to modernize facilities and ultimately to delay its plans to expand in the U.S. market.

As another British company found, the integration management team should also pay particular attention to any locations where the acquired company is not currently in compliance with all environmental regulations. It was not until the postmerger integration period that the company fully understood the potential costs associated with the installation of new equipment to ensure compliance with clean water legislation.

***Manufacturing Planning Processes***.  At the same time that it is reviewing manufacturing facilities, the postmerger integration team should examine manufacturing planning processes because their quality is often a relatively accurate overall indicator of the facilities' efficiency. There are four key functions that the team should analyze:

1. *Production planning*.  Traditionally manufacturing organizations have done a very poor job of production planning, particularly when it is based on sales forecasts. Even when it is based on historical trends, production planning is often inaccurate. The integration management team should pay particular attention to whether the acquired company has a slow-moving, relatively rigid manufacturing environment requiring a relatively long planning horizon or whether it has a flexible, nimble manufacturing environment with shorter production plans.

2. *Materials ordering*.  If the planning function is about estimating the quantities of product to be produced, then materials ordering is about having the right materials on hand when they are needed by production. The two functions need to work together because inaccurate production planning results in stock outages, overages, production delays, higher manufacturing costs, and lower margins. The integration management team, then, should pay particular attention to how well the two functions work together, as well as to the historical accuracy of the materials ordering function.

3. *Order entry*.  The critical question for the integration management team to ask is: *Does the manufacturing facility build to stock or to order?* If it builds to stock, then the manufacturing organization may lack the discipline and the agility needed to operate effectively in today's competitive environment where customer service and high quality standards are critical. If this is the case, then the acquiring company may be forced to spend additional money and time retooling the organization to make it more competitive.

4. *Quality control.* The general guideline that the integration management team should follow is that the more inspectors and process checkers it encounters onsite, the worse the quality and the higher the associated manufacturing costs will be. The key indicator the team should examine is *first-run yield* or the percentage of time the product goes through the manufacturing process without any inspection, rework, or expedition. If the team finds that the first-run yield is low (under 70 to 80 percent), then the manufacturing processes of the acquired organization may be out of control and may require significant reorganization.

***Manufacturing Operations.*** Manufacturing operations are another area that the integration management team should reexamine. During its review, the team should focus on four areas: (1) technology, (2) manufacturing processes, (3) inventories, and (4) setup or changeover times. The first step that the team should take is to determine the age of the manufacturing technology in the acquired organization because older technology is less efficient and has a lower first-run yield. Consequently, if the integration management team finds that the technology of the acquired company is not competitive, it will have to be replaced, thus increasing the costs of the acquisition.

When examining manufacturing processes, the team should review these key indicators: efficiency, quality, and cost, such as cycle time; cost per unit of output; first-run yield; and the ratio of throughput time to value-added time. Inventories should be examined in three areas: (1) raw materials, (2) work in process, and (3) finished goods. If any of them are excessively high for industry standards, then the team should spend additional time reviewing manufacturing costs, scrap, and lead time because they may be noncompetitive.

If the manufacturing function produces many different products, then the integration management team should also review setup or changeover time, which is the amount of time required to prepare equipment and processes to produce different products. Setup is a valuable measure of a manufacturing operation's agility, a highly desirable competitive advantage in today's market. As shown by the experience of a British food company when it acquired several private-label food manufacturers in the United States, improved setup time does not always require the modernization of equipment or processes. A review of a food packing operation in New York revealed an extremely long changeover time for a particular line of specialty food products. Further examination indicated that it was because the products were kosher, thus requiring considerable special attention.

***The Purchasing Function and Suppliers.*** With the current emphasis on just-in-time inventories and supplier/manufacturer partnerships, the integration management team should give special consideration to the effectiveness of both the purchasing function and the suppliers. The team should look for best practices, such as empowered buyers with high thresholds of purchasing authorization; the use of credit cards for the purchase of high-velocity, low-cost items; and electronic data interchanges to eliminate purchase orders and invoices. The team should also look for evidence of frequent reviews of the supply base and the establishment of partnerships with key suppliers. Such relationships help eliminate the need for incoming inspections, thus reducing manufacturing time and costs. If these best practices are not found, then the integration management team should target areas for improvements in operating efficiency.

*Staffing Resources.* In most cases the staffing analysis conducted prior to an acquisition focuses almost entirely on senior management expertise. The postmerger staffing analysis, however, should focus on middle and supervisory levels, as well as on equipment operators. Key questions that the integration management team should ask cover not only staffing levels and types of expertise, but also employee empowerment and labor relations:

- Are staffing levels appropriate for the volume of work, or is overtime the norm?
- Do facilities managers have the appropriate skills and levels of experience for their assignments?
- Are manufacturing engineers located with production, or are they on the mezzanine or near executive offices?
- Are equipment operators empowered to make decisions and to solve problems related to the manufacturing process?
- Is an appropriate amount of ongoing training provided?
- Is there an effective working relationship between management and bargaining units?

After the integration management team has completed its review of all manufacturing operations, it should develop an integration plan that focuses on maximizing value through the elimination of unnecessary manufacturing facilities and the consolidation of other facilities that provide duplicate services. Consideration should also be given to reductions in the cost of parts and materials and other opportunities for synergy. The plan should define specific targets for cost saving and should explain any other benefits of consolidation. In addition, the plan should identify areas where old technology should be replaced, processes should be modified, and staffing must be changed. The plan should also define all training requirements and provide a timetable for all implementation activities.

### Key Lessons from Previous Experience

- Review premerger objectives for synergy to ensure that they are still valid.
- Make sure that market demand is fully understood before building new manufacturing facilities.
- Be sure to achieve compliance with environmental regulations before an acquisition is completed.
- Understand that manufacturing efficiency is essential for competition in today's global market.

- Implement best practices in purchasing to improve operating efficiency.
- Duplicate and excess capabilities should be eliminated to improve efficiency.
- Remember that staffing in manufacturing operations involves more than just the right expertise; it also means locating staff in the right areas, empowering them to make decisions, and providing ongoing training.

## Human Resources

Recent trends in management practices and increasingly competitive market conditions have had a dramatic impact on both the role and the position of the human resources department in global organizations. During the early 1980s, many British companies established large, highly centralized HR departments that provided a broad array of services to operating units around the world. These departments were responsible for conducting climate surveys; assessing the effectiveness of key managers; developing, hiring, succession, and staffing plans; and providing training assistance. Even more important, they devised and implemented global strategies for improving organizational effectiveness. Senior HR executives were involved in essentially all key strategic decisions, including acquisitions.

Since the beginning of the 1990s, however, these same global companies have downsized their corporate HR functions and decentralized nearly all their responsibilities. The objective of the new model is to attract, develop, and retain high-potential talent in all global markets through the use of standardized systems with local adaptations. Consequently, one of the primary functions of the corporate HR function is to identify key corporate positions, describe the skills required to perform them, and compile succession plans for each one. Similarly, the corporate function works with the regional offices to identify potential high performers, determine their developmental needs, and track their progress. Unilever has implemented a multitiered system that relies heavily on input from regional managers but that is centrally coordinated. Based on extensive global experience, the company developed a list of culturally transferable competencies, such as entrepreneurial drive and the ability to lead and develop others, which it uses to apprise and to identify talent from around the world. Potential high performers are categorized according to talent, experience, and mobility. The corporate office works with the regional offices to ensure that these individuals receive both a variety of work experience and education. The in-company international training college, which is open to all managers, provides some of the educational experiences.

To establish an effective HR function after an acquisition, the integration management team should analyze the HR services offered by the acquired company, not just determining whether they are adequate to meet the acquiring company's overall goals but also deciding whether they offer any unique value that can be incorporated into the new organization. Key areas for consideration are benefits programs, compensation, hiring, succession planning, training and organizational development, performance evaluation, HR information systems, new employee orientation programs, and expatriate management. With the exception of benefits programs, which require specialized expertise, the HR information system, and some limited support in organizational development, corporate guidelines today generally specify that managers within individual operating units should perform most other functions. Expatriate management is also a very specialized function and can be placed in either the newly acquired company or the corporate office, depending on where there is the greatest amount of expertise.

Although the policies and procedures of newly acquired companies should still be examined to determine how congruent they are with those of the acquiring organization, in many instances the acquired organization is allowed to observe different holidays and working hours. Regulations concerning various types of leave may also vary according to the customs of the local community.

In developing an integration plan for the HR function, the integration management team should consider the most effective way to provide services that are responsive to the needs of the local market while still maintaining low staffing levels. Special consideration should be given to the identification and the development of new management talent. The integration management team should also consider whether the HR function should be staffed with expatriates or local personnel. In more and more instances today, global companies are deciding to staff HR positions with local managers. As in other functional areas, the need for an interface between information systems should be reviewed and training should be provided in the use of the system.

### Key Lessons from Previous Experience

- Highly centralized HR departments are expensive and not always responsive to local conditions.
- The role of the HR function is being redefined in many organizations.
- Operating units can most effectively perform hiring and training.
- Cultural imperialism in the HR function should be avoided.
  - Recruit local nationals, including those in emerging markets.
  - Recruit internally.
  - Adjust job competency requirements to accommodate local conditions.
  - Provide adequate budgets for training and development in all markets.
  - Avoid large differences in compensation for expatriates and local nationals.
- Expatriate management is a highly specialized function requiring knowledge of many different operating environments, as well as the home country.
- Effective global organizations have formalized systems for defining key management competencies and identifying high-potential management talent throughout their operations.

# Checklist: Critical Postmerger Integration Considerations

I.  General considerations.
    A.  Objectives for making the acquisition, especially, the anticipated time frame for cost reductions and growth.
    B.  Previous experience in acquiring firms in the United States.
    C.  Similarity of the organization being acquired to the acquiring company.
    D.  Size of the two organizations being merged.
    E.  Identification or reaffirmation of core competencies of organization being acquired.
    F.  Resources available to devote to the acquisition.
        1.  Financial resources.
        2.  Human resources.
        3.  Outside consultants.
    G.  Availability of strong leadership to effectively articulate the benefits of the merger.
    H.  Appointment of team to manage the postmerger integration period.
        1.  Appropriate mix of skills and management styles.
        2.  Cultural sensitivity.
        3.  Continuity of team members.
        4.  Expatriate orientation and reentry programs.
        5.  Safeguards to ensure that lessons learned from team, including outside consultants, are not lost to the organization.
        6.  Clear understanding of the strategic intent of the merger, e.g., growth, new market penetration, increased efficiency.

II. Communications.
    A.  Immediate action.
        1.  Damage control strategy for information leaks and rumors.
        2.  No unnecessary speculation about what might happen.
        3.  Acknowledgment of bad news.
        4.  Clear indication of who is in charge.
            a.  Whether the CEO of the acquired firm will be retained.
            b.  Who will make key decisions concerning the integration of the two organizations.
        5.  Emphasis on the ongoing need for change.
    B.  Commitment to open communications.
    C.  Development of new corporate identity and company name.

    D.  Preparation of short- and long-term communications plan.
1. What the community outside the acquired firm should know.
2. Employee surveys to determine key perceptions, morale, and communications styles.
3. Identification of national cultural differences in communications styles: match of communication styles and audiences.
4. Identification of key messages to be disseminated.
5. Development of outcome measures for evaluating the effectiveness of key messages.
6. Identification of specific audiences.
7. Identification of appropriate media for each audience and message.
   a. Personal letters, road shows, question-and-answer sessions, web sites, newsletters and videotapes for key messages.
   b. Ongoing briefings and forums to reinforce critical values, beliefs, and behavior.
   c. News releases, letters, and briefings for the outside community, the government, and shareholders.
   d. Employee orientation sessions for new hires and current employees.

III.   Overall organization structure.
    A.  General considerations.
1. Redesign of overall organizational structure to consider:
   a. Global versus traditional multinational paradigm.
   b. Centralization versus decentralization.
   c. Extent to which the acquisition will be integrated into the acquiring organization.
   d. Appropriate amount of local autonomy.
   e. Responsiveness to local, national, and global markets.
   f. Elimination of duplicate functions and processes.
   g. Control processes.
   h. Information processes.
   i. Efficient transfer of knowledge and organizational learning.
2. Plan for implementing the new structure.
   a. Geographic location of specific functions.
   b. Timing.
   c. Training.
    B.  Postimplementation review to determine the strengths and weaknesses of the new structure and make changes, as necessary.
1. Resistance to change.
2. Additional opportunities for synergy and enhanced effectiveness.

IV. Postmerger implementation of functional areas.
    A. Information systems.
        1. Positioning of IS change as a strategic business initiative.
        2. Extent to which the acquiring and the acquired companies will be integrated.
        3. Degree of centralization versus decentralization desired.
        4. Inventory of hardware.
            a. Owned versus leased.
            b. Location.
            c. Use.
            d. Reliability.
            e. Age.
            f. Capacity.
        5. Inventory of software, including both mainframe and departmental applications.
            a. Purpose.
            b. Users.
            c. Databases accessed by each application.
        6. Analysis of communications and networks.
            a. Voice and data communications equipment.
            b. Local-access networks (LANs) and wide-access networks (WANs).
            c. Number and location of terminals and microcomputers that permit network access.
        7. Review of technical support available.
            a. Vendor agreements.
            b. Documentation.
            c. Training materials and assistance.
            d. Systems development and operations standards.
            e. Determination of business requirements and IS needed to support them.
        8. Assessment of systems compatibility.
        9. Development of implementation plan.
            a. Ability of systems to support strategic objectives and to enhance value of new organization.
            b. Identification of highly visible champion of IS changes.
            c. Continued user support.
            d. Customized development versus off-the-shelf systems of software.
            e. Staffing requirements.
            f. Timetable for implementation.

B. Finance.
1. Extent to which the acquiring and the acquired companies will be integrated.
2. Degree of centralization versus decentralization desired.
3. Review of existing financial controls and systems.
   a. Budgets.
   b. Plans.
   c. Cost systems.
   d. Operating procedures.
   e. Reports.
   f. Flow charts.
4. Review of credit and collection functions.
5. Analysis of existing information systems.
   a. Compatibility.
   b. Centralized versus decentralized user capability.
6. Identification of potential philosophical differences.
   a. Disclosure of information.
   b. Planning viewpoint—short range versus long.
7. Development of integration plan.
   a. Common reports and reporting intervals.
   b. Common procedures.
   c. IS interface.
   d. Development or purchase of new systems.
   e. Staffing requirements.
   f. Timetable for implementation.
C. Sales.
1. Extent to which the acquiring and the acquired companies will be integrated.
2. Degree of centralization versus decentralization desired.
3. Analysis of existing products/services.
   a. Duplicate items.
   b. Gaps in offerings.
   c. Products in development and their strategic fit.
   d. Compatibility or conflict with existing items.
   e. Strengths and weaknesses.
   f. Potential legal issues.
   g. Government regulations.
4. Review of sales forecasting techniques and systems.
5. Review of sales systems and capability.
   a. Sales approach used.
   b. Potential philosophical differences in approaches to sales.

(1) Customer oriented.

(2) Revenue driven.

(3) Profit driven.

   c. Management of sales force.

   d. Staffing levels.

   e. Depth of expertise.

   f. Review of distribution channels and systems.

(1) Overall considerations.

    (a) Impact of industry consolidation.

    (b) Locations.

    (c) Stability.

    (d) Opportunities for synergy and new market penetration.

(2) Accessibility to markets.

(3) Warehousing.

(4) Shipping.

   g. Review of current customer-service functions.

(1) Key accounts.

(2) Procedures.

(3) Turnaround time on orders.

(4) Turnover of customer accounts.

   h. Development of integration plan.

(1) How to restructure to capture value and to plan for future growth.

(2) Potential rationalization of product lines and distribution channels.

(3) Staffing.

(4) Training.

(5) Technology.

(6) Customer service.

(7) Sales strategies.

(8) Timetable for implementation.

D. Marketing.

  1. Extent to which the acquiring and the acquired companies will be integrated.

  2. Degree of centralization versus decentralization desired.

  3. Review of all markets.

   a. Similarities and differences.

   b. Levels of maturity.

   c. Possible areas of conflict.

   d. Stability versus seasonality.

   e. Legal issues and other special circumstances.

   f. Cultural differences in foreign and domestic markets.

4. Identification of all marketing support services.
    a. Advertising—agency or in-house.
    b. Market research.
    c. Public relations.
    d. Printing and publications.
5. Review of current staffing.
    a. Types of unique expertise available.
    b. Duplicate areas of expertise.
    c. Location of staff.
6. Analysis of all existing marketing strategies.
    a. Image.
    b. Advertising.
    c. Other promotional activities.
7. Development of implementation plan.
    a. How to capture maximum value and to plan for growth.
    b. Centralization versus decentralization of marketing support.
    c. Staffing requirements.
    d. Ongoing provision of services, especially web-based functions.
    e. Image.
    f. IS requirements.
    g. Timetable for implementation.

E. Manufacturing.
  1. Opportunities for cost reduction and increased efficiency.
  2. Extent to which the acquiring and the acquired companies will be integrated.
  3. Degree of centralization versus decentralization desired.
  4. Inventory of facilities.
      a. Location.
      b. Age and condition.
      c. Adequacy of space for desired manufacturing processes.
      d. Potential for expansion.
      e. Potential duplication.
      f. Potential overcapacity.
      g. Equipment.
          (1) Suitability.
          (2) Adherence to standards.
          (3) Maintenance requirements.
      h. Environmental regulations.
  5. Review of manufacturing planning processes.
      a. Production.
      b. Materials ordering.
      c. Order entry.

      d.  Quality control.

  6.  Analysis of manufacturing operations.

      a.  Technology.

      b.  Processes.

      c.  Equipment.

  7.  Analysis of purchasing function and suppliers.

      a.  Stability.

      b.  Proximity.

      c.  Importance.

      d.  Lead time.

      e.  Quality assurance procedures.

  8.  Review of staffing resources.

      a.  Types of expertise available.

         (1)  Management.

         (2)  Engineering.

      b.  Adequacy of resources.

         (1)  Staffing levels.

         (2)  Skills.

         (3)  Training programs.

  9.  Development of integration plan.

      a.  Potential consolidation of manufacturing processes and facilities.

      b.  Degree of centralization versus decentralization desired.

      c.  Ongoing production without interruption.

      d.  Staffing.

      e.  Timetable for implementation.

F.  Human resources.

  1.  Extent to which the acquiring and the acquired companies will be integrated.

  2.  Degree of centralization versus decentralization desired.

  3.  Analysis of services offered.

      a.  Staffing.

      b.  Training/orientation.

      c.  Benefits.

      d.  Compensation.

      e.  Performance reviews.

      f.  Career planning.

      g.  Expatriate management.

      h.  Organization development.

  4.  Relationships with labor unions.

  5.  Review of human resources IS.

  6. Analysis of compensation and benefits programs.

  7. Review of policies and procedures.

   a. Holidays.

   b. Leave.

   c. Work hours.

   d. Attendance.

   e. Recruiting.

  8. Development of implementation plan.

   a. Staffing.

   b. IS.

   c. Timetable for implementation.

V. People.

 A. Identification of the types of resources needed for the immediate postmerger period and for the long term—skills and competencies.

 B. Analysis of human resources available in acquired company—strengths and weaknesses versus needs.

  1. Management expertise.

  2. Technical expertise.

  3. Language skills.

  4. Any unique expertise of strategic importance.

  5. Global perspective.

 C. Identification of personnel to be eliminated.

  1. Timing—as soon as possible to avoid speculation.

  2. Severance packages.

 D. Identification of key personnel to be retained.

  1. Communication of their value to new organization.

  2. Plan to bind them to organization—stock options, bonuses, and new responsibilities.

 E. Identification of key personnel to be transferred from elsewhere in the organization or hired from outside the organization.

 F. Harmonization of performance appraisal, compensation, and benefits programs.

 G. Training and development.

  1. Short term.

  2. Long term.

VI. National and organizational culture.

 A. Profile of the organizational culture of the acquiring company.

 B. Profile of the organizational culture of the acquired company.

 C. Identification of the critical differences in the two organizational cultures.

    D.  Identification of the differences in the national cultures of the acquiring and the acquired companies, including implications for:
1. Planning and scheduling.
2. Morale and productivity.
3. Negotiations.
4. Management style.
5. Recruiting and selection processes.
6. Performance appraisal and reward systems.
7. Organizational structure.
8. Authority.

    E.  Demonstrated knowledge of and respect for national cultural differences.

    F.  Definition of the desired culture of the postmerger organization.

VII.  Mission, values, and common language.
    A.  Evaluation of common values and identification of areas of potential conflict.
    B.  Development of common strategic vision.
    C.  Development of common values statement.
    D.  Communication of mission and values to all employees.
    E.  "Walking the talk"—management of the postmerger period according to key values.

# References

## PART ONE: CRITICAL ISSUES IN PLANNING AND IMPLEMENTATION

### Books

*Cases in Corporate Acquisitions, Buyouts, Mergers, & Takeovers.* Detroit: Gale, 2000.

*Cross-Border M&A: A Guide to Global Strategic Direct Investment for Asian Companies.* Hong Kong: Asia Law & Practice, 1997.

*Cross-Border Mergers and Acquisitions and Development.* New York: United Nations, 2000.

*The Euromoney Global M&A Handbook 1998.* London: Euromoney Publications Ltd., 1998.

*Getting Things Done in the International Marketplace.* Chicago: American Bar Association, 1996.

*Handling High-Tech M&As in a Cooling Market.* New York: Practising Law Institute, 2001.

*Harvard Business Review on Mergers and Acquisitions.* Boston: Harvard Business School Pub. Corp., 2001.

*International Mergers & Acquisitions: Review 2000/2001.* London: Euromoney Publications, 2001.

*Mergers & Acquisitions.* 2d ed. New York: Wiley, 1994.

*Unlocking Shareholder Value: The Keys to Success: Mergers & Acquisitions, a Global Research Report.* Forth Worth, Tex.: KPMG, 1999.

*World Business: The Global Perspective.* New York: KPMG Peat Marwick LLP, 1995.

Aw, M. S. B., and R. A. Chatterjee. *The Performance of UK Firms Acquiring Large Cross-Border and Domestic Takeover Targets.* Cambridge: Judge Institute of Management Studies, 2000.

Begg, P. F. C., and Jason Haines. *Corporate Acquisitions and Mergers.* The Hague: Kluwer Law International, 1999.

Bishop, Matthew, and J. A. Kay. *European Mergers and Merger Policy.* New York: Oxford University Press, 1993.

Brittan, Leon. *Europe as a Global Partner—Trade and EMU in the New Millennium.* Edinburgh: Manchester University of Manchester, 1997.

References compiled by Donald Schnedeker with the staff of the Johnson Graduate School of Management Library, Cornell University.

Brown, Meredith M. *International Mergers and Acquisitions: An Introduction*. The Hague: Kluwer Law International, 1999.

Camesasca, Peter D. *European Merger Control: Getting the Efficiencies Right*. Antwerpen: Intersentia-Hart, 2000.

Caywood, Clarke L., and Raymond P. Ewing. *The Handbook of Communications in Corporate Restructuring and Takeovers*. Englewood Cliffs, N.J.: Prentice Hall, 1992.

Child, John, David Faulkner, and Robert Pitkethly. *The Management of International Acquisitions*. Oxford, U.K.: Oxford University Press, 2001.

Climan, Richard E., Michael J. Egan, and David M. Silk. *Doing Deals, 2001: Understanding the Nuts and Bolts of Transactional Practice*. New York: Practising Law Institute, 2001.

Cooke, Terence E. *International Mergers and Acquisitions*. Oxford: Basil Blackwell, 1988.

Cooper, Cary L., and Alan Gregory. *Advances in Mergers and Acquisitions*. New York: JAI, 2000.

Copeman, Sue. *Strategic Mergers and Acquisitions in the Global Insurance Industry*. London: Pearson Professional Ltd, 1997.

Cosh, A. D., and Alan Hughes. *Takeovers*. 3 vols. Aldershot, U.K. Ashgate, 1998.

Czinkota, Michael R., and Masaaki Kotabe. *Trends in International Business: Critical Perspectives*. Malden, Mass.: Blackwell, 1998.

Dewhurst, John. *Buying a Company: The Keys to Successful Acquisition*. London: Bloomsbury, 1997.

Freund, Caroline L., and Simeon Djankov. *Which Firms Do Foreigners Buy?: Evidence from Korea*. Washington, D.C.: World Bank Financial Sector Strategy and Policy Department Financial Economics Unit, 2000.

Fumagalli, Gina. *International Mergers & Acquisitions Review 2000/2001*. London: Euromoney Publications, 2000.

Gaughan, Patrick A. *Mergers, Acquisitions, and Corporate Restructurings*. New York: Wiley, 2001.

Gregory, Alan. *Strategic Valuation of Companies*. London: Financial Times/Prentice Hall, 1999.

Gup, Benton E. *Megamergers in a Global Economy: Causes and Consequences*. Westport, Conn.: Quorum Books, 2001.

Higgott, Richard A., and Nicola Phillips. *The Limits of Global Liberalisation: Lessons from Asia and Latin America*. Warwick, U.K.: University of Warwick, 1998.

Holmström, Bengt, and Steven N. Kaplan. *Corporate Governance and Merger Activity in the U.S.: Making Sense of the 1980s and 1990s*. Cambridge, Mass.: National Bureau of Economic Research, 2001.

Hubbard, Nancy. *Acquisition Strategy and Implementation*. Rev. ed. New York: Palgrave, 2001.

Marren, Joseph H. *Mergers & Acquisitions: A Valuation Handbook*. Homewood, Ill.: Business One Irwin, 1993.

Millerchip, Chris. *International Acquisitions*. London: Practical Law Company Ltd., 2001.

Morris, Joseph M. *Mergers and Acquisitions: Business Strategies for Accountants*. 2d ed. New York: Wiley, 2001.

Neven, Damien J., and Lars-Hendrik Röller. *The Scope of Conflict in International Merger Control*. London: Centre for Economic Policy Research, 2000.

Pagell, Ruth A., and Michael Halperin. *International Business Information: How to Find It, How to Use It*. 2d ed. New York: AMACOM, 1999.

Pearson, Barrie. *Successful Acquisition of Unquoted Companies.* 4th ed. Gower Publishing Co., 1999.

Picot, Gerhard. *Mergers & Acquisitions in Germany.* 2d ed. Yonkers, N.Y.: Juris Publishing, 2000.

Pitofsky, Robert. *EU and U.S. Approaches to International Mergers: Views from the U.S. Federal Trade Commission.* Washington, D.C.: U.S. FTC, 2000.

Rappaport, Alfred. *Creating Shareholder Value: A Guide for Managers and Investors.* Rev. ed. New York: Free Press, 1998.

Reed, Stanley Foster. *The M&A Deskbook and Dictionary.* New York: McGraw-Hill, 2001.

Rowley, J. W., and Donald I. Baker. *International Mergers: The Antitrust Process.* 3d ed. London: Sweet & Maxwell, 2001.

Rugman, Alan M. *International Business: Critical Perspectives on Business and Management.* London: Routledge, 2002.

Schleier, Curt. *How to Think Like the World's Greatest Masters of M&A: Business Lessons from Sumner Redstone, Sanford Weill, John Chambers, Michael Armstrong, and Other Empire Builders.* New York: McGraw-Hill, 2000.

Shull, Bernard, and Gerald A. Hanweck. *Bank Mergers in a Deregulated Environment: Promise and Peril.* Westport, Conn.: Quorum Books, 2001.

Smith, Gordon V., and Russell L. Parr. *Intellectual Property: Licensing and Joint Venture Profit Strategies.* 2d ed. New York: Wiley, 1998.

Taqi, S. J. *Acquisition Strategy in Europe.* Geneva, Switzerland: Business International S.A., 1987.

Thompson, Samuel C. *Business Planning for Mergers and Acquisitions.* 2d ed. Durham, N.C.: Carolina Academic Press, 2001.

Tolchin, Martin, and Susan J. Tolchin. *Buying into America: How Foreign Money Is Changing the Face of Our Nation.* Rev. ed. Washington, D.C.: Farragut Publishing, 1993.

Törnroos, Jan-Åke, and Jarmo Nieminen. *Business Entry in Eastern Europe: A Network and Learning Approach with Case Studies.* Helsinki: Aleksanteri-Instituutti, 1999.

Weston, J. Fred, and Samuel C. Weaver. *Mergers and Acquisitions.* New York: McGraw-Hill, 2001.

White, David. *Mergers & Acquisitions in Global Financial Institutions.* London: Datamonitor PLC, 1999.

Wright, Mike, and Ken Robbie. *Management Buy-Outs and Venture Capital: Into the Next Millennium.* Northhampton, Mass.: Edward Elgar Publishing, 1999.

Zabihollah, Rezaee. *Financial Institutions, Valuations, Mergers, and Acquisitions: The Fair Value Approach.* New York: Wiley, 2001.

## Articles

Garette, Bernard. "Alliances Versus Acquisitions: Choosing the Right Option." *European Management Journal* 18 (February 2000): 63–69.

Kral, Kenneth H. "Mergers & Acquisitions." *International Tax Review* (July/August 1998): 13–17.

Luscombe, Patricia. "Strategic Value Sought in Middle-Mkt. M&As." *National Underwriter* 103 (August 2, 1999): 6.

McCann, Joseph E. III. "The Growth of Acquisitions in Services." *Long Range Planning* 29 (December 1996): 835–841.

Mukherjee, Arijit, and Sarbajit Sengupta. "Joint Ventures Versus Fully Owned Subsidiaries: Multinational Strategies in Liberalizing Economies." *Review of International Economics* 9 (February 2001): 163–180.

Van Oldenborgh, Marita. "Court with Care." *International Business* (April 1995): 20–22.

## PART TWO: LEGAL ASPECTS

## Books

*Acquisitions, Mergers, Spin-Offs, and Other Restructurings.* New York: Practising Law Institute, 1993.

*EC Merger Control: Ten Years On. Papers from the EC Merger Control 10th Anniversary Conference Held in Brussels in September 2000 under the Auspices of the European Commission Directorate General for Competition and the International Bar Association.* London: International Bar Association, 2000.

*From Notification to Approval: Global Competition Law and Practice.* London: PLC Publications, 1999.

*Getting the Deal through 2000: Merger Control: The International Regulation of Mergers and Joint Ventures, 2000.* 4th ed. London: Law Business Research, 1999.

*Getting the Deal Through: The International Regulation of Mergers and Joint Ventures, 2001.* London: Law Business Research, 2000.

*Getting the Deal through a Competition Review: The Merger Review Process in the U.S. and Abroad.* Chicago: American Bar Association, 1995.

*Getting Things Done in the International Marketplace.* Chicago: American Bar Association, 1996.

*Global Counsel Competition Law Handbook.* London: PLC Publications, 2000.

*Horizontal Merger Guidelines.* Washington, D.C.: U.S. Department of Justice, 1997.

*Merger Review and Market Access.* Paris: OECD, 1999.

*Mergers and Acquisitions Handbook.* 2d ed. London: Practical Law Company, 2001.

*Survey of Worldwide Antitrust Merger Notification Requirements. 2001.* Washington, D.C.: White & Case, 2001.

Brittan, Leon. *European Competition Policy: Keeping the Playing-Field Level.* London: New York, 1992.

Choper, Jesse H., John C. Coffee, and Ronald J. Gilson. *Cases and Materials on Corporations.* 5th ed. Gaithersburg, Md.: Aspen Law & Business, 2000.

Climan, Richard E., Michael J. Egan, and David M. Silk. *Doing Deals, 2001: Understanding the Nuts and Bolts of Transactional Practice.* New York: Practising Law Institute, 2001.

Finbow, Roger J., and A. Nigel Parr. *UK. Merger Control: Law and Practice.* London: Sweet & Maxwell, 1995.

Forry, John I. *Foreign Investment in the U.S.: A Practical Guide.* 3d ed. London: BNA International, 1989.

Freeman, Peter, and Richard Whish. *A Guide to the Competition Act 1998.* London: Butterworths, 1999.

Genadio, Monica. *The Asia Law Guide to Mergers & Acquisitions: The Definitive Guide to Global Strategic Direct Investment for Asian Companies.* Hong Kong: Asia Law & Practice Ltd., 1998.

Ginsburg, Martin D., and Jack S. Levin. *Mergers, Acquisitions, and Buyouts: A Transactional Analysis of the Governing Tax, Legal, and Accounting Considerations.* June 2001. New York: Panel Publishing, 2001.

Greene, Edward F. *Current SEC and Cross-Border M&A Developments.* New York: Practising Law Institute, 2000.

Harroch, Richard D. *Partnership & Joint Venture Agreements.* New York: Law Journal Press, 1992 [looseleaf].

Hoffman, Scott L. *The Law and Business of International Project Finance: A Resource for Governments, Sponsors, Lenders, Lawyers, and Project Participants.* 2d ed. Ardsley, NY: Transnational Publishers, 2001.

Jones, Christopher, F. Enrique Gonzales-Diaz, and Colin Overbury. *EEC Merger Regulation.* London: Sweet & Maxwell, 1992.

Lowenfeld, Andreas F., and David R. Tillinghast. *International Economic Law.* Rev. 2d ed. New York: M. Bender, 1989.

Newkirk, Thomas C. *Some International Issues in the United States Securities and Exchange Commission's Enforcement Program.* London: International Bar Association, 1995.

Oesterle, Dale A. *The Law of Mergers and Acquisitions.* St. Paul, Minn.: West Group, 1999.

Prager, Bruce J., and Keith D. Shugarman. *Successful Premerger Notification: Basic Problems and Practical Solutions.* Chicago: American Bar Association, 1995.

Raybould, D. M., and Alison Firth. *Comparative Law of Monopolies.* London: Boston, 1991.

Rivas, José. *The EU Merger Regulation and the Anatomy of the Merger Task Force.* London: Boston, 1999.

Rowley, J. W., and Donald I. Baker. *International Mergers: The Antitrust Process.* 3d ed. London: Sweet & Maxwell, 2001.

Verloop, Peter. *Merger Control in the EU: A Survey of European Competition Laws.* 3d rev. ed. The Hague: Kluwer Law International, 1999.

Whalley, Michael, and Franz-Jörg Semler. *International Business Acquisitions: Major Legal Issues and Due Diligence.* 2d ed. The Hague: Kluwer Law International, 2000.

Whish, Richard, and B. E. Sufrin. *Competition Law.* 4th ed. London: Butterworths, 2000.

## Articles

Angwin, Duncan. "Mergers and Acquisitions across European Borders: National Perspectives on Preacquisition Due Diligence and the Use of Professional Advisers." *Journal of World Business* 36 (spring 2001): 32–57.

Cabell, John. "The Structure of the International Deal." *Folio: the Magazine for Magazine Management* 29 (April 1, 2000): 29–30.

Cabell, John T. "The 'Asset' Test." *Folio: the Magazine for Magazine Management* 28 (April 1, 1999): 21–22.

Chamberlain, James R. "Getting the Deal Approved: Multinational Merger Filing Obligations." *Private Investments Abroad—Problems & Solutions in International Business* 39 (1996): 3–21.

Gotts, Ilene Knable, and Sarah E. Strasser. "International Pre-Merger Notification Requirements." *The Practical Lawyer* 44 (October 1998): 65–74, 76–82.

## PART THREE: ACCOUNTING AND TAX ASPECTS

## Books

*Business Combinations: Proposed International Accounting Standard.* London: International Accounting Standards Committee, 1997.

*Disclosures about Segments of an Enterprise and Related Information: FASB Statement 131.* New York: KPMG, 1999.

*Methods of Accounting for Business Combinations: Recommendations of the G4+1 for Achieving Convergence.* Norwalk, Conn.: Financial Accounting Standards Board of the Financial Accounting Foundation, 1998.

*Revisions to International Accounting Standards: IAS 16, Property, Plant and Equipment, IAS 28, Accounting for Investments in Associates, IAS 31, Financial Reporting of Interests in Joint Ventures.* London: International Accounting Standards Committee, 1998.

*Studies on Accounting Information and the Economics of the Firm.* Chicago: Institute of Professional Accounting Graduate School of Business University of Chicago, 2001.

Arnold, Brian J., and Neil Brooks. *Tax Administration and Litigation.* Toronto, Ont.: Osgoode Hall Law School of York University [Professional Development Programme], 2000.

Arnold, Brian J., and Michael J. Mcintyre. *International Tax Primer.* Boston: Kluwer Law International, 1995.

Feinschreiber, Robert, and Margaret Kent. *International Mergers & Acquisitions: A Country by Country Tax Guide.* New York: Wiley, 2002.

Freeman, Louis S. *Tax Strategies for Corporate Acquisitions, Dispositions, Spin-Offs, Joint Ventures, Financings, Reorganizations & Restructurings 2000.* New York: Practising Law Institute, 2000.

Freeman, Louis S., and David F. Nitschke. *Tax Planning for Domestic & Foreign Partnerships, LLCs, Joint Ventures, & Other Strategic Alliances, 2001.* New York: Practising Law Institute, 2001.

Hennell, Alison, and Mary Moore. *Making an Acquisition.* London: Faculty of Finance and Management, The Institute of Chartered Accountants in England and Wales, 2000.

Herring, Hartwell C. *Business Combinations and International Accounting.* Cincinnati, Ohio: South-Western Thomson Learning, 2002.

Morris, Joseph M. *Mergers and Acquisitions: Business Strategies for Accountants.* 2d ed. New York: Wiley, 2001.

Orsini, Larry L., John P. McAllister, and Rajeev N. Parikh. *World Accounting.* New York: M. Bender, 1987.

Posin, Daniel Q. *Basic Federal Income Tax: Selected Code and Regulations.* Gaithersburg, Md.: Aspen Law & Business [annual].

Posin, Daniel Q. *Corporate Tax Planning: Takeovers, Leveraged Buyouts, and Restructuring Supplement.* Boston: Little Brown, 1990.

Thompson, Samuel C. *Taxable and Tax-Free Corporate Mergers, Acquisitions, and LBOs.* St. Paul, Minn.: West Publishing, 1994.

Thompson, Samuel C. *Taxation of Business Entities: C Corporations, Partnerships, and S Corporations: Including International Considerations.* 2d ed. St. Paul, Minn.: West Group, 2001.

## Articles

Alty, Derek. "Canada." *International Tax Review—Mergers & Acquisitions Supplement,* (2001): 22–30.

Ayearst, James. "Canada." *International Tax Review* (July/August 2000): 17–24.

Bock, Volker. "Germany." *International Tax Review* (July/August 2000): 31–36.

Cheng, Rita H. "Target Shareholders' Returns: The Effect of Diversity in Accounting Standards and Tax Treatments in Cross-Border Acquisitions." *Journal of Accounting and Public Policy* 16 (spring 1997): 35–62.

Cullen, Pat. "Ireland." *International Tax Review—Mergers & Acquisitions Supplement* (2001): 42–49.

De Jong, Chris E. "The Netherlands." *International Tax Review—Mergers & Acquisitions Supplement* (2001): 73–82.

Douvier, Pierre-Jean. "France." *International Tax Review* (July/August 2000): 25–30.

Eerdmans, Paul. "Netherlands." *International Tax Review* (July/August 2000): 48–54.

Ekkel, Mark R. "Australia." *International Tax Review* (July/August 2000): 5–10.

Endres, Dieter. "Germany." *International Tax Review—Mergers & Acquisitions Supplement* (2001): 32–40.

Faber, Peter, and Arthur Rosenbloom. "Managing under the New Tax Law." *Inc* 8 (November 1986): 89–91.

Herinckx, Yves. "New Tax Rules for Belgian Acquisitions." *International Tax Review* 8 (March 1997): 4.

Orlando, Marios. "Brazil." *International Tax Review* (July/August 2000): 11–16.

Penney, Mark. "United Kingdom." *International Tax Review* (July/August 2000): 55–60.

Reyes, Rocky. "Philippines." *International Financial Law Review* (2001): 87–91.

Rosenbach, Georg. "Introduction." *International Tax Review—Mergers & Acquisitions Supplement* (2001): 3–11.

Schreier, Douglas B. "United States." *International Tax Review—Mergers & Acquisitions Supplement* (2001): 94–108.

Seijido, Eva. "United States." *International Tax Review* (July/August 2000): 63–72.

Solano, Manuel. "Mexico." *International Tax Review* (July/August 2000): 43–47.

Tajima, Ryuichi. "Japan." *International Tax Review* (July/August 2000): 37–42.

Torrione, Henri. "Switzerland." *International Tax Review—Mergers & Acquisitions Supplement* (2001): 84–92.

Wiseberg, Stanley C. "Global Overview." *International Tax Review—Mergers & Acquisitions Supplement* (2001): 13–20.

## PART FOUR: FINANCIAL ASPECTS

## Books

Altman, Edward I., and Roy C. Smith. *Firm Valuation and Corporate Leveraged Restructuring.* New York: Salomon Brothers Center for the Study of Financial Institutions, Leonard N. Stern School of Business, New York University, 1991.

Altman, Edward I., and Roy C. Smith. *Highly Leveraged Restructurings. A Valid Role for Europe.* New York: New York University Salomon Center, 1991.

Bierman, Harold. *Increasing Shareholder Value: Distribution Policy, a Corporate Finance Challenge.* Boston: Kluwer Academic Publishers, 2001.

Britton, Anne, and John Burnup. *Essentials of Finance for Mergers.* Harlow, U.K.: Financial Times/Prentice Hall, 2000.

Buchanan, Bruce S., Robert Lamb, and Roy C. Smith. *Professional Responsibility: Markets, Ethics and Law.* 7th ed. Boston: Pearson Custom Publishing, 2000.

Clark, Peter J., and Stephen Neill. *The Value Mandate Maximizing Shareholder Value across the Corporation.* New York: AMACOM, 2000.

Diamond, Walter H., Dorothy B. Diamond, and John E. Sullivan. *Global Guide to Investment Incentives and Capital Formation.* New York: Aspen Publishers, 2000.

Glantz, Morton, and Thomas L. Doorley. *Scientific Financial Management: Advances in Intelligence Capabilities for Corporate Valuation and Risk Assessment.* New York: AMACOM, 2000.

Karatzas, Ioannis, and Steven E. Shreve. *Methods of Mathematical Finance.* New York: Springer, 1998.

Klein, William A., and John C. Coffee. *Business Organization and Finance: Legal and Economic Principles.* 7th ed. New York: Foundation Press, 2000.

Mills, Roger W. *The Use of Shareholder Value Analysis in Acquisition and Divestment Decisions by Large UK Companies.* London: Chartered Institute of Management Accountants, 1998.

Nevitt, Peter K., and Frank J. Fabozzi. *Project Financing.* 7th ed. London: Euromoney Books, 2000.

Pratt, Shannon P. *Cost of Capital: Estimation and Applications.* New York: Wiley, 1998.

Smith, Roy C. *The First European Merger Boom Has Begun.* St. Louis, Mo.: Center for the Study of American Business, Washington University, 1991.

Smith, Roy C., *Restructuring Japanese Financial Institutions.* New York: New York University Salomon Center, 1999.

Smith, Roy C., and Ingo Walter. *Global Banking.* New York: Oxford University Press, 1997.

Smith, Roy C., and Ingo Walter. *Global Financial Services: Strategies for Building Competitive Strengths in International Commercial and Investment Banking.* New York: Harper Business, 1990.

Smith, Roy C., and Ingo Walter. *Global Patterns of Mergers and Acquisition Activity in the Financial Services Industry.* Fontainebleau, France: Insead, 1996.

Smith, Roy C., and Ingo Walter. *Risks and Rewards in Emerging Market Investment.* New York: New York University Salomon Center Leonard N. Stern School of Business, 1997.

Walter, Ingo, and Roy C. Smith. *High Finance in the Euro-Zone: Competing in the New European Capital Market.* London: Financial Times/Prentice Hall, 2000.

Weston, J. Fred, and Samuel C. Weaver. *Mergers and Acquisitions.* New York: McGraw-Hill, 2001.

## Articles

Loree, David, Chun-Chung Chen, and Stephen Guisinger. "International Acquisitions: Do Financial Analysts Take Note?" *Journal of World Business* 35 (fall 2000): 300–313.

Smith, Roy C. "Planning Your Global Financial Strategy." *The Journal of Business Strategy* 9 (September/October 1988): 8–11.

Smith, Roy C. "Restructuring Japanese Financial Institutions." *The Washington Quarterly* 22 (summer 1999): 181–193.

Smith, Roy C., and Ingo Walter. "Europe's Merger Boom Begins." *Financier* 15 (August 1991): 6–20.

## PART FIVE: JOINT VENTURES

### Books

*Financial Reporting of Interests in Joint Ventures.* New York: International Federation of Accountants, 2000.

*International Joint Ventures & Strategic Alliances in 2001.* Mechanicsburg, Pa.: Pennsylvania Bar Institute, 2001.

Berger, Simon. *International Joint Ventures: A Practical Guide.* London: Financial Times/ Prentice Hall, 1999.

Campbell, Dennis, Susan Meek, and Wilson Chu. *International Joint Ventures, Mergers, and Acquisitions.* Ardsley, N.Y.: Transnational Publishers, 2000.

Child, John, and Yanni Yan. *Predicting the Performance of International Joint Ventures: An Investigation in China.* Hong Kong: Chinese Management Centre, University of Hong Kong, 1999.

Detjen, David W. *United States Joint Ventures with International Partners.* Yonkers, N.Y.: Juris Publishing, 2000.

Gutterman, Alan. *A Short Course in International Joint Ventures: Negotiating, Forming, and Operating the International JV.* Novato, Calif.: World Trade Press, 2001.

Gutterman, Alan S. *International Joint Ventures: Negotiation, Formation, and Operation.* London: Euromoney, 1997.

Kidd, John. *Venturing Jointly: Oriental & Occidental Perceptions.* Birmingham, U.K.: Aston Business School Research Institute, 1999.

Li, J. T. *Managing International Business Ventures in China.* New York: Pergamon, 2001.

Luo, Yadong. *Partnering with Chinese Firms: Lessons for International Managers.* Aldershot, England: Ashgate, 2000.

Matthews, Clifford. *Managing International Joint Ventures: The Route to Globalizing Your Business.* London: Kogan Page, 2001.

O'Brien, Clare. *International Joint Ventures, 2001.* New York: Practising Law Institute, 2001.

Rao, M. B. *Joint Venture: International Business with Developing Countries.* New Delhi: Vikas Publishing House Distributors UBS Publishers' Distributors, 1999.

Ross, Alfred J. *International Joint Ventures, 2000.* New York: Practising Law Institute, 2000.

Yan, Aimin, and Yadong Luo. *International Joint Ventures: Theory and Practice.* Armonk, N.Y.: M. E. Sharpe, 2001.

### Articles

Anonymous. "Tips for Remote Joint Ventures." *The Internal Auditor* 55 (April 1998): 54.

Bleeke, Joel, and David Ernst. "The Way to Win in Cross-Border Alliances." *Harvard Business Review* 69 (November/December 1991): 127–135.

Brannen, Mary Yoko. "Partnering across Borders: Negotiating Organizational Culture in a German-Japanese Joint Venture." *Human Relations* 53 (April 2000): 451–487.

Chen, Sheng-Syan et al. "Investment Opportunities, Free Cash Flow, and Market Reaction to International Joint Ventures." *Journal of Banking and Finance* 24 (November 2000): 1747–1765.

Fey, Carl F. "Strategies for Managing Russian International Joint Venture Conflict." *European Management Journal* 17 (February 1999): 99–106.

Fey, Carl F. "Success Strategies for Russian-Foreign Joint Ventures." *Business Horizons* 38 (November/December 1995): 49–54.

Fraser, Jill Andresky. "Deciding When a Joint Venture Makes Sense." *Inc* 16 (November 1994): 138.

Griffith, David A. "Knowledge Transfer as a Means for Relationship Development: A Kazakhstan-Foreign International Joint Venture Illustration." *Journal of International Marketing* 9 (2001): 1–18.

Groot, Tom L. C. M., and Kenneth A. Merchant. "Control of International Joint Ventures." *Accounting, Organizations and Society* 25 (August 2000): 579–607.

Hyder, Akmal S. "Managing International Joint Venture Relationships: A Longitudinal Perspective." *Industrial Marketing Management* 29 (May 2000): 205–218.

Johnson, James P. "Multiple Commitments and Conflicting Loyalties in International Joint Venture Management Teams." *International Journal of Organizational Analysis* 7 (January 1999): 54–71.

Kvint, Vladimir. "Don't Give Up on Russia." *Harvard Business Review* 72 (March/April 1994): 62–70.

Kvint, Vladimir. "Moscow Learns the Language of Business." *Journal of Accountancy* 170 (November 1990): 114–118.

Kvint, Vladimir. "Vladimir Kvint Responds: Now Is the Time to Do Business in Russia." *Harvard Business Review* 72 (May/June 1994): 42–43.

Li, Ji, Kevin Lam, and Gongming Qian. "Does Culture Affect Behavior and Performance of Firms? The Case of Joint Ventures in China." *Journal of International Business Studies* 32 (2001): 115–131.

Li, Jiatao. "Building Effective International Joint Venture Leadership Teams in China." *Journal of World Business* 34 (spring 1999): 52–68.

Loree, David, Chun-Chung Chen, and Stephen Guisinger. "International Acquisitions: Do Financial Analysts Take Note?" *Journal of World Business* 35 (fall 2000): 300–313.

Luo, Yadong, Oded Shenkar, and Mee-Kau Nyaw. "A Dual Parent Perspective on Control and Performance in International Joint Ventures: Lessons from a Developing Country." *Journal of International Business Studies* 32 (2001): 41–58.

Makino, Shige. "Matching Strategy with Ownership Structure in Japanese Joint Ventures." *The Academy of Management Executive* 13 (November 1999): 17–28.

Makino, Shige, and Kent E. Neupert. "National Culture, Transaction Costs, and the Choice between Joint Venture and Wholly Owned Subsidiary." *Journal of International Business Studies* 31, no. 4 (2000): 705–713.

Mandell, Mel. "Joint Ventures." *World Trade* 6 (December 1993): 46–48.

Merchant, Hemant. "Configurations of International Joint Ventures." *Management International Review* 40 (second quarter 2000): 107–140.

Millington, Andrew. "Transnational Marketing Joint Ventures: A Viable Market Penetration Strategy in the EU?" *European Management Journal* 17 (December 1999): 635–644.

Ott, Ursula F. "Termination and Endgame Scenarios in International Joint Ventures." *Global Business and Economics Review* 2 (December 2000): 172–184.

Reece, Richard. "Successful Joint Ventures in Russia." *World Trade* 11 (August 1998): 42–44.

Roy Chowdhury, Indrani, and Prabal Roy Chowdhury. "A Theory of Joint Venture Life-Cycles." *International Journal of Industrial Organization* 19 (March 2001): 319–343.

Shaughnessy, Haydn. "International Joint Ventures: Managing Successful Collaborations." *Long Range Planning* 28 (June 1995): 10–17.

Steensma, H. Kevin. "Explaining IJV Survival in a Transitional Economy through Social Exchange and Knowledge-Based Perspectives." *Strategic Management Journal* 21 (August 2000): 831–851.

Sulzer, Alessandra. "The Business of Cooperation: Peace and Profit through Joint Ventures." *Harvard International Review* 23 (summer 2001): 34–36.

Tatoglu, Ekrem. "Strategic Motives and Partner Selection Criteria in International Joint Ventures in Turkey: Perspectives of Western Firms and Turkish Firms." *Journal of Global Marketing* 13 (2000): 53–92.

# PART SIX: VALUING COMPANIES AND NEGOTIATING TRANSACTIONS

## Books

*Cybervaluation 2000: Internet Business Valuation, Trends, and Analysis:* 1999 *Transactions.* Washington, D.C.: Bond & Pecaro, 2000.

*Financial Statements Included in Written Business Valuations.* New York: American Institute of Certified Public Accountants, 1999.

Abrams, Jay B. *Quantitative Business Valuation: A Mathematical Approach for Today's Professionals.* New York: McGraw-Hill, 2001.

Arrow, Kenneth Joseph. *Barriers to Conflict Resolution.* New York: Norton, 1995.

Campbell, Ian R., and Howard E. Johnson. *The Valuation of Business Interests.* Toronto: Canadian Institute of Chartered Accountants, 2001.

Clark, Kenneth A., and Karen F. Copenhaver. *Structuring, Negotiating, & Implementing Strategic Alliances, 1999.* New York: Practising Law Institute, 1999.

Clark, Peter J., and Stephen Neill. *Net Value: Valuing Dot-Com Companies: Uncovering the Reality behind the Hype.* New York: AMACOM, 2000.

Collins, Andrew, and John T. Murphy. *Negotiating International Business Acquisitions Agreements.* London: Sweet & Maxwell, 1997.

Cornell, Bradford. *Corporate Valuation: Tools for Effective Appraisal and Decision Making.* New York: McGraw-Hill, 1993.

Damodaran, Aswath. *The Dark Side of Valuation: Valuing Old Tech, New Tech, and New Economy Companies.* Harlow, U.K.: Financial Times/Prentice Hall, 2001.

Dewhurst, John. *Buying a Company: The Keys to Successful Acquisition.* London: Bloomsbury, 1997.

Evans, Frank C., and David M. Bishop. *Valuation for M&A: Building Value in Private Companies.* New York: Wiley, 2001.

Fogg, Blaine V., and Theodore J. Kozloff. *Negotiating Corporate Acquisitions: Public &*

*Private 2000 [Doing Deals in the New Millennium].* New York: Law Journal Seminars, 2000.

George, Joan M., and Gary M. Hoffman. *Intellectual Property Issues in Structuring Deals & Drafting Agreements: A Satellite Program.* New York: Practising Law Institute, 2001.

Ghauri, Pervez N., and Jean-Claude Usunier. *International Business Negotiations.* Amsterdam, N.Y.: Elsevier Science, 1999.

Gregory, Alan. *Strategic Valuation of Companies.* London: Financial Times/Prentice Hall, 1999.

Guterl, Joseph N. *Valuation of Closely Held Businesses.* New York: Aspen Law & Business, 1997.

Gutterman, Alan. *A Short Course in International Joint Ventures: Negotiating, Forming, and Operating the International JV.* Novato, Calif.: World Trade Press, 2001.

Hawkins, George B., and Michael A. Paschall. *CCH Business Valuation Guide.* Chicago: CCH Inc., 1999.

Kasper, Larry J. *Business Valuations: Advanced Topics.* Westport, Conn.: Quorum Books, 1997.

Kling, Lou R., and Eileen Nugent Simon. *Negotiated Acquisitions of Companies, Subsidiaries, and Divisions.* New York: Law Journal Seminars-Press, 1994.

Kramer, Roderick Moreland, and David M. Messick. *Negotiation as a Social Process.* Thousand Oaks, Calif.: Sage, 1995.

Link, Albert N., and Michael B. Boger. *The Art and Science of Business Valuation.* Westport, Conn.: Quorum, 1999.

Marren, Joseph H. *Mergers & Acquisitions: A Valuation Handbook.* Homewood, Ill.: Business One Irwin, 1993.

Martin, Thomas John. *Valuation Reference Manual: Putting a Price Tag on a Business When You're Buying, When You're Selling, When You're Valuing.* Locust Valley, N.Y.: Business Owner, 2000.

Mitchell, David, and Garrick Holmes. *Making Acquisitions Work: Learning from Companies' Successes and Failures.* London: Economist Intelligence Unit, 1996.

Palepu, Krishna G., Paul M. Healy, and Victor L. Bernard. *Business Analysis & Valuation: Using Financial Statements: Text & Cases.* 2d ed. Cincinnati, Ohio: South-Western College Publishing, 2000.

Pratt, Shannon P. *Business Valuation Body of Knowledge: Exam Review and Professional Reference.* 2d ed. New York: Wiley, 2001.

Pratt, Shannon P. *Business Valuation Discounts and Premiums.* New York: Wiley, 2001.

Pratt, Shannon P. *The Market Approach to Valuing Businesses.* New York: Wiley, 2001.

Pratt, Shannon P., Robert F. Reilly, and Robert P. Schweihs. *Valuing a Business: The Analysis and Appraisal of Closely Held Companies.* 4th ed. New York: McGraw-Hill, 2000.

Pratt, Shannon P., Robert F. Reilly, and Robert P. Schweihs. *Valuing Small Businesses and Professional Practices.* 3d ed. New York: McGraw-Hill, 1998.

Reilly, Robert F., and Robert P. Schweihs. *Handbook of Advanced Business Valuation.* London: McGraw-Hill, 1999.

Rosenbloom, Arthur H. *Due Diligence for Global Deal-Making.* New York: Bloomberg Press, 2002.

Sayer, Stephen. *Negotiating International Joint Venture Agreements.* London: Sweet & Maxwell, 1999.

Trugman, Gary R. *Understanding Business Valuation: A Practical Guide to Valuing Small to Medium-Sized Businesses.* New York: American Institute of Certified Public Accountants, 1998.

West, Thomas L., and Jeffrey D. Jones. *Handbook of Business Valuation.* 2d ed. New York: Wiley, 1999.

Wise, Richard M., Jay E. Fishman, and Shannon P. Pratt. *Guide to Canadian Business Valuations.* Scarborough, Ont.: Carswell, 1993.

Yegge, Wilbur M. *A Basic Guide for Valuing a Company.* 2d ed. New York: Wiley, 2001.

Zabihollah, Rezaee. *Financial Institutions, Valuations, Mergers, and Acquisitions: The Fair Value Approach.* New York: Wiley, 2001.

## Articles

Cellich, Claude. "Contract Renegotiations: The Neglected Phase of the Process." *International Trade Forum* (1999): 11–15.

Chu, Wilson. "Getting What You Bargained For." *International Corporate Law* (March 1995): 14–16.

Evans, Frank C. "Tips for the Valuator." *Journal of Accountancy* 189 (March 2000): 35–41.

Kahan, Stuart. "A Firm's Worth." *The Practical Accountant* 32 (August 1999): 30–38.

Keeney, Jennifer. "What's It Worth to You?" *FSB: Fortune Small Business* 11 (September 2001): 105 108.

Kroll, Karen M. "Valuing Asia's Bargains." *Industry Week* 249 (January 10, 2000): 49–50.

Paik, Yongsun. "Negotiating with East Asians: How to Attain 'Win-Win' Outcomes." *Management International Review* 39 (second quarter 1999): 103–122.

Rosenbloom, Arthur H., "Pricing Companies for Transactions in Central and Eastern Europe." *Journal for Corporate Growth* (spring 1992).

Rosenbloom, Arthur H., and Stephen H. Haimo. "Look Before You Leap: Checklists for Making Deals in Emerging Markets." *Directorship* (October 1997).

## PART SEVEN: SPECIAL TOPICS

### Books

Blair, Margaret M. *The Deal Decade: What Takeovers and Leveraged Buyouts Mean for Corporate Governance.* Washington, D.C.: Brookings Institution, 1993.

Blair, Margaret M., and Thomas A. Kochan. *The New Relationship: Human Capital in the American Corporation.* Washington, D.C.: Brookings Institution Press, 2000.

Buchel, Bettina. *International Joint Venture Management: Learning to Cooperate and Cooperating to Learn.* New York: Wiley, 1999.

Cauley De La Sierra, M. *Managing Alliances and Acquisitions in Latin America.* London: Economist Intelligence Unit, 1999.

Caywood, Clarke L., and Raymond P. Ewing. *The Handbook of Communications in Corporate Restructuring and Takeovers.* Englewood Cliffs, N.J.: Prentice Hall, 1992.

Caywood, Clarke L. *The Handbook of Strategic Public Relations & Integrated Communications.* New York: McGraw-Hill, 1997.

Child, John, David Faulkner, and Robert Pitkethly. *The Management of International Acquisitions.* Oxford: Oxford University Press, 2001.

Daniel, Teresa A., and Gary S. Metcalf. *The Management of People in Mergers and Acquisitions.* Westport, Conn.: Quorum Books, 2001.

Eneroth, Kristina, and Rikard Larsson. *The Human Side of Strategic Change.* Armonk, N.Y.: M. E. Sharpe, 1996.

Ferenczy, Ilene H. *Employee Benefits in Mergers and Acquisitions.* New York: Aspen Publishers, 2000.

Gertsen, Martine Cardel, Anne-Marie Søderberg, and Jens Erik Torp. *Cultural Dimensions of International Mergers and Acquisitions.* Berlin, N.Y.: Walter DeGruyter, 1998.

Harris, Phillip R., and Robert T. Moran. *Cultural Differences in Business: Understand and Appreciate People from Different Cultures.* Anderson, S.C.: Tavenner Publishing, 1997.

Harris, Phillip R., and Robert T. Moran. *Managing Cultural Differences.* Houston, Tex.: Gulf Publishing, 1991.

Hutchinson, Kevin. *Readings in Organizational Communication.* Dubuque, Iowa: Wm. C. Brown Publishers, 1992.

Jandt, Fred Edmund. *Intercultural Communication: An Introduction.* 3d ed. Thousand Oaks, Calif.: Sage, 2001.

Jandt, Fred Edmund, and Paul Pedersen. *Constructive Conflict Management: Asia-Pacific Cases.* Thousand Oaks, Calif.: Sage, 1996.

Jandt, Fred Edmund, and Derrick J. Taberski. *Intercultural Communication Workbook.* 2d ed. Thousand Oaks, Calif.: Sage, 1998.

Kochan, Thomas A., and Michael Useem. *Transforming Organizations.* New York: Oxford University Press, 1992.

Kotter, John, and James Heskett. *Corporate Culture and Performance.* New York: Free Press, 1992.

Lang, Nikolaus S. *Intercultural Management in China: Strategies of Sino-European and Sino-Japanese Joint Ventures.* Wiesbaden, Germany: Deutscher Universitätsverlag, 1998.

Layne, Judy. *Forging New Families: An Overview of Mergers and Acquisitions in the Context of Organizational Change.* Kingston, Ont.: IRC Press, 2000.

Li, J. T. *Managing International Business Ventures in China.* New York: Pergamon, 2001.

Locke, Richard M., Thomas A. Kochan, and Michael J. Piore. *Employment Relations in a Changing World Economy.* Cambridge, Mass.: MIT Press, 1995.

Luo, Yadong. *Partnering with Chinese Firms: Lessons for International Managers.* Aldershot, England: Ashgate, 2000.

Matthews, Clifford. *Managing International Joint Ventures: The Route to Globalizing Your Business.* London: Kogan Page, 2001.

Moran, Robert T., and John Riesenberger. *The Global Challenge.* London: McGraw-Hill, 1994.

Morosini, Piero. *Managing Cultural Differences: Effective Strategy and Execution across Cultures in Global Corporate Alliances.* Oxford: Elsevier Science, 1999.

Phillips, Nicola. *Innovative Management: A Pragmatic Guide to New Techniques.* London: Pitman Publishing, 1993.

Phillips, Nicola, and Richard A. Higgott. *Global Governance and the Public Domain: Collective Goods in a 'Post-Washington Consensus' Era.* Coventry, U.K.: University of Warwick, 1999.

Pritchett, Price. *Culture Shift: The Employee Handbook for Changing Corporate Culture.* Dallas, Tex.: Pritchett & Associates, 1994.

Pritchett, Price. *The Employee Guide to Mergers and Acquisitions.* Dallas, Tex.: Pritchett & Associates, 1987.

Pritchett, Price, and Ron Pound. *The Employee Handbook for Organizational Change.* Plano, Tex.: Pritchett & Associates, 1996.

Pritchett, Price, Don Robinson, and Russell Clarkson. *After the Merger—the Authoritative Guide for Integration Success.* Rev. ed. New York: McGraw-Hill, 1997.

Rahim, M. Afzalur. *Managing Conflict: An Interdisciplinary Approach.* New York: Praeger, 1989.

Schweiger, David M. *M&A Integration: A Framework for Executives and Managers.* New York: McGraw-Hill, 2002.

Treacy, Michael, and Fred Wiersema. *The Discipline of Market Leaders.* New York: Addison Wesley, 1995.

Wolf, Ronald Charles. *Effective International Joint Venture Management: Practical Legal Insights for Successful Organization and Implementation.* Armonk, N.Y.: M. E. Sharpe, 2000.

## Articles

Bagli, Charles."Snapple Is Just the Latest Case of Mismatched Reach and Grasp." *New York Times,* March 29, 1997, sec. 1, p. 33, col. 4.

Beard, Myron. "Developing an Effective Strategy for International Mergers and Acquisitions." *International HR Journal* (winter 1999): 22–30.

Burke, Warner, and Peter Jackson. "Making the SmithKline Beecham Merger Work." *Human Resource Management* 30, no.1 (spring 1991): 69–87.

Cantoni, Craig. "Mergers and Acquisitions: The Critical Role of Compensation and Culture." *ACA Journal* (summer 1996): 38–45.

Cossey, B. "Systems Assessment in Acquired Subsidiaries." *Accountancy* (January 1991): 98–99.

"DaimlerChrysler: Marital Problems." *Economist,* October 14, 2000, pp. 76–79.

Eig, Deogun, and Jonathan Eig. "Nestle Nears an Accord to Acquire Ralston Purina for about $10 Billion." *Wall Street Journal,* January 15, 2001, Major Business News, A3.

Drucker, Peter. "The Five Rules of Successful Acquisition." *Wall Street Journal,* October 15, 1981, p. 28.

Feldman, Mark. "Disaster Prevention Plans after a Merger." *Mergers and Acquisitions* (July/August 1995): 31–36.

Fuller, Jane. "Urge to Merge IS Gathering Force." *Financial Times,* January 28, 1999, p. 23.

"Is Standardized Global IS Worth the Bother?" *Financial Times,* March 1, 1999, Survey Section, p. 3.

Kubilus, Norbert. "Mergers and Acquisitions: Their Impact on the IS Department." *Information Systems Management* (spring 1991): 54–61.

Kubilus, Norbert. "Acquired and Abandoned." *Information Strategy: The Executive's Journal,* (winter 1991): 33–40.

Lawrey, Richard. "The Role of HR in Multi-Country Acquisitions." *Benefits & Compensation International* 31 (July/August 2001): 14–22.

Leighton, Lawrence. "How Culture Clashes Can Ambush the Unwary Buyer Going Abroad." *Mergers and Acquisitions* (March/April 1993): 26–29.

Li, Ji, Kevin Lam, and Gongming Qian. "Does Culture Affect Behavior and Performance of Firms? The Case of Joint Ventures in China." *Journal of International Business Studies* 32 (2001): 115–131.

Li, Jiatao. "Building Effective International Joint Venture Leadership Teams in China." *Journal of World Business* 34 (spring 1999): 52–68.

Lohr, Steve. "Behemoths in a Jack-Be-Nimble Economy." *New York Times*, September 12, 1999, sec. 4, p. 1, col. 2.

"Merger Brief: The DaimlerChrysler Emulsion." *Economist*, July 19, 2000, pp. 67–68.

Potgieter, Leon. "International Mergers and Acquisitions: Don't Overlook the HR Issues." *Benefits & Compensation International* 25 (May 1996): 18–22.

Risberg, Anette. "Employee Experiences of Acquisition Processes." *Journal of World Business* 36 (spring 2001): 58–84.

Shrivastava, P. "Post-Merger Integration." *Journal of Business Strategy* 7 (1986): 65–76.

Sorkin, Andrew. "Europeans Are Setting Merger Sights on U.S. Targets." *New York Times*, July 5, 2000, sec. C, p. 4, col. 1.

Uchitelle, Louis. "As Mergers Get Bigger, So Does the Danger." *New York Times*, Sunday, late edition, February 13, 2000, sec. 3, p. 4, col. 6.

Warner, Joan, John Templeman, and Robert Horn. "The World Is Not Always Your Oyster: Why Cross-Border Mergers So Often Come to Grief." *Business Week* (October 30, 1995), pp. 132–133.

Zweig, Phillip, Judy Kline, Stephanie Forest, and Kevin Gudridge. "The Case Against Mergers." *Business Week* (October 30, 1995).

## ADDITIONAL REFERENCES

### Books

*Acquisitions Yearbook.* New York: New York Institute of Finance [annual].

*Harvard Business Review on Mergers and Acquisitions.* Boston: Harvard Business School Pub. Corp., 2001.

Gregory, Alan, and Steve McCorriston. *Foreign Acquisitions by UK Limited Companies: Long-Run Performance in the U.S., Continental Europe and the Rest of the World.* Exeter, U.K.: Department of Accounting and Finance, University of Exeter, 2000.

Ingles, David. *Mergers and Acquisitions in the Chemical Industry.* London: Informa Chemicals, 2000.

*Mergers and Acquisitions.* Philadelphia: MLR Enterprises, 1965.

Pan, Yigang. *Equity Ownership in International Joint Ventures: The Impact of Source Country Factors.* Hong Kong: Chinese Management Centre, Hong Kong University, 1999.

### Articles

"International Mergers and Acquisitions Special Issue." *Journal of World Business* 36 (spring 2001).

Moon, Chul W. "Impact of Organizational Learning Contexts on Choice of Governance Mode for International Strategic Combinations." *Journal of High Technology Management Research* 10 (spring 1999): 167–202.

Reuer, Jeffrey J. "Downside Risk Implications of Multinationality and International Joint Ventures." *Academy of Management Journal* 43 (April 2000): 203–214.

Reuer, Jeffrey J. "Parent Firm Performance across International Joint Venture Life-Cycle Stages." *Journal of International Business Studies* 31 (first quarter 2000): 1–20.

Sim, A. B. "Determinants of Stability in International Joint Ventures: Evidence from a Developing Country Context." *Asia Pacific Journal of Management* 17 (December 2000): 373–397.

Sinha, Uday Bhanu. "International Joint Venture, Licensing and Buy-Out under Asymmetric Information." *Journal of Development Economics* 66 (October 2001): 127–151.

Steensma, H. Kevin. "Explaining IJV Survival in a Transitional Economy through Social Exchange and Knowledge-Based Perspectives." *Strategic Management Journal* 21 (August 2000): 831–851.

Ueng, C. Joe, Seung H. Kim, and C. Christopher Lee. "The Impact of Firm's Ownership Advantages and Economic Status of Destination Country on the Wealth Effects of International Joint Ventures." *International Review of Financial Analysis* 9 (2000): 67–76.

Zeira, Yoram. "Equity International Joint Ventures (EIJVS) and International Acquisitions (IAs): Generic Differences in the Pre- and Post-Incorporation Stages." *Management International Review* 39 (fourth quarter 1999): 323–352.

# Index